The Magic Garden Explained

The Internals of
UNIX® System V Release 4
An Open Systems Design

The Magic Garden Explained

The Internals of
UNIX® System V Release 4
An Open Systems Design

Berny Goodheart
Tandem Computers Pty Ltd
Sydney, Australia

James Cox
Tandem Computers Ltd.
Stockley Park, United Kingdom

PRENTICE HALL

New York   London   Toronto   Sydney   Tokyo   Singapore

Acquisitions Editor: Andrew Binnie
Production Editor: Fiona Marcar
Cover design: The Modern Art Production Group, Prahran, VIC; from an original painting "The Magic Garden" by James H. Evans.
Printed in Australia by Star Printery Pty Limited

3 4 5 98 97 96 95 94

ISBN 013 098138 9

National Library of Australia
Cataloguing-in-Publication Data

Goodheart, Berny
   The magic garden explained: the internals of UNIX System V Release 4.

   Bibliography.
   Includes index.
   ISBN 0 13 098138 9.

   1. UNIX (Computer file). I. Cox, James .II. Title.

005.43

Library of Congress
Cataloging-in-Publication Data

Goodheart, Berny
   The magic garden explained: the internals of UNIX System V
   Release 4, an open-systems design / Berny Goodheart & James Cox.
   p.   cm.
   Includes bibliographical references and index.
   ISBN 0-13-098138-9
   1. Operating systems (Computers)   2. UNIX System V (Computer file)
I. Cox, James .II. Title.
QA76.76.063G6633 1993   93-23385
005.4'3--dc20   CIP

Prentice Hall, Inc., *Englewood Cliffs, New Jersey*
Prentice Hall Canada, Inc., *Toronto*
Prentice Hall Hispanoamericana, S.A., *Mexico*
Prentice Hall of India Private Ltd, *New Delhi*
Prentice Hall International, Inc., *London*
Prentice Hall of Japan, Inc., *Tokyo*
Prentice Hall of Southeast Asia Pty Ltd, *Singapore*
Editora Prentice Hall do Brasil Ltda, *Rio de Janeiro*

PRENTICE HALL

A division of Simon & Schuster

The MAGIC Garden

One might wonder what **The MAGIC Garden** has in common with UNIX. Have the authors lost their minds?

> **magic 1:** *an extraordinary power or influence seemingly from a supernatural source.* **2:** *any natural power or art seeming to have miraculous results.* **3:** *control of natural forces by the direct action of objects, materials, or words considered supernaturally potent.* **4:** *the elixir of life.*

> **garden 1:** *an open environment furnished with tables and chairs and serving refreshments — See BEER.* **2:** *a rich well-cultivated region.* **3:** *variety of cat that is technically known to fanciers.*

UNIX is magical since, like a garden, it keeps growing and sprouting new hybrids each spring as if nothing but nature itself can destroy it.

Note from the authors: Yes, we have lost our minds. Be forewarned: you will lose yours too.

FOREWORD

John R. Mashey

Just over twenty years ago (1973), I started work at Bell Laboratories, arriving in the Programmer's Workbench department the same week as our new Digital PDP-11/45. This magnificent 248-Kbyte minicomputer ran an early version of the UNIX operating system, and although it often strained a bit under the load of 16 (and later 24) users, it was still a fine experience. We had 64KB of code, and 64KB of data per program, and access to a variety of 300-baud printing terminals. Of course, this "UNIX machine" was often viewed askance by Digital's Customer Engineers, as well as by some of our mainframe-oriented compatriots, who often doubted the use of smaller computers, especially ones with oddly-named operating systems.

In those years, there existed but a few dozen of UNIX systems, and a "release" was accomplished by driving up to Murray Hill, NJ, logging onto the "research" machine, and making a tape of anything new that looked interesting. Since documentation consisted of the Manual and a few short memoranda, learning most often depended on reading code, which fortunately was elegant, short, and accessible.

In those twenty years, many things have changed. For example, this Foreword is being written on a Silicon Graphics workstation more than 100X faster than that PDP-11/45, with 64MB of memory, and I don't even have to share it with anyone. Still, much of its code is still written in C, and it certainly runs a version of the UNIX system.

At least one more thing has not changed. There has long been a somewhat mysterious connection between the UNIX system and the folks Down Under. For whatever reason, there were often Australian computer scientists around Bell Labs, or doing interesting things with the UNIX system very far away. A bit later came John Lions' wonderful booklets explaining the innards of the UNIX system.

"The Magic Garden Explained" carries on that fine tradition in at least two ways. First, at least one of the authors is Australian. Second, it provides a detailed and comprehensive look at the innards of an important and popular version of the UNIX system, in this case UNIX System V Release 4.

Of course, current UNIX systems are far more complex than in the early days, and it takes a great deal more time and effort to make the innards understandable.

I enjoyed reading this book, and even after twenty years, I still learned plenty from it. You will, too.

John R. Mashey
Silicon Graphics
Mountain View, CA
November 1993

CONTENTS

Foreword   vii

Contents   ix

Preface   xxi

Acknowledgments   xxvii

Part 1 Overview   1

Chapter 1   **BACKGROUND AND HISTORY**   3
   1.1   Genealogical history of UNIX   3
      1.1.1   Before UNIX   3
      1.1.2   The Epoch   3
      1.1.3   First edition   5
      1.1.4   Research UNIX   5
      1.1.5   The first port of UNIX   6
      1.1.6   Seventh Edition   8
      1.1.7   Berkeley UNIX (BSD)   9
      1.1.8   AT&T UNIX System III & Microsoft XENIX   9
      1.1.9   AT&T UNIX System V   10
      1.1.10   AT&T UNIX System V Release 2   10
      1.1.11   AT&T UNIX System V Release 3   11
   1.2   Politics and the battle for standards   12
      1.2.1   The user's dilemma   12
      1.2.2   SVID   12
      1.2.3   POSIX   13
      1.2.4   X/Open   13
   1.3   AT&T UNIX System V Release 4   15
      1.3.1   UNIX International   15
      1.3.2   Univel UnixWare   18
      1.3.3   Novell UNIX System V Release 4   18
      1.3.4   Summary   19
Chapter 2   **CONCEPTS AND FACILITIES**   20
   2.1   Introduction   20
   2.2   Philosophy   20
      2.2.1   The user interface   21

	2.2.2	The user's credentials	22
	2.2.3	The privileged user	22
	2.2.4	User programs and commands	23
2.3		The UNIX kernel	24
	2.3.1	Kernel software organization	25
	2.3.2	Kernel source code organization	26
2.4		The UNIX file system	27
	2.4.1	File system structure	29
	2.4.2	Mountable file systems	30
	2.4.3	Storage devices for file systems	31
	2.4.4	File system interface	32
	2.4.5	File system types	33
2.5		Files	34
	2.5.1	Regular files	35
	2.5.2	Directories	35
	2.5.3	Special files	36
	2.5.4	Links	37
	2.5.5	Symbolic links	38
	2.5.6	Named pipes	38
	2.5.7	Memory mapped files	39
	2.5.8	File removal	39
	2.5.9	File names	39
2.6		Descriptor management	40
	2.6.1	File and record locking	41
2.7		I/O redirection	42
2.8		Resource limitations	44
2.9		Quotas	45
2.10		Security	45
	2.10.1	Process execution rights	45
	2.10.2	File protection	46
2.11		Devices	47
	2.11.1	Device drivers	47
	2.11.2	User process interface	47
2.12		System initialization	48
2.13		Networking & communication services	51
	2.13.1	STREAMS	51
	2.13.2	TCP/IP	53
	2.13.3	Transport level interface (TLI)	56
	2.13.4	Remote procedure call (RPC)	57
	2.13.5	External data representation (XDR)	57
	2.13.6	Sockets	58
	2.13.7	STREAMS-based pipes	59
	2.13.8	UUCP	59
2.14		File sharing	60
	2.14.1	Networked file system (NFS)	62
	2.14.2	Remote file sharing (RFS)	63

2.15   User access   63
        2.15.1   Service access facility (SAF)   63
2.16   Extended Fundamental Types (EFT)   64
2.17   Exercises   65

Part 2   UNIX Internals   67

Chapter 3   MEMORY MANAGEMENT SUBSYSTEM   69
3.1   Introduction to the memory subsystem   69
        3.1.1   Virtual memory   69
        3.1.2   Structure of a page   71
        3.1.3   Associative memory cache   71
3.2   Demand paging   74
        3.2.1   Page stealing   76
3.3   Segmentation and regions   78
3.4   The hardware independent layer   80
        3.4.1   Structure of physical memory   80
        3.4.2   Initializing the page system   81
        3.4.3   The *page* structure   83
        3.4.4   Page list management   84
        3.4.5   *vnode* pages   85
        3.4.6   Anonymous pages   85
        3.4.7   The *as* structure   86
        3.4.8   The *seg* structure   86
        3.4.9   The *segvn_data* structure   87
        3.4.10   The *anon* structure   88
3.5   Paging system procedures   89
3.6   Hardware dependent layer   92
        3.6.1   Segment operations   93
        3.6.2   HAT layer data structures   96
        3.6.3   HAT layer support functions   102
3.7   Demand paging   105
        3.7.1   Exception handling   105
        3.7.2   Low-level routines   106
        3.7.3   The *pagefault( )* function   106
        3.7.4   The *utlbmiss* function   107
        3.7.5   Page fault examples   108
3.8   Page out and swapping   110
        3.8.1   Page stealing variables   111
        3.8.2   The *pageout* process   112
        3.8.3   The swapper process   115
        3.8.4   Swap space management   117
3.9   Non-paged memory allocation   119
        3.9.1   Memory allocation strategies   121
        3.9.2   *kmem_alloc( )* and *kmem_free( )*   122

	3.9.3	*kmem_fast_alloc( )* and *kmem_fast_free( )*	127
	3.9.4	*rmalloc( )* and *rmfree( )*	128
3.10	Memory related system calls		129
	3.10.1	Stack growth, *brk* and *sbrk*	132
	3.10.2	*memcntl* and *plock*	134
	3.10.3	*mprotect* and *mincore*	138
3.11	Exercises		139

Chapter 4   PROCESS MANAGEMENT SUBSYSTEM   141

4.1	Introduction to the process management subsystem		141
	4.1.1	Concurrency	142
	4.1.2	Flow of execution	142
4.2	The process image		143
	4.2.1	Format of an executable on disk	143
	4.2.2	Process memory model	145
	4.2.3	Context of a process	145
	4.2.4	The *user-area*	146
	4.2.5	Process image in *user* address space	146
	4.2.6	Process image in *system* address space	147
	4.2.7	Processor registers	150
4.3	The structure of a process		153
	4.3.1	The *user* structure	153
	4.3.2	The *proc* structure	154
4.4	Process states		155
	4.4.1	Functional state	155
	4.4.2	Execution state	157
4.5	Context switching		159
4.6	Process scheduling		160
	4.6.1	Priority classes	160
	4.6.2	Process time-slice	161
	4.6.3	Priority class independent variables	161
	4.6.4	Priority dispatch queues	162
	4.6.5	Priority class independent functions	163
	4.6.6	Priority class groups	166
	4.6.7	Priority class dispatch parameter tables	168
	4.6.8	System-class	169
	4.6.9	Real-time class	169
	4.6.10	Time-shared class	171
	4.6.11	Class dependent interface	174
	4.6.12	Class dependent functions	175
	4.6.13	Sleeping processes	180
	4.6.14	Algorithm *sleep( )*	183
	4.6.15	Stopped processes	188
	4.6.16	Algorithm *wakeprocs( )*	188
	4.6.17	Algorithm *setrun( )*	190
4.7	User-level context switching		191

4.8		The system clock	192
	4.8.1	Clock interrupt service routine	192
	4.8.2	Priming the clock	195
	4.8.3	Callout tables	196
	4.8.4	Alarm calls	197
	4.8.5	Process execution-time statistics	199
	4.8.6	System-wide statistics	200
	4.8.7	System-wide process accounting	200
	4.8.8	Enforcing CPU resource limits	201
	4.8.9	Profiling	202
	4.8.10	Keeping time	204
	4.8.11	High resolution interval timers	206
4.9		Process execution modes	209
	4.9.1	Transferring to *kernel-mode*	210
	4.9.2	Interrupt, trap and exception handling	212
	4.9.3	Saving and restoring the environment	213
	4.9.4	System call traps	214
	4.9.5	The *sysent[]* table	215
	4.9.6	Exception traps	216
	4.9.7	Interrupts	216
	4.9.8	Returning to *user-mode* in *systrap()*	218
	4.9.9	*longjmp()* and *setjmp()*	220
4.10		Signals	221
	4.10.1	Signal posting	221
	4.10.2	Algorithm *sigtoproc()*	225
	4.10.3	Handling signals	225
	4.10.4	System calls for signals	226
	4.10.5	Algorithm *ssig()*	233
	4.10.6	Getting signal information	233
	4.10.7	Execution errors and signals	235
	4.10.8	Signal processing	236
	4.10.9	Algorithm *psig()*	238
	4.10.10	System calls for posting signals	240
4.11		User, process, process group and session relationships	241
	4.11.1	Parents, children and siblings	241
	4.11.2	Process identification (PID)	243
	4.11.3	Process groups and job control	245
	4.11.4	Sessions	248
	4.11.5	Process credentials	249
4.12		Process creation	252
	4.12.1	Algorithm *fork1()*	253
	4.12.2	Algorithm *newproc()*	253
4.13		Program execution	258
	4.13.1	Algorithm *exece()*	259
	4.13.2	Program flow of execution	261
	4.13.3	Dumping core	262

	4.13.4	Algorithm *core( )*	262
4.14	Shared libraries		263
	4.14.1	Statically-linked-libraries	263
	4.14.2	Statically-linked-shared-libraries	264
	4.14.3	Dynamically-linked-shared-libraries	264
4.15	Process termination		265
	4.15.1	Transition phases of process termination	265
	4.15.2	Algorithm *exit( )*	266
	4.15.3	Waiting for a process	269
	4.15.4	Algorithm *waitid( )*	270
	4.15.5	Algorithm *freeproc( )*	271
4.16	Process suspension		273
4.17	System operation		273
	4.17.1	System initialization	273
	4.17.2	System shutdown and reboot	277
4.18	Exercises		279

Chapter 5	**I/O SUBSYSTEM**		**282**
5.1	Introduction		282
5.2	The new buffer cache		283
	5.2.1	Overview of the new buffer cache	283
	5.2.2	New buffer cache data structures	285
	5.2.3	Functions in the new buffer cache	285
5.3	The old buffer cache		288
	5.3.1	Overview of the old buffer cache	288
	5.3.2	Old buffer cache data structures	288
	5.3.3	Buffer allocation and freeing	290
	5.3.4	Buffer mapping: *bmap( )* operations	291
	5.3.5	Reading and writing buffers	292
5.4	File I/O support functions		292
	5.4.1	Page I/O low level functions	293
5.5	Read and write file I/O		296
	5.5.1	Data structures for *read* and *write*	296
	5.5.2	The *read* and *write* system calls	297
	5.5.3	The *readv* and *writev* system calls	298
5.6	Device drivers		299
	5.6.1	Special files	300
	5.6.2	Driver functions	301
	5.6.3	Device driver data structures	301
	5.6.4	Device driver *open* function	304
	5.6.5	Device driver *close* function	306
	5.6.6	Device driver interrupt service routine	306
5.7	Block device drivers		307
	5.7.1	Device driver *strategy* function	308
	5.7.2	Block device *read* and *write* functions	309
	5.7.3	Raw disk I/O	309

5.7.4	The *physiock( )* function	311
5.8	Character device drivers	313
5.8.1	Character device *read* and *write* functions	313
5.8.2	Device driver *ioctl* function	313
5.8.3	Character device *poll* function	316
5.9	The *mmap* system call	319
5.9.1	Block device and regular file *mmap*	322
5.9.2	Character device *mmap* function	323
5.10	Example character driver: mm	325
5.11	The Device Driver Interface and Driver Kernel Interface	327
5.11.1	DDI/DKI section 2	329
5.11.2	DDI/DKI section 3	330
5.11.3	DDI/DKI section 4	333
5.12	Exercises	333
Chapter 6	**FILE MANAGEMENT SUBSYSTEM**	335
6.1	Introduction to the file management subsystem	335
6.2	Associating with a file	336
6.2.1	The process open file table	336
6.2.2	The system open file table	337
6.2.3	File allocation operations	340
6.2.4	File descriptor allocation	341
6.2.5	File descriptors inherited from the parent	342
6.2.6	The *open* and *creat* system calls	344
6.3	The file system independent *vnode*	345
6.3.1	Allocating a *vnode*	346
6.3.2	*vnode* operations	346
6.3.3	File system type dependent *vnodeops* functions	348
6.4	File and record locking	357
6.4.1	Advisory locking	358
6.4.2	File and record locking in the *vnode*	358
6.4.3	Mandatory locking	359
6.4.4	Lock resource and accounting	360
6.5	The virtual file system	360
6.5.1	Virtual file system switch table (VFSSW)	362
6.5.2	File system type dependent VFS operations	363
6.6	The UNIX file system hierarchy	369
6.6.1	Mountable file systems	370
6.6.2	The system's VFS mount list	373
6.6.3	The *vnodes* association with the *vfs* structure	376
6.6.4	The *mount* and *umount* system calls	376
6.7	The directory name lookup cache	378
6.8	Pathname resolution	381
6.8.1	The *pathname* data structure	381
6.8.2	Pathname resolving functions	381
6.9	The special file system (*specfs*)	384

6.9.1	The shadow-special-vnode (*snode*)	385
6.9.2	The *fifo* file system (*fifofs*)	388
6.10	Concept of the *inode*	388
6.10.1	Layout of the file and *inode* on disk	390
6.11	The /*proc* file system (*procfs*)	392
6.11.1	/*proc* implementation	393
6.12	Exercises	398

Part 3 Additional Facilities 401

Chapter 7	**STREAMS**	403
7.1	Introduction	403
7.2	STREAMS data structures	409
7.2.1	STREAMS messages (*msgbs*)	409
7.2.2	STREAMS *queue* structures	412
7.2.3	The *module* structures	416
7.2.4	Initialization of module data structures	418
7.3	STREAMS modules	418
7.3.1	Open procedures	420
7.3.2	Put procedures	421
7.3.3	Service procedures	422
7.3.4	Message processing	423
7.3.5	Processing *ioctl*	424
7.3.6	Flush handling	430
7.3.7	Close procedures	432
7.4	STREAMS drivers	433
7.4.1	Configuration and linking	434
7.4.2	Driver open	434
7.4.3	Driver close	436
7.4.4	Driver input	437
7.4.5	Driver output	438
7.5	Multiplexors	441
7.5.1	Building the multiplexor	442
7.5.2	Multiplexor data structures	444
7.5.3	Multiplexor open	447
7.5.4	Multiplexor write side	447
7.5.5	Multiplexor read side	452
7.5.6	Multiplexor close	453
7.6	STREAMS utility functions	454
7.6.1	STREAMS memory allocation functions	456
7.6.2	Queue manipulation functions	459
7.6.3	Flow-control functions	460
7.7	STREAMS memory management	461
7.7.1	allocb( ) and esballoc( )	461
7.7.2	Comparison of old and new allocation schemes	462

7.8		STREAMS scheduling and flow-control implementation	464
	7.8.1	Flow-control variables	464
	7.8.2	Flow-control procedures	465
	7.8.3	The STREAMS scheduler	468
7.9		Operation of the stream head	469
	7.9.1	Stream head data structures	469
	7.9.2	Limiting STREAMS memory	472
	7.9.3	Opening a stream	473
	7.9.4	Opening a clone device	474
	7.9.5	Writing to a stream	476
	7.9.6	Reading from a stream	477
	7.9.7	Stream *ioctl*	482
	7.9.8	*putmsg* and *getmsg*	487
	7.9.9	Polling a stream	489
	7.9.10	The *Strinfo* array	493
	7.9.11	*qattach( )* and *qdetach( )*	497
7.10		STREAMS-based pipes and FIFOs	497
	7.10.1	FIFO operations	498
	7.10.2	Pipe operations	500
7.11		STREAMS terminals	502
	7.11.1	Using *ldterm*	503
	7.11.2	Job control	505
	7.11.3	The *straccess( )* function	508
7.12		Implementation of *ldterm*	508
	7.12.1	Data structures in *ldterm*	508
	7.12.2	*ldterm* read side	509
	7.12.3	*ldterm* write side	511
	7.12.4	*ldterm ioctl*	511
	7.12.5	Character input	511
	7.12.6	Special character I/O	513
	7.12.7	Flow-control	513
	7.12.8	VMIN & VTIME input	514
7.13		Other terminal issues	516
	7.13.1	Pseudo terminals	516
	7.13.2	Intelligent controllers	518
7.14		STREAMS networking support	519
	7.14.1	Transport service interface	519
	7.14.2	Socket interface	521
	7.14.3	Transport layer interface	523
7.15		STREAMS module configuration	526
7.16		Exercises	526
Chapter 8		**INTERPROCESS COMMUNICATION**	528
8.1		Introduction to interprocess communication	528
	8.1.1	IPC operation permissions	529
8.2		Semaphores	530

	8.2.1	Semaphore initialization and control	532
	8.2.2	Using semaphores	534
8.3	The implementation of semaphores		535
	8.3.1	Semaphore support functions	539
	8.3.2	Semaphore initialization	540
	8.3.3	Semaphore allocation	540
	8.3.4	Semaphore operations	540
	8.3.5	Semaphore undo	541
8.4	Message queues		543
	8.4.1	Message initialization and control	543
	8.4.2	Using messages	544
8.5	The implementation of message queues		545
	8.5.1	Message initialization	548
	8.5.2	Message allocation	549
	8.5.3	Message operations	549
8.6	Shared memory		551
	8.6.1	Shared memory data structures	551
	8.6.2	Using shared memory	553
8.7	The implementation of shared memory		555
	8.7.1	Initialization and control of shared memory	557
	8.7.2	Attaching shared memory	559
	8.7.3	Detaching shared memory	559
8.8	Exercises		559
Chapter 9	**CRASH**		561
9.1	Introduction to crash		561
9.2	Getting started		563
9.3	Symbols		565
9.4	Processes		568
	9.4.1	The proc command	571
	9.4.2	Hints for the proc command	574
	9.4.3	The u command	576
	9.4.4	Hints for the u command	582
	9.4.5	The as command	583
9.5	Kernel stack		585
	9.5.1	C Language stack	585
	9.5.2	The kernel stack layout	589
	9.5.3	Kernel stack commands	590
	9.5.4	Kernel stack hints	591
9.6	Files		594
	9.6.1	The file command	595
	9.6.2	Examining *vnodes*	595
	9.6.3	Examining *inodes*	596
	9.6.4	Mounted file systems	599
9.7	Memory		601
	9.7.1	Memory configuration commands	601

	9.7.2	Virtual memory commands	603
	9.7.3	The map command	604
	9.7.4	Memory hints	605
9.8	STREAMS		605
	9.8.1	STREAMS memory	606
	9.8.2	Queues and streams	610
	9.8.3	STREAMS terminals	614
	9.8.4	STREAMS hints	618
9.9	Miscellaneous commands		619

Appendix A System call error codes   622

Appendix B filock structure   626

Appendix C siginfo structure   627

Appendix D strevent structure   628

Appendix E Streams D3DK functions   629

Appendix F Crash commands   632

Appendix G IEEE POSIX Suite   636

BIBLIOGRAPHY   638

INDEX   642

PREFACE

I take the view, and always have done, that if you cannot say what you have to say in twenty minutes, you should go away and write a book about it.

— Derek Charles Moore-Brabazon

The first generally available text describing the internals of the UNIX operating system was published in the form of an excellent and very popular book called *The Design of the UNIX Operating System* [Bach 1986]. It was based on UNIX System V Release 2. Following this, another popular book called *The Design and Implementation of the 4.3BSD UNIX Operating System* [Leffler, McKusick, Karels, Quarterman 1988] described the internals of the Berkeley Software Distribution's (BSD) variation of UNIX. In between these publications, UNIX System Laboratories Inc, (USL) released a new version of the UNIX operating system which combined System V, BSD, and some XENIX features into a single UNIX operating system called **UNIX System V Release 4.**

This book follows in the footsteps of both of those books and offers a thorough, authoritative examination of the various techniques, algorithms, and structures used in the UNIX System V Release 4 *core* operating system (the kernel), how it manages system resources, and how it provides hardware and software services for programmers and users alike.

This book is not about to teach you how to use the UNIX system nor is it a book exclusively for programmers, and there are some prerequisites required of the reader. The following is assumed throughout the text: you have experience with a structured programming language (preferably the C Language [Kernighan, Ritchie 1978]); you have experience with the UNIX system as a user or administrator. This is not mandatory but it would be beneficial since, except for a discussion of the *crash(1M)* program, no other user-based programs or commands are discussed.

Like many other subjective and specialized UNIX books, such as *UNIX Network Programming* [Stevens 1990], *The UNIX Programming Environment* [Kernighan, Pike 1984], *UNIX System Administration* [Nemeth, Snyder, Seebass 1989], and of course *UNIX Curses Explained* [Goodheart 1991], this book is also subjective and specialized, since its topic specifically describes the internal design of the UNIX System V Release 4 Kernel. It provides a technically oriented description of how the UNIX System V Release 4 operating system functions.

This book has various uses. It is detailed and complex enough for use as a university course textbook for either first or second level computer science graduates studying operating systems. It is also explanatory enough for the casual reader and for short education courses on computer operating system subjects. For sophisticated application developers, it will help develop intuition; for system administrators, it describes the meaning and use of tuneable parameters, and how to use and understand the **crash** command; for academics, it provides a case study of the application of general operating system principles. However, its greatest use is as an aid to system engineers and programmers involved with porting and supporting the UNIX System V Release 4 operating system. Programmers involved in implementing device drivers will find this book invaluable — although it does not cover in detail the wizard-art of device driver design since specialized texts such as *Writing UNIX Device Drivers* [Pajari 1992] and *Writing A Unix Device Driver* [Egan, Teixeira 1988] are already available for this purpose.

Exercises are provided at the end of each chapter. For some of the exercises, the answers can be found in the pages of this book. Other more difficult questions may require a certain level of ingenuity and there are some more advanced questions that even provide a topic for further research and investigation. The more difficult questions are marked with an asterisk. The more asterisks, the more difficult the question is likely to be.

The UNIX System V Release 4 source code is the property of Novell, Inc. and is copyright protected by a number of institutions such as AT&T, the Microsoft Corporation, the University of California at Berkeley (UCB) and Sun Microsystems, Inc. Source code is distributed by license only, from Novell, Inc. UNIX Systems Group (USG). Publishing the source code, or any part of it, is illegal since it would render it into the public domain. Therefore, it is not within the scope of this book, nor permissible, to publish original source code extracts from the operating system. Where it is necessary to explain an algorithm in such detail, we have used a C-like pseudo code in place of the original source code. However, procedures retain their original function names and function calling syntax corresponding to their use within the kernel. If you can gain access to the source code (i.e., if your institution has a source code license) we strongly recommend that you reference it while using this book. However, the book is instructive and explanatory enough to be read without it.

As an additional aid to reading this book we have used a consistent format throughout the text: system calls, C Library calls programmed at the user level, kernel based structures and variables, and any other semantics used within the C programming language are shown in *italics*, and procedure names other than system calls are identified by a trailing pair of parentheses. Some examples of this are: *open, close, clock(), sleep(), read, fclose(), strcmp(), struct proc, u.u_procp*. C-like pseudo code examples are shown in `constant-width`. Commands and user-based programs such as **ps(1)**, **link(1M)** and **sleep(1)** are shown in **Helvette bold** with parentheses, the information contained in the parentheses corresponds to the UNIX system documentation section of the manual supplied with the operating system. File names are shown in italics and are given as full hierarchical path names. For example, */etc/passwd* and */usr/share/lib/locale*. C Language include-files, are shown in italic but are shown as they would be used in a C program. For example, *sys/user.h* and *<sys/proc.h>*. All other text is shown in Times Roman.

The UNIX System V Release 4 kernel is elegantly designed, although it is also very complex. With this in mind we have tried to describe the algorithms and concepts it involves in the simplest possible way, by paying as much attention to basic detail without actually describing each individual line of the source code. To do this we have split the UNIX Kernel into four basic sub-systems:

- The memory management subsystem
- The process management subsystem
- The I/O subsystem
- The file management subsystem

We have tried to explain the system in a logical form by using diagrams and figures in a building-block fashion to explain how each sub-system is constructed, how each sub-system interconnects and communicates with the others, and how the various data structures and algorithms within each sub-system are manipulated as the system executes them. Once the basic concepts of each sub-system are understood, then understanding the system as a complete functioning operating system will become easier.

The word "UNIX" can nowadays refer to a number of past and present versions and variants of the UNIX operating system. Since this book is written about the USL UNIX System V Release 4 version of the operating system, references to the word "UNIX" will refer to that version unless otherwise stated. Furthermore, this book is based on the USL UNIX System V Release 4.0.3 distribution.

Although almost all of the UNIX System V Release 4 kernel is hardware independent, some areas of the kernel remain dependent on hardware architecture. These areas have been placed into well-defined interfaces within the kernel and are discussed in the text. However, in order to give implementation examples of these areas we chose to discuss the MIPS architecture.

The structure and organization of the book consists of nine chapters split up into three parts. Part 1 provides a high level overview of the concepts and facilities provided by the operating system, Part 2 delves deep into the core operating system's internal workings, and Part 3 discusses additional facilities that we felt needed to be described separately:

Part 1

- *Chapter 1* — describes the evolution and history of the UNIX operating system up to and including USL UNIX System V Release 4. Among some of the discussions are the differences in UNIX System releases and versions, the emerging standards effecting its continued evolution, and the new features provided with the UNIX System V Release 4 Kernel.

- *Chapter 2* — offers a general introduction to the operating system concepts, a description of the facilities it provides, and a brief description of the system call interface. Succeeding chapters in the book assume that the reader is familiar with the concepts discussed in this chapter. Thus, it provides the groundwork for understanding the rest of the book.

Part 2

- *Chapter 3* — describes the memory management system. It distinguishes the operating systems hardware dependent layer from the hardware independent layer. It covers the virtual memory system, demand paging, paging arrangements, hashing and caching techniques, swapping, memory related system calls, memory exception handling and memory allocation and deallocation techniques.

- *Chapter 4* — describes the process management system. It discusses the structure of a process, the context of a process, the structure of the user area, the format of an executable, the system and user address space, process execution modes and states, CPU interrupt priority levels, preemption, CPU scheduling, class dependent and independent context switching, priority classes and queues, dispatch queues, sleep and wakeup mechanisms, the system clock and interval timer, callout tables, signal posting and handling, interrupt and exception handling, processor execution levels, process groups, the system call interface, process creation, termination and synchronization, process overlay schemes and system initialization and shutdown.

- *Chapter 5* — describes the I/O subsystem. It discusses the communication methods between process and device, responsibilities of the I/O subsystem, block and character devices, device switch tables, system buffer cache, the device driver interface, and I/O control (*ioctl*) service.

- *Chapter 6* — describes the file management subsystem — the responsibility of the file subsystem, mount lists and in-core inode tables, the user open file table and system file table, file and record locking, the file system independent vnode, the shadow special vnode, the virtual file system, the special file system, the */proc* file system, and the virtual file system switch table.

Part 3

- *Chapter 7* — covers the STREAMS subsystem and includes an introduction to streams, streams components and modules, multiplexed streams, streams mechanisms and manipulation methods, stream based pipes, streams system call interface.

- *Chapter 8* — describes the interprocess communication system, including the shared memory, semaphore and message queue facilities.

- *Chapter 9* — covers the only user-based application in the book — an introduction to *crash(1M)*, a utility for inspecting a core-image of the kernel.

The development of this book has been truly cosmopolitan; James lives in England and I live in Australia. Our day time employment requires much overseas travel so apart from the very early mornings, late late nights, non eventful vacation time, weekends and public holidays spent in "book-space" at home, we have spent many a night working either in-flight, in-hotel, in-bar and in some circumstances, in-taxicab! Parts of the book were conceived in Australia, New Zealand, England, Sweden, Germany, Holland, France, Singapore, Hong-Kong, South Korea, Taiwan, Canada, USA, and even China.

Since we were both 10 hours apart, the development cycle was not at times so easy. We communicated by e-mail or by telephone, and even in some circumstances by air-mail. By far e-mail worked best. However, while I wrote, James slept and while James wrote I slept — it was painstakingly slow at times. Daylight saving time was no help either; if it was summer time in England, the time difference between us was 9 hours, if it was summer time in Australia (eastern), the time difference was 11 hours — that extra hour in bed was much missed. To add further difficulty, I was often communicating with the folks at USL in New Jersey — they are a mere 18 hours ahead of my clock but one day behind in reality. But our efforts have paid off.

Bug fixes and comments

Every effort has been made to remove typographical bugs and errors. However, writing a book of this nature is likened to the design of a very large software project — neither are ever completely free of bugs.

If you find a bug or wish to suggest improvements or pass comment about any other error found in the book, please send electronic mail to:

svr4book-support@books.prenhall.com.au

ACKNOWLEDGMENTS

Several people around the globe have helped enormously with this book. Their ideas, critique, suggestions, reviews, contributions, encouragement, information, improvements, formidable fact checking, in some circumstances unfailing good humour, beer-tasting sessions (they know who they are !!) and excellent Thai food have been the brawn for its conception.

Some contributions to our work came from people who we have never met and probably never will. We are grateful, nonetheless, to everyone who helped.

There were many, however, who took part more directly. Among them, we want especially to thank:

The staff at Prentice Hall Australia. In particular: Andrew Binnie (Editorial Director) who is the very best in the business — we are both personally indebted to you. Fiona Marcar (Editorial Manager) for being so helpful and for yet another brilliant production; Chris Richardson (Editorial Assistant) for coordinating everything — talk about multi-tasking!

A humble thanks to Gillian Gillett (Editor). She did it again: fast, clear and thorough, what more could we say; she was given a humongous manuscript but with her enthusiasm, honest criticism, and meticulous eye for errors, she did the impossible — twice!

Several people helped put the history section together. In particular we would like to thank: Professor John Lions (Department of Computer Science, University of New South Wales) and Tony McGrath (Uniq Professional Services). Both were indefatigable sources of information.

Many reviewers spent their precious play time reviewing parts or all of the manuscript and we would like to acknowledge them for their effort. In particular, we would like to thank: John Brazier (Brazier Systems & Consultants Ltd, UK), Warren Simon (Computer Telephone Integration Pty Ltd, Sydney), Mr D M Lyons (Department of Computer Science, University of Essex, UK), Ben Golding (Connect.com.au Pty Ltd, Sydney), Pauline van Winsen (Uniq Professional Services, Sydney), Michael Paddon (Iconix Pty Ltd, Melbourne), Peter Chubb (Softway Pty Ltd, Sydney) and John Hall (McDonald Douglas, UK).

We would like to extend our warm appreciation for the support of our employer: Tandem Computers Incorporated. In particular we would like to thank: Ray Villareal (Director of Asia Operations), Peter Lloyd, Steve Young, and the bloke with the funny accent, Rhod Davies. We would also like to acknowledge Michael John, Marcus Bain, Martin Sullivan and Paul Gundry — all old time hackers whose seemingly insignificant contribution played an important role. Also, John Hanrath and Ron Maxwell of AT&T who gave us the inspiration.

On behalf of the UNIX system community, we would like to extend special gratitude to Novell, Inc. and UNIX System Laboratories, Inc. for upholding the philosophy and allowing this book to be published. In particular, we want to acknowledge: Steven R. Breitstein, Elka Grisham, Dick Hamilton, George Holober, Bill Klinger, Burt Levine, Chris Schoettle, and Sandy Tannenbaum.

Above all, our greatest appreciation is offered to our wives and children who have put up with a less than normal domestic life and an almost zero social life during the book's two year development. They truly deserve more than just a mention — without their support and encouragement, this book would not have been possible. So, starting with our dear lovely wives, here's to the Goodheart family: Peppy, Natalie, Benjamin and Melisah; and to the Cox family: Kathy, Joanne, Rhian, Christopher, Alexander and Phillip.

Finally, no amount of appreciation can be placed into words about our mentors,* Dennis and Ken, without whom there would be no magic in our garden.

Berny M. Goodheart

James H. Cox

---

*   *See: Roget's Thesaurus, Class IV Division II Note 540*
     "mentor &c (adviser)".

PART 1

Overview

CHAPTER 1

Background
and history

All our ancient history, as one of our wits remarked, is no more than accepted fiction.

— Voltaire

1.1 Genealogical history of UNIX

UNIX is not a new operating system, in fact it is one of the oldest. It was well established before MS-DOS and CP/M. At the time of writing this book, the UNIX operating system is 24 years old. Much about its origin and pedigree is already known since it has been documented so many times in so many different ways. However, a brief background of its evolution is included here.

1.1.1 Before UNIX

In 1965 the Massachussets Institute of Technology (MIT) and the General Electric Company (GEC) joined together to develop a new, innovative and rather ambitious operating system called MULTICS [Organick 1972]. Its goal was to be a multi-user, interactive operating system, servicing a large community of users with copious amounts of computational power and data storage. In the days when batch-oriented systems prevailed this was certainly an innovative concept, for in the 1960s huge printouts, punched cards and endless waiting were a natural pastime. Shortly after, the Computing Science Research Center at Bell Laboratories became involved in the project. But in 1969 this research group decided that to develop MULTICS would take a lot longer than expected, and possibly even years to deliver, and so Bell Laboratories pulled out of the joint development venture.

1.1.2 The Epoch

It all started in 1969 when Ken Thompson was working on a Honeywell 635 running the GECOS system (General Electric Company Operating System) which was used during the development of MULTICS. Thompson wrote a game called "Space Travel" in FORTRAN, which simulated the positions and motions of planets in the

3

solar system by rotation and revolution, and supported a space ship that could be maneuvered between planets.

At the same time Thompson, Dennis Ritchie and others at Bell Laboratories were attempting to improve their programming environment and came up with a proposal for a new file system. Shortly after, Thompson wrote a kernel and programs to simulate this proposed file system and implemented them on a GE-645 computer. This new file system allowed Thomson to store his game source files in a hierarchical directory structure similar to that used in the MULTICS project. But Thompson was not very happy with the result of his "Space Travel" game since it did not run very well on the GE-645; it was a time sharing system and not very efficient. The jerky response from the game and the fact that it was so expensive to run (apparently $75 a game — in 1969 that was a lot of money) prompted Thompson to look for a replacement. He found one, a hardly-used PDP-7 in the corner of a room. Weighing just over half a ton, it was an eighteen bit machine with 4096 words of memory and a teletype, it provided a good graphic display and was a good contender. It seemed obvious at the time that this was not only a better machine for his game, but also cheaper to run. However, its programming and development environment was not very good, and it was too cumbersome to move his space game between the GECOS system and the PDP-7 since it had to be cross-assembled and of course in those days paper-tape had to be hand-carried between machines to exchange data. In view of this, Thompson and Ritchie decided to move the game onto the PDP-7. Soon after that, Thompson, finished with his game, decided to implement the file system that he had designed and simulated earlier. From this work was born the first version of UNIX although at that time the operating system had no name. But it included an early version of the UNIX file system which used *inodes*, a process subsystem with memory management and support for two users in a time sharing environment, a command interpreter (although at this time the Bourne shell [Bourne 1978] had not been invented), and for manipulating the file system, a small set of utility programs. During this time, the GE-645 system was used for development and cross-compiling between the two machines was required, but as soon as an assembler became available for the PDP-7, the system could fundamentally support itself.

The name "UNIX" came about after Brian Kernighan, another member of the team at Bell Laboratories, wittily named their two user system "UNICS", an acronym for "Uniplexed Information and Computing System" that was also a pun on their involvement in the MULTICS project. Shortly after, "UNICS" became "UNIX".

The first real user of the UNIX system was the patent department at Bell Laboratories. However, there were a few problems: the PDP-7 was not theirs (it was only a borrowed machine), it was grossly underpowered, and it failed to support the growing demand of the computer research group. Thus in 1971, the first assembler version of UNIX was ported to a PDP-11/20. It supported even more users and included a text formating system called *roff* written in PDP-11/20 assembler.

1.1.3 First edition

The first of many to come, it was called "First Edition" UNIX and named after its documentation system published in November 1971 (the tradition of naming releases of the UNIX system after each new edition of the documentation still continues at Bell Laboratories. The current version of UNIX is the "Tenth Edition"). Thompson set out to create a FORTRAN compiler for the new system but instead created, with the help of Ritchie, a new language called B, an interpretive language derived from Martin Richards' BCPL language [Richards 1969]. Soon after, in 1972, the "Second Edition" was released which included pipes and a kernel written in the B Language. However, B suffered several limitations: it was typeless, and only supported a single machine word data type (although other object types could be accessed via function calls or special operators). Because of B's limitations, Ritchie, whose forte was programming languages, went on to develop C, and in 1973 Thompson and Ritchie rewrote the UNIX system using the C language. By this time there were about 25 installations of the UNIX system and a UNIX systems group was initiated at Bell Laboratories to provide internal support for what was now "Fourth Edition" of the operating system.

In July 1974 Thompson and Ritchie described the UNIX system in a paper that was published in the computer science research journal, Communications of the ACM [Ritchie, Thompson 1974]. This paper marked the beginning of the UNIX system's prominence. Academics all over the world began to take interest in this new operating system which soon promoted a "Fifth Edition", made available free (apart from media and documentation costs) inclusive of source code to universities for educational purposes; recipients included the University of California at Berkeley (UCB), and the University of New South Wales (UNSW) in Sydney Australia. This paved the way for various new enhancements and development projects. Meanwhile, another group from Bell Laboratories, called the Programmer's Workbench (PWB), ran a version of UNIX that was enhanced to support a larger user base. In particular it serviced a number of large software projects, one of which bore the now famous Source Code Control System (SCCS).

1.1.4 Research UNIX

In 1975 the "UNIX Time-Sharing System, Sixth Edition", commonly known as "V6" or "Research UNIX", was released and for the first time made available outside Bell Laboratories through the Western Electric Company. By this time, most of the UNIX system was written in C. In those days it was unheard of to write operating system software in such a high level language since it was perceived that if you want to extract the best performance from your hardware you had to write your programs in assembler. However, C was soon known by many to be the next best thing to assembler. The C Language compiler itself, because of its relatively small size, could be easily ported to a wide variety of computer hardware. It was rich with functionality, easier to read, non-restrictive, easy to learn, and so efficient that system programmers soon gave up programming in assembler.

In 1976 Ritchie produced the *stdio* (Standard I/O) library, a reworked version of Mike Lesk's Portable C Library [Ritchie 1977]. This was a major step forward for both UNIX and the C language since it allowed programmers to write code without having to hard-code hardware dependencies. This meant that programs written in C on one system could be recompiled on another so long as it supported the C language, even if the underlying hardware architecture was different — essentially it promoted the design of portable code.

At about the same time, Thompson visited the University of California at Berkeley (UCB) while on sabbatical. While there, he installed V6 on the campus's PDP-11/70. Shortly after, Bill Joy and Chuck Haley became graduates there.

1.1.5 The first port of UNIX

In a small industrial town called Wollongong, about 80km south of Sydney, Australia, a new breed of UNIX was brewing. During 1975-6, Professor Juris Reinfelds was offered a foundation chair at the University of Wollongong. His mission was to set up a computer science department. This eventually led to the employment of a previous work associate and friend, Richard Miller from Canada who took up the position of Tutor in Computing Science. Richard had once reimplemented Juris' 20,000 line interactive graphics language called SIGMA and produced a more efficient 2,000 line version with fewer bugs. The mainframe computer facility in the practical laboratory was neither cost-effective nor flexible enough for easy use so Richard's first mission was to set up a student laboratory whereby a number of students could work on a computer system using their own terminals. In 1976, the University of Wollongong allocated a small amount of funds to establish the facility.

Juris visited Professor Murray Allen and Dr John Lions at the UNSW to see how they managed their computing science facility. He was impressed by the computer environment set up there (a PDP-11/40 running V6 UNIX). Seeing that a PDP-11 was required, Juris visited DEC with the possibility of buying one. Unfortunately, (or as it turned out, fortunately) his department's low budget forced him to look elsewhere. Eventually, Juris purchased an Interdata 7/32 (later renamed Perkin-Elmer). It was considerably cheaper than a PDP-11, showed similar performance, and was a 32 bit machine. However, the immediate environment was limited. The Interdata operating system (Operating System Multi Tasking — OSMT/32) used a partitioned architecture. Each program ran in its own partition of memory. To run a program, one had to load it into a partition, then pass control to that program. With 10 students it became a very laborious task setting up 10 terminals, so Richard wrote a terminal handler called MOTH (Miller's Own Terminal Handler). The scenario was to boot OSMT and load MOTH into a partition. MOTH would then open each terminal and start a command line interpreter.

Some time later, Juris and Richard decided that UNIX could, perhaps be ported to the Interdata 7/32. So as a challenge, Juris suggested to Richard that he should port UNIX to the 7/32 with the help of his students. It would be good practical work for the students and would provide a good example for their discipline in computing science. They applied for a UNIX licence which arrived on November 9, 1976. However, their copy of the source code did not arrive with it so they set off to UNSW to view it there and to see how they were going to attempt the port.

The first major task was to get a C compiler onto the Interdata 7/32 to compile the UNIX source. At that time, the only C compiler available was Ritchie's but it was tied very closely to the PDP-11 architecture. Nevertheless, it was a start, and so Richard had to find a way to bring the C compiler source across to the Interdata 7/32. The problem was, the Interdata 7/32 had no tape drive and there was no common disk format between the Interdata 7/32 and the PDP-11. Thus, to exchange data between the machines required the following scenario: Richard took a tape dump of the C compiler from UNSW to the Interdata office in Sydney where they had a tape drive. The data was then copied from the tape onto a disk pack and brought back to Wollongong. Richard then set about modifying the C compiler source by using the local line editor. The changes were then loaded onto disk and taken back to Interdata where it was loaded onto tape. The tape was then taken to UNSW where the C compiler was assembled and then cross-assembled back to Interdata assembler. The binary was then reloaded onto tape, taken back to Interdata, loaded onto a disk pack and taken back to Wollongong for testing. Fortunately, it took Richard only two passes of this incredible data exchange journey (if only *ftp* was available then). By January 1977, Richard had a working C compiler which was successfully compiling itself. The following month, a rudimentary UNIX kernel was ported to the Interdata 7/32, it ran without terminal drivers or interrupt handling and consisted of about 8 commands and a very basic shell.

The result of Richard's work was a hybrid UNIX system based on Version 6 from Bell Laboratories running on top of OSMT/32. UNIX was loaded into a partition and the device driver interface was replaced with direct calls to the OSMT operating system. This was required so that students could still have access to the Interdata 7/32 assembler (CAL) and BASIC interpreter. But effectively, Richard had created the first port of UNIX. There were four users of the system: Juris, Richard and two students, Ross Nealson and Tony McGrath (the "eager young cub scout" as he was then named). Unfortunately, Ross died later of cancer. In July 1977, the first port of UNIX was put into production in the Computing Science Laboratory. The students put the system under heavy load and its success was immediate.

In November 1977, John Lions at the University of New South Wales produced two booklets: *A Commentary On The UNIX Operating System* and *UNIX Operating System Source Code, Level Six* [Lions 1977]. These papers were the course notes for an operating system class. Their contents consisted of almost the entire Sixth Edition source code with a line by line commentary including a limited set of device drivers. Both booklets were prepared initially for students who attended John's class, but towards the end of 1978, Bell Laboratories took over their distribution and eventually they were withdrawn from publication.

Up to this stage, AT&T had their hands tied behind their back because of a 1956 Consent Decree which had been signed with the Federal Government's Justice Department. The Decree banned AT&T from entering the commercial computer market so they could neither advertise, market, nor support the system in adherence to the terms of the Decree. However, in 1977 AT&T relaxed its licensing policies so that outside companies could distribute binary forms of the UNIX system to the commercial sector. The first company to seize this opportunity was Interactive Systems Corporation of Santa Monica, California who enhanced the system by adding an office automation system. Interactive Systems became the first value added reseller (VAR) of the UNIX system. By this time there were approximately 500 installed systems.

1.1.6 Seventh Edition

Richard Miller later went to the USA to discuss his port with Ken and Dennis at Bell Research Labs. It was not long after that they purchased an Interdata 8/32 (the next model up from Richard's 7/32) which was conveniently placed next to their PDP-ll. Since PDP-11s were inexpensive and pretty powerful for that era, almost all earlier versions of UNIX ran on them. However, UNIX's capabilities on the PDP-11 were limited because of its architecture. It was a 16 bit machine and the average program ran in only 8K bytes of memory (although the maximum user program size was 64K bytes, the kernel ran in 20k of it!). Furthermore, programs could address only 128k bytes of memory and so developing large programs was difficult. However, the 32 bit architecture overcame many of these constraints. Thus, Ken and Dennis decided to embark on a full blown 32 bit port of UNIX using their new Interdata machine. This led Dennis to extend his C Language to incorporate features such as the *union*, and the explicit data types *short*, *long*, and *unsigned int*. This allowed programmers to write programs using the 32 bit architecture. Additionally, there were several other features discovered such as improved and expanded initialization, bit fields, macros and conditional compilation, the use of registers, globals, and so on.

This prompted a real tidy-up of the UNIX code to make it more portable. Up until then the UNIX code, although written in C, was heavily tied to the PDP-11/45 which used a memory management unit (MMU) using a split 64k instruction and 64k data address space. Thus, the memory management routines were rewritten together with the device driver interface so that UNIX could be more easily ported to other architectures. This resulted in the release of Seventh Edition UNIX.

Seventh Edition UNIX (or "Version 7" as it was commonly called) was released in 1979 and included a full featured K&R C compiler known as PCC (Portable C Compiler), and a new command interpreter known as *sh* or the "Bourne shell" after its author, Steve Bourne [Bourne 1978] (K&R is common UNIX jargon referencing Kernighan and Ritchie's definitive book "The C Programming Language", often referred to as "The Bible" [Kernighan, Ritchie 1978]). There were many other new features including a suite of new device drivers.

Soon after the release of Version 7, Dennis went to Australia to attend a conference and took with him the V7 code which was ported onto an Interdata 8/32 at the University of Melbourne. Robert Elz and Richard Miller later reverse-engineered the port and got it running on the Interdata 7/32 in Wollongong.

According to Juris, Dr Doug McIlroy, the head of the UNIX Research Group at Bell Laboratories said:

We here at Bell Laboratories were truly dumbfounded when this visitor from an unknown school in Australia reported his elegant procedure and remarkable success. Our own people took considerably longer to move UNIX to an Interdata machine, not because they were not as clever but because they had a different objective: a portable UNIX, rather than a UNIX port. But I think they'd have blinked before undertaking the heroic effort that Richard Miller did, and he did not even have a UNIX computer to port from. [Reinfelds 1990].

1.1.7 Berkeley UNIX (BSD)

At the University of California at Berkeley (UCB), some of the Bell Laboratories research team including Ken spent their sabbatical teaching UNIX and taking part in local research. Subsequently, they generated a lot of interest about the UNIX system among several graduate students and professors. This promoted a new breed of UNIX gurus, one of which was Bill Joy. Bill Joy put together several pieces of software which he collated for general distribution. He called it the "Berkeley Software Distribution". It consisted of the complete Version 6 UNIX operating system, and several other pieces of software including a Pascal compiler and his own **ex** editor which later became known as **vi**. There is some belief that the Version 6 UNIX port that formed part of the BSD 1.0 distribution was the "all-known-bugs-free" version produced by Ian Johnstone and derived from the UNSW. 2BSD was a serious attempt at rewriting the V6 kernel.

The Computer Science Department at Berkeley had access to a number of VAX computers and consequently Seventh Edition UNIX was ported to one and was given a new name, "32/V", after its 32 bit architecture. With the introduction of 32 bit machines (particularly the VAX-11/780), it paved the way for UNIX to expand its functionality. New facilities were introduced into the UNIX kernel such as demand paging and virtual memory, and this resulted in a version of UNIX called 3BSD after Berkeley's previously released PDP-11 versions, 1BSD and 2BSD.

Facilities such as these prompted the Department of Defense Advanced Research Project Agency (DARPA), who had evaluated UNIX's memory management on the VAX as well as the VAX's native operating system VMS, to fund further research, specifically in the area of communications. What resulted from this was Transport Control Protocol/Internet Protocol (TCP/IP) for UNIX. UNIX took a vital turn in its evolution from then on.

Bell Laboratories set up a reciprocal arrangement with Berkeley allowing them to redistribute sources for their version of UNIX, providing that their customers also obtained, or previously held, a source code license from Bell Laboratories. In 1980 Berkeley released 4BSD.

1.1.8 AT&T UNIX System III & Microsoft XENIX

In 1978, soon after the release of Version 7, the Research Group at Bell Laboratories handed over UNIX to the UNIX Support Group (USG). USG was limited to providing internal support only and subsequently they released several versions of UNIX at Bell Laboratories. However, outside Bell laboratories, UNIX development continued. Commercial interest became more prolific and many companies and institutions started to take an interest in the UNIX system because it was relatively easy to port to new and evolving hardware platforms. During that same period, silicon chip manufacturing methods were also maturing, resulting in lower priced and yet more powerful chip-sets. With the cost of manufacturing a computer system being reduced, the availability of an already developed operating system, and the government's growing interest in the UNIX system, it became a more viable business proposition to manufacture and sell UNIX computer systems. This sparked off a number of companies specializing in porting the UNIX system. One such company was the UniSoft Corporation who produced a version of UNIX called UniPlus+. Additionally, the Microsoft Corporation and The Santa Cruz Operation (SCO) joined forces to produce the XENIX system. All this interest resulted in UNIX being installed in thousands of sites and of course it was ported to several other hardware architectures such as Zilog's Z8000, Intel's 8088 and Motorola's 68000.

1982 saw the first version of UNIX released from USG outside Bell Laboratories. It was called "UNIX System III" and incorporated features from Version 7, PWB, V/32 and others. Shortly after, a number of BSD based M68000 systems were being produced and SCO released XENIX System III.

1.1.9 AT&T UNIX System V

System IV was never released outside AT&T but in an attempt to move into the software market in early 1983, AT&T announced the release of UNIX System V, and to the surprise of the UNIX community they also announced their intentions to provide support for it and for any other future releases of UNIX System V. More important, AT&T announced that this release of the operating system would also be upwards compatible with future releases of AT&T UNIX System V. The System V kernel incorporated numerous new features although essentially it was just an enhanced System III with performance improvements such as hash tables and data caches. However, new system services were also introduced such as semaphores, message queues and shared memory.

1.1.10 AT&T UNIX System V Release 2

USG was transformed into the UNIX System Development Laboratories (USDL). In 1984 USDL released UNIX System V, Release 2 (SVR2). Numerous sub-releases of SVR2 saw the introduction of facilities such as record and file locking, copy-on-write, and demand paging as opposed to the more traditional swapping memory management techniques (although the System V implementation of demand paging was not based on the Berkeley paging system). By this time, UNIX was installed in approximately 100,000 sites around the world and was fast becoming the operating system of first choice.

Table 1.1: *Recent UNIX System V kernel developments*

1982	System III	Named pipes The run queue
1983	System V	Hash tables Buffer and *inode* caches Semaphores Shared memory Message queues
1984	System V Release 2	Record and file locking Demand paging Copy on write
1987	System V Release 3	Inter Process Communication (IPC) Remote File Sharing (RFS) Enhanced signal operations Shared libraries File System Switch (FSS) Transport Layer Interface (TLI) STREAMS communication facility
1989	System V Release 4	Real time processing support Process scheduling classes Enhanced signal processing Dynamically allocated data structures Extended open file facilities Virtual Memory management (VM) Virtual File System capabilities (VFS) Berkeley Fast File System (UFS) Enhanced STREAMS Preemptive kernel File system Quotas Driver Kernel Interface facilities (DKI)

1.1.11 AT&T UNIX System V Release 3

In 1987 AT&T Information Systems (AT&T-IS — a group within USDL) released System V Release 3 (SVR3) and within the numerous sub-releases of this version of UNIX we saw the introduction of Inter Process Communication (IPC) facilities, Remote File Sharing (RFS), enhanced signal operations, shared libraries, the File System Switch (FSS), the Transport Layer Interface (TLI), and the first release of the STREAMS communication facility. There were also some performance and security enhancements although many of these security enhancements were at the user level. By the end of 1987, there were an estimated 750,000 UNIX installations and 4.5 million users.

1.2 Politics and the battle for standards

The last version of SVR3 was version 2. AT&T System V Release 4 (SVR4), however, was almost a total rewrite of the System V kernel and in the following section we take a look at the developments that led up to the release of SVR4, and at why AT&T embarked on such a huge project, and how it has gained public acceptance.

1.2.1 The user's dilemma

Having looked briefly at the history and evolution of the UNIX operating system, it is apparent so far that UNIX has emerged as a portable operating system, that is, it is easily ported to various hardware architectures. Rich in functionality, it is a multi-tasking, multi-user operating system that is efficient and powerful, elegant, yet simple. However, there lies one major dilemma for UNIX users: which version or variant of UNIX should they base their application on?

While UNIX had emerged as the de facto standard for multi-user operating systems, it is by no means the basis for a public standard. In the late 1980s UNIX was owned by AT&T, and AT&T's own licensees were and still are the vendors who compete for AT&T's own UNIX business. Then there were the other variants. For example, Sun Microsystems, Inc. with their enhancements to the BSD variation of the UNIX operating system cornered a huge part of the graphical workstation market, and Microsoft's PC based variation, XENIX, also had a large following. XENIX was at one time installed on more systems than any other version of UNIX. Up-and-coming features such as MIT's X Window System, Sun Microsystems, Inc. Networked File System (NFS), and many others, were and still are designed on BSD based variants of the operating system.

The success of System V led many vendors to emulate System V on their 4.2BSD systems. In other instances, vendors of System V based computer systems were emulating 4.2BSD systems. Some even provided both environments. Also, many BSD features have been adopted by System V such as the vi(1) editor, the *curses(3X)* package, directory manipulation facilities, and so on.

Thus, users started to turn to the standards organizations in the hope that an organizational body would define a single version of the UNIX operating system that is compliant with 4.xBSD, Microsoft XENIX and UNIX System V so that the user does not have to worry about which version of the operating system to choose.

1.2.2 SVID

In 1985 AT&T published a two-volume document called the *System V Interface Definition* (SVID). This copyrighted but non-proprietary publication (often referred to as "the purple book", named after the color of its cover) documented the SVR2 interface in a codified form. The document offered a standard which defined the UNIX system library and command interface. In addition to the SVID, AT&T also provided the System V Verification Suite (SVVS), a set of utilities and programs which verify if a system conforms to the SVID. The purpose of this document was to specify an operating system environment that allows users to create hardware independent application software.

AT&T took their SVID very seriously. Consequently, vendors were allowed to give their version of UNIX the label "System V" only if it conformed to the SVID. This proved to be difficult for many vendors since adding enhancements or modifying the operating system could prevent their version of UNIX passing the SVVS conformance tests. The effect was that a vendor had the choice of either supplying a compliant UNIX System V operating system that was void of the enhancements users required, or supplying a UNIX system that didn't comply with the SVID standard but didn't attract users because of the worry of being locked in to a particular vendor's version of UNIX. Thus, users started to turn to other emerging organizations and standards such as POSIX and X/Open.

1.2.3 POSIX

In 1986 the Institute of Electrical and Electronic Engineers (IEEE) Committee formed its "Trial-Use" standard 1003.1, the first emerging standard for a portable operating system for computer environments. AT&T at this time retained UNIX as a proprietary name and so the name POSIX (Portable Operating System based on UNIX) was adopted. The committee, known as the POSIX committee, largely derives from the UniForum Committee (formally known as /usr/group Standards Committee [UniForum 1989]) who adopted an earlier /usr/group proposal for a portable operating system standard. Since its inauguration, the POSIX committee has proposed a number of specifications for a standard and there are at present 10 subcommittees (see Table 1.2) whose aim is to produce an International Standards Organization (ISO) standard for a portable operating system environment. In 1988 "Draft 13" was published and was balloted as a *full-use* version of the standard later adopted by ISO. POSIX offers a potential solution to users who require conformance to a standard product recognized by a formal standards body. POSIX is still evolving and at the time of this writing, there are only four fully approved standards in the POSIX suite (Table 1.3). However, in the coming years it is highly likely that other already approved POSIX projects will become standard [UniForum 1993]. A list of the approved POSIX projects proposed for ISO standards approval is given in Appendix G.

1.2.4 X/Open

The X/Open consortium was formulated in 1984 as an international non-profit based organization, by five independent European computer manufacturers. It is not a standards-setting organization but rather a consortium whose purpose is to bring together computer system vendors who have an interest in developing an open, Common Applications Environment (CAE) based on de facto and international standards. The goal of the X/Open CAE is to "provide a comprehensive development and run-time environment for portable application software".

Table 1.2: *Subcommittees of the POSIX Technical Committee*

Distributed file systems
Network interface
Internationalization
Security
Performance measurements
Realtime
Super-computing
Usability
Transaction processing
C++

Table 1.3: *Approved POSIX standards (as of this writing)*

Standard	Description
IEEE P1003.1	POSIX Application/Operating System Interface
IEEE P1003.3	General Test Methods
IEEE P1003.5	Ada Bindings for P1003.1
IEEE P1003.9	FORTRAN-77 Bindings for P1003.1

Table 1.4: *X/Open XPG3 component specification*

Source code transfer	IPC	ADA Language
Window Manager	Transport Interface	PC Inter-working
ISAM	SQL	Terminal Interface
COBOL Language	FORTRAN Language	PASCAL Language
Internationalization		
System calls & libraries	Commands & utilities	C Language
Hardware		

In a similar fashion to AT&T's SVID, the X/Open consortium published in 1988 its X/Open Portability Guide (XPG) [X/Open 1988] which offers a specification that defines the interfaces of the CAE and integrates the series of environment components required by a portable application. The most recent XPG specification is XPG3 which defines interfaces ranging from system utilities to networking services (see Table 1.4).

Again, in a similar fashion to AT&T's SVVS, the X/Open consortium provided an X/Open conformance test suite called VSX, currently VSX3. These tests (5,500 of them) verify that a system's software environment conforms to the X/Open specification. Upon completion of these tests, a conformance report is generated to identify the degree of conformance. The report is then used to determine if a vendor's system is qualified for the XPG3 branding program. Products that successfully pass the tests can then bear the X/Open Brand as a symbol of conformance to the X/OPEN CAE.

Compared to AT&T's SVID, the X/Open CAE has catered for several areas that go beyond AT&T's effort to provide a standard. The XPG addresses some areas not included in the SVID — for example, window interfaces, data management, relational databases, commands and utilities and so on. The CAE also adopts the policy that it will always recognize public standards. Thus, it fully supports the POSIX standard, indeed it incorporates many of the specifications from the original POSIX draft. Figure 1.1 shows the genealogy of UNIX system implementations and standards.

1.3 AT&T UNIX System V Release 4

The dilemma of which UNIX system to choose was compounded by the proliferation of standards: UNIX System V, 4.xBSD or Microsoft XENIX? SVID, X/Open or POSIX? Finally, in 1989 AT&T — the licensee of all versions of UNIX, and whose operating system is the base for all the aforementioned standards — produced the UNIX System V Release 4 (SVR4) operating system which offered to compound everything (see Figure 1.2).

1.3.1 UNIX International

In December 1988 a group of companies convened to form a non-profit organization called "UNIX International" (UI). Since several variants of UNIX system standards were evolving, vendors were perturbed at the likelihood of having to support a multitude of different UNIX operating systems, and the market made it obvious that a single operating system standard was a prerequisite for building a common application interface. This was the motive for the creation of UNIX International.

UNIX International has offered to be responsible for "directing the evolution of UNIX System V, the industry-standard open operating system for multi-user computing", and has provided "the structure for the entire UNIX System community to participate directly in defining the direction of UNIX System V".

Members of UI (of which AT&T is a corporate member) come to a consensus over a set of requirements and specifications for future versions of System V. These specifications are passed on to AT&T's UNIX Software Operation (USO) who code, test and license the new version of the operating system. Requirement proposals are solicited from its members and other standards organizations such as X/Open and POSIX. In 1990, UNIX International released the UNIX System V Road Map, which outlined the requirements for the future development of UNIX System V.

Figure 1.1: *UNIX System Genealogy: Implementations and Standards[1]*

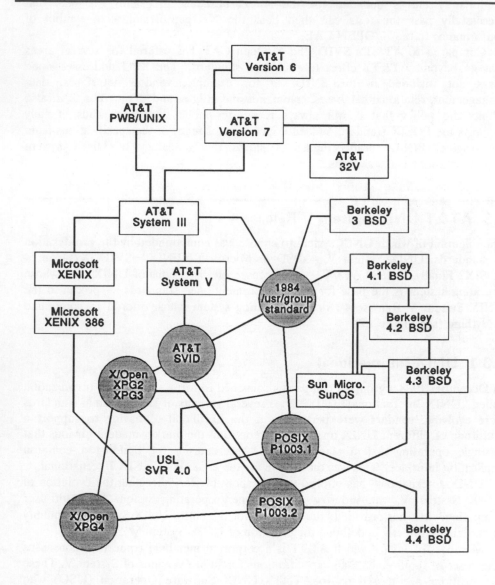

Figure 1.2: *Features of AT&T UNIX System V Release 4*

TCP/IP   BSD
C shell
Sockets
Job control
Symbolic links
4.3BSD signal enhancements
Berkeley fast file system (UFS)
Multiple groups and file ownership
Selection of commands and system calls

vnodes
Open Look   SunOS
Memory mapped files
Networked File System (NFS)
Remote Procedure Call (RPC)
External Data Representation (XDR)

Shared libraries
Enhanced signals   System V.3
File System Switch (FSS)
Remote File Sharing (RFS)
Transport Layer Interface (TLI)
STREAMS communication facility
Inter Process Communication (IPC)

Source code compatibility   XENIX
80386 Binary compatibility

Korn shell
Real time   NEW in System V.4
Service access facility
STREAMS enhancements
Virtual File System (VFS)
Multi National Language Support (MNLS)

1.3.2 Univel UnixWare

In April 1991 AT&T announced its intentions to sell off a proportion of its software company, UNIX System Laboratories, Inc. (formerly USO) in an effort to establish it as an independent company. Novell, Inc. the largest supplier of PC based networking products, bought a large percentage of USL's offering in an effort to move into the UNIX desktop market. In October of the same year, the two companies revealed plans for a joint venture.

In December 1991 USL and Novell, Inc. formed Univel, a joint venture to deliver a desktop version of UNIX System V Release 4, tightly coupled with Novell's NetWare operating system. Just under a year later, Univel's first product, UnixWare, began shipping.

1.3.3 Novell UNIX System V Release 4

In June 1993 the UNIX operating system's commercial acceptance took an even bigger step forward when AT&T announced the sale of UNIX System Laboratories, Inc. to Novell, Inc. Although seen as a boost to UNIX (since it improved the chances of it becoming a major player in desktop computing), the reaction from the UNIX community of Novells strategy was one of wary. Concerned for its future, users sparked rumours that Novell would limit UNIX's openness (particularly in the light that it was now owned by a single vendor). However, in October 1993 Novell announced its release of the UNIX trademark and conformance certification to X/Open Co. Ltd. The announcement was met with open arms by all major UNIX system vendors.

Figure 1.3: *Convergence of UNIX versions and standards*

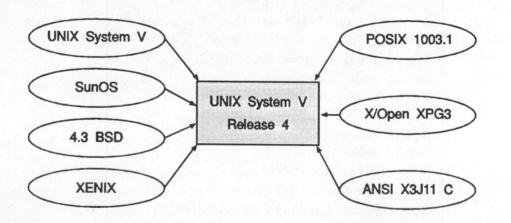

1.3.4 Summary

The differences between SVR3 and SVR4 are many. SVR4 merges four of the most popular derivatives of the UNIX system into a single standard operating system that provides backwards compatability to all four versions. The four operating systems (Figure 1.3) are: Berkeley Software Distribution 4.3 (4.3BSD), AT&T UNIX System V Release 3, SunOS and Microsoft XENIX System V.

SVR4s power and flexibility is what makes it unique amongst operating systems. It has evolved by the efforts of both commercial and academic interests, and has taken more than two decades in the making. It is the largest unification of UNIX system variants to cross the industry and represents a firm assurance of the continued success of the UNIX system. The fact that it has probably taken millions of man-hours to produce during its 20+ year evolution means that no commercial institute could possibly hope to repeat its complex elements of design.

CHAPTER 2

Concepts
and facilities

Unix is simple and coherent, but it takes a genius (or at any rate, a programmer) to understand and appreciate the simplicity.

— Dennis M. Ritchie

2.1 Introduction

This chapter provides a high-level overview of the facilities provided by the UNIX operating system. Most of the concepts discussed in this chapter must be understood before you proceed with the much more detailed discussions in following chapters.

If you are an experienced UNIX user, you will no doubt be familiar with the concepts discussed in the earlier parts of this chapter. However, unless you understand them fully, the rest of this book may be difficult to follow. For this reason, we have provided it.

2.2 Philosophy

It has been said that "Onions and UNIX have two things in common; they both have shell-like structures, and both cause tears to flow from those who look beneath the surface". The first part of this statement is true (see Figure 2.1), and to the uninitiated, the second part could well be true also. But hopefully this book will help wipe those tears away.

The basic philosophy of UNIX is "to build upon the work of others". Like an onion, the UNIX system is built up from layers, with each layer representing a building block that can be used to build other building blocks, and so on. This is in fact one of the very reasons why UNIX has gained such popularity. Most programs and commands supplied with the UNIX system can be used in combination with each other to build other tools, and complex mechanisms can be built up from a single line of commands to perform vast assortments of functions.

Figure 2.1: *A high-level perspective of the UNIX architecture*

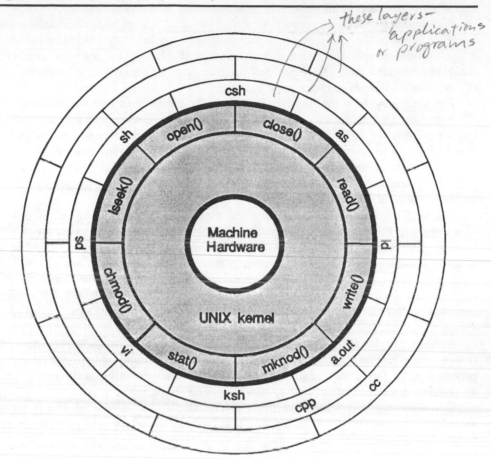

*these layers—
applications
or programs*

2.2.1 The user interface

Users interact with the UNIX operating system through application programs that are often called utilities.

One such utility is called **ttymon(1M)**, which simply monitors an inactive terminal, waiting for a user to come along and request the use of the system. A user must first logon to the system by typing his or her *account name* and *password*. The **login(1)** program, started by **ttymon** uses a list of account names and encrypted passwords maintained in files, to confirm that a user logging into the system is legitimately registered to do so. Once successfully logged in, the user is usually given a utility with which to type commands. A utility such as this is called a command-line interpreter.

Each user of the system is given a *home* directory which forms part of the hierarchical structure of directories in the UNIX file system. When a user logs in, he is given immediate access to his home directory and any other files and directories in it. He may create, remove or modify files as he sees fit. Thus, the user's home directory is his own, private hierarchical directory structure.

The command-line interpreter is called a *shell*. It provides an interactive interface between the user and other user programs. A facility provided by the shell is a built-in interpretive command-language that allows the user to construct complex command lines. Its high-level programming language also allows the user to combine commands to create new programs.

The shell provides a method by which the user can interact with the resources of the computer system, such as other programs and files, devices and communication facilities. Typically, the shell displays a prompt on the terminal screen which signifies that it is ready to be told what command to execute next (reminiscent of the saying "I am at your command, O master"). The user types commands at the prompt (called a command line) and the shell promptly carries them out, usually by calling on the services of other programs.

The shell's low-level primitives allow the user to manipulate the input and output of a program. For example, it is possible to redirect the output of a program so that instead of displaying the information on the terminal screen it is directed to a file. It is also possible to take the output of a command and use it as input to another. Another feature of the shell is its ability to run programs (or jobs) in the background. Features such as these, combined with the shell's built-in programming language, allow the user to construct his or her own shell programs (called *shell scripts*).

Although the shell provides a relatively simple interface for the novice user, its power and flexibility allows the experienced user to build simple yet complex procedures. In fact, many administrative tasks are done by using shell-scripts, such as shutting down the system, adding new users and so on.

UNIX System V Release 4 supports several shells, one of which is the program called */bin/sh*; we call it a *shell* because it is typically the outer-shell layer above the kernel (see Figure 2.1).

2.2.2 The user's credentials

The kernel identifies a user by a unique integer called a User ID (UID). A user is also a member of a group of users identified by an integer called a Group ID (GID). Both these variables are stored within the user-area of each running process (see § 4.2.4) and can be set by the *setuid* and *setgid* system calls. For security reasons, the kernel imposes strict rules governing the use of these system calls. The **login** process is generally responsible for setting the UID and GID for the user's login shell. These variables are then inherited by other processes created by the user which are subsequently used by the kernel to validate such things as file access permissions, program execution permissions, and so on.

2.2.3 The privileged user

The only user that specific code is included for in the kernel is the user whose effective or real UID is equal to zero. This user is called the *super-user* or *root* and is given privileges to override all file access and execution permissions imposed by the system. The super-user is given the power to create, modify, or remove any file administered by the system. More important, he or she is given control of the system as a whole and can initiate such operations as shutting the system down or even inadvertently destroying it with a single command!

In view of this, it is hoped (and, more important, assumed by the kernel) that the person who has access to the system as super-user knows what he or she is doing. Typically this user is responsible for supervising the UNIX facility, and thus, will already be familiar with basic UNIX operating system administration procedures. The super-user will have such responsibilities as maintaining the security of the system, configuring the system, adding and deleting users, maintaining regular backups and so on.

Apart from the super-user, the kernel makes no provision to single out any other user (i.e., those users with UIDs which are not equal to zero). All other users are treated equally and are given privileges to access only those files whose access permissions allow them to.

In addition to access and execute permissions, the kernel imposes a resource management policy which limits what operating environment a user process may work in. Such limitations include maximum file creation size, maximum number of shared memory slots, maximum allowed disk-space-usage and so on. Although these limitations are configurable (or tuneable, as is said in the UNIX world), the super-user is usually exempt from such limitations and can thus override most of them during normal system use.

2.2.4 User programs and commands

Applications or programs such as those shown in the outer layers of the diagram in Figure 2.1 (the *shell*, for example) are executable files. That is, they are stored as files in a file system and are constructed in a form which the UNIX system recognizes as runnable programs containing machine instructions. Executable programs are generated by a compiler which takes a text file containing a high level language source program of some sort, and produces from it a machine runnable object or executable.

Compilers are very specific and will only accept and recognize a grammar they have been specifically designed for. There may be many types of compiler on a UNIX system, each for a specific language. Since almost all of the UNIX operating system and the user programs supplied with it are written in the C language, this is the standard language used for writing other programs on the UNIX system. Thus, a C language compiler is provided as a standard feature of the UNIX system.

Previously we learned that programs can be intermixed or combined with each other to produce other tools. The C compiler (better known as the program **cc**) is a good example of this concept. The **cc(1)** program calls on the services of other programs such as the C preprocessor (**cpp(1)**), assembler (**as(1)**) and link editor (**ld(1)**) before finally generating a runnable program.

A compiler is also responsible for checking the syntax of a program code. For example, it will fail to produce a final executable if there is a grammatical error in the text. Additionally, a compiler can produce a final executable only if there are no unresolved references to routines or variables specified within the program. In such cases it may be necessary to instruct the compiler to link into the program a library of routines to resolve these references. This again emphasizes the building block philosophy of UNIX, since UNIX is supplied with a vast range of libraries containing functions for different purposes which can be linked into a program. There are libraries containing mathematics functions, screen manipulation functions, networking functions, and many more. A programmer merely has to reference the required function in his program and link the relevant library containing it into his program at compile time. The internals of how the function works are totally transparent, indeed the programmer need not know how it is implemented, only how it is supposed to be used.

Source code compatibility

Libraries such as those discussed are standard across all implementations of UNIX System V Release 4. Thus it is easy to transport a program in source code form, from one UNIX system to another, and recompile it to produce an exact functioning copy on the new system, regardless of the possible differences in hardware architecture.

2.3 The UNIX kernel

A computer system is symbiotic in the sense that its hardware and its software are totally dependent upon one another and neither is of any use without the other. At the center of the diagram in Figure 2.1 is the machine hardware. It entails peripheral devices, processors, memory, hard disks and other bits of electronics which collectively form the computer engine. However, without software to manipulate it, the engine itself is useless. The software that performs this task is called the operating system; in UNIX terminology it is called "the UNIX kernel". The UNIX kernel is the low-level support software that interacts with the hardware to provide a defined set of services for user programs.

The basic services provided by the kernel are as follows:

- *System initialization* — the operating system has to incorporate a facility to start up and initialize itself. The system provides a "bootstrap" facility so that a copy of the UNIX kernel can be loaded into the machine memory and start running. This facility is usually only required when the computer hardware is first turned on.

- *Process management* — UNIX provides a facility to manage the creation, termination and control of processes. Since UNIX is a multi-processing operating system, the kernel ensures that every running process is given a fair share of system execution time and resources so that it can simulate the execution of all processes in parallel.

- *Memory management* — a process can run only if it resides in physical memory. However, a process's address space may be restricted to the amount of physical memory installed in the computer hardware. To help overcome this, the UNIX kernel implements a virtual-memory machine. The system provides mechanisms to multiplex individual virtual-address spaces for processes and map virtual-addresses to physical addresses at runtime. Thus, conceptually, a process has no memory restrictions other than those imposed by the operating system.

- *File system management* — a UNIX file system is normally an organized hierarchy of directories containing files, and the UNIX system maintains many types of files. Some may contain data or ASCII text, others may be special files representing hardware devices. There are object files, executable files and so on. File systems typically reside on a physical medium such as a hard disk and are accessed via system services. There are several file systems supported by UNIX System V Release 4. However, the system is independent of file system type and it is flexible enough to incorporate a number of file system structures.

- *Communication facilities* — the kernel provides many communication facilities such as: inter-process communication, inter-machine communication (networks) and communication between devices and processes.

- *Programmatic interface* — to enable a process to access the services of the operating system the kernel provides a set of system calls (or hooks) furnished as a subroutine library stored in the file system.

2.3.1 Kernel software organization

The source code for the kernel software as licensed from UNIX System Laboratories, Inc. is distributed for a particular processor type. The greatest portion of the operating system is written in the C language and is easily transportable to other architectures. However a small portion of the distributed software is machine dependent and contains a mixture of C and processor specific assembler. Porting the UNIX system kernel to another machine architecture requires the low-level machine dependent parts of the kernel to be rewritten in an assembler for that particular machine's processor type. However, the machine dependent parts of the kernel are cleverly isolated from the main body of the kernel code and are relatively easy to construct once their purpose is understood. The machine dependent parts of the kernel include:

- Low-level system initialization and bootstrap.
- Fault, trap, interrupt and exception handling.
- Memory management: hardware address translation.
- Low-level kernel/user-mode process context switching.
- I/O device driver and device initialization code.

The rest of the UNIX kernel is extremely transportable and is largely made up of the system call interface that application programs request services from.

2.3.2 Kernel source code organization

The source code for the system is usually stored in the directory */usr/src/uts/machine* where *machine* is a symbolic name referring to a particular machine architecture. For example, **3b2**, **i386**, **mips**, and so on. Within this directory are other directories containing C source code and assembler, making up the kernel software:

- *boot* — contains the source code for bootstrapping the UNIX kernel. The bootstrap procedure is responsible for locating the disk containing the boot block partition (track 0). The boot block typically contains two programs for bringing the system into operation. The first program called **mboot** is brought into execution by the machine's microcode. This first stage boot procedure simply loads the second stage boot program called **boot** which is responsible for loading the kernel (*/stand/unix*) into memory and transferring control to the start address of it. The kernel starts, runs through its auto-configuration and internal data structure initialization procedures, and finally starts the UNIX system environment.

- *os* — mainly contains the source code for the management of processes and files. It includes the code for process accounting, system call interface, file descriptor manipulation, process manipulation, management of credentials, real time clock routines, common error and exception handling, signal manipulation, scheduling and swap system, stack, physical memory and virtual memory manipulation, inter-process communication system, hash and caching algorithms, system buffer manipulation, STREAMS system and other facilities that make up the general parts of the system kernel.

- *sys* — contains all the C language include files (or header files) for the operating system. They define each data structure used as well as some global variables and other data type definitions. It is a common practice for structures like *struct foo* to be defined in a file named *foo.h*. For example, *struct user* is defined in a file called *user.h*, *struct proc* is defined in a file called *proc.h*.

- *fs* — contains the source code for specific file system dependent subsystems. For example, the file management subsystems for *nfs, rfs, proc, ufs, s5* and others reside here. It also contains the code for *vfs* and *vnode* management.

- *io* — contains the source code for the I/O management subsystem and its device drivers. There are several generic device drivers supplied with the operating system but many of these require modification to suit a specific hardware platform.

- *disp* — contains the source code for the dispatch low-level process switching operations. It includes the code for the class specific real-time and time-shared routines as well as the class specific priority scheduling algorithms.

- *exec* — contains the source code for reading in an executable file and starting the execution of it. It also includes the code that manipulates *COFF* and *ELF* file formats.

- *vm* — contains the source code that handles the memory and virtual memory management subsystems.

- *debug* — contains the source code for the kernel debugging subsystem.

- *master.d* — contains files and directories that describe the system configuration. Almost all the various tables defined in the UNIX kernel are tuneable and are changed by modifying a constant called a *tuneable parameter*. These tuneable parameters are normally found in a file called *kernel* in this directory.

- *ml* — contains the machine dependent portions of the operating system and may contain a mixture of C programs and assembler files.

2.4 The UNIX file system

A file system provides a convenient method for organizing and storing files. All files under the UNIX operating system, no matter what their type, reside in a *file system*.

The UNIX file system is a tree-like structured organization of directories and files (see Figure 2.2). The *root* of a UNIX file system tree is signified by the character "/" (known as *slash*). A file can be uniquely identified by specifying its *absolute* (or full) pathname with respect to "/". For example, the full pathname for the shell program is */bin/sh*. A pathname that is not preceded with a slash is called a *relative pathname* and signifies that the file is found in the current *working* directory.

A process identifies a file by associating itself with the file corresponding to its specified pathname. Additionally, a process's notion of its root directory is the highest point in the file system tree that the process can access. This is usually the root of the entire UNIX file system but may be somewhere within the file system tree if a *chroot* system call has been made. The directory specified in the *chroot* system call then becomes its root or "/" of the file system tree and the process cannot see outside this area even if the file system tree extends beyond it.

The kernel associates two directories with every running process: the *current working directory*, signified by the file name "." (known as *dot*), and the current working directories *parent directory*, signified by the file name ".." (or *dot-dot*). A process changes its current working directory with the *chdir* system call. For example, the call:

```
chdir("..");
```

makes the current working directory for the process change to its parent directory (or the next level up the tree towards the root). The top level directory is always its own parent directory.

The UNIX system provides many utilities to manipulate files and directories in a file system. An example of some of these utilities is given in Table 2.1. The UNIX file system is organized into a well-known directory structure that remains consistent across all versions of UNIX System V Release 4. All the commands depicted in

Figure 2.2: *File system directory structure*

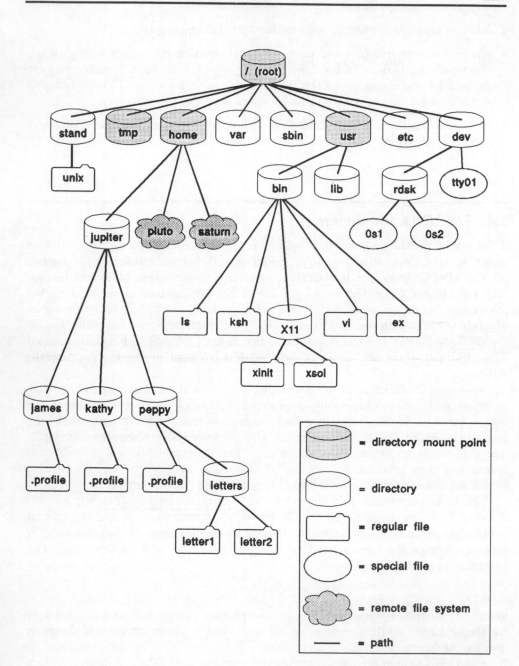

Table 2.1: *Example of file and directory manipulation commands*

Command	Description
cp	Copy files
rm	Remove files
mv	Rename (move) a file
mkdir	Create a new directory
rmdir	Remove a directory
ls	List the contents of a directory
cat	Print or list a file's contents
chown	Change the access mode of a file

Table 2.1, along with the many other system utilities supplied with the operating system, are situated in well-defined places within the UNIX file system hierarchy.

2.4.1 File system structure

A file system normally resides on a disk or other fixed medium that is block structured. Apart from the hierarchy of directories and files stored in a file system, there are also reserved areas used specifically for administration.

The actual layout of a file system depends on what type of file system it is because the UNIX System V Release 4 kernel is independent of a file system's structure. There are several different types of file system supported by the operating system. However, we will discuss these in more detail later. For now, we will discuss the two most commonly known file systems: the traditional UNIX System V file system called *s5*, and the *ufs* file system derived from the BSD universe. The *s5* file system uses a *flat* file system containing four specific sections. A *ufs* file system uses a sequence of sections that are repeated throughout the disk partition (see Figure 2.3). In both cases, a single boot-block is reserved at the beginning of the file system:

- *boot block* — this area contains bootstrap programs that bring the UNIX system into operation. On *s5* file systems, if the file system is not a bootable file system (i.e., not a root file system), then this area is still present, but left unused.

- *Super block* — the super block is used purely as an area for administering the file system as a whole. It contains the list of free-blocks and *inodes* (information nodes) that are assigned to files, and other administrative information. A *ufs* file system has multiple copies of the super block to improve file system integrity. Each copy of the super block is 8192 bytes in size and only one super block is used while the file system is mounted. The critical information within each super block is static, so it does not change during file system use. A copy of the super block may be used as a backup if the primary super block is corrupt or inconsistent at the time of mounting.

- *Cylinder group block* — a cylinder group contains a number of *inodes* specified in the *ilist* for the cylinder group, and a number of data blocks pertinent to them.

The size of the cylinder group block is dependent on the file system size.

Currently, this is implemented only on *ufs* type file systems. To improve disk accessing efficiency, the *ufs* file system attempts to allocate *inodes* and data blocks from the same cylinder group.

- *ilist* — the maximum number of files that can be created in a file system depends on the number of *inodes* available. Thus, a file system with, say, 100 megabytes of unused disk space but with only one *inode* available, will allow the creation of only one more file, regardless of its file size.

  The *ilist* is the list of *inodes* configured into a file system. An *inode* is used to store information pertinent to a file such as its access permission modes, the time it was created, updated and last modified, the UID and GID of its creator and so on. *Inodes* are file system implementation specific. The concept of *inodes* is discussed in § 6.10.

- *Data blocks* — the rest of the file system is devoted to the actual data blocks used by files within it. In the case of the *ufs* file system, an attempt is made to place the data blocks in cylinder groups. The physical size of each data block is dependent on how the file system was formated with **mkfs(1M)**. Depending on the file system's type, it may be formated in 512, 1024, 2048, 4096 or 8192 byte blocks.

2.4.2 Mountable file systems

Files in a UNIX file system are accessible only if the file system is mounted. Files in an unmounted file system are not seen by the operating system and so do not form part of the file system tree.

File systems are mounted with the *mount* system call and can be mounted onto any directory. A directory used as a place to mount a file system onto is called a *directory mount point*. A file system classed as *dirty* (i.e., corrupt or inconsistent) cannot be mounted until it is repaired. The system provides utilities for checking the consistency of a file system and can attempt to repair them on request. One such utility is called **fsck(1M)**, which does a pretty thorough job.

Programs wishing to obtain status information about a file system may do so using the *statvfs* and *fstatvfs* system calls. Both of these system calls replace the UNIX System V Release 3 *statfs* system call, although it is still provided in a subroutine library for backwards compatibility.

Normally, a directory mount point is an empty directory, although the system does not require that it should be. However, once a file system is mounted onto a directory mount point, files that were accessible in the directory before the file system was mounted remain inaccessible until the file system is unmounted again via the *umount* system call.

File systems cannot be unmounted while they are *busy* (i.e., being used). A file system is classed as busy if a process is associated with it, or if any files stored in it are open. Therefore, it can be seen that the root file system can never be unmounted and so is always present. During system startup, the kernel automatically mounts the root file system onto an in-core mount point (§ 6.6.1).

Figure 2.3: *ufs and s5 file systems on disk*

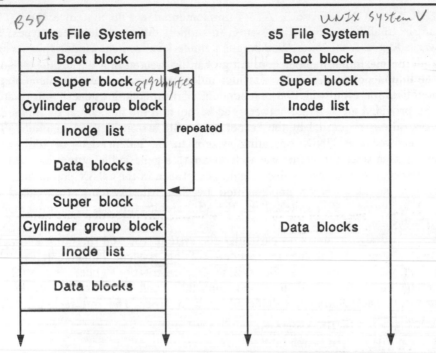

Thus, the root file system is the starting-point for all file systems, other file systems may be mounted onto it, and other file systems may be mounted onto directory mount points within those mounted file systems. A file system, once mounted, becomes part of the overall UNIX file system tree and is always referenced with respect to the root file system.

2.4.3 Storage devices for file systems

A typical UNIX installation supports several file systems on several devices, and a single device may contain many file systems. Typically, a single device such as a hard disk is partitioned into several individual logical devices, each containing a separate file system. However, the UNIX system gives the user an illusion that there is one file system only, although it may consist of several individual file systems which collectively form one virtual file system. For example, /usr normally resides on its own partition as a separate file system, so it usually exists as a separate disk or as a separate partition on a disk.

A file system is initialized to a clean, empty state and space is set aside for all the files and directories that can be created within it. No system calls are supported for either formatting or organizing a device into a file system. Utilities such as **format(1M)**, **fmthard(1M)** are used to format a hard disk and **mkfs(1M)** is used to create a file system. They perform these operations by writing directly to the device.

2.4.4 File system interface

In UNIX System V Release 3, AT&T implemented a File System Switch (FSS) mechanism to allow the operating system to support different file system types. The FSS was adopted from Peter Weinberger's *inode* level switch. Under this scheme, the *inode* is split into two parts consisting of a file system dependent portion and a file system independent portion. The dependent portion contains implementation dependent information while the independent portion contains generic information. The FSS provided an interface between the kernel and the file system by forwarding *inode* operations requested by the kernel to the file system dependent *inode*. This scheme allowed the UNIX operating system to be independent of file system implementation since the kernel was only aware of a generic file system independent *inode*. However, this scheme failed to gain acceptance in the UNIX community who preferred a similar scheme implemented by Sun Microsystems, Inc. called the Virtual File System (VFS) switch. Thus, the VFS architecture has been implemented in UNIX System V Release 4.

The VFS design assumes no particular file system type and therefore allows the operating system to become independent of file system implementation. The underlying mechanisms of a file system implementation under the VFS are completely hidden from both user and application and there are no system calls provided for manipulating a specific file system type. The interface uses three components:

- A Virtual File System switch table — *struct vfssw vfssw[]*
- A Virtual File System structure — *struct vfs*
- A Virtual inode structure — *struct vnode*

The VFS table contains an element for each configured file system type, and each element describes what operations can be done to the file system while it is active. A VFS structure is allocated for each active (i.e., mounted) file system. It describes the operations that can be done within the file system itself. A *vnode* structure is allocated for each active file of the whole UNIX file system tree. A *vnode* describes the operations that can be done to a file (or object) within a file system. The kernel's generic abstraction of a file is, therefore, represented by a *vnode*; it is the focus of all file activity taking place in the kernel. The file system implementation is responsible for specifying the *vnode* operations. Thus, the kernel does not care about a file's domicile or construction. It leaves those responsibilities to the file system's implementation.

By using this scheme, the kernel is independent of file or file system type since system services such as *read, write, open, close*, and others, perform their actions on a file via its corresponding *vnode* operations. The kernel cares only about the management of these data structures. How the individual operations are implemented is of no concern to the kernel. The file system dependent functionality is handled by each individual file system but the kernel hides the dependencies from the user and provides a consistent interface to all file systems. The user need not know what type of file system he is using even if the underlying file system architectures are totally different in character. For example, both a locally resident disk based file system and a remote file system accessible over a network are presented to the user as a single virtual file system.

A detailed discussion of the VFS and VFS operations is given in § 6.5.

2.4.5 File system types

The VFS interface provides a facility for allowing a number of various file system types to coexist on the same installation. The traditional UNIX System V file system (known as the *s5* file system), which is the standard file system used in previous releases of the UNIX System V operating system, is now just one of the many different file systems supported under UNIX System V Release 4. The modular design of the VFS allows for the incorporation of various file system types, even those yet to be developed, and the installation of a new file system can now be done with nearly as much ease as installing a device driver.

Among the several file systems supported by UNIX System V Release 4 are those which provide access to remote resources such as Sun Microsystems, Inc., Networked File System (NFS).

The default file system used by UNIX System V Release 4 is the Berkeley Fast File System (FFS) [McKusick, Joy, Leffler, Fabry 1984], now called the UNIX File System (UFS). UFS is a far more efficient file system and provides enhancements such as:

- *255 byte file names* — previous releases of UNIX System V allowed only 14 bytes for a file name.

- *8192 byte blocks* — support for up to 8k byte block structured file systems is now provided allowing fast disk I/O transfers. The traditional UNIX System V file system supports only 512, 1024 or 2048 byte block structured file systems with a default of 1024 byte blocks.

- *multiple super blocks* — multiple copies of the super block provide backups against super block corruption.

Although the traditional UNIX System V file system is still supported in UNIX System V Release 4, it has now been reimplemented to suit the VFS architecture. The standard distribution of UNIX System V Release 4 comes with the following file system types, although for some of them installation is optional:

- *s5* — the traditional UNIX System V file system supported in earlier releases of the UNIX System V operating system from AT&T.

- *ufs* — the default and preferred file system used in UNIX System V Release 4. *ufs* was derived from Sun Microsystems, Inc. SunOS file system, which was in turn derived from the Berkeley fast file system (FSS).

- *nfs* — adopted from Sun Microsystems, Inc. SunOS operating system, *nfs* is the now commonly known Networked File System (NFS), which facilitates the sharing of files and directories across a network of heterogeneous computer systems with potentially different hardware architectures and/or operating systems.

- *rfs* — the Remote File Sharing (RFS) system was introduced in UNIX System V Release 3. While NFS was designed by Sun Microsystems, Inc., RFS was designed by AT&T, although conceptually they both provide the same types of facility. That is, they both facilitate the sharing of files across a network. However, RFS requires the computer system to be running UNIX System V Release 3.0 or a later version of the operating system.

- *specfs* — this new file system type provides a common interface to all special files described in the */dev* directory.

- *fifofs* — this new file system uses the VFS to implement STREAMS based First In First Out (FIFO) files (also known as *pipes*).

- *bfs* — stands for "*boot* file system". It contains all the necessary support utilities for bringing the UNIX operating system (the kernel) into operation. Its purpose is to allow a quick and simple booting procedure and so it is a very simple flat file system consisting of a single directory.

- */proc* — this file system type provides access to the address space image of each active process in the system. It is typically used by debugging and tracing utilities.

- */dev/fd* — this file system provides a convenient method for referencing open file descriptors. For example, the files */dev/fd/0, /dev/fd/1* and */dev/fd/2* can be used to reference file descriptors 0, 1, and 2 (*stdin, stdout* and *stderr*).

A more detailed discussion of file system related subjects is given in Chapter 6. For now, it is only important to realize that a file system may not necessarily be in the form of a traditional UNIX file system.

2.5 Files

Conceptually a file consists of a contiguous stream of bytes terminated by an end-of-file. However, in its physical manifestation a file may contain a series of blocks on disk or tape or even a RAM resident disk. Furthermore, the data blocks that belong to a file may be stored randomly across the media leaving potential holes free to be used by other files. A file may not necessarily be stored on magnetic media. It was not so long ago that files were stored as a series of holes punched into paper tape. A file may also manifest itself as a remote resource, i.e., not being part of the computer system that the user is logged into.

Since UNIX System V Release 4 provides support for a number of different file system types, for the purpose of the following sections we will discuss only those files used in a *traditional* UNIX file system. That is, a file system that resides on a locally fixed disk and contains the normal, everyday files and directories the user will be working with.

Under the UNIX operating system all I/O is performed through a file interface. Any program that has the ability to read or write to a file can, conceptually, read or write to everything and anything.

A UNIX file system may contain six different types of file:

- Regular files
- Directories
- Special files
- Named pipes (FIFO)
- Links
- Symbolic links

2.5.1 Regular files

A regular file (also known as an *ordinary file*) contains arbitrary data in zero or more data blocks stored within a file system. These files may simply contain ASCII text, or binary data. Individual applications may store their files in a specific format. For example, a database application may store records within a file in a format that is known only to the database application itself. There is no structure imposed by the operating system about how a regular file must be made up. The only exception is that a binary executable file (a program for building a process image) must be stored in *a.out* form (§ 4.2.1). However, even an *a.out* file is stored as a regular file. Unlike other operating systems, the UNIX operating system makes no distinction between regular files containing different forms of data.

Data blocks belonging to a regular file may not necessarily reside on disk in a contiguous order. However, the UNIX operating system hides this side effect from the user and presents a file as if it were a contiguous stream of bytes; the user does not need to be concerned with a file's underlying storage structure.

2.5.2 Directories

Directories are special types of files since they provide the mapping between the names of files and the files themselves. As a result of this, the structure of directories defines the structure of the file system as a whole.

The format of a directory is *flat*. That is, it consists of a table of entries each containing two distinct fields: an *inode* number, and a file name used to symbolically reference that *inode*. For example, the command **ls -ai** can be used to list the contents of the current directory (see **ls(1)**). Here is an example of its output:

inode number	File name
59	.
757	..
69	file_A
66	file_B
66	B_again
43	another_dir

Every entry in the directory table is used to map a file name to its corresponding *inode*. In the above example, the file named "file_B" is represented by *inode* number 66. File "B_again" has the same *inode* number as "file_B" — thus it is hard-linked to it (i.e., it is the same file but it has its own directory slot). The entry named "." represents the *inode* entry for the present working directory. The entry named ".." represents the *inode* entry for this directory's parent directory. Thus, to locate either the current or parent directory, the user can reference either "." or ".." respectively.

The file named "another_dir" is a directory type file although it is represented as a flat file in this directory. That is, it contains a sequence of bytes much like any other regular file. However, unlike a regular file, a directory cannot be written to by users although several utilities allow the super-user to manipulate them, such as the file system debugger, **fsdb(1M)**. However, it should be understood that most utilities that are available to manipulate directories (or file systems) are file system specific. For example, **fsdb** is specifically for use on an *s5* type file system. Directories that are manipulated with such utilities are done so via the raw device interface of the file system.

The only system calls available for use with directories are:

- *mkdir* — make a new directory
- *rmdir* — remove an empty directory
- *getdents* — read contents of a directory file

Thus, a directory type file cannot be written to. On the other hand, directory type files can be read freely by any process provided that it is privileged to do so.

2.5.3 Special files

Special files contain no data. Instead, they provide a mechanism to map physical devices to file names in a file system. Each device supported by the system, including memory, is associated with at least one special file. Special files are created with the *mknod* system call and have associated software incorporated into the kernel called *device drivers*. When a request to read or write to a special file is made it results in a direct activation of its associated device driver, which is responsible for passing data between its controlling process and associated physical device. For example, consider the following two commands:

```
$ cp /etc/passwd /tmp/garbage
$ cp /etc/passwd /dev/console
```

The first command simply copies the contents of the file */etc/passwd* to a file called */tmp/garbage*, effectively overwriting the file if it already existed, or creating it if it did not. However, the second command copies the file */etc/passwd* to the file */dev/console* which is the associated special file for the physical console terminal. The contents of the file */etc/passwd* will be displayed on the console screen.

There are two types of special files: *block-special* and *character-special*. A block-special file is associated with a block structured device such as a disk, which transfers data to the machine's memory in blocks, typically made up of 512, 1024,

4096 or 8192 bytes. The *mount* system call requires a block-special file, so a file system is stored on a block-special device. A character-special file is associated with any device that is not necessarily block structured. An example of character-special type devices are: terminals, system console, serial devices, and streaming tape drives. There are also some character-special files associated with disk drives.

When data is transferred via the block-special interface, the system buffers the data in an internal buffer cache. At specified intervals, the system updates the device by writing those portions of the buffer cache marked to be written. The system calls *sync* and *fsync* can be used within a user program to force the system to flush its buffer cache to the device, thereby synchronizing the disk and buffer cache. A problem with this design is that data integrity may suffer if the system should crash before the buffer cache and device are synchronized. So if the UNIX system fails, it is possible for unwritten data to be lost. More important, if the buffer cache contained blocks of data that belonged to the super block of a file system, then the file system could be left in an inconsistent state — in the worse case, it could be beyond repair!

Data transferred via the character-special interface is passed directly between device driver and controlling process without going through the system buffer cache. Hence, this form of device interface is often referred to as the *raw interface*.

2.5.4 Links

The UNIX file system provides a facility for linking files together with different file names. This facility is called *linking*. The purpose of linking files together is to allow a single program to administer different names. When the program is invoked, it can base its actions on its calling name given on the command line. An advantage of this is that there is only one copy of the program stored in the file system, which often results in a saving of valuable disk space. A good example of this is the UNIX visual screen editor **vi**. The **vi** program can operate in five different modes depending on its invocation name. Thus, it is programmed to check for **ex**, **edit**, **vi**, **view** and **vedit**. These five files are stored on the file system as individual files yet there is only one copy of its associated data blocks stored on the disk. This can be seen with the following two commands:

```
$ ls -i /usr/bin/vi
   372 /usr/bin/vi
$ ncheck -i 372 /dev/dsk/sc0d0s5
/dev/dsk/sc0d0s5:
372    /usr/bin/edit
372    /usr/bin/ex
372    /usr/bin/vedit
372    /usr/bin/vi
372    /usr/bin/view
```

Note that the third argument to **ncheck** (in our case it is */dev/dsk/sc0d0s5*) specifies the special file associated with the */usr* file system where these files are stored.

Previous releases of UNIX System V only allowed files to be *hard* linked (see **ln(1)**) by using the *link* system call. A hard link is a file that can only be linked to another file in the same file system. When a hard link is created, a new directory entry is made using the same *inode* number as the one that it is to be linked to. No data blocks or *inode* are reserved for it.

2.5.5 Symbolic links

A new file linking facility is provided with UNIX System V Release 4, which facilitates *soft* linking of files across file systems. This new facility is called a *symbolic link* and is implemented using the system call *symlink*. A symbolic link is a data file containing the name of the file it is supposed to be linked to. We say "supposed to be", because a symbolic link can be created even if the file it is supposed to be linked to does not exist. With symbolic links, both a directory entry and new *inode* are created. Additionally, a single data block is reserved for it containing the full pathname of the file it references.

Many system calls traverse a symbolic link file until the real file is found, then perform the actions expected of the system call on the real file. Thus, linked files do not have to reside on the same file system. The advantage of this is seen best when a file system is low in space but a new software package expects to be installed in it. A directory can be made on another file system which is then symbolically linked to the name of the expected installation directory.

There are three other system calls associated with symbolic links. Their purpose is to access the information relevant to the link itself as opposed to the file or directory it references. They are as follows:

- *readlink* — read the pathname of the file or directory that the symbolic link references. This information is stored within the symbolic link's associated data block.

- *lstat* — similar to the *stat* system call but is used, instead, to obtain information about the link itself.

- *lchown* — similar to the *chown* system call but is used, instead, to change the owner and group of the link itself.

2.5.6 Named pipes

A pipe is an interprocess communication facility. A pipe file is a special file that buffers up data received in its input so that a process that reads from its output receives the data on a first-in-first-out (FIFO) basis. No data is associated with a pipe special file although it does use up a directory entry and *inode*. Under UNIX System V Release 4, pipes are implemented using STREAMS communications modules (see Chapter 7).

2.5.7 Memory mapped files

A by-product of the new UNIX System V Release 4 Virtual Memory (VM) architecture is the ability to map the contents of a file (or device) as a series of bytes within a process's virtual address space. Once mapped into its address space, a process simply accesses the information as memory locations.

A more detailed explanation of the Virtual Memory system architecture is given in Chapter 3, and memory mapped files are discussed in § 5.9.

2.5.8 File removal

The *unlink* system call is used to remove a directory entry so that the file is removed from the file system. In practice, data blocks associated with a removed file remain intact. However, their associated data block pointers are reassigned, they are placed on the super block's free list ready to be assigned to another file.

In the case of a file with associated hard links, its associated data block pointers remain untouched until all associated links are removed. Thus, a file named A can be hard linked to file B. If file A is then removed, file B will still remain and it will contain the data associated with file A. If the file to be removed is a symbolic link, then the file it references remains intact but the symbolic link itself is removed.

With executable *a.out* files, the kernel locks those files that have associated process images resident (§ 4.2) Therefore, such files cannot be removed until their associated processes terminate. If a process has a file open for use, the *unlink* system call will remove the file but the space it occupies will remain intact until all references to the file are closed.

Directory type files are removed with the *rmdir* system call although they can be removed with the *unlink* system call if the user has super-user privileges. However, it is hoped that this person knows what he or she is doing. The preferred method for removing a directory type file is with *rmdir* since this system call will fail if the directory is not empty.

2.5.9 File names

The size of a file name is very much dependent on what has been imposed by the file system's directory structure implementation. The *s5* file system is limited to a maximum file name size of 14 bytes. The *ufs* file system uses a maximum file name size of 255 bytes.

Note that the *NAME_MAX* constant defined in */usr/include/limits.h* specifies that all file names, regardless of file system type, consist of 1 to *NAME_MAX* characters. The default value for *NAME_MAX* is 14 characters but on some implementations it is set to 255. Note that since this is not a tuneable parameter it cannot be reconfigured. However, it is meant to be a constraint for applications that wish to be portable. That is, if filenames are kept within this limit the application will work on almost all file system types. It is currently unused in the kernel although it may be used in future releases of the system. Thus, the maximum size of a file name remains file system dependent. For more information see *pathconf(2)*.

All file names are NULL terminated character strings and may consist of any character value except NULL (\0) or ASCII "/". Since the shell reserves the characters "*, [,]," and "?" for file name expansion, it is not good practice to name any files that use them. Nor is it good practice to name a file beginning with a dash "-" since most commands expect arguments beginning with this character. Consider files named -z and foo in the current directory. The command to remove all files in the current directory is rm *. Since the shell expands this to rm -z foo, the command will fail because rm does not understand the argument -z.

2.6 Descriptor management

To access a file, a program must first open it for reading or writing. This is done by using the open system call which returns a descriptor subsequently used to identify the file within the program code.

A descriptor is an unsigned integer. In its simplest form a descriptor is a logical representation of an object being manipulated. Once a descriptor is obtained, it is subsequently used to pass as a parameter to other system calls such as read, write, ioctl and close.

The kernel maintains a table of open descriptors used on a per process basis. It uses the integer value of a descriptor as an index into the process's, private descriptor table, which translates it into an internal representation of the object being manipulated (§ 6.2).

The following system calls cause a descriptor table to be either updated or created:

- open — opens a file for reading, writing or both. There is also an option to create the file if it does not already exist. Upon successful opening of the file, a file descriptor is returned.

  A file may be opened for reading or writing by multiple processes, so different processes accessing the same file may have inconsistent data since each may have a different idea about the contents of the file. The last process to close a file is the last one to complete any modifications to it. (See also "File and record locking" in § 6.4.)

- creat — create a file or prepare to overwrite its contents. Note that we have not misspelled creat. Historically, this system call has always lacked a trailing "e". A file descriptor is returned upon the successful creation of the file.

- pipe — creates a bidirectional interprocess communication channel in which two separate flows of data can be managed. Note that the system call pipe is different to the named pipe stored as a file in a file system, although it provides a similar type of service. In the case of the pipe system call, a pipe has no associated name, and cannot be opened for use with the open system call.

  The pipe system call sets up two descriptors that are bidirectional streams. Both streams are opened for reading and writing. If data is written to descriptor

A, data is available for reading from descriptor B. Similarly, if data is written to descriptor B, then data is available for reading from descriptor A. Data is always read from a stream on a first-in-first-out (FIFO) basis.

- *dup* — is used by applications for I/O redirection. It must be passed an already open descriptor, which it attempts to duplicate. The descriptor returned from *dup* is a copy of the original descriptor which inherits much of the same information as its partner. The main difference between the two descriptors is that the new descriptor is given a different integer value. They both index into the same open file (or pipe), they share the same file pointer, and inherit the same access modes set into the file's *inode* (§ 6.2.4).

- *fcntl* — facilitates the control over open files. One of the functions it provides resembles the *dup* system call but also facilitates the sharing of any record-locks the passed file descriptor maintained.

- *fork* — the function of the *fork* system call is discussed in § 4.12. For now, it is only important to understand that its purpose is to create a new process. When a process is created with *fork* it is given a copy of every descriptor its parent had open at the time of creation. As with the *dup* system call, these file descriptors share the same file pointer and so on. However, unlike *dup*, the integer value of each descriptor inherited from its parent is the same as that in the parent's descriptor table, but because it is a new process the kernel maintains a fresh descriptor table for it.

- *close* — disassociates a process from an open descriptor. When all descriptors associated with the open file have been closed, the file is said to be *freed*.

- *exit* — the *exit* system call cleans up a process's execution environment and then terminates it. While doing this, it automatically closes all descriptors the process has open.

In general, a process is assigned the lowest value descriptor available. The only exception is with the *fcntl* system call, which allows a process to obtain a descriptor whose value is the lowest available but is also greater than or equal to that specified in its function calling parameters.

2.6.1   File and record locking

UNIX System V Release 4 provides the system call *fcntl* for locking a file for exclusive use by a process. This service also provides a facility for placing locks on segments (or records) within a file. Locks placed on or within a file are not inherited by child processes. Thus, the *fork* system call results in locks being cleared for the new child. This prevents deadlock situations where both parent and child may wait for a file to become unlocked. If the child tries to access a file that has been previously locked by its parent, access will be denied until the lock is removed.

2.7 I/O redirection

By default, each running process is automatically assigned three file descriptors, one each for *stdin, stdout* and *stderr*. These file descriptors are normally associated with the terminal (or console) that the user is using (see Table 2.2).

Table 2.2: *Default open file descriptors assigned to a process*

Name	Descriptor	Data direction	Default Use
stdin	0	Keyboard input	Standard input
stdout	1	Console output	Standard output
stderr	2	Console output	Standard error output

In the case of *stdin, stdout* and *stderr*, these descriptors are mapped to the default input, output, and error output that the process inherited from its parent process via the *fork* and *exec* system calls (§ 4.13). However, the kernel makes no assumptions about these descriptors or any others. They exist simply because they are inherited from the **ttymon(1M)** process, which is the program responsible for configuring terminals and login processes. **ttymon** opens the terminal for reading and obtains descriptor 0; similarly it opens the terminal for writing and obtains descriptor 1. It then does a *dup* on descriptor 1 to obtain descriptor 2.

As an example of their use, consider the program example in Figure 2.4 which simply reads from *stdin*, writes to *stdout* and sends errors to *stderr*. Note that this is not a very well written program since it uses non-portable constructs, but it serves as a good example.

Since the UNIX I/O interface is designed to allow processes to ignore the underlying structure of a file, a process may simply open a file and use its descriptor to read or write data to it. It does not have to concern itself about what type of file it is. For example, the file may be a regular file stored in a file system, it could be a device whose interface node is also stored in a file system, then again, it could be a software pipe managed by the operating system. Additionally, processes are freed from concerning themselves with the complex I/O operations that the kernel handles for them. Thus, it is relatively simple for a process to redirect a file descriptor without concerning itself with how it is done internally by the kernel. Hence, the UNIX operating system lends itself unpretentiously to truly portable applications. The shell is a good example of this since it implements a programming language that caters for all forms of I/O redirection.

Take for example the following command line:

```
$ cat < /etc/passwd | grep gallio
```

For simplicity, the left arrow "<" means *take input from*, the bar or pipe "|" means *copy output of process to input of another*.

To explain how the shell re-maps descriptors to achieve I/O redirection between individual commands specified in the above command line example, we will dissect it into individual portions, as follows:

Figure 2.4: *Default file descriptor use*

```
#include <fcntl.h>

char error[] = "Error\n";

main()
{
    char mybuf[512]; /* buffer for I/O */
    int count; /* # of bytes transferred */
    while((count = read(0,mybuf,512)) > 0)    /* stdin */
        if(write(1,mybuf,count) != count) {   /* stdout */
            count = -1;
            break;
        }

    if(count < 0) {
        /* we should use perror()
         * but for this example we
         * are demonstrating the use of
         * stderr
         */
        write(2,error,sizeof(error));           /* stderr */
        exit(1);
    }
    exit(0);
}
```

cat < /etc/passwd   Instead of **cat** reading from the keyboard (i.e., *stdin* or
descriptor 0), the shell arranges for descriptor 0 to be re-mapped, so that the file
pointer associated with descriptor 0 is pointing to the file */etc/passwd*. It does this
by first forking a new process which proceeds to *close* descriptor 0 so that it is
free to be allocated on the next call to *open*. The new process then opens the file
/etc/passwd for reading. The *open* system call returns a new file descriptor with
a value of 0 since it is the lowest value descriptor available. Thus, when **cat** is
finally executed and reads from descriptor 0, it will be reading data from the file
/etc/passwd instead of the keyboard.

| grep gallio   The shell allows output from one program to be the input of
another. It does this by implementing a software pipe using the *pipe* system call.
By default, the **cat** program writes its output to *stdout* which is descriptor 1.
However, the command line specifically requests the shell to copy the output of
the **cat** program to the input of the **grep** program. Thus, the shell must arrange to
remap descriptor 1 also, so that instead of the **cat** program writing to its default
stdout, it writes to the input descriptor of the software pipe. It does this by first

closing descriptor 1 and then calling the *pipe* system call which obtains two file descriptors that are numbered 1 and 3.

The **grep** program, in this case, simply reads from its *stdin* (descriptor 0) and searches for the word "gallio". If it finds a line containing the word, it writes the line to *stdout* (descriptor 1). In view of this, the shell must arrange to remap descriptor 0 for the **grep** program so that it reads from the output of the software pipe which was previously set up. However, the software pipe's output descriptor's value is currently 3. To overcome this, the shell forks another process for the **grep** program which inherits a copy of all open descriptors in its parent. The new process then closes descriptor 0 (its default *stdin* channel) and uses the system call *dup* on descriptor 3 (the output descriptor of the pipe). This results in a new descriptor being allocated to the new process which is a duplicate of descriptor 3. Since descriptor 0 is now free (from the previous close), it is the descriptor returned by *dup* that now becomes the new processes *stdin* channel. Now, when **grep** reads from *stdin* it will be reading from the software pipe instead of the keyboard.

The first process created then *execs* the **cat** program (see *exec* in § 4.13.1) so that the address space of the new process is overlaid with a new process image obtained from the **cat** program in the file system. Similarly, the second new process *execs* the **grep** program.

It can be seen that by using a careful mixture of *open, close, fork, exec, pipe* and *dup,* process I/O redirection and interprocess communication can be relatively easy to implement in a program, providing one knows what one is doing!

2.8 Resource limitations

The operating system imposes specific limitations on a process's ability to consume certain system resources. The system calls *ulimit, getrlimit* and *setrlimit* provide facilities for getting and setting the current process resource limits. They affect the following resources:

- Maximum size of core file creation.
- Maximum amount of CPU usage in seconds.
- Maximum amount of memory usage.
- Maximum file creation size.
- Maximum number of open file descriptors.
- Maximum size of process stack.
- Maximum size of memory mapped file address space.

A process may set a resource limit to any value providing it is lower than or equal to its current hard limit. A process may irreversibly lower a resource hard limit although super-user (or a process with an effective UID equal to zero) may raise it so long as it is not raised past a system imposed hard limit.

2.9 Quotas

The traditional UNIX System V file system (s5) gives users the freedom to use up file system resources as required. Thus, a user could in fact use up all the resources of a file system by allocating all of its available space to files and directories, but this is undesirable for most installations. In an attempt to restrict the user's working environment, the designers of the Berkeley Fast File System implemented a quota mechanism and this is available for use with the ufs file system under UNIX System V Release 4.

The quota system imposes limits on the number of inodes and disk blocks that a user may allocate. Quota arrangements can be made for individual users for each individual ufs file system. Thus, a user's quota may be set differently on different file systems. A process with an effective UID equal to zero may use the quotactl system call. It provides control of quotas for a specific ufs file system. System Administration utilities such as **quota(1M)** make use of this system call. Note that the quota mechanism is optional and some manufacturers omit it from their version of the operating system.

2.10 Security

The UNIX system uses a simple, yet effective scheme for managing a process's ability to associate itself with a file or system service. A three-level file protection scheme is used to test whether a process wanting to associate itself with a file can do so. Additionally, certain system calls are reserved for use by the super-user only, and others render different actions if the user is not the super-user. This section discusses the kernel's in-built security system and the effects imposed on the user.

2.10.1 Process execution rights

Every running process has an associated real user ID, effective user ID, and saved user ID state. These values are set with the setuid system call. Similarly, a process has an associated real group ID, effective group ID, and saved group ID state which are set with the setgid system call. For the rest of this section we will collectively call these states process ID states.

When a user logs in to the system, the **login(1)** program, once satisfied that the user is allowed to use the system, forks a new process and execs the user's desired login shell. But before doing this, it sets the process ID states for the newly forked process from the information obtained about the user stored in the /etc/passwd and /etc/group files. Once these process ID states are set, the new process is restricted to specific rights. For example, the process is granted permission to access a file only if the files access modes allow it to. Similarly, it can execute the file (program) only if it is granted execute permission. These process ID states are handed down to other processes that the process creates. Thus, all programs executed by a user are imposed with the same restrictions. However, in some circumstances a process can change its rights by using the *setuid* and *setgid* system calls. There are also some circumstances where the system will change the rights of a process automatically.

Consider the following situation: the file */etc/passwd* is marked for read-only by anyone. That is, anyone can read the file but not write to it. If a user who does not have super-user privileges tries to modify the file, the request to write to it will be rejected. This poses a potential problem to joe_user who wants to change his password. The program */bin/passwd* is used to change a user's password. But how does joe_user change his password if he does not have write permission on the */etc/passwd* file? The system overcomes this sort of problem by allowing executable files to be set-user-ID or set-group-ID on execution. When a process executes a program such as this, the kernel automatically changes the access rights to the UID of the file in the case of set-user-ID, or the GID of the file in the case of set-group-ID. The */bin/passwd* program belongs to super-user but it is also set-user-ID on execution. When joe_user executes it he becomes super-user for the short duration that */bin/passwd* executes. Thus, he successfully changes his password since super-user overrides all access permissions.

For both user and group IDs, the real ID is the true ID of the executing process. The effective ID is its current executing ID. A process that execs a program that is either set-user-ID on execution or set-group-ID on execution will change its user or group IDs to the owner or group of the file before execution begins. This has no effect on the calling process, so when the process terminates and control is passed back to the parent process the real IDs are resumed.

If the process is executing with super-user privileges (i.e., its effective UID is 0), it can change its user process ID states so that it continues executing with the privilege of another UID. On the other hand, if the calling process is not executing with super-user privileges, it can only change its effective UID back to its real user ID. The *setgid* system call has the same effect but changes the group ID.

2.10.2 File protection

The UNIX system maintains file access permissions for all files and directories in the file system. A process can access a file only if its permission modes allow it to do so.

We have already learned that every process has an associated owner that is identified by its UID. We also learned that every file in a UNIX file system has an associated *inode*. It is important to realize that files and file names are in this case not the same. In the case of *hard linked* files, several file names may represent the same file and be associated with the same *inode*. However, for every active *inode* managed by the system, there is only one file. Most of the information stored within a file's *inode* is obtained by using the *stat* or *fstat* system calls. The kernel uses the information in the *inode* and other information obtained from the process's address space, to confirm whether the process is legitimately allowed to access the file associated with the *inode*. Each file belongs to a specific user (or account), and within each *inode* is a string of bits specifying the file's accessibility. They are interpreted in Table 2.3.

Table 2.3: *File access and execution modes*

Octal bit-mask	Description
04000	Set-user-ID on execution
020n0	Set-group-ID on execution if *n* is 7, 5, 3 or 1. Enable mandatory file or record locking if *n* is 6, 4, 2 or 0
01000	Save text (swap) image after execution; also called the *sticky* bit
00400	File may be read by owner
00200	File may be written to or modified by owner
00100	File may be executed by owner or searched by owner if a directory
00040	File may be read by all users in the group
00020	File may be written to or modified by all users in the group
00010	File may be executed by all user in the group or searched by all users in the group if a directory
00004	File may be read by all users
00002	File may be written to or modified by all users
00001	File may be executed by all users or searched by all users if a directory

2.11 Devices

All devices on a computer system running the UNIX operating system are accessible if they have associated special files stored in the file system and associated device drivers linked into the kernel. Pseudo devices such as RAM resident disks and pseudo terminals are accessible in the same way. Pseudo devices have no associated physical device, they simply emulate one, in one way or another.

2.11.1 Device drivers

Every device driver must support an *open* and *close* subroutine. In most cases a driver will also be furnished with a *read* and *write* subroutine. A device driver can also provide an *ioctl* routine for facilitating control over the device when a process uses the *ioctl* system call. Device drivers are discussed in § 5.6.

2.11.2 User process interface

A process uses the same system calls: *open, close, read* and *write,* to access either a regular file or a special file. The kernel determines from the file type whether it is to pass control to the subroutine associated with the device defined by the device driver. Thus, if a process opens a regular file for reading, the *open* and *read* system calls issued by the executing process will be handled by the built-in kernel provided *open* and *read* subroutines. However, if the file is a special file the kernel passes control to the *open* and *read* subroutines defined in the special file's associated driver (see Figure 2.5).

A special file has an associated *major* and *minor* number. The kernel uses the *major* number to index into a list of configured device driver tables, aptly named *device switch tables*. If the file is block-special, the kernel uses the *major* number to index into *bdevsw[]*. Similarly, if the file is character-special, the kernel uses the *major* number to index into *cdevsw[]*. Both *bdevsw[]* and *cdevsw[]* are arrays of structures whose elements point to the relevent device driver subroutines. A device driver may be implemented in such a way that it can process both character and block-based I/O. In this case, the driver will have a structure element reserved in both *bdevsw[]* and *cdevsw[]* (see § 5.7 and § 5.8).

There is only one device driver per block or character major number. For example, both */dev/tty* and */dev/swap* may use major number 6. Since */dev/tty* is a character-special file, and */dev/swap* is a block-special file, they can both use the same major number, although they are both associated with different device drivers. In both cases, the *minor* number is passed as a parameter to the relevant function in the device driver. The device driver is free to interpret the minor number as it sees fit, although in most cases it uses it as a port number. In this way, a single device driver can control several physical device interfaces.

2.12 System initialization

UNIX System V Release 4 uses two disk partitions for bringing the system into operation:

- *boot* — contains programs that find the partition containing the */stand* file system, selecting the file within it called *unix* and loading it into the machine's memory for execution. It is important to realize that the boot partition is not a file system and the procedure for booting UNIX is very much vendor dependent. Thus, the programs in this partition will almost definitely be different for each individual port of the operating system.

- *stand* — contains a *bfs* type file system mounted on */stand*. It is a simple flat file system containing the minimal number of files needed to bring the UNIX system into operation.

Both the *boot* and *stand* partitions must reside on the same disk although any disk can be used. Obviously, the *root* partition must also be accessible, otherwise the boot procedure will fail to bring UNIX into operation. The default installation places both partitions on the first available fixed disk.

A *bfs* file system is a special-purpose one although it is still made with the **mkfs(1M)** utility as are other file system types. Its purpose is to facilitate a very fast and simple boot procedure. It contains a single directory containing the necessary

Figure 2.5: *Logical view of path followed to open a special file*

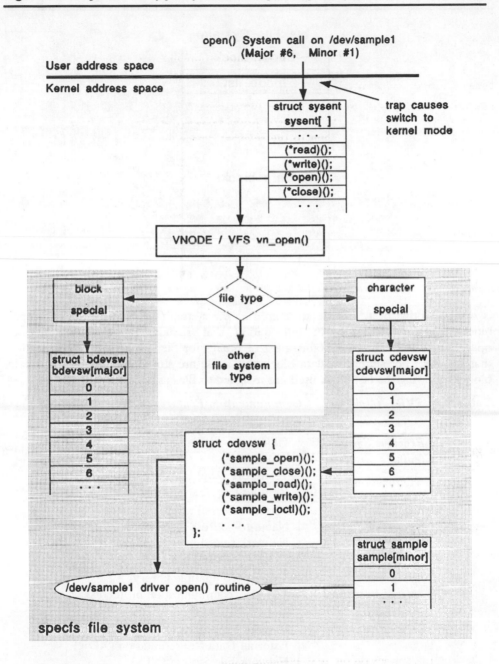

stand-alone programs and files required to bring the system up as quickly and as simply as possible. The *bfs* file system does not support the *mkdir* or *mknod* system calls, so only regular file types can be created in it. The structure of a *bfs* file system

Figure 2.6: *Structure of a bfs file system on disk*

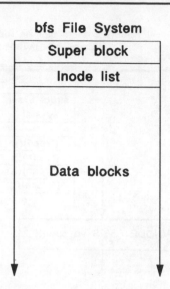

is similar to that of a 512 byte structured *s5* file system (see Figure 2.6). The super block contains administrative information that remains static during normal operation. The *inode* list contains a list of *inodes* for files in the data block section that follows. For simplicity, data blocks for a file are stored contiguously and data blocks following the last block used are assigned to files as necessary.

Table 2.4: *SVR4 Networking & Communication Features*

Previous System V features	UUCP STREAMS Transport Level Interface (TLI) Remote File Sharing (RFS)
New features from AT&T	Service Access Facility (SAF) Name-to-address mapping Network selection STREAM-based pipes
New features derived from BSD	Sockets (compatible library) TCP/IP (communication protocols)
New features derived from SunOS	**inetd** Remote Procedure Calls (RPC) External Data Representation (XDR) Network File System (NFS)

2.13 Networking & communication services

Many of the changes and enhancements to UNIX System V Release 4 have been made to incorporate the networking features of BSD and SunOS (see Table 2.4). This section outlines those features and discusses the basic facilities they provide. A more detailed discussion of their implementation is provided in later chapters.

2.13.1 STREAMS

In early releases of the UNIX system, communication facilities were implemented using single character I/O, mainly because I/O was only ever performed through devices such as modems and terminals. Since these devices were comparatively slow compared to other compute-intensive tasks required of the operating system, performance and modularity were not the main issue then. Support for other devices, protocols, operating modes, and so on, came in later versions of the operating system, but they were still bound to single character I/O.

With the advent of networking protocols such as the US Defense Advanced Research Project Agency's (DARPA) Transmission Control Protocol/Internet Protocol (TCP/IP), IBM's Systems Network Architecture (SNA), Open Systems Interconnection (OSI), X.25, and others, it became obvious that there was a need to incorporate them into a single framework. However, developers were hindered by the lack of standard interfaces supported by the UNIX system necessary for developing such diverse functionality. In addition to this, several up and coming protocols were based on a layered organization. This meant that functionality was required not only at the application level but also at the transport level. In other words, extensive modifications were required within the kernel as well as at the device driver level.

To relieve this problem, developers implemented new facilities as demand for them grew, even though the UNIX system lacked a standard I/O interface system. This resulted in several different I/O mechanisms using similar facilities, but because they were developed as individual projects, none of them were compatible with each other and they required several different, individual interfaces.

Traditionally, the UNIX I/O subsystem requires the design and installation of a new device driver for each new device added to the system. The problem with this scheme is that functionality required by a new device driver is often already implemented in an existing device driver, yet there is no way for them to share the common code. Unfortunately, the overlap between them often produced multiple implementations using the same functionality. So, obviously a system by which device driver designers can share common code was required.

To overcome these limitations, AT&T provided the STREAMS subsystem which offers a flexible and modular mechanism for implementing device drivers and communication protocols. STREAMS was originally written by Dennis Ritchie in 1984 and was first released with the Networking Support Utilities (NSU) package of UNIX System V Release 3.

Figure 2.7: *Logical view of a Simple STREAMS interface*

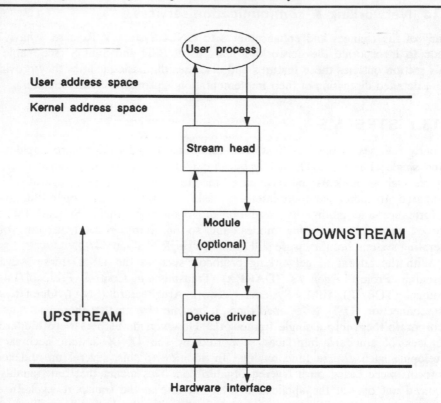

In UNIX System V Release 3, STREAMS was initially introduced as a framework for implementing all existing character I/O. However, with the release of UNIX System V Release 4, the STREAMS implementation has been extended to include a Device Driver Interface (DDI) and Driver Kernel Interface (DKI) to provide a scheme for interfacing between the kernel and device driver and at the same time provide an easy way to port existing device driver source code. Thus, STREAMS is used for implementing all character I/O under UNIX System V Release 4. In fact, the entire terminal interface sub-system, as seen in earlier releases of the UNIX system, has been rewritten to make use of it. In addition to this, *pipes* have been re-implemented using STREAMS mechanisms.

Put simply, STREAMS is a general purpose suite of tools consisting of a set of system calls, kernel routines and kernel resources, and is implemented in such a way that it provides standard interfaces for character based I/O within the kernel, and between the kernel and its associated device drivers. Collectively, these tools and interfaces provide a flexible facility for developing UNIX system communication services.

The STREAMS architecture is completely open-ended. That is, it does not impose a specific network or protocol architecture. It is fully compatible with the traditional UNIX I/O interface — a process simply accesses a stream as it would any other device driver by accessing its special file node in the file system with the system calls *open, close, read, write* and *ioctl.*

In its simplest form, a stream is a full-duplex data transfer path between a controlling process in user address space and a device driver in kernel address space (see Figure 2.7).

When a process opens a streams device by using the *open* system call, the kernel associates a stream head with the driver. The process then communicates through the stream head as if it were a normal device driver. The stream head itself is responsible for processing system calls made by the user process on the stream device. When the process writes to the device, the stream head passes the data *downstream* towards the device driver. Similarly, when the process reads from the device, the device driver passes data *upstream* towards the stream head. A stream such as this simply transfers data unmodified between the user process and device. There is no processing done between them. However, data passed in any direction may be subjected to processing before it reaches its destination if it passes through one or more streams modules linked between the stream head and driver. A streams module is a self-contained processing module representing a defined set of in-kernel functions to be carried out on data as it flows through the stream. For example, a module may simply transform lowercase characters to uppercase. A more complex module may envelope outbound data into packets or remove the envelope on inbound data by depacketizing it.

A streams module is independent of any other modules linked into the stream. Its job is to receive data, process it, then pass it on along the stream. The data may be intercepted by another module for additional processing, and so on, until eventually, depending on the direction of data flow, the data is passed to the stream head or driver.

The STREAMS sub-system uses messages to pass data between modules and the stream head and driver. A message consists of a set of message blocks each containing three data structures: a header, a data block, and a data buffer.

Interfaces to STREAMS devices are implemented in the file system just as other devices. That is, they have associated special files with *major* and *minor* device numbers. Streams are dynamically allocated and the first process to open a STREAMS device causes its construction. Other processes that open the same device will share the same stream since there is only one stream constructed per *minor* device. Once created, a stream remains intact until the last process associated with it issues the *close* system call. The last close causes a stream to be dismantled.

The implementation of STREAMS, as well as the semantics and use of its associated system calls, are discussed in Chapter 7.

2.13.2 TCP/IP

To place TCP/IP into perspective, a brief discussion of the Department of Defence (DOD) internetworking protocols is presented first. Although this discussion is not necessarily kernel-related, we feel that it is required since TCP/IP is the most common transport protocol used by communication facilities on the UNIX operating system. It provides a good basis for understanding where TCP/IP is used and how it fits into the UNIX I/O interface.

In a network, computer systems (hosts) are connected together by a physical medium such as a cable; the most common form, called *Ethernet*, uses a coaxial cable known as an *ether*. Whatever network connection method is used, its purpose is to enable the connecting hosts to communicate with each other.

Figure 2.8: *Internetworking host 1 and 2 via networks and gateways*

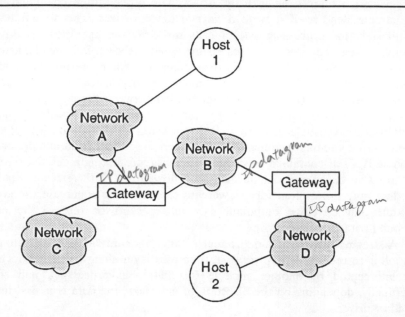

A network is responsible for transporting messages, called *frames*, between each physical connection. The size of a frame very much depends on the network technology. A frame is constructed of a *header* and the data to be communicated. The header holds control information that is used by the network interface of each connecting host. When a host interface wishes to send a message to another host interface, it fills a frame header with the destination host interface address, and adds the data portion to it. The frame is then placed on the network to be transmitted. The receiving host interface extracts the data portion and passes it to its operating system for additional processing.

There are many different types of network technologies. The problem is that few of them can *internetwork* with each other. In 1969, in an effort to fix this, the Department of Defense Advanced Research Project Agency (DARPA) sponsored a project to find a way to unify all networks into a common framework, and came up with a single virtual network called *Internet*. The Internet uses a series of gateways to interconnect independent networks or domains (see Figure 2.8). Each individual host on a network is identified by a unique address called an *Internet address*.

To resolve the differences in network technology frame formats, a universal data packet was defined, called an *Internet Protocol* (IP) datagram, which is similar to a network frame in that it contains a header and a data portion. However, the IP datagram forms the data portion within the network frame. In other words, the network frame encapsulates the IP datagram so that it can be transmitted through the Internet. All hosts, gateways and networks on the Internet must be able to comprehend IP datagrams. Thus, a host connected to a local network, which in turn is connected to the Internet, can exchange IP datagrams with any other host on the Internet.

The Internet service is *connectionless*. That is, communicating hosts do not tie up a physical connection for private use. This is because datagrams are not processed in any particular order, but are processed independently of each other to allow the Internet to share its resources efficiently amongst connecting hosts. Unfortunately, this means that the service offered by the Internet is *unreliable* since packets may be delivered out of order or become lost, duplicated or even scrambled. Thus, delivery cannot be guaranteed. An IP datagram that resolves this problem is the Transmission Control Protocol (TCP). TCP offers a *reliable delivery service* by transforming the datagram into a full-duplex data stream. It does this by using *acknowledge or retransmit*. If the sending host does not receive an acknowledgement within a specified amount of time, it assumes that the datagram has failed to reach its destination and so retransmits it.

There are many protocols used in IP datagrams and each protocol is used for a different purpose. Some must be implemented by all hosts, others are either recommended or optional. The complete IP family is usually referred to as TCP/IP, signifying the two most commonly used protocols: Transmission Control Protocol/Internet Protocol. We will not discuss these or other Internet protocols further, since they are the subject of a book within itself [Comer 1988]. It is sufficient to understand that TCP/IP is the most common transmission protocol used by UNIX communication services. Some services, in fact, depend on it.

Table 2.5: *Universal protocols of the Internet*

Protocol	Description
TCP	Transmission Control Protocol
UDP	User Datagram Protocol
ARP	Address Resolution Protocol
RARP	Reverse Address Resolution Protocol
IP	Internet Protocol
ICMP	Internet Control Message Protocol
FTP	File Transfer Protocol
TFTP	Trivial File Transfer Protocol

Under UNIX System V Release 4, TCP/IP is implemented as a suite of STREAMS modules, and the Transport Level Interface (TLI) is the predominant application interface. Therefore, the interface between an application and the transport mechanism is the TLI, and an application that uses the TLI can use TCP/IP.

2.13.3 Transport level interface (TLI)

The TLI, often referred to as the "Transport Layer Interface", is modelled after layer 4 of the International Standards Organization (ISO) 7 layer model. The model defines a reference model of networking functions separated into 7 areas as shown in Figure 2.9. The purpose of this model is to provide a standard for interconnecting machines over a network, which are independent of manufacturer. The reference model is used to describe network protocols, and for each of the seven layers specified in the reference model, the standard defines what functionality a layer must provide. The seven layers are described as follows.

- *Layer 1: Physical Layer* — the transmission medium such as an Ethernet cable or other device. It is responsible for transmitting raw data across the network.

- *Layer 2: Data Link Layer* — the device driver level, also referred to as the ARP and RARP layers in the TCP/IP protocol. It is responsible for encapsulating and decapsulating the data while correcting errors occurring in the physical layer.

- *Layer 3: Network Layer* — responsible for handling intermediate network functions such as finding a relay through which to route communications if no direct connection is available between the host and destination. This is the IP and ICMP layers in the TCP/IP protocol.

- *Layer 4: Transport Layer* — the TCP or UDP layer in either TCP/IP or UDP/IP protocols. It is responsible for hiding the transport service by piecing fragmented data messages together so that it looks like a single message to the upper levels. It also handles errors in packet transmission such as *acknowledge or retransmit.*

- *Layer 5: Session Layer* — responsible for controlling the conversation between the communicating transport layers. NFS uses this layer for Remote Procedure Calls (RPC). Procedure calls can be made across the network to a machine acting as a server.

- *Layer 6: Presentation Layer* — responsible for managing the presentation of information being communicated. NFS implements its External Data Representation (XDR) at this level. XDR translates data into a form that is understood by all machines on the network.

- *Layer 7: Application Layer* — the interface between communicating applications such as **telnet, rlogin** and **mail**.

The TLI is an interface between an application and the mechanism used to transfer communicated data across a network. It defines how a process accesses the services of a protocol in a manner that eliminates the need for an application to know the underlying transport level mechanism. It is used to build communications and network services that must adapt to the ISO/OSI model.

Under UNIX System V Release 4, the TLI is implemented using the STREAMS I/O message interface. However, there are no system calls specifically set aside for use with the Transport Level Interface. The programmatic interface is implemented

Figure 2.9: *Open Systems Interconnect (OSI) reference model*

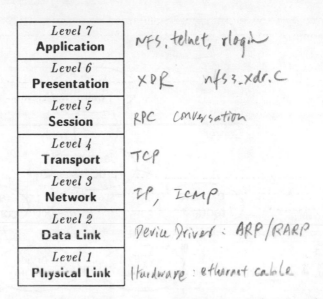

Level 7 **Application**	NFS, telnet, rlogin
Level 6 **Presentation**	XDR nfs3_xdr.c
Level 5 **Session**	RPC conversation
Level 4 **Transport**	TCP
Level 3 **Network**	IP, ICMP
Level 2 **Data Link**	Device Driver : ARP/RARP
Level 1 **Physical Link**	Hardware : ethernet cable

as a suite of user-level functions stored in a library (*/usr/lib/libnsl_s.a*) that must be linked into a program. Typically, an application uses the interface to interact with a protocol used by the TLI. Examples are Remote Procedure Call (RPC) protocol, TCP, IP, and so on.

2.13.4 Remote procedure call (RPC)

The RPC package was introduced by Sun Microsystems, Inc. in 1984 as part of their NFS platform. The Remote Procedure Call specification [RFC 1057] details a procedure call oriented protocol for accessing the services of a remote machine. It is built on top of an External Data Representation (XDR) protocol, also distributed as part of the NFS package.

The RPC package was designed to be transport independent, so it fits nicely into the OSI model and its implementation is similar to that of the TLI under UNIX System V Release 4 (see Figure 2.10). The RPC protocol is an interprocess communication facility that allows programmers to write client-server based applications that request services at various levels from a server machine.

There are no system calls provided by the operating system for RPC services. Programs must be linked with a user-level library (*/usr/lib/librpcsvc.a*) to make use of them.

2.13.5 External data representation (XDR)

XDR is a separate platform although it forms part of the Sun RPC package. Its purpose is to take care of the differences between communicating machine

Figure 2.10: *Remote Procedure Call IPC*

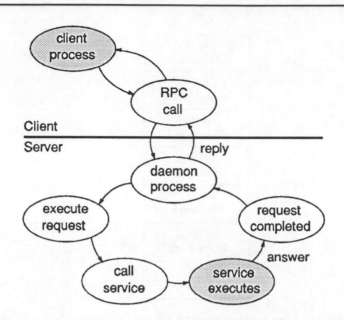

architectures, allowing them to communicate without worrying about implementation-defined data abstractions. The XDR specification [RFC 1014] defines a standard method of representing standard data types. For example, it hides the differences in byte ordering, structure alignment, represented data types, and so on. The XDR fits into the ISO model at the presentation layer and is typically used by applications which need to describe their data format. Both the RPC and the NFS protocols make use of this service.

2.13.6 Sockets

Sockets were introduced in 1982 with the 4.1aBSD operating system. In its simplest form, a socket is an interprocess communication (IPC) method. In other words, it is a facility for allowing a process to communicate with another process that may be running locally or on a remote machine. In use, it is a networking interface similar in functionality to the TLI.

In the BSD environment, sockets are implemented as a set of five system calls: *socket, bind, listen, connect* and *accept.* However, like the TLI, sockets under UNIX System V Release 4 are implemented with the STREAMS I/O message interface, the four previously mentioned BSD system calls are implemented as a suite of user level functions archived in a compatibility library (*/usr/lib/libsocket.a*) which must be linked into a program.

Under UNIX System V Release 4, the SVID defines the TLI as the transport mechanism for networking interfaces. Thus, the TLI library of routines are the prefered ones to use when writing communications-based applications. Despite this, sockets are provided for backwards compatibility with existing socket-based applications. However, programmers are encouraged to make use of the TLI rather than sockets when writing new applications. (See "Sockets Migration and Sockets-to-TLI Conversion" — § 4-1 in [AT&T 1990f].)

Figure 2.11: *Logical view of a STREAMS-based pipe*

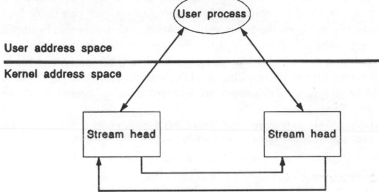

2.13.7 STREAMS-based pipes

Under UNIX System V Release 4, pipes are implemented using the STREAMS system. When a *pipe* system call is made, two streams are created. However, unlike a STREAMS-based driver, there is no associated device driver. The two stream heads are effectively joined together so that data passed at either end can be read from its opposite end (see Figure 2.11). Thus, pipes are implemented as bidirectional interprocess communication channels in which two separate flows of data can be managed. Pipes are discussed in detail in § 7.10.

2.13.8 UUCP

UUCP, which stands for UNIX-to-UNIX Copy program, was the first networking application supplied with the UNIX system. It was first developed in 1976 and supplied outside AT&T with Version 7 UNIX in 1978, and it is still widely used in many installations around the world today. UUCP is implemented as a suite of user applications that operate in batch mode. It is typically used between UNIX systems that are directly connected to each other via dial-up modes on a telephone line. We will not discuss this facility further, since it is implemented at the user level. The kernel has no special functionality included for it.

2.14 File sharing

In the same way that locally fixed disk-based file systems are supported, UNIX System V Release 4 also supports two types of remote file system. That is, it supports two methods for accessing files stored on remote machines connected to each other over a network. They are: the Remote File Sharing (RFS) system from AT&T, and the Networked File System (NFS) from Sun Microsystems, Inc.

File sharing is a method by which multiple computer systems can share files over a network. There are many methods for implementing such a scheme, but under the UNIX operating system file sharing is generally implemented as mountable remote file systems. That is, a remote file system is mounted just like any other file system type using a directory mount point within the UNIX file system tree. Once mounted, the files stored in a remote file system are presented to a process as if the files reside on a locally fixed disk.

Consider the example in Figure 2.12. Two UNIX systems are connected to each other over a network. In this case, the client is called "Sally" and the server "Harry". They are both configured the same except that Sally's resources for the directories *share* and *X11* are stored on Harry's machine and are mounted as remote file systems, whereas on Harry's machine the directories *share* and *X11* are resources stored within its own locally fixed disks.

Figure 2.12: *Sharing resources between two machines*

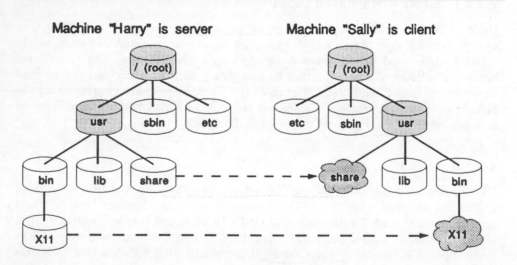

There are advantages and disadvantages to this scheme. There is only one copy of the resource stored on a single machine (Harry). Thus, there is a saving of expensive disk space, and only one backup required. However, accessing the remote resource will be slower than if it was stored on a locally available disk. Users on Sally also depend on the availability of the network, the other machine's hardware, and the other machine's operating system. Should either of these fail then the remote resource will cease to be available. In general, however, such implementations are very efficient and extremely reliable, so the advantages far outweigh the disadvantages.

A remote file system is not necessarily a file system per se, although it can be. A machine acting as a server advertises the directories in its local file system hierarchy which clients are allowed to access. A client then uses that directory as a remote file system by mounting it onto a local directory mount point. Any files and directories within that directory hierarchy are then accessible by the client. Thus, the scheme allows for applications on either the server or the client to access the directory and its contents, without knowing where they reside.

The two remote file system types, RFS and NFS, use the *client-server* model. A machine acting as a client accesses files stored on a machine acting as a server. A machine acting as a server offers its resources to clients and the scheme is flexible enough to allow a single machine to act as both client and server. Since both RFS and NFS are file system types, they are both implemented under the VFS subsystem (see § 6.5).

Table 2.6: *Differences between RFS and NFS*

AT&T Remote File Sharing (RFS)
Advantages
• Ability to share files with another UNIX system • Supports UID and GID file mapping • Offers fast access of files by caching data on the client • Applications need not know where the remote files are stored • Allows the sharing of special files and named pipes • Independent of transport provider
Disadvantages
• Requires UNIX System V Release 3 or higher

SunOS Networked File System (NFS)
Advantages
• Ability to share files with another computer system • Heterogeneous operating environment (any operating system) • Available on many operating systems • Applications need not know where the remote files are stored • Stateless design provides a more robust recovery scheme
Disadvantages
• Requires TCP/IP for transport provider • Does not preserve UNIX System semantics • Error handling is clumsy because of stateless design

2.14.1 Networked file system (NFS)

Sun Microsystems, Inc. introduced NFS in 1985 as part of their Open Network Computing (ONC) offering. With Sun's contribution to the design of UNIX System V Release 4, NFS became an official part of the UNIX System V Release 4 distribution.

NFS was originally designed to be completely transportable to other operating system environments and machine architectures. It is currently implemented by more than 200 manufacturers around the world. There are both commercial and public domain versions of NFS on machines ranging from notebook computers to super computers.

The design of NFS required portions of the 4.2BSD file system interface to be rewritten. This resulted in the implementation of the Virtual File System (VFS) and *vnode* interfaces. These changes, which have now been incorporated into the UNIX System V Release 4 file system interface, led to extensive modifications to AT&T's System V kernel. It could be said that NFS is probably responsible for the greatest portion of the changes and enhancements made to the UNIX System V kernel.

The NFS design is built from three main parts: a protocol, a server, and a client. The NFS protocol uses the Remote Procedure Call (RPC) primitives, which are built on top of the External Data Representation (XDR). A client requests the service from a server using the RPC protocol.

Figure 2.13: *NFS as seen from the OSI/ISO reference model*

Level 7 **Application**	NFS	
Level 6 **Presentation**	XDR	
Level 5 **Session**	RPC	
Level 4 **Transport**	TCP	UDP
Level 3 **Network**	IP	
Level 2 **Data Link**	Logical	
Level 1 **Physical Link**	Ethernet	

2.14.2 Remote file sharing (RFS)

RFS (often referred to as the Remote File System) was introduced by AT&T in UNIX System V Release 3. Functionally, it is presented to the user and application in the same way that NFS is. That is, it provides transparent access to remote files. However, its implementation is totally different. Its main disadvantage is that it is only implemented on machines running the UNIX operating system. However, unlike NFS, RFS preserves the full UNIX file system semantics by allowing processes to access all types of files over a network including special files and named pipes. It also allows file and record locking on remote files.

Just as NFS uses an RPC protocol, RFS uses a STREAMS-based message protocol which in turn is based on the UNIX system calls. Each operation defined for an RFS *vnode* uses these primitives to communicate across the network to a server machine where the real file is stored.

The design of RFS employs network independence. That is, it is independent of transport provider (i.e., physical network mechanism). More important, RFS can run over multiple transport providers at the same time, so it can operate over a wide variety of commercially available protocols without modification. Some examples of transport providers that can be used with RFS are TCP/IP and AT&T's STARLAN NETWORK. On the other hand, NFS is dependent on TCP/IP as its transport provider.

2.15 User access

Users generally access the system via a terminal connected to a serial port. However, it has become increasingly popular for users to access the system using a remote machine over a local or wide area network. This section details the access procedures.

2.15.1 Service access facility (SAF)

Prior to UNIX System V Release 4, there were two types of access methods: if the user was using a terminal, then the **getty(1M)** program provided access to the system; if the user was accessing the system across a network, then a network connection monitor such as **inetd(8)** provided access by first validating the network address of the requestor, then passing control to the requested service such as **rlogin(1)** or **rsh(1)**.

Both these and other access methods proved to be clumsy in operation since there were several sets of individual facilities to administer, and so UNIX System V Release 4 introduced a new facility called the Service Access Facility (SAF) which provides a single consistent facility for administering all external access points to the system.

A program that is under the control of the Service Access Facility is called a *port monitor.* It simply monitors external access points such as serial ports for activity.

Currently there are three types of port monitor supported under UNIX System V Release 4, although the SAF system has been designed to incorporate other port monitors if they are required. Specific applications may supply their own port monitor which can be installed by either user or application. The three port monitors supplied with the system are as follows:

- *ttymon* — replaces **getty(1M)** used in previous releases of UNIX System V. Unlike **getty,** which was executed for each configured serial port on the system, a single process called **ttymon(1M)** is used. This program is a STREAMS-based application which makes use of the *poll* system call. *poll* provides a mechanism by which a program can monitor a number of open file descriptors waiting for certain events to take place. Thus, **ttymon** opens each active serial port configured, and waits for activity on them. If input is received, it starts the service required for that port — usually the **login** program.

- *listen* — "listens" on a network for service requests. Once a request is received and accepted, it invokes the service required to respond to the request. It is used with any connection-oriented network that conforms to the Transport Level Interface (TLI) such as AT&T's Remote File Sharing (RFS) system.

- *inetd* — uses a configuration file that specifies configured services and the names of programs to provide the services. While listening on a TCP/IP network for connections, if a connection is established, then **inetd** invokes the relevant server program to provide the service to the requestor.

2.16 Extended Fundamental Types (EFT)

In an effort to remain compatible with earlier versions of the UNIX operating system, UNIX System V Release 4 introduces a concept called *Extended Fundamental Types* (EFT). Basically, there are a number of kernel data structures that have been modified to suit 32 bit architectures, and so certain data items that were originally defined as *short* (usually 16 bits) have been enlarged to *unsigned long* (usually 32 bits). To effect this, UNIX System V Release 4 defines the preprocessor variable called _STYPES. C programs that require compatibility with UNIX System V Release 3 kernel data structures must define _STYPES before including any header files, otherwise EFT will be assumed by the compiler. Note that EFT affects only a few programs, in particular those that need to include any of the following header files: *fcntl.h, ipc.h, msg.h, sem.h, stat.h, stream.h, stropts.h, strsubr.h, utsname.h* and *mkdev.h*.

2.17 Exercises

2.1   What is the difference between a named pipe and a pipe system call?

2.2   Name a file system that can never be unmounted and explain why not.

2.3   Name the system call that is used to create and format a file system.

2.4   What is the difference between a *busy* and a *dirty* file system? How does it affect their operation?

2.5   A process is currently associated with a file, but the file is subsequently removed by another process. What happens to the file's data?

2.6   Name the three components of the file system interface.

2.7   What is the difference between a hard link and a soft link?

2.8   How does a process associate itself with the Transport Layer Interface (TLI)?

2.9   What file system is likely to be used to store a character-special file?

2.10   Why is it not possible to create a directory on a *bfs* file system?

2.11   What method is used to pass data between STREAMS modules?

2.12   What is the difference between a network frame and an IP datagram?

2.13   Name the two most common Internet Protocols used by UNIX communication facilities.

2.14   What is a transport provider?

2.15   What is common between RPC, TLI, and sockets?

2.16   How does a process request the services of the operating system?

2.17*   Using three system calls — *open*, *close* and *read* — write a C program to calculate the amount of memory installed on your UNIX installation.

PART 2

UNIX Internals

CHAPTER 3

Memory management subsystem

There is a wicked inclination in most people to suppose an old man decayed in his intellects. If a young or a middle aged man, when leaving a company, does not recollect where he laid his hat, it is nothing; but if the same inattention is discovered in an old man, people will shrug and say, "His memory is going".

— Samuel Johnson

3.1 Introduction to the memory subsystem

A major concern for any operating system is the method by which it manages a process given the restrictions imposed by the amount of physical memory installed in the computer hardware. It must be determined where the process will be placed in main memory, and how memory is allocated to it as it grows and shrinks during its execution. One problem that is familiar to all operating systems is what to do when memory becomes scarce.

To overcome these and other memory management problems, UNIX System V Release 4 has adopted a concept called *virtual memory* [Moran 1988].

3.1.1 Virtual memory

Microprocessors of the late 1970s and early 1980s, such as the Intel 8080 and the Zilog Z80, provided the programmer with an address space of 64k bytes. A program running on one of these processors used direct physical addresses to access code and data. That is, when a program referenced a data item at address A it corresponded directly to physical address A in physical memory. This direct mapping meant that the programmer had to know which areas within the machine's memory could be physically addressed. In particular, the programmer had to arrange that the program code and data avoided any "holes" in the given address space (see Figure 3.1).

The 64k address space, and the direct mapping of program addresses to physical memory locations, also meant that the physical size of a program itself was limited to 64k. It was only possible to run larger programs by using *overlay schemes* or by

69

Figure 3.1: *Holes and sparse memory*

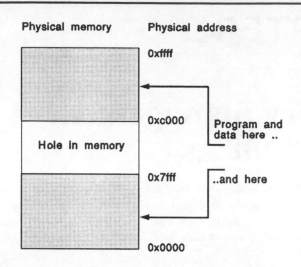

bank switching alternative areas of memory.

It is much more convenient to ignore the physical layout of the machine's memory, and work instead with an idealised or *virtual* machine. A program can then be written to reference virtual addresses for both its code and data. This scheme allows the programmer and the compilation system to choose addresses that are convenient to work with, rather than those forced by the hardware architecture. Furthermore, a hole in memory can be ignored when using a virtual addressing scheme, since the restrictions imposed by physical memory are invisible to both programmer and program.

A virtual addressing scheme gives the illusion that there is more memory available than is physically installed in the machine. This allows the operating system to run a program that is larger than physical memory. In order to run, however, a program must reside in physical memory and it must generate real addresses for both its code and data. Therefore, a translation mechanism is needed to convert virtual memory addresses to physical memory addresses at run time, but to be practical, the translation mechanism must not provide any significant run time overhead.

Virtual memory is implemented using a *multiple-level* (or *hierarchical-storage*) scheme (see Figure 3.2). That is, the parts of a program that will not fit into main memory are held on secondary storage devices such as locally attached disks, or remote disks accessed over a network.

During program execution, the portions of code and data that are not being used can be placed into secondary storage. The swapping between main memory and secondary storage is explained in § 3.8.

Figure 3.2: *Multiple levels of storage*

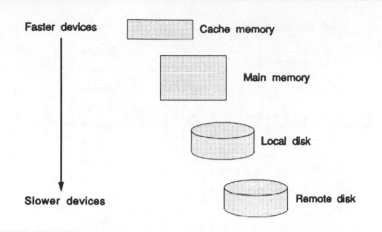

3.1.2 Structure of a page

Physical memory is divided into fixed-size pieces called *pages* and each page maps to a range of physical addresses. The size of a page differs between processor type but 4k bytes is typical. For each physical page of memory there is an entry in a *page map*.

As a process runs, it references code and data by using virtual addresses that are transparently translated to physical addresses. In order to map a virtual address to a physical memory address, a *mapping function* is used. It takes a virtual address and applies it to an *address map* to yield the physical address. A virtual address consists of two parts: a *virtual page number* and an *offset* within that page (see Figure 3.3). The virtual page number and offset must be converted to a *physical page number* (also referred to as the *page frame number*) and offset at run-time. Using a combination of software and hardware techniques, a virtual address is looked up in a page table to yield a physical page number. This is then combined with the offset to produce a real address in physical memory (see Figure 3.4).

The virtual addressing scheme allows the virtual address space to be larger than the physical address space. However, physical pages are not always available for every virtual address reference. To overcome this problem, the page table contains a flag (typically called a *valid bit*) for each page indicating whether the page is currently in main memory or not. If the page is not in main memory then it is inactive and the memory management system keeps information about where in secondary storage the page is kept. When non-resident or inactive pages are referenced, a process must wait until the memory management system brings the page into physical memory. How this is done is described fully in § 3.8.

3.1.3 Associative memory cache

The page table is a data structure that is usually held in physical memory. Each time a virtual page is referenced it must be looked up in this table to yield its

Figure 3.3: *Components of a virtual address*

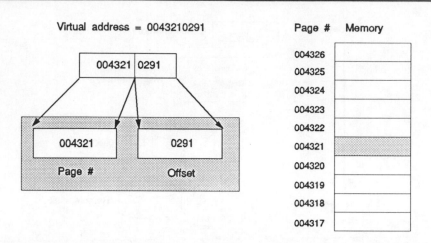

Figure 3.4: *Translation of virtual to physical address*

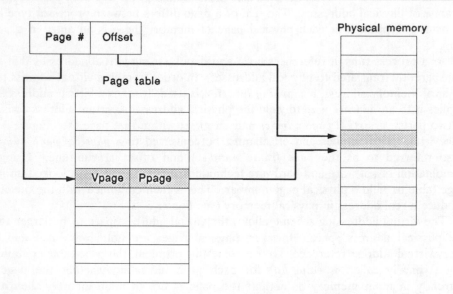

corresponding physical address. Searching this table every time the operating system needs a virtual page could be very time-consuming, so as an alternative, the page table is stored in *associative memory* (see also [Cheng 1987]). This type of memory is often built into the processor chip.

The function of associative memory is to yield the physical address corresponding to a given virtual address. An advantage of using associative memory instead of physical memory is that it can be searched much faster. However, due to the lack of real-estate on the CPU for memory of this type, on-chip associative memory is

Figure 3.5: *Associative memory*

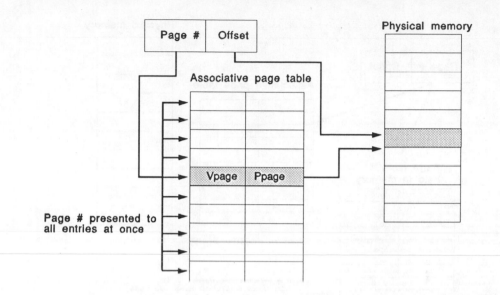

limited to a small area. The MIPS R3000 has 64 entries of on-chip associative cache memory, referred to as the *translation lookaside buffer* (TLB). Figure 3.5 shows how virtual addresses are translated with an associative memory.

Large associative memories are currently not practicable. Therefore many implementations adopt a combined approach: a portion of the page table is held in associative memory, and the remainder is held in physical memory. When the virtual to physical mapping is done the associative memory cache is searched first. If the address is not found in the cache, then the page table is searched instead. The information found is then placed in the associative memory cache in the hope that it will speed up future references to this virtual address (see Figure 3.6).

An alternative method used on the Intel 80386 processor is *linear* or *direct translation* mapping (see Figure 3.7). This form of address translation avoids the need for an associative memory cache because the location of the page table entry can be calculated directly from the virtual page number. The virtual address is split into three parts:

- a page directory number;
- a virtual page number;
- an offset within the virtual page number.

The page directory number is an offset into a *page directory table* which is used to find a corresponding page table. The virtual page number is then used as an offset into that page table. The item found there contains the information about the physical page, and is combined with the offset to yield the physical address of the data.

Figure 3.6: *Combined associative and physical memory cache*

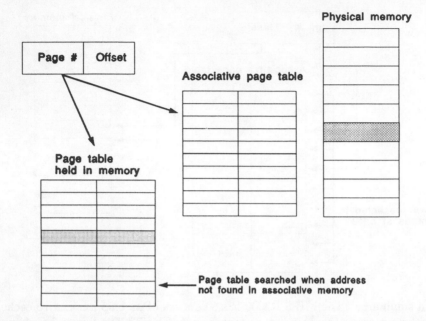

The Intel 80386 processor does not use an associative memory to perform page translation. However, it still has a cache memory which it uses for page translation. Confusingly, this memory is sometimes referred to as the translation lookaside buffer [Intel 1987]. This cache memory holds the translation information about the most recently used pages and so accessing the cache memory is much faster than accessing main memory. However, this cache is not used in the same way as the previously described associative memory. In the MIPS R3000 implementation, operating system code explicitly loads translation information into the TLB, but on the Intel 80386 the cache is loaded automatically by the processor hardware.

3.2 Demand paging

During the initial stages of process execution, only a small amount of physical memory is used: some physical memory is needed to hold administrative data structures such as the *proc* and *user* structures (see *fork* in § 4.12) but the code and initialized data areas associated with the process remain stored in the file from which the program is being run, and the stack and uninitialized data areas are adjusted during its execution.

Page creation and allocation for a process is done in a *lazy* fashion. That is, a page is created and allocated to a process only as it is referenced by the currently running process. This lazy creation of pages is called *demand paging*.

Figure 3.7: *Direct translation mapping*

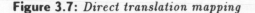

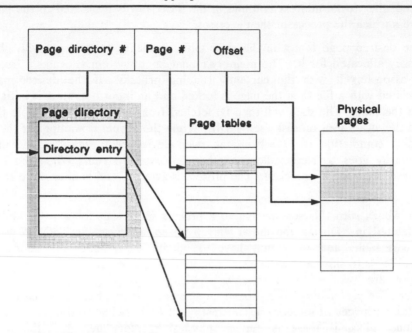

When demand paging is used pages are created only for those parts of the process that actually execute. Those parts of a process that never run remain in secondary storage. For example, the portion of the program that contains error handling code will not be executed if no errors occur. This scheme makes better use of main memory since memory that is not actively used by one process is available for use by others.

Each process has a set of pages that must be in main memory to ensure "efficient" working. This is referred to as its *working set*. When a process accesses an address that is not part of its working set, a *page-fault* occurs so that the page containing the address can be read in to memory and attached to the processes address space. On a machine that uses an associative cache for virtual address translation (such as the MIPS R3000), the procedure for bringing a page into memory (called *paging-in*) is as follows:

- The process references an address. The processor looks up the virtual address in the associative memory but it is not found.

- The execution of the currently running process is suspended and an exception is generated (also called a *fault* or *trap*). On the MIPS R3000 this is called a *TLB miss exception*, meaning that the virtual address was not in the cache.

- The exception handler searches the page tables to see if there is an entry corresponding to the virtual address that was not found in the associative memory. If one is found, then the translation information for this page is placed in the associative memory. The instruction that caused the *TLB miss* is then re-executed. The virtual address is once more looked up in the TLB but this time around, the virtual address is found in the TLB and is translated to the physical address which the processor then accesses.

- If the desired page is not in the page table, it means that there is no physical memory allocated for it. The memory management system allocates a free page and associates it with the currently running process. If the desired page is associated with a file then the page is locked and an input operation is initiated to fetch the data. The data will then be fetched from either the executable file, or from the swap area on disk (see § 3.8). While the kernel is waiting for the data, pending completion of I/O from the swap device or file system, the process voluntarily goes to sleep, allowing other processes to run. When the data is received, the page is unlocked. The process is awoken, and is once more ready to run.

One drawback with this scheme is that a process must wait for a page while it is being faulted in. During the initial startup phase, a process is likely to generate many page-faults and so it may have to initiate many input operations. This overhead leads to slow startup times and an increased number of disk operations.

There are two solutions to this problem: *clustering* and *prefetch*. The procedure for prefetching, as its name implies is an attempt to pre-fetch (or bring in) additional pages of memory in anticipation of them being used in later stages of execution. Thus, if there is enough physical memory available, the memory management system will bring in other pages at the same time as the desired page, and often in a single I/O request. If these pages are subsequently referenced by the process, then a significant gain in performance is made since fewer input operations are required.

When a paging implementation uses clustering (also referred to as *klustering*), physical pages are grouped together and manipulated as a single logical unit (a cluster). An advantage of grouping pages together in this way is that there is less administrative overhead. The page tables can be made smaller, and more data can be transferred with each I/O request. A side effect of clustering is that the memory management system automatically prefetches pages adjacent to the desired page.

Clustering can also be used when the page size of a machine is small, but the virtual memory size is large. For example, on early Digital Equipment Corporation (DEC) VAX series machines, the page size was 512 bytes. To simulate larger pages, the 4.1BSD version of UNIX running on the VAX introduced page clustering. To reduce the overhead of administering small pages, a 2k byte logical page scheme was used, with each page consisting of four 512 byte physical pages.

3.2.1 Page stealing

At some point the operating system will want to bring a page in from secondary storage, but it will have no free physical memory pages available. The operating system overcomes this problem by *page stealing*. This is done by a system process called *pageout* (also called the *page stealer* or *pagedaemon*).

The *pageout* process looks at pages that are already allocated to a process and steals some of them so that they can be used by other processes. The *pageout* process is initiated when the number of free pages falls below its minimum configured threshold. It keeps stealing pages until the number of free pages reaches a maximum configured threshold. (The operation of *pageout* is described in § 3.8.2.)

The page stealer must decide which pages are the ideal ones to steal. The best page to steal is the one whose next reference will be at the furthest point in the future. However, in practice, this is hard to achieve, and so a different method is used.

The simplest page stealing strategy is called *First-in First Out* (FIFO). Under this scheme, the page that has been in memory the longest is the one to be freed. The disadvantage of this scheme is that all pages are eventually stolen regardless of how often they are accessed.

An alternative scheme is called *Least Recently Used* (LRU). Whenever a page is accessed, it is given a time stamp. The page stealer then takes the pages with the earliest time stamps until there are enough free pages available. The LRU algorithm is expensive to run because a page must be time stamped every time it is referenced, so as a result, LRU is rarely used.

The most commonly used method, and the method used in UNIX System V Release 4 UNIX, is called *Not Recently Used* (NRU) or *clock*. This method is similar to LRU but simpler to operate. Each page has a *modified* and a *referenced* bit. Initially, both bits are set to zero, but when a page is referenced, its reference bit is set. Similarly, when a page is modified, its modified bit is set. When the page stealer looks for pages to steal, it first selects those that have not been referenced. If that does not yield enough pages, then it selects those that have been referenced but not modified. Finally, if neither is available, it selects pages that have been both referenced and modified.

Sooner or later, most of the pages will have their reference bits set, so the page stealer periodically goes through memory clearing the reference bits of every page. This procedure resembles the sweep of a hand around a clock, which is why this algorithm is called *clock* (but must not be confused with the *clock( )* function described in § 4.8).

After selecting the pages to steal, those pages that have not been modified are placed directly on a freelist. The page stealer invalidates these pages and clears any associative memory entries pointing to them. Stolen pages are placed at the back of the freelist so that they can be reclaimed by their original owner. Pages that have been modified (also known as *dirty pages*) are first written to disk before being placed on the freelist. Dirty pages may be reclaimed by their rightful owner if the page is referenced before it is written to disk.

Under heavy load, it is possible for a process to have less than its working set in main memory. This can lead to excessive paging. The load is such that a working page is stolen, but the process immediately needs it to be paged back in again. This is repeated for all active processes in the system. Such a state is known as *thrashing*; the system spends almost all its time paging in and paging out instead of processing.

If the system is thrashing, whole processes can have their pages stolen. That is, the system may swap whole processes to secondary storage. If this is done with sufficient processes, it reduces the thrashing. However, if a system is constantly thrashing or swapping processes in and out then it is evident that the system does not have enough physical memory installed.

3.3 Segmentation and regions

Under UNIX System V Release 4 the address space of a process is divided up into different sections called *segments* or *regions*. A segment is a contiguous portion of the virtual address space. A segment provides a convenient method for allowing a process to share a portion of its address space with other processes. It also allows the operating system to protect a process's address space so that the process itself cannot alter it. Figure 3.8 shows how a process is split into segments.

Figure 3.8: *Segments of a process*

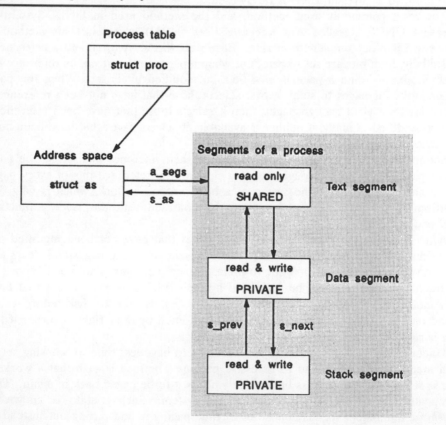

The address space of a process contains the following different types of segment:

- *Text* — contains the executable code (or machine instructions) for a process. It is usually marked read-only so that a process cannot alter its own code, or have it altered by others. A text segment can be shared amongst many processes that execute the same code. For example, there may be many users running the program **vi** at the same time. The operating system will place the code for **vi** in a text segment that is shared amongst all the processes executing it.

- *Data* — holds the data used and modified by a process during its execution. A data segment is usually marked for read and write. However, it is never shared with other processes. If this segment was sharable, then a process may inadvertently alter the data of another process, leading to chaos!

- *Stack* — contains the process stack. It is marked read and write, and like the data segment it is not shared with other processes.

Figure 3.9: *Shared memory*

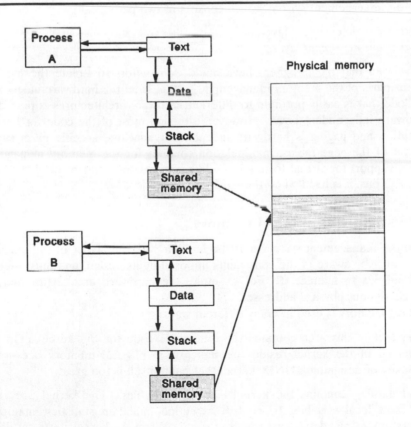

There are two other types of segment that may be used:

- *Shared memory* — this area of memory is accessible to other processes, they can write data into the shared memory segment and have it read by other processes. A shared memory segment can be mapped to different virtual addresses within the address space of each process (see Figure 3.9).

- *Mapped file* — mapped file segments are used to map portions of files into the address space of a process. Normally, to access a file a process must issue both *read* and *write* system calls. By mapping a file into a process's address space its contents can be manipulated simply by using pointers (see § 5.9).

3.4 The hardware independent layer

Under UNIX System V Release 4, virtual memory and segmentation are handled by the memory management system, which consists of two parts:

- the *hardware independent* layer;
- the *hardware dependent* layer.

It can be seen that the designers have made every effort to isolate the hardware dependent parts of the memory management system from the hardware independent parts. Code that is easily portable to different hardware architectures is placed into the hardware independent layer. However, although most of the code for handling segmentation and paging is hardware independent, machine specific parts such as the format of the page tables, manipulation routines for the memory management hardware, support for virtual to physical address translation, and so on, is hardware dependent. Thus, it is handled by the hardware dependent layer.

3.4.1 Structure of physical memory

The memory management system must be familiar with the layout of the machine's memory, must be aware of the constraints imposed by its design, and must maintain suitable policies to manage it. For example, the hardware architecture may not support contiguous physical addresses.

Physical memory is used in many different ways:

- *Kernel text* — this area contains the executable code for the kernel. On most systems all of the kernel resides permanently in physical memory because the complexity of designing a UNIX kernel that pages itself is too great.

- *Kernel data* — contains the kernel's private variables. The kernel uses many global and local variables to control execution, maintain statistics, manipulate pointers to dynamic data structures, and so on. When the kernel starts, an area of physical memory is reserved for kernel static data. This memory area also resides permanently in physical memory.

- *Kernel dynamic data* — wherever possible, the designers of UNIX System V Release 4 have used dynamically allocated data structures to hold kernel data. For example, each active process is given a *proc* structure that is dynamically allocated from a memory pool. Under previous releases of UNIX System V, all *proc* structures were stored in a fixed sized array (called the *process table*) that was allocated at boot time. The advantage of dynamically allocating *proc* structures is that memory is not wasted when only a few processes are running. Under the fixed scheme, if there are fewer processes active than the total number of slots available in the process table, then the memory assigned to the unused slots in the table is wasted.

   Memory allocation for all dynamic data structures is handled by the kernel's dynamic memory allocation routines: *kmem_alloc()* and *kmem_free()* (see § 3.9.2). All dynamically allocated kernel data structures remain permanently in memory until deallocated. That is, they are not paged.

- *User pages* — the remaining memory in the system is allocated as pages. These pages are referred to as *user pages*; they are the pages used by programs running in user-mode.

Figure 3.10: *Example layout of physical memory*

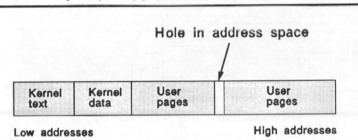

Hole in address space

| Kernel text | Kernel data | User pages | | User pages |

Low addresses   High addresses

3.4.2 Initializing the page system

The kernel cannot assume that the memory layout of each machine will be the same, so the method used to describe the areas of memory to the kernel is hardware dependent. In particular, the kernel needs to know exactly which areas of memory will be used to contain the *user pages*. For example, on the implementation shown in Figure 3.10, user pages are split into two groups that start after the kernel data area. A table called *pageac_table[]* is used to hold the information about which areas of memory are to be used for user pages. Each entry in the table is a *pageac* structure (Table 3.1). The interesting fields in the *pageac* structure are:

- *firstpfn* — holds the page frame number of the first page in the area. It can be thought of as the address of the start of the area.

- *num* — holds the number of pages in the area. By using these two fields, the operating system can calculate the start and end addresses.

Table 3.1: *Struct pageac*

Element	Description
*struct pageac *panext*	Pointer to the next *pageac* structure in the list
unsigned num	Number of pages in this segment
unsigned firstpfn	Page frame number for the first physical page in the area
unsigned endpfn	1 greater than the page frame number of the last page in the area
*struct page *firstpp*	Pointer to the *page* structure for the first page in the area
*struct page *endpp*	Sum of *firstpp* and *num*

Figure 3.11: *The pageac table*

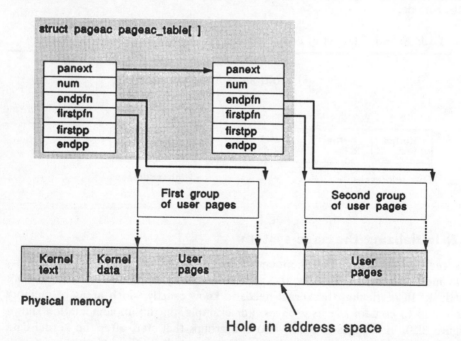

Physical memory

Hole in address space

Each *pageac* structure in the *pageac_table[]* describes the contiguous blocks of physical memory that will be used for user pages. The table makes it easy to accommodate gaps in physical memory. The use of a table also gives a measure of machine independence; the table is set up in a machine specific way, but once initialized, it is passed as a parameter to the machine independent page initialization routines.

As the operating system starts up, the function *mlsetup( )* is called to set up the machine dependent data structures, which in turn sets up the kernel memory management data structures. For example, it may need to inspect the hardware registers to find out how much physical memory is installed. From this information it can initialize the *pageac_table[]* (Figure 3.11).

3.4.3 The *page* structure

The kernel's generic abstraction of a physical page of memory is described by the *page* structure (see Table 3.2). There is one *page* structure for each physically configured page of memory. A *page* structure describes the location and current state of its associated page as the system manipulates it. These structures allow the kernel to maintain information for every physical page of memory in the system. The fields of the *page* structure are described as follows:

- *p_lock* — a page is locked when an operation is in progress. A locked page cannot be freed by or stolen from a process that is using it.

- *p_want* — the page is wanted. When a page is locked or in transit (see below) and another process wants to use it, it marks the page as wanted and then goes to sleep pending the event that the page becomes unlocked. When that event takes place, the process wakes and marks the page locked to obtain its exclusive use.

- *p_free* — the page is free. That is, it is currently on the freelist.

- *p_intrans* — the page is "in transit", this means that an I/O operation is pending for the page. When an output operation is pending, the page cannot be stolen from the process. If it was, then data for the page that had been recently changed would be lost.

- *p_gone* — the page has been released but has not yet been put on the freelist.

- *p_mod* — a copy of the hardware modified bit is kept within the page structure so that the operating system can determine which pages have to be written to the disk. It also helps the page stealer decide which pages are good to steal.

- *p_ref* — a copy of the hardware reference bit is also stored within the page structure. When a page is referenced, this bit is set. Like the *p_mod* bit, the *p_ref* bit is used by the page stealer to determine which pages are good to steal.

- *p_pagein* — if this bit is set, it indicates that the page must be brought in from secondary storage, but the data in the page is not yet valid.

- *p_age* — this bit helps the page stealer to determine which pages to steal.

- *p_vnode* — when a page belongs to a text segment or a mapped file, *p_vnode* points to the *vnode* associated with the file that the data in the page originated.

- *p_hash* — the pages associated with a *vnode* are kept on a *hash list*. The *p_hash* pointer points to the next page in the list. The hash list allows the operating system to find the physical pages for a *vnode* quickly.

Table 3.2: *Struct page (page_t)*

Element	Description
unsigned p_lock:	Set when this page is locked
unsigned p_want:	Set when this page is wanted
unsigned p_free:	Set when this page is free
unsigned p_intrans:	Set when this page is in transit (pending I/O)
unsigned p_gone:	Set when this page has been released
unsigned p_mod:	Software copy of hardware modified bit
unsigned p_ref:	Software copy of hardware reference bit
unsigned p_pagein:	Set when this page is being paged in, data not valid
unsigned p_nc:	Set when this page must not be cached
unsigned p_age:	Used by page stealer
unsigned p_nio :	Number of pending I/O requests
*struct vnode *p_vnode*	Logical *vnode* this page is associated with
unsigned p_offset	Offset into *vnode* for this page
*struct page *p_hash*	Hash list for this page
*struct page *p_next*	Next page in freelist
*struct page *p_prev*	Previous page in freelist
*struct page *p_vpnext*	Next page in *vnode* list
*struct page *p_vpprev*	Previous page in *vnode* list
caddr_t p_mapping	Pointer to HAT information
unsigned short p_lckcnt	Count of page data locks
unsigned short p_cowcnt	Count of copy-on-write locks
short p_keepcnt	Count of processes keeping this page

- *p_next, p_prev* — these two pointers link the page in a doubly linked list. If the page is free, these pointers hook it into the list of free pages. If the page is in transit, they hook it into an I/O list so that the I/O operation can be applied to all pages on the list in a single I/O request.

- *p_mapping* — points to the Hardware Address Translation (HAT) information for the page.

- *p_keepcnt* — a count of the number of processes that want to keep this page in memory. If the keep count is greater than zero, the page will not be stolen. It is used for temporarily locking the page in memory.

- *p_lckcnt* — the lock count is used to lock a page permanently in memory. The count is incremented in response to the *plock* or *memcntl* system calls. A permanently locked page will never be stolen by the page stealer.

3.4.4 Page list management

Each *page* structure in the system represents a physical page. At any one time, a *page* structure may reside on any of the following lists:

- *Vnode hash list* — each mapped or executing file is described by a *vnode*. Pages associated with a *vnode* are chained together in two ways. First a doubly linked list is used to chain together all pages associated with the *vnode* so that the operating system can find all the pages associated with it. Secondly, pages are attached to hash lists pointed to by the *vnode*, allowing the system to access a page quickly when a page-fault occurs.

- *Freelist* — chains together all pages that are free and thus are available to be allocated to processes. Pages become free in response to the page stealer freeing them. Additionally, pages are freed when a process terminates.

- *Cache list* — similar to the freelist, but the data in the pages on this list remains valid. Pages are usually put on the cache list by the page stealer. When a page is wanted, and if it is on the cache list, then it can be reused. For example, a page may be stolen by the page stealer who places it on the cache list. The process may then reuse the page before the operating system allocates it to another process. Thus, a cached page can be reassigned to a process without the need to bring in the data for the page from secondary storage.

    In some implementations there are multiple freelists and cache lists maintained by the operating system. For example, one list may contain "normal" pages, whilst another may contain "DMA" pages (i.e., pages suitable for DMA).

3.4.5 *vnode* pages

When a page is attached to a hash list associated with a *vnode*, it is called a *vnode page* (because of the association with the *vnode*, they are also thought of as *named pages*). Being associated with a *vnode* in this way means that the data in the page originated from a file. Such pages are usually text pages. That is, they hold data that remains unmodified during process execution. Since text pages do not change, the memory management system does not need to allocate swap space for them. When they have to be paged in, the operating system simply reads them directly from the associated file.

3.4.6 Anonymous pages

Anonymous pages are the opposite of *vnode pages*, that is, they have no association with their original *vnode*. Anonymous pages are writeable, and are given to a process for its data and stack segments. As the data and stack segments of a process grow, the operating system assigns more anonymous pages to it. However, an anonymous page always retains its association with the *vnode* of its swap device. Pages are written to and read from their swap device by using the *vnode* operations (see § 6.3.2) appropriate for the swap device. Since the *vnode* is associated with a file, it means that any file type can be used as a swap device. It also means that the same functions that are used to fault pages in from a file can be used to fault pages back in from the swap device.

The memory management system uses four main data structures to handle anonymous pages. They are: *as*, *seg*, *segvn_data* and *anon* and are discussed in the following sections.

3.4.7 The *as* structure

Every process has an *as* structure (Table 3.3) which is used to describe its virtual memory *address space*. The *as* contains pointers to the hardware address translation (HAT) information and to a list of segments that are associated with the process's address space. The fields of interest in the *as* structure are:

- *a_segs* — points to the list of segments attached to the process.

- *a_seglast* — segments in a process's address space are linked together in a circular list and when the kernel needs to search for a segment associated with a particular address, it starts here; there is a good chance that the specified address will fall within the last segment referenced, so the kernel keeps a cached copy of the last referenced segment in *a_seglast*.

- *a_size* — gives the size of the processes virtual address space.

- *a_rss* — measures how much physical memory the process is currently using (i.e., its resident set size).

- *a_hat* — is a hat data structure containing pointers to the implementation specific data structures used for hardware address translation (see § 3.6.2).

Table 3.3: *Struct as*

Element	Description
struct seg *a_segs	Pointer to the first segment in this address space
struct seg *a_seglast	Pointer to the last segment referenced
size_t a_size	The size of this address space
size_t a_rss	Amount of physical memory used
struct hat a_hat	HAT information

3.4.8 The *seg* structure

The address space of a process is divided up into *segments*, (Under UNIX System V Release 3, segments were referred to as *regions*.) and each segment is managed by its own *seg* structure (see Table 3.4). Segments for a process are chained together on a doubly linked list which is attached to the address space of the process (see Figure 3.8). The fields of interest in the *seg* structure are:

- *s_base* — gives the base (or starting) virtual address of the segment. When a page-fault occurs, the operating system uses this field to determine which segment the fault occurred in.

- *s_size* — gives the size of the segment in bytes. By using a combination of starting virtual address and size, the operating system can determine whether an address falls inside or outside a segment. If it falls outside, the operating system generates an error and terminates the process (*SIGSEGV*).

- *s_as* — is a back pointer to the *as* structure containing this segment.

Table 3.4: *Struct seg*

Element	Description
addr_t s_base	Virtual address of the start of the segment
unsigned s_size	The size of the segment, in bytes
struct as *s_as	Back pointer to address space
struct seg *s_next	A pointer to the next segment in the same address space
struct seg *s_prev	Pointer to previous segment
struct seg_ops *s_ops	Segment operations
void *s_data	Pointer to segment specific information

- *s_next, s_prev* — pointers to the next and previous segments in the current address space.

- *s_ops* — each *seg* structure holds a pointer to a *seg_ops* structure (see Table 3.8) containing a set of function pointers defining the operations that can be done to the segment. For example, segments can be duplicated, freed, mapped, and so on. These routines differ between implementations and segment types. Each pointer is initialized to point to the function that will carry out the operation. When the operating system wants to carry out an operation, it calls the function via its associated *seg_ops* pointer. (Segment operations are described in § 3.6.1)

- *s_data* — is a pointer to a private data structure for this segment used by the hardware dependent layer. Usually it points to a *segvn_data* structure.

3.4.9 The *segvn_data* structure

Most active segments in the system are *segvn* segments and are associated in some way with a *vnode*, or anonymous memory. These segments are described by the *segvn_data* structure (Table 3.6), which contain the following fields:

- *pageprot* — if this value is non-zero, it indicates that pages in the segment each have their own protection bits. That is, if the process wants to perform an operation on a page, the page itself is checked to see if the operation is allowed.

- *prot* — if *pageprot* is zero, the segment as a whole has a set of protection bits given by this field. *prot* is a bitmask that specifies which operations are allowed on the segment. There are separate bits for read, write or execute code. If the appropriate bit is set, the operation is allowed. These protection bits are checked each time the segment is accessed. If access is disallowed, the user process

Table 3.5: *Struct segvn_data*

Element	Description
unsigned char pageprot	True if pages are individually protected
unsigned char prot	Segment protection
unsigned char maxprot	Maximum segment protection
unsigned char type	Type of sharing carried out
struct vnode *vp	Pointer to *vnode* this segment is associated with
unsigned offset	Offset into *vnode*
unsigned anon_index	Index into *anon* structure map in *amp*
struct anon_map *amp	Anonymous map pointer
struct vpage *vpage	Individual page information
unsigned swresv	True if swap is reserved for this segment

terminates with a protection violation error. For example, if the process attempts a write operation on a segment that does not have the write bit set, the process is killed.

- *type* — indicates how the segment is shared. If the value is *MAP_PRIVATE* (defined in *<sys/mmap.h>*), all changes that take place within the segment are private to it. Alternatively, if the value is *MAP_SHARED*, any changes made to the pages are seen by other segments that share them.

- *vp* — is a pointer to a *vnode*. It is used by the operating system when it has to find the *vnode* pages associated with the segment.

- *amp* — points to the map for the anonymous pages associated with the segment (see the next section).

- *swresv* — a flag indicating whether swap space has been reserved for the segment.

Table 3.6: *Struct anon_map*

Element	Description
u_int refcnt	Reference count for this map
u_int size	Size in bytes mapped by the *anon* array
struct anon **anon	Array of *anon* pointers
u_int swresv	Swap space reserved for this *anon_map*

3.4.10 The *anon* structure

The *anon_map* structure (see Table 3.6) for a segment allows the operating system to find the anonymous pages associated with it. Anonymous pages for a segment occupy successive virtual addresses and descriptors for the pages are held in an array called *anon*. Each successive element in the array maps to a successive block of virtual addresses. Items in this array are *anon* structures (Table 3.7) whose elements are:

- *an_refcnt* — contains a count of the number of segments that are associated with this *anon* structure.

- *an_page* — contains a pointer to the *page* structure (see Table 3.2) associated with this anonymous page. Note that this pointer is invalid if the page has been stolen from the process. When the kernel dereferences this pointer it always checks whether the page it points to is the expected page.

- *an_next* — *anon* structures are dynamically allocated from a pool. This field points to the next free structure in the freelist.

Table 3.7: *Struct anon*

Element	Description
int an_refcnt	Reference count
*struct page *an_page*	Pointer to associated page
*struct anon *an_next*	Pointer to next item in freelist
*struct anon *an_bap*	Back pointer to anonymous array

3.5 Paging system procedures

There are many procedures within the memory management subsystem that manipulate data structures such as those described in previous sections. This section outlines the procedures that are of interest.

- *as_alloc()*, *as_free()* — dynamically allocate and free *as* structures.

- *as_segat()* — finds the segment corresponding to a particular virtual address within a process's address space. It searches the list of segments attached to the address space and returns a pointer to the segment containing the desired virtual address.

- *as_map()* — allocates a *seg* structure and inserts it into the linked list of segments in the process's address space (the segments are sorted by virtual address). The segment initialization function is then called to set up the *s_data* and *s_ops* fields, and *as_map()* calls either *segvn_create()* or *segdev_create()* depending on the segment type being operated on. *segvn* segments are described in § 3.6.1, and *segdev* segments are described in § 5.9.2.

- *as_fault()*, *as_faulta()* — handle hardware page-faults, and are called directly by the kernel fault handling code. They look up the segment in which the fault occurred, and call the hardware dependent fault handling function within the HAT layer. *as_fault()* handles page-faults synchronously. That is, the page is faulted-in immediately, whereas *as_faulta()* is used to start I/O on pages asynchronously.

Figure 3.12: *Algorithms for anon_alloc( ) and anon_decref( )*

```
anon_alloc( )
input: none
output: pointer to anon structure
{
  struct anon *a;
  a = swap_alloc(); /* get swap space and anon structure */
  initialize the new anon structure
  set reference count to 1
  return a pointer to it
}

anon_decref( )
input: pointer to struct anon
output: none
{
    if (reference count == 1) {
        /* free resources.. */
        if( physical page attached )
            free the page
        decrement reference count
        free the slot in swap space
    }
    else
        decrement reference count
}
```

- *seg_alloc( ), seg_free( )* — dynamically allocate and free *seg* structures.

- *seg_attach( )* — places a segment into the linked list of segments attached to the process's address space. Segments within an address space are sorted by address.

- *anon_alloc( )* — allocates a new anonymous page, usually when the data segment of a process has to be extended, or a copy-on-write page has been written to. Since anonymous pages are always associated with a swap device, *swap_alloc( )* (Figure 3.12) is called to establish the swap space for it. The page is then initialized and its address is returned to the caller (see § 3.8.4).

- *anon_zero( )* — allocates a private zero-filled anonymous page. It is usually called when anonymous pages for a segment are first created. *anon_alloc( )* is called to reserve swap space and allocate the anonymous page. It then attempts to reserve enough memory for it using *page_get( )* (see below).

- *anon_decref( )* — decrements the reference count of an anonymous page (Figure 3.12). If the reference count falls to 1, the anonymous page is freed and its swap space is given up.

- *anon_free( )* — frees a list of anonymous pages. It is called after a process dies to free the anonymous pages in each of its segments. All pages to be freed are passed to *anon_decref( )*.

- *anon_getpage( )* — retrieves an anonymous page. Usually it is called when a page-fault occurs and the page is not mapped through the associative memory. It checks the page pointer in the supplied *anon* structure, which is termed "reasonable" if it points to a page that has the same *vnode* and offset as the *anon* structure. If not, it means that the page has been stolen, and so must be reclaimed from swap space or the *vnode*. If the page is in transit, *anon_getpage( )* waits until the input operation has completed. If the page is on the freelist, it is removed. If the page pointer is not reasonable, it means that the page has been stolen or else not yet referenced, so the page is brought in directly from the *vnode*, which may refer to the original file from which the program was executed, or to its associated swap area. Finally, the page pointer in the *anon* structure is set to point to the physical page (see Figure 3.13).

- *anon_private( )* — implements anonymous page "copy-on-write" (see Figure 3.14). Two processes can refer to the same page, and have read/write access to it. However, when it is first written, the page must be copied, and the copy given to the writing process. *anon_private( )* implements the copy after the hardware has determined that a "copy-on-write" fault has occurred. It allocates a new anonymous page, copies the data from the old page, then gives the new page to the writing process. Finally, it decrements the reference count on the original page.

The key functions in the paging system implementation are described as follows:

- *page_reclaim( )* — ensures that the page is marked as no longer free, and sets up the corresponding *anon* structure to point to the page (see Figure 3.15).

- *page_find( )* — searches the *vnode* hash lists to see if it already contains the page corresponding to the desired *vnode* and offset. If it does, the page is returned, otherwise a null pointer is returned. This routine is called when the desired page is not in memory, and the page is associated with a *vnode* (see Figure 3.16).

- *page_get( )* — attempts to reserve a number of free pages for a specified number of bytes (see Figure 3.17). If there are not enough pages in memory, it initiates a pageout and the process sleeps until the pageout completes. There is no guarantee that the process will ever wake up and find the required number of pages. This can happen when higher priority processes are scheduled first and they take the memory. However, if the process wakes up, and there are enough free pages, they are taken from the freelist and returned to the caller.

In Figure 3.18 all the data structures are brought together to give a high-level view of how the hardware independent layers of the memory management system fit together.

Figure 3.13: *Algorithm for anon_getpage( )*

```
anon_getpage( )
input: anon structure map
       segment pointer
       pointer to store retrieved page
output: found pages, error code
{
  while structure is locked
      sleep ( anon unlocked )
  lock anon structure
again:
  if (page pointer in mapped anon structure looks reasonable) {
    if( page is in transit ) {
      /* Wait for page input from swap */
      page_wait( )
      goto again
    }
    if( page is on freelist )
      reclaim page

    /* marks page as ''kept'' */
    increase reference count
  }
  else
    /* Page can be re-fetched direct from vnode */
    VOP_GETPAGE(...)

  assign the retrieved page
  unlock page
}
```

3.6 Hardware dependent layer

In this section we look at the hardware dependent layer of the memory management system, which is known as the Hardware Address Translation (HAT) layer. Its purpose is to manage the basic operations on segments and to provide a set of machine specific functions that support segment operations.

The procedures described in the following sections are heavily machine dependent. When they were written the programmer had to know in detail the processor and memory management hardware of the computer that they would run on. The following sections refer to their implementation on a computer system using the MIPS R3000 processor. For further information about this processor architecture see [Kane, Heinrich 1992].

Figure 3.14: *Algorithm for anon_private( )*

```
anon_private( )
input: anonymous map
       segment pointer
       original page
output: new page
{
  new page = anon_alloc( )  /* Allocate swap space */
  if( new page is  NULL )
      error, out of swap space

  /* See if page still exists in system */
  look up page using page_lookup( )
  if ( page not found )
      allocate new page frame  /* usual case */
  else
      it was still there, so use it

  attach page to new anon structure
  copy contents of original page
  decrement reference count on original page
  return new page
}
```

Figure 3.15: *Algorithm for page_reclaim( )*

```
page_reclaim( )
inputs: page to reclaim
output: none
{
  if( page on freelist ) {
      mark page as in use
      if( page is anonymous )
        point corresponding anon structure at the page
  }
}
```

3.6.1 Segment operations

As discussed in § 3.3, the address space of a process is divided into segments, each of which, is represented by a *seg* structure containing a set of private pointers to functions that operate on the segment. Whenever the hardware independent layer has to operate on a segment, it calls the function pointed to in the *seg* structure by using the indirect function call mechanism of C. This is illustrated in Figure 3.19.

Figure 3.16: *Algorithm for page_find( )*

```
page_find( )
input: vnode, offset
output: pointer to page
{
  current_page = start of vnode hash list
  while( current_page not NULL ) {
    if( vnode, offset of current page match ) {
      /* found it */
      page = page_reclaim( current_page )
    }
    else
      /* we missed it */
      alter ''page miss'' count
  }
  return page
}
```

There are 17 operations defined for a segment, and they are referenced via their associated function pointers defined in a *seg_ops* structure (see Table 3.8). Of special interest is *(*fault)( )* since it performs the bulk of the work. Normally, all segments encountered in the operating system are *vnode* segments (*segvn*), so the *(*fault)( )* field will have been initialized to point to the *segvn_fault( )* function which is described as follows:

- *segvn_fault( )* — called by the page-fault mechanism to bring in pages from secondary storage to main memory. If the pages are *vnode* pages, it calls the *vnode* routines (such as *VOP_GETPAGE( )*) to bring them into memory. If the pages are anonymous, it uses the various *anon* functions to access the data.

  If *segvn_fault( )* detects an access error, it returns a failure code. The user process that is running will be killed with either a *SIGSEGV* or a *SIGBUS* signal, depending on the failure code.

  segvn_fault( ) uses a private array called *pl[ ]*, containing eight *page* structures. It holds information about the pages that are being paged in from secondary storage.

- *segvn_faultpage( )* — this function is only ever called by *segvn_fault( )* to process each individual page. It handles three distinct cases:

  - A reference is made to an anonymous page that has to be created and initialized with zeros.

  - A reference is made to a *vnode* page that has to be read in from the associated file.

Figure 3.17: *Algorithm for page_get( )*

```
page_get( )
input: byte count, flags
output: list of pages big enough to hold byte count
{
  npages = number of pages needed to hold byte count
  if( npages > largest allowed request )
    return empty list

  /* Work out how many free pages we want in the system */
  reqiredfree = npages + minimum allowed number of free pages
  while( freepages < requiredfree ) {
    if( CANWAIT flag NOT set ) {
      /* return what we already have.. */
      return listofpages
    }

    initiate pageout to create free pages
    sleep( pageout completed )
  }

  update freemem
  if ( freemem < required amount of freemem ) {
    /* maybe memory was allocated while we slept above */
    initiate pageout
  }

  while( npages-- ) {
    pull pages from freelist
    add to return list
  }
  return list
}
```

- A reference is made to a copy-on-write page. A new page is created, and a copy of the original data is written into it.

In all three cases, after the page has been found, the support functions of the HAT layer are called to set up the page tables and associative memory entries for the page.

Figure 3.18: *Memory management system data structures*

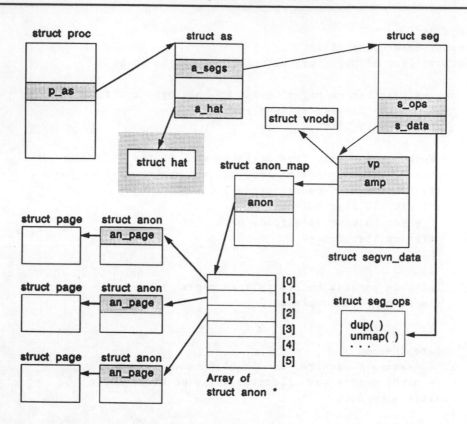

3.6.2 HAT layer data structures

The data structures in the HAT layer described here support the paging system used on an implementation for the MIPS processor. The HAT layer functions will be different on other implementations.

On the MIPS processor, the paging system makes use of a 64-entry associative page table. The page tables used by a process are held in kernel memory and the operating system allocates pages to hold the page tables. These are called *page table pages* or more simply *page wrappers*. The page table pages hold *page table entries*. Page table entries are used to hold information about the physical page, such as its address and its protection fields. The structure of the page table entry reflects precisely the hardware page table information.

On the MIPS processor the page table pages are accessed by using kernel virtual addresses. (This area of the processor address space is called *KSEG2*.) This brings three main benefits. Having them in kernel address space means that the process cannot directly alter its page tables — if it did, chaos would ensue. Secondly, by using virtual addresses the kernel can swap the page tables for a process out to disk when memory gets low. Thirdly, by using virtual addresses, the page tables can be

Figure 3.19: *Indirect function call for segment operation*

```
/* Part of declaration of seg_ops
 * unmap is a pointer to a function
 * returning integer
 */
struct seg_ops {
   ...
   int     (*unmap)();
   void    (*free)();
   ...
} ;

/* S points to the seg_ops field */
struct seg_ops *s ;

/* Indirect function call */
result = (*s->unmap)( seg, addr, count ) ;
```

Table 3.8: *Struct seg_ops (segment operations)*

Function	Operation
int (*dup)( )	Makes an exact copy of a segment
int (*unmap)( )	Unmaps the segment from the address space
void (*free)( )	Similar to unmap, but also deletes all the resources used by the segment
faultcode_t (*fault)( )	Handles a page-fault
faultcode_t (*faulta)( )	Pre-fetches pages
void (*unload)( )	Frees any address translation associated with pages
int (*setprot)( )	Sets protection for a range of pages in the segment
int (*checkprot)( )	Says what protection bits are set for the segment
int (*kluster)( )	Checks if it is sensible to perform pre-fetch
u_int (*swapout)( )	Swaps out pages from a segment
int (*sync)( )	Writes modified pages back to swap or to mapped file
int (*incore)( )	Checks if pages are in physical memory
int (*lockop)( )	Locks pages mapped by the segment
int (*getprot)( )	Returns the protection bits for a range of pages
off_t (*getoffset)( )	Converts address to offset relative to start of segment
int (*gettype)( )	Returns the type of the page
int (*getvp)( )	Gets the *vnode* pointer associated with the segment

Figure 3.20: *Algorithm for segvn_fault( )*

```
segvn_fault( )
inputs: segment in which the fault occurred
        address at which the fault occurred
        length of area to bring in (usually 1 byte)
        fault type
        operation type
{
 if( operation type not permitted on this segment )
   return illegal access error

 /* Check to see if anon map is needed */
 if( there is no associated vnode )
   allocate anon map structure
 if( it is a private segment AND
     the operation is write or it is a protection fault )
   allocate anon map structure

 initialize pl[] to be empty

 if( there IS an associated vnode ) {
   if ( no associated anon map OR
        no associated anon pages OR
        associated anon page is missing ) {
     /* then we have to get the page from the vnode
      * because it is an anon page that is initially
      * brought in from the vnode (i.e., the file)
      */
     call VOP_GETPAGE to fill pl[] from the vnode
 }

 for( one address in each page to be faulted ) {
   call segvn_faultpage( segment, address, pl, ... )
 }
 return
}
```

grown if necessary. (In practice, one page table page holds 512 page table entries, enough to map a process 2Mb in size, so each process uses few page table pages.)

Each address space in the operating system is represented by an *as* structure (see Table 3.3) which contains a pointer called *a_hat*, which points to the HAT specific information. The interesting fields of the *hat* structure (see Table 3.9) are described as follows:

Figure 3.21: *Algorithm for segvn_faultpage( )*

```
segvn_faultpage( )
inputs: segment, page and offset
outputs: error code
{
 if( operation type not permitted on this segment )
   return illegal access error

 if( no associated vnode OR
     no anonymous page ) {
   /* We need to create anonymous page */
   page = anon_zero( ) ;
   hat_memload(page) ; /* See text */
   return ;
 }

 if ( there is anonymous page )
   page = the anonymous page
 else
   page = vnode page from the pl array

 if ( page is NOT copy-on-write ) {
   hat_memload(page) ;
   return ;
 }
 else { /* It is copy-on-write */
   hat_memload(page) ;
   /* Lock page in memory */
   /* Create copy of the page */
   pagep = anon_private( page ) ;
   hat_memload(pagep) ;
   return ;
 }
}
```

- *h_pid* — the TLB entries in the associative memory all have a 6 bit field called the Address Space Identifier (ASID). The *h_pid* field is a copy of the ASID to use for this address space.

- *h_hash* — this array is a hash table containing the page table pages for the process. There are 32 entries, each holding a circular linked list of page table pages. When the kernel needs to find the page tables that belong to an address space, it searches this table. Each page in this hash list contains *pte* structures which are described below.

Table 3.9: *Struct hat (hat_t)*

Element	Description
unsigned h_pid	ASID field for the MIPS TLB
*page_t *h_hash[32]*	Pointers to the page tables for this address space
pte_t h_wptbl[5]	Wired *TLB* entries
caddr_t h_tlbhi_tbl[5]	Wired *TLB* entries upper part
int h_nwired	Wired entries in use in lower part

- *h_wptbl, h_tlbhi_tbl* — the associative cache (the TLB) on the R3000 processor has 8 *wired* or fixed TLB entries. The fixed TLB entries are not overwritten during the normal course of events. The first three of these entries are reserved to point to the user-area and the kernel stack of the currently running process. The remainder are available, and are used to hold mappings for page table pages. When a page table page is referenced, the mapping information for the page is placed in a *wired* TLB entry. Putting the page table mappings into the fixed entries means that once they have been set up, there will be no further TLB faults caused by accessing the page tables. When a context switch occurs, and the process whose address space contains this *hat* structure becomes the currently running process, the entries from these fields are reloaded into the wired entries of the *TLB*. As a result, the number of *TLB miss* faults that occur after a context switch are reduced. The field *h_wptbl* holds the *TLB lo* information which consists of the page frame number and the hardware protection bits. The other field *h_tlbhi_tbl*, holds the *TLB hi* information which consists of the virtual page number and the ASID.

- *h_nwired* — holds the number of wired entries that this address space has in use.

Each process has a page table associated with it. Part of the page table is held in associative memory (the *TLB* on the MIPS processor) and the rest is held in page tables in memory. Each page of the process, whether it is held in memory or not, has a page table entry associated with it. Page table entries held in memory are represented by a *pte* structure (see Table 3.10).

A *pte* is either valid or invalid. If its associated physical page is present in memory, and it contains the correct data, it is valid. Otherwise, the fields of the *pte* are zero and it is invalid. If a process associated with a page dies or the page is stolen, the physical page no longer needs to exist in memory, so the *pte* structure is filled with zeros; this operation is called invalidating the *pte*. The act of making a *pte* contain valid data is called *mapping* the page, and invalidating a *pte*, is called *un-mapping* a page.

Three distinct parts comprise a *pte* structure: the hardware bits, the software bits and the link field. The hardware bits are a direct copy of the bits in the *TLB* registers in the processor. If the bit is set in the *TLB*, the corresponding bit will be set in the *TLB* entry when it is loaded. The software bits are used by the kernel to implement extra facilities not provided by the processor — for example, support for referenced, written, and locked pages. Finally, the link field is used to chain page table entries together. The fields in the *pte* structure are described below. The first group of fields represent the hardware bits, which are stored in a 32 bit word and are directly loaded into the *TLB* registers.

- *pg_pfn* — holds the 20 bit page frame number, that is, the physical page number that is being mapped.

- *pg_n* — corresponds to the *N* bit in the *TLB*. This bit marks the page as non-cacheable. If it is set, the processor will always access memory directly instead of going first to the onboard cache. This facility is used by device drivers when they map registers or on-board memory into the address space.

- *pg_d* — the dirty bit. When this bit is clear, and the processor tries to write to the page, a trap occurs. The kernel detects this trap and can then perform copy-on-write operations, or detect writes to read-only pages and so on. If *pg_d* is set, no trap occurs when the page is modified.

Table 3.10: *Struct pte (pte_t)*

Element	Description	
unsigned pg_pfn	20 bit page frame number	
unsigned pg_n	Page is non-cacheable	
unsigned pg_d	Page is dirty	Hardware bits
unsigned pg_v	Page is valid	
unsigned pg_g	Ignore ASID field in *TLB*	
unsigned pg_r	Page is referenced	
unsigned pg_w	Page is writeable	Software bits
unsigned pg_l	Page is locked	
unsigned pg_f	Force *TLB* miss	
*struct pte *pg_next*	Pointer to next *pte*	Link field

- *pg_v* — the valid bit. If this bit is set, the *TLB* entry is valid and can be used. If it is not set, the entry is invalid, and a *tlbmiss* will occur if the page is accessed. For example, when the page stealer takes a page from memory, it clears the valid bit in any *TLB* entries that reference the page. When the process next accesses the page, a trap occurs, and the kernel brings the page back into memory.

- *pg_g* — the global bit. If this bit is set, the processor does not compare the ASID field in the *TLB* entry. *pg_g* is set for all pages that map kernel virtual addresses, it means the kernel does not need to save and restore values of the ASID when it wants to access kernel pages.

- *pg_r* — the software referenced bit. When it is set, the page has been referenced.

- *pg_w* — the writeable bit. If set, the kernel will allow the process to write to the page. Otherwise, a write to the page will force the process to be killed with a segmentation violation.

- *pg_l* — the locked bit. If set, the *pte* is locked, which means that the fields in the *pte* cannot be changed. In particular, the associated physical page cannot be stolen by the page daemon, and the physical page cannot be moved.

- *pg_next* — this field is a pointer to a *pte* structure. Each page in the system can be mapped by many processes. That is, a page can appear in the address space of many processes. For example, when five users are running the **vi** editor, there will be five processes that access the pages of the **vi** program. The kernel uses the *HAT Data* field in the *page* structure to link together all the *pte* structures that map the particular page. When the page is stolen, the kernel follows the chain of *pte* structures from the *HAT Data* field and marks them all as invalid.

Figure 3.22 shows the relationships between the page table pages, the *page* structure and the *pte* structure.

Figure 3.22: *HAT layer data structures*

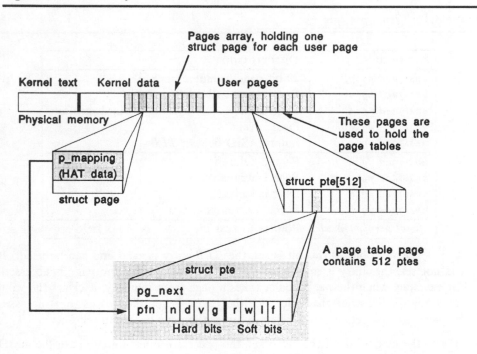

3.6.3 HAT layer support functions

The HAT layer support functions are called by the segment operation functions to perform the machine dependent operations on pages and page tables. To illustrate how the HAT layer interacts with the processor hardware we present a description of *hat_pteload( )*. This is followed by a brief summary of other HAT layer functions.

Figure 3.23: *Algorithm for hat_pteload( )*

```
hat_pteload( )
input: segment page belongs to
       virtual address to map
       pointer to the page to map
       page frame number
{
  pte = hat_getpte( ) ;
  if ( pte is valid ) {
    if( pte->pg_pfn == page frame number ) {
      /* update the ref and
       * mod bits in the page structure
       */
      lock pte if necessary
      set pte writable bit if necessary
      return
    }
    else {
      /* pfn does not match expected pfn so... */
      PANIC( page mapping changed unexpectedly )
    }
  }
  /* The pte was invalid, so set it up */
  pte->pg_pfn = page frame number
  set pte valid bit
  /* link onto the struct page.. */
  hat_inmap( )
  return
}
```

The algorithm for *hat_pteload( )* is shown in Figure 3.23. It calls the function *hat_getpte( )* to return the appropriate *pte* structure that is used to represent the corresponding *page* structure. If the *pte* is valid, the corresponding data in the *page* structure is updated. Otherwise, the fields of the *pte* structure are set up to match the page frame number and the current state of the page.

- *hat_getpte( )* — returns a pointer to the *pte* that will be used to map a given virtual address. If the page table page has not yet been allocated then *hat_getpte( )* allocates the page table page.

- *hat_inmap( )* — links a *pte* into the list of *ptes* that map a particular page.

- *hat_demap( )* — removes a *pte* from the list of *ptes* that map the page.

- *hat_init( )* — initializes any data structures used by the HAT layer functions.

- *hat_alloc( )* — initializes the HAT fields in an *as* structure.

- *hat_free( )* — removes all the *ptes* associated with an address space. The function is called when an address space is being deleted. All the *ptes* associated with the *hat* structure for the address space are set to zero (that is, they are invalidated). If there are any page table pages associated with the address space, they too are freed.

- *hat_swapin( ), hat_swapout( )* — on the MIPS implementation these functions do nothing. On other systems they are used to swap in or swap out the HAT layer resources associated with the address space. On the MIPS implementation, the swap in happens as a side effect of *hat_pteload( )*. *hat_swapout( )* happens as a side effect of *pageout* stealing a page from a process.

- *hat_pageunload( )* — when a page is freed, this function is called to invalidate all the *ptes* associated with it. Once invalidated, future references to it cause a page-fault. The page is then brought back from secondary storage.

- *hat_unload( )* — similar to *hat_pageunload( )*, but it unmaps all the pages within a specified range of addresses, rather than unmapping a single page.

- *hat_chgprot( )* — changes the protections on a specified range of virtual addresses. This function is used, for example, to change read-only pages into writable pages.

- *hat_pagesync( )* — the *pte* structure contains a copy of the hardware and software bits that describe the state of the physical page. For example, the pg_d, pg_v and pg_g bits in the *pte* structure. Some of these bits are also held in the *page* structure. *hat_pagesync( )* copies the necessary hardware and software bits from the *pte* into a *page* structure.

- *hat_memload( )* — sets up a page table entry for a given page.

- *hat_dup( )* — when an *as* structure is being duplicated, *hat_dup( )* is called to duplicate any necessary *hat* data structures.

- *hat_map( )* — sets up page table entries so that the area of the file specified in an *mmap* system call (§ 5.9) has virtual addresses set up in the address space of the calling process.

- *hat_unlock( )* — unlocks *ptes*; the *ptes* are locked when I/O operations are in progress.

- *hat_getkpfnum( )* — used by the Driver-Kernel Interface (see § 5.11). It returns the page frame number that corresponds to a particular virtual address.

- *hat_exec( )* — when an *exec( )* operation is performed, this function performs the special processing to copy the stack segment of the old process image into the stack segment of the new one.

3.7 Demand paging

So far in this chapter we have examined the whole virtual memory system in a top-down fashion. In this section, we examine the bottom layer, and see how the processor and the bottom layers of the kernel implement virtual memory. At the lowest level, there are processor *exceptions* which are similar to interrupts, and the low-level support routines that handle them. The exceptions are described in the following subsections.

The exception processing and the exception handlers are complicated and hard to understand. Therefore, the last sub-section provides some worked examples of typical paging situations.

3.7.1 Exception handling

On the MIPS R3000 processor there are 20 possible *exceptions*. When an exception occurs, normal processing is suspended, and special code to handle the exception is executed. Of the 20 exceptions, we will look at three: *TLB Refill, TLB Invalid* and *TLB modified*. These three exceptions enable the operating system to provide demand paged virtual memory.

Consider the following example: a TLB Invalid exception occurs because the process attempts to access a virtual address whose TLB entry is currently invalid (the valid bit is not set in the TLB entry). The processor switches into kernel-mode, aborts the currently executing instruction and jumps unconditionally to an exception handling routine. This routine then determines the exact cause of the exception. On the MIPS implementation a common exception handling routine is called. It determines the cause of the exception and in turn calls an exception specific handling routine to service it. The following processor registers are used:

- *EPC* — the processor contains a register called the *exception program counter*. The EPC holds the address where normal processing is to be resumed after the exception has been processed. Usually, this is the address of the instruction that caused the exception.

- *Cause* — the cause register indicates the cause of the exception.

- *BadVAddr* — when a TLB exception occurs, indicating that a virtual address does not have a valid translation in the TLB, this register is filled with the address that failed. This allows the kernel to see which virtual address did not work, and to set up a mapping for it.

The three exceptions are:

- *TLB Refill* — occurs a virtual address is referenced with no matching TLB entry. To handle this exception, the kernel tries to put the *pte* that maps the virtual address into the TLB. The processor provides a special vector for this exception. When it occurs, the assembler routine *utlbmiss* is called. *utlbmiss* is fundamental to the operation of the virtual memory, and its operation is described later.

- *TLB Invalid* — occurs when a virtual address in the TLB is accessed and its valid bit is not set. The valid bit is cleared if the virtual address does not exist, or the page is not in memory. The kernel will also clear the bit if it wants to force a trap when the page is referenced (this is done to simulate the referenced bit). When this exception occurs, the common exception handler is called which in turn calls *VEC_tlbmiss* (discussed later).

- *TLB Modified* — occurs when a virtual address is referenced that has the valid bit set, but does not have the writeable bit set in its TLB entry (that is, an attempt is made to write to a page that is not marked as writeable). When this exception occurs, the kernel checks if the page is marked copy-on-write, or read-only. If it is marked copy-on-write, the physical page is duplicated. If the page is marked read-only, then the process is terminated with a segmentation violation signal (*SIGSEGV*).

If the process voluntarily goes to sleep pending some event after the exception has been processed, a context switch occurs before returning to user-mode. Otherwise the process resumes processing at the address held in the EPC register.

3.7.2 Low-level routines

In the MIPS kernel there are five key routines that implement the lowest levels of the paging system. The assembly language routines *exception*, *VEC_tlbmod* and *VEC_tlbmiss* handle the TLB Invalid and TLB Modified exceptions. When an exception occurs, the *exception* routine is executed and it in turn calls *VEC_tlbmiss* or *VEC_tlbmod* depending on the exception type. These functions then set up the stack and call the C Language function *pagefault( )* (they set up the stack so that *pagefault( )* thinks it was called from another C Language routine with five parameters).

The assembly language routine *utlbmiss* handles the TLB Refill exception, and its operation is described in § 3.7.4.

3.7.3 The *pagefault( )* function

The *pagefault( )* function, as its name implies, does most of the processing necessary to handle a page-fault. If possible it sets up the TLB to map the virtual address. If not, it calls *as_fault( )* to bring in the page from secondary storage. *pagefault( )* is called with five parameters, of which the following three are interesting:

- *ep* — a copy of the EPC register, so that *pagefault( )* can determine where the page-fault occurred.

- *code* — a copy of the processor cause register, so that *pagefault( )* can determine exactly which exception it was called from.

- *vaddr* — the bad virtual address (BadVAddr) that caused the exception (see below).

The operation of *pagefault( )* breaks down into four major sections:

- *Handle a null pointer reference* — when a user tries to use a null pointer to access data, the process is normally terminated with a segmentation violation. However, on some implementations, a page of zeros is mapped at address zero. This means that dereferencing a null pointer yields the value zero instead of a segmentation violation error. In this case *pagefault( )* calls *as_map( )* to create a fake page of zeros in the processes address space. Some implementations map the *ELF* header at address zero. So dereferencing a null pointer yields the string "\117ELF\001\002\001\002......" (see § 4.2.1).

- *Determine if read or write* — the *code* parameter is examined to determine whether the operation is a read, write, or a copy-on-write.

- *Handle page table page fault* — if *pagefault( )* is called because there was no TLB entry found for a page table page, there will, in fact, have been a double exception. The first because the user-mode virtual address was not in the TLB, the second because the page table page virtual address was not in the TLB. *utlbmiss* saves the original bad virtual address on the kernel stack; this is used later by *pagefault( )* to determine the failing user-mode virtual address.

  The *pte* for the page table page is looked up. If the corresponding page is not in memory, then *as_fault( )* is called to bring in the page table page from secondary storage. Once the page is in memory, a TLB entry is set up for it. Now that the page table page is resident in memory, the *pte* for the user page can be looked up.

- *User-mode page fault* — if the user page is valid and present in memory, then a TLB entry is set up for it, and *pagefault( )* returns. If the page is not in memory, or a copy-on-write operation is in progress, *as_fault( )* is called to bring the page in from secondary storage.

3.7.4 The *utlbmiss* function

utlbmiss is an assembly language function that is called whenever the user program accesses a virtual address that has no TLB entry. When the virtual address is accessed, a *TLB Refill* exception is raised, and *utlbmiss* is called.

There are two distinct modes of operation for this function:

- *Page table present in memory* — the easier of the two cases. The referenced bit is set in the page table entry and the function simply jumps to the exception program counter address. That is, it attempts to return from the exception. This generates a second *TLB Refill* exception. However, a second *TLB Refill* that occurs when the first is still being processed causes transfer to the common exception handler. The common exception handler calls *pagefault( )*, which in turn sets up a TLB entry for the failed address.

- *Page table not present in memory* — in this case the page table page is not present in memory or the TLB, so a second *TLB Refill* exception occurs. Since the exception occurred within the *TLB Refill* handler, the common exception

Figure 3.24: *Algorithm for pagefault( )*

```
pagefault( )
input: copy of exception program counter
       copy of cause register
       user virtual addr that caused exception
{
  if( zero virtual address ) {
    map in page of zeros at address zero
  }

  if( page table page-fault ) {
    calculate the bad user specified address
    if ( page table page not in memory )
      as_fault( page table page ) /* bring it into memory */
    set up TLB entry for this page
    vaddr = user_vaddr   /* Fall through to user page handling */
  }

  if( vaddr is user page ) {
    if ( page not present or not valid or copy-on-write) {
      as_fault( ... ) /* bring the page into memory */
    }
    set referenced bit and valid bit in pte
    set modified/write bits as needed
    set up TLB entry for the page
    return
  }
}
```

handler is called. This calls *VEC_tlbmiss* which in turn calls *pagefault( )* to set up a TLB entry for the page table page and also for the original user-mode virtual address.

After *pagefault( )* has done its work, the kernel returns from the exception. The exception may cause the process to sleep while it waits for a page to come in from secondary storage. In this case, a context switch will occur, and a different process will run.

3.7.5 Page fault examples

This section gives examples of the page-fault and exception mechanisms. In each case, the execution flow is described, showing how the basic facilities of the processor are used to implement demand paged virtual memory. The examples are simple to begin with but increase in complexity.

• A reference is made to a virtual memory location that is mapped in the TLB and the physical page is present in memory. In this case, the processor executes an instruction that references a user virtual address and the virtual address is looked up in the TLB. A TLB entry is found that matches the referenced virtual address, so the valid bit is set. The processor gets the physical page number from the TLB entry, and then retrieves the data from a physical memory address.

• A reference is made to a virtual memory location that is not mapped in the TLB, but the page tables and the physical page are in memory. The processor executes an instruction that references a user virtual address and the virtual address is looked up in the TLB, but in this case, no entry is found, so a *TLB Refill* exception occurs. The processor switches into kernel-mode and executes *utlbmiss*. The reference bit in the corresponding page table page is set, and *pagefault( )* is called to set up a TLB entry for the user page. Since the process does not need to sleep waiting for a page to be delivered, user-mode processing continues.

• A reference is made to a virtual memory location that is not mapped in the TLB, and although the page table pages are present, the physical page is not. The same steps as before are carried out, and *pagefault( )* is called. *pagefault( )* looks up the *pte* for the requested page and finds that the *pte* is invalid, so *as_fault( )* is called to bring in the page from secondary storage. It in turn calls *segvn_fault( )* to bring in the page from the *vnode* associated with the file or swap area. This operation must sleep while the page is being read in. While the process sleeps, other processes run. Once the page is resident in memory, the process is woken up and the execution of *pagefault( )* continues. The fields of the *pte* are updated, and a TLB entry is set up for the page. The user process then continues executing the original instruction that caused the *TLB Refill* exception.

• A reference is made to virtual memory location that is not mapped in the TLB. The page table page is not present, nor is the physical page. The processor executes an instruction that references a user virtual address and the virtual address is looked up in the TLB. In this case, there is no TLB entry that matches the virtual address, so a *TLB Refill* exception occurs. The processor enters kernel-mode and executes *utlbmiss*. The address of the *pte* is calculated, and *utlbmiss* attempts to read the data from the *pte* so that it can set the referenced bit. However, the page table page containing the *pte* is not present in memory, so a second *TLB Refill* exception occurs. As a result of this, the common exception handler is called and it in turn calls *pagefault( )*. *pagefault( )* sees that the bad virtual address was in a page table page, and so calls *as_fault( )* to bring the page table page in from secondary storage. After the page table page has been brought in, a TLB entry is set up. If possible, it is set up in one of the wired TLB entries, so that the mapping will always be present when this process is running. Otherwise, the mapping is set up in one of the normal TLB entries.

After the mapping for the page table page is set up, the original failed user virtual address is calculated, and processing continues as described in the previous example.

Figure 3.25: *Paging variables*

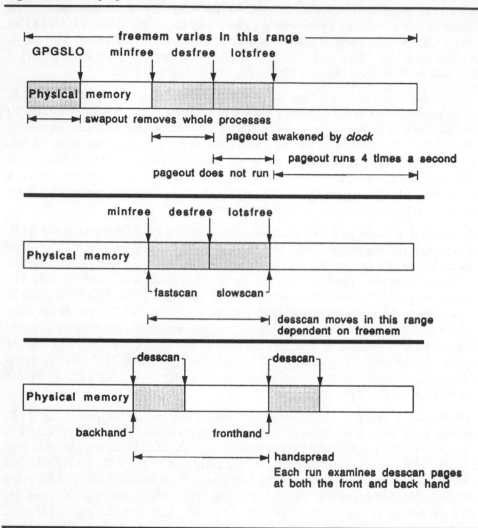

3.8 Page out and swapping

When available memory in the system gets low, the *pageout* process is called upon to create some free pages. In general, processes do not voluntarily give up pages, so *pageout* must steal them.

When the free memory available to the operating system falls below a threshold called *lotsfree*, *pageout* is run 4 times per second. If the memory falls below a lower threshold, called *desfree*, *pageout* is run from every cycle of *clock( )* (see *clock( )* in § 4.8.1).

Under UNIX System V Release 4, *pageout* uses the NRU algorithm, as described in § 3.2.1. Each time *pageout* runs, it examines a certain number of pages with both its front and back clock hands. Pages that are referenced by the front hand of the clock have their referenced bits cleared. Otherwise, pages that are referenced that have their referenced bit cleared are stolen from their associated process and put onto the page freelist. Stolen pages that are modified are first written to the swap area before being freed.

The designers of UNIX System V Release 4 made *pageout* so that it would not impose a great overhead on the system — the code is limited to prevent the operating system from spending too much time in the *pageout* process. The imposed limits are specified by many kernel variables. These variables and their relationships with each other are described in the next section. The operation of *pageout* and its related functions are described in § 3.8.2.

3.8.1 Page stealing variables

The kernel variables that control the operation of *pageout* are shown in Figure 3.25. They are described as follows:

- *minfree* — holds the absolute minimum of free memory in the system. When free memory is below this limit, the operating system makes every effort to get back above it. By default, *minfree* is set to be 3% of memory.

- *desfree* — holds the amount of memory that the operating system wants to have free at all times. When the amount of free memory falls below this limit, *pageout* is called from each cycle of *clock( )*. By default, *desfree* is set to 6.25% of memory.

- *lotsfree* — if the amount of free memory is greater than this amount, *pageout* is not run. If the amount of free memory is between *lotsfree* and *desfree*, *pageout* is run 4 times a second. The amount of pages scanned varies between *slowscan* and *fastscan*.

- *slowscan* — if *pageout* is running and the amount of free memory is equal to *lotsfree*, *slowscan* pages are examined on each run of *pageout*.

- *GPGSLO* — this tuneable parameter controls the memory level at which the swapper process (*sched*) comes into action. If memory falls below this level, the complete set of pages for a process are freed.

- *fastscan* — when *pageout* is running and the amount of free memory is equal to *desfree*, *fastscan* pages are examined on each run of *pageout*. If the amount of free memory lies between *desfree* and *lotsfree*, the number of pages scanned by *pageout* lies between the values *slowscan* and *fastscan*. (The amount of pages to scan is linearly interpolated between the two values.)

- *desscan* — this value is set somewhere between *slowscan* and *fastscan*, depending on the amount of free memory. It is the number of pages for which *pageout* must clear the referenced bit.

- *nscan* — each time *schedpaging* is called (see § 3.8.2), this value is set to zero. Every time that *pageout* clears the referenced bit, this value is incremented. *Pageout* keeps running while *nscan* is less than *desscan*.

- *maxpgio* — *pageout* attempts to limit how much data it writes to disk. This variable holds the number of pages that can be written to swap space during a run of *pageout*. When *maxpgio* pages have been written to disk, *pageout* stops running. This prevents *pageout* from queueing too many disk writes.

- *fronthand* — is the front hand of the clock, which indexes into the array of pages. When *pageout* is run, the page at the front hand has its reference bit cleared. Any page pointed to by the front hand that already has its referenced bit set, is freed.

- *backhand* — holds the back hand of the clock. Any page pointed to by the back hand that has its referenced bit clear, is freed.

- *handspread* — holds the distance between the front and back hands of the clock. If the spread is wide, there is a longer time between clearing the referenced bit and the page being stolen. If the spread is narrow, the time is less.

3.8.2 The *pageout* process

The *pageout* process is created by the kernel when the operating system boots (see § 4.17.1). This process can never be killed since it is a system process, and it always runs in kernel-mode. The kernel always creates this process with the process ID 2, and with the name *pageout*. (You can see it when you list processes with the **ps(1)** command.)

The four kernel functions that support the operation of *pageout* are as follows:

- *pageout( )* — manages the front and back hands of the clock. Whenever it runs, it examines *desscan* to see how many pages it must process (see Figure 3.26). A page is classed as processed if *pageout* is able to clear its referenced bit, or if the page is freed. If a page is free, locked, or has I/O in progress, *pageout* will not clear the reference bit, nor will it increment the count. It is conceivable that *pageout* can examine all the pages in memory, but never achieve the target of *desscan* pages with their referenced bits cleared. If this condition was not checked, *pageout* would run forever, and the system would appear hung. Therefore, if *pageout* detects that it has scanned the whole of memory twice, but has still not processed *desscan* pages, it gives up and goes back to sleep.

   Every time *pageout* wakes up, it frees the pages on the buffer-cleaned list called *bclnlist*. However, the variables *nscan* and *desscan* limit *pageout* by ensuring that a maximum of *desscan* pages are processed in each quarter second period.

- *schedpaging( )* — is called from the *callout[]* table (see § 4.8.3). Each time *schedpaging( )* is called, it checks the amount of free memory available to the kernel. If free memory is below *lotsfree*, *pageout* is woken up. Just before it completes, *schedpaging( )* adds an entry for itself in the *callout[]* table scheduling itself to be run again.

   schedpaging( ) is not the only function that will wake up the *pageout* process. It will also be woken up by *clock( )* or by *page_get( )* if they detect that the

Figure 3.26: *Algorithm for pageout( )*

```
pageout( )
inputs: none
outputs: none
externals: desscan initialized by schedpaging( )
          nscan set to zero every quarter sec by schedpaging
{
  initialize front and back clock hands
loop:
  if the buffer-cleaned list is not empty {
    free pages from the buffer-cleaned list
    goto loop
  }
  go to sleep until woken up by schedpaging( )

  while (nscan < desscan AND freemem < lotsfree) {
    examine page at the front hand with checkpage( )
      clear reference bit in page if the
      page is at the front hand, and increment nscan
    examine page at the back hand with checkpage( )
      if the page is at the back hand and referenced
      dont increment nscan /* cant free it yet */
    /* in both the above cases, if the referenced bit
     * is clear then the page is written to disk
     * if it is dirty, and nscan is incremented.
     * i.e., it is paged-out */
    increment front and back hands
    if the front hand is at the end of the pages array
      point the front hand at the first page
    similarly, wrap back hand if necessary

    increment a loop counter
    if the loop counter is too high
      /* then we went through too many cycles of the pages array
       * without nscan reaching desscan. Defensive measure
       * is to break the possible never ending while-loop.
       */
      goto loop
  }
  goto loop
}
```

Figure 3.27: *Algorithm for checkpage( )*

```
checkpage( )
input: pointer to page
       indicator of front or backhand
outputs: 0: if page cannot be freed
         1: if page can be freed
{
  if the page is free, locked, I/O in progress, or kept in memory
    return 0 ;

  clear reference and modified bit for page in
  the TLB cache and page tables

  if the page is at the back hand and it was referenced
    we cant free it, because it was recently referenced
    so return 0 /* dont increment nscan */

  if the page is at the front hand and it was referenced
    clear the reference bit and return 1  /* increment nscan */

  /* page is not referenced recently, so write it. */
  if the page is dirty and it has a vnode pointer {
    write page to secondary storage
    VOP_PUTPAGE( page, page->inode ) ;
    /*
     * page will be freed from buffer-cleaned after
     * the putpage operation completes
     */
    return 1 /* increment nscan */
  }

  /* Page is not modified, so just free it */
  unmap page from TLB cache
  return page to the freelist
  return 1 /* increment nscan */
}
```

amount of free memory has fallen below *desfree*.

Whenever *pageout* frees a dirty page, the page must be written to disk before it can be reused by another process. Disk writes occur asynchronously. That is, *pageout* initiates a disk transfer but does not wait for it to finish. Eventually, the disk pages will be written to disk. Once the output operation is complete, the disk driver attaches the I/O buffers to the buffer-cleaned list.

- *cleanup( )* — examines the buffer-cleaned list and frees any I/O buffers and associated *page* structures. Whenever *pageout* runs, it calls *cleanup( )* to free any pages available from earlier write operations. The pages on the buffer-cleaned list are ideal candidates for reuse because they have already been written to disk.

- *checkpage( )* — is called by *pageout* for each page that is scanned. It examines pages at the front hand and at the back hand. If the page is at the front hand, and is eligible, its reference bit is cleared. *checkpage( )* (see Figure 3.27) returns 1, to indicate to *pageout* that *nscan* must be incremented. If the bit is clear when *checkpage( )* is called, it initiates the write to disk.

3.8.3 The swapper process

Before the advent of demand paged virtual memory, operating systems swapped out whole processes from memory to disk to make room for other processes that want to run. These are called swapping systems. Historically, UNIX was a swapping system and the swapping was carried out by a special process called the *swapper* or the *scheduler*. Under UNIX System V Release 4, there is still a swapper process, it has the name *sched* (short for scheduler) and always runs as process 0.

There are times when memory load is so high that *pageout* cannot maintain a large enough freelist. When memory falls below the threshold set by *GPGSLO*, *sched( )* is invoked. It in turn calls the process class dependent function *CL_SWAPOUT( )* to select a process to swap out to secondary storage (see § 4.6.12). The function *swapout( )* is then called to free all the pages associated with the process. The *SLOAD* bit in this process's *proc* structure is cleared indicating that the process has been swapped and is no longer eligible to run.

Some time later, *sched( )* will run again. If the amount of free memory is above *GPGSLO*, the class dependent function *CL_SWAPIN( )* is called to select a process to swap back into memory. The *SLOAD* bit of the chosen process is set, making it eligible to run again. As this process runs, its pages are faulted back in, in the usual way.

There are two functions that support the operation of the process swapper. They are described as follows:

- *sched( )* — has two distinct modes of operation (Figure 3.28): swap in mode and swap out mode. In swap in mode, it calls the process class dependent *CL_SWAPIN( )* function to select a process to swap in. Under conditions of low load, all processes are swapped in, and *CL_SWAPIN( )* will not be able to find any more eligible processes. At this point, *sched( )* sleeps. When *clock( )* is invoked (see § 4.8.1), it checks the amount of free memory in the system and if free memory is below *GPGSLO* then *sched( )* is awoken. When *sched( )* wakes up, it starts again from the beginning.

  If there are no more processes to swap in, but free memory is less than *GPGSLO*, *sched( )* changes to swap out mode. The class dependent *CL_SWAPOUT( )* function is called to select a process to swap out. If a process is suitable to be swapped out, the function *swapout( )* is called to free all the

Figure 3.28: *Algorithm for sched( )*

```
sched( )
inputs:none
outputs:none
{
swap_in_mode:
  for each priority class
    nominates a process to swap in
  if there is no nominated process or the nominated
    process is already in memory
  {
    goto swap_out_mode if freemem is less than GPGSLO
    otherwise there is nothing to swap in so go to sleep
    goto swap_in_mode when awoken by clock()
  }

  /* We have a process to swap in.. */
  if freemem is greater than GPGSLO
  {
    swap in the nominated process's user-area
    mark the process SLOAD /* loaded in memory */
    /* Try again */
    goto swap_in_mode if freemem is still greater than GPGSLO
  }

swap_out_mode:
  for each priority class
    nominate a process to swap out
  if the nominated process is suitable /* see text */
    swap out the nominated process's user-area
    goto swap_in_mode
  }
  go to sleep until awoken by clock
  goto swap_in_mode
}
```

---

pages associated with it. A process is a suitable candidate for swapping if it is not a system process, it is not locked in memory, it is not already swapped, and it has no I/O operations pending on it via the */proc* file system.

After freeing the pages, *sched( )* sleeps. It stays asleep until awoken by *clock( )*, or until awoken by another process. Once *sched( )* runs again, it starts from the beginning in swap in mode.

There is a possibility of thrashing in *sched( )*. The process just swapped in could be the one selected to be swapped out at the next run. To avoid this, *sched( )* keeps a record of the last process it swapped in. When it calls *CL_SWAPOUT( )* it passes the most recently swapped in process as parameter. This gives *CL_SWAPOUT( )* the hint that this process should not be selected this time for swapping out.

- *swapout( )* — is called by *sched( )* to remove all the pages from the address space of the process via *as_swapout( )*. This in turn calls the segment specific swapout functions for all the segments that comprise the address space. In general, these are *vnode* segments, and the function *segvn_swapout( )* is invoked.

  segvn_swapout( ) scans all the pages in the segment. Pages that are locked, marked as being kept in memory, or marked as having a copy-on-write operation in progress are not removed. Any pages that are not dirty are returned to the freelist, and dirty pages are written to swap space before being freed.

3.8.4 Swap space management

When memory pages are swapped out to disk, the kernel must keep track of where the pages were put in the swap area. The management of swap space is simpler under UNIX System V Release 4 than in previous versions because only the anonymous pages have to be swapped. This allows the kernel to maintain a simple mapping between anonymous pages and swap space on the disk: there is one anonymous page for each page-sized block of swap space.

Under UNIX System V Release 4 there must be at least one disk partition or file allocated to swap space. Additional swap areas can be added and removed dynamically as the system runs. With previous releases of the UNIX Operating System, disk partitions had to be reserved for swap space, but under UNIX System V Release 4, a disk file may also be used as swap space. This increases the flexibility of the swapping mechanism. Further flexibility is provided by the use of *vnodes*. The *vnode* mechanism allows any file system that supports swapping to be used to hold a swap file. Of particular interest to workstation manufacturers is the support for swapping provided by NFS; the swap partition of a diskless workstation can be held in an NFS file held on a remote networked server.

When the system administrator adds a swap area, the number of pages that can be stored in that area are calculated. The kernel uses a *swapinfo* structure (Table 3.11) to keep track of each swap area in use. The *swapinfo* structure contains a pointer (*si_anon*) to point to an array of *anon* structures that represent each consecutive page of storage in the swap area. Each *swapinfo* structure also maintains an *anon* structure freelist. When the memory management system needs an *anon* structure, it is taken from the freelist of one of the swap areas. The relationship of these data structures used for swap management is shown in Figure 3.29.

Each of these *anon* structures is associated with a particular page-sized block of swap space on the disk: the first is associated with the first page-sized block in the swap area, the second with the second page-sized block, and so on. Under earlier versions of UNIX, such as System V.3 or 4.3BSD, allocation of swap space was much more complicated. The swap management strategies of these operating

Figure 3.29: *Swap management data structures*

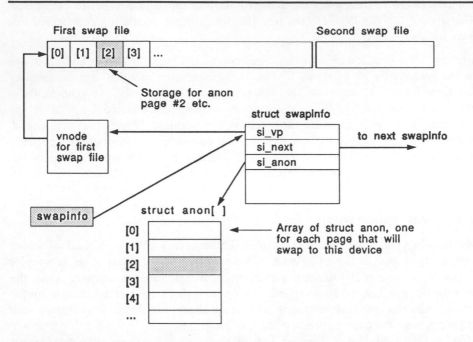

systems are described in Chapter 9 of [Bach 1986] and Chapter 5 of [Leffler, McKusick, Karels, Quarterman 1988].

The following section describes how swap space is manipulated (i.e., added or removed). It also describes how pages associated with swap space are swapped in and out, and how the *swapinfo* structure is used to describe where a swap area is located.

When swap space is being added to the system via the *uadmin* system call, the system ensures that the swap area requested is large enough to accommodate the requested number of swap blocks and also that the start and end offsets are aligned on a page boundary. If the new swap area is associated with a regular file, the kernel writes data into each block of the file. So if 32M bytes of swap space are requested, the kernel ensures that the file size is 32M bytes so that there is enough space for all the pages to be held in the swap area. After allocating the file blocks, the *anon* structures are allocated and linked into the *swapinfo* structure associated with the swap area and all the *anon* structures are placed onto the freelist for the new swap area.

When a new anonymous memory page is being established, the function *swap_alloc( )* (Figure 3.30) uses an elegant method to spread the anonymous pages across all swap areas. Each time an *anon* is allocated from the swap area, a counter is incremented. When the counter reaches a fixed upper limit, the counter is set to zero, and the next swap area is used. All swap partitions are searched until a free *anon* structure is found.

Table 3.11: *Struct swapinfo*

Element	Description
*struct vnode *si_vp*	*vnode* for this swap device or file
*struct vnode *si_svp*	*snode* for this swap device
uint si_soff	Starting byte offset in file
uint si_eoff	Ending byte offset in file
*struct anon *si_anon*	Pointer to *anon* array for this swap space
*struct anon *si_eanon*	Pointer to end of anon array
*struct anon *si_free*	*anon* free list for this swap space
int si_allocs	Number of consecutive allocs from this area
*struct swapinfo *si_next*	Pointer to the next swap area
short si_flags	Swap deletion lock flags
ulong si_npgs	Number of pages of swap space
ulong si_nfpgs	Number of free pages of swap space
*char *si_pname*	Swap file name

When an anonymous page must be written to disk, the *vnode* associated with it is obtained, and the *vnode* specific *VOP_PUTPAGE()* function is called to write the data.

3.9 Non-paged memory allocation

Many of the dynamic data structures used by the kernel need a memory allocation procedure that can deal with blocks of memory in sizes of less than one page. For example, segment descriptors are typically only a few bytes long, yet still have to be dynamically allocated and freed. Under UNIX System V Release 4, the kernel's memory allocation and memory freeing routines are called *kmem_alloc()* and *kmem_free()*. These will be discussed in this section. For a detailed description of the various memory management techniques in use today, see Chapter 7 of [Deitel 1984].

The memory allocator procedure needs an area of memory it can use to satisfy memory allocation requests. This area of memory is referred to as the "arena" or "pool". The kernel memory allocator uses data structures to keep track of which pieces of its pool are currently allocated and freed. In UNIX System V Release 3 the free areas of the pool were accounted for by using an array of *map* data structures (see Table 3.13) and each *map* structure contained the address of the start of the free area and its size. This array is called *map*. Initially a map contains a single *map* structure, which contains the address of the start of the memory pool and its size. This single entry indicates that the whole memory pool is free, and ready to be allocated. When the memory allocator routine is called, it searches for a free block big enough to satisfy the memory request. The map entry is altered to reflect the reduced size and the new start point of the free area, as shown in Figure 3.31. A

Figure 3.30: *Algorithm for swap_alloc()*

```
swap_alloc( )
inputs: none
output: pointer to anon structure
{
  loop through all swap areas starting with
    the current swap area
  {
    get next free anon from the swap area
    if anon is NULL
      /* No space in swap area so use next one */
      continue

    increment allocation count
    if allocation count reaches fixed upper limit
      /* use next swap area */
      continue

    return anonptr
  }

  /* If we get here, we visited all swap partitions,
   * but found no free pages
   */
  return  NULL
}
```

---

pointer to the newly allocated space is then returned to the caller. Figure 3.32 shows the situation after 3 blocks have been allocated. Assume that the routine that allocated block 2 gives it back because it is no longer needed, blocks 1 and 3 are still in use. The memory deallocator needs to allocate a new map entry to represent this free block. A new map entry is taken, the pointer is set to the start of block 2 and its length is altered to reflect its size.

After some time, it is possible that block 3 will also be deallocated. This results with block 2, block 3 and a large contiguous free area. The memory deallocator notices this, and coalesces the 3 free blocks into one big one. It then deletes the map entry for block 2 which gives, once more, the same situation as that shown in the bottom half of Figure 3.31. However, over time, this fixed size map entry algorithm causes memory to become very fragmented. The more fragments of memory there are, the more map entries are needed. Furthermore, if the map table is too small, the deallocator runs out of map entries. Without a map entry, the deallocator cannot represent the free block, so it becomes "lost forever". The solution is to increase the size of the map table. UNIX System V Release 3 uses multiple memory pools — for example, in the shared memory, semaphore and interprocess

Figure 3.31: *Simple memory allocator (initialization)*

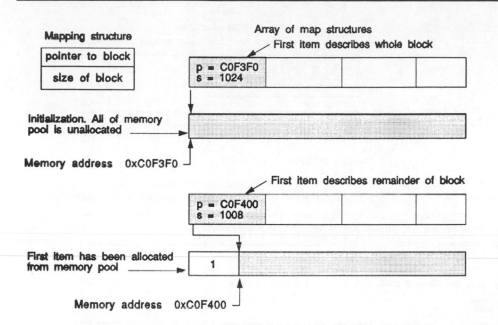

communication subsystems.

The map-based memory allocation functions are provided in UNIX System V Release 4 via the functions *rmalloc( )* and *rmfree( )* described in § 3.9.4.

3.9.1 Memory allocation strategies

To satisfy a memory request, the memory allocator can choose one of three strategies for deciding which free block to allocate:

- *First fit* — in this case, the memory allocator searches the freelist for the first block that is big enough to satisfy the request. This has the advantage of being very efficient, and is used in UNIX System V Release 3 implementations.

- *Best fit* — with this method, the memory allocator allocates the memory segment with the size closest to that required. This has the advantage that the chunk of memory left over will be the smallest possible, so memory wastage is minimized.

- *Worst fit* — in this case, the memory allocator allocates the largest chunk of memory available to it in order to satisfy the request. This seemingly strange choice has the benefit that the chunk of memory left over will be quite large — possibly large enough to satisfy another memory request.

An alternative scheme is the *buddy system* [Knuth 1968]. In this system, allocated block sizes must be to the power of 2 (i.e., 4, 8, 16, 32 bytes and so on). There is also a minimum allocation size, say 8 bytes. Blocks are manipulated in pairs; each

Figure 3.32: *Simple memory allocator (memory request)*

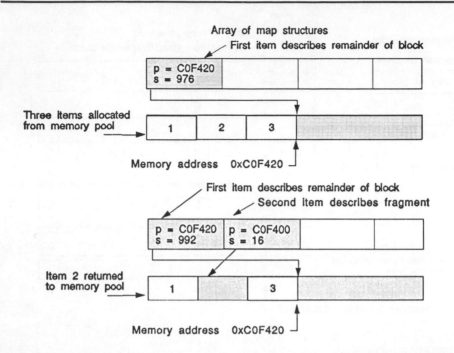

block has a partner or buddy (an American colloquial term meaning "friend" or in some circumstances, "foe"!). A memory pool starts out as a fixed size — for example, 4096 bytes. Associated with a pool is a bitmap which represents the allocation status (or the availability) of each minimum sized block in the pool.

In order to allocate a block, larger blocks are repeatedly split in half until a block of the correct size is yielded. For example, suppose a request is made for a 32 byte block, the allocator takes the 4096 byte block and splits it into two blocks each measuring 2048 bytes. The first block remains free, and the second is divided into two 1024 byte blocks, and so on, until a 32 byte block is yielded, which is allocated to the caller — its partners (or *buddy's*) block of 32 bytes remains free. The bits representing the allocated block are then configured in the bitmap. A subsequent request for 32 bytes would take the free 32 byte block, which is the buddy of the original. If a subsequent request was made for 64 bytes, the buddy's 32 byte block would be left, and the neighbouring 64 byte block would be used instead.

When the initial 32 byte block is freed, the memory allocator checks if its buddy is free. If it is, the 2 blocks are coalesced into a single 64 byte block and the process continues, possibly resulting with the original 4096 byte block.

3.9.2 *kmem_alloc( )* **and** *kmem_free( )*

UNIX System V Release 4 uses the buddy system with the addition of freelists and a "lazy" compaction scheme for deallocated blocks. Multiple memory pools are used and each pool is one page in size. For example, on the MIPS implementation each pool is 4096 bytes.

There are two variations of the kernel memory allocation and deallocation routines; *kmem_alloc( )* and *kmem_free( )* — used for ordinary memory allocation requests, and *kmem_fast_alloc( )* and *kmem_fast_free( )* — used for "fast" memory allocation requests. *kmem_fast_alloc( )* and *kmem_fast_free( )* are optimized for performance reasons by using fixed size buffers.

There are three data structures for managing the memory pools used by *kmem_alloc( )* and *kmem_free( )*: the *bpool* structure, for managing buffer pools; the *flist* structure, for managing lists of free buffers; and the *fbuf* structure, for chaining together individual buffers in a freelist. These structures are summarized in Table 3.12.

Table 3.12: *Structures for kmem_alloc( )*

struct bpool (bufpool)	
Element	Description
unsigned char *bp_startp	Start address of buffer
unsigned bp_inuse	Count of largest buffers in use
unsigned bp_status	Status of the pool
unsigned *bp_bitmapp	Pointer to bitmap information
unsigned bp_expmin	Exponent of smallest buffer class (the size of all classes is a power of 2)
unsigned bp_expmax	Exponent of the largest buffer class in this pool
struct flist (freelist)	
Element	Description
freebuf *fl_nextp	Pointer to first item in the freelist
freebuf *fl_prevp	Pointer to last item in the freelist
unsigned fl_slack	Variable used for coalescing by *kmem_free( )*
unsigned fl_mask	Mask for bitmap
unsigned fl_nbits	Number of bits to set/clear in one operation
struct fbuf (freebuf)	
Element	Description
freebuf *fb_nextp	Pointer to next free buffer
freebuf *fb_prevp	Pointer to previous free buffer
unsigned fb_mask	Mask for setting bitmap
bufpool *fb_poolp	Pointer to the buffer pool this buffer is in
unsigned fb_state	Status of buffer: is it delayed or not
unsigned *fb_mapp	Pointer to corresponding word in bitmap

Figure 3.33 shows the data structures used to manage the memory pools and the blocks within them. Two types of pools are used: a small pool is used to allocate small memory requests, and a large pool is used to allocate large memory requests. In the case of a memory request that is larger than the size of a physical page (4096 bytes on the MIPS implementation), memory requests are satisfied by directly

allocating memory pages. In either case, the memory allocator uses freelists to hold all the pool blocks of a particular size.

Figure 3.33: *Initial state of memory pool*

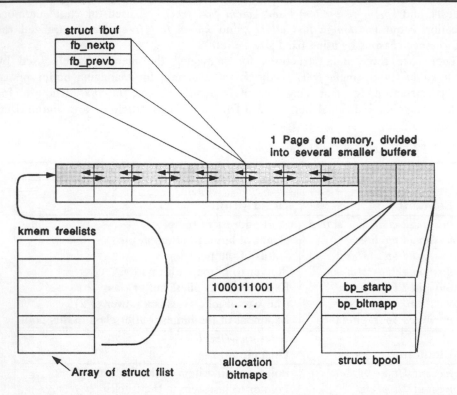

Before the first *kmem_alloc( )* request is made, the operating system allocates a pool and initializes it, as shown in Figure 3.33. A pool is split into a number of smaller buffers. Two of them are needed for administrative use. The first buffer is used to hold the *bpool* structure information. This contains a pointer to the freelists, a pointer to the bitmaps, and a count of how many of the largest blocks in the pool are allocated. (Once the count goes to zero, the whole pool is freed.) The second buffer is used to hold the allocation bitmaps for all the buffers in the pool.

The remaining blocks are all "freed" and linked into the freelist for the buffers in the pool. Each free buffer can be used to store management data for the memory allocator, and each one is overwritten by an *fbuf* structure which is used to maintain the pointers to the next and previous buffers on the list as well as pointers to the pool and the allocation bitmaps.

When a block is freed, the memory deallocator checks if its buddy is free and if necessary, proceeds to coalesce the blocks. This procedure is time-consuming and can lead to efficiency problems when buffers of the same size are repeatedly allocated and deallocated — the processor may spend much of its time repeatedly breaking up 4k byte buffers into 32 byte chunks, and then reforming them again. To

Figure 3.34: *Algorithm for kmem_alloc( )*

```
kmem_alloc( )
input: requested size, flags
output: pointer to allocated block
{
 compute which memory pool to work with /* small or large */
 if (request size is bigger than sizeof page)
   allocate directly from memory pages

again:
 compute freelist big enough to satisfy memory request

 if ( freelist contains a buffer ) {
  if (buffer in use or using largest buffer size in the pool)
    use next buffer by increasing buddy coalescing counter by 2
  else {
    use its buddy and increase buddy coalescing counter by 1
    mark buffer as allocated in bitmaps
  }
  increment buffer count for this freelist
  return the buffer
 }
 else { /* all buffers on the freelist are used up */
  sz = size to allocate; /* Break up a larger buffer */
  while ( sz != max possible buffer size ) {
    sz *= 2   /* try next size up */
    freelist = freelist for 'sz' sized blocks
    if ( there is a free buffer ) {
      split buffer until it is the right size
      return the correct sized buffer
    }
  } /* End while */
 }
 if ( we successfully allocated a new pool )
  goto again
 else {
  go to sleep awaiting for memory to become available
  when awoken goto again
 }
}
```

Figure 3.35: *Algorithm for kmem_free( )*

```
kmem_free( )
input: pointer to block to free, size of block to free
output: none
{
 if ( block size is bigger than sizeof page )
    block was allocated as a page, so free it directly

 compute which memory pool to work with /* small or large */
   then find the correct freelist for this block size
 if ( buddy coalescing count >= 2 OR maximum sized buffer ) {
  /* The biggest buffers can't be coalesced, and we don't
   * coalesce smaller ones when the count is high
   */
  reduce buddy coalescing count by 2
  mark buffer as delayed
  return it to head of freelist
  if ( all largest buffers have been freed
       AND this was not the most recent pool allocated ) {
    return the pool to the operating system
  }
 }
 else {
  mark buffer as free
  try to coalesce buffer with its buddy

  if ( buddy coalescing count == 0
       AND next buffer on freelist is delayed ) {

     if ( the buddy of this buffer is delayed ) {
        /* it will still be marked as allocated in the bitmap */
        clear bitmap entry for buddy of this buffer
        remove next buffer from freelist
        check delayed buffers on the freelist for coalescing
     }
  }
  else
   set buddy coalescing count to zero
    /* Next free will force coalesce.*/
 }
}
```

avoid this problem, the UNIX System V Release 4 deallocator uses a "lazy" coalescing scheme.

When the pool is created, each block in the pool is marked as allocated in the bitmap. Each freelist has a count associated with it and as blocks are allocated, the count is incremented for that freelist; as they are deallocated, the count is decremented. The deallocator attempts to coalesce blocks only when the count falls below a minimum (UNIX System V Release 4, uses the value of 2). Additionally, when the deallocator notices that all the blocks in a pool are free, it returns the pool to the operating system. The algorithms for *kmem_alloc( )* and *kmem_free( )* are shown in Figures 3.34 and 3.35.

When *kmem_free( )* wishes to return a pool to the operating system, it cannot simply give back the page containing it because the buffers in the pool are still attached to the freelists.

To return pools to the operating system, the system process *kmdaemon* is used. A process is used rather than a function because the processing of the pool is time-consuming, and the processing of a free pool is not urgent, thus it can afford to wait until *kmdaemon* is rescheduled.

When *kmem_free( )* has a pool to release, it places a pointer to the pool being freed onto an idle list and then wakes up *kmdaemon* to free it. A pool consists of a group of free buffers linked together. When *kmdaemon* runs, it scans the idle list for each pool to free. *kmem_alloc( )* can be called from interrupt level and consequently *kmdaemon* needs to manage interrupts.

When a pool has all its entries free, *kmdaemon* scans the freelist and unlinks each buffer from that freelist (again *kmdaemon* must manage interrupts). The page that forms the pool is returned to the operating system page pool for use by other processes. *kmdaemon* eventually goes back to sleep until another pool is to be released.

3.9.3 *kmem_fast_alloc( )* and *kmem_fast_free( )*

The kernel uses dynamic allocation for most of its data structures — for example, for the *anon*, *as*, and *proc* structures, and so on. While the system is running, many requests to allocate and free data structures such as these are made. Data structures are defined with a fixed size so that each request for a particular data structure type is always the same. The routines *kmem_fast_alloc( )* and *kmem_fast_free( )* provide facilities for managing these fixed-sized requests. They have the advantage of being simpler and quicker to run than *kmem_alloc( )* and *kmem_free( )*.

Multiple memory pools are used, and each request on a pool is always the same size. Each memory pool is maintained as a simple linked list, and allocations are made by taking an item from it. When all items in the list are used, *kmem_alloc( )* is used to add more to it. Note that memory acquired in this way is never returned via *kmem_free( )*.

Figure 3.36: *Use of the map structure*

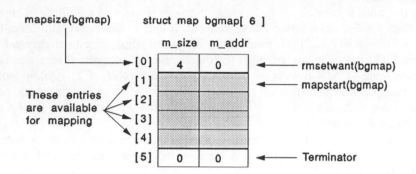

Table 3.13: *Struct map*

Element	Description
unsigned long m_size	Size of this chunk of memory area
unsigned long m_addr	Address of first byte in this area

3.9.4   *rmalloc( )* and *rmfree( )*

The functions *rmalloc( )* and *rmfree( )* manipulate *map* structures (Table 3.13). A *map* structure holds the information about an area of free memory.

An *allocation map* is an array of *map* structures (see Figure 3.36). The first and last elements in the allocation map are reserved for use by the allocation routines themselves. The *m_size* field of the first element specifies how many empty slots are in the mapping array and its *m_addr* field specifies how many processes are asleep, waiting for memory to become available. The last entry in the map is a terminator indicating the end of the array; its *m_size* and *m_addr* fields are set to zero.

When a subsystem wishes to use *rmalloc( )* and *rmfree( )*, it must first provide a mapping array and a memory buffer. The mapping array can be statically or dynamically allocated; the memory buffer is usually dynamically allocated by using *kmem_alloc( )*. The following support functions are provided to manipulate the mapping array:

- *rminit( )* — initializes the mapping array. It takes two arguments, a pointer to the array and its size. It initializes the fields in the array as shown in Figure 3.36. This function is called before calling *rmalloc( )*. It sets up the map so that it has a single map entry pointing at the entire memory buffer.

- *rmsetwant( )* — indicates that a process is waiting to allocate memory from the buffer. It is called when *rmalloc( )* fails to allocate memory.

- *rmwant( )* — is called to check if any processes are waiting for memory. If there are, it calls *wakeprocs( )* to wake any processes sleeping on a map.

Figure 3.37 gives an example of how these functions are used, and how a function sleeps when it wants memory. The example demonstrates a typical use of *rmalloc( )* and *rmfree( )*. In the example, the functions shown are called from a fictitious device driver called *dvr*. The driver initializes the map when it is first used, and allocates a buffer whenever it is reading data from the device.

rmalloc( ) and *rmfree( )* are described as follows:

- *rmalloc( )* — is called with two arguments: the map to allocate from, and the size of buffer requested. The system allocates space from the memory map on a first-fit basis and coalesces adjacent space fragments when space is returned to the map by *rmfree( )*. A pointer to the allocated space is then returned.

- *rmfree( )* — deallocates a block of memory. It is called with three parameters: the map into which the block is being deallocated, the size of the block, and a pointer to the start of the block being freed. The operation of *rmfree( )* is summarized in Figure 3.38. The map entries are held in the array in order of the address of the block being mapped. The function coalesces adjacent fragments as it returns the block. If it causes the number of fragments in the map to exceed the number of map entries specified by *rminit( )* (see § 3.9.4), the following warning message is displayed on the console:

> WARNING: rmfree map overflow *map*. Lost *size* items at *addr*

Where the words in italics are: the *map* address, the *size* of the deallocated buffer, and the address that was lost (*addr*). If this message occurs on your system, it means that the memory activity is causing too much fragmentation. If possible, the appropriate map size should be increased. (The map sizes are usually configurable parameters.) The map in question can be found using the **ds** command in **crash(1M)** (see § 9.3). Give the **ds** command the map address reported in the error, and it will give the name of the table in which the error occurred. The name of the table will give you a good hint about which parameter to increase.

3.10 Memory related system calls

The address space of a running process rarely stays fixed in size; a process dynamically allocates the required memory needed and frees it again when it is no longer required. Thus, processes often grow and shrink in size as they run. The following operating system facilities are used to grow and shrink a process:

- *malloc(3X)* — this function and its related *calloc( )*, *realloc( )*, and *free( )* functions are provided in the C library and are used by programmers for dynamic memory allocation. These functions use the system calls *brk* and *sbrk* to grow or shrink the data segment of the process.

Figure 3.37: *Using rmalloc( ) and rmfree( )*

```
/* Data structure definitions */
#define DVRPOOLSIZE 4096              /* Total memory in the pool */
struct map dvrmap[ DVRMAPSIZE ] ;

/* Initialization function -- called when driver first opened */
dvr_mapinit( )
{
  caddr_t dvrbuf ;
  if( (dvrbuf = kmem_alloc(DVRPOOLSIZE, KM_SLEEP)) == NULL ) {
    /* Out of memory, return error to caller */
    return 0 ;
  }
  /* Initialize the map */
  rminit( dvrmap, DVRMAPSIZE ) ;
  /* This makes the first free map entry point to the entire pool */
  rmfree( dvrmap, DVRPOOLSIZE ) ;
  return 1 ;
}


/*  Part of driver read routine - allocates buffer, copies it
 * to user space, deallocates buffer
 */

dvrread(..)
{
  caddr_t dvrbuf ;

  /* Try to allocate buffer, sleep if not possible..*/
  while( (dvrbuf = rmalloc( dvrmap, 256 ) ) == NULL ) {
    rmsetwant(dvrmap) ;
    sleep(dvrmap, PZERO+1) ;
  }
  copy data from device into dvrbuf
  copy dvrbuf to user space

  /* Free the buffer.. */
  rmfree(dvrmap,  256, dvrbuf ) ;
  return ;
}
```

Figure 3.38: *Operation of rmfree( )*

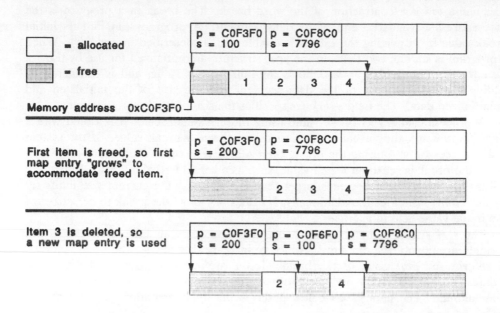

- *brk, sbrk* — these system calls can be called directly by a running process and are used to alter the size of the data segment of a process.

- *Stack growth* — as a process runs its stack grows to hold the information about currently active functions and to hold the local variables of those functions. Stack growth is handled by the kernel function *grow( )*. The *grow( )* function is not a system call, but it is called implicitly by processes as they run. It is related to *brk*, and so it is described here.

- *Shared memory* — changes the size of a process. When a running process attaches itself to a shared memory segment, it grows in size and has an extra segment of memory attached to its address space. Shared memory is described with other interprocess communication facilities in Chapter 8.

- *mmap* — this system call also attaches a new segment to a process, and is used to access the contents of a file. It is described with other I/O facilities in Chapter 5.

Since UNIX System V Release 4 is expected to be used in real-time processing environments, it must guarantee real-time response times. So the operating system must provide a greater degree of memory control than its predecessors — processes cannot afford to have their pages stolen. If the page must be brought in from secondary storage, it will increase the response time dramatically. To allow a process to control which parts of memory can and cannot be paged, the operating system provides the *memcntl* and *plock* system calls.

The sections that follow describe the use and implementation of the memory-related system calls.

3.10.1 Stack growth, *brk* and *sbrk*

The name *brk* is a contraction of the word break. The break in a program is the first address beyond the end of its data segment. A program can find its initial break value by inspecting the external variable *end*, as described in *end(3C)*. When a program is started, two fields in the *proc* structure are initialized for use by the *brk* system call. The field *p_brkbase* holds the initial break value, and is calculated by adding the base address of the data segment and the size of the initialized and uninitialized data. The field *p_brksize* specifies the size of the break segment.

A process changes its break value using the *brk* system call. It is called with a single argument: the virtual address to use as the new break value. If the system call is successful at altering the break, then zero is returned. The system call might fail if the break is set to an illegal value, such as a kernel virtual address. It will also fail if the data segment becomes larger than is allowed by the current size limits set by the *ulimit* system call. Additionally, *brk* does not allow the break to be set below the initial value held in *p_brkbase*.

The *sbrk* system call is used to change the break incrementally. It is called with a single argument: the amount by which to increase or decrease the break address. It returns the new value of the break. If the argument is positive, the break is increased by that amount and the process grows in size — otherwise it shrinks by that amount. The paragraphs below describe the implementation of these system calls.

- *brk* — the pseudo-code for *brk* is shown in Figure 3.39. The function calculates the new size of the data segment. If it is being grown, then *as_map( )* is called to create a new *segvn* segment. The start address of the segment is set to the old break value, and the size of the new segment is the amount by which the data segment must grow. *as_map( )* creates a new segment and attaches it to the process. The arguments to *as_map( )* indicate that it must call *segvn_create( )* to initialize the new segment, and that the pages in the segment should be zero-filled and created when they are first accessed. When *segvn_create( )* executes, it cheats! It detects that the new segment is adjacent to the existing data segment, and that it is the same type. As a result, it deletes the new segment, and increases the size of the old segment to accommodate the growth.

  If the segment is shrinking, the function *as_unmap( )* is called to reduce the size of the segment so that it represents a smaller area of memory. Resources that are used, such as pages, page tables, or anonymous page pointers, are released.

- *sbrk* — usually implemented as a C library function. Internally, it uses a variable *_curbrk* to hold the current break value. This is initialized to the value of *end* (i.e., the initial break value). When *sbrk* is called, it adds the value of its argument to the value of *_curbrk* to yield the new virtual address of the break. It calls *brk* with this new address, and if it is successful, then *_curbrk* is updated with the new break address, and the value is returned to the caller. Otherwise, *_curbrk* is left unchanged and -1 is returned.

Figure 3.39: *Algorithm for brk( )*

```
brk( )
input: virtual address for the new break value
output: 0 or error code
{
  if( new break address < p_brkbase OR
      new data seg size > ulimit value )
    error ENOMEM

  if( data segment must grow ) {
    /* Call as_map to create a new segment adjacent
     * to the existing data segment. Size of the
     * two segments will be the new break size
     */
    call as_map to create a new segvn segment
    if( as_map failed )
      return
    increase p_brksize
  } else {
    /* Segment is shrinking */
    call as_unmap to destroy mapping area no longer used
    decrease p_brksize
  }
  return 0
}
```

- *grow( )* — when a process starts to execute, the stack segment is initialized (it is usually set to the size of a page). As the process runs, the amount of stack needed may grow, and if it does, it may eventually point outside of the initial segment. This causes a page-fault because the new page is not mapped into the address space of the currently running process. It also causes a segmentation violation because the stack pointer now points outside the bounds of the stack segment. Normally, accessing an address that is outside a segment causes the kernel to kill the process with a segmentation violation signal, *SIGSEGV*.

  However, the kernel detects that the process is trying to grow its stack, so the process is not terminated. Instead, the function *grow( )* is called to extend the stack segment. It usually increases the stack segment by one page but the actual number of pages is machine dependent (defined by the constant *SINCR*).

  The function *grow( )* calculates the amount by which the stack must grow. It checks that the new stack falls within the bounds defined by *ulimit*. If the stack exceeds this limit, the process is terminated with *SIGSEGV*. Otherwise *as_map( )* is called to grow the stack segment. This works in the same way as *brk*: a new segment is attached adjacent to the existing stack segment. The function *segvn_create( )* is called to initialize the new segment. It, in turn, sees that the two segments are adjacent, and that they have the same type, so it coalesces the two segments into one larger segment.

Table 3.14: *Plock commands*

Command	Description
TXTLOCK	Locks the process's text segment in memory
DATLOCK	Locks the process's data segment in memory
PROCLOCK	Locks the entire process in memory
UNLOCK	Removes all locks

3.10.2   *memcntl* and *plock*

The system calls *memcntl* and *plock* are used to lock areas of a process into memory. The *plock* system call was provided with UNIX System V Release 3, but is carried over into UNIX System V Release 4 to maintain backwards compatibility. However, under UNIX System V Release 4, *memcntl* is the preferred interface. Both these system calls rely on the memory management function *as_ctl( )* to perform the low-level locking operation on the pages of the process. This in turn uses the segment specific locking operation. These functions and the *segvn* locking function, *segvn_lockop*, are described in the following paragraphs.

- *plock* — allows the process to lock a particular segment once. It is called with a single parameter summarized in Table 3.14. If *plock* is called to lock the segment for a second time, it fails with the *EINVAL* error code.

  plock uses the *u_lock* field in the user-area to describe which segments have already been locked. When it is called, it first checks the user-area to see if the segment is already locked. If it is, the system call fails. The processing corresponding to the four different arguments is as follows:

- *TXTLOCK* — the function *as_ctl( )* is called to lock all pages in the address space that are marked readable and executable, and that are not in shared-memory segments. (Shared-memory segments are those used to hold memory referenced by the system calls *shmat*, *shmget*, *shmop*, and so on.)

- *DATLOCK* — the function *as_ctl( )* is called with parameters that tell it to lock pages that are readable, writeable and executable, and that are not in shared-memory segments. This set of pages will include all those in the stack segment and data segments.

- *PROCLOCK* — to lock the entire process, *plock* first locks the user-area in memory. This is done by setting the *SLOCK* bit in the *p_flag* field of the *proc* structure. The text and data segment are then locked. Note that *PROCLOCK* leaves shared-memory segments unlocked; they are locked via the *shmctl* system call, described in Chapter 8.

- *UNLOCK* — the process is unlocked in almost the same way as it is locked. The system call uses the *u_lock* bit field in the user-area to determine which segments were locked. For each locked segment it calls *as_ctl( )* to unlock the pages that it locked previously. The bits in *u_lock* are cleared to show that the segment is now unlocked.

- *memcntl* — provides finer control over which parts of memory are locked. *plock* is rather crude since it simply locks everything that looks like code or data. *memcntl*, on the other hand allows you to specify exactly which parts of the process's address range are locked or unlocked. This system call takes six arguments:

  - *addr* — the address at which to start locking or unlocking. The address must be aligned to a page boundary or the system call will fail.

  - *len* — the length of data to be operated on. The operation will be carried out on all pages in the interval *addr* to *addr + len*.

  - *cmd* — specifies the operation to carry out (see Table 3.15).

Table 3.15: *Memcntl commands*

Command	Description
MC_LOCK	Lock all matching pages in page range
MC_LOCKAS	Lock all matching pages in address space
MC_SYNC	Write to backing store all pages in range
MC_UNLOCK	Unlock matching pages in range
MC_UNLOCKAS	Unlock all matching pages in address space

- *arg* — provides an argument that is used by some of the commands described in Table 3.15.

- *attr* — this bit-field is used to specify selection criteria for pages that are being operated on by *memcntl*. If it has the value zero, then all pages will be operated on. If it is non-zero, then only those pages with the given attributes will be operated on. The attributes are summarized in Table 3.16.

- *mask* — this value is always set to zero. It is reserved for future use.

When *memcntl* runs, it first checks that the arguments are valid and consistent with each other. The paragraphs below describe the processing carried out for each of the different commands.

- *MC_LOCK* — locks all pages in the given address range that have the given attribute. The *arg* argument is unused, but must be set to zero to maintain compatibility with future releases. The values of the arguments *addr*, *len*, *cmd*, and *attr* are passed directly to *as_ctl( )*. The effect is that *as_ctl( )* locks the pages in the given address range whose attributes match those specified in the *attr* argument.

Table 3.16: *Memcntl page attributes*

Attribute	Description
SHARED	Page is part of a shared-memory segment
PRIVATE	Page is not part of a shared memory segment
PROT_READ	Page is readable
PROT_WRITE	Page is writeable
PROT_EXEC	Page is executable
PROC_TEXT	Private pages that have read and execute permission
PROC_DATA	Private pages that have read, write and execute permission

- *MC_LOCKAS* — locks all pages in the address space of the process that have the given attributes. The page range arguments are ignored, but should be set to zero. The *arg* parameter must have one or both of the following bits set: *MCL_CURRENT* or *MCL_FUTURE* (defined in *<sys/mman.h>*). If *MCL_CURRENT* is set, then all pages in the address space that match the attributes are locked into memory. If *MCL_FUTURE* is set, then any pages added later to the address space are also locked. When locking the address space, the user-area is locked, and *as_ctl( )* is called. The values of *addr*, *len*, *cmd*, *attr* and *arg* are passed directly to *as_ctl( )*. The arguments *addr* and *len* must be set to zero when the system call is made. The zero values for the address and length tell *as_ctl( )* that it must apply the operation to all pages in the address space that have the given attribute.

- *MC_SYNC* — as with the previous case, the arguments are passed directly to *as_ctl( )*. The arguments tell *as_ctl( )* to write back any modified pages to disk.

- *MC_UNLOCK* — again, the arguments are passed to *as_ctl( )* and the matching pages in the page range are unlocked.

- *MC_UNLOCKAS* — the user-area is unlocked, and the system call arguments are passed directly to *as_ctl( )*, which unlocks all matching pages in the address space.

- *as_ctl( )* — is called to apply the memory control operation on segments in the address space of the process that issued the *memcntl* system call. The parameters to the function specify the address space, the address range over which to operate, and the operation to perform. The control flow in this function takes one of the following three paths:

  - If the operation is carried out across the entire address space (e.g. *MC_LOCKAS*), each segment in the address space is looked up. For each of the segments, the segment-type specific locking function is called. For example, the locking function for a segment *s* is held in the field *s->s_ops->lockop*.

  - If the operation specifies an address range, the segment-type specific locking function is called to carry out the necessary operation for each segment that is encompassed by that range.

- If the operation is *MC_SYNC*, the pages that have been changed must be written back to disk. This is achieved by calling the segment-specific synchronization function.

Figure 3.40: *Algorithm for segvn_lockop( )*

```
segvn_lockop( )
inputs: segment to lock
        address range to lock
        attributes of pages to lock
{
  attr =  attributes of pages to lock
  if( attr is non zero ) {
    if( SHARED bit set in attr, and segment is private )
      return ; /* Segments have different types */
    if( SHARED bit not set in attr, and segment is shared )
      return ; /* Segments have different types */
  }
  for( each page in the address range ) {
    if( page protection matches attr OR attr is zero ) {
      if( locking the page ) {
        call segvn_faultpage to get the page into memory
        increment p_lckcnt field in this page
      } else {
        lookup page
        if( page is present in memory )
          decrement p_lckcnt field
      }
    }
  }
  return
}
```

Most segments in the operating system are *segvn* segments. The locking operation on this segment type is *segvn_lockop( )* (Figure 3.40), which is called with seven parameters, five of which are described as follows:

- *seg* — points to the segment on which the function is operating.

- *addr, len* — specify the range of addresses over which the operation applies.

- *attr* — gives the attributes that a page must have in order to be considered by *segvn_lockop( )*. The page attributes are described in Table 3.16. If *attr* is zero, all pages in the segment are operated on by this function.

- *op* — describes the operation to perform. Its value is either *MC_LOCK* or *MC_UNLOCK*.

3.10.3   *mprotect* **and** *mincore*

The system call *mprotect* is used to alter the page protections that apply to pages in a given address range. It is possible to alter pages so that they are readable, writeable or executable. *mprotect* is called with the following arguments:

- *address* — specifies the address at which to start applying the protection.

- *len* — specifies the length of the address range. All pages in the range *address* to *address + len* are altered.

- *protection* — specifies the protections to apply. If the value is *PROT_NONE*, the page is inaccessible. Otherwise, this value is a bitmask constructed from the values: *PROT_READ*, *PROT_WRITE*, or *PROT_EXEC*.

mprotect looks up each page in the specified range and for each page, the segment-specific protection function is called to set the protection for the page. (The protection function for a segment *s* is given by the field *s->s_ops->setprot*.)

This system call is both powerful and dangerous; it is possible to make the text segment writeable, so that a process can alter its own program code as it runs. For example, some COBOL compilers allow a running program to dynamically load other COBOL subprograms. This is done by making the text segment writeable, writing the subprogram into the text segment, and making it read-only once more. However, if it is done incorrectly, or if it is done accidentally, the program will crash. The risk to other programs is, however, limited. When a read-only page is made writeable, it is converted into a copy-on-write page, and swap space is reserved for it. This means that when a process alters its own executable code, it will not affect other processes executing the same program.

The *mincore* system call is used to check which pages in a given address range are in memory. It takes three parameters:

- *address* — specifies the start address for the check.

- *len* — specifies the length of the address range to check.

- *vector* — an array of characters. There must be one element in the array for each page being checked. If the page is resident, the bottom bit in the corresponding array entry is set.

The information returned in the vector is correct only at the time the system call was made. If the system is under heavy load, the information returned may be out of date because the pages may have been stolen from the process.

This system call operates by calling the segment-specific *incore* function, which is called for each page in the segment that falls within the specified address range. For *segvn* segments, a page is deemed to be resident if there is a *page* structure that maps to the particular virtual address.

3.11 Exercises

3.1   Describe the mechanism used to address more memory than is physically installed in the computer.

3.2   Describe the parts that constitute a virtual address.

3.3   What steps are taken to convert a virtual memory address into a physical memory address, and why is this conversion necessary?

3.4   Describe what happens when a reference is made to a page that is not present in physical memory.

3.5   What is the purpose of the page stealer (*pageout*), and why does it place pages into a cache list?

3.6   Describe the benefits of dividing the address space of a process into segments.

3.7   Which segments would you expect to find in all processes? What other segment types are possible?

3.8   The kernel checks that virtual addresses referenced by a running process fall within the bounds of its segments. When and how are these checks performed, and what is the benefit of forcing a program to stay within these bounds?

3.9   A program such as **vi** is typically run by many people simultaneously. How does the kernel manage this without keeping many different copies of the same program in memory?

3.10   Describe the use of copy-on-write pages.

3.11   What is the purpose of the *page* structure?

3.12* What is the difference between *vnode* pages and *anonymous* pages? How does this difference improve the efficiency of the operating system?

3.13   What is the purpose of the *seg_ops* structure?

3.14   Describe what is meant by the term "page-fault" and what actions take place when one occurs.

3.15   What is the effect of a system that is thrashing? What steps are taken to reduce it?

3.16   Describe the different algorithms used for non-paged memory allocation.

3.17** The functions *kmem_alloc( )* and *kmem_free( )* are used to manage the kernel memory pool. Write your own program that implements these two functions and simulates an operating system making memory requests. Compare the performance of two different implementations of *kmem_alloc( )*. For example, compare the implementation of first-fit with best-fit. Which algorithm is faster? Which algorithm results in the least memory wastage during normal operation? When memory is exhausted, which algorithm allocates the most memory?

3.18** Write a program that grows its stack as far as possible. How much space has been allocated to it? Modify the program so that it uses *sbrk* to increase its data segment size as far as possible. How much space has been allocated to it? Use these programs to test whether the operating system implementation has a single overall limit for the size of your program, or whether there are separate limits for the stack and data segments.

3.19 What facilities are provided under UNIX System V Release 4 to lock segments of a process in memory? Describe the circumstances in which a process would lock a particular part of its address space in memory.

3.20* Write a C program that prints the addresses of its stack, data and code segments. What happens if the program attempts to read or write an address outside these segments?

CHAPTER 4

Process management subsystem

It looked insanely complicated, and this was one of the reasons why the snug plastic cover it fitted into had the words DON'T PANIC printed on it in large friendly letters.

— Douglas Adams, *The Hitch Hiker's Guide to the Galaxy*

4.1 Introduction to the process management subsystem

At the heart of the UNIX operating system is the *process subsystem*. It is responsible for the correlation of all tasks requested by human beings and machine. Its purpose is to coordinate everything that is required to manage the life of *processes*. Its tasks include:

- *Process life-cycle* — a process's life-cycle includes its creation, execution and termination.

- *Scheduling* — processes are placed on run queues and their execution schedule is based on their class and priority level.

- *Switching* — once executing, a process is given a fair share of CPU time based on its class and priority level. The process subsystem must decide how long a process is allowed to use the CPU and when to switch in another.

- *Timing* — the system must keep track of process execution time by monitoring the time that a process takes to run. It must also monitor the hardware clock to keep track of the real system time.

- *Memory usage* — the process subsystem must coordinate with the memory management subsystem so that main memory can be allocated and deallocated as required to new and existing processes.

- *File subsystem coordination* — the process subsystem must coordinate with the file subsystem so that processes can associate themselves with files in the file system hierarchy. It must also be able to locate a file and read it into memory for execution.

141

- *Exception handling* — an address or exception fault that occurs during process execution requires a signal to be posted to the process. Processes may also post signals to other processes. Thus, the process subsystem must perform the signal posting and receiving.

4.1.1 Concurrency

The UNIX system provides a *multi-tasking* environment. A *task* is termed as the execution of a *process* in its own address space. The operating system gives the illusion that several processes execute simultaneously, but there is really only one process executing at any one time. There is also only ever one instance of a program executing, either the currently running process or the kernel itself, because in most implementations of UNIX there is only one processor and it can execute only one set of instructions at a time. Therefore, UNIX can be seen as a single executing program that is user programmable, or self-modifying at runtime.

4.1.2 Flow of execution

When a user program is executing, it is given control of the computer system and is restricted only by what has previously been set up as reserved by the kernel. For example, when a user program requires the services of the operating system, it transfers control to the operating system via a system call which is usually implemented as a hardware trap. The trap causes the transfer of CPU modes from user-mode to kernel-mode. Once this transition takes place, the kernel is then executing on behalf of the process and the user process is suspended until the kernel is ready to pass control back to it. Therefore, it can be seen that a process or task forms part of the overall *flow* of execution (see Figure 4.1).

It is sometimes difficult to tell the difference between a process and a program. A process is said to be the *execution* of a program. Yet there may be more than one instance of a process running on the system but only one instance of the program stored in the file system. Consider the following example:

```
$ grep foobar /etc/* &
$ grep foobar /etc/*
```

The ampersand at the end of the first command line tells the shell to execute the command in the background. Since there is no ampersand at the end of the second command line, the user would have to wait until the command completes. In this example, there are two instances of the process *grep* but there is only one instance of the program *grep*.

Figure 4.1: *Flow of execution*

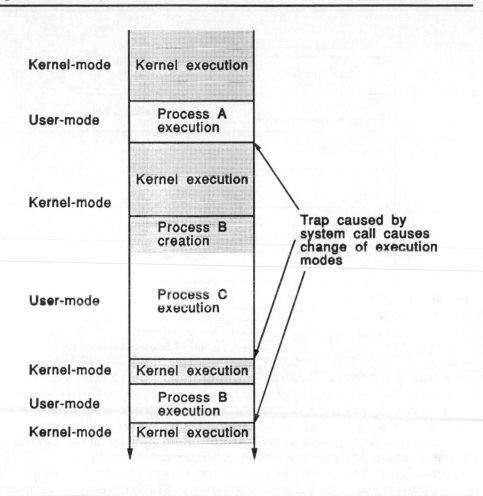

4.2 The process image

From the user's point of view, a process is the execution of an executable file stored in the file system. However, the kernel's view of a process is very much more complicated. This section discusses the image or view of a process as seen by the kernel.

4.2.1 Format of an executable on disk

Executable files created by the compilation system are called *a.out* files, because the default link editor and assembler output is a file called *a.out*. Within each *a.out* file is a *header*. The *header* holds the information about the format and structure of the program within the file.

Figure 4.2: *Logical view of an executable a.out file*

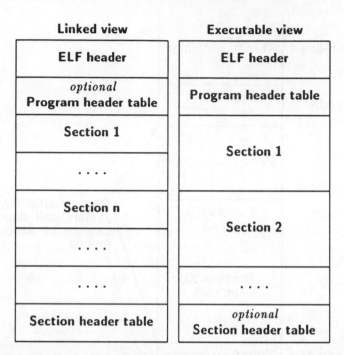

Prior to UNIX System V Release 4, *a.out* format files on System V versions of UNIX used the *Common Object File Format* (COFF). COFF is supported in UNIX System V Release 4, although a new *a.out* format is introduced called *Extensible Linking Format* (ELF). An *a.out* file's format is described by a header which resides at the beginning of the file. The header contains all the information the kernel requires to create a process image (i.e., execute the program).

Although both ELF and COFF object formats contain similar information, the information is stored in the file in different formats. ELF is the default format used for an *a.out* file in UNIX System V Release 4. (For more information about COFF, see [Gircys 1988]. For more information about ELF, see [Nohr 1993]).

ELF *a.out* files are built up from various *sections* which are described within the header. These sections describe the organization of the different portions of an executable as stored in the file on disk. The stored format of an *a.out* file is called the *linked view* (a program). As individual *segments* of the file are loaded into memory for execution, the format of the *a.out* file within memory is called the *executable view* (a process); see Figure 4.2.

Sections are used to hold information such as program header table, instructions, data, symbol table, relocation information, line numbers and so on. Files used to build up a process image must contain a program header table. However, intermediate object files are not required to have this information.

Sections and segments have no specified order within an *a.out* file. Only the ELF and COFF headers have fixed positions and sizes. The order and positions of the sections are described within the header.

Although there are two *a.out* formats officially supported by the operating system, the kernel is flexible enough to accommodate other executable object formats as they become available (see *execsw[]* in § 4.13.1).

4.2.2 Process memory model

Every process runs in its own address space on a virtual machine. That is, a process behaves as if all the resources of the machine are available for its exclusive use. The concurrent or parallel execution of multiple processes is achieved by switching different processes in and out every few milliseconds. Thus, the operating system gives the illusion that multiple processors are employed to do the work.

The operating system differentiates a user process from a system process. System processes are responsible for administering the system as a whole and perform housekeeping chores such as allocating memory, switching user processes in and out, swapping pages of memory between secondary storage, and so on. So a system process can be classed as a procedure rather than a process. User processes carrying out instructions generated by their own code are said to be operating in *user-mode*. User processes executing instructions that belong to the operating system are said to be operating in *kernel-mode*. A user process enters kernel-mode when it makes a system call, generates an exception (fault), or when an interrupt occurs such as that produced by the system clock. In kernel-mode, because the process executes kernel code, it is given full use of the processor and so can execute privileged instructions. The virtual memory system allows the kernel to access the code and data of any process, but not vice versa. The only thing that a process operating in user-mode can do to the kernel is request services from it through the system call interface. On the other hand, the kernel has the power to access the entire address space of any process.

From the point of view of a C program, a process's address space is a linear, flat, addressable area of memory starting at address zero and extending to a fixed address boundary set by both hardware and operating system. However, inside the kernel, a process's address space is divided into specific segments called *text, data, bss* and *stack*. These areas are explained later.

4.2.3 Context of a process

A process may be executing in user-mode, executing in kernel-mode, or not even executing at all, but rather, in a state of suspension. For example, it may be waiting for the completion of an I/O operation, or in a "ready to run" state — that is, placed in a scheduling queue waiting to be given a portion (or slice) of CPU time. The context of a process is a snapshot of its current run-time environment. It includes its address space, stack space, virtual address space, register set image such as program counter, stack pointer, general purpose registers, program status register, and so on. It also includes a snapshot image of its associated kernel data structures such as the *user* and *proc* structures, and any other system variables the operating system requires to manipulate the process at any given time. You could say that the context of a process is an image of a virtual machine. At any one time during its execution, a process runs in the context of itself and the kernel runs in the context of the *currently running process*.

4.2.4 The *user-area*

Every process has an associated *user-area* (sometimes referred to as the *u* area or *u* block). The user-area is defined by the *user* structure. It contains all the necessary information about a process that does not need to be referenced while the process is idle. The kernel only ever accesses one user-area, the one belonging to the currently running process. The user-area is only ever used or referenced while the process is running (i.e., actually using the CPU). If a user-area does not belong to the currently running process, it is stored along with the rest of its process image. It may remain in main memory, or be swapped or paged out to secondary storage if memory becomes scarce.

The user-area of a process is accessible only to the kernel and so is not addressable by a user program. (There is one exception: a parent process making use of the *ptrace* system call can modify a child process's user-area although the child process is stopped first.)

The user-area holds all the information relevant to a process's execution environment. It holds information such as who the process belongs to (i.e., its real and effective user and group IDs), the number of open files, its signal disposition, the number of shared memory segments, a pointer to its *proc* structure (see § 4.3.2), program invocation arguments, accounting information, and so on.

4.2.5 Process image in *user* address space

The image of a process in user address space is built up from both the user-area as described above, and the sections described in the executable *a.out* file (recall *execution view* in § 4.2.1). These two components form the *user program image*.

The following logical segments are set up in the user address space within the virtual memory system when the kernel loads an *a.out* file into memory for execution (see Figure 4.3):

- *text* — contains the program's machine instructions, which are often referred to as program code.

- *data* — contains initialized variables: external, global and static. Some implementations use this area to hold uninitialized static variables also.

- *bss* — contains uninitialized variables (*bss* came from the IBM 7090 assembly language and stood for "block started by symbol" but could be thought of as a "basic static storage" area). During process execution, both *data* and *bss* sections are usually referred to as a single *data* segment.

- *stack* — this segment is automatically expanded as required (refer to the *brk* system call § 3.10.1). It is used to hold locally allocated variables and parameters passed to functions.

Figure 4.3: *The user-area within the user program image*

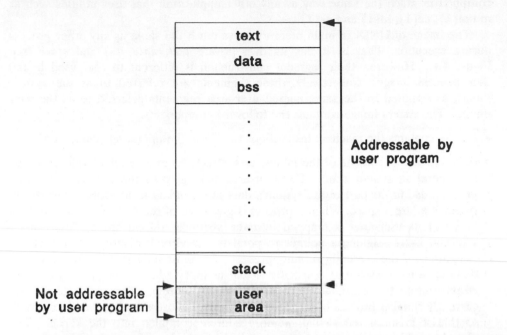

A process has two stacks: a *user stack* for use while executing instructions in user-mode, and a *kernel stack* for use while executing instructions in kernel-mode. The kernel stack is used by the kernel while operating in the context of the process. The user stack consists of *frames* or *activation records* which are pushed when the process makes a procedure call and popped on return. Locally allocated variables are also pushed during procedure execution and popped when the procedure terminates.

When the process makes a system call, a frame is pushed just like any other function call. System calls are stored in a library and are linked into a program at compile time. They are written in machine assembly language and contain specially encoded trap instructions. When executed, the trap generates an interrupt which results in a switch to kernel-mode execution. In kernel-mode, the process executes instructions from the kernel text and makes use of the kernel stack. The kernel stack is explained in detail later.

- *user-area* — as previously described, it is an area set aside for the kernel to use for controlling the process during its life-cycle.

4.2.6 Process image in *system* address space

The UNIX kernel itself is a program much like any other. It is a large C program that is compiled into an executable *a.out* file. It is stored as a file within the file system called */stand/unix*. No special utilities are required to generate it. It is compiled in much the same way as any other application that uses utilities such as **make(1)**, **cc(1)**, **ld(1)** and **as(1)**.

The image of UNIX in main memory looks much the same as any other process during execution. That is, it has its own private *text, data, bss* and *stack* (see Figure 4.4). However, their segment construction is different to that used in the user process image. Collectively, these segments are referred to as the *system image*, as opposed to the same named user-area segments referred to as the *user image*. The system image contains the following components:

- *text* — contains the machine instructions that form the operating system code.

- *data and bss* — consists of the tables, lists, structures and variables referenced by the operating system code. The user-area belonging to the *currently running process* also forms part of the system's data area, and so it also forms part of the system's address space. When a process is given use of the CPU (called *switching in* § 4.5) its user-area is mapped into the system's address space. This can be achieved by reassigning a pointer to point to the virtual memory address of the user-area for the currently running process. On most implementations, however, the user-area is placed at a specific virtual memory address assigned by the link editor during the compilation of the operating system. The user-area of the currently running process is mapped to this global address during a context switch so that it exists at the virtual memory address compiled into the kernel. The global variable *struct user u* is then used within the kernel to reference the user-area of the currently running process. For example, to reference the *proc* structure for the currently running process the kernel may reference *u.u_procp*.

- *kernel stack* — like the user stack, the kernel stack also consists of *frames* or *activation records*. A frame is pushed when the process enters kernel-mode, when its context is switched out, or when it invokes a kernel function in kernel-mode. The frame is subsequently popped off the stack when the process returns to user-mode, when its context is switched back in, or when it returns from a function made in kernel-mode.

  In the case of function calls made by the kernel on behalf of an executing process in kernel-mode, activation records are used for local variable allocation and parameter passing. They are pushed on function invocation, and popped on return to the caller.

  In the case of a context switch, the kernel pushes an activation record on the stack when a process is context switched out. When the process is later switched back in, the kernel pops it back off again. In this case, an activation record contains a saved copy of the processor registers used by the process (see process control block (PCB) § 4.3.1).

  Since there is only one copy of the kernel residing in memory, all processes execute the same kernel code. Thus, each active process must have its own private kernel stack. Although each process has its own stack, the kernel must be able to restore the contents of the kernel stack and the stack pointer so that it can reinstate the execution of a process in kernel-mode. By pushing and popping

Figure 4.4: *Logical view of user-area in system address space*

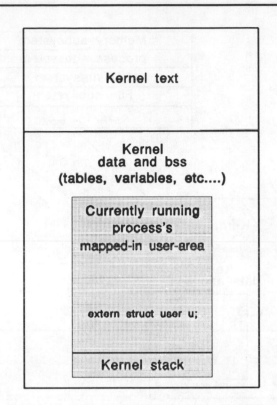

activation records on and off the kernel stack in this way, the kernel can rebuild a process's execution environment when its context is switched in to become the currently running process. When the process returns to user-mode, the last activation record on the kernel stack is popped. Thus, in user-mode execution, the kernel stack is always empty.

The placement of the per-process kernel stack is implementation dependent although it is usually allocated its own portion of the virtual address space. Some implementations use a variable in the user area to store its location. For example, on the AT&T Intel 80386 implementation, the *user* structure contains a field called *u_stack* which contains the virtual memory address of the process's kernel stack.

In summary, the image of a process as seen by the kernel includes the mapped in image of the currently running process (i.e., the *user program image*), the total *system image*, and the current state of the *processor registers*. Taken altogether they fabricate the overall execution of a process. These three components form a snapshot of the *total process image* (see Figure 4.5) which is referred to as its context.

Figure 4.5: *Logical view of the total process image*

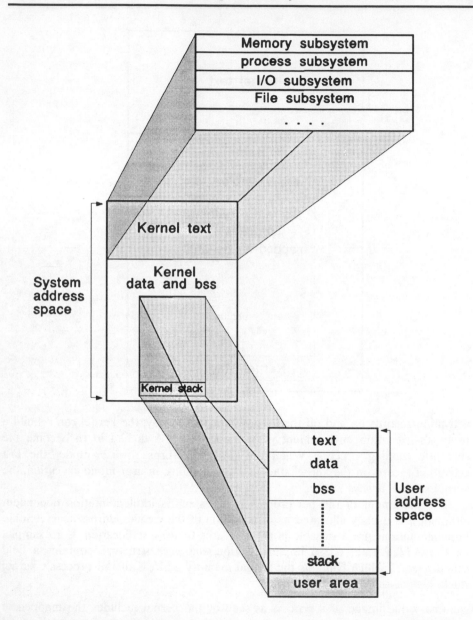

4.2.7 Processor registers

The kernel's use of processor registers is basically the same for all implementations of the operating system, although the amount and type of registers available to it obviously depends on what is provided by the processor design. Although implemented differently, some registers are common to almost all processors and their use by the kernel is described as follows:

- *General Purpose Data Registers* — contain data manipulated by the process during its execution. In general, register usage is specified by the operating system implementation. These registers typically contain temporary expression evaluations, integer and pointer return values, function calling parameters, and so on.

- *Scratch Registers* — used for intermediate expression evaluation results such as the return value generated by function calls.

- *Program Counter (PC)* — contains the virtual memory address of the instruction that the CPU will execute next.

- *Processor Status Register (PS)* — has many names: Program Status Word (PSW) register, cause register, flag register, control register, system register, and so on. On the MIPS R3000 processor, it is implemented as two 32 bit registers — *status* and *cause* — which are incorporated within the on-chip System Control Coprocessor (known as CP0). On the Intel 80386 processor it is implemented as a single 32 bit register called the *flags* register.

  The PS register may be implemented as a class of registers. In general it is split into sections which represent different conditions. Specific bits in the registers are set or unset when certain conditions or events occur. For example, if a register overflows the carry bit is set, or the result of a computation is signed or equalled zero. The status register is also consulted for its mode of operation (user-mode or kernel-mode on the R3000, unprotected-mode or protected-mode on the 80386), and processor execution level (i.e., interrupt level). Since the kernel operates in the context of the currently running process, the PS register contains the current hardware status in relation to that process.

- *Frame Pointer (FP)* — bonds together a chain of activation records into a single activation record called a frame. The order of elements within a frame are processor dependent as is the direction of stack growth. Neither will be discussed here.

- *Stack Pointer (SP)* — contains the virtual memory address of the uppermost element of the stack. If the process is executing in user-mode, the stack pointer points to the process's private user stack. If the process is executing in kernel-mode, then the stack pointer points to the process's kernel stack.

- *Memory Management Registers* — the kernel requires a set of registers that translate virtual memory addresses into physical memory addresses. On both the MIPS R3000 and Intel 80386, mapped virtual addresses are translated into physical addresses using an on chip Translation Lookaside Buffer (TLB).

- *Floating point registers* — the IEEE Standard 754 specifies a standard for binary floating point arithmetic. The installation of a floating-point co-processor adds several floating point registers to the system for use with floating point operations. During a context switch, the operating system must also make provisions for saving a copy of these registers along with the CPU registers.

Figure 4.6: *Process related data structures*

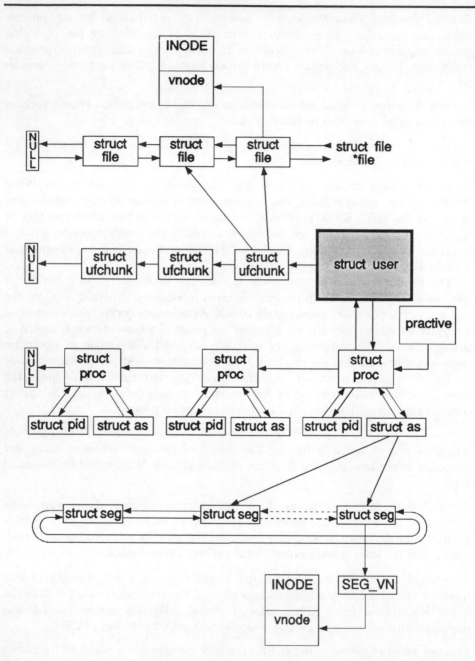

4.3 The structure of a process

So far we have discussed the image of a process. However, the image of a process is only a logical view. The actual structure of a process as managed by the system is very much more complex.

There are several data structures that describe the context and state of a process (some of which are shown in Figure 4.6). This section will discuss the structure elements that are relevant to the process management subsystem.

As previously mentioned, the *user* structure belonging to a process is only ever used or referenced while the process is active. Thus, it is only ever needed when the process is the currently running process and is otherwise stored in main memory or swapped out to disk. However, some data structures must remain memory resident — for example — data structures shared amongst processes, and *proc* structures associated with active processes.

Table 4.1: *Variables used in a MIPS R3000 user structure implementation*

Category	Field	Description
register context	u_pcb	Process control block save area used during context switch
stack	u_sub	Upper bound address of user stack
	u_userstack	Address of user stack
memory resident	u_procp	Pointer to *proc* structure
	u_ap	Pointer to command line argument list
vnode	u_cdir	Pointer to *vnode* for current directory
	u_rdir	Pointer to *vnode* for root directory
a.out	u_tsize	Text size
	u_dsize	Data size
	u_ssize	Stack size

4.3.1 The *user* structure

The *user* structure is the area that is re-mapped (either in or out) during a context switch. It contains the process's current hardware register state at the time the context switch took place. Thus, the execution of a process is not stopped, it is just suspended until its context is switched back in again.

Some of the fields in the *user* structure that are of interest are shown in Table 4.1. The *user* structure is very much implementation dependent because the implementor must decide what context switching arrangements the system will use. The implementor must also provide the assembler routines required to perform the low-level context switch itself. Since the user structure holds an image of the current execution state of the process, it is an obvious place for the implementor to store context-related machine information such as its current register status, program counter, stack pointer, and so on. Such information is normally stored within the process control block (PCB). For example, in the MIPS implementation, all the process's context-related machine information is stored in the PCB (Table 4.2) and the PCB is the very first element in the *user* structure. The implementation uses a fixed virtual address for the user-area within the kernel's address space, and so it is a simple matter of re-mapping the virtual addresses of the PCB structures when switching between processes. Since the rest of the *user* structure information for the process is stored below the PCB area, the user-area is automatically mapped when the PCB area is mapped. (Note that some implementations use a pointer in the user-area to point to the virtual address of the kernel stack stored within the process's address space.)

Table 4.2: *MIPS R3000 registers saved in the Process Control Bock*

Register	Description
S0	
S1	
S2	
S3	Saved registers
S4	
S5	
S6	
S7	
SP	Stack pointer
FP	Frame pointer
PC	Program counter
SR	Status register

The address space of a process is described by its associated *as* structure which is indirectly locatable from the *user* structure via its associated *proc* structure pointer (*u.u_procp->p_as*). For more information on how a process's address space is managed, see Chapter 3.

Since the kernel executes in the context of the currently running process, the kernel's current execution state is derived from the contents of the PCB in the user-area of the currently running process. Thus, both user-mode and kernel-mode machine execution states are saved in the user-area during a context switch.

4.3.2 The *proc* structure

Each active process has one associated *proc* structure which is accessible by referencing the *u_procp* pointer in the user-area.

The *proc* structure belonging to an active process must remain memory resident because it contains information that may have to be referenced by the kernel even if that information belongs to a process that is not currently running. For example, consider the currently running process posting a signal to another process. Since the receiving process is not currently running, there is no guarantee that its *user* structure is memory resident. Therefore, the kernel stores pending signals for the receiving process in that process's associated *proc* structure. Since a process can post a signal to any process including itself, all *proc* structures in the active list must remain memory resident.

The scheme for allocating *proc* structures in UNIX System V Release 4 is different to that used in previous releases of UNIX System V where the system allocated a fixed number of *proc* structures at boot time. In UNIX System V Release 4, *proc* structures are allocated dynamically. As a process is created, the kernel allocates memory for a new *proc* structure and places it into the list of active processes. When the process terminates, the kernel removes it from the active list. Table 4.3 lists the fields of interest in the *proc* structure.

All *proc* structures are chained together on a linked list headed by *practive* (process active list). The system maintains the active list so that kernel procedures can search the list (using *p_next*) for a particular *proc* structure.

The *proc* structure also contains a pointer to its associated *cred* structure (*p_cred*). There is one *cred* structure per process. It contains the process's *credentials* — its real and effective user and group execution IDs.

There are two pointers to *pid* structures in a *proc* structure. *p_pidp* points to the *pid* structure containing process ID information, and *p_pgidp* points to the *pid* structure containing process group ID information. These will be discussed in more detail later.

4.4 Process states

A process has two associated states: a *functional* state and a hardware *execution* state. The functional state describes its current running condition as an active process as managed by the operating system. The execution state describes its current hardware status. Both states are discussed in the following sections.

4.4.1 Functional state

A process can be in only one state (Figure 4.7). During a process's life-cycle its current active state is specified as a value in the *proc* structure field *p_stat*. The process states are described in Table 4.4.

All processes are created by the system call *fork* which initially marks a process as *SIDL*. *fork* then attempts to allocate resources for the newly created process and duplicates its parent environment. If successful, *fork* marks the process *SRUN* and places it on a dispatch queue ready to be given use of the CPU.

A process may voluntarily go to sleep by calling the kernel routine *sleep( )*. A process goes to sleep pending an event. Going to sleep means that it gives up the use of the CPU, causing a context switch. For example, a process normally goes to sleep when it must await the completion of I/O. The *sleep( )* routine is invoked with a wait channel and a scheduling priority value. It marks the process as *SSLEEP* and assigns the passed wait channel to *p_wchan*. When the process is awakened it is

Table 4.3: *Fields in the proc structure (proc_t)*

Category	Field	Description
Miscellaneous	p_segu	Pointer to the u structure
	p_next	Pointer to the next *proc* structure in active list
	p_stat	Current status of process
	p_flag	Bitmask containing runtime flags
	p_exec	Pointer to file *a.out vnode*
Identifiers	p_cred	Pointer to the credentials information
	p_pidp	Pointer to Process ID (PID) information
	p_pgidp	Pointer to Process Group ID (PGID) information
	p_sessp	Pointer to session information
Scheduling	p_pri	Scheduling priority value
	p_cpu	CPU usage
	p_cid	Process scheduling class id
	p_clproc	Pointer to process class specific data structure
	p_clfuncs	Pointer to class specific functions
Synchronization	p_wchan	Event-channel for sleeping processes
	p_wcode	Current wait code
	p_wdata	Current wait return value
Process list management	p_parent	Pointer to the parent process
	p_child	Pointer to the first child process
	p_sibling	Pointer to the next sibling on the chain
	p_link	Link pointer for sleep and dispatch queue hash chains
Signals	p_clktim	Pending alarm clock time
	p_cursig	Current signal being handled by process (if any)
	p_hold	Signals being held
	p_sig	Pending signals for this process
	p_ignore	Signals being ignored
	p_whystop	Flag saying why the process stopped
	p_whatstop	Flag saying what caused it to stop
Memory management	p_brkbase	Base address of heap
	p_brksize	Size of the heap
	p_stkbase	Base address of stack
	p_stksize	Size of stack
	p_ubptbl	In-core page-table information
	p_as	Pointer to process's address space (*as*) structure
Per process accounting	p_utime	User-mode execution time
	p_stime	Kernel-mode execution time
	p_cutime	Sum of child's user-mode execution time
	p_cstime	Sum of child's kernel-mode execution time

Figure 4.7:  *Process states*

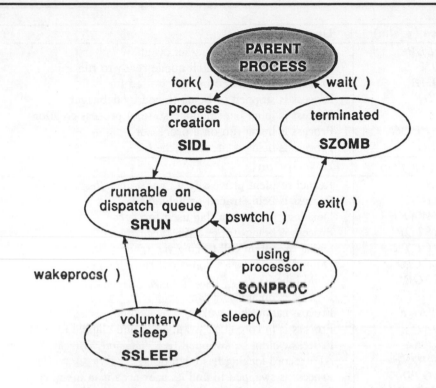

marked *SRUN*. (Sleeping and waking processes are discussed in § 4.6.13).

A process marked as *SONPROC* means that it is the currently running process. A terminated process is marked *SZOMB* (a zombie process) until its parent process receives its termination status via the *wait* system call (§ 4.15.4).

Additional information about a process's *functional* status is stored in a bitmask in the *proc* structure *p_flag* field. These flags are set and cleared by the kernel during process execution. They are shown in Table 4.4, and their use is described throughout this chapter.

4.4.2 Execution state

A context switch can only occur in kernel-mode. But since the kernel operates in the context of a process, a context switch between processes requires the saving and restoring of hardware execution states for both kernel and user-mode contexts. For this reason the user-mode state of a process is placed in the *user* structure.

Since the *user* structure is the area that is context switched, the kernel-mode execution state at the time the context switch takes place is described in the PCB save area in the *user* structure. The saved user-mode state of a process executing in kernel-mode is stored on the kernel's stack. When a process in user-mode executes a system call, it transfers execution to kernel-mode. This transfer of execution modes

Table 4.4: *Process states and flags*

State (*p_stat*)	Description
SSLEEP	Process is asleep pending an event
SRUN	Process is on the dispatch queue ready to run
SZOMB	Process is terminated but not waited for
SSTOP	Process is stopped or being traced by debugger
SIDL	Process is in an intermediate state of process creation
SONPROC	Process is being run on a processor
SXBRK	Process is being context switched
Flag (*p_flag*)	**Description**
SSYS	Kernel resident process (e.g., *pageout, fsflush, sched*)
STRC	Process is being traced or debugged
SPRWAKE	Deadlock prevention flag used for */proc*
SPRSTOP	Process is being stopped via */proc*
SPROCTR	Signal or system call tracing via */proc*
SPROCIO	Doing I/O via */proc*, so do not run
SPRFORK	Child inherits */proc* tracing flags
SPROPEN	Process is open via */proc*
SNWAKE	Process cannot be awakened by a signal
SLOAD	Process is in core (i.e., swapped in and eligible to run)
SLOCK	Process cannot be swapped (e.g., *pageout, fsflush...*)
SLKDONE	NFS record-locking has been done
SULOAD	Process is swapped in and its user-area is in memory
SRUNLCL	Set process running on last */proc* close
SNOSTOP	Not allowed to stop process while it sleeps
SPTRX	Process is exiting via *ptrace(2)*
SASLEEP	Process is suspended within a call to *sleep( )*
SUSWAP	User-area is in the middle of being swapped in or out
SUWANT	Waiting for user-area swap to complete
SEXECED	Process has exec-ed
SSWLOCKS	Process has swap locks
SXSTART	*setrun( )* by *SIGCONT* or *ptrace( )*
SPSTART	*setrun( )* by */proc*
SJCTL	*SIGCHLD* sent when children stop/continue (job control)
SNOWAIT	Children never become zombies
SVFORK	Process in the middle of a *vfork( )*
SVFDONE	*vfork( )* child waits for parent to release address space

causes the system trap handlers to save the process's current user-mode execution context. As a result of this an activation record is built onto the kernel stack containing the saved vectors (stack pointer, program counter, scratch registers, and so on) of the process so that they can be resumed later when the process returns to user-mode. Other process-related structures, such as *proc, as, pid,* and so on, must remain memory resident.

4.5 Context switching

The multi-tasking UNIX operating system simulates multiple processors by providing each task (process) with its own virtual processor. During any instance of execution, the operating system assigns the real processor with a virtual processor to run its task. To maintain such an illusion, the operating system frequently switches the service of the real processor to a virtual processor. Since task scheduling policies vary between operating system implementations, the processor allows the operating system to choose its own policy for scheduling the execution of tasks. However, the real core of the task switching is left to the processor itself. The scheduling policy used by the UNIX System V Release 4 operating system is discussed later. First we will discuss the method used to implement the task switch itself.

The procedure of switching the service of the CPU from one process to another is called a *context switch*. During a context switch, the kernel saves the context of the currently running process and resumes the context of the next process that is scheduled to run. When the kernel *preempts* a process, its context is saved. When the kernel schedules it to run again, its context is restored and it continues to execute again as if it had never actually stopped.

The context of the currently running process is saved when any of the following happens:

- The process in user-mode executes a system call causing a change of execution mode from user-mode to kernel-mode.

- A *trap* is generated perhaps as a result of a system hardware generated interrupt (i.e., the system clock or a peripheral device), a software generated interrupt, or an exception fault such as a bus error, segmentation fault or floating point exception, divide by zero, and so on. A trap can occur in either user-mode or kernel-mode.

- The process voluntarily goes to sleep pending the availability of a resource or event.

- The kernel preempts the currently running process which results in a context switch.

Since most processor designs support their own task switching facilities the context switch implementation is machine dependent. For this reason, the low-level parts of the context switch implementation are left for the operating system implementors. The result is that the actual context switch is written in machine assembly language. However, the formalities for implementing the actual context switch are basically the same for all implementations. We will discuss these in detail in the following sections.

There are three issues related to context switching:

- The context switch must be done efficiently. The time taken to switch one process out and the next one in must be in the order of a few microseconds. Since most of the time taken to carry out the context switch is sacrificed in saving and restoring the context of processes, it is important that the amount of information to be saved is reduced to an absolute minimum. Otherwise the performance of the operating system suffers considerably and gives a poor response to users.

One effective method of producing faster context switches is to re-map the virtual address of the new running process's *user* structure into an address that the kernel knows about (i.e., the address of the global *user* structure *u*). This method requires only the re-mapping of an address instead of copying the data into some area of storage and it is the method used in UNIX System V Release 4.

- Since many data structures are shared amongst processes, there must be a consistent method for allowing data access between them. The only obvious answer is to store these data structures in memory.

- Since the system manages multiple processes, each of which assumes that it is the only process running on a virtual machine, the system must choose a scheme in which all processes are given a fair share of CPU time. This is discussed in the following section.

4.6 Process scheduling

Preemptive operating systems can interrupt a running task and suspend its execution while a task of higher priority is being executed. Preemption guarantees response to short tasks at the price of some overhead [Hansen 1973]. Obviously, preemptive kernels are more complex in design since they must keep track of several tasks that are in a different stage of execution. Additionally, a single processor can service only one task at a time even though several tasks may be simultaneously executing. Thus, a task must be assigned a time-quantum (or time-slice) for when it can use the CPU. When the time-quantum expires, the operating system must switch to another task, and so on in perpetual motion. It is also the responsibility of the process scheduler to select the next highest priority task to run.

The UNIX System V Release 4 process scheduling mechanism incorporates many features that have not been previously seen in earlier releases of the System V kernel. Prior to UNIX System V Release 4, all processes were time-shared [Ritchie, Thompson 1974] and subject to the same selection criteria. That is, all scheduled processes were placed on a single *run queue* and brought into service according to their *priority level*. The process with the lowest priority level was the next process to be given the use of the CPU.

4.6.1 Priority classes

UNIX System V Release 4 introduces the notion of *priority classes* and supports two types, although the design is flexible enough to incorporate new priority classes into the scheme as they become available. The two officially supported priority class types provide support for *time-sharing processes* and *real-time processes*, and a dynamic process selection scheme is used to determine which process will get to use the CPU next. This new selection scheme allows some flexibility in the choice of process priorities.

In UNIX System V Release 4, all processes belong to a particular process priority class. Each priority class supported by the system has an associated set of *class dependent* routines that calculate the priority level of a process and determine which *priority queue* to place it onto. These routines decide how a process is scheduled to run. Instead of a single *run queue*, there are now multiple *priority queues*, one for each priority value used by the system. In addition to this, the kernel's process selection code (the *class independent* routines) now selects a process from the highest valued priority queue, as opposed to the lowest priority level used in previous versions of the operating system.

In general, a time-shared process is subjected to a *round-robin* approach similar to that used in earlier versions of UNIX System V. That is, every process is eventually given use of the CPU, although some processes may get to use the CPU before others depending on their operating characteristics. However, a real-time process is given a higher precedence and is guaranteed to be selected to run before any time-shared process. Furthermore, in order that a real-time process can be guaranteed maximum response time, many well defined preemption points are placed throughout the kernel.

4.6.2 Process time-slice

A *time-slice* is the amount of time that a process is given to use the CPU before it calls either *swtch( )* or *pswtch( )* to switch the CPU to another process — these routines are responsible for enacting a context switch and will be discussed in more detail later.

A process's allotted time-slice depends on its priority class and priority level. The time-slice may be short, long, or even infinitely long. A real-time process may hog the CPU forever! The value of a process's time-slice is decided by the priority class dependent functions. The *proc* structure variable *p_pri* is used to store the process's current priority value — the higher its value, the higher its priority, and the faster it is given the CPU.

4.6.3 Priority class independent variables

The scheduling algorithms use several variables to coordinate context switching. They are shown in Table 4.5 and will be discussed in the following sections.

The *runrun* and *kprunrun* variables are used as flags. *runrun* is set by the process to tell the kernel that it should call *swtch( )* at its earliest convenience. The kernel can switch out a process running in user-mode at any time, in favor of a higher priority runnable process. However, a process running in kernel-mode can only be switched out if the operating system code specifically asks it to do so, so that in certain instances a process cannot be preempted. In such cases the *runrun* flag is used to tell the operating system that it should call *swtch( )* as soon as possible. The trap handling code usually checks the *runrun* flag before returning from kernel-

Table 4.5: *Class independent variables*

Variable	Description
int runrun	Set to cause preemption
int kprunrun	Set to preempt at next kernel preemption point
int curpri	Priority of current process (i.e., *u.u_procp->p_pri*).
int maxrunpri	Priority of highest priority active queue
int srunprocs	Total number of loaded, runnable processes waiting to be scheduled
int idleswtch	Flag set while idle in pswtch( )
int npwakecnt	Non-preemptive wake-up flag
*proc_t *curproc*	Pointer to the currently running process (i.e., *u.u_procp*)
*dispq_t *dispq*	Pointer to array of dispatch queues indexed by *p_pri*
*ulong *dqactmap*	Points to an array of *dispq* active bitmaps, 1 per dispatch queue

mode to user-mode and also when entering kernel-mode from user-mode as a result of a system call. If the flag is set, *preempt( )* is called. *preempt( )* first calls the class dependent preemption routine to recalculate the current process's new priority value and which dispatch queue it is to be placed on. Finally it calls *swtch( )* to cause a context switch (*preempt( )* is discussed in detail later).

There are many well-defined preemption points within the operating system code. The *kprunrun* (kernel preemption runrun) flag is set if kernel preemption points are enabled. This flag is similar to *runrun* except that it tells the kernel that implicit calls to *preempt( )* will be made only if the *kprunrun* flag is set. If *runrun* is set but *kprunrun* is not set, then preemption takes place only as the kernel returns to user-mode. Thus, *kprunrun* is only ever set within the real time class specific kernel code.

curpri and *curproc* are set within *pswtch( )* and reference the priority level of the newly switched process and the process to be switched in. Once the context switch takes place, *curpri* becomes the same as *u.u_procp->p_pri*, and *curproc* becomes *u.u_procp*.

4.6.4 Priority dispatch queues

The kernel maintains a *priority dispatch queue* for each priority value in the system and they are held together in an array of dispatch queues called *dispq[]*. Each element within *dispq[]* is a *dispq* structure (Table 4.6).

Each *dispq* structure consists of a linked list of runnable *proc* structures (i.e., with *p_stat* marked *SRUN*) each linked together via their *p_link* member. Each *proc* structure in the queue has the same *p_pri* value that is used to index into *dispq[]*. The queue is managed by two pointers: *dq_first* points to the first process in the priority queue and *dq_last* points to the last process in the queue (see Figure 4.8).

The scheduling algorithms select the process with the highest priority to use the CPU next. Since all processes on a dispatch queue have the same *p_pri* value, the algorithms simply index into the *dispq[]* array to gain access to the dispatch queue with the highest priority. Whichever process is first in that dispatch queue is scheduled to use the CPU.

The variable *maxrunpri* contains the current maximum *p_pri* value. This value is used to index into *dispq[]*. *maxrunpri* changes its value as the queues are manipulated, and is dependent on the highest process priority value. The system call *priocntl* allows a user-level program to change its *p_pri* value providing it has sufficient permission to do so.

Table 4.6: *Struct dispq (dispq_t)*

Element	Description
*struct proc *dq_first*	Pointer to first process in the queue
*struct proc *dq_last*	Pointer to last process in the queue
int dq_sruncnt	Number of in-core processes in the queue

The variable *srunprocs* stores the total number of loaded (in-core), runnable processes held on the combined priority dispatch queues. The *dispq* structure member *dq_sruncnt* stores the number of processes in the queue with the *SLOAD* bit set in *p_flag*. If *SLOAD* is set, the process is loaded in memory and eligible to run. As it runs, its pages are faulted in, in the usual way (see § 3.2).

To speed up the selection algorithms, the system uses a bitmap (*dqactmap*) consisting of a single bit per configured element in *dispq[]*. If a bit is non-zero, the element within *dispq[]* corresponding to the bit position is active — in other words, there is a *proc* structure active on that dispatch queue. If a bit is zero, the queue corresponding to that element is empty. The most significant bit in *dqactmap* coincides with the highest priority dispatch queue configured.

4.6.5 Priority class independent functions

The following class independent functions are used by the system to manage dispatch queues and processes, regardless of the process's priority class:

- *setbackdq()* and *setfrontdq()* — places a process on the back or front of the dispatch queue corresponding to its current priority.

- *dispdeq()* — removes a process from its priority dispatch queue.

- *dq_sruninc()* and *dq_srundec()* — increments or decrements the dispatch queue's *dq_sruncnt* when a process on a dispatch queue is made schedulable or un-schedulable by resetting the *SLOAD* or *SPROCIO* flags. *srunprocs* and *maxrunpri* are updated accordingly.

- *preempt()* — preempts the currently running process by calling its class dependent function to deduce which dispatch queue it should be placed on. *swtch()* is then called to force a context switch to take place.

Figure 4.8: *Priority dispatch queues*

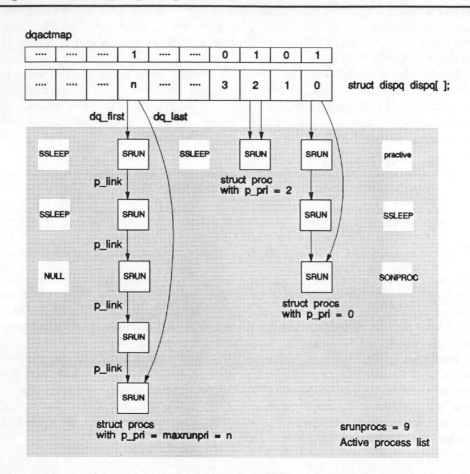

- *PREEMPT( )* — a macro that simply tests to see if *kprunrun* is set. If it is, then *preempt( )* is called.

- *pswtch( )* — selects the next highest priority process to run (Figure 4.9). The selected process must also be loaded into memory (i.e., marked *SLOAD*). If the parent process has set *SNOWAIT* and the process is a zombie, the process is removed from the process list. If the process is marked *SONPROC*, it is using the processor and so it must give up the CPU and be replaced by another process. If this happens it is marked *SRUN* again and placed back into a dispatch queue signifying that it is ready to be scheduled again. Once a process has been selected it is removed from its dispatch queue and marked *SONPROC*. The variables *curpri* and *curproc* are set to coincide with the new process. The *runrun*, *kprunrun* and *npwakecnt* variables are set to zero, since their purpose is to tell the system to call *pswtch( )*.

Figure 4.9: *Algorithm for pswtch( )*

```
pswtch()
input:  none
output: none
{
    update system statistical information

    if(process is in state SZOMB) {
        free remaining memory used by process
        if(process is marked SNOWAIT) {
            free up resources used by the process and
            remove the process from the active process list
        }
    } else if(process is in state SONPROC)
        set process to state SRUN

    raise processor interrupt priority to block all interrupts
    zero runrun, kprunrun and npwakecnt
    find the highest priority loaded (SLOAD), runnable process
    remove the process from its dispatch queue
    increment srunprocs
    set process to state SONPROC
    set curpri and curproc to reference this process
    reset processor priority level to previous level
}
```

- *swtch( )* — the context of the currently running process is saved in its associated user-area process control block. *pswtch( )* is called to select the next process to run. The selected process's context is resumed from its saved PCB. This involves mapping in the process's user-area and memory management information such as hardware registers and virtual memory mapping translation information. The mapping in of the user-area replenishes the system stack, register set, and program counter of the selected process, so it begins to execute from where it left off within *swtch( )*.

  On the MIPS R3000 processor, *swtch( )* uses two low-level assembler routines called *save( )* and *resume( )* (see Figure 4.10). Both routines manipulate the PCB area. *save( )* saves the current processor state in the PCB of the process being switched out. *resume( )* maps in the user-area of the newly selected process and restores the processor registers from its PCB. Upon return from *resume( )*, the newly selected process becomes the currently running process and its user-area is automatically mapped into the virtual memory address of the system's global user-area. The newly mapped in process continues executing its instructions without knowing it had been previously context switched out.

Figure 4.10: *Algorithm for swtch( )*

```
swtch()
input:  none
output: none
{
    save(curproc context in pcb)

    pswtch(); /* find the next process to switch in */

    /* curproc now set to resumed process here */

    resume(restore context for curproc from its pcb)

    /* restored process resumes execution here */
}
```

4.6.6 Priority class groups

All processes are arranged into specific *priority class* groups, and each group is categorized by its own scheduling characteristics which are determined by the class dependent functions provided with each process priority class type.

When a process is created, it inherits its parent's priority class scheduling characteristics, which include its priority class and priority value within that class. The process remains in that class unless it is changed as the result of a user-mode request using the *priocntl* system call.

The class dependent functions determine a process's priority value. This value is made available to the class independent functions as a global priority value. The highest valued priority is chosen by the scheduler. Thus, the scheduler always runs a process from the highest global priority dispatch queue.

UNIX System V Release 4 is independent of process priority class and provides for the installation of new priority class types as they become available. All installed priority class types are configurable with the exception of the system-class. Table 4.7 lists the priority class types (and their default global priority values) that are provided with the operating system. We will discuss each priority class implementation later on in this section.

Each priority class is described in a *class* structure. An array of *class* structures called the *class table* (*struct class class[ ]*) consists of one *class* structure per priority class configured in the system. Table 4.8 lists the elements in the class structure. The relationship between a process and a priority class is made through specific *proc* structure members described in Table 4.9.

The *proc* structure member *p_cid* is used to index into the table. Both *class* and *proc* structures have pointers which point to the *classfuncs* structure for that particular priority class type. This structure consists of a number of pointers to the priority class dependent functions.

Table 4.7: *Priority class types*

Priority Class	Scheduling Sequence	Global Value
	first	159
Real-time	.	.
	.	.
	.	.
	.	100
	.	99
System	.	.
	.	.
	.	.
	.	60
	.	59
Time-shared	.	.
	.	.
	last	0

Table 4.8: *Struct class (class_t)*

Element	Description
char *cl_name	String containing the priority class name
void (*cl_init)( )	Pointer to the class initialization function called at boot time
struct classfuncs *cl_funcs	Pointer to the structure containing function pointers to the class dependent functions

Table 4.9: *Struct proc related priority class members*

Element	Description
id_t p_cid	An integer used to index into the class[] table for the class to which the process is associated with
_VOID *p_clproc	Pointer to a class dependent data structure defined by the priority class dependent functions
struct classfuncs *p_clfuncs	Pointer to the same classfuncs structure described in the priority class table

The *cl_init* function pointer in the class structure points to a class specific initialization routine. This is called by the scheduler initialization routine *dispinit( )* at boot time (§ 4.17.1). Each *proc* structure contains a pointer (*p_clproc*) to its class dependent data structure, defined by the priority class dependent functions. Figure 4.11 shows how these data structures and tables are linked together.

Figure 4.11: *Priority class groups*

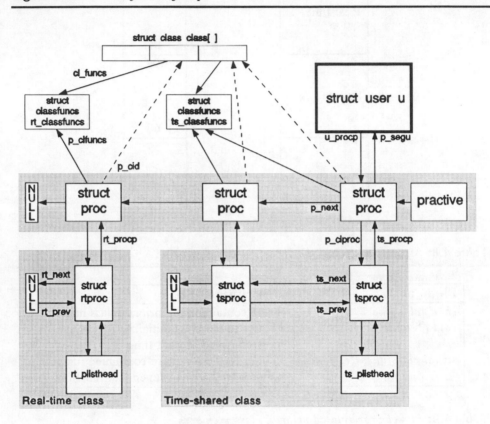

4.6.7 Priority class dispatch parameter tables

Each priority class type maintains its own specific table to describe the characteristics of process priority levels for processes running in that specific priority class. The tables contain structures, one for each supported priority level, and they are aptly named *dispatch parameter tables*.

These tables are built from configurable (tuneable) tables in the *master.d* files of the kernel build directory. They may be adjusted as the administrator sees fit. A program called **dispadmin(1M)** allows the administrator to change or retrieve scheduler information in the running system.

The definition of a dispatch parameter table is class dependent and its purpose is simply to specify the default dispatch configuration of processes running at a specific priority level in a specific priority class. The supported priority classes and their dispatch parameter tables are explained in the following sections.

4.6.8 System-class

System-class processes such as *pageout, fsflush,* and *sched* use a fixed priority policy. The system-class is reserved for kernel use only and is not configurable. The priority scheme is set up within the kernel code and remains at that priority level throughout system operation. System-class processes and kernel-mode processes have nothing in common. A user process running in kernel-mode runs with its own scheduling characteristics — it is not in the system-class.

4.6.9 Real-time class

Real-time class processes also use a fixed priority scheduling policy. Real-time process priorities remain fixed unless the user changes them. A real-time process can literally take over the machine. Since system-class processes must compete against user processes for use of the CPU, real-time applications must be configured correctly so that the kernel is given the processing time it needs for normal system operation. While there is a process on a dispatch queue that is in the real-time class, no other system or time-shared class process is scheduled. Thus, a real-time process always has a higher priority than any system-class or time-shared class process.

Figure 4.12: *Real-time class dispatch parameter table*

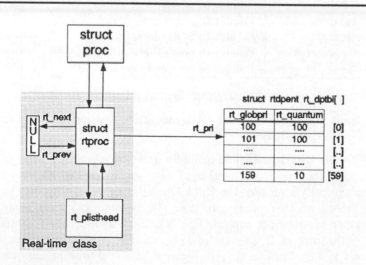

The real-time dispatch parameter table is called *rt_dptbl[]*. It is an array of *rtdpent* structures, one for each priority level (see Table 4.10 and Figure 4.12).

Table 4.10: *Struct rtdpent (rtdpent_t)*

Element	Description
int rt_globpri	Default global priority (from 100 - 159)
long rt_quantum	Default time-quantum (slice) for this level specified in clock ticks

The *rt_pri* member of the real-time class specific data structure (*rtproc*) offsets into *rt_dptbl[]* to reference the priority level parameters for that process. The *proc* structure member *p_clproc* points to the class specific data structure. In the case of a real-time process, it points to an *rtproc* structure (see Table 4.11). This structure contains specific data and information used by the real-time class dependent functions.

Table 4.11: *Struct rtproc (rtproc_t)*

Element	Description
long rt_pquantum	Time-quantum assigned to this process
long rt_timeleft	Time remaining in time-quantum
short rt_pri	Priority level (offset into *rt_dptbl[]*)
ushort rt_flags	Flags: $RTRAN$ — process has run since last swap out, $RTBACKQ$ — process is placed on the back of its dispatch queue when next preempted.
*struct proc *rt_procp*	Pointer to process in the active list.
*char *rt_pstatp*	Pointer to *p_stat* in *rt_procp*
*int *rt_pprip*	Pointer to *p_pri* in *rt_procp*
*uint *rt_pflagp*	Pointer to *p_flag* in *rt_procp*
*struct rtproc *rt_next*	Pointer to next *rtproc* in list
*struct rtproc *rt_prev*	Pointer to previous *rtproc* in list

The members of the *rtdpent* structure are explained as follows:

- *rt_globpri* — holds the default global class independent priority level. Higher values get to use the CPU first.

- *rt_quantum* — holds the default time-quantum (or time-slice) for that priority level. This specifies the maximum number of *clock-ticks* that can elapse while a process with this priority level uses the CPU. Once this time-quantum has passed, the scheduler selects another process to run. The system clock ticks away at a predefined number of times per second. This is defined as a constant named *HZ* (after Hertz — the unit of frequency) in *sys/param.h*. A clock tick occurs *HZ* times per second (§ 4.8). For example, in Figure 4.12 a real-time process running at priority 159 is assigned 10 clock ticks, a process running at priority 100 is assigned 100 clock ticks, and so on. These values depend on the system configuration.

By default, a time-shared process that switches to become a real-time process is given the lowest configured *rt_dptbl* priority, unless it specifies differently when the change is made.

Figure 4.13: *Time-sharing class dispatch parameter table*

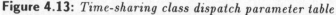

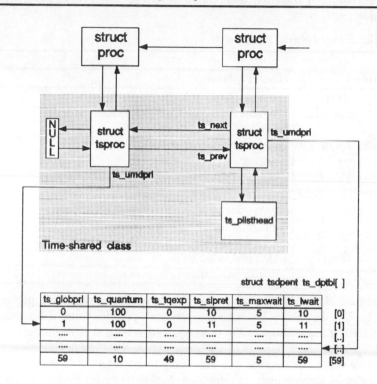

4.6.10 Time-shared class

Prior to UNIX System V Release 4, all processes were time-shared, and by default the UNIX System V Release 4 configuration assigns all processes to the time-shared class. The scheduling configuration can be changed so that an application will run in real-time mode if required. However, a process running in time-shared mode will remain in that mode unless it is changed to become a real-time process with the *priocntl* system call. In general, the default scheduling configuration suits most installations. However, if an application is governed by strict timing constraints, then it may be necessary to configure it to run in real-time mode.

The time-sharing policy objective is to schedule each process fairly and efficiently. That is, each time-shared process must be given a fair share of CPU without affecting the responsiveness of the system to interactive processes and users. To effect this approach, the time-sharing scheduling mechanisms use a dynamic priority allocation scheme to assign time-quanta of different lengths. Thus, it adapts to a process's operating characteristics.

The priority value assigned to a time-sharing process is calculated from two proportional values made up from a kernel part and a user provided part. The user provided part of the priority value is based on a scheme similar to the *nice(2)* value as seen in earlier releases of the UNIX system V operating system. Thus, only a user process with an effective user ID of zero (i.e., super-user) can increase its priority value.

Table 4.12: *Struct tsdpent (tsdpent_t)*

Element	Description
int ts_globpri	Default global priority (from 0 - 59)
long ts_quantum	Default time-quantum (slice) for this level specified in clock ticks
short ts_tqexp	Assigned value to *ts_cpupri* when this process's time-quantum expires
short ts_slpret	Assigned value to *ts_cpupri* upon returning to user-mode after a sleep
short ts_maxwait	Maximum number of consecutive seconds that the process can run in its allocated time-quantum before assigning *ts_lwait* to *ts_cpupri*.
short ts_lwait	Assigned value to *ts_cpupri* if *ts_dispwait* exceeds *ts_maxwait*

The kernel part of the priority value allows the scheduler to govern a process's usage of the CPU. It does this by lowering the process's priority value if it consumes long periods of CPU time without going to sleep, and raising it if the process frequently goes to sleep after short periods of CPU use. Thus, a CPU hogging process is given a low priority which means that it is less likely to be selected to use the CPU while higher priority processes exist. In contrast, low priority processes are given longer time-slices than higher priority processes. So, even though a low priority process does not run as often as a higher priority process, when it is finally selected to run it is given a larger portion of CPU time. Hence, a process is given a larger time-quantum as the kernel portion of the priority value decreases.

Like the real-time priority class, the time-sharing priority class dependent functions maintain a time-sharing dispatch parameter table (Figure 4.13). The table is called *ts_dptbl[]* and contains one *tsdpent* structure per configured priority level (see Table 4.12). The table is tuneable by configuring the *ts* master file in the *master.d* directory. This file specifies the default values used in the time-sharing priority class table. The table is used to calculate a process's priority value according to its CPU usage. As its priority value is deduced, it is mapped to a system global priority value in the range that the class independent functions understand (i.e., between 0 and 59). The *tsdpent* structure members are explained as follows:

- *ts_globpri* — holds the global priority value for processes running at this priority level (i.e., the value assigned to *p_pri* in the *proc* structure).

- *ts_quantum* — specifies the default number of clock ticks that a process running at this level is allowed to consume before *runrun* is set to tell the kernel to preempt the current process.

- *ts_tqexp* — the kernel portion of the priority value assigned to a process running at this level when its time-quantum has expired. This value is assigned to *ts_cpupri* in the process's associated *tsproc* structure.

- *ts_slpret* — the value assigned to *ts_cpupri* when a process running at this level returns to user-mode after going to sleep pending some resource or event. Sleeping processes are given a high priority so that they are scheduled to run again as soon as the resource becomes available or the event takes place. The priority value assigned to a sleeping process is fixed to that specified in *ts_slpret* until such time that the process begins to run again. Thus, processes that frequently volunteer to go to sleep run at high priority levels.

- *ts_maxwait* — the maximum number of consecutive seconds that the process running at this level is allowed to consume. If this time-quantum expires before *ts_quantum*, then the process obviously is not hogging the CPU and so it is given a higher priority.

- *ts_lwait* — the priority value to assign to *ts_cpupri* if *ts_maxwait* seconds expire.

In the case of a time-shared process, the *proc* structure pointer *p_clproc* points to the process's private time-sharing class specific data structure called *tsproc* (see Table 4.13). This data structure is used by the time-sharing class dependent functions to calculate the process's global priority value. The *tsproc* structure members are explained as follows:

- *ts_timeleft* — the number of clock ticks remaining in the process's time-quantum at its current priority level.

- *ts_cpupri* — the kernel portion of the process's priority value assigned to *p_pri*.

- *ts_uprilim, ts_upri* — the upper limit and current value of the process's user supplied portion of the priority value. These two variables are modifiable by the user application by using the *priocntl* system call. Their purpose is to allow the process to control (to some degree) its scheduling characteristics.

- *ts_umdpri* — the variable used to index into the time-shared class parameter table (*ts_dptbl[]*) so that the priority level parameters can be referenced to deduce the system wide global priority value for the process. Both *ts_cpupri* and *ts_upri* are added together to formulate the index value.

- *ts_nice* — provided for backwards compatibility of the *nice* system call. It contains the current nice value for the process and has an overall effect on the resultant priority value deduced by the time-sharing class dependent functions. The default value used by the system is 20, the maximum and minimum values imposed by the system are 39 and 0 respectively. The *nice* system call allows the process to change its priority value. The higher the specified value, the lower the priority. However, only processes with an effective user ID of zero can lower their

Table 4.13: *Struct tsproc (tsproc_t)*

Element	Description
long ts_timeleft	Remaining time in process's time-quantum
short ts_cpupri	Kernel portion of priority value
short ts_uprilim	User modifiable — priority value limit, set with *priocntl*
short ts_upri	User modifiable — current user portion of priority value
short ts_umdpri	Offsets into *ts_dptbl[]* to find the global priority level
char ts_nice	Nice value (for backward compatibility)
unsigned char ts_flags	Operational flags
short ts_dispwait	Number of seconds since start of current time-quantum (not reset upon preemption)
*struct proc *ts_procp*	Pointer to process's *proc* structure
*char *ts_pstatp*	Pointer to *p_stat* in *proc* structure
*int *ts_pprip*	Pointer to *p_pri* in *proc* structure
*uint *ts_pflagp*	Pointer to *p_flag* in *proc* structure
*struct tsproc *ts_next*	Link to next *tsproc* on *tsproc* list
*struct tsproc *ts_prev*	Link to previous *tsproc* on *tsproc* list

current nice value (i.e., request a higher priority value). Under UNIX System V Release 4, the *nice* system call has an effect on time-sharing processes only. It is recommended that the *priocntl* system call be used in place of *nice*.

- *ts_flags* — set as follows: *TSKPRI* — the process is currently running at kernel priority level, and *TSBACKQ* — the process should be placed on the back of its dispatch queue when appropriate.

- *ts_dispwait* — the number of seconds that have elapsed since the process started its current time-quantum. If this value exceeds *ts_maxwait*, it is given a higher priority value (specified in *ts_lwait*).

4.6.11 Class dependent interface

So far we have discussed the class independent kernel code and the class dependent related structures and tables. However, we have yet to discuss the interface between them.

The priority value assigned to a process is calculated by the priority class dependent functions. In the case of a real-time process, the real-time class dependent functions are responsible. Similarly, the time-shared class dependent functions are responsible in the case of time-shared processes. However, the class independent kernel code uses a single interface scheme for all configured priority class types. It does this by using a set of macros prefixed with *CL_* to call the necessary class dependent function, without knowing the class type. These macros use either the *proc* structure member *p_clfuncs* or the *class* structure member *cl_funcs* to call the relevant class dependent function with its required arguments. For example, to call the class dependent *preempt( )* function, the kernel class independent code must call the function pointed to by *cl_preempt( )*, which is a member of the process's associated *classfuncs* structure. To do this, the kernel uses the *CL_PREEMPT( )* macro which is defined in a way that is similar to the following example:

```
#define CL_PREEMPT(classfuncs, argument) \
    (*(classfuncs)->p_clfuncs->cl_preempt)(argument)
```

Since the priority class dependent functions are called from various places within the kernel's class independent code, as well as from other areas of the operating system, it is obvious (even if just for readability) that a set of macros such as these are required. There is, in fact, one macro per function pointer defined in the *classfuncs* structure, and they are defined in */usr/include/sys/class.h* (see Table 4.14).

Table 4.14: *Struct classfuncs and related functions (classfuncs_t)*

classfuncs element	Related macro	Real-time function	Time-shared function
int (*cl_admin)( )	*CL_ADMIN*	*rt_admin*	*ts_admin*
int (*cl_enterclass)( )	*CL_ENTERCLASS*	*rt_enterclass*	*ts_enterclass*
void (*cl_exitclass)( )	*CL_EXITCLASS*	*rt_exitclass*	*ts_exitclass*
int (*cl_fork)( )	*CL_FORK*	*rt_fork*	*ts_fork*
void (*cl_forkret)( )	*CL_FORKRET*	*rt_forkret*	*ts_forkret*
int (*cl_getclinfo)( )	*CL_GETCLINFO*	*rt_getclinfo*	*ts_getclinfo*
void (*cl_getglobpri)( )	*CL_GETGLOBPRI*	*rt_getglobpri*	*ts_getglobpri*
void (*cl_parmsget)( )	*CL_PARMSGET*	*rt_parmsget*	*ts_parmsget*
int (*cl_parmsin)( )	*CL_PARMSIN*	*rt_parmsin*	*ts_parmsin*
int (*cl_parmsout)( )	*CL_PARMSOUT*	*rt_parmsout*	*ts_parmsout*
int (*cl_parmsset)( )	*CL_PARMSSET*	*rt_parmsset*	*ts_parmsset*
void (*cl_preempt)( )	*CL_PREEMPT*	*rt_preempt*	*ts_preempt*
int (*cl_proccmp)( )	*CL_PROCCMP*	*rt_proccmp*	*ts_proccmp*
void (*cl_setrun)( )	*CL_SETRUN*	*rt_setrun*	*ts_setrun*
void (*cl_sleep)( )	*CL_SLEEP*	*rt_sleep*	*ts_sleep*
void (*cl_stop)( )	*CL_STOP*	*rt_stop*	
void (*cl_swapin)( )	*CL_SWAPIN*	*rt_swapin*	*ts_swapin*
void (*cl_swapout)( )	*CL_SWAPOUT*	*rt_swapout*	*ts_swapout*
void (*cl_tick)( )	*CL_TICK*	*rt_tick*	*ts_tick*
void (*cl_trapret)( )	*CL_TRAPRET*		*ts_trapret*
void (*cl_wakeup)( )	*CL_WAKEUP*	*rt_wakeup*	*ts_wakeup*

4.6.12 Class dependent functions

This section contains a discussion of both the real-time and time-sharing class dependent functions. However, the interface is designed to be independent of their implementation. This section details what each of these functions is required to do and where they are used in the kernel.

Each priority class implementation must define its own *classfuncs* structure and assign its member function pointers to its own class dependent functions. If the class does not require a specific function defined in the *classfuncs* structure, it must nevertheless assign an appropriate function to do the minimum required of it. In most cases, such functions either do nothing or return an error value to the effect that it is not supported. The functions that form the *classfuncs* structure members are explained in their macro form as follows:

- *CL_ADMIN* — used by the *priocntl* system call to get or reset the class dependent dispatch parameter tables on the running system. Only super-user may change them.

- *CL_ENTERCLASS* — allocates a class specific data structure for the process (pointed to by *p_clproc*) and initializes it according to the parameters supplied in its arguments. It is also used when a process wishes to change its current priority class to that of another (i.e., from time-shared to real-time and vice versa). This function is normally called only as a result of a *priocntl* system call. However, during the initialization of the system the operating system calls *newproc( )* to start **init(1M)**, and in turn calls on the services of *CL_ENTERCLASS( )* to place **init** into its correct scheduling class. Other than for **init**, *newproc( )* never calls this function. Remember that a newly created process inherits its parent's priority class. Thus, *fork* does not need to call this function, although it uses *CL_FORK( )* to allocate the new process's class dependent structure. Both *fork( )* and *newproc( )* are discussed in § 4.12.

- *CL_EXITCLASS* — called when the kernel wants to remove a process from its associated priority class. It must remove the class dependent data structure associated with the process from its list and free the memory used by it. Since each process is given its own private class dependent data structure, the one associated with the process can now be removed. Thus, as a process terminates — for example, as a result of an *_exit* system call — *CL_EXITCLASS* is called as part of the process destruction.

  A process can change its priority class by using the *priocntl* system call. Suppose a time-sharing process wishes to change to a real-time process. *priocntl* must call *CL_ENTERCLASS* to create the new *rtproc* structure and associate it with the process, and it must remove the *tsproc* structure previously associated with it by calling *CL_EXITCLASS* to cause its destruction.

- *CL_FORK* — all processes are created with the *fork* system call. Thus, a process must call *fork* to create a new process. A process that creates a new process is called a *parent process*, and the newly created process is its *child process*. We will discuss *fork* later, but for now it is only important to realize that all *child* processes inherit their *parent's* priority class characteristics, and *fork* calls *CL_ENTERCLASS* to initialize a *child* process's class dependent data structure.

- *CL_FORKRET* — once *fork* has initialized the new process, it marks it *SRUN* which tells the kernel that it is on the dispatch queue in a ready to run state. The *fork* system call has now completed its task but must call *CL_FORKRET* before returning to user-mode. This is because there are now two related processes, both with the same priority values (since the child inherited the priority values of its parent), and the system must decide which to run first: the parent or child. Such decisions are priority class dependent. Thus, the *CL_FORKRET* function is called to make the decision.

    In the case of a real-time process, the child is simply placed on the back of the priority dispatch queue and will eventually (hopefully) be scheduled to run (usually when the parent gives up the CPU).

    In the case of a time-sharing process, the child is also placed at the back of its priority dispatch queue. However, the child will run first so that it gets a chance to *exec* its new program image. This saves the system from doing unnecessary copying of *copy-on-write* pages since the child's address space now reflects the new program image. To do this, the *ts_forkret( )* function simply marks *tsproc->ts_flags* with *TSBACKQ* and sets *runrun*. The *TSBACKQ* flag arranges for the process to be placed at the back of the priority dispatch queue when *preempt( )* is next called; and remember that *runrun* tells the kernel to call *preempt( )* at its earliest convenience.

- *CL_GETCLINFO* — used by the *priocntl* system call to obtain the class specific information for a given class type. This function simply obtains the maximum configured user priority value for that class. This is the only information that is class specific. All other information is obtainable by the system without consulting the class dependent functions.

- *CL_GETGLOBPRI* — called to obtain the global scheduling priority value for the process. The function must validate the user portion of the priority value to make sure that it fits within the range configured for its priority class. It then obtains from its class dependent despatch parameter table, the global value associated with its class dependent value.

- *CL_PARMSGET* — called by *priocntl* to get the class dependent scheduling parameters of the process. In the case of a real-time process, the information obtained is the process's class specific priority value (*rtproc->rt_pri*) and time-quantum (*rtproc->rt_pquantum*). The information obtained from a time-sharing process is its user supplied priority value (*tsproc->ts_upri*) and its current limit (*tsproc->ts_uprilim*). Note that these values returned by this function remain class specific — they are not translated to their global scheduler priority values.

- *CL_PARMSIN* — called by *priocntl* when the user wants to set the class specific scheduling parameters of the process to the ones supplied by the user. Before making the request, *priocntl* calls *CL_PARMSIN* to validate the user supplied parameters and to check if the user has enough permissions to set them.

- *CL_PARMSOUT* — called by *priocntl* when the user wants to obtain the process's scheduling parameters. Once again, the function may check permissions and perform any necessary processing before the information is passed back to the user. In the case of a time-sharing process, this function does nothing but return success. For a real-time process, the process time-quantum is obtained and converted to nanoseconds (as opposed to clock ticks which are machine dependent and would be useless information unless the user is privy to the value of HZ on his or her installation).

- *CL_PARMSSET* — called by *priocntl* when the user wants to set the scheduling parameters of a process. *priocntl* first calls *CL_PARMSIN* to check that the user has enough permissions to set the parameters of the target process and to check that the specified parameters are within range. It then calls *CL_PARMSSET* to set them.

- *CL_PREEMPT* — called by *preempt()* before calling *swtch()*. The priority class of the currently running process to be preempted must decide where the process is to be placed on the dispatch queues. In both real-time and time-sharing cases, the process is moved to its appropriate place within its queue by using the class independent *setbackdq()* and *setfrontdq()* functions. The system-class function always moves the process to the front of its queue.

- *CL_PROCCMP* — used by *priocntl* when the user requests class or class-specific information (by using the *PC_GETPARMS* switch — see *priocntl(2)*) about a process or set of processes. If the user specifies a set of processes to *priocntl*, the criteria for selecting a process from the set is class specific (they may be in different classes). This function is a tool that simply compares two processes of the same class to see if they are in the same priority level. It is simply a hack to save looping through the list of processes to find the process that best fits the selection criteria.

- *CL_SETRUN* — a process that sleeps is placed onto a sleep queue (§ 4.6.13). *CL_SETRUN* is called by *setrun()* to put back the process that has been sleeping onto its dispatch queue. Both real-time and time-sharing functions place the process at the back of its dispatch queue. In the case of a real-time process, both *runrun* and *kprunrun* are set to cause preemption.

- *CL_SLEEP* — called by the kernel *sleep()* routine when a process voluntarily goes to sleep. In contrast to *CL_SETRUN*, *CL_SLEEP* is called to do whatever is appropriate before the process is put to sleep (i.e., give up the CPU). In the case of a real-time process, the function simply sets the *RTRAN* bit in *rtproc->rt_flags* which signifies that the process has used the CPU since it was last swapped out and so can be swapped out again if the scheduler sees fit. In the case of a time-sharing process, *tsproc->ts_flags* is marked *TSKPRI* (running at kernel priority) and the process is given a special kernel priority so that it is given a better chance to run quickly when it wakes up again.

- *CL_STOP* — if the process is stopped (*SSTOP*), the kernel's *stop()* routine calls *CL_STOP* so that any specific class dependent processing can be done to the process. The time-sharing function does nothing, it is simply a null function. The real-time function sets *RTRAN* if the process being stopped is the currently running process. A process can be stopped for a number of reasons, such as *job control* (§ 7.11.2).

- *CL_SWAPIN* — called by the scheduler (*sched( )*). Its purpose is to nominate (or select) a process within its class, with the highest priority to be swapped in. The process must be both runnable (*SRUN*) and unloaded (not *SLOAD*), and it must not be marked *SUSWAP* because this signifies that the process is currently undergoing a swap in or swap out anyway. Real-time processes are never unloaded, and their user-areas are never swapped, they are locked in memory until they terminate. There is, however, an *rt_swapin( )* function. Its purpose is to scan through its *rtproc* list to find a process that is both runnable and "loaded".

- *CL_SWAPOUT* — in contrast to *CL_SWAPIN*, this function is called by *sched( )* to ask the class dependent routines to nominate a process to be swapped out. The function must choose the lowest priority process to swap out. In the case of a time-sharing process, the function will nominate a process that is sleeping or stopped before nominating the lowest priority process. The process is not nominated for obvious reasons if it is marked with any combination of *SSYS* (kernel resident process), *SLOCK* (process cannot be swapped), *SUSWAP* (process is already being swapped), *SPROCIO* (currently doing I/O through /proc), *SSWLOCKS* (process is locked from being swapped) or *SZOMB* (process is for all purposes a dead process), or if the process has just been swapped in.

   The real-time process does the same checking although it also tests the *SIDL* (process is in intermediate stages of creation) flag. In this way, a real-time process is guaranteed to be fully loaded during its creation. Since a real-time process's user-area cannot be swapped, there is no point in testing for *SUSWAP*. If the process is not marked *RTRAN*, it has not run since it was last swapped out, so there is no point in selecting it either. If however, a process is successfully selected by *rt_swapout( )*, it sets a flag to tell the scheduler to try to swap out the pages of the process that it has nominated, but not to swap out its user-area or mark it unloaded.

- *CL_TICK* — the kernel function *clock( )* calls this function if the currently mapped in process is marked *SONPROC*. Its purpose is to determine if the currently running process's time slice has elapsed. If it has, its time-quantum is recalculated and adjusted as necessary and the process is placed onto the back of its dispatch queue. The *runrun* flag is then set (*kprunrun* also in the case of a real-time process) to tell the system to call *swtch( )* as soon as it sees fit. When *clock( )* returns to *ttrap.s*, the *runrun* flag is checked. If it is set, it checks the mode of execution that the process was running in (via the PS register). If the mode was user-mode, *preempt( )* is called to select the next process to run, the currently running process is switched out, and the newly selected process is switched in.

   The time-sharing function does no time-quantum recalculation if the process is running at kernel priority (marked *TSKPRI*). The real-time function recalculates a process's time-quantum only if it has one (i.e., if it is not set to *RT_TQINF* — meaning infinity).

- *CL_TRAPRET* — called from within *ttrap.s*. As a process returns to user-mode after operating in kernel-mode as the result of a trap or system call, *ttrap.s* calls *CL_TRAPRET* to do any last-minute class dependent adjustments to the process's priority value.

  In the case of the time-sharing function, if the process is currently running at kernel priority (i.e., marked *TSKPRI* — meaning the process went to sleep) it is assigned an appropriate user mode priority and time-quantum. If that means lowering the process's priority below that of the highest priority active queue (i.e., less than *maxrunpri*), *runrun* is set to cause preemption. If, however, a non-preemptive wake-up has occurred since the process was last switched, then *runrun* is not set because doing so may defeat the non-preemptive wake-up procedure. If the process is not marked *TSKPRI*, nothing is done. The real-time function is a null function since real-time processes are never given kernel priorities — their priority level is fixed unless changed with *priocntl*.

- *CL_WAKEUP* — called from *wakeprocs( )* when a process awakes from its sleep. The class dependent function must decide where the process must go on its dispatch queue and also if there must be any adjustment to its time-quantum and priority level. The function is passed a *preempt* flag which it may choose to ignore. In the case of the real-time function, the process is given a fresh time-quantum and placed at the back of its dispatch queue. If the awoken process has a higher priority than the currently running process, both *runrun* and *kprunrun* are set. The time-sharing function does the same except that it does not set *runrun* (and for obvious reasons does not set *kprunrun* either) because a non-preemptive wake-up may have occurred and setting *runrun* may defeat the non-preemptive wake-up procedure.

4.6.13 Sleeping processes

A process goes to sleep voluntarily pending the availability of some resource or event, without which it cannot continue any further. It puts itself to sleep with the kernel *sleep( )* function and is awoken by *wakeprocs( )* when the event or resource it is waiting for becomes available. Thus, *sleep( )* and *wakeprocs( )* form an internal synchronization scheme that allows the system to share its resources amongst multiple processes. Rather than hold up the CPU, a process that must wait, for whatever reason, puts itself to sleep. Some examples of this are:

- An *inode* is locked — the process must wait for the *inode* to become free.

- The process is reading from an empty pipe or writing to a full one — the process must block until the reader reads from the pipe or the writer writes to it, depending on the condition.

- Waiting for the completion of I/O — for example, disk I/O is slow compared to the execution speed of the processor, so a process that issues a disk I/O request has to wait for the disk to complete its task before it can continue. In this case the device driver puts the process to sleep until the I/O request has completed.

Eventually the disk interrupts the system, and the device driver's interrupt handling code calls *wakeprocs( )* to wake the process up.

- Waiting for terminal input — a process such as the user's login shell waits for the user to enter data at the keyboard. The process goes to sleep until the user types a key, at which time the terminal device driver interrupt routine buffers the input and awakes the sleeping process (the shell) to read it. The terminal, typically operating at 9600 baud, runs much slower than the CPU, so the process will sleep and wake up many times during character input from the terminal.

- Waiting for memory — a process that accesses a virtual memory address that is not yet loaded encounters a *page fault* (Chapter 3). The process must sleep until the contents of the page are read in.

When a process goes to sleep, it is said to be *sleeping on an event*. There are two types of event that a process may sleep on: events that allow the process to be awakened by a signal, and events that cause signals to be ignored. A process that chooses to sleep on an event that ignores signals will sleep indefinitely until that event takes place.

Since real-time class priority levels (100—159) are higher than system priority levels (60—99), assigning a system priority level to a real-time process would lower its priority, defeating the real-time class priority mechanism. Thus, processes that belong to the real-time class remain at their set priority level even when they sleep. However, a time-sharing process is assigned a *system priority* while it sleeps.

Since the system (default) priority levels are between 60 and 99 inclusive, and normal (non-sleeping) time-sharing priority levels are between 0 and 59 inclusive, a process that is assigned a system priority while it sleeps will be scheduled to use the CPU more quickly than other non-sleeping time-sharing processes when it wakes up.

System priorities are described in *ts_kmdpris[]*, which is an array of integers built from a configurable (tuneable) table in the *master.d/ts* directory. This array contains 40 contiguous numbers representing the system class priority levels. The default configuration is as follows:

```
int ts_kmdpris[] = {
        60,61,62,63,64,65,66,67,68,69,
        70,71,72,73,74,75,76,77,78,79,
        80,81,82,83,84,85,86,87,88,89,
        90,91,92,93,94,95,96,97,98,99
};
```

The system divides these values into ranges called *system priority levels*, and each system priority level equates to an *event-type*. A process that wishes to sleep must decide what kind of event that it wants to sleep on. Table 4.15 lists these event-types and their corresponding values. The shaded area of the table shows which event-types cause signals to be ignored.

The system uses mnemonics such as *TTIPRI* to pass to sleep as a parameter. This is the event-type that the process wishes to sleep on. Its value forms the basis for recalculating the process's system priority level.

Table 4.15: *System priority levels*

Sleep parameter	Parameter value	Global priority value	Description
PSWP	0	99	Swapper priority
PMEM	0	99	Locked memory
PINOD	10	89	Locked *inode*
PRIBIO	20	79	Block I/O
PZERO	25	74	Signal level
PPIPE	26	73	Empty or full pipe
PVFS	27	72	Wait for unmount of file system
TTIPRI	28	71	Terminal input
TTOPRI	29	70	Terminal output
PWAIT	30	69	Wait for *SIGCHLD*
PSLEP	39	60	Pause for signal

The variable *ts_maxkmdpri*, also defined in the *master.d/ts* directory, holds the highest kernel-mode priority value (i.e., event-type) that may be passed as a parameter to *sleep( )*. In most cases, it is defined as follows:

```
short ts_maxkmdpri = (sizeof(ts_kmdpris)/4) - 1;
```

Thus, *ts_maxkmdpri*, in most cases, would be equal to 39 and (not by coincidence) it is also equal to *PSLEP*. A problem may occur if the *sizeof(int)* is greater than 4 bytes. Furthermore, no checking is done to see if the passed parameter to sleep is greater than the defined value of *PSLEP* (39). Thus, unless a device driver writer is careful to specify an event-type with a value that lies between 0 and 39, there is a good chance that the system will panic.

The highest system global priority level that a process can run at is configurable via the system tuneable parameter named *MAXCLSYSPRI*. The lowest value that this parameter can be is 39. Any value below this has no effect since the system-class initialization function (*sys_init( )*) will automatically set it to 39 at boot time. The system-class dependent routines require this value to be at least 39 for kernel resident processes. The default value for this tuneable parameter is 99. A value higher than this may have a negative effect on the overall performance of the system. In most cases, there should be no need to modify it.

The global priority assigned to a sleeping process is based on the event-type passed as a parameter to sleep, but the class dependent functions are responsible for calculating it (if necessary) and assigning it. Within *ts_sleep( )*, the new priority value is calculated by subtracting the value of the passed event-type parameter from *ts_maxkmdpri*, and then using the result to index into *ts_kmdpris[ ]*. For example, if the passed parameter is *PRIBIO + 1*, the new priority level for the process is calculated as follows:

```
*tsproc->ts_pprip = ts_kmdpris[ts_maxkmdpri - (PRIBIO + 1)]
    == ts_kmdpris[18]
    == 78
    == proc->p_pri
```

As well as an *event-type*, a process that calls *sleep( )* must also supply a unique *event-identifier*. The most common method is to supply the address of a data structure in the system's address space that is somehow related to the procedure making the call. Thus, the call:

```
sleep((caddr_t)p, PZERO - 1);
```

tells the system to put the process to sleep with a system priority of 75 (i.e., ignore signals) using the address of the *proc* structure *p* as the event-identifier. The type *caddr_t* is used to cast *p* into a system address.

Another name for *event-identifier* is *wait-channel* and the *proc* structure member *p_wchan* is used to save the sleeping process's wait-channel when the process goes to sleep. Otherwise, this structure member is zero (i.e., after it has been awoken by *wakeprocs( )*).

Sleeping processes are placed on a sleep queue called *sleepq[]*. *sleepq[]* is an array of *sleepq* structures that simply contain forward and backward pointers to *proc* structures. All *proc* structures in the queue are marked *SSLEEP* and their *p_wchan* members are set to their assigned event-identifiers. However, contrary to what one might think, the forward and backward pointers are not used to link the *proc* structures in a doubly linked list. The *proc* structures on the sleep queue are linked together by using their *p_link* members in the same way that processes on the dispatch queues are linked together. The forward and backward pointers in the *sleepq* structure are used to maintain lists of sleep queues whose *proc* structures are associated with one or more similar events (see Figure 4.14).

To find which sleep queue to place a process onto, *sleep( )* hashes the passed wait-channel to obtain an integer value representing its appropriate queue. The resulting value is then used to index into *sleepq[]*. By using this scheme, the system can gain quick access to processes sleeping on an event when that event takes place.

In most cases, there is only one process on any given sleep queue since it is rare for multiple processes to use the same kernel address. The process that locks a resource usually frees it again before a process requiring the same resource is scheduled to run. However, some processes go to sleep by using different wait-channels, but their wait-channel addresses hash to the same sleep queue (Table 4.16).

4.6.14 Algorithm *sleep( )*

The kernel address passed to *sleep( )* as the event argument is not written to or read from; it is simply a unique identifier which is mutually known and used by related functions that call the *sleep( )* and *wakeup( )* mechanisms. The address is simply

Figure 4.14: *Sleeping process queue*

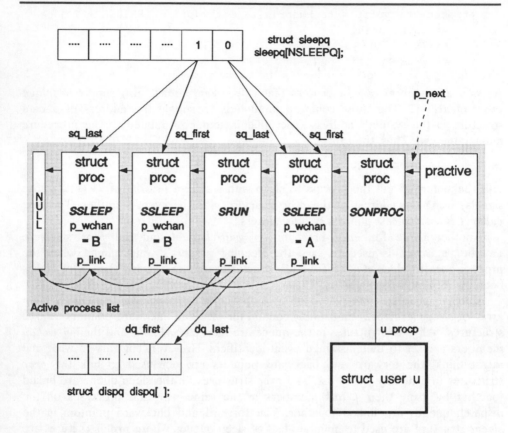

Table 4.16: *Sleep queue collision*

Sleep queue	Event address	Sleep queue	Event address	Sleep queue	Event address	Sleep queue	Event address
0	e0000000	8	d0114a44	14	d00c3874	20	d00c1aa4
1	d0089008	10	d00c3450	18	d013ac96	21	d00c32a8
3	d00c3a1c	12	d00b7460	19	d00c3c98	21	d01362ac
8	d00c3e40	12	d1016064	19	d014a498	21	d01624a8

used as an abstraction of the event the process wants to sleep on. The mapping of system address to event relies on the mechanism by which the event the process is put to sleep on also maps to the same address that the process will be woken up on when the event takes place.

The *sleep()* algorithm is shown in Figure 4.15. The process is first marked *SSLEEP* and placed onto a hashed sleep queue. If the process elects to ignore signals while sleeping (*event-type* < *PZERO*), it is marked *SNWAKE* to tell the

Figure 4.15: *Algorithm for sleep( )*

```
sleep()
input: event — kernel address to sleep on
       event-type — kernel mode priority
output: 0 — if event successfully takes place
        1 — if signal is caught and PCATCH is set
        none — if signal is caught and PCATCH is not set
{
    raise processor interrupt priority to block out interrupts
    mark process status as SSLEEP
    assign event to process wait channel
    place process on the sleepq indexed by its hashed event

    if(event-type allows signals) {
        unset SNWAKE
        call issig() to check for signals
        if(signals pending) {
            take process off its sleep queue
                and change its state to SONPROC
            goto psig
        }
        if(not on the sleepq)
            goto finish

        /* process must still be asleep here */
        wakeup the scheduler if it is sleeping
        call class specific sleep routine
        /* possible new priority level set here */
        do context switch
        /* execution resumes here when process wakes up */

        call issig() to check for signals
        if(signals pending)
            goto psig
    }

    else  /* sleep for this process ignores signals */
    {
        mark process p_flag SNWAKE
        call class specific sleep routine
        /* possible new priority level set here */
        do context switch
        /* execution resumes here when process wakes up */
    }
```

```
finish: /* return to caller */

    unset SNWAKE
    resume processor interrupt priority level

    return (0);

psig: /* process signals */

    resume processor interrupt priority level

    if(event-type specified PCATCH)
        return(1);

    longjmp(non-local jump to previously saved context);
}
```

---

kernel that it must not be awakened by a signal. The class dependent sleep function is then called (*CL_SLEEP()*) to do any required class dependent processing. In the case of a time-shared process it will result in a system-class priority being assigned to it.

The process is now asleep pending the event specified in the function calling parameters. But rather than hold up the CPU while waiting for the event to take place (which might be never!), a context switch is requested to switch in another process to use the CPU. When the event that the process is sleeping on eventually occurs, the process is awakened by *wakeprocs()* (§ 4.6.16) and placed back onto a dispatch queue ready to be scheduled use of the CPU again. When finally switched in, it continues within sleep just after the point where the context switch occured. At this point, *SNWAKE* is cleared, and *sleep()* returns zero to the caller to signify that the event successfully took place.

Processing is more complicated if the process elects to allow signals to be processed while sleeping (*event-type* >= *PZERO*). The *SNWAKE* flag is cleared; this signifies that the process allows the processing of signals during its sleep.

The signal disposition for the process is checked. This is done by a function called *issig()* (see § 4.10.8). By default, *issig()* processes pending signals, but if the calling function specified *PNOSTOP* in the event-type argument, *issig()* will not process them (see Table 4.17). If, however, the process is being stopped then *issig()* indirectly calls *stop()* to stop the process. This results in the process entering the stopped state (*SSTOP*) although it still remains on its sleep queue. Such a condition causes a context switch to take place and the process gives up the CPU. Eventually, the process is awoken by *wakeprocs()* (Figure 4.16), which simply removes processes sleeping on a specified event from their sleep queue and marks them *SRUN* (it also clears their *p_wchan* members). It then places them onto a dispatch queue ready to be scheduled. However, while the process is context switched out, it is possible for it to receive signals, so its signal disposition may change before it is context switched back in again. Therefore, on return from *issig( )*, *sleep( )* must check if there are pending signals, and if there are, and the process is still on a sleep queue, the process must be woken up (recall that it elected to sleep while allowing signals to interrupt it). The process is taken off its sleep queue and placed back onto the CPU (i.e., re-marked *SONPROC*). It is now the currently running process. Since, *sleep( )* was interrupted by a signal, it either returns a 1 to the caller if it specified *PCATCH* (this normally results in the caller returning *EINTR* — interrupted system call), or arranges for the process to be placed back into user-mode directly. This is done by calling *longjmp( )* (§ 4.9.9), which does a non-local jump back to a saved state in *systrap( )* resulting in the system call activation frames being popped back off the system stack, and returning error to the user program.

If *issig( )* cannot find any signals to process, but the process is still on a sleep queue, then it can be deduced that there were no signals pending for the process and it also remains asleep.

The scheduler's global *runin* variable is checked. If it is set, the scheduler is asleep and must be woken up. The scheduler stays asleep until awoken by *clock( )* or until a process goes to sleep. So, if *runrun* is set at this point, *wakeprocs( )* is called to wake the scheduler up.

Having thoroughly checked for signals, *sleep( )* is now ready to place the process into bed until its specified event takes place; a context switch is requested and the process gives up the CPU in favor of another. Once again, when the process is next switched in (after being awoken by *wakeprocs( )*), it resumes execution at the place where the context switch took place. But even though the process is now awake, it is still being processed within *sleep( )*. Again, *issig( )* is called to see if the process received a signal while it slept. If there is a pending signal, then the process is subject to the same conditions as if signals were pending before. That is, *sleep( )* must either return 1 if *PCATCH* is set or *longjmp( )* back to *systrap( )*.

The necessity to check for signals twice within *sleep( )* is to save a race condition. Suppose that a signal is set for the process as it enters *sleep( )* and the event-type specified by the caller allows signals to interrupt it. If *sleep( )* does not check for signals before actually putting the process to sleep (i.e., context switching it out), and no more signals are posted for it, the process may never wake up. So when the process is finally awoken with *wakeprocs( )*, signal checking must be done again.

Table 4.17: *Sleep event-type modifiers*

Constant	Description
PCATCH	Do not *longjmp( )*, instead, return 1 if signal is caught
PNOSTOP	Not safe to stop process within *sleep( )*

In the previous discussion, we referenced two constants that need further explanation. They are listed in Table 4.17. These constants can be ORed with the event-type parameter passed to *sleep( )*.

It is sometimes necessary for the kernel to resume execution in kernel-mode after the process is awoken by a signal instead of doing a *longjmp( )* back to the saved environment in *systrap( )* which results in a return to user-mode. The point of doing a *longjmp( )* is to return the process to user-mode after failing to complete the system call that it was executing. A *setjmp( )* is done to save the context of the process when it enters kernel-mode as the result of a system call. The system cannot assume that a system call will not be interrupted during its execution. Thus, a *setjmp( )* is done to apprehend the possibility of a *longjmp( )* if the system call goes to sleep and is subsequently interrupted. All system calls that need to sleep set the *PCATCH* bit in the event-type. If the sleep is interrupted, then a 1 is returned instead of doing a *longjmp( )*. This allows the system to return the *EINTR* error code. For example:

```
if(sleep((caddr_t)kernel_address, PRIBIO | PCATCH))
        return (EINTR);
```

A discussion of stopped processes is given shortly. For now, it is only important to understand where *PNOSTOP* is used.

During the execution of critical areas of the kernel code where the kernel must put the process to sleep (for example, waiting for a buffer to become available), the kernel sometimes sets *PCATCH* so that *sleep( )* returns 1 on receipt of a signal but it also sets *PNOSTOP* so that the process is not stopped within *issig( )*.

4.6.15 Stopped processes

A process is never stopped purposely by the kernel. A process is "stopped" only if it receives a signal to stop (i.e., *SIGSTOP*), if its parent requests it to stop via the *ptrace* system call, or in response to a requested stop via */proc*. For example, a debugger may issue an *ioctl* system call on */proc* to set a trap in the child process to stop it (see *proc(4)*). Once set, the process is stopped when an "event of interest" occurs — for example, every time the child enters kernel-mode via a system call (*systrap( )*) or returns to user-mode when the system call finishes.

When stopped, the process enters state *SSTOP*. A context switch takes place and control is eventually passed back to the parent to continue its interrogation; it may choose to make the process runnable again (see *proc(4)* — reference *PIOCSTOP*, *PIOCWSTOP* and *PIOCRUN*).

4.6.16 Algorithm *wakeprocs( )*

In order for a process to wake up, the *event* argument must be specified with the same system address that was used to put the process to sleep. The *preempt-flag* argument specifies whether a preemptive or non-preemptive wake-up should be done.

After raising the processor interrupt level to mask out interrupts, *wakeprocs( )* (Figure 4.16) uses the event argument to hash into the sleep queue. Once obtained, the queue is traversed and processes with a *p_wchan* value equal to the passed event argument are processed. Although rare, there may be more than one process asleep using the same wait-channel (event), so the whole queue must be searched. Each process that matches the selection criteria is taken off the sleep queue and its

Figure 4.16: *Algorithm for wakeprocs( )*

```
wakeprocs()
input:  event — same kernel address used to put
                process to sleep.
        preempt-flag — indicating preemptive or
                non-preemptive wakeup
output: none
{
    raise processor interrupt priority to block all interrupts
    hash on event to find appropriate sleep queue

    for(each process on the queue with matching event) {

        take the process off the sleep queue and
        place it on an appropriate dispatch queue

        mark the process SRUN
        call class specific wakeup function
        /* possible runrun and kprunrun set here */
        /* if the process is in Real-time class */

        if(process is NOT loaded in memory (!SLOAD))
            invoke the scheduler
    }
    request preemption if this process priority level is greater
        than the currently running process priority level and
        preempt-flag says do a preemptive wakeup

    reset processor priority level to what it was prior
            to invocation of this routine

}
```

p_wchan member is zeroed. Processes that are marked *SSTOP* are subjected to no further processing here, since they are set running elsewhere (see § 4.10.2). Only processes marked *SSLEEP* are processed further. Assuming that the process is in state *SSLEEP*, it is re-marked *SRUN*. If the wake-up is non-preemptive, *npwakecnt* is incremented. This tells the time-sharing class dependent routine not to set *runrun*.

In almost all cases where sleeping processes are awoken, *runrun* is set to cause preemption. However, if the calling process does not want to be preempted, it sets a flag to stop a preemptive wakeup taking place. Non-preemptive wake-ups are used only when it is vital to limit the context switching between cooperating processes.

Now that the process is awake, it must be placed onto a dispatch queue. The class dependent wake-up routine is called since it is responsible for calculating the process's appropriate priority level and time-quantum. It must also decide which dispatch queue the process is to be placed onto.

Remember that only time-shared sleeping processes are assigned a kernel priority level. If the process is time-shared, then it is assigned an appropriate user-mode priority level according to its current kernel priority level. The point of having a kernel priority during its sleep is to allow the process to run as soon as possible after *wakeprocs( )* has been called. However, the process is not set running immediately by *wakeprocs( )* although it will run soon after if *runrun* is set.

Arrangements are made to swap in the process or preempt it. If the process is not loaded into memory (*SLOAD*) and the scheduler is asleep, a flag is set so that the scheduler is set running with *setrun( )* to swap the process in. If, on the other hand, the process is marked *SLOAD* and the process's priority level is higher than that of the currently running process, and this is a preemptive wake-up, then *runrun* is set to cause preemption. If the process is a real-time process, *runrun* may already be set; remember that the real-time class dependent routine will have set both *runrun* and *kprunrun* if the process's priority level is higher than that of the currently running process.

If *runrun* and especially if *kprunrun* are set, the process will probably run as soon as the next call to *pswtch( )* is made. We say "probably" because if there are higher priority processes on the dispatch queue, it will have to wait its turn, although this is extremely rare. In most cases, *runrun* will be set. This is especially true for time-sharing processes because the currently running process usually runs at a priority level between 0 and 59, but a time-sharing process that has slept runs at a priority level between 60 and 99.

Incidentally, in previous versions of UNIX System V, this function was called *wakeup( )* and it is still provided for backwards compatibility. It takes a single argument: the wait-channel (or event) that the process is sleeping on. Under UNIX System V Release 4, *wakeup( )* simply calls *wakeprocs( )* with the *preempt-flag* set to *PRMPT*.

4.6.17 Algorithm *setrun( )*

The function *setrun( )* (Figure 4.17) is used much the same way as *wakeprocs( )* with the main difference being that *wakeprocs( )* potentially wakes up several processes whereas *setrun( )* wakes up only one.

The kernel often has to wake up a process without waking up other processes (especially the scheduler). There are often many processes on the active process list, but only one process is given the CPU. The operating system normally has many processes asleep waiting on some event, so the *sleep-wakeprocs* algorithm is probably the one most often used by the operating system.

The kernel wakes up the sleeping scheduler on its own in *sleep( )* before doing a context switch, and in *wakeup( )* if the process is not yet loaded. To do this *setrun( )* is called to set the scheduler running, perhaps to swap-in or swap-out a process as necessary.

Figure 4.17: *Algorithm for setrun( )*

```
setrun()
input:  proc — pointer to the process to run
output: none
{
    raise processor interrupt priority to block all interrupts

    if(process is SSLEEP or SSTOP)
        take process off the sleepq
    else if(process is SRUN) {
        reset processor priority level to what it was prior
            to invocation of this routine
        return;
    }

    if(process is SSTOP)
        possibly wakeup parent process and return

    mark process SRUN

    call class specific setrun routine to put the process on
        a chosen dispatch queue

    if(process is NOT loaded in memory (!SLOAD)) {
        if(the scheduler is asleep)
            setrun(the scheduler process)
    } else if( this process priority level is greater than
            the currently running process priority level)
            set runrun

    reset processor priority level to what it was prior
            to invocation of this routine

}
```

4.7 User-level context switching

Two system calls are provided by the operating system for implementing user-level context switching between multiple *threads* of controlled execution in a process. They are: *getcontext* and *setcontext*. The user context manipulated by these system calls is described in *ucontext(5)* and includes the context of the process's machine registers, signal mask and execution stack.

The system call *getcontext* saves a copy of the current user context and then returns to the calling function. *setcontext* is called to resume execution at the point where the context was originally saved. It is assumed that the context passed to *setcontext* was obtained by an earlier call to *getcontext*. In other words, program execution resumes as if the original call to *getcontext* had just returned. For obvious reasons, *setcontext* does not return unless the context to resume is invalid.

Multi-threaded processes are often referred to as Light Weight Processes (LWP) since they use less system resources. However, it should be made clear that threads are not separate processes. They are a method of achieving concurrency from within a process. Multiple threads within a process have the same process ID and share a common user address space, so they tend to use fewer system resources, although a multi-threaded process may not necessarily run faster than a single threaded one.

It is important to realize that the operating system can only see a process as a whole, since it has no concept of multiple threads of execution being manipulated within it. Therefore, the scheduling of multiple threads is not done by the operating system and the user-mode process must assume this responsibility.

4.8 The system clock

An important fact about computer systems is that they are clock driven. A hardware clock carefully measures time and sends out regularly spaced signals that make things happen. Just as the CPU is the brain of a computer system, the hardware clock is the heart of it. Devices such as the microprocessor that depend on the hardware clock are literally controlled by it, since the clock signal initiates the operation to be performed. The hardware clock is, therefore, the mover of the system and in modern computer systems it is quite common for the microprocessor to be driven at its highest specified clock-rate so that it can achieve its maximum possible throughput.

Like the hardware, the operating system software must also keep track of time so that it can schedule the use of the CPU to processes fairly, while providing numerous time-related system services to user programs. This section discusses those system services and the "system clock", which fabricates the operating system's heartbeat mechanism.

4.8.1 Clock interrupt service routine

Clock interrupts are posted at a high processor interrupt level (typically Interrupt level 15). The hardware clock interrupt mechanism is very hardware dependent and so we will not go into any great detail about it. It is sufficient to say that the operating system calls the function *clkstart( )* from *main( )* to start the clock interrupt mechanism. It is left to the implementor to decide how this is achieved, but it is usually done by poking some specific value into an address that programs the interval timer and starts it running.

The hardware clock is programmed to interrupt the CPU at a fixed, hardware-dependent number of times (or ticks) per second (typically 100). The kernel uses the interrupt to mark time by implementing a *clock interrupt service routine*.

Figure 4.18: *Algorithm for clock( )*

```
clock()
input: pc — Program counter (instruction pointer)
       ps — Processor status register (or word)
output: none
{
   re prime the clock so that it will interrupt again

   service timeout() requests in the callout table
   update current process CPU usage accounting information

   enforce CPU resource limits - send SIGXCPU to current
      - process if it exceeds its tunable CPU limit threshold.

   call class specific CL_TICK() routine
   request context switch if process time quantum
      - has exhausted

   increment lbolt /* # of elapsed ticks since system boot */
   increment the time of day and adjust the time as necessary

   /* Primary cycle operations */
   if(one second has elapsed) {
      increment time

      traverse active process list {
         if(process has pending alarm clock)
            decrement alarm time and send process SIGALRM
               - if its alarm time expires
      }

      wake up fsflush if tunable age of delayed write
         - buffers has expired
      wake up scheduler if it is asleep
      wake up pageout if free memory is low
   }
}
```

Like any other interrupt (or event) that occurs while the system is functioning, the hardware clock interrupt generates a hardware trap in kernel-mode which results in a particular routine within *ttrap.s* being called. In the case of a clock interrupt, that routine is the *clock interrupt service routine.*

In previous versions of UNIX System V, the clock interrupt service routine directly invoked a function called *clock( )* to do clock and time-related processing.

However, in order to implement the BSD interval timer-related system calls such as *getitimer( ), setitimer( )* and *gettimeofday( )*, a high resolution timing mechanism is required. The result is that *ttrap.s* now calls *clock( )* (Figure 4.18) via the high resolution clock interrupt handling code in *clock_int( )* (Figure 4.19). We will discuss the services and mechanisms of the high resolution interval timer later. But first, we will discuss the mechanisms of *clock( )*.

To avoid being interrupted by other interrupt generating devices, the clock runs at a high processor interrupt level and while a clock interrupt is being serviced, other interrupts are masked out (blocked). But this means that other interrupt generating devices, such as disk, terminal, and network controllers, will not be serviced if they generate an interrupt while the clock interrupt is being serviced. This may have all sorts of implications. Furthermore, if the *clock_int( )* and *clock( )* mechanisms do not complete execution before the next clock interrupt occurs (usually within 100th of a second), the next clock interrupt will be missed. If clock interrupts are missed then the system's idea of the time will be incorrect, so the clock servicing routines must complete their execution in the fastest time possible.

As we mentioned earlier, under UNIX System V Release 4 *clock( )* is indirectly called by *ttrap.s* via *clock_int( )*. Each time *clock( )* is invoked it performs a number of time-related chores that will be discussed in detail in the following sections. They are as follows:

- Re-prime the clock.
- Service callout-table *timeout( )* requests.
- Maintain system and user time statistics.
- Keep track of time.
- Implement the date.
- Enforce CPU resource limits.
- Record memory use of the currently running process.
- Update profiling information.
- Post alarm signals to processes requesting them.
- Wake up the *fsflush* daemon to write out delayed write buffers, pages marked dirty, *inode* cache, and so on.
- Wake up the scheduler to swap-in or swap-out a process as necessary.
- Wake up the *pageout* daemon if memory gets too low.

The predetermined number of times per second (*ticks*) that the hardware clock interrupts the processor is defined as a global constant called *HZ*. It is normally set to 50, 60 or 100Hz. The MIPS implementation uses the value 100.

Once primed, the hardware clock interrupts the processor *HZ* times per second. Certain operations performed by *clock( )* are done for each *tick* of the clock, and these are called secondary or minor cycle operations. Others are done for each completed cycle of *HZ* (i.e., each second), and these are called primary or major cycle operations.

The interrupt service routine for the clock in *ttrap.s* passes the current PS and PC register values to *clock_int( )* on invocation. These in turn are passed on to *clock( )* after processing any high resolution interval timers. Before *clock_int( )* is called, the user-mode registers are saved for the currently running process just as

Figure 4.19: *Clock interrupt handling*

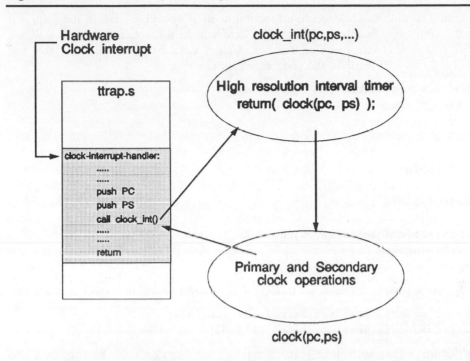

they are for any other interrupt trap. They are restored on return from *clock( )* so that execution resumes at the point of interruption. Thus, it can be seen that clock interrupts occur without the user being aware of them.

Both *clock( )* and *clock_int( )* operate in kernel-mode, and because of this they require the PS register to be passed as a parameter. This register is consulted to deduce the mode of execution that the process is currently running with (i.e., user or kernel-mode). The PC register contains the next instruction to be executed. This register is consulted to see if the CPU is either waiting for I/O completion or in an idle condition (nothing to process). This information is used to update the system statistical information for the running system.

4.8.2 Priming the clock

The clock is started in *main( )* (§ 4.17.1). Once started it interrupts the processor accordingly. However, on some implementations the hardware clock must be reprimed each time *clock( )* is called — in such cases, the hardware clock interrupt itself makes the hardware clock stop. The fact that *clock( )* relies on the hardware to interrupt the CPU means that the low-level clock priming mechanism is hardware dependent. But if the clock needs to be reprimed, it is usually done by writing to a special register in the CPU. Once reprimed, the processor will be interrupted again on the next tick of the hardware clock.

4.8.3 Callout tables

If a kernel routine has to execute a function at some specified time in the future, it uses the *timeout( )* function. This routine arranges for a function to be called with a specified argument in a specified number of clock ticks. For example, if a table has to be aged every 60 seconds, the code may look like this:

```
typedef struct table {
   time_t age;
   ...
} TABLE;

TABLE table;

update_table()
{
   timeout(update_table, 0, 60 * HZ);
   table.age += 60;
}
```

Or suppose a process wants to go to sleep for a known period of time. For example:

```
timeout(wakeup, (caddr_t)kernel_address, 30);
sleep((caddr_t)kernel_address, PRIBIO);
```

In order for a timeout to take place, the timed-out function must be triggered into operation when the specified number of clock ticks expires. However, there may be many instances of functions to timeout, so the system must keep them in a table to process appropriately. To do this, the system implements a *callout[]* table; its size is configurable via a tuneable parameter in the file system *master.d* directory. Each element configured in the callout-table is a *callo* structure (Table 4.18).

As a *timeout( )* routine is requested, a *callo* structure in the callout-table is constructed for it. Its position in the callout-table array depends on its requested triggering time. The system organizes the callout-table into sorted triggering order, with the first entry, *callout[0]*, being the earliest timeout entry to trigger.

Table 4.18: *Struct callo*

Element	Description
int c_time	Elapsed time
int c_id	Timeout id
caddr_t c_arg	Argument to pass to function
*void (*c_func)( )*	Function to be called on timeout

The triggering is initiated by *clock( )*. Since the first entry of the callout-table contains the earliest timeout to trigger, a test need only be done to see if this entry's absolute time has elapsed. If it has, then a programmable interrupt is generated which results in another trap. This time, the programmable interrupt handler in *ttrap.s* calls the kernel function *timein( )* to trigger (or call) the required function with its specified argument. The callout-table is then readjusted so that the first element in the table (which is the first entry, since it was the earliest to be triggered) is taken up by the next earliest timeout (this is done within *timein( )*).

When *timeout( )* is called, it returns an integer. This integer value is stored in the *callo->c_id* field which can later be used by *untimeout( )*. The function *untimeout( )* is used to stop the timeout occurring. The callout-table is simply re-adjusted so that the un-timed-out function is either replaced by another timeout entry or zeroed.

The reason why *clock( )* does not call the function directly, as opposed to generating another interrupt, is to prevent the clock interrupt mechanism from being masked from itself. While the *clock( )* function is executing, the processor execution level is set to mask out all other interrupts. If *clock( )* called the timed-out function directly, and that function took too long to complete, then all other interrupts (including clock interrupts) occurring during its execution would be masked also, so *clock( )* usually pokes a machine instruction to generate a programmable (software) interrupt. Since the clock interrupt level is at a higher priority than the programmable interrupt, the clock interrupt is always serviced first.

From this it can be seen that the system may service several clock interrupts (and any other interrupts with a higher priority than the programmable interrupt) before the system finally gets around to servicing the interrupt that results in calling the timed-out function. If this happens, the time at which the function was expected to be triggered may have expired. Although this has no effect on the timeout scheduling mechanism, it can be seen that scheduling a timeout cannot be fully relied on. In practice, however, the timeout usually occurs on time but in the worse case it may occur a few clock ticks later than expected.

4.8.4 Alarm calls

In contrast to *timeout( )*, which allows a kernel routine to schedule an internal timeout to trigger a function, the system provides a similar service to the user with an *alarm* system call. With this service a process can schedule an alarm signal to be posted to itself at some time in the future. Note that the granularity of the *alarm* system call is specified in seconds as opposed to *timeout( )* which uses clock ticks. The *alarm* system call, however, uses a very much simpler scheme. The *proc* structure member *p_clktim* is set to equal the number of seconds specified by the user at the time the system call was made. When *clock( )* performs its primary cycle operations (on each second), the active process list is scanned. For each process with a non-zero *p_clktim* member, the *p_clktim* member is decremented. A test is then done to see if the time has expired (reached zero). If it has, the process is simply sent an alarm signal (*SIGALRM*).

For the process to make use of this service, it must define an interrupt handler in its program code which will be brought into action on receipt of an alarm signal. Since the number of seconds to trigger is simply assigned to *p_clktim*, a call to *alarm(0)* turns the alarm call off. Figure 4.20 shows an example program making use of this facility.

Figure 4.20: *using the alarm( ) system call*

```
#include <stdio.h>
#include <setjmp.h>
#include <sys/signal.h>

jmp_buf env; /* non-local goto saved environment */

int alarm_handler()
{
   longjmp(env,1);
}

main()
{
   extern alarm_handler();
   char buff[30];
   char *p = &buff[0];

   *p = '\0';

   /* set up the alarm and handler */
   signal(SIGALRM,alarm_handler);
   alarm(30);

   if(setjmp(env))
      /*
       * message if user does not enter
       * data within 30 seconds
       */
      strcpy(p,"Your 30 seconds are up!\n");

   else {
      /* ask user for input */
      printf("Enter some characters within 30 seconds: ");
      fgets(p,30,stdin);
      alarm(0);
   }

   /* print the result */
   printf("%s",p);

}
```

4.8.5 Process execution-time statistics

Two members are used in the *proc* structure for process execution time statistics. They are *p_utime* and *p_stime*. On each invocation of *clock( )* (i.e., every tick), these variables are updated depending on the process's mode of execution. For example, if the process is executing in kernel-mode at the time of the clock interrupt, then the *p_stime* variable is incremented. Similarly, if the process was executing in user-mode, then *p_utime* is incremented. To allow a process to analyze these statistics, it provides the *times* system call. This service also provides similar statistical information for terminated children so long as they were waited for (using *wait*, for example) by the parent. The sum of the child's user and kernel-mode execution time is kept in the *proc* structure members *p_cutime* and *p_cstime* respectively.

Figure 4.21: *Program to extract system-wide statistical information*

```
#include <stdio.h>
#include <nlist.h>
#include <fcntl.h>
#include <unistd.h>
#include <sys/types.h>
#include <sys/sysinfo.h>

/*
 * our information structure
 */
typedef struct inf {
   long i_wait,i_kern,i_user,i_idle, i_sxbrk,
   w_iowait, w_swap, w_physio;
}INF;

/*
 * build the nlist table
 */
struct nlist nl[]= {
   {"sysinfo",0L,0,0,0,0},
   {"",0L,0,0,0,0}
};

main()
{
   INF inf;
   int fd;

   if(nlist("/stand/unix",nl) < 0) {
      fprintf(stderr, "/unix: no name list\n");
      exit(1);
```

```
   }

   if((fd = open("/dev/kmem", O_RDONLY)) < 0) {
      perror("/dev/kmem");
      exit(1);
   }

   if(lseek(fd, nl[0].n_value, SEEK_SET) == -1) {
      perror("lseek");
      exit(1);
   }

   if(read(fd,&inf,sizeof(INF)) != sizeof(INF)) {
      perror("read");
      exit(1);
   }

   printf("Execution mode\n");
   printf("WAIT=%ld, KERNEL=%ld, USER=%ld, IDLE=%ld, SXBRK=%ld\n",
      inf.i_wait,inf.i_kern,inf.i_user,inf.i_idle,inf.i_sxbrk);
   printf("Wait status\n");
   printf("I/O=%ld, SWAP=%ld, PHYSIO=%ld\n",
      inf.w_iowait,inf.w_swap,inf.w_physio);
   exit(0);

}
```

4.8.6 System-wide statistics

In contrast to per process execution time statistics, the operating system maintains system-wide execution statistics by updating counters for its mode of execution in a structure called *sysinfo*. This information is updated on each tick of the clock. The program in Figure 4.21 demonstrates the type of information captured and how it can be extracted from the running system.

4.8.7 System-wide process accounting

The operating system provides the *acct* system call for system-wide process accounting. Once enabled, an account record is written into a log-file whenever a process terminates. The information written is gathered from several data structures that were associated with the process during its execution. This information can later be used for generating customer billing reports based on system resource use. Table 4.19 lists the information written.

The *user* structure member u_mem holds an account of the number of pages of memory currently claimed by its associated process. If the process is marked *SONPROC* when *clock( )* is called, this variable is updated to show the number of pages used by the currently running process. The process must be marked *SONPROC* so that a true indication of the process's in-core page count can be made. If the process is not marked *SONPROC*, it may have some of its pages swapped out to secondary storage.

Table 4.19: *System-wide process accounting information*

Derived	Element	Description
struct user	*u_comm*	Name of the program for the account
	u_start	Process start time (relative to 00:00:00 UTC, January 1, 1970)
	u_ticks	Elapsed number of clock ticks
	u_mem	Number of memory pages (clicks) used
	u_ioch	Number of characters transferred
	u_ior + u_iow	Number of blocks read or written
	u_acflag	Account flags (append)
struct sess	*s_dev*	Device number associated with tty
struct cred	*cr_ruid*	User ID of invoker
	cr_rgid	Group ID of invoker
struct proc	*p_utime*	User-mode execution time
	p_stime	Kernel-mode execution time

4.8.8 Enforcing CPU resource limits

During the discussion of the process scheduling algorithms, we mentioned several times that a process's use of the CPU mostly depends on its given time-quantum. Time-quantums are measured in multiples of system clock *ticks*. For example, if *HZ* is 100, then a *tick* is:

$$1000/100 = 10 \text{ milliseconds.}$$

Thus, in the worst case, the operating system will context switch at around 100 times per second (in this case). Fortunately, a process will voluntarily give up the CPU several times between each clock tick while waiting for I/O to complete after issuing a system call. However, a process that does not relinquish the CPU before its time quantum expires can at best run a full 10 milliseconds (in this case) before it is interrupted by the hardware clock interrupt (this assumes that the process runs entirely in user-mode).

If CPU resource limits are enforced for the currently running process when *clock( )* is called, and the process's combined user and kernel-mode execution time has exceeded its imposed CPU resource limits (soft or hard), then the process is sent a *SIGXCPU* signal. *SIGXCPU* can be caught or ignored by the process. By default, if the signal is not caught or ignored then a *core image* is dumped into a file in the file system (§ 4.13.3). However, if the process ignores the *SIGXCPU* signal, it continues executing, although it will be sent a *SIGXCPU* for each clock tick that occurs while the process is mapped in as *curproc*. For more information about resource limits imposed by the operating system see § 2.8.

4.8.9 Profiling

The system provides a method by which a process can measure and compare how much user and kernel-mode time is spent during kernel procedure execution. It does this by implementing a *kernel profile driver* which is used to monitor the individual execution of kernel procedures. To use the kernel profiler, a process must first upload a list of sorted kernel addresses to the driver. The list must be sorted to enable the kernel to do a binary search, and the addresses are used internally to build a list of addresses to be sampled. This is done by opening */dev/prf* and then writing a *namelist* to it. The namelist is built from a list of symbols stored in the symbol-table of an *a.out* object. In most cases the namelist is extracted from */stand/unix* so that it contains a list of valid symbols used in the running system. The maximum size of the namelist depends on a tuneable parameter (*PRFMAX*) defined in the *master.d* directory.

Having loaded the driver, profiling must be switched on by issuing an *ioctl* call with the correct argument to turn profiling on. Once loaded, with kernel profiling enabled, the *clock( )* routine invokes the profiler driver interrupt routine passing both PS and PC registers. If the mode of execution (specified in PS) is user-mode, the profiler increments an internal counter for user-mode execution. If the mode of execution is kernel-mode, the profiler does a binary search of the pre-loaded internal namelist to locate the counter corresponding to the address of the procedure associated with the value found in the PC. If the captured value of the PC matches an entry in the internal namelist, its associated counter is incremented.

To read the sampled data, the process issues a *read* system call by using the file descriptor returned from the previous *open* on */dev/prf*.

The operating system provides a set of utilities for use with the kernel profiler. These utilities use the mechanisms detailed above and they are shown in Table 4.20. For more information on how to use these programs, see § 8 in [AT&T 1990g].

Table 4.20: *Kernel profiler utilities*

Program	Description
prfld	Load the profiler driver
prfstat	Turn on/off profiler sampling
prfdc	Profiler data capture to log file
prfsnap	One time snapshot data capture to log file
prfpr	Print data in captured log file

To allow a process to do profiling at user-mode execution level, the system provides a system call named *profil*:

```
profil(buff, bufsiz, offset, scale);
```

Since this profiling mechanism is separate from the kernel profiling driver it does not depend on its installation. However, the *profil* system call is complex to use and so it is rarely used directly. In almost every case requiring process profiling, the user invokes the C compiler with the '-p' option which directs the compiler to link in the code to generate profiling information. If the resulting *a.out* file is invoked and subsequently terminates without error, a file called *mon.out* is created. An execution profile can then be generated from the data stored in this output file with the **prof(1)** command.

The *profil* system call parameters are explained as follows:

- *buff* — points to the address of an area of memory in user address space.

- *bufsiz* — specifies the size in bytes of the area that *buff* points to.

- *offset* — the virtual address of a user subroutine (typically, *main( )*). The value *offset* is subtracted from the value in the captured program counter (PC).

- *scale* — the resultant value (PC - *offset*) is multiplied by *scale*.

Table 4.21: *Struct prof in the user structure*

Element	Reference	Description
short *pr_base	u.u_prof.pr_base	Buffer base
unsigned pr_size	u.u_prof.pr_size	Buffer size
unsigned pr_off	u.u_prof.pr_off	Program counter offset
unsigned pr_scale	u.u_prof.pr_scale	Program counter scaling

As mentioned previously, for each clock tick the hardware clock interrupt service routine indirectly calls *clock( )*. In *clock( )*, the PS register is examined to determine the current mode of execution. If the mode is user-mode, *clock( )* examines the *u.u_prof.pr_scale* structure member to see if it is set and if it is, a variable is set so that *clock( )* will return non-zero to *ttrap.s*. When it does return non-zero, the hardware clock interrupt service routine will know that profiling is enabled and so it will call the kernel function *addupc( )* to update the profiling information in the current process's user-area. This function is implementation dependent since it requires the manipulation of the program counter. The *user* structure contains a structure with members for each parameter of the *profil* system call (Table 4.21). Note that a *scale* value of zero turns profiling off.

Each entry in *buff* acts as a counter for events that take place at that particular address. The kernel offsets into *buff* with the following calculation:

```
buff_index = (PC - offset) * scale
```

If the resulting value matches an entry in *buff*, that entry is incremented.

Table 4.22: *Variables used by clock to mark time*

Variable	Description
time_t time	Number of seconds since midnight 1/1/1970
clock_t lbolt	Number of ticks since system boot
timestruc_t hrestime	Structure containing number of seconds and nanoseconds since midnight 1/1/1970
timedelta	Number of ticks per second adjustment

4.8.10 Keeping time

The operating system uses a number of variables for keeping time (Table 4.22) and provides the user with three time-related system calls. We will discuss these shortly, but first a discussion on the UNIX notion of time.

UNIX has always maintained time as the number of seconds elapsed since midnight of Thursday the 1st of January 1970. Whether or not this date and time has any bearing on its birthday is a matter for further investigation. Nevertheless, it has been chosen as the base for calculating the time on all UNIX system implementations.

The system call *time* returns the time in seconds, expressed as a long integer since Universal Coordinated Time (UTC) 00:00:00 1/1/1970. It does this by returning the value for seconds stored in *hrestime* (Table 4.22) which is incremented for each tick of the hardware clock.

In contrast to getting the time, the *stime* system call is used to set it. In this case, *hrestime* is set to that specified in the passed parameter. This is the system call used to set the system's internal notion of the time and date. Besides setting *hrestime*, the value passed to *stime* is used to set the hardware's notion of the time and date. This usually requires that an area of non-volatile RAM is written to. For example, on PC implementations of the operating system the battery backed-up CMOS chip is updated. However, internally, the kernel maintains time in microseconds. That is, its notion of time is the number of microseconds since UTC 00:00:00 1/1/1970.

We previously learned that the clock ticks away at a predefined number of *ticks* per second defined by the constant *HZ*. Another constant that is used is *TICK*. It defines the number of nanoseconds in a tick. For example, on the MIPS implementation a *TICK* is 10,000,000 — 10 milliseconds, so there are 100 *TICKs* in a *tick* and *HZ* number of *ticks* in a second.

Table 4.23: *Struct timestruc (timestruc_t)*

Element	Description
long tv_sec	Count of seconds
long tv_nsec	Count of nanoseconds

When *clock( )* is called it must update the internal notion of the time of day by incrementing a variable for each tick of the clock. Two variables are used and they are stored in the global *hrestime* structure. The nanosecond counter is incremented *n* number of nanoseconds per tick (*n* is the sum of *TICK* and *clock-drift* — see below), and the seconds counter is incremented when the nanosecond counter reaches 1000000000 (i.e., when one second has elapsed). When the nanosecond counter reaches 1000000000, it is decremented by 1000000000 and the seconds counter is incremented. This would normally leave the nanosecond counter with a value of zero (see Figure 4.22).

The reason why the nanoseconds counter does not always fall to zero is to allow for any adjustments that may have been made to the clock by a process using the *adjtime* system call. If the clock has not been adjusted by *adjtime*, then the nanosecond counter is always incremented by a *TICK* (10000000) for each tick of the clock. If, however, adjustments have been made, *clock( )* must take suitable measures to adjust the clock. This may mean slowing it down (more ticks per second) or speeding it up (fewer ticks per second). To do this, the system maintains two variables called *timedelta* and *tickdelta*. Within *clock( )*, the *timedelta* variable is tested. If it is non-zero, it means that adjustments have been made by *adjtime* and so the clock must be adjusted. The amount of adjustment is stored in *tickdelta*. This variable stores the amount of skew (in milliseconds) that must be applied to render the correct number of ticks per second that the internal clock should be using. Both variables are set by a process using *adjtime* and initially they are set to zero.

Figure 4.22: *Incrementing the time*

```
/*
 * The clock time is incremented on each clock tick
 */
increment the count of nanoseconds by TICK +/- clock-drift
/* TICK is typically 10 milliseconds (10000000) */
/* clock_drift is user defined by adjtime(2) */

if(the count is >= 1000000000) {
    decrement the count by 1000000000 nanoseconds
    increment the count of seconds
    set a flag to do one second (Primary) clock operations
}
```

You might wonder at first if there is ever a need to adjust the clock since crystal controlled oscillators are almost exclusively used to implement hardware clocks nowadays, and they are not only extremely reliable but accurate and stable too. Why is it then that the hardware clock cannot be relied upon, since it can be assumed that it will always be correct?

While it is true that the hardware clock is always accurate, there is no guarantee that two computers connected over a network will agree on the time. Thus, *adjtime* is provided so that any number of machines in a local area network can have their own internal clock adjusted as necessary.

The system call *adjtime* is derived from 4.3BSD and is primarily intended for use in a Local Area Network (LAN) to synchronize the internal clocks of cooperating machines. This is done with a daemon process called *timed*. All hosts on the network act as a slave except one which is configured as the master time server. The master obtains the time set in each slave and computes an overall average time. It then applies a correction value to each host's clock so that they all agree on an average network time.

4.8.11 High resolution interval timers

To comply with 4.3BSD, UNIX System V Release 4 provides the set of functions described in Table 4.24 but these functions are not implemented as system calls per se, although there is a special system call entry point that is indirectly called by them. They are provided by compatibility libraries documented under section 3 of [AT&T 1990a].

Table 4.24: *4.3BSD emulated system calls*

Function	Description
getitimer(3C)	Get value of interval timer
setitimer(3C)	Set value of interval timer
gettimeofday(3C)	Get the date and time
settimeofday(3C)	Set the date and time

The special system call entry point for these functions will not be discussed here. We will, however, discuss the high resolution interval timer implementation which is used to implement these services under UNIX System V Release 4.

Table 4.25: *Interval timer types*

Type	Description
ITIMER_REAL	Decrements the interval timer using real time. When the timer expires, a *SIGALRM* is posted to the process.
ITIMER_VIRTUAL	Decrements the interval timer only when the process is running in user-mode. When the timer expires, a *SIGVTALRM* is posted to the process.
ITIMER_PROF	Decrements the interval timer for both user-mode and kernel-mode execution of the process. When the timer expires, a *SIGPROF* is posted to the process.

The system provides each process with the ability to set an interval timer using three different but related interval timer types. The three interval timers are defined in *sys/time.h* and are described in Table 4.25. An interval timer is set with *setitimer(3C)*, and *getitimer(3C)* can be used to retrieve a timer's current value:

```
int getitimer(int which, struct itimerval *value);
int setitimer(int which, struct itimerval *value,
          struct itimerval *ovalue);
```

An interval timer is described by the *itimerval* structure (Table 4.26). The function argument *which* specifies the interval timer type. By using the function *setitimer( )*, the argument *value* specifies the configuration of the interval timer *which*. Assuming that an interval timer has already been previously requested, it can be reconfigured at any time with subsequent calls to *setitimer( )*, in which case *ovalue* is filled by *setitimer* with the previous interval timer configuration (as long as *ovalue* is not passed as (struct itimerval *)NULL).

An interval timer configuration is dependent on what is set in the *itimerval* structure pointed to by *value*; *it_value* specifies the timer expiration. If *it_interval* is non-zero, its specification is used to reload *it_value* when the timer expires. A subsequent call to *setitimer( )* with *it_value* set to zero disables the timer. Thus, it can be seen that the scheme is flexible enough to allow a process to set a one-time interval timer, or to keep resetting it when the interval timer expires.

Table 4.26: *Struct timeval and itimerval*

Structure	Element	Description
struct timeval	*long tv_sec*	seconds since 00:00:00 1/1/70
	long tv_usec	microseconds
struct itimerval	*struct timeval it_interval*	timer interval
	struct timeval it_value	current value

With these functions a process can set an alarm call by using a resolution of time that is higher than it would be if the system call *alarm* was used, since the lowest resolution that *alarm* can operate with is one second. By using *setitimer( )* a process can reduce the resolution to that used by the system clock (i.e., one tick). In addition to this, a process can set an interval timer that gives a timeout resolution to one microsecond.

We learned earlier that the clock interrupt service routine in *ttrap.s* calls *clock_int( )* which in turn is responsible for calling *clock( )*. It is in *clock_int( )* that high resolution timers are processed.

The high resolution timer code is divided into two parts. One part provides the generic high resolution timer service to processes that have set interval timers with the real time clock (*ITIMER_REAL*). It decrements all currently active timers on each occurrence of a hardware clock interrupt regardless of what process is currently running. The other part provides an interval timer service on a per process execution basis. It also uses the real time clock interrupt mechanism, but decrements only the timers set for the currently running process. In other words, if the process is not *curproc*, any set interval timers for that process remain untouched until that process is context switched in.

Figure 4.23: *Algorithm for clock_int( )*

```
clock_int()
input: PC and PS registers
output: return value from clock()
{
 /* process high resolution timer list first for all  */
 /* processes that have set them (ITIMER_REAL)  */
 while( there is an expired high-resolution timer ) {
    decrement its time
    remove its entry from the active list
    call the function to process the event
    /* for example psignal() to post */
    /* the appropriate signal        */

    if(the alarm was repetitive)
        arrange for another timeout later
    else
        free its related interval timer data structure
 }

 /* update timer variables -- see Table 4.28 */
 if(currently running process is in user-mode)
    update process virtual time and user virtual time counter
 else if(kernel is not idle)
    update process virtual time counter

 /* Now process the currently running processes */
 /* private interval timer list  */
 while(there is an expired interval timer) {
    decrement its time
    remove its entry from the active list
    call the function to process the event
    /* for example psignal() to post */
    /* the appropriate signal        */
    if(the alarm was repetitive)
        arrange for another interval timeout later
    else
        free its related interval timer data structure
 }

 return( clock(pc,cs) );  /* tell UNIX to tick */
}
```

Table 4.27: *Interval timer variables*

Structure	Element	Description
struct proc	*timer_t *p_italarm[0]*	*ITIMER_VIRTUAL* timer list
	*timer_t *p_italarm[1]*	*ITIMER_PROF* timer list
struct user	*clock_t u_uservirt*	user-mode execution counter
	clock_t u_procvirt	user and kernel-mode execution counter

The service is flexible enough to allow the user to set an interval timer that decrements while the process is executing in user-mode only (*ITIMER_VIRTUAL*), or while executing in either user or kernel-mode (*ITIMER_PROF*). The latter is primarily intended for profiling the execution of a program. Note that a process setting an interval timer using *ITIMER_PROF* must be prepared to restart uncompleted system calls. Since the timer may expire while executing in kernel-mode, it can interrupt system call execution.

Several circular doubly linked lists maintain the interval timers (Figure 4.24), with each interval timer type having its own active-list and free-list. Active interval timers of type *ITIMER_REAL* are queued on a global list headed by a variable called *hrt_active*. The other two interval timer lists are maintained in the process's associated *proc* structure and are headed by the two pointers in the *p_italarm[]* array. As a timer expires, it is put back on its original freelist.

Two variables in the *user* structure are used as time-counters (Table 4.27) and are incremented depending on the processes mode of execution.

4.9 Process execution modes

We have already learned that the kernel operates in the context of the currently running process and that a process runs in the context of itself. We have also learned that a process executes in one of two modes: user-mode or kernel-mode. When a process executes its own code it operates in user-mode. When it executes kernel code it operates in kernel-mode. When executing in kernel-mode, the kernel is able to execute privileged instructions and has access to privileged data. A process executing in user-mode is prohibited from executing these instructions and can access data only within its own assigned address space. A process is switched to kernel-mode when any of the following happens:

- It calls on the services of the operating system via the system call interface.
- An interrupt is generated during user-mode execution.
- The process in user-mode generates a fault (exception). Examples of this are: violation of its address space, growth of stack, floating point exceptions, page not present exceptions, and so on.

In contrast to this, a process is returned to user-mode when:

Figure 4.24: *Interval timer list management*

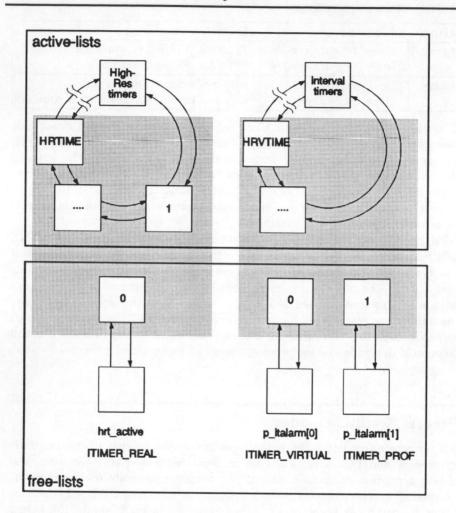

- The operating system has finished servicing a system call made by the user.
- The interrupt which interrupted user-mode execution has been serviced.
- An exception, once serviced, allows user-mode processing to be continued.

This section describes the mechanisms for making the transition between the two execution modes.

4.9.1 Transferring to *kernel-mode*

The transition between user and kernel-mode can be broken down into two specific groups, described as follows:

Figure 4.25: *Transferring process execution modes to kernel-mode*

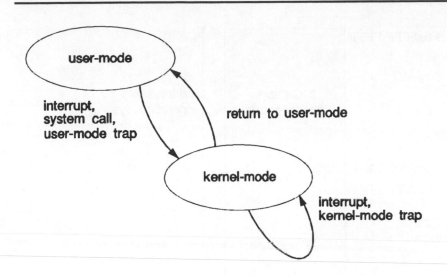

- *internal synchronous events* — such as system call invocation and traps generated or made by the program during its execution. When an event of this type occurs, execution is transferred to specific functions in the operating system that run in kernel-mode. These functions have the power to terminate the process or modify its execution environment. For example, if the process generates a "bus error", the process may be killed. Such a condition means that the process is never returned to user-mode execution since it is terminated. The system would simply free all memory and data structures associated with it and then choose another process to run instead. Another example is "growth of stack" error. If the operating system finds that there is no room to push an activation record onto the stack, a fault is generated which results in a hardware trap. This may extend the stack for the process to accommodate more activation records without the process even knowing that the fault occurred (§ 3.10.1).

- *External asynchronous events* — any non-process-related events that occur during the process's normal execution. Examples of this are: interrupts generated by external I/O devices, and hardware clock interrupts.

The transfer from user-mode to kernel-mode and vice versa is done by switching the mode of execution in the processor. The processor normally operates in user-mode until an asynchronous or synchronous event occurs which results in the processor being switched to kernel-mode. The processor then remains in kernel-mode until the operating system executes an instruction to restore user-mode execution. The two operating environments are separated from each other but only kernel-mode is privileged enough to access both user and kernel-mode address spaces. Thus, a process executing in user-mode cannot gain access to the kernel-mode address space since it is not addressable. This provides adequate protection to the operating

Figure 4.26: *MIPS R3000 virtual addressing scheme*

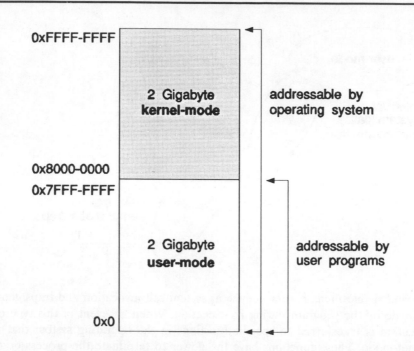

system which operates only in kernel-mode. As an example of this, consider the MIPS R3000 virtual addressing scheme in Figure 4.26. The MIPS R3000 has an addressing range of 4 Gigabytes which is split into two specific areas: 2 Gigabytes for use by users and 2 Gigabytes for use by the kernel. In user-mode, a user program is given a single uniform virtual address space which is addressable from 0 thru 0x7FFFFFFF inclusive. In kernel-mode, this area is also addressable allowing the kernel access to user data. However, the kernel also has an extended address space which ranges from 0 thru 0xFFFFFFFF inclusive.

4.9.2 Interrupt, trap and exception handling

Many processors provide hardware support for handling interrupts and traps by saving execution state information automatically. They may also provide several vector addresses to which control is transferred in response to exceptions. Although it may seem that these facilities offer benefits, they often add complexity to hardware besides reducing the overall flexibility of the operating system design. Thus, to simplify hardware design and to give operating system implementors more flexibility, most of the newer processors on the market leave such tasks for the operating system designers to implement in software.

UNIX is a good example of this: when an interrupt occurs, a hardware trap is generated and control is passed to a predetermined interrupt service routine. It is the operating system implementors who determine which interrupt servicing routine the interrupt is vectored to. The resulting interrupt handler to which control is passed on is then responsible for determining the processing requirements for that specific interrupt. The operating system implementors are also left to decide what state information should be saved and where it is stored when an interrupt occurs. The result of this approach is that the operating system can be made portable to many processors. All that has to be done is to code the low level interrupt and exception handling routines for the particular processor that UNIX is being ported to.

Interrupts are generated from two sources: from a software interrupt programmed by a component of the operating system (such as a timeout), or from a hardware interrupt generated by a device when it requires attention. Exceptions or (faults) are generated when an instruction executed in either user or kernel-mode encounters an error condition such as the "growth of stack" error mentioned previously. Each interrupt source and each exception type is identified by an operand that is used to invoke the servicing routine associated with the prevailing interrupt or exception. Exceptions are generally handled by the processor; it defines the numbers used for the exception handling routines. However, interrupt numbers are generally left for the operating system implementation.

When an interrupt or exception is detected by the processor, the normal flow of instruction execution is suspended. In the case of an exception, the instruction that caused the exception is aborted. The processor, if not already in kernel-mode, is forced into kernel-mode so that it can respond to the event. Control is then passed to the interrupt handler by jumping directly to its designated interrupt or exception servicing routine.

So that execution can return to the point where the interruption took place, the interrupt or exception handler saves a copy of the current environment.

4.9.3 Saving and restoring the environment

Whenever a transition from user-mode to kernel-mode takes place, the kernel must ensure that the current user-mode environment is saved so that it can later be restored to allow the process to resume execution in user-mode. The method for this is implementation dependent but is usually done by a trap handler in *ttrap.s*, which saves several registers such as the PS, SP and PC in the PCB. In the case of a system call, the state of the general purpose data registers for the process will already have been pushed on the user-stack when the system call was made in user-mode as a result of the C language function calling procedure. These will be restored on return from the system call in user-mode. The PS and PC are then loaded with the destination vector. The PC contains the function address to which control is passed. For example, in the case of an interrupt control is passed on to the relevant interrupt handler. Similarly, in the case of a system call trap, control is passed on to *systrap( )* to determine which function will provide the processing required by the system call. When the kernel has finished servicing the interrupt, trap, or system call, it restores the previously saved vector from the process's PCB. The PS contains the previous mode of execution, in this case, user-mode, so that when the saved PS is restored execution returns to user-mode. Restoring the PC

Figure 4.27: *System call trap to kernel-mode*

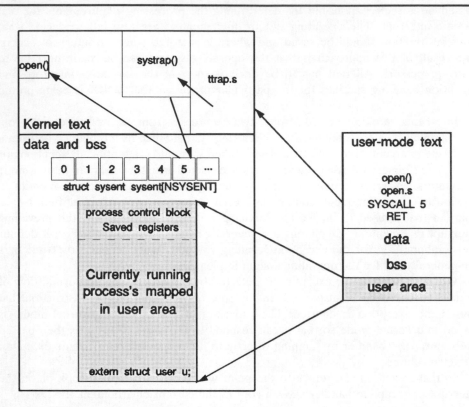

resumes execution at the point that the process entered kernel-mode. If the transition occurred because of a system call, execution continues at the next instruction after the instruction that caused the transition to kernel-mode. Thus, the system call usually returns to its calling function. In the case of an interrupt or fault, execution continues from where the process was interrupted.

4.9.4 System call traps

Traps and interrupts can occur while the process executes in user or kernel-mode. However, system calls can only be invoked while the process executes in user-mode (Figure 4.27). All system calls are assembler routines which are compiled into object form and stored in a library in the file system. They are linked into the target executable by the link loader **ld(1)** at compile time just like any other library functions the program might use. When a process makes a system call, the invoked system call executes a special assembly language instruction which transfers the processor execution mode to kernel-mode (often referred to as supervisory mode). For example, on the MIPS R3000 processor, the instruction is called a *SYSCALL*; on an AT&T 3B2 the instruction is called a *GATE*. In response to this instruction, a system call *trap* occurs. This results in the immediate and unconditional transfer to kernel-mode and the system call trap handler usually found in *ttrap.s* is brought into action. The operand of the instruction will later be used to identify the system call handler in the *sysent[]* table within *systrap()*. All system calls are subject to the same procedure.

Table 4.28: *Struct sysent*

Element	Description
char sy_narg	Number of arguments
char sy_flags	If set to *SETJUMP*, it means *systrap()* should do a *setjmp()* before calling the handler
*int (*sy_call)()*	System call service handler

4.9.5 The *sysent[]* table

The *sysent[]* table consists of one initialized *sysent* structure (Table 4.28) per system call. By indexing into the table with the number specified in the *SYSCALL* instruction operand, *systrap()* can locate the function pointer that points to the system call service handler. The arguments passed as parameters to the system call may be saved in the process's PCB area, presumably by *ttrap.s* when the user-mode to kernel-mode transition took place. We say "presumably", because, as mentioned earlier, this mechanism is implementation dependent. Within *systrap()*, the *user* structure member *u_arg[MAXSYSARGS]* is populated with the value of each argument that the user-mode process specified at the time the system call was made. To do this, the *sy_narg* member of the indexed *sysent* structure is used. This variable contains the number of arguments that the handler expects to be passed to it as parameters. The *u_ap* member is then set to point to the argument list which is passed as a parameter to the handler when it is called. In addition to this, *systrap()* constructs and initializes a return value structure which is also passed to the system call handler. The structure is a union *rval* (Table 4.29), and is used for manipulating return-value parameters passed by reference to system call handlers. The system call fills the structure accordingly when it returns through *systrap()* after it has done with processing. For example, the *pipe* system call (§ 7.10.2) is called as follows:

```
int pipe(fd);
int fd[2];
```

The argument *fd[]* represents the desired file descriptors that pipe obtains for connecting two streams together. Within the *pipe* system call, the *rval_t* structure passes back the two file descriptors to the user process requesting them. When *pipe* is finished and returns to user-mode via *systrap()*, this information will appear as the values returned by the system call.

Table 4.29: *Union rval (rval_t)*

Element		Description
struct r_v	*int r_v1*	First *int* return value
	int r_v2	Second *int return* value
off_t r_off		Used for returning values of type *off_t*
time_t r_time		Used for returning values of type *time_t*

4.9.6 Exception traps

An exception or fault is generated when a process executing in either user-mode or kernel-mode causes an error condition that can only be corrected by the operating system. For example, if the process causes a divide by zero or floating point exception, the operating system must take action to handle the situation. Another example is "growth of stack" or a memory fault.

When an exception occurs, a hardware trap is generated bringing the trap handler in *ttrap.s* into action. As with a system call trap, the current user-mode registers are saved and control is transferred to a designated handling routine.

As mentioned previously, a trap can occur in either user-mode or kernel-mode and so there are different handling routines for each mode of execution. For example, if the processor is in user-mode when the exception is generated, then *u_trap( )* is called. Similarly, *k_trap( )* is called to handle kernel-mode exceptions.

A stack exception means that the stack could be corrupt, so the processor, if in user-mode, is switched to kernel-mode execution so that the stack fault can be serviced. Stack exceptions have their own handling functions, which are highly implementation dependent. Typically, there are two stack exception handlers: one for servicing a user-mode stack exception and another for servicing a kernel-mode stack exception. Nothing can be done about a kernel-mode stack exception. It must be assumed that the kernel stack is corrupt and so the system must be stopped (paniced — see § 9.1). In the case of a user-mode stack exception, the complete process state is saved in the PCB. The PS, SP and PC are then revectored so that execution is transferred to the user-mode stack exception handler, which in turn calls *grow( )* to extend the user-stack (see § 3.10.1).

4.9.7 Interrupts

Interrupts may be generated at any time and usually have nothing to do with the execution of the currently running process. An interrupt literally means that the processor's instruction flow is interrupted. Devices such as the hardware clock, disk drives, network controllers, and async controllers (to name but a few) can all interrupt the processor, and usually do so when they require attention.

The servicing of interrupts is machine dependent because each processor uses different interrupt servicing mechanisms and it defines the interrupt mechanisms available for the operating system. For example, the MIPS R3000 processor supports six hardware interrupt input lines for devices, and two software interrupts that are programmable.

Figure 4.28: *Typical interrupt level scheme (implementation dependent)*

High interrupt priority level	7	Machine exceptions
	6	Hardware clock
	5	Disk controller
	4	Network controllers
	3	Async controller
Low interrupt priority level	2	Software programmable

Each interrupt has an associated number that is used as a reference to its interrupt priority level. The value determines whether the interrupt is allowed to interrupt the processor or not. The processor runs at a specific interrupt priority level. Interrupts that occur with interrupt priority levels lower than the processor's current interrupt priority level are ignored. This scheme enables the operating system to mask out specific interrupts by changing the current priority level of the processor. The higher the interrupt priority level, the more important the interrupt, which means that it is more likely to be serviced by the processor. For example, the clock is usually given a high interrupt priority level and programmable interrupts tend to have the lowest (Figure 4.28). The lowest priority level is zero. When the processor is executing in user-mode, the processor's interrupt priority level is set to zero. Thus, all interrupts are able to interrupt the processor at this level since they all have higher interrupt priority levels.

Interrupts are handled by interrupt vectoring routines within *ttrap.s*. As an interrupt occurs, the processor's instruction stream is suspended, the PC, PS and SP are saved and then reloaded with the vector of the interrupt handler in *ttrap.s*. These interrupt handling routines are responsible for servicing the interrupt.

Whenever the kernel finds it necessary to mask out interrupts, say, for example, when manipulating critical sections of code or data structures, it sets the processor interrupt priority level to a level that prevents it from being interrupted. As soon as the critical section has passed and there is no longer a concern of being further interrupted, it changes the processor interrupt priority level back to its previous priority level.

A set of functions named *spl* allow the kernel to set the processor priority level. Each routine returns the current interrupt level so that the value can be saved and reset later. Since these routines manipulate the processor's execution environment, they are usually implemented in machine assembler so they are very implementation dependent. Table 4.30 lists the typical *spl* functions implemented.

As an example of how they are used, consider the *tty* driver. While servicing an interrupt, the driver's interrupt handler masks out other similar interrupts so that it can complete servicing the current interrupt. It usually sets *spltty( )* so that other interrupts generated by the terminal are ignored. When the current interrupt has

Table 4.30: *Functions to set processor interrupt level (implementation dependent)*

Functions	Description
int spl0( )	All interrupts are acknowledged
int spl1( )	Mask out software clock interrupts
int spl6( )	Mask out scheduler clock interrupts
int spl7( )	Mask out all interrupts
int splall( )	Same as *spl7( )*
int splbio( )	Mask out block device interrupts (e.g., disk/tape)
int splclock( )	Same as *spl6( )*
int splhi( )	Same as *spl7( )*
int spltty( )	Mask out asynchronous device interrupts (e.g., terminals)
int splstr( )	Set interrupt level to protect STREAMS code
void splx(x)	Restore previously saved interrupt level *x*

been serviced the device driver calls *splx( )* to reset the previous interrupt level to allow further interrupts generated by the terminal to be serviced. If, however, a higher level interrupt occurs while servicing the terminal interrupt, that interrupt is serviced elsewhere, but execution is eventually returned to the *tty* driver interrupt handler where it continues without knowing that a higher level interrupt occurred.

4.9.8 Returning to *user-mode* in *systrap( )*

When a system call is finished processing, it returns through *systrap( )* (Figure 4.29) which updates the PCB area with the system call return values found in the return value structure *rval_t*. If the system call returned with an error, then *systrap( )* arranges for *errno* to be set and the *errno* code is stored in place of the system call return value in the PCB area.

Some system calls arrange for *setjmp( )* to be called before the system call handler is invoked (see Table 4.31). This is done in order to save the current context in case of an aborted or interrupted system call. In such cases, control is passed back to the saved context in *systrap( )*, via *longjmp( )* (see also § 4.6.14). Execution then resumes just after the call to *setjmp( )* in *systrap( )* giving the illusion that the system call had never been called. This scheme also allows the operating system to silently restart an interrupted system call if required to do so (see *SA_RESTART* in § 4.10.4). Generally though, a system call is interrupted when an asynchronous event occurs — for example, the user presses the keyboard sequence for *quit*. If the signal causing the interruption is caught by the process, then after processing the signal in the interrupt handler the system call returns *EINTR* (the error code for interrupted system call).

Before returning to user-mode, certain housekeeping chores are done. *systrap( )* checks the system call type. If it was a *vfork* then the child is given a chance to *exec* its new program image. The process is put to sleep, allowing its new child to run first; this can save the system from unnecessary copying of copy-on-write marked page tables.

Figure 4.29: *Algorithm for systrap( )*

```
systrap()
input: none
output: none
{
   find the system call entry in the sysent[] table

   collect the system call arguments and arrange
     - them in a u_ap to pass to the system call handler

   construct and initialize a return value structure /* rval_t */

   if required, call setjmp() for the system call
   /* process will resume here if the system call was interrupted */

   if ( interrupted system call ) {
      error = EINTR;

      if(signal caused system call to be silently restarted)
         error = ERESTART

      set error in pcb /* for errno */

   } else {
      call the system call handler routine
      get system call return values from rval_t and
      - set them in the pcb
   }

   /* returned from system call at this point */

   if(the system call was a vfork())
      wait for the child to exec its new program image

   request context switch another process if runrun is set
   process any pending signals

   return to user-mode via trap return handler in ttrap.s

   /* should be impossible to reach here */
}
```

Table 4.31: *System calls that automatically call setjmp( ) on invocation*

read	*readv*	*write*	*writev*	*open*	*close*
ioctl	*creat*	*sigpause*	*msgctl*	*getpmsg*	*putmsg*
pipe	*signal*	*sigset*	*sighold*	*sigrelse*	*sigignore*
msgget	*msgrcv*	*msgsnd*	*shmat*	*shmctl*	*shmdt*
shmget	*semctl*	*semget*	*semop*	*uadmin*	*fcntl*
getmsg	*putpmsg*	*poll*	*sigsuspend*	*waitid*	*waitpid*
pause	*sync*	*ptrace*			

If *runrun* is set, it means that a request has been made to switch in another process, thus *systrap( )* satisfies the request by preempting another process to run. Additionally, if signals are pending for the process, *systrap( )* arranges for them to be processed.

When *systrap( )* is complete and ready to pass control back to user-mode, it does not return to the system call trap handler from where it was originally called. Instead, it calls a trap return handler (which is usually defined in *ttrap.s* although this is implementation dependent).

For both synchronous and asynchronous events, the trap return handler is responsible for restoring user-mode. But before returning to user-mode, final checks are done to see if signals were posted or if *runrun* was set at interrupt level, since these events may have taken place after they had been tested for. This may require further processing before finally returning the process to user-mode. If no further processing is required, the hardware registers are populated with the information stored in the PCB which includes the restoration of the PS, SP and PC, and the program continues in user-mode from where it left off.

4.9.9 *longjmp( )* and *setjmp( )*

In some circumstances the kernel must abort its current thread of execution and return control to a previously saved context — for example, when handling an interrupted system call, as described in the previous section. To do this, the kernel uses the following two functions:

- *setjmp( )* — saves the current context. The method used to save the context is implementation dependent. In most cases, however, the system saves the values of several processor registers in the user-area associated with the currently running process (usually an array of integers called *u_qsav*). Note that there is room for only one context save.

- *longjmp( )* — restores a previously saved context. This is the kernel's "non-local goto" function. It loads the previously saved context from the user-area set up by *setjmp( )* and arranges for *setjmp( )* to return 1. Processing then continues at the original point where *setjmp( )* was called.

4.10 Signals

Signals inform a process of the occurrence of an event. Events can be broken into two categories:

- *Error events* — generated by the process executing. For example, if the process references an illegal area of memory a hardware trap is generated and the trap exception handler posts a segmentation violation signal (*SIGSEGV*). Similarly, if the process executes an illegal instruction it is sent *SIGILL*, or if the process exceeds its CPU resource limits it is sent *SIGXCPU*.

- *Asynchronous events* — occur externally to the process executing but have some relation to it. For example, the death of a child (*SIGCHLD*) or parent process, or the receipt of a signal sent by another process. The tty device driver may also post a signal to a process. For example, it may post *SIGHUP* to the process if the terminal line it is associated with, hangs up. If the process has set an alarm the kernel will post *SIGALRM* to it when its programmed alarm time expires.

All signals are ultimately sent to a process by the kernel. However, a process may request that a signal be sent to another process (or itself) by using the *kill* or *sigsend* system calls. These will be discussed later.

Any signal (Table 4.32) can be sent to a process, but the method by which they are received and processed depends on the process's signal disposition and defined set of actions to be taken in response to them. However, the action to be taken on receipt of a specific signal is determined at the time the signal is delivered. A signal is said to be delivered when the receiving process handles the signal. The signal handling mechanisms are not aware of how a signal is generated; they are aware only that a signal is pending and must be processed.

A process that wishes to perform some action on receipt of a specific signal can define a signal handler to be invoked in the context of the user process when the signal is delivered. This scheme, to a user-mode process, is similar to interrupt handling in the kernel. That is, a process can define individual interrupt handlers for each of the signal types that are catchable and specific signals can be masked out if required.

The following sections discuss the mechanisms and algorithms used to implement signals, and how they are posted, received and processed by both the kernel and user process.

4.10.1 Signal posting

When a signal is posted to a process, a bit is set within *p_sig* in the *proc* structure. Each signal type has a specific value (Table 4.32). To send a signal, the kernel simply sets the bit in *p_sig* corresponding to the signal being sent. From then on, and until the signal is processed by the receiving process, the signal is said to be *pending*. This interval is really so short that a process cannot detect it. At some future time during the execution of the process, a check is made to see if there are

Table 4.32: *Signals — a signal marked † means that it is new to System V*

Signal	Value	Description	Default Action
SIGHUP	1	Hangup	exit
SIGINT	2	Interrupt	exit
SIGQUIT	3	Quit	core
SIGILL	4	Illegal instruction (not reset when caught)	core
SIGTRAP	5	Trace trap (not reset when caught)	core
SIGIOT	6	IOT instruction	core
SIGABRT	6	Used by abort, replace SIGIOT in the future	core
SIGEMT	7	EMT instruction	core
SIGFPE	8	Floating point exception	core
SIGKILL	9	Kill (cannot be caught or ignored)	exit
SIGBUS	10	Bus error	core
SIGSEGV	11	Segmentation violation	core
SIGSYS	12	Bad argument to system call	core
SIGPIPE	13	Write on a pipe with no-one to read it	exit
SIGALRM	14	Alarm clock	exit
SIGTERM	15	Software termination signal from kill	exit
SIGUSR1	16	User-defined signal 1	exit
SIGUSR2	17	User-defined signal 2	exit
SIGCLD	18	Child status change	ignore
SIGCHLD †	18	Child status change (POSIX)	ignore
SIGPWR	19	Power-fail restart	ignore
SIGWINCH	20	Window size change	ignore
SIGURG †	21	Urgent socket condition	ignore
SIGPOLL	22	Pollable event occurred	exit
SIGIO †	22	Socket I/O possible (SIGPOLL alias)	exit
SIGSTOP †	23	Stop (cannot be caught or ignored)	stop
SIGTSTP †	24	User stop requested from tty	stop
SIGCONT †	25	Stopped process has been continued	ignore
SIGTTIN †	26	Background tty read attempted	stop
SIGTTOU †	27	Background tty write attempted	stop
SIGVTALRM †	28	Virtual timer expired	exit
SIGPROF †	29	Profiling timer expired	exit
SIGXCPU †	30	Exceeded cpu limit	core
SIGXFSZ †	31	Exceeded file size limit	core
NSIG	32	Valid signals range from 1 to NSIG-1	
MAXSIG	32	Size of u_signal[]	

any pending signals for it. If there are, they are processed as necessary.

Signals are always checked before returning from kernel-mode to user-mode. For example, if the process executes a system call, then signals are checked in *systrap( )* just before returning to user-mode. Similarly, they are checked when an interrupt or exception occurs within the interrupt or exception handler before returning the process to user-mode. They are also checked if the process voluntarily goes to sleep in kernel-mode with an event type greater than *PZERO* (i.e., allowing signals to interrupt the sleep). In each case, if the check proves that signals are pending for the currently running process, they are processed before the process is allowed to return to user-mode.

The range of valid signals supported by UNIX System V Release 4 is between 1 and *NSIG*, which is 32. This fits nicely into a 4 byte integer, and *p_sig* is typically 4 bytes long (an unsigned long on a 32 bit machine) with each bit position representing a signal type. Since there is only one bit for each signal type in *p_sig*, it is obvious that signals cannot be queued there. So once a bit position is set for a signal, any other signal with the same value that is posted to the process will overwrite the same bit position. Thus, a process has no way of knowing how many signals of a particular type have been sent to it.

A signal can be *posted* to a process only by the process that is currently running. But since the receiving process may have been paged out, it is necessary to store pending signal information for the receiving process in that process's associated *proc* structure. This is the only part of the process's image guaranteed to be memory resident. In contrast to this, a process can process (or *handle*) its pending signals only while it is the currently running process executing in kernel-mode.

With the exception of processes that run with a real or effective user ID of zero (i.e., super-user), a process can post a signal to another process only if that process has the same real or effective user ID as itself.

In summary, a process that is not currently running can only receive signals from the currently running process. A process that is currently running can, on the other hand, both send and receive signals. Any process is allowed to send a signal to itself but it must have permission to send a signal to another process. A process can arrange to catch or ignore certain signals, but some signals cannot be caught. However, the kernel can send any signal to any process at any time whether the receiver is the currently running process or not.

There are several functions that the kernel can use to post a signal to a process, but the function ultimately called by them all is called *sigtoproc( )* (Figure 4.30). Thus, *sigtoproc( )* is responsible for doing the actual signal posting. In general, the kernel uses the function *psignal( )* to post a signal to a process, but it, in turn, simply calls *sigtoproc( )* to do the work. There is no functional difference between the two functions.

To post a signal to a process group, the kernel uses a function called *signal( )*. That is, all processes within a process group will be sent the signal. Note that the *signal( )* function in this case is an internal function that has no relation to the *signal* system call, which will be discussed later. The function *signal( )* is passed the process group ID and the value of the signal to send to all processes in that group. Within *signal( )*, the process group ID is used to hash into a table to obtain a

Figure 4.30: *Algorithm for sigtoproc( )*

```
sigtoproc()
input: p — pointer to process's associated proc structure
       sig — signal value to send to process
output: none
{
  if signal is SIGCONT  {
    /* stopped process has been continued */
    turn off default stop bits set in p_sig
    mark process SXSTART
    wake the process up
  }

  return if signal is being ignored /* SIGKILL cannot be ignored */
  set the bit for ''sig'' in p_sig  /* post the signal */

  if the process is asleep (SSLEEP) {
    return if the process cannot be awakened by a signal
      - or the signal is being held
    else wake the process up
  }

  if the process is stopped or being traced by a debugger {
    if the process is on a sleep queue at an interruptable priority
      /* the signal will be seen when the process  */
      /* receives SIGCONT so don't wake it up here */
      remove process from its sleep queue
  }

  if it is the currently running process
    /* make sure that signals posted to it from interrupt level */
    /* are received before returning it to user mode           */
    set u.u_sigevpend in the user area
}
```

---

pointer. The pointer points to a linked list of *proc* structures representing each related process in the group. The resulting pointer and the signal value are both then passed to *pgsignal( )* which traverses through the linked list to obtain the process ID of each process in the group. For each process found, *psignal( )* is called with arguments that include the found process ID and signal value to be sent. Within *psignal( )*, *sigtoproc( )* is called to finally post the signal to the process.

4.10.2 Algorithm *sigtoproc( )*

The ultimate purpose of this function is to set the bit representing the signal in the process's *p_sig* member, and to wake up the process (assuming, of course, that the process is sleeping at an interruptable priority) so that the signal can be handled by it.

A debugger wishing to restart a stopped process may send it a *SIGCONT* signal — meaning continue execution. In this case, *sigtoproc( )* clears the default stop-bits in *p_sig* and the process is marked *SXSTART* so that the kernel knows that the process is ready to continue; the process is then woken up and set running.

If the signal is being ignored by the process (remember that *SIGKILL* cannot be caught or ignored — this is true even for a process that is stopped), *sigtoproc( )* just returns and the signal is not posted. Otherwise, the bit representing the signal is set in *p_sig* and the signal is officially posted.

If the process is asleep when the signal is posted (*SSLEEP*), and the sleep is interruptable, the process is woken up and set running. However, if the process is sleeping at an uninterruptable priority, or if the signal is being blocked, *sigtoproc( )* simply returns since there is nothing more that it can do.

If the process is not asleep but is nevertheless, on a sleep queue marked *SSTOP*, then instead of waking it up, it is simply taken off its sleep queue — the signal will be noticed and handled when the process next receives *SIGCONT*.

Finally, the currently running process may have been posted a signal while servicing an interrupt in kernel-mode. If the signal was posted on return to user-mode within the interrupt trap handler, it is possible that the check for pending signals has already been done. But the kernel never allows a process to return to user-mode without checking for signals. So if the process is the currently running process, *sigtoproc( )* sets a flag (*u_sigevpend*) in the user-area to ensure that the signal is handled before the process leaves kernel-mode.

4.10.3 Handling signals

A process maintains several variables to describe its current signal disposition and processing actions. Some are stored in the *user* structure, while others are stored in the *proc* structure (see Table 4.33).

The mask variables in the *proc* structure describe how a process reacts to signals as they are posted to it. For example, if the process is ignoring a specific signal, then the bit representing that signal will be set in *p_ignore*. Similarly, if the process is blocking a specific signal, then the bit for that signal in *p_hold* will be set. When a signal is posted to a process, the kernel uses these variables to determine what action the receiving process must take for the signal. For example, in the case of *p_ignore*, the kernel must determine whether the signal should be posted or ignored.

If *p_cursig* is non-zero, its value represents the signal currently being handled by (or delivered to) the process. When a process handles a pending signal, the signal becomes the current signal. In other words, it is moved from *p_sig* to *p_cursig*.

A table named *u_signal[MAXSIG]* describes the actions to take on receipt of a signal. This table and several other variables used to process signals are stored in the

Table 4.33: *Per process signal variables*

Struct	Element	Description
proc	*p_sig*	Mask of signals pending to this process
	p_sigmask	Mask of tracing signals for */proc*
	p_hold	Mask of signals held for this process
	p_ignore	Mask of signals ignored by this process
	p_siginfo	Mask of signals causing signal handler to receive more information (see *sigaction*)
	p_sigqueue	Pointer to the queue of siginfo structures
	p_curinfo	Pointer to current signal information
	p_cursig	Most current signal being handled
user	*u_signodefer*	Mask of signals deferred when caught
	u_sigaltstack	Alternate stack for signals
	u_sigonstack	Mask of signals taken on an alternate stack
	u_sigresethand	Mask of signals reset when caught
	u_sigrestart	Mask of signals that restart interrupted system calls
	u_sigoldmask	Mask of signals used by *sigsuspend*
	u_sigflag	Boolean used by *sigsuspend*
	u_sigmask[MAXSIG]	Mask of signals held while in catcher
	u_signal[MAXSIG]	Disposition of signals

user structure. Since they are not referenced unless the process is running, they can be safely paged out while another process runs. Each entry in *u_signal[]* represents the action to be taken for a specific signal. For example, *u_signal[SIGINT - 1]* describes the action to be taken upon receipt of *SIGINT*. These actions are user programmable. Assuming signal *n*, they can be specified as follows:

- *Default* — upon receipt of the signal, take the default action.

- *Ignore* — ignore the signal.

- *Handle* — upon receipt of the signal, execute a specified function handler.

4.10.4 System calls for signals

Signal handling services under UNIX System V Release 4 have been adopted from the POSIX specification. However, their implementation remains compatible with signal handling services found in earlier versions of UNIX System V and 4BSD. These signal system calls allow a process to manage, alter or inspect its signal disposition and are described briefly as follows:

- *signal and sigset* —

```
void (*signal(int sig, void (*disp)(int))) (int);
void (*sigset(int sig, void (*disp)(int))) (int);
```

Both of these functions change the disposition of any signal specified in the argument *sig* except *SIGKILL* or *SIGSTOP*. The disposition of *SIGKILL* and *SIGSTOP* always remain with their default values and cannot be changed. If the process tries to change the disposition of these signals, the system call will fail and *errno* is set accordingly. However, if the process tries to block them (*SIG_IGN*), the system silently accepts the request although the request is ignored. Thus, these signals are always guaranteed to be delivered to the process even if the process thinks it has programmed them to be ignored.

The argument *disp* may be *SIG_DFL*, *SIG_IGN* or the address of a signal handling function in user address space. A call to *signal* is the same as calling *sigaction* with *sa_flags* set to *SA_RESETHAND | SA_NODEFER*. The *sigaction* system call is discussed later. When the *signal* system call is used, and the specified signal is caught, the system resets that signal's disposition to its default value before passing control to the user specified signal handler. Therefore, on entry to the signal handler the signal is reset. As far as the kernel is concerned, the signal has been serviced at this point. Once the signal is serviced, any other signal of the same type will take the default action unless a further call to *signal* is made to arrange a different disposition (with the exception of *SIGILL*, *SIGTRAP* and *SIGPWR*, which are never reset).

The *sigset* system call is similar to *signal*. However, with *sigset*, if *disp* is the address of a handling function, then before executing the specified signal handler on receipt of the signal, the system first arranges for other signals of the same type to be masked out while the handler executes. When the handler returns, the disposition of the signal mask for the process is reset so that it is the same as it was before the signal was handled. If *disp* is *SIG_HOLD* (defined in */usr/include/sys/signal.h*), the action taken by this system call is the same as that taken by *sighold* (see below).

Note that neither of these functions are described in the POSIX standard. Programmers writing POSIX compliant programs should use *sigaction* instead.

- *sigprocmask* —

```
int sigprocmask(int how, const sigset_t *set, sigset_t *oset);
```

Every process inherits a copy of its parent's signal mask and the signal mask is defined by the variable *p_hold* within the process's associated *proc* structure. Each non-zero bit in *p_hold* represents a signal type that is currently being blocked from being delivered to the process.

To comply with POSIX, UNIX System V Release 4 now supports *signal-sets* evident in the data type *sigset_t*, which is used to hold a set of signals of some form. In general, an application does not need to know the construction of *sigset_t*. Furthermore, a program should not depend on its underlying construction. A set of library routines that operate with this data object are provided with the operating system. For more information about these functions see *sigsetops(3C)*. With these functions an application can build a signal set for this and other signal system calls to allow it to change or inspect its signal mask. The system call is controlled by the argument *how* as follows:

- *SIG_BLOCK* — the set of signals pointed to by *set* are added to the process's signal mask.
- *SIG_UNBLOCK* — the set of signals pointed to by *set* are removed from the process's signal mask.
- *SIG_SETMASK* — the process's current signal mask is overwritten with the set of signals described in the area pointed to by *set*.

If *oset* is not NULL, the contents of the current signal mask are copied into the area pointed to by *oset* before the signal mask is modified.

- *sigsuspend* —

      int sigsuspend(const sigset_t *set);

The process's current signal mask is overwritten with the set of signals described in the area pointed to by *set*. The process is then suspended with *pause( )* until such time that it is awoken by a signal. However, before this is done, a copy of the current signal mask is saved in the user-area (*u_sigoldmask*) so that it can be restored later when *sigsuspend* returns. This is done by setting a flag (*u_sigflag*) to tell *psig( )* (discussed later) not to overwrite the saved signal mask. At some time the process will be awoken by a signal (unless it is killed, in which case, none of the following occurs). Within *psig( )*, which is called to deliver the signal to the process, *u_sigflag* is tested. If it is already set it is simply reset to zero again, ready for next time. However, the flag being set indicates to *psig( )* that it must not overwrite the contents of *u_sigoldmask* which holds a copy of the saved signal mask (saved by *sigsuspend*). Otherwise, if *u_sigflag* is zero, *u_sigoldmask* is overwritten with the contents of *p_hold*. On return from *sigsuspend* the saved signal mask in *u_sigoldmask* is restored so that the process's signal mask reflects the same signal mask that existed before this system call was called. Obviously, if the process is terminated, *sigsuspend* does not return.

- *sigaltstack* —

      int sigaltstack(int stack_t *ss, stack_t *oss);

Although this service is not a POSIX specified function, it is derived from the 4.3BSD *sigstack( )* system call. In previous versions of UNIX System V signals were always handled by using the process's normal run-time stack. Under UNIX System V Release 4 the *sigaltstack* system service allows a process to specify an alternate stack to be used when handling signals. A program that manages fixed sized run-time stacks can now reliably handle signals on an alternate stack.

The argument *ss* points to a structure of type *sigaltstack* (Table 4.34) which describes the alternate stack environment. On return from the *sigaltstack* system call, the new stack specified in *ss* takes effect. If *oss* is not NULL, the old stack environment is stored in the area it points to.

When a process is first created, *u_sigaltstack* is set to *SS_DISABLE* and *u_sigonstack* is zero. The *sigaction* system call can be used to tag a signal to an alternate stack frame by setting a bit corresponding to the signal that is handled on the alternate stack in *u_sigonstack*.

Table 4.34: *Struct sigaltstack (stack_t)*

Element	Description
int *ss_sp	Stack pointer base address
int ss_size	Size of the stack
int ss_flags	SS_ONSTACK — process is using alternate stack. Attempts to change it while the process executes will fail. SS_DISABLE — there is no current alternate stack.

Table 4.35: *Struct sigaction*

Element	Description
int sa_flags	Flags that modify delivery of the signal
void (*sa_handler)()	SIG_IGN, SIG_DFL, or address of function
sigset_t sa_mask	Set of signals to be blocked while executing handler

- *sigaction —*

```
int sigaction(int sig, const struct sigaction *act,
    struct sigaction *oact);
```

This system call overcomes the limitations of previous releases of the operating system where the only system call supported for signals was *signal*. With *signal*, it was common for C programmers to code the first statement in their signal handler to call *signal* again so that the signal handler could react to further signals while handling the current one. This method was very unreliable since the scheme is prone to race conditions in which signals are sometimes missed. Consider the following program extract:

```
1    catch_sigquit( ) {
2
3         signal(SIGQUIT, catch_sigquit);
4         . . .
5    }
6
7    main( ) {
8         signal(SIGQUIT, catch_sigquit);
..        . . .
..    }
```

A *SIGQUIT* signal arriving at line 2 will cause the process to exit and perhaps leave a *core dump* in the file system. However, there is no fault in this program, just a timing problem. The *signal* system call causes the system to reset the signal to its default action before passing control to the handler. The default action for *SIGQUIT* is to exit and dump core. Therefore, if a *SIGQUIT* signal is currently being handled by the signal handler, and the current flow of execution is at line 2, another *SIGQUIT* signal taken at this point will take the default action.

Unfortunately, when using *signal*, there is no way to block a signal from interrupting a signal handler already in mid-execution from a previously delivered signal. This method of programming is not recommended, although in earlier versions of UNIX this was the only method.

To overcome these problems, UNIX System V Release 4 implements the POSIX defined function *sigaction( )*. This function uses a structure called *sigaction* (Table 4.35) which defines the action (*act*) to be taken when *sig* is delivered to the process. The current actions are saved in *oact* before the new actions take place. The argument *sig* can be any signal specified in Table 4.32. However, *EINVAL* is returned if the specified signal is either *SIGKILL* or *SIGSTOP*.

The POSIX standard defines only *SA_NOCLDSTOP* to be used with the *sa_flags* member although UNIX System V Release 4 defines additional switches that can be logically ORed together. They are as follows:

- *SA_ONSTACK* — the bit representing *sig* is set in *u_sigonstack*. If an alternate stack has been set up with *sigaltstack*, the process will be operating on that stack when *sig* is handled. If no alternate stack has been declared, *sig* is handled on the process's normal stack.

- *SA_RESETHAND* — causes the automatic resetting of signal *sig*. If *sig* is not *SIGILL, SIGTRAP* or *SIGPWR*, the bit representing *sig* is set in *u_sigresethand*. When *sig* is next handled by the process, the disposition of the signal (*u_signal[sig - 1]*) is reset to *SIG_DFL*. Therefore, while executing the signal handler a further delivery of *sig* will interrupt the handler — i.e., the signal is not blocked.

- *SA_NODEFER* — the bit representing *sig* is set in *u_signodefer*. When *sig* is next handled by the process, further signals of the same type will interrupt the handler. Normally, the kernel automatically blocks further signals of the same type while a similar signal is being handled so long as the disposition of the signal was set with *sigset* or *sigaction*.

- *SA_RESTART* — the bit representing *sig* is set in *u_sigrestart*. Once set, if a signal of type *sig* is caught during the execution of a system call, that system call is transparently restarted. If the bit representing *sig* is not set in *u_sigrestart* (default case), and the signal is caught, the interrupted system call returns *EINTR*.

- *SA_SIGINFO* — the bit representing *sig* is set in *p_siginfo*. Normally, when a signal handling function is invoked as the result of delivery of a specified signal, the only argument passed to the handler is the signal number. If *SA_SIGINFO* is set and the signal *sig* is caught, the handling function is given three arguments. Additionally, if another signal of type *sig* is received it is queued. The three arguments passed to the signal handler are: the signal number *sig*, a pointer to a *siginfo* structure, and a pointer to a *ucontext* structure. The *siginfo* structure contains information about why the signal was generated. We will discuss this in more detail later. The *ucontext* structure contains a copy of the user context at the time the signal was delivered. The context can be restored with *setcontext* (§ 4.7).

- *SA_NOCLDWAIT* — if *sig* is *SIGCHLD*, the process's *p_flag* member is marked *SNOWAIT*, meaning that all child processes will exit without leaving a zombie. Furthermore, if any process-related zombies exist, they are removed before *sigaction* returns to the calling process. If the calling process subsequently calls the *wait* system call, *wait* will block until all children have terminated. *wait* then sets *errno* to *ECHILD* and returns -1 to the caller. The *wait* system call is discussed in § 4.15.3.
- *SA_NOCLDSTOP* — if *sig* is *SIGCHLD*, then *SIGCHLD* will not be posted to the process until all its children terminate. However, if a child is stopped or started as the result of job control, then the signal is posted.

In most cases, *sigaction* has to be called once only in the program to set up the signal handler and the actions to be taken on receipt of the signal.

Within the kernel, the body of processing done by *sigaction* is carried out by a function called *setsigact( )*. Its purpose is to install the signal handler for the signal being described (i.e., set up *u_signal[sig - 1]*), and to arrange for specific bits to be set or unset for the signal according to the flags stated in *sa_flags*. For example, if *sa_flags* is set to *SA_SIGINFO* and a signal handler is specified, then the bit representing *sig* in the *p_siginfo* mask is set.

- *sigpending* —

      int sigpending(sigset_t *set);

This system call allows a process to identify the signals that were sent to it but were not delivered because its signal mask caused them to be blocked. The signals that are blocked and pending are placed into the area pointed to by *set*.

- *sighold* —

      int sighold(int sig);

The signal *sig* is added to the process's signal mask.

- *sigrelse* —

      int sigrelse(int sig);

The signal *sig* is removed from the process's signal mask.

- *sigignore* —

      int sigignore(int sig);

The signal *sig* is set to the *SIG_IGN* disposition.

- *sigpause* —

      int sigpause(int sig);

The signal *sig* is removed from the process's signal mask and the process is suspended until a signal is received or the process is terminated (see *pause* in § 4.16).

Figure 4.31: *Algorithm for ssig( )*

```
ssig()
input: sig — signal type to operate on and signal action
       func — address of function handler
output: zero on success, EINVAL on error
{
  if(sig is out of range or non-maskable (i.e., SIGKILL))
    return EINVAL

  switch(system call type) {
    case sighold:
      add signal to signal mask /* p_hold */
      return success
    case sigrelse:
      remove signal from signal mask
      return success
    case sigpause:
      remove signal from signal mask then pause()
      /* never reaches here */
    case sigignore:
      remove signal from signal mask
      set func to SIG_IGN
      break
    case sigset:
      if(signal is currently being blocked)
         set return value to SIG_HOLD
      else
         set return value to previous action /* u_signal[] */
      if(func is SIG_HOLD)
         add signal to signal mask and return success
      remove signal from signal mask
      break
    case signal:
      set return value to previous action  /* u_signal[] */
      break
    default:
      return EINVAL
  }
  call setsigact() to place the new signal action into the
    user area u_signal[sig -1] and adjust user area variables
    u_sigresethand and u_signodefer
}
```

4.10.5 Algorithm *ssig( )*

The following system services: *signal, sigset, sighold, sigrelse, sigignore* and *sigpause*, are implemented via a single system call entry point called *ssig( )* (Figure 4.31). This function is called from *systrap( )* via each system calls associated *sysent[ ]* function pointer. The function arranges for specific bits to be set or cleared within the process's signal mask *p_hold*. It then calls the function *setsigact( )* to carry out the operations required by the POSIX standard. Note that the *signal* system call is provided for backwards compatibility of the same system call in previous versions of the operating system although it does not perform any actions associated with new POSIX compliant signal system calls.

The arguments expected by *ssig( )* are: a pointer to the system call argument list, and a pointer to a return value structure (*rval_t*). The system call itself expects in its arguments: an integer representing the signal type, and the action to take for that signal (for *signal* and *sigset* only). The value of the signal passed to *ssig( )* by the user is stored in the low-order byte of the signal, and the system call number (used to index into *sysent[ ]*) is stored in the high-order byte.

4.10.6 Getting signal information

We mentioned earlier that a process can arrange for a signal handling function to receive three arguments. One of these includes a pointer to a structure of type *siginfo_t*. By using the information in this structure, a process can obtain an explanation of why the signal was generated. Another system call that uses a similar scheme is *waitid*. This system call suspends the process until one of its children changes its state. When this happens, *waitid* returns, after setting a pointer to a *siginfo_t* structure containing the explanation for why the child changed its state (§ 4.15.4).

The *siginfo* structure is complicated because it is made up of a union of several data abstractions. Thus, it is best shown in its coded form as it is defined in <sys/siginfo.h>. Please refer to Appendix C for a listing of that file.

The information in the structure always contains the following variables:

```
int si_signo;   /* generated signal number */
int si_errno;   /* non-zero errno number */
int si_code;    /* reason/cause code */
```

The value of *si_signo* represents the signal type that was generated. If *si_errno* is non-zero, its value represents an *errno* code (Appendix A provides a listing of the error number codes). The *si_code* variable contains a cause-code. A program should first read *si_signo* to find out how to interpret *si_code*. If *si_code* is less than or equal to zero, then the signal was generated by a process running in user-mode. This means that the *siginfo* structure contains the following additional information:

```
pid_t si_pid;   /* Process ID of sending process */
uid_t si_uid;   /* User ID of sending process */
```

If *si_code* is greater than zero then its interpretation depends on the signal received

Table 4.36: *Interpretation of si_code in siginfo structure*

Generated Signal	Cause Code	Description or Reason
SIGILL	*ILL_ILLOPC*	Illegal opcode
	ILL_ILLOPN	Illegal operand
	ILL_ILLADR	Illegal addressing mode
	ILL_ILLTRP	Illegal trap
	ILL_PRVOPC	Privileged opcode
	ILL_PRVREG	Privileged register
	ILL_COPROC	Coprocessor error
	ILL_BADSTK	Internal stack error
SIGFPE	*FPE_INTDIV*	Integer divide by zero
	FPE_INTOVF	Integer overflow
	FPE_FLTDIV	Floating point divide by zero
	FPE_FLTOVF	Floating point overflow
	FPE_FLTUND	Floating point underflow
	FPE_FLTRES	Floating point inexact result
	FPE_FLTINV	Invalid floating point operation
	FPE_FLTSUB	Subscript out of range
SIGSEGV	*SEGV_MAPERR*	Address not mapped to object
	SEGV_ACCERR	Invalid permissions for mapped object
SIGBUS	*BUS_ADRALN*	Invalid address alignment
	BUS_ADRERR	Non-existent physical address
	BUS_OBJERR	Object specific hardware error
SIGTRAP	*TRAP_BRKPT*	Process breakpoint
	TRAP_TRACE	Process trap point
SIGCHLD	*CLD_EXITED*	Child has exited
	CLD_KILLED	Child was killed
	CLD_DUMPED	Child terminated abnormally
	CLD_TRAPPED	Traced child has trapped
	CLD_STOPPED	Child has stopped
	CLD_CONTINUED	Stopped child had continued
SIGPOLL	*POLL_IN*	Data input available
	POLL_OUT	Output buffers available
	POLL_MSG	Input message available
	POLL_ERR	I/O error
	POLL_PRI	High priority input available
	POLL_HUP	Device disconnected

and the value of the cause code identifier, *si_signo* shown in Table 4.36. For more information about *siginfo*, see *siginfo(5)*.

Figure 4.32: *Algorithm for u_trap( )*

```
u_trap()
input: none
output: none
{
  /*
   * called by the kernel trap handler when a trap
   * occurs while operating on the user stack
   */

  inspect the program status word (PSW)
  fill the siginfo structure with reason for the fault

  add the signal to p_sigqueue
  post the signal to the process

  if(issig(process_signals))
      psig()

  update profiling information
  call trap_ret(); /* return to user mode in trap_ret */

  /* impossible to get here */
}
```

4.10.7 Execution errors and signals

When an exception or fault is generated or, in fact, when any of the conditions described in Table 4.36 occur, a trap is generated so that the kernel can handle the situation. For example, if a program in user-mode tries to execute an illegal instruction, its instruction stream is halted and the system posts *SIGILL* to the process. In a case such as this the program would generate an exception error resulting in a user-mode to kernel-mode trap. The kernel's trap handler in *ttrap.s* results in calling *u_trap( )* since the trap occurred while operating on the user stack. Within *u_trap( )* (Figure 4.32), a *siginfo* structure is constructed and queued in the *proc* structure associated with the ailing process. The signal is then posted to the process. The information in the *siginfo* structure explains why the signal was generated.

Signal information structures are queued onto *p_sigqueue* by a function called *sigaddq( )*. The information is stored in the *proc* structure although the fault can occur only while the process executes. The queue maintains only one *siginfo* structure per signal type. Thus, if a *siginfo* structure already exists on the queue with the same signal number as the one being generated, the one on the queue is replaced by the new *siginfo* structure. Naturally, ignored signals are ignored and are not queued.

A process using the *sigaction* system call with the *SA_SIGINFO* switch for a particular signal will enable those signals to be reliably queued for the process, allowing a signal handler to find out why the signal was generated. This information is generated at the time the signal is posted. The signal information structure is removed from the queue when it is handled by the process i.e., within *issig( )*.

4.10.8 Signal processing

So far we have discussed how signals are posted to a process. This section discusses how they are processed (or handled) by the receiver.

There are five signal handling scenarios:

- *terminate* — the process is forced to *exit*. In all cases, a *SIGKILL* signal cannot be caught, ignored or held. It always forces a process to *exit*. Note that a *core image* (§ 4.13.3) is not written to the file system on receipt of this signal.

- *exit* — the process *exits* on receipt of the signal. By default, a process receiving one of the following signals will make it exit (via the same path as the *_exit* system call), and a *core image* of the executing process will be written to the file system: *SIGQUIT, SIGILL, SIGTRAP, SIGIOT, SIGEMT, SIGFPE, SIGBUS, SIGSEGV, SIGSYS, SIGXCPU,* and *SIGXFSZ*.

- *ignore* — the process ignores the signal and no action is taken. The following signals are ignored by default: *SIGCONT, SIGCHLD, SIGPWR, SIGWINCH,* and *SIGURG*. A process wishing to catch a signal on the death of its child (*SIGCHLD*) must use the *wait* system call. It is not possible for a process to ignore *SIGKILL* or *SIGSTOP*.

- *handle* — the process has arranged to pass control to a specified handling function on receipt of the signal. In general, once a process has handled a signal the signal is reset so that another signal of the same type can be received. However, the following signals, once received, can never be reset: *SIGILL, SIGTRAP,* and *SIGPWR*.

- *stop* — by default, a process is stopped on receipt of one of the following signals: *SIGSTOP, SIGTSTP, SIGTTOU,* and *SIGTTIN*. However, a process cannot catch, ignore or hold the *SIGSTOP* signal.

As mentioned earlier, in order for a process to handle signals that are pending for it, it must be mapped in as the currently running process executing in kernel-mode.

Signals are checked and handled as a process returns to user-mode from kernel-mode via a trap handling function — for example, *systrap( ), u_trap( )* and *k_trap( )*, and within the kernel's interrupt handling routines. Furthermore, if the process voluntarily goes to sleep at an interruptable priority level, signals are

Figure 4.33: *Algorithm for issig( )*

```
issig()
input: why — flag to indicate if only testing for
       signals, or if processing is to be done also.
output: integer — zero if no signals or the lowest numbered
       signal pending that is neither ignored or blocked
{

next_sig:
  get the next non-ignored non-held pending signal from p_sig

  if(there is no pending signal)
    return 0

  if ( the signal is ignored ) {
    remove its info structure from the signal queue
    goto next_sig
  }

  if only testing for pending signals
    return sig

  remove signal from p_sig
  make it current in p_cursig

  /* no point in keeping it on the */
  /* queue since it is current now */
  remove it from the queue

  return sig

}
```

checked before and after a context switch within *sleep( )*. Remember that signals are checked twice within *sleep( )* if the process sleeps at an interruptible priority level (§ 4.6.14).

The most frequent method used for checking signals within the kernel code is as follows:

```
        if(ISSIG(proc, why))
            psig();
```

The function *ISSIG( )* is actually a macro defined in *proc.h*. It results in calling *issig( )* (Figure 4.33) after conducting a few simple sanity checks — *issig( )* is not necessarily an expensive function to execute but there is no need for unnecessary calls to it. For this reason, a macro is used to check first that there are, in fact, signals to process before calling *issig( )* to possibly process them.

The purpose of *issig( )* is to find the next lowest signal posted to the process that is neither ignored nor blocked. The *why* argument is the only argument passed to *issig( )*. It tells the function that the caller is either testing only for signals and so no signal processing is to be done, or that it should process a pending signal if it is found. In other words, if the caller specifies that it is only testing for signals, all that *issig( )* must do is return zero if there are no signals, or non-zero (the lowest signal number) if there are. On the other hand, if the caller specifies that a pending signal should be processed, then a signal that is found is dealt with — its corresponding bit in *p_sig* is cleared and the signal number is placed into *p_cursig* since this is the current signal being handled. The signal information structure for the posted signal is then removed from its queue and placed onto *p_curinfo*. The signal number is eventually returned to the caller, telling it that a signal was found and possibly processed. The calling function, satisfied that a signal is pending, normally calls *psig( )* to deliver the signal.

4.10.9 Algorithm *psig( )*

psig( ) is responsible for carrying out the action specified by the current signal (*p_cursig*) — for example, invoking its signal handler. When *psig( )* (Figure 4.34) is called, the bit corresponding to the signal in *p_sig* is already clear, and the current signal number is stored in *p_cursig*. An explanation for the signal being generated is stored in *p_curinfo*. This information is later used by *sendsig( )* to fill in a *siginfo* structure which is passed to the user-mode signal handler for inspection (see *SA_SIGINFO* in § 4.10.4).

If *SIGKILL* is pending when *psig( )* is called it is serviced first since this signal takes precedence over all others.

If the signal's disposition is not set to its default action, *psig( )* assumes that the user has organised for it to be handled. It also assumes that the signal is not being ignored, for if it were, *issig( )* would have failed and *psig( )* would not have been called.

psig( ) holds signals that aren't already being deferred. So any signals that are received by the process that are of the same type are automatically blocked while the current signal is being serviced.

Eventually, the signal is passed to *sendsig( )* which is responsible for building an activation record for the signal handler on the user stack — note that *sendsig( )* is machine dependent. If the user used the *sigaction( )* system call and specified *SA_SIGINFO* in the *sa_flags* member of the *sigaction* structure argument, it means that the user has requested the handler to receive additional information about why the signal was generated. In this case, the bit corresponding to the signal in *p_siginfo* will be set. If this is so, then *sendsig( )* arranges for a *siginfo* structure to be passed as the second argument to the handling function. *sendsig( )* also saves a copy of the user context (*ucontext_t*) and passes that to the handling function as its third argument (see *sigaction* for more information).

Figure 4.34: *Algorithm for psig( )*

```
psig()
input: none
output: none
{
  if( SIGKILL is pending )
    set current signal to SIGKILL
    /* SIGKILL overrides all other signals */

  /* assume that the signal is not ignored */
  if( not default disposition for the signal ) {
    if( the signal is not being deferred )
        hold and block out further signals of this type
        - during handler execution

    call sendsig() to execute user specified signal handler
    /* signal handler returns here */

    free memory associated with any set siginfo structure
    clear p_cursig and p_curinfo

    if sendsig() failed to build a stack frame for signal handler
        set current signal to SIGSEGV
    else
        return /* success - signal is posted */
  }

  /* process must be killed */

  create a dump file in the file system if the current signal
    - dumps core /* i.e., SIGSEGV */

  free memory associated with any set siginfo structure
  clear p_cursig and p_curinfo

  call exit() to end process and tidy up execution environment
}
```

If an alternate stack is arranged for the signal handler to operate on, it is set up before the process is returned to user-mode to allow the handling function to execute. When the handling function returns, execution continues at the point in the process's instruction stream where it was interrupted by the signal.

Once the signal has been processed, *psig( )* tidies up. This involves resetting *p_cursig* and freeing any memory that may be associated with a *siginfo* structure for the now posted signal. If *sendsig( )* failed to build a stack frame for the handling function, the current signal is set to *SIGSEGV*. *SIGSEGV* defaults to dumping core (see § 4.13.3), so in this case the process is automatically *core dumped* and *exit( )* is called to tidy up the execution environment and terminate the process (§ 4.15.2).

4.10.10 System calls for posting signals

Three system calls are provided by the operating system to allow a process to send a signal to a process or a group of related processes. They are *kill, sigsend* and *sigsendset*. However, *sigsend* and *sigsendset* are implemented under one system call handler in the kernel called *sigsendsys( )*. The system call *sigsend* is not in fact a system call per se, but a C library function that directly calls *sigsendsys* after building a *procset_t* structure from the user-supplied arguments (we will discuss this in detail shortly). Thus, there are really only two entry points for all three of these system calls: *kill* and *sigsendsys*. To make things even more complicated, both system call handlers call an internal function named *sigsendset* to finally perform their services. Throughout the following discussion we will refer to *sigsend* and *sigsendset* as *sigsendsys* unless stated otherwise.

The traditional UNIX System V system call for this type of service is *kill* and under UNIX System V Release 4 this system call is by far the simplest to use. However, it is less versatile than *sigsendsys*. Note, however, that *kill* and *sigsendsys* do not form part of the POSIX standard, although *kill* is required by the standard C Language. Thus, if you are writing portable C programs you should use *kill*. The semantics for *kill* are as follows:

```
int kill( pid_t pid, int sig );
```

In general, the argument *pid* specifies the process ID of the process to send signal *sig*. However, many switches to this system call depend on the value of *pid*. For example, if *pid* is zero, then *sig* is sent to all processes whose process group ID is equal to the calling process. For more information, see *kill(2)*.

The system call *sigsendset* is an alternate system call for sending a signal to "sets" of processes:

```
int sigsendset( procset_t *psp, int sig );
```

The argument *psp* points to a *procset* structure (Table 4.37) which may seem complex at first sight but is really very simple to use. Rather than explain how it is used, we have presented an example. We have emulated the *kill* system call by using *sigsendset* (see Figure 4.35). Note that in our example a macro called *setprocset( )* is used which takes as its arguments a set of values with which to populate a *procset_t* structure. This macro is also defined within *<sys/procset.h>*. Incidentally, the constant *P_MYPID* is defined in *<sys/types.h>*. An *id* of *P_MYPID* means that the value of *id* is taken from the calling process's PID.

Table 4.37: *Struct procset (procset_t)*

Element		Description
idop_t	p_op	Specifics the operation to be performed on both left and right sets of processes
idtype_t	p_lidtype	ID type of the left set of processes
id_t	p_lid	ID of the left set of processes
idtype_t	p_ridtype	ID type of the right set of processes
id_t	p_rid	ID of the right set of processes
Type	**Enumeration**	**Description**
idop_t	POP_DIFF	Set difference: processes in left set and not in right set
	POP_AND	Set disjunction: processes in both left and right sets
	POP_OR	Set conjunction: processes in either left or right set or both sets
	POP_XOR	Set exclusive-or: processes in either set but not both
idtype_t	P_PID	*sig* is sent to process ID
	P_PPID	*sig* is sent to the parent process of process ID
	P_PGID	*sig* is sent to all processes with process group ID
	P_SID	*sig* is sent to all processes with session ID
	P_CID	*sig* is sent to all processes with scheduling class ID
	P_UID	*sig* is sent to all processes with an effective user ID
	P_GID	*sig* is sent to all processes with an effective group ID
	P_ALL	*sig* is sent to all processes (ID is ignored)

4.11 User, process, process group and session relationships

The system uses several data structures to bond a relationship between the user, his or her working environment, the device in which he or she is logged on to, the process and its children, and the process itself. These data structures are referenced by pointers in the *proc* structure (Table 4.38) discussed in the following sections.

4.11.1 Parents, children and siblings

All processes are children, and as with humans, all those that have born children are parents. If a process does not create a child then obviously it is not a parent. A process creates a child by calling the *fork* system call (discussed later).

Technically speaking, there is only ever one child per process — the first-born. All other children created by a parent are known as siblings. However, as far as the user is concerned, all processes created by a parent are children. There is no distinction between the first-born or last-born child.

The bond between parent, child and sibling is made by using three pointers defined in the *proc* structure (Table 4.38) so that a process maintains its own linked

Figure 4.35: *An implementation of kill(2) using the sigsendset system call*

```
#include <sys/types.h>
#include <sys/signal.h>
#include <sys/procset.h>
#include <sys/errno.h>

extern int errno;

int kill( pid, sig )
pid_t pid;
int sig;
{
    procset_t psp;
    idtype_t  idtype;
    id_t      id;

    if(sig < 0 || sig >= NSIG) {
        errno = EINVAL;
        return -1;
    }

    if (pid > 0) {
        idtype = P_PID;
        id = (id_t)pid;
    }
    else if (pid == 0) {
        idtype = P_PGID;
        id = (id_t)getpgrp();

    }
    else if (pid == -1) {
        idtype = P_ALL;
        id = P_MYID;

    }
    else { /* uap->pid < -1 */
        idtype = P_PGID;
        id = (id_t)(-pid);
    }

    setprocset( &psp, POP_AND, idtype, id, P_ALL, P_MYID );
    return sigsendset( &psp, sig );
}
```

Table 4.38: *Various pointers in the proc structure*

Element	Description
struct pid *p_pidp	Process ID information
struct pid *p_pgidp	Process group ID information
struct sess *p_sessp	Session information
struct cred *p_cred	Credentials information
struct proc *p_pglink	Process group chain link
struct proc *p_parent *struct proc *p_child* *struct proc *p_sibling*	Process group list management

list of its children and siblings.

The example in Figure 4.36 shows eight processes split up into three process groups. The first group consists of processes 1, 2, 3 and 5, the second group consists of processes 2, 4 and 6, and the third group consists of processes 6, 7 and 8. The parent of the first group is process 1, the parent of the second group is process 2, and the parent of the third group is process 6. In all three groups, only the parent's *p_child* member is assigned and it points to the first-born. All other children are linked via their *p_sibling* members. Additionally, each process has a pointer, *p_parent*, which links directly to its parent process. Unless a sibling has a child of its own, its *p_child* member is *NULL*. Finally, the parent process of each group and the last process in the chain of each group have *NULL p_sibling* pointers, so the kernel can go through a process group list starting with *p_child* and on through each sibling with *p_sibling*. If either of these pointers is equal to *NULL*, the end of the list has been reached.

All processes in the running system are connected to each other by process group lists such as those shown in Figure 4.36.

4.11.2 Process identification (PID)

All processes are given a unique integer called a Process ID (PID), which is used by both kernel and user to identify a process. For example, the *kill* system call requires in its calling parameters the PID of the process to send the signal to. Similarly, the kernel's *psignal( )* function also needs to know the PID of the process it must send the signal to.

PIDs range between 0 and 29,999 inclusive and the system assigns them from an incremental counter called *mpid*. If the counter reaches *MAXPID* (30,000) it is reset to the value stored in *minpid* (discussed in a moment).

When a process is created, a new PID is assigned to it. The value for the PID is taken from the value stored in *mpid*. If it is found that a process already exists (active, swapped, zombie, or otherwise) with the same PID as the value in *mpid*, the system simply increments *mpid* until a free PID is found. Once a PID has been assigned to a process, that process owns the PID and remains with it throughout its life until it is fully terminated. The system never changes a PID once assigned, nor

Figure 4.36: *Relationship between parent, child and sibling*

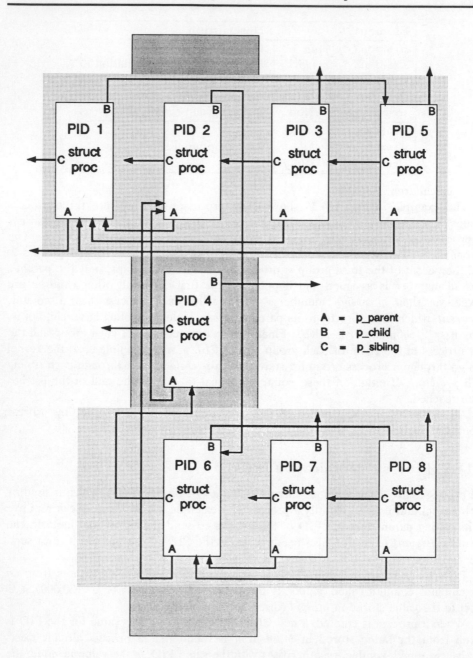

are there any system calls to allow the user to change a PID.

The four system processes: *sched, pageout, fsflush* and *kmdaemon*, are the first processes to start when the system boots (§ 4.17.1). They are assigned PIDs 0-3 inclusive and remain running for as long as the operating system runs. For each system process started at boot time, the variable *minpid* is incremented. Thus, the value of *minpid* is typically 4 although it is implementation dependent since some vendors may also start their own system processes at boot time. From this, it can be seen that the range of PIDs assigned by the system during normal operation is really between *minpid* and *MAXPID-1* inclusive.

When the system assigns a PID to a process, it does so by allocating it a *pid* structure (Table 4.39). The process's *p_pidp* member is then set to point to this area which holds, among several other pieces of information, the process's unique PID (*pid_id*).

Table 4.39: *Struct pid*

Element	Description
unsigned int pid_prinactive :1	Process active flag
unsigned int pid_pgorphaned :1	Process is orphaned flag
unsigned int pid_ref :6	Reference counter
unsigned int pid_prslot :24	Index into */proc* table
pid_t pid_id	Unique process ID
*struct proc *pid_pglink*	Assigned if a process group leader
*struct pid *pid_link*	Link for chain of hashed *pid* structures

To save the kernel from recursively scanning through each *pid* structure each time a *pid* is to be referenced, the system maintains an array of *HASHSZ* (64) *pid* structure pointers called *pidhash*. Each element in the array forms the head of a linked list which the system hashes onto (modulo 64), using the PID as the index:

```
#define HASHPID(pid)      ( pidhash[( pid & ( HASHSZ - 1 ) )] )
```

Each *pid* structure in a list is linked via its *pid_link* member. Thus, to find the *pid* structure for a given PID, the system first hashes the PID to find the correct list and then traverses through it using *pid_link*.

4.11.3 Process groups and job control

The kernel often has to identify processes that are related to each other by a common ancestor. Such processes are collectively called a *process group*. The kernel needs to identify processes in a process group so that they can all be notified of certain events — for example, signals generated by the terminal driver (and presumably by the user). Such signals are delivered to all processes in a group. For example, if the user presses the *delete* key, then *SIGINT* is generated and delivered to all processes that are multiplexed to the user's login device. Such processes are all part of a single login session (discussed in a moment) and form part of a process group. Similarly, a job-control-stop (*SIGTSTP*) generated at the terminal is delivered to all processes running in the background (§ 7.11.2). Consider the following command line:

```
% cat myfile.nr | pic | tbl | troff -ms | lp &
```

By using the **csh(1)**, these processes (**cat, pic, tbl, troff** and **lp**) are arranged into their own process group. The user is presented with another command line prompt to work with while these processes execute concurrently in the background.

If the user presses the Control-Z keyboard sequence, the terminal driver posts a *SIGTSTP* to the process group. The result is that all processes in that process group are suspended. The user can restart them at any time by typing the command interpreter sequence to bring them back into the foreground, which makes the terminal driver post *SIGCONT* to the process group.

Process groups are also used by the terminal driver to determine whether a process has permission to read or write to a terminal. When a process tries to write to the terminal, the terminal driver tests the calling process to see if it is in the same process group as the shell controlling the terminal. If not, access may be denied. Since background processes run in a different process group, the **csh** can control them. Background processes trying to write to the terminal generate *SIGTTIN*, while background processes trying to read from the terminal generate *SIGTTOU* if the *TOSTOP* bit is set (§ 7.11.2). The **csh** receives this signal and determines its actions accordingly. Thus, process groups are used exclusively for the distribution of signals to a group of related processes.

A process group is headed by a *process group leader*. The PID of the process group leader is also referred to as the *Process Group ID* (PGID). There is no variable set aside to hold the PGID, although from the user's point of view all processes belonging to a process group are referenced by it (we shall see why in a moment). The distinction between PID and PGID is done via pointers in the *proc* structure. The *p_pidp* pointer points to the process's private *pid* structure containing its own unique PID. The *p_pgidp* pointer points to the process group leader's *pid* structure containing its PID which also happens to be the group's PGID. Thus, a process inherits its PGID from its parent and processes within a process group retain their own unique process ID in addition to their hypothetical PGID.

Processes that are ancestors of a login shell are related by being in the same process group. They normally have the same PGID as their parent, although as we shall see later a process sometimes changes its PGID to that of another.

Processes in a group are linked together on a circular linked list headed by the process group leader. The group leader is the common ancestor. Its pointer, *pid_pglink*, points to the first process in the process group list. All other processes in the group list are linked together via their *p_pglink* members (Figure 4.37).

We previously mentioned that the kernel uses the *signal( )* function to send a signal to a group of processes. One parameter required by this function is the PGID of processes that the signal will be sent to. To find each process in the group, the PGID is hashed to find its associated *pid* list. The list is then searched until a matching *pid_id* is found. It can be assumed that the *pid* structure containing the matching *pid_id* belongs to the process group leader. By using this, the kernel can traverse the list posting the specified signal to each process found. Of course, the

Figure 4.37: *Tracing a process group ID*

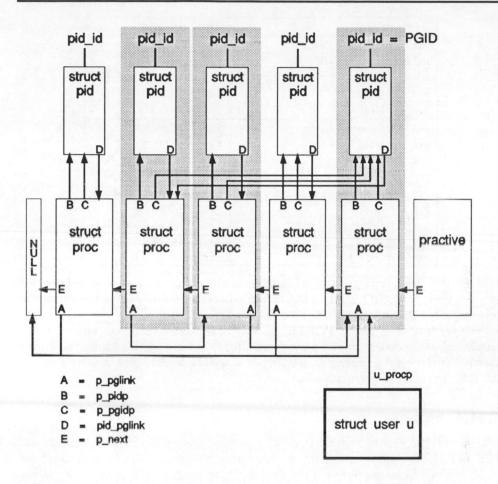

action taken upon delivery depends on how the individual process handles the signal.

The example in Figure 4.37 shows the process group leader as the *currently running process*. Its *pid* structure member *pid_pglink* points to the first *proc* structure in the group. If it points to the *proc* structure belonging to itself the process is the only one in the group. In the example, this is not the case. Thus, each following *proc* structure in the group is linked via its *p_pglink* member. The last *proc* structure in the group points back to the process group leader.

If a process group leader terminates before its children, then each of its children is sent *SIGCHLD*. By default, this signal is ignored, but because the parent has died, they become orphaned (*pid_pgorphaned* is non-zero). An orphaned process is automatically adopted by Process 1 (**init**; see § 4.17.1) so its parent process ID (*p_ppid*) becomes equal to 1.

A process can change its PGID with the *setpgid* or *setpgrp* system calls (see Table 4.40). *setpgid* is used to set the PGID of process *pid* to *pgid*. If both *pid* and

Table 4.40: *Various ID getting and setting system calls*

System Call	Description
int setuid(uid_t uid)	Set user ID
int setgid(gid_t gid)	Set group ID
int setpgid(pid_t pid, pid_t pgid)	Set process group ID
pid_t setpgrp( )	Set process group ID
pid_t setsid( )	Set session ID
uid_t getuid( )	Get real user ID
gid_t getgid( )	Get real group ID
uid_t geteuid( )	Get effective user ID
gid_t getegid( )	Get effective group ID
pid_t getppid( )	Get parent process ID
pid_t getpid( )	Get process ID
pid_t getpgid(pid_t pid)	Get process group ID
pid_t getpgrp( )	Get process group ID
pid_t getsid(pid_t pid)	Get session ID

pgid are the same, then process *pid* becomes a process group leader. If *pid* is equal to zero, then the PGID is set to the calling process's PID. If *pgid* is zero, then the process with a PID of *pid* becomes the process group leader.

setpgrp is used to set the PGID to the PID of the calling process. However, this system call is dependent on the process not already being a session leader (described shortly). If the calling process is not already a session leader, then *setpgrp* releases the calling process's control terminal.

4.11.4 Sessions

A session is the relationship between all processes that multiplex to a login device. The user's login shell is usually the *session leader*, so a session leader is the ancestor of all processes created during a login session. The program responsible for *forking* and *execing* the user's login shell (see **ttymon(1M)**) arranges for the login shell to run in its own session and process group (by default, a session leader is also a process group leader; however, it should be understood that a process group leader is not necessarily a session leader). A session structure, *sess*, describes the controlling terminal and user environment associated with a process that runs on that login device (Table 4.41).

A process is associated with one session only via its *p_sessp* pointer. As with process group information, session information is inherited from its parent when the process is created. All processes in a session have *p_sessp* pointers that point to their parent's session structure, but only one session structure exists for all processes in that session (see Figure 4.38). As well as describing the characteristics of the device and the user controlling it, the session structure also maintains a pointer to the *pid* structure containing the session ID for all processes in the session. It also contains a pointer to the special file's *vnode* structure (§ 6.3), and a pointer to the

Table 4.41: *Struct sess (sess_t)*

Element	Description
short s_ref	Reference count
short s_mode	tty's current permissions
uid_t s_uid;	tty's current user ID
gid_t s_gid;	tty's current group ID
ulong s_ctime	tty's modification time
dev_t s_dev;	tty's device number
*vnode_t *s_vp*	tty's *vnode*
*struct pid *s_sidp*	Session ID info
*cred_t *s_cred*	Allocation credentials

credentials structure describing the user associated with the session (discussed in a moment).

The reason for having yet another pointer to a *pid* structure within the session structure is to allow the use of a *Session ID* (SID) which is used by the *setsid* system call. Since all processes in a single session have their *p_sessp* pointers pointing to their parent's session structure, the parent's *p_sessp->s_sidp* pointer points to the *pid* structure containing the parent's PID. Like the PGID, this integer is also used as the SID. The system call *setsid* can be used by a process that is not already a process group leader to set the PGID and session identification (SID) of the calling process to the calling process's PID. If successful, the calling process's controlling terminal is released.

When a user logs off the system, his login shell terminates. However, there may be other processes running in the background that are multiplexed to the same device that the user was logged in to. The system uses the SID to relate to processes that are associated with a login device. Since the user has logged off, each of these processes must be notified of the event. The system sends *SIGHUP* to all processes in the process group to signify that the user has finished his session.

The kernel implements a single system call handler called *setpgrp( )* to handle all of the following system calls: *setpgrp, setsid, setpgid, getpgrp, getsid* and *getpgid*. At the user level, these system calls set a flag so that the correct channel of processing performed corresponds to the system call being called.

For more information on the semantics and use of these system calls, refer to Section 2 in [AT&T 1990a].

4.11.5 Process credentials

Each process has a pointer to a *cred* structure called *p_cred* (Table 4.42). This data structure contains the *credentials* of the process while it executes (Figure 4.39). By default, a process executed by a user is executed in the context of that user. In other words, a process executes with specific access permissions. However, the access bits in the *a.out* file's *inode* specify whose context the program will execute with. For example, if the file's *inode* specifies that the file is to be executed with an effective

Figure 4.38: *Tracing a session ID*

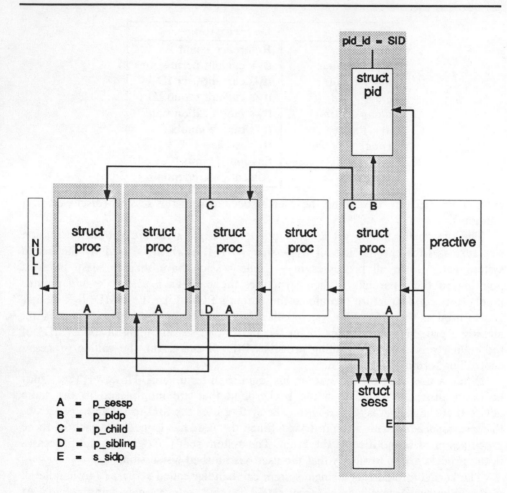

A = p_sessp
B = p_pidp
C = p_child
D = p_sibling
E = s_sidp

user ID set to the owner of the file, then the system must arrange permission for that program to act as if the owner of the file is executing it. This paradigm is called *Set User ID* or SUID on execution, and was patented by Dennis Ritchie in 1979 [Ritchie 1979]. A similar scheme is also used for the Group ID, and is called *Set Group ID* or SGID.

The User ID (UID) and Group ID (GID) of a process are inherited from its parent when it is created. These values are obtained from the */etc/passwd* file and are set up at the beginning of a session (typically by the login procedure). They are handed down to each process in a session and default to the user and group IDs of the session leader. These are referred to as the *real* user and group IDs. By default, the *effective* user and group IDs are set to the *real* user and group IDs on execution. However, if the file's access permissions specify that the file is to be executed with SUID or SGID, the effective user and group IDs are set to the owner

Figure 4.39: *Pointers to the credentials structure*

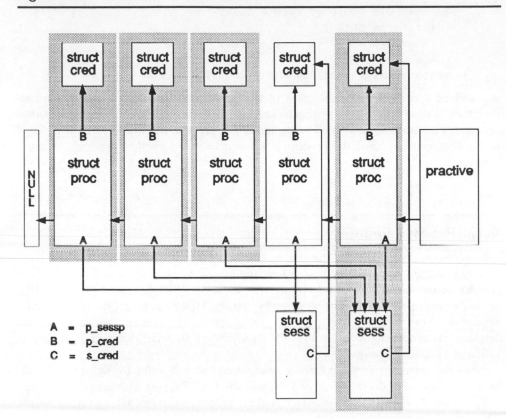

A = p_sessp
B = p_cred
C = s_cred

Table 4.42: *Struct cred (cred_t)*

Element	Description
ushort cr_ref	Reference count
ushort cr_ngroups	Number of groups in *cr_groups*
uid_t cr_uid	Effective user id
gid_t cr_gid	Effective group id
uid_t cr_ruid	Real user id
gid_t cr_rgid	Real group id
uid_t cr_suid	Saved user id (from *exec*)
gid_t cr_sgid	Saved group id (from *exec*)
gid_t cr_groups[1]	Supplementary group list

or owner's group of the file during its execution. The algorithm is as follows:

```
exec_UID = real UID
exec_GID = real GID
```

```
if( file is SUID )
    exec_UID = UID of file's owner
if( file is SGID )
    exec_GID = GID of file's owner

execute using exec_UID and exec_GID
```

As well as specifying the credentials of the process as it executes, the credentials structure is also used by the system to enforce the permission requirements of other services. For example, it is used to decide if the process is allowed to send a signal to another process, or if the process is allowed to share another process's memory segment.

4.12 Process creation

All processes are created by the system call called *fork* except for system processes that are started from *main( )* at system initialization. A system call called *vfork*, derived from 4.3BSD, is also provided for creating new processes in a way that makes efficient use of the virtual memory system. However, note that *vfork* may be removed from future releases of the operating system because system implementation changes to the operating system are showing that *fork* is almost as efficient as *vfork* anyway.

For the purposes of the following discussions, we will refer to both system calls as *fork* unless stated otherwise, and we will discuss "Process Management" related subjects only. Further discussions related to process creation are discussed in the "Memory Management" section.

There is no way to create a process other than using *fork*. The new process is called a *child* (although it may be a *sibling*; § 4.11.1). The child is given its own *proc, user, cred* and *pid* structures and possibly a *sess* structure if it is a new session leader. Almost all of the variables and data structures associated with the parent are inherited by the child. That is, the system automatically initializes the child's data structures from the contents of its parent's. Certain accounting variables in the child's user-area are initialized, the child's unique PID is assigned to it, and the child's parent-PID (PPID) is initialized.

Once the new process is created, its *swappable* image is almost an exact mirror of its parent. This includes the *text, data* and *stack* segments. The system achieves this by giving the child a copy of its parent's page tables. However, the actual pages of data are not copied. Instead, the parent's page tables, and the child's data and stack pages are marked copy-on-write, and both parent and child share the parent's pages (the text page is never modified, thus it does not need to be marked as such). If either parent or child attempts to modify a copy-on-write page, a protection fault occurs which results in the page then being copied to a newly allocated page of memory. This scheme prevents unneccessary copying of pages every time a process is *forked*. Supposing the child calls *exec* (§ 4.13) immediately after the *fork* — there is no need to copy the parent's pages since the data space of the child will reflect the new program image. This is discussed in more detail later.

When the *fork* system call returns to user-mode, there are two processes instead of one and both processes continue execution from the point where *fork* returns, giving the illusion that both processes have just called *fork*. The next instruction executed by both processes is the one that comes after returning from the *fork* system call in the user text.

The novice C programmer often finds this system call confusing, but it is really quite simple. It should be assumed by the programmer that *fork* creates a child process in the image of its parent except that its own PID and its parent's PID differ. In a C program, *fork* returns the PID of the child to the parent, and it returns zero to the child. Therefore, the printf( ) statement within the braces of the following example is executing in the context of the child:

```
printf("parent here\n");

if( fork() == 0 ) {
    printf("child here\n");
}

printf("parent here\n");
```

This paradigm allows the program to determine easily whether it is executing as the parent or the child after calling *fork*, by testing the system call return value.

4.12.1 Algorithm *fork1( )*

Like all other system calls, the *fork* system call handlers are called by *systrap( )* via their system call entry points in the *sysent[ ]* table.

The internal system call handlers for both *fork( )* and *vfork( )* are named after their user-mode system call library names. However, both functions do nothing else but call *fork1( )* to do the actual processing. Thus, *fork1( )* is the common routine for handling both system calls (see Figure 4.40).

The function of *fork1( )* (see Figure 4.41) is to call *newproc( )* to do the process creating tasks. Upon successful completion of *newproc( )*, both parent and child processes return to *fork1( )*, which in turn returns to *fork( )* or *vfork( )*, and then back to *systrap( )*, and finally back to user-mode via the trap return handler in *ttrap.s*. Note that *newproc( )* returns 1 in the context of the child and zero in the context of the parent, whereas, the *fork* system call does the opposite. That is, it returns zero in the context of the child and non-zero (the PID of the new child) in the context of the parent. When *fork* returns to user-mode, the user-mode library function, *fork.s* translates the return information generated by the system call in kernel-mode to the calling function in the user text in user-mode.

4.12.2 Algorithm *newproc( )*

Both *fork( )* and *vfork( )* eventually call *newproc( )* via *fork1( )*. *newproc( )* is the kernel's version of *fork* which performs the many tasks required to create a new

Figure 4.40: *fork( ) and vfork( ) flow of execution*

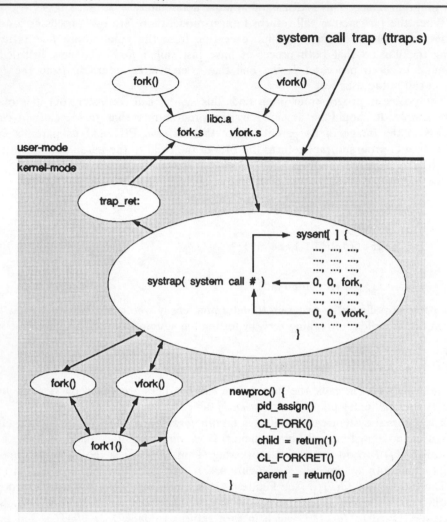

process. *newproc( )* is passed a conditional flag (Table 4.43) which directs the processing and indicates who the caller is. For example, if *newproc( )* is called from within *main( )* of the kernel's text, the new process being created is a system process initialized during system boot. In this case, the flag passed to *newproc( )* is *NP_SYSPROC* or *NP_INIT*. Once the system is running, however, *newproc( )* is generally only ever called as the result of a *fork* or *vfork* system call. The flag *NP_FAILOK* tells *newproc( )* that a failure to create the child should require just a clean-up and a return of -1 to the calling process. If this flag is not set, the system is paniced (halted) leaving a message on the system console.

The algorithm for *newproc( )* is shown in Figure 4.42. A system tuneable parameter called *NPROC* specifies the maximum number of active processes the

Figure 4.41: *Algorithm for fork1( )*

```
fork1()
input: rvp — pointer to a return value structure
output: zero on success, EAGAIN on error
{
    int error = 0;

    increment system accounting for fork system calls

    switch( newproc(&error) ) {
        case 1: /* child */
            setup return value r_val1 to PPID
            setup return value r_val2 to 1 /* meaning child */
            initialize child's accounting information in the user area
            break;

        case 0: /* parent */
            setup return value r_val1 to new PID
            setup return value r_val2 to 0 /* meaning parent */
            break;

        default: /* newproc failed */
            error = EAGAIN
            break;
    }
    return(error);
}
```

system can run at any one time. Another tuneable parameter called *MAXUP* specifies the maximum number of active processes a user (not super-user) can run with at any one time. The system must determine if the user can *fork* a new process given his or her restricted environment and the overall resources of the system. It does this by maintaining a global variable called *nproc* which is incremented for each successful call to *newproc()*, and decremented for each successful call to *freeproc()* (§ 4.15.5). *nproc* is never allowed to go beyond the configurable maximum. If an attempt is made to go beyond *NPROC*, the *fork* fails. Interestingly, a similar test is done for *MAXUP*. If the user tries to *fork* too many processes, the fork fails. However, rather than keep a count of active processes per session, the test is done for all active processes that are running by that user even if they are split up into different login sessions. For example, assume that *MAXUP* is, say, 64. A user can login to several terminals but will only be allowed to run 64 processes in total between all his login sessions.

Assuming that the calling process is allowed to create a new child, a new *proc* and *pid* structures are allocated to it. A function called *procdup()* is called to

Figure 4.42: *Algorithm for newproc( )*

```
newproc()
input: flags — conditional processing flags (see Table 4.43)
       pidp — pointer to area for storing new PID of child
      perror — pointer to area to store error value
output: 0 on success in parent process
        1 on success in child process
        -1 on error
{

  if maximum number of active processes in system are running
     - or if not super user and maximum number of processes for
     - this process running
     return error

  allocate memory for new proc and pid structures
  assign next unused PID from mpid /* for child's p_pid */
  insert the new process into /proc directory entry
  hash the PID onto pidhash /* see section 4.11.2 */
  mark the new process SIDL and place it on the practive list
  mark child SLOAD /* loaded in core */
  increment nproc

  inherit the following from parent:
     credentials,
     signal information,
     job control flags, /* SJCTL | SNOWAIT */
     session information,
     parents stack information,
     cpu priority level and priority class

  set p_clktim to zero /* do not inherit pending alarm() time */
  add child to parent's process group

  if( the new child is a system-process ) {
     mark child SSYS | SLOCK so that it cannot be swapped
     set p_exec to NULL /* no associated a.out file */
  } else
     inherit parent's a.out file

  if( child is not a system process )
     inherit /proc signal and system call tracing flags
  else
     initialize child's signal mask
```

```
    call priority class dependent CL_FORK() routine
    place child on parent's child-sibling list

    /* parent's open files are available to the child */
    for ( each open file in parent (u_nofiles) )
        increment open file reference count /* f_count */

    increment reference count in vnode for both
      - current and root directory

    /* call procdup() to duplicate parent's memory image in child */
    /* procdup is machine dependent */
    switch( procdup( child, parent ) ) {
        case 0: /* PARENT RESUMES HERE */
            break;

        case 1: /* CHILD RESUMES HERE */
            /* child is switched in for first time in procdup() */
            child has PID of parent in pidp
            inherit semaphores and shared memory segments from parent
            return success in child

        default: /* fork failed */
            reverse engineer all of the above
            return error
    }

    /* PARENT PROCESS ONLY AT THIS POINT */

    mark child SRUN /* child is queued and ready to run */

    call CL_FORKRET() to decide if parent or child is to run first
    parent returns PID of child in pidp

    if( child is not a system process )
        increment reference count in vnode for a.out program file

    return success in parent
}
```

duplicate the parent process's memory image in the child so that it can resume execution in *procdup( )* (as did its parent) the very first time it is switched in. Thus, it must arrange for the child to look as though it had been context switched out with *swtch( )*.

Table 4.43: *Conditional flags for newproc( ) (defined in <sys/proc.h>)*

Constant	Description
NP_FAILOK	Do not panic if process cannot be created
NP_NOLAST	Do not use last process slot
NP_SYSPROC	System (resident) process
NP_INIT	This is the /sbin/init process
NP_VFORK	Share address space — vfork
NP_SHARE	Share address space — asyncio

procdup( ) is very machine dependent since it must manipulate the hardware registers. A copy of all the registers are saved and the address space is duplicated. If the system call is a *vfork*, the address space is shared between parent and child and so there is no copying to be done. The child's context is built; this may involve saving a copy of the memory address unit (MAU) registers and duplicating the parent's *ufchunk* list (§ 6.2.1). Finally, the child's PCB area is populated. In particular, the register for storing the function return value is set to 1, so that processing continues in *newproc( )* for the child. The child's *p_flag* is marked *SULOAD* to signify that the process is now on a dispatch queue. *procdup( )* returns 0 to signify to *newproc( )* that it is the parent returning.

4.13 Program execution

When *fork* is used to create a new process it is created with the image of its parent. The child, for all intents and purposes, is a clone of its parent, sharing its *text, data,* and even its *stack.* In most cases, however, the purpose of creating a new process is to invoke a new program. Thus, the program image of the child stored in memory must somehow be overlaid with the image of a desired program stored in a file within the file system.

The UNIX operating system provides a set of related system calls for invoking a new program image (Table 4.44). They are commonly refered to collectively as *exec.* The calling parameters for each of the *exec* system calls are different. However, they all require at least one parameter which specifies the program's name (possibly its full pathname). Other parameters specify the invocation arguments in different forms.

In the kernel, however, there is a single system call handler for all *exec* system calls called *exece( )*. Other *exec* system calls are implemented as library functions that are linked into the final executable at compile time. All these library functions eventually call the kernel's *exece( )* handler (see *exec(2)*). In the following discussion we will refer to the *exec* family of system calls collectively as *exec* unless specified otherwise. Since *exec* interacts with the file subsystem to obtain its program image, it is often necessary to refer to functions that are described in Chapter 6.

Table 4.44: *exec system calls*

System call
execl
execv
execle
execve
execvp
execlp

When *exece( )* overlays the current program image with a new program image, it overlays only the *text*, *data* and *stack* segments (i.e., the user address space). Almost all the original process's internal execution environment remains intact. The user structure, *proc* structure, PID, SID, PGID, and so on remain the same. However, the process's page tables are reorganized to suit the memory requirements of the new program image. It is important to understand that the *process* remains the same; only the *program* associated with it is replaced. It should also be understood that because the program has been replaced, its instruction stream has changed. Thus, a successful *exec* system call can never return because the original user address space has been overlaid with a new user address space, which in turn means that a new stack has been allocated and overlaid also.

4.13.1 Algorithm *exece( )*

The name of the file containing the desired program to execute is passed to *exec* by the calling process as an argument. With this file name, *exece( )* (Figure 4.43) looks up the pathname of the specified file and converts it to a *vnode* (see *lookuppn( )* in § 6.8.2). The *vnode* (§ 6.3) provides the information for locating the data blocks that belong to the file. The system call arguments and environment variables are saved so that they can be placed into the new execution stack and passed to the new executing process as parameters to *main( )*. The file is then opened for reading and its magic number is read in. The magic number is stored in the first few bytes of the file's header and tells *exece( )* what type of file the executable is. It uses the magic number to locate the index of its associated *exec* handling function (*exec_func*) in the *execsw[ ]* table (discussed in a moment). If the executable object file is *setuid* or *setgid* on execution, the credentials of the process are set to reflect the files new operating owner.

The *execsw[ ]* table contains an array of *execsw* structures (Table 4.45). Each structure defines how a specific executable object is handled. An executable object is a file that is laid out (or formated) in such a way that the system recognizes it as a program. The magic number of the file is unique, and represents the file's format. The only executable objects that UNIX System V Release 4 supports at present are *ELF* or *COFF* file formats, or executable text files (shell scripts). However, the design is flexible enough to incorporate newer executable object formats into the operating system as they become available. Executable text files are interpreted text

Figure 4.43: *Algorithm for exece( )*

```
exece()
input:  uap — pointer to area containing argument list
        rvp — pointer to a return value structure
output: zero on success
        non-zero on error and errno is set
{
  store the system call arguments and environment variables
  look up path name and convert into vnode to get file

  if( no permission to access file )
    return EACCES

  open the file for reading and read in its magic number
  set setid flag if the file is setuid or setgid on execution

  for each entry in the execsw[] table
    if( entry has matching magic number ) {
      invoke the exec handling function
      break
    }

  if( no matching magic ) /* file is not executable */
    return ENOEXEC

  if( setid flag is set ) {
    reset resource limits for this process to defaults
    /* file is executed with UID or GID of owner */
    initialize cred structure to reflect the file owner
    /* the process now runs with the file owner's credentials */
  }

  save a copy of the file name in u.u_comm for accounting

  copy saved system call arguments and environment variables
    into new stack

  return 0
}
```

files. If the first two bytes of the file are "#!" followed by a full pathname, that pathname is used as the command interpreter.

The *exec* handling function (*exec_func*) interprets the contents of the file, and updates the process's program image accordingly. This may include:

- Reading the *a.out* section header (if there is one).
- Interpreting the "#!", if the file is text.
- Loading and setting up any required shared objects.
- Deallocating the old program's *text, data* and *stack*.
- Loading the new program's *text, data,* and *bss* from the *a.out* file and building the new user program image.
- Building a new execution stack.
- Setting up the execution environment for the new program.

Table 4.45: *Struct execsw*

Element	Description
short *exec_magic	Unique magic number of object type
int (*exec_func)()	*exec* system call handling function
int (*exec_core)()	*core image* file handling function

A copy of the newly execed program's file name is stored in the user-area (*u.u_comm*) for accounting purposes. The previously saved system call arguments and environment variables are copied onto the new stack. They become *argv[]* and *envp[]* (see below). The signal actions for signals are set to their default action, and the register set is arranged so that the process starts in *main()* when it returns to user-mode.

4.13.2 Program flow of execution

When a process is started, it begins in function *main()* and the system arranges to pass three parameters to it on the stack. They are:

- *int argc* — contains the number of entries in *argv*
- *char *argv[]* — list of command line parameters
- *char *envp[]* — list of environment variables ("variable = value" form)

A process can examine these variables to direct its program flow. By convention, the system always arranges for *argc* to start at 1 and *argv[0]* to contain the program's invocation name. *argc* is then incremented for each argument given on the command line. This facility is useful if the file associated with the program is linked to another file. The program can be invoked either by its real program name or by its link name. By inspecting *argv[0]* the program can find out its invocation name and direct its execution accordingly. Similarly, the program can also read its list of environment variables and direct program execution according to their values.

A discussion of the programming environment under UNIX System V Release 4 is the subject of a book in itself. There are many books covering this subject and so we refer you to them for further information — see, for example, [Kernighan, Pike 1984].

4.13.3 Dumping core

The term "dumping core" refers to the kernel creating a memory image dump (core) of the execution of the process in the current directory. The file is called *core* as is the internal function (*core( )*) that creates it.

The only place in the kernel where a decision is made to core-dump the current process is in *psig( )* (§ 4.10.9). However, the decision is governed exclusively by the execution behaviour of the program itself. The current process is *core dumped* if it receives a signal that has its default action set to *core dump* (see Table 4.32). This usually occurs when the process attempts to execute an illegal instruction (*SIGILL*) or violates its address space (*SIGSEGV*). Programs that go out of control can sometimes be killed by typing the sequence of keys at the keyboard to make the program *quit*. When this happens, the terminal driver posts *SIGQUIT* to the process. Unless the program maintains a handler for *SIGQUIT*, the process is *core dumped* and terminated.

The point of creating a *core* file is to allow later inspection of the memory image of the process at the time it received the signal. Utilities such as **sdb(1)** allow the user to debug a program symbolically at the source code level using the dumped *core file* for post mortem analysis.

Figure 4.44: *Algorithm for core( )*

```
core()
input:   filename — pointer to the name of the core file
         procp — pointer to the current process's proc structure
         credp — pointer to the current process's cred structure
         rlim — pointer to the current process's resource limits
         sig — signal number to assign to u_sysabort
output: 0 if success
        non-zero on failure
{
  obtain vnode for "core" file
  check permission to write to file
  loop through execsw[] table to find matching a.out type {
    /* u.u_execid == execsw[n].exec_magic */
    call (execsw[n].exec_core)(vnode, procp, credp, rlim, sig)
  }
  close( vnode )
  return
}
```

4.13.4 Algorithm *core( )*

The format of a core file is dependent on the program's associated a.out file type. For example, a program executed from a COFF a.out file will create a COFF core file. Similarly, a program executed from an ELF a.out file will create an ELF core file. The two core file types are entirely different and require a different set of tools to debug them with.

A COFF core file image simply consists of a copy of the process's user structure followed by its data and stack segments. An ELF core file image is somewhat more complex. It consists of an ELF header containing a magic number and number of section headers, a number of program headers describing the characteristics of each segment in the process's address space (defined in *<sys/elf.h>*), a *prstatus* structure (see Table 6.20), a *prpsinfo* structure (defined in *<sys/procfs>*) containing information for the *ps(1)* command, followed by a dump of each of the segments in the process's address space.

The function responsible for performing a *core dump* is *core( )* (see Figure 4.44). Thus, *psig( )* calls *core( )* if the action specified by the signal causes it to do so.

The first thing that *core( )* does is check that the process has enough permission to create the *core file* in the current directory. Assuming that permission is granted, a pointer to a *vnode* is obtained which is used to describe the file that the *core image* will be written to. Since the executable image of an executable file differs between *a.out* file formats, the *core( )* function calls the *core* handling function (*exec_core( )*) in *execsw[]* for the *a.out* file type. This function performs the final *core dump* in the file system.

A number of deciding factors affect the creation of the *core file*. For example, if the process has exceeded its resource limits, the *core* handling function must decide how much, if any, of the *core image* to save. For this reason, the *core( )* function is passed several arguments which are in turn passed to the *core* handling function.

4.14 Shared libraries

We will not go into any great detail about the C Language compilation system under UNIX System V Release 4 (for more information see [AT&T 1990c]). We will, however, discuss to some extent why and how libraries are linked into an *a.out* executable before we describe the *Dynamic link loader* and *shared objects*.

In the following discussions, the term "object" refers interchangeably to all functions, variables, data structures, symbols, and so on that can be referenced externally in a C program.

The term "link editing" or "link loading" refers to the procedure by which a referenced object in a program module is connected with another module containing its definition. For example, the function *scanf( )* is normally connected with its definition in the standard C Library *libc.so*.

4.14.1 Statically-linked-libraries

Several hundred C Library functions are provided with the operating system in the form of archive libraries. These libraries can be linked into an executable on demand, during compilation. If a referenced object is not directly locatable in the program code, the link loader (**ld(1)**) can be instructed to search a list of libraries to find it. Once located, the object is linked into the target executable. This procedure is repeated until all references to objects in the program have been resolved. Quite often this means that several executable files are maintained with duplicate copies of the same object. There are several problems with this scheme:

- Since objects are often duplicated in executables (for example, *printf(3S)*, *strcat(3C)* and so on), the system requires large amounts of disk space that is unnecessarily wasted.

- Memory may be utilized unnecessarily if several processes execute the same function loaded into different text segments.

- If a library function is changed, all executables that use that function will have to be recompiled and relinked with the version of the new updated library function.

4.14.2 Statically-linked-shared-libraries

UNIX System V Release 3 introduced *statically-linked-shared-libraries*. As with statically-linked-libraries, a copy of the referenced shared-object is incorporated into the target executable at link time by the link loader. However, all objects in a statically-linked-shared-library are assigned with a fixed virtual address. The link loader connects external referenced objects to their definition in the library by assigning their virtual addresses when the executable is created. Thus, a library function remains fixed onto its virtual address even if the function is changed. If several *a.out* files reference the same library object, and that object is changed, then only the object has to be re-compiled, not the *a.out* files. However, this scheme requires a shared library developer to understand a process's address space (specifically for the target machine) and to know which virtual addresses are free to be used by new shared functions within it.

4.14.3 Dynamically-linked-shared-libraries

With the release of UNIX System V Release 4, a new shared-object concept is introduced in the form of *dynamically-linked-shared-libraries* (see also [Peacock 1991]). In this scheme, instead of assigning fixed virtual addresses to externally referenced functions during *a.out* creation, the system assigns them at run-time. When using a dynamically-linked-shared-library, the entire library contents are mapped into the process's virtual address space. However, there is only one copy of the library code loaded in memory, although it may be mapped onto a different virtual address for each process that uses it.

Since many processes share a single copy of the library in memory, the memory pages associated with it must be marked read-only. To overcome this limitation, the system makes use of the copy-on-write scheme. If a process writes to a page in a shared object, the system assigns a copy of the page to the process which it can modify freely without affecting other users of the page. The benefits of dynamically-linked-shared-libraries are described as follows:

- Library routines are stored in a single file on the disk instead of being duplicated in several *a.out* files as well as in the library itself.

- There is only one copy of the *text* for a shared library in main memory.

- *text* and *data* symbols are located at dynamically assigned virtual addresses at run-time. Absolute memory addresses are calculated for a process by the *dynamic-link-loader* at run-time.

- Since external references are linked at run-time, shared objects can be updated without re-linking executables that depend on them.

- *text* and *data* memory pages associated with a shared library can be paged in and out in the same way that other memory pages are paged.

4.15 Process termination

All processes terminate via the same path as the _*exit* system call, which will be discussed in this section. This is so even if the process does not explicitly call _*exit*. A process is terminated for any of the following reasons:

- The process voluntarily calls _*exit*.
- The process handles (receives) a signal set for its default action.
- The process *returns* from or finishes executing *main( )*.

The internal function handler for _*exit* is called *exit( )*. For the rest of this discussion, we will refer to the latter unless we state otherwise. For more information on the use and semantics of the _*exit* system call, see *exit(2)*.

4.15.1 Transition phases of process termination

In order to understand how this function operates, we must first understand how processes are terminated.

When a process terminates via _*exit* it enters an intermediate stage of termination called a *zombie* state (*SZOMB*) — see Figure 4.45. A zombie process has no swappable image and so for all intents and purposes it is dead. However, a *proc* structure is still maintained for it and is partially overlaid with time accounting information for the parent to inspect with *times* (§ 4.8.5). *exit( )* cleans up the remaining parts of the process's execution environment by deallocating its user-area, *data, stack* and any non-shared portions of *text* area. Therefore, *exit( )* terminates a process but not completely; complete annihilation occurs when the parent subsequently uses the *wait* system call.

exit( ) informs the parent about the death of its child by posting *SIGCHLD* to it. By default, a process ignores *SIGCHLD*. This means that the parent is not normally aware of its delivery. If the parent maintains a signal handler for *SIGCHLD* the signal can be caught. However, with this method there is no way to find out why the

Figure 4.45: *Phases of process termination*

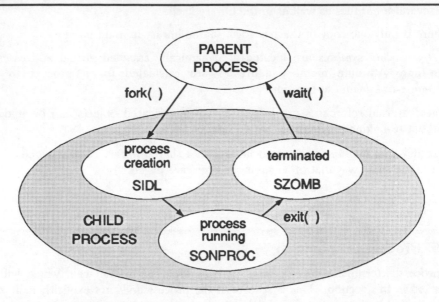

child died or, in fact, which child died (assuming there is more than one). To overcome this problem, the system provides a family of system calls, which for the time being, will be referred to collectively as *wait*.

Assume that a parent has at least one active child process. If it calls *wait*, it is automatically put to sleep at an interruptable sleep priority ($PWAIT$), waiting for a $SIGCHLD$ signal. When the parent receives $SIGCHLD$, the *wait* system call collects status information from the dead child (zombie), then frees its associated *proc* structure. The process is now non-existent. Therefore, it can be seen that the parent is responsible for conducting the final burial ceremony for its child.

The status information obtained by *wait* contains enough information to detect which child died (i.e., its PID), and the exit value that the child passed to *_exit* (if any). However, a problem remains: what if the parent does not wait for its children to die before the parent itself is terminated? If this happens the child's *proc* structure remains allocated. To overcome this problem, the system arranges for process 1 (*/sbin/init*) to inherit the defunct process since, after all, this is the mother of all other processes.

4.15.2 Algorithm *exit( )*

The trap handler for the *_exit* system call is called *rexit( )*. *rexit( )* is called as a direct result of an *_exit* system call via *systrap( )* from *sysent[]*. As with other system call handlers, *rexit( )* is passed a pointer to the user-mode system call arguments and a pointer to a return value structure. However, the return value structure is not used since *_exit* never returns. The only thing *rexit( )* does is directly call *exit( )* to do the actual processing.

Figure 4.46: *Algorithm for exit( )*

```
exit()
input:   why — integer specifying why the process is exiting
         what — integer specifying what caused it to exit
output: none — does not return
{
  zero alarm clock
  set action for all signals to ignore
  delete all pending signals
  deallocate any queued siginfo structures
  decrement all reference counts on file structures
  close all open files
  cancel any set high resolution timers

  if( this process is a session leader ) {
    send SIGHUP to all processes in the group
    and deallocate vnode for controlling terminal
  }

  deallocate file descriptor ufchunks
  unlock previously locked text or data segments
  clean up shared memory and semaphore environments
  setup wait status information and return value for waiting parent
  update accounting file /* mem usage, time.... */
  release the virtual memory information for the process
  deallocate process's credentials structure

  give all children/siblings spawned by the exiting
    process to /etc/init

  release the vnode associated with a.out file
  mark the process SZOMB /* now a zombie process */
  update proc structure with reason why process is exiting and what
   - caused it to exit /* parent can collect this info with wait()
  post death of child signal (SIGCHLD) to the parent

  /* call class specific exit routine */
  CL_EXITCLASS()
  /* switch in another process */
  swtch()

  /* never gets here */
}
```

Since *exit( )* is also called from other parts of the operating system, the designers had to provide a common interface for all functions that need it, including *systrap( )*. The end result is *exit( )*. However, to satisfy *systrap( )*, *exit( )* is called from within *rexit( )*. Thus, *rexit( )* is the trap handler.

exit( ) (see Figure 4.46) requires two integer arguments called *why* and *what*. The argument *why* specifies why *exit( )* was called (see Table 4.46). This value is assigned to *p_wcode*. The argument *what* is only ever non-zero when called from *rexit( )*. It is the status value that was passed to the *_exit* system call in user-mode. Within *exit( )*, the *p_wdata* field is set to this value. This combined information is stored in the *proc* structure for the parent process to investigate with *wait*. The value passed to *_exit* is an arbitrary value between 0 and 255. It has no use within the kernel. Its purpose is to allow a parent process in user-mode to evaluate the success or failure of its child. By convention, a status code of zero means that the process terminated normally, and a non-zero status value (typically 1 or sometimes 255) means that an error occurred. As far as the kernel is concerned the *_exit* system call, when called like this:

$$\_exit( );$$

is perfectly legal, since the kernel will still assign *what* to *p_wdata* even if it contains garbage.

Table 4.46: *Reasons why a child exits or stops*

Constant	Description
CLD_EXITED	Child has exited
CLD_KILLED	Child was killed
CLD_DUMPED	Child has *core-dumped*
CLD_TRAPPED	Traced child has stopped
CLD_STOPPED	Child has stopped on a signal
CLD_CONTINUED	Stopped child has continued

exit( ) begins by turning off the alarm clock and resetting all signals to their default actions. While doing this, all pending signals are discarded (*p_sig* is zeroed) and any queued *siginfo* structures are de-queued. Following this, all open files are closed and any high resolution timers are cancelled. If the process is a session leader, *SIGHUP* is sent to all processes in the session group to tell them that the session leader has terminated. All dynamically allocated memory for file descriptors (*ufchunks*) is freed (*ufchunk* is discussed in § 6.2.1). Text or data segments in the process's address space that were previously locked with the *plock* system call are unlocked (§ 3.10.2). References to the current directory and root directory *vnodes* are released. Semaphores are undone, and the process is detached from any previously maintained shared memory segments (semaphores and shared memory are discussed in Chapter 8). *exit( )* then sets up the child status information for the (assumed) waiting parent (see below). If accounting is enabled, a record is written to the accounting file. The virtual address space for the process is released and its *p_as* member is zeroed. The credentials structure for the process is then deallocated.

Time accounting is adjusted for the process to be used by the *times* system call (§ 4.8.5). If the process has any children of its own, they are given to process 1 — the ultimate ancestor. The *vnode* associated with the *a.out* containing the process's program image is released. Since the address space of the process is given up, the process is now a zombie and so *exit( )* marks the process *SZOMB*. The reason why the process exited and its status value (passed to *exit* as an argument) are placed into the *proc* structure for the parent to analyze with *waitid*. Finally, *SIGCHLD* is sent to the parent, and the class dependent routine *CL_EXITCLASS( )* is called to remove the process from its associated priority class. The next process is then switched in to use the CPU (hopefully the parent).

At this point, it can be seen that the process is terminated. Its address space has been freed from both user and kernel address space. However, the operating system maintains a *proc* structure for it containing status and time accounting information to be evaluated at the parent's leisure.

4.15.3 Waiting for a process

There are a number of ways to investigate a stopped or terminated child, but in all cases, the parent that owns the child must *wait* for it to *exit*. We will discuss these methods in this section.

Three system calls are provided by the operating system for allowing a parent process to investigate why a child is not able to run any more: *wait, waitid[1]* and *waitpid*. However, there are only two system call handlers: *wait( )* and *waitsys( )*. The internal function that performs processing for all wait system calls is *waitid( )*. Figure 4.47 describes how these system call interfaces are interrelated.

The situation where a process exits leaving behind a non-runnable zombie has already been discussed. However, there are many reasons why a process may not be able to run. For example, the process may have been stopped by a job control signal, or stopped for a debugger to trace, or terminated by the kernel because it violated its address space or executed an illegal instruction, and so on. For whatever reason the child is stopped or terminated, the *proc* structure variable *p_wcode* contains the code that explains why (Table 4.46). This variable is updated accordingly by the function that causes the stoppage or termination. For example, the system call handler *rexit( )* calls *exit( )* with the argument *why* set to *CLD_EXITED*. Within *exit( )*, this is assigned to *p_wcode* for later inspection by the parent using one of the *wait* system calls.

All *wait* system calls eventually result in a call to the internal *waitid( )* function to carry out processing for them. For this reason, we will discuss only the *waitid( )* function in any detail (see *wait(2)* and *waitid(2)*). For now, it is only important to understand that *wait* and *waitpid* are generalized versions of *waitid* but with less

---

1 *Programmers writing POSIX compliant C programs should be aware that the waitid( ) function does not form part of the current POSIX standard.*

functionality. Both system calls can be used to obtain status information about the stopped or terminated process, which can be analyzed further by using the macros defined in *wstat(5)*.

waitid( ) suspends the calling process by putting it to sleep until a child is ready to be waited for or until one of its children changes state. If no children are found, then *waitid( )* fails and returns *ECHILD* to the calling process. If a child marked as *SZOMB* (zombie) is found, then its *proc* structure is freed and the information it contains is returned to the parent in a *siginfo_t* structure (see Appendix C) that the parent must set aside space for. In the case of the *wait* and *waitpid* system calls, this information is transformed into a single integer (*stat_loc*) that is returned to the parent for inspection.

4.15.4 Algorithm *waitid( )*

With the *wait* system call, it is not possible to specify which child to wait for. However, with *waitid*, it is possible to wait for a particular child, or any child within a particular process group, or any child regardless of its PID or PGID. Furthermore, by logically OR-ing some constants together (Table 4.47) and passing them to *waitid* to direct its flow of execution, the programmer has several options — for example — the event to wait for (or not to wait for) can be specified.

The system call handler for the *waitid* and *waitpid* system calls is called *waitsys( )* (see Figure 4.47). The *wait* system call, on the other hand, has its own system call handler called *wait( )*. In both cases, however, *wait( )* and *waitsys( )* call *waitid( )*. Thus, *wait* eventually calls upon *waitid( )* to do processing on its behalf in the same way that *waitid* and *waitpid* do via *waitsys( )*. Interestingly, the *waitid* system call and the *waitid( )* kernel function both use the same function calling parameters.

waitpid is a more general version of *waitid* and is similar in operation to the BSD *wait3(2)* system call. Like *wait*, the status information is passed back by *waitpid* as an integer that can be analyzed by using the macros defined in *wstat(5)*.

waitid( ) searches through the process's child-sibling list for all children that match the selection criteria specified in its function calling arguments. If there are no children, *ECHILD* is returned. For each child that is found, the reason why it is being waited on is sought by consulting its *p_wcode* member. Depending on the options specified in its calling arguments, a *siginfo_t* structure is constructed for the calling process to analyze. Within the structure is placed the status information of the child being waited for.

If children exist on the child-sibling list but none of them match the specified selection criteria, the parent is put to sleep at a sleep priority level of *PWAIT* (interruptable) until the child wakes it up. Of course this means that other signal types will also wake up the sleep. Some time later (presumably), the child is stopped or terminated, or it voluntarily exits via the *_exit* system call. As a result the parent receives *SIGCHLD* and processing continues within *waitid( )* where it was originally put to sleep. Within *waitid( )*, the child-sibling list is searched from the beginning again. This time, a child matching the selection criteria is found. If the child was killed, suffered a *core dump*, or simply exited, the process will be in a

Figure 4.47: *Wait, waitid, and waitpid flow of execution*

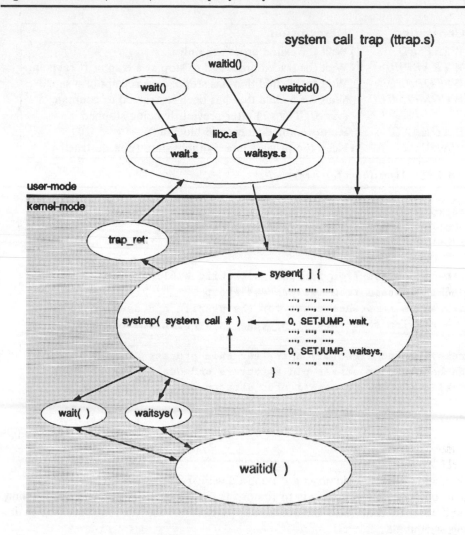

zombie state; *freeproc( )* is then called to free the remaining portions of the dead child's *proc* structure.

4.15.5 Algorithm *freeproc( )*

The function *freeproc( )* (Figure 4.48) is mostly called by *waitid( )*, but it may also be called by *setsigact( )*.

Remember that the *sigaction* system call has a switch (*SA_NOCLDWAIT*) that allows the calling process to tell the system not to create zombie processes when its children die. Within *setsigact( )* (the system call handler for *sigaction*), the process is marked *SNOWAIT*, meaning that all child processes will exit without leaving a

Table 4.47: *Options for the waitid system call, and the kernel's waitid() function*

Constant	Description
WEXITED	Wait for exited processes only
WTRAPPED	Wait for traced processes to stop at a trap or breakpoint
WSTOPPED	Wait for a child that has stopped on receipt of a signal
WCONTINUED	Wait for a child that has been instructed to continue (via SIGCONT) after previously being stopped
WNOHANG	Return immediately (non-blocking)
WNOWAIT	Keep the process in a waitable state (non-destructive)

Figure 4.48: *Algorithms for freeproc()*

```
freeproc()
input:  p — pointer to proc structure to free
output: none
{
  detach process from its parent's child-sibling list
  detach process from its process group
  decrement reference count for the session and deallocate
    - session structure if process is session leader

  remove /proc directory entry for this process
  un-hash the process's pid structure and deallocate it
  deallocate the process's proc structure

  decrement nproc /* user has one less procs running */
}
```

zombie, and all existing zombies are removed with *freeproc()*.

The purpose of *freeproc()* is to remove the child from its parent's child-sibling list and then to deallocate the remaining portions of the process specified in its calling arguments.

The child is detached from its process group and session and its */proc* directory entry is removed. Its PID is given up and its *pid* structure is deallocated — the PID is free to be assigned to another process. Finally, its *proc* structure is removed from the *practive* list, memory used by it is freed, and *nproc* is decremented to signify that the user has one less active process. At this point, the process is history.

4.16 Process suspension

By far, the simplest system call implemented in the operating system is *pause*. The process is simply put to sleep at the lowest sleep priority level (*PSLEP*) until it is awoken by a signal.

This function never actually returns because the sleep is interrupted by a signal that results in an interrupted system call. This in turn results in a *longjmp( )* back to *systrap( )* from whence it was called. Since the system call is interrupted, *errno* is set to *EINTR* and the system call returns -1 to the calling process in user-mode.

There is no successful completion return value and the current signal actions remain in effect for the process. For this reason, if the signal delivered causes the process to terminate or *core dump*, then obviously *pause( )* does not return at all. On the other hand, if the signal is ignored the *pause* remains in effect. If the signal is caught, then on return from the signal handler execution resumes as though *pause* had just returned.

The internal function handler for *pause* is called *pause( )* — what a surprise! What may not be a surprise is that *pause* is not its only caller. The *sigsuspend* and *sigpause* system calls also use the internal version of *pause( )*.

4.17 System operation

This section discusses how the system is brought into operation and how it is shut down again. Note that most of the concepts discussed are very implementation dependent since interaction with hardware is often required. For this reason, we have given a generic overview. However, the basic methods are the same for all implementations.

4.17.1 System initialization

When a computer system is first powered up it is just a dumb piece of electronics that has no program. The machine must somehow locate a binary image of a boot program from some storage device and load it into its memory for execution. The CPU instruction stream must then be vectored to the first address in memory where that program is loaded. The program then begins to execute. This procedure is often referred to as *bootstrapping* and it applies to any computer system, not necessarily a computer system running UNIX.

Almost all modern computer systems are implemented with non-volatile RAM storage devices for storing the machine's firmware bootstrap program. This program is the code responsible for locating a specific track on a specific disk and loading the program stored there into the machine's memory for execution (typically, track zero on disk zero). It is now quite common to find a computer system supporting elaborate boot programs by using-menu driven console monitors to interactively select from several devices and partitions to bootstrap. Once the device and partition are located, the program stored at that location is loaded into memory and executed. This program is often referred to as the operating system bootstrap program and its location is often referred to as the boot partition or boot sector (note the boot partition is not a file system).

On computers running the UNIX operating system, the boot sector usually contains two programs for bringing the system into operation. The first program is brought into execution by the machine's microcode. It builds a runtime stack containing the device, partition and kernel file name used to locate the binary image of the UNIX kernel in the file system. In a similar way to the C Language *argc, argv* argument passing paradigm, this information is passed to a second boot program historically called *boot. boot* is responsible for loading the operating system into memory and transferring control to its start address. However, this procedure is not as simple as it reads.

The UNIX kernel is much like any other program in that it is stored in an *a.out* file within a UNIX file system. Therefore, supplied only with device, partition and file name (the UNIX program image — i.e., */stand/unix*), the boot program must be able to locate the file within the file system of the given device/partition, and then know how to read the file (*a.out*) into memory and set it going.

In many implementations of the operating system, this is done by a function called *mlsetup()* (machine level set up). Its job is to make sure that everything is initialized properly before starting the kernel proper. The boot program calls *mlsetup()* to do low-level machine specific initialization in readiness for the operating system. This usually includes disabling hardware interrupts, making sure that the virtual address translation mechanisms supported by the CPU are set up and initialized, placing the CPU into protected-mode (kernel-mode), and carrying out any other chores necessary to make the hardware environment acceptable to the kernel software. *mlsetup()* may also have to initialize the hardware dependent software environment. For example, the page tables have to be set up, and the kernel's virtual address space must be constructed and initialized.

At this point the operating system is almost ready to be started. But before this is done, several global variables and data structures must be initialized. The function *dispinit()* is called to run through the scheduler initialization (Figure 4.49). The high-resolution timer and interval timer data structures are then initialized. Following this comes the construction and initialization of the first process (process 0 — the scheduler). A *pcb, user* and *proc* structure are allocated to it and its page tables are built. After these structures are initialized, the process is marked *SONPROC* and its flag's member is marked *SLOAD* and *SSYS*. However, this process has no *text, data* or *bss* yet, and it is not using the CPU. Finally, the initialization of the pid and process tables (*pidhash* and *procdir*) is done. At this point, the first process exists on the *practive* list and *mlsetup()* is complete. The boot program now calls *main()* in the kernel text and the UNIX system starts.

Within *main()*, final machine dependent startup procedures are carried out, usually by a function called *startup()*. However, some implementations may place the machine dependent startup code within *main()* itself. The *startup()* code may be used, for example, to initialize peripheral devices, DMA controllers and so on.

Figure 4.49: *Algorithm for dispinit( )*

```
dispinit()
 input: none
 output: none
{
   for (each configured process priority class )
     call its class specific initialization functions.
   /* dispq */
   if( cannot allocate memory for the dispatcher queue headers )
      panic("Can't allocate memory for dispatcher queues.")
   /* dqactmap */
   if( cannot allocate memory for the active queue bitmap )
      panic("Can't allocate memory for dispq active map.")
   set total number of loaded, runnable processes to zero
   set priority of highest priority active queue to -1 /* none */
}
```

There are numerous kernel data structures, variables, lists and modules to be initialized before the system starts up. Therefore, besides hardware initialization, final software initialization is carried out from *main( )*, by calling each module's initialization routine. For example:

- initialize the high resolution timer freelist
- initialize the interval timer's freelist
- initialize the buffer I/O system and device hash buffer lists
- initialize the system's open file table
- initialize the STREAMS subsystem
- initialize each configured virtual file system type *vfs* structure
- initialize the Interprocess Communication System
- initialize the directory name lookup cache
- initialize the kernel memory allocator (*kmdaemon*)

The UNIX *utsname* structure must also be initialized. This structure contains the version and release of the operating system and machine hardware. Since it may need to consult the firmware for machine information, this is usually machine dependent. The system hardware clock or programmable interval timer may need priming so that the system *clock( )* routine is regularly interrupted at each *tick*. Finally, interrupts are enabled.

A *cred* structure is allocated and assigned to the current process (which has not really started yet). All initialization functions are called for device drivers to allow them to conduct any final initialization. For example, the hard disk device driver may need to initialize the SCSI controller card, or a RAM disk device driver may need to allocate and reserve enough memory for its pseudo disk. The amount of memory installed in the system is known at this point so the paging constants for the clock algorithm can be initialized to set the scan rate, paging threshold and other parameters of the paging subsystem — for example, *lotsfree, desfree, minfree, maxpgio, fastscan, slowscan* and *handspread* (§ 3.8.1).

Figure 4.50: *Example of a system boot banner*

```
****************************************************************
              UNIX(R) System V Release 4.0 Version 3.0
         Copyright (c) 1984, 1986, 1987, 1988, 1989  AT&T
                       All Rights Reserved
****************************************************************

Bunyip² Valley Computer Corporation BVIX Version 1.0
Total real memory  = 7995392
Available memory   = 4438912
```

At this point, the virtual file system operation *VFS_MOUNTROOT()* is called to mount the file system containing the root file system. The root file system type is normally described by a configurable parameter called *rootfstype* (default is the *ufs* file system). However, if this variable is not set, the whole virtual file system switch table (*vfssw[]*) is scanned until a file system supporting the *VFS_MOUNTROOT()* operation is found. If none is found, there is no point in continuing. A message is printed to the console saying "vfs_mountroot: cannot mount root", and the system is paniced. For more information about the virtual file system and the virtual file system mountroot operations see § 6.5.2.

The UNIX System release banner is displayed showing various pieces of information including copyright and proprietary notices (Figure 4.50). This information is printed to the console. The amount of available memory shown by the system banner indicates the total amount of physical memory left after the operating system has been loaded and initialized.

The swap partition is configured into the system. Then comes the initial call to *schedpaging()* which constantly brings itself into operation 4 times per second via a timeout to keep track of free memory (§ 3.8.2).

newproc() is then called to fork a new process which will be used to overlay with */sbin/init*. Unlike other system processes, */sbin/init* is built from the image of an *a.out* file stored in the file system. Thus, the program instructions for this program must be read into a *text* segment and the process must then be converted into a system process as though it originally formed part of the kernel text itself. In addition to this, the new process's *bss* and *stack* segments must be built. However, since the *text, bss* and *stack* segments for process 0 are non-existent, the normal *exece()* calling mechanisms cannot be used. Therefore, it is necessary to hand-craft

---

2 *A "Bunyip" is a legendary wild beast that lives in the outback bush of Australia. Most Australian nippers are warned about the dangers of the Bunyip.*

the *exec* of */sbin/init* in machine assembler. The code for doing this is referred to as *icode* and it is defined in a file called *misc.s.* The procedure for execing */sbin/init* is as follows:

- An address space data structure is allocated and initialized for holding the user address space of the new process (see *as_alloc( )* in § 3.5).

- A text segment is allocated and mapped into the process's address space for holding the *icode* (see *as_map( )* in § 3.5).

- The *icode* is copied from a known fixed virtual memory address into the newly created text segment.

- Finally, a stack segment is allocated and assigned to the process's address space.

The *icode* will be executed in user-mode when process 1 is next switched in to use the CPU. When it runs, the first thing it does is build a run-time stack to use as *argv, argc* and *envp* for exec-ing the new program image. *argv[0]* holds the string */etc/init* which is hard coded into the *icode* (*/etc/init* is symbolically linked to */sbin/init* within the file system). The *icode* then calls *exece( )* with the arguments that it built on the run-time stack. From then on, Process 1 is subject to scheduling much like any other process except that it is a System class process so it runs at a higher priority than other time sharing processes (see § 4.6.8).

Following the spawning of */sbin/init* comes the forking of *pageout, fsflush,* and the *kmdaemon* processes. The procedure for this is much simpler than for */sbin/init* since the code for each of these system processes is built into the kernel text. For each of the aforementioned, *newproc( )* is called to create a new process. Some accounting information is initialized, and the program's related function is called to do the work of the process. That is, *pageout* calls *pageout( )*, *fsflush* calls *fsflush( )*, and *kmdaemon* calls *kmem_freepool( )*.

At this point, as far as the kernel is concerned, the system is operating. The rest of the system initialization (if any) is done in user mode by */sbin/init* and mainly depends on what has been defined in the */sbin/inittab* file. For more information on this subject, see init(1M).

4.17.2 System shutdown and reboot

Once the system is up and running, at any given time during its operation it is in one of eight possible run levels (as described by init(1M)). However, these run levels are a user-mode concept understood by */sbin/init* only. As far as the kernel is concerned, the process responsible for the life and well-being of all other processes is */sbin/init*. The kernel does not care about any other process (except, of course, other system processes) and it does not understand run levels.

There is, however, a system call called *uadmin* (see Figure 4.51) that provides a limited administrative environment at user-mode level and is intended to be used by the super-user only:

```
int uadmin(int cmd, int fcn, mdep)
```

Figure 4.51: *Algorithm for uadmin( )*

```
uadmin()
input:   uap — pointer to area containing argument list
         rvp — pointer to a return value structure
output: zero on success of a root file system remount
         otherwise this system call should not return
{
   switch( cmd argument ) {
      SHUTDOWN:
         hold all signals /* don't want to be killed */
         send SIGKILL to /sbin/init process
         /* wait for init to die */
         put the current process to sleep until awoken by a SIGCHLD
         for( each process on the practive list )
             send SIGKILL to the process and wait for it to die
         sync all mounted file systems
         unmount all mounted file systems except root
         wait for any asynchronous writes to finish.
         unmount the root file system
         /* fall through */

      REBOOT:
         /* action depends on system call argument "fcn" */
         halt or reboot the system
         /* NEVER GETS HERE */

      REMOUNT:
         remount the root file system
         break;

      SWAPCTL:
         /* implement swap control system call */
         swapctl(uap, rvp);
         break;
   }
}
```

With this system call, a process with super-user privileges can initiate a system shutdown or a system reboot. Additional facilities give the administrator control of the virtual swap device, and there is a facility for remounting the root file system (normally only used during system initialization after the root file system has been repaired with *fsck(1M)*). The virtual swap device facilities are used by the *swapctl* system call which is actually implemented as a C Language function that simply calls *uadmin*. Thus, *uadmin* supports an additional runtime switch that directs processing for *swapctl*. The virtual swap device is discussed in § 3.8.4.

The argument *mdep* is machine dependent and has no official use. Vendors wishing to implement their own system administration facilities via *uadmin* may do so by making use of *mdep*. For more information on the semantics and use of this system call, see *uadmin(2)*.

To shutdown the system, the administrator invokes */sbin/init* with a specified run level of zero, usually via a shell script such as */usr/sbin/shutdown*. On receipt of the instruction to shutdown, */sbin/init* is invoked to send a *SIGINT* signal to process 1 which catches the signal and interprets it to mean change state to run level zero. This causes Process 1 to re-examine the */sbin/inittab* file for entries that describe the actions to be done at the change of state to run level zero. The course of actions for a specified run level entirely depend on that described in the */sbin/inittab* file. Generally, the entry for run level zero invokes *uadmin(1M)*. *uadmin(1M)*, in turn, calls the *uadmin* system call to tell the kernel to shut the system down.

4.18 Exercises

4.1** Write a program that lowers its CPU resource limits below its currently set threshold, say for a maximum of 10 seconds execution. In your program define a signal handler that is brought into action on receipt of a SIGXCPU signal. Write the program to test for three cases: the signal is neither caught nor ignored; the signal is caught; the signal is ignored. Compare the results and explain what happens in each case.

4.2** Assume that a variable called *p_alarmid* exists in the *proc* structure definition and that no checking is done for alarm signals in *clock()*. Suppose we re-implemented the *alarm* system call by using the C code example shown in Figure 4.52. Will this work? If so, what are the implications? For example, will it be more or less accurate, and will it provide any performance overhead? What happens if the program terminates before the alarm signal is delivered?

4.3 Explain the use of the *p_link* member in the *proc* structure.

4.4 Write a function to emulate the BSD *gettimeofday* system call.

4.5** Write a simple device driver that allows a process, through the use of an *ioctl()* call, to arrange for an alarm signal to be sent to itself after a specified number of milliseconds.

4.6 Describe the differences between a *task*, a *program*, and a *process*?

4.7 At what time are sections of an executable *a.out* read into memory?

4.8 Two variables are used to flag preemption; *runrun* and *kprunrun*. Why are there two variables and how do they affect the preemption algorithms?

Figure 4.52: *alarm() implementation — see exercise question 4.2*

```
alarm(seconds)
time_t seconds;
{
    extern sendalarm();
    register struct proc *p = u.u_procp;

    if(!seconds) {
        if(p->p_alarmid)
            untimeout(p->p_alarmid)
    } else
        p->p_alarmid = timeout(sendalarm, p, seconds * HZ);
    return(0);
}

sendalarm(proc)
register struct proc *p;
{
    p->p_alarmid = 0;
    psignal(p,SIGALRM);
}
```

4.9 In *sleep()*, signals are checked if the specified event-type allows signals to be caught. Why is it necessary to check for signals twice?

4.10 When is a sleeping process taken off its sleep queue?

4.11 While a process sleeps it is normally marked *SSLEEP*. But under what circumstances would a queued, sleeping process not be marked *SSLEEP*? What would its state be?

4.12* Using the *setitimer(3C)* function, implement an alarm call function that operates with a parameter of milliseconds instead of seconds.

4.13 During the intermediate stages of process creation, what state is the process in and when is the transition made to *SRUN*?

4.14 Name the three scheduling classes used by the class independent code. Name their priority class order.

4.15 When is a real-time process marked *TSKPRI*?

4.16 Since a process executes on a virtual machine, why is it necessary for the system to maintain separate user and kernel stacks?

4.17 In the pseudo code example of *systrap()* given in Figure 4.29, the comment at the end of the function says:

```
/* should be impossible to reach here */
```

Why is this?

4.18   Describe the pointers in the *proc* and *pid* structures which the system uses to locate processes belonging to a process group.

4.19   Which structure holds the process group ID (PGID) for a set of processes belonging to a process group? What is the structure element called ?

4.20   When does the system check whether signals are pending for a process? When does the receiving process take delivery of a signal?

4.21   An exiting process sends *SIGCHLD* to its parent and the parent (assumed to be waiting with *wait*) receives the signal and collects its status information. What happens if the parent receives a signal other than *SIGCHLD*? Is the zombie process removed from the active process list?

4.22   There are two variables that can be referenced to access the current process's *proc* structure in the kernel code. What are they?

4.23   If a process *execs* a new program image, what happens to its old *proc* structure?

4.24   Describe how the set user ID mechanism allows a process to safely execute with another user's privileges.

CHAPTER 5

I/O subsystem

Wedlock, indeed, hath oft compared been
To public feasts where meet a public rout,
Where they that are without would fain go in
And they that are within would fain go out.
— Sir John Davies, 1569-1626

5.1 Introduction

The purpose of the I/O subsystem is to transfer data between device and process, and vice versa. I/O to and from a process can be thought of as occurring at a high and a low level; the high level is concerned with moving data between user address space and kernel address space, the low-level is concerned with moving data between kernel address space and physical hardware devices. The I/O subsystem must interact with other subsystems. For example, when data is to be written to disk, the high-level I/O functions copy the data from user space to kernel space. The data is then passed to the file management subsystem, which decides where and on which disk the data is to be written. The low-level I/O functions are then called by the file management subsystem to write the data to disk.

Under UNIX System V Release 4 there are three distinct types of I/O that a process can perform. The first two of these are described in this chapter, the third is the subject of Chapter 7. They are:

- *File I/O* — read and write data to and from a file held on a file system. At the high level, the data transfer is handled by the *segmap* virtual memory segment operations. At the low level, it is handled by *block device drivers*.

- *Character I/O* — read and write data to and from a device. Data is passed directly to the low-level *character device driver*, and the driver talks directly to the physical device. However, a character driver makes use of the high-level I/O functions to copy data between user and kernel space.

- *STREAMS-based I/O* — similar to character I/O, but the STREAMS mechanism gives device driver writers greater flexibility. Chapter 7 describes the STREAMS subsystem.

5.2 The new buffer cache

Under UNIX System V Release 3, all I/O operations on files within a file system used a buffer cache; it gave faster access to files by buffering recently used disk blocks in memory. This buffer cache is still used in UNIX System V Release 4 for certain types of file operations. The buffer cache in UNIX System V Release 3 is referred to as the *old* buffer cache, and its operation is described in § 5.3.

The location of data in a file is characterized by its offset from the beginning of the file referenced by its *vnode*. In the following sections this is referred to as a *vnode/offset*. File access to a *vnode/offset* is achieved by using the virtual memory segment type called *segmap*, which is similar to the *segvn* segment type described in Chapter 3.

The *segmap* method of accessing a file is referred to as the *new* buffer cache. The following sections describe the operation of this new buffer cache. Later sections show how the I/O subsystem uses the new buffer cache to perform file I/O operations.

5.2.1 Overview of the new buffer cache

In Chapter 3 we saw how the address space of a process is divided into segments. Each segment has a particular segment type, although a running process mainly uses *segvn* segments. This segment type implements the basic paged memory model.

The new buffer cache provides a similar function: it implements a paged memory access model to reference blocks of a file. The page size used by the new buffer cache is machine dependent and is determined by the constant *MAXBSIZE*. For example, on the MIPS R3000 processor, a page size is 8k bytes, which corresponds to the largest file system block size supported. To support the new buffer cache, the kernel maintains its own address space, that is, there is an *as* structure used for kernel virtual memory, which means that part of the kernel pages itself. One of the segments in the kernel's address space is the *segkmap*. It is the generic kernel mapping segment, and is used to provide paged virtual memory access to areas of files. This segment, and its relationship to the other data structures in the new buffer cache, is shown in Figure 5.1.

The I/O subsystem maintains an array of *smap* structures. They are used to map a particular *vnode/offset* into a kernel virtual address. Each *smap* structure maps *MAXBSIZE* consecutive disk locations into a corresponding block of kernel virtual addresses. The structure has fields that describe which *vnode/offset* is mapped by the *smap*. The index of the structure in the array implies the kernel virtual address at which the *vnode/offset* is mapped.

The following example gives an overview of how a portion of a file is mapped into virtual memory. Suppose a process issues two *read* system calls to read consecutive bytes from a file. The first byte is at offset 2048 in the file, the second at 2049. The process issues the *read* system call which is subsequently passed to the file system dependent read operation (see VOP_READ() in § 6.3.3), which then calls the function *segmap_getmap( )* (§ 5.2.3) to set up the mapping of the *vnode* and the offset 2048. This function searches for an *smap* structure that already maps this *vnode/offset*. If one is not found, a new one is allocated and initialized for it. The function returns the kernel virtual address at which the *MAXBSIZE* block is mapped. The file system dependent *read* function then copies the data from the kernel virtual address to the correct user virtual address. However, the first access to this kernel virtual memory address will cause a page fault because the page containing the data is not yet in memory. The kernel page fault handler will call a segment type specific function to read the page in from disk. This in turn, calls the file system dependent read page function (*VOP_GETPAGE()*) to read the data in. Subsequent accesses to offsets within the block will not normally cause a page fault because the pages containing the data are already resident in physical memory.

Writes to a file proceed in a similar fashion. After the data has been written, the *smap* structure is freed by the file system dependent write function. When the structure is freed, the file system dependent *VOP_PUTPAGE()* function is called to write the data back to the file. The following sections describe the details of these functions and their associated data structures. For more information about *vnode* operations, see Chapter 6.

Figure 5.1: *Segmap data structures*

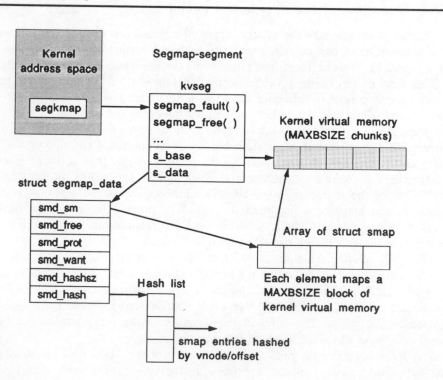

5.2.2 New buffer cache data structures

Two data structures are used by the new buffer cache to map disk blocks into kernel virtual memory: *segmap_data* and *smap* (see Table 5.1). The fields of the *segmap_data* structure are described as follows:

- *smd_sm* — is an array of *smap* structures. When the kernel virtual memory segment (*struct seg segkmap*) is initialized, the starting (or base) address of the segment is assigned to a kernel virtual address. The segment is also given a certain size. For example, the size may be arbitrarily set to say, one third of the amount of paged memory in the system. An array of *smap* structures is then allocated, one for each *MAXBSIZE* block of virtual memory in *segkmap*. This array is called *smd_sm*.

- *smd_free* — entries in the *smd_sm* array that are not in use are chained together on this freelist.

- *smd_hashsz* — counts the elements in the hash list array.

- *smd_hash* — when the I/O subsystem needs to look up the *smap* corresponding to a particular *vnode/offset* it uses a hash function. All the *smap* items that hash to the same place are chained together in a doubly linked list. If there is no entry corresponding to the desired *vnode/offset* a new *smap* is allocated.

An *smap* is used to map a particular *vnode/offset* to a kernel virtual address. The index of the *smap* in the *smd_sm* array is used to calculate the kernel virtual address. The kernel virtual memory segment starts at the address *segkmap->s_base*, and each *smap* maps a chunk of virtual memory with a size of *MAXBSIZE*. If the index of the *smap* in the array is x, then the kernel virtual address of the *vnode/offset* is:

```
kvaddr = segkmap->s_base + ( x * MAXBSIZE )
```

The fields in the *smap* structure are:

- *sm_vp* — pointer to the *vnode* mapped by this item.

- *sm_off* — offset being mapped in the file referenced by the *vnode*.

- *sm_hash* — all *smaps* that hash to the same address are linked together by using this pointer.

- *sm_next, sm_prev* — *smaps* are linked together on the freelist by using forward and backward pointers. When an *smap* is placed on the freelist, its *sm_vp* and *sm_off* fields are not cleared, and it remains on the hash list. This allows it to be reclaimed if it is reused shortly after. The *sm_vp*, *sm_off* and *sm_hash* fields are altered only when the *smap* is allocated to a new *vnode/offset*.

5.2.3 Functions in the new buffer cache

Three functions are used to implement the new buffer cache. Understanding their operation is vital to understanding how the new buffer cache works. They are:

Table 5.1: *Struct segmap_data and struct smap*

struct segmap_data	
Element	**Description**
struct smap *smd_sm	The array of *smaps*
struct smap *smd_free	Pointer to head of freelist
unsigned char smd_prot	Smap protections
unsigned char smd_want	Someone wants an *smap*
unsigned smd_hashsz	Size of the hash table
struct smap **smd_hash	Hash lists
struct smap	
Element	**Description**
struct vnode *sm_vp	The *vnode* being mapped
unsigned sm_off	Offset in *vnode* being mapped
short sm_refcnt	Reference count
struct smap *sm_hash	Next item in hash list
struct smap *sm_next	Next item on freelist
struct smap *sm_prev	Previous item on freelist

Figure 5.2: *File I/O fragment*

```
kvaddr = segmap_getmap( segkmap, vnode_pointer, offset ) ;
err = uiomove( .,.,.,uio_p ) /* Move the data to/from user space */
segmap_release( segkmap, kvaddr, flag ) /* Release the buffer */
```

- *segmap_getmap( )* — sets up a kernel virtual address that maps a block of the file.

- *uiomove( )* — copies the data between user and kernel virtual address space.

- *segmap_release( )* — releases the page mapping associated with the block.

An example of how a file system implementation might use these functions to say, read a block of data from a file into the kernels virtual address space is shown in Figure 5.2. These three calls are repeated for all chunks of data being read or written. They are described as follows:

- *segmap_getmap( )* — maps a *vnode/offset* to a kernel virtual address. It is called with three parameters:

  - *seg* — pointer to the segment in which the *vnode/offset* is being mapped. This is always a segment in the kernel address space pointed to by *segkmap*.

  - *vnode* — pointer to the *vnode* being accessed.

  - *offset* — the offset into the file being accessed.

segmap_getmap( ) returns the kernel virtual address to which the block containing the specified *offset* was mapped. The operation always maps a chunk from the file of *MAXBSIZE* bytes. The offset is rounded to the beginning of the mapped file block that contains the offset.

If the specified *vnode/offset* is found, then the reference count is incremented and the kernel virtual address calculated. Otherwise, it must take a new *smap* structure from the freelist.

Before the new mapping is set up, *hat_unload( )* is called to free all hardware mappings to the kernel virtual address mapped by this *smap* (see § 3.6.3). As a side effect of this, any data that has been changed will be written back to the original file. This design ensures that a buffer mapping persists as long as possible, and that disk writes are performed at the last possible moment. Delaying the update as long as possible gives the highest probability that a page will be reused without having to be read back from disk.

- *uiomove( )* — copies the data between user and kernel address space. The direction of the copy (to or from kernel address space) is described by the *uio_segfly* member in the *uio* structure passed down to *uiomove( )* as one of its arguments (see Table 5.5). This function is described in more detail in *uiomove(D3DK)* (see [AT&T 1990e]).

- *segmap_release( )* — once the data has been transferred, its associated *smap* structure is returned to the freelist with *segmap_release( )*. It has three parameters:

  - *seg* — the segment holding the virtual address. This is always *segkmap*.

  - *vaddr* — the mapped virtual address of the buffer to be returned to the freelist.

  - *flags* — describe how the mapped block is to be freed (see Table 5.2).

Table 5.2: *Flags for segmap_release( )*

Flag	Description
SM_WRITE	Associated pages must be written back
SM_ASYNC	Write the pages asynchronously (i.e., do not wait for output to complete)
SM_FREE	Return the associated pages to the freelist
SM_INVAL	Invalidate the page, so it will not be cached
SM_DONTNEED	Its associated *smap* structure is not likely to be needed soon, so put it at front of freelist

In addition to these function calls, the paging mechanism calls *segmap_fault( )* to fault-in a block from disk when a page fault occurs on a virtual address in the kernel virtual memory segment. It, in turn calls *VOP_GETPAGE( )*, which calls *hat_pteload( )* to set up the page address translation. The operation of *segmap_fault( )* is much simpler than *segvn_fault( )* (described in § 3.6.1) because it does not have to allocate swap space for pages in a *segmap*.

5.3 The old buffer cache

The functions described in this section describe the *old* buffer cache mechanism. This buffer cache and its associated functions will already be familiar to you if you have studied the internals of previous versions of UNIX System V. The old buffer cache mechanism forms an integral part of the I/O subsystem, and has been carried across into UNIX System V Release 4; and so, for completeness, it is described here.

5.3.1 Overview of the old buffer cache

As we saw in the previous section, the *segmap* operations provide a mechanism for reading data blocks from a file. However, not all data held in a disk file is arbitrary; some of it is *inode*, file, directory or other administrative information and the old buffer cache mechanism is used to access it. For example, the file system function used to read data from the disk, (*VOP_GETPAGE()*) converts a *vnode/file* offset into a disk address and then calls the low-level disk driver to read the data from the device. The old buffer cache provides the set of functions that perform the *vnode/file* offset to disk block address mapping. Additionally, it also implements a cache for holding recently used disk blocks.

5.3.2 Old buffer cache data structures

The mainstay of the old buffer cache is the *buf* structure. It holds a block of disk data and other information needed to pass data between the low-level disk driver and high-level functions such as *VOP_GETPAGE()*. The important fields in this data structure are shown in Table 5.3, and are summarized as follows:

Table 5.3: *Struct buf (buf_t)*

Element	Description
unsigned b_flags	Buffer state flags
struct buf *b_forw, *b_back	Hash list pointers
struct buf *av_forw, *av_back	Freelist pointers
o_dev_t b_dev	SVR3-style major/minor number
unsigned b_bcount	Count of bytes to be transferred
caddr_t b_addr	Memory address of data buffer
daddr_t b_blkno	Address of block in disk partition
struct proc *b_proc	Pointer to process doing I/O
struct page *b_pages	Pointer to pages for paged I/O
long b_bufsize	Size of data buffer
int (*b_iodone)()	Function called when I/O completes
struct vnode *b_vp	Pointer to its associated *vnode*

Table 5.4: *Buffer flags*

Element	Description
B_WRITE	Write data to disk
B_READ	Read data from disk
B_DONE	I/O operation has finished
B_ERROR	I/O operation failed due to error
B_BUSY	Buffer is in use, not on freelist
B_WANTED	Processes will be awoken when buffer is freed
B_ASYNC	Write buffer, but do not wait for I/O to complete
B_DELWRI	Write buffer only when it gets reallocated
B_FREE	Free pages when I/O operation complete
B_INVAL	Buffer data is not valid
B_HEAD	Buffer is really a hash list header
B_AGE	Buffer has not been accessed recently
B_PAGEIO	Write pages from *b_pages*

- *b_flags* — is a bitmap that describes the status of the buffer. There are 33 values specified for this variable, and the important ones are summarized in Table 5.4.

- *b_forw, b_back* — a buffer is held on a hash list so that it can be easily looked up. The hashing algorithm is based on the values of the *b_dev* and *b_blkno* fields. The fields *b_forw* and *b_back* are used to link the buffer to its hash list.

- *av_forw, av_back* — these fields are used to link the buffer onto a freelist. When a buffer is freed, it is placed at the end of the freelist and its hash pointers are left unchanged; this allows the buffer to be reclaimed if necessary. While the buffer is in use, these fields can be used as private list management variables by device drivers. For example, a SCSI device driver may use them to chain together I/O requests destined for the same disk.

- *b_dev* — holds the major and minor device number of the device special file to which the data being transferred is associated.

- *b_bcount* — specifies how many bytes should be read or written.

- *b_addr, b_bufsize* — in earlier releases of UNIX System V, the *b_addr* field pointed to a 512 byte data buffer. Under UNIX System V Release 4, the I/O block size is file system dependent, so this field points to a dynamically allocated data block whose size is given by *b_bufsize*.

- *b_iodone* — holds a pointer to a function that will be called when the I/O operation on the buffer has completed. Although the *ufs* and *s5* file system implementations do not use this facility, other file system implementations do. It allows the file system software to be notified when an I/O operation has completed.

The hash lists on which the buffers are placed are described by a *hbuf* structure, which contains three fields:

- *b_flags* — a buffer-flags field that only ever has the *B_HEAD* bit set. This indicates to the buffer allocator that this is a hash list header and not a bona-fide buffer.

- *b_forw, b_back* — pointers used to link the first buffer in the hash list onto the list.

The following global variables are used by the old buffer cache:

- *hbuf[]* — an array of *hbuf* structures that hold buffer hash lists. Its size is governed by the tuneable parameter *NHBUF*. The larger the value, the more hash lists are available, and the shorter the search time for a buffer. The default value of *NHBUF* is 64, which means that 64 hash lists are used for buffer-cache lookup. Each of the hash lists in the array are initially set up to be empty.

- *bfreelist* — this *buf* structure is used as the head of the buffer freelist, and when a buffer is no longer being used, it is linked onto it. The field *bfreelist.b_bufsize* holds the total amount of memory that can be allocated to the buffer cache. It is initialized by dividing the amount of system memory by the tuneable parameter *BUFHWM* (buffer high water mark). For example, if *BUFHWM* has the value 4, it means that one quarter of the available memory can be consumed by the buffer cache. The freelist pointers are initialized to indicate that there are no buffers on the freelist. Subsequent calls for buffers will use *kmem_alloc()* to allocate buffer headers and buffer data up to the memory limit given in *bfreelist*.

- *bhdrlist* — this list is similar to *bfreelist*, but it holds only buffer headers. That is, it holds *buf* structures that have invalid *b_addr* fields.

- *pfreelist* — this buffer cache is used for raw (physical) I/O operations. The number of buffers in this list can be configured by the system administrator through the *NPBUF* parameter. *pfreecnt* specifies how many buffers are on *pfreelist*. Each raw disk I/O request uses one of these buffers for the duration of the I/O (see § 5.7.3 for a discussion of raw disk I/O).

5.3.3 Buffer allocation and freeing

There are two functions used to allocate buffers: *getblk()* and *geteblk()*. They both make use of *getfreeblk()* to physically allocate memory for the buffers, and *brelse()* is subsequently used to free them. These functions are described as follows:

- *getblk()* — is called with three parameters: the device on which the disk block resides, the block number within that device, and the size of the buffer required. The buffer hash list is searched giving one of the following three results:

  - The buffer is found with the *B_BUSY* bit set in its flags. This means that the buffer is allocated to another process performing I/O to the same disk location. The buffer is marked as *B_WANTED*, and the process goes to sleep until the buffer becomes free.

- The buffer is found, and is not busy. The buffer is removed from the freelist and returned to the caller with the B_AGE bit cleared.

- The buffer is not found so *getfreeblk( )* is called to create one.

- *geteblk( )* — allocates an empty buffer (one that has no device or block number association). It is called with a single parameter specifying the size of the buffer to allocate. It calls *getfreeblk( )* repeatedly, until a buffer is returned.

- *getfreeblk( )* — the functions *getblk( )* and *geteblk( )* call this function to physically allocate a buffer. As a side effect of attempting to allocate the buffer, the buffer freelist is cleaned. All buffers with the B_AGE bit set are removed from their hash list. The data part of the buffer is returned to the operating system via *kmem_free( )*, and the header portion is placed back onto the *bufhdr* freelist. If there is not enough memory available to satisfy a request, buffers are removed in the same way as B_AGE buffers, until there is enough. The new buffer is allocated by taking a header from the *bufhdr* freelist and thereafter using *kmem_alloc( )* to allocate its data part.

- *brelse( )* — once a buffer is no longer needed (for example when the I/O operation has completed), it is returned to the buffer pool with *brelse( )*. If the buffer is marked B_WANTED, any processes sleeping on the buffer are awoken. If the buffer has the B_AGE bit set, it is placed at the front of the buffer freelist, otherwise it is placed at the end. This improves the chance of the buffer being reused by a later I/O operation.

5.3.4 Buffer mapping: *bmap( )* operations

The *bmap( )* function calculates disk addresses of data blocks by converting a logical block number into a disk address. Note that each file system type defines its own *bmap( )* function although file system types that are not disk-based, such as *nfs* and *rfs*, have no need for one.

For most file system types the logical block number is found by dividing the file offset by the file system block size. The *bmap( )* functions take this logical block number and returns its disk address.

For example, the *ufs* file system defines *ufs_bmap( )* as its private *bmap( )* function. It operates in two distinct modes:

- *read mode* — if the requested logical block number is in a direct-block associated with the file, the disk block number is read from the *inode* itself (see § 6.10.1). If the requested logical block number is in an indirect-block, the indirect-block must be read from the disk or from the buffer cache. From this, the disk address of the required block can be found.

    If a logical block number beyond the end of a file is requested, a hole is returned. All reads from a hole return zeros.

- *write mode* — if the write occurs to a block that is already part of a file, the disk address is looked up in the direct or indirect-blocks of the *inode*.

When a file is extended, file system dependent functions are called to allocate a new disk block. The block is filled with zeros and its disk address is returned to the caller.

Under previous releases of UNIX System V, the *bmap( )* functions took part in most file I/O operations. Under UNIX System V Release 4, *bmap( )* is used mainly by the *VOP_GETPAGE( )* and *VOP_PUTPAGE( )* functions. *VOP_GETPAGE( )* uses *bmap( )* to indicate whether a read is being performed at a hole in the file system. If it is, it creates a page filled with zeros, instead of reading the data from the disk. *VOP_PUTPAGE( )* uses *bmap( )* to extend the file and fill it with zeros. When a page is written beyond the end of a file, *bmap( )* creates the blocks, and *VOP_PUTPAGE( )* is called to write the data.

5.3.5 Reading and writing buffers

The functions *bread( )* and *bwrite( )* are called by *bmap( )* to read and write buffers. However, these functions are *not* called for normal paged I/O. Instead, the function *pageio_setup( )* and its derivatives are used (see § 5.4.1).

- *bread( )* — has three arguments: the device to read from, the disk address of the block to read, and the size of the block to read. It calls *getblk( )* to search the buffer cache. If the buffer is not found, it calls the device driver *strategy( )* function (see § 5.7.1) to read the block from the disk.

- *bwrite( )* — This function takes a single argument, the buffer to be written. The buffer contains the information about which device and block number must be used. The device driver *strategy( )* function is called to write the buffer to the disk. If the buffer has the *B_ASYNC* flag set, the function returns immediately, or else it sleeps waiting for the output to complete.

5.4 File I/O support functions

The functions *VOP_GETPAGE( )* and *VOP_PUTPAGE( )* form the heart of the file I/O mechanism. Almost all file I/O operations are performed by them. Each file system type defines its own *getpage( )* and *putpage( )* functions which are responsible for transferring pages of data between kernel address space and the file on disk.

The pages contain the data for a particular *vnode*, starting at a particular offset in the file and extending for a certain length. The functions defined by the *ufs* file system for *getpage( )* and *putpage( )* are described as follows:

- *ufs_getpage( )* — called by the upper levels of the operating system to get pages of data from a file. For example, it is called by *segvn_fault( )* and *segmap_fault( )* after a page fault has occurred.

    ufs_getpage( ) calls *ufs_getapage( )* (see Figure 5.3) to read each individual page in a specified range. *ufs_bmap( )* is used to find out if a hole in the file is being accessed. If it is, *ufs_getapage( )* allocates a page and initializes it to zeros.

Normally, a section of a file is being accessed so *ufs_getapage( )* allocates a page to hold the requested page. Once allocated, *ufs_getapage( )* initiates the input operation by calling the device driver *strategy( )* function. If the read is synchronous, *ufs_getapage( )* waits for the input to complete, otherwise it returns once the read has been initiated.

- *ufs_putpage( )* — called when pages of data must be written back to a file. Only dirty (modified) pages are written to the disk. When a page is to be written the device driver *strategy( )* function is called to physically write the data to its device. Generally, a page that is written to disk is cached and can be reclaimed by a program before it is reallocated. However, in some circumstances, it is necessary to dissociated the page from its *vnode* and mark it invalid. This means that the data within the page becomes invalid and thus it will not be reclaimed. If the page is referenced again, the data will be read in from disk. For example, when a file system is unmounted all the pages for the *vnodes* associated with open files on the unmounted file system must be invalidated. Since the *vnodes* themselves are no longer valid, all pages associated with them are also invalid.

  By default, disk writes are performed synchronously. That is, the currently running process will be put to sleep until the write is complete. However, it is possible to direct *ufs_putpage( )* (via a flag argument) to do asynchronous writes; the process will not be put to sleep during the write and will continue processing even if the I/O transaction has not completed. The *pageout* process calls *ufs_putpage( )* in this way when pages are being stolen from a process.

  ufs_putpage( ) (Figure 5.4) makes use of low-level functions to perform both synchronous and asynchronous I/O; these functions are described shortly.

5.4.1 Page I/O low level functions

Low-level I/O is carried out by the following five functions: *pageio_setup( )*, the device driver *strategy( )* function, *biowait( )*, *biodone( )*, and *pageio_done( )*. They are described by as follows:

- *pageio_setup( )* — allocates a buffer header by calling *kmem_alloc( )*.

- *strategy( )* — is the low-level block device driver function that carries out the read or write operation (see also § 5.7.1). When performing paged I/O, the driver *strategy( )* function is passed a buffer that was allocated by *pageio_setup( )*. The buffer will already have its *B_PAGEIO* bit set, and *b_pages* will point to the data. However, when performing I/O on behalf of *bread( )* and *bwrite( )*, the driver *strategy( )* function is passed a buffer from the buffer cache that has the *B_PAGEIO* bit clear, and the data is pointed to by *b_datap*.

- *biowait( )* — is used for synchronous writes. A write operation is initiated, and *biowait( )* is called. When it returns, the caller can assume that the write has completed. *biowait( )* puts the process to sleep until such time that the *B_DONE* bit is set. If the *B_PAGEIO* bit is set, it returns the pages to the page freelist.

Figure 5.3: *Algorithm for ufs_getapage()*

```
ufs_getapage()
inputs: vnode/offset for data to read
        length of data to read
outputs: pages are read in as a side effect
{
  struct buf *iobuffer

tryagain:
  call ufs_bmap /* are we are addressing a hole in the file */
  decide whether to do a read-ahead

  if( page_find( vnode, offset ) is NULL ) {
    /* page is not already in memory */

    if( accessing a hole in the file ) {
      allocate a page /* this may sleep if memory is low */
      initialize page to zeros
    }
    else {
      allocate a list of pages into which we read the data
      lock all pages in the list
      call pageio_setup to initialize iobuffer
      get device major number from vnode pointer
      call device's strategy function with iobuffer as argument
    }

    if( performing read ahead )
        do the above steps for the read-ahead page
    wait for io to complete on first page
    call pageio_done for iobuffer
    wait for io to complete on read-ahead page
    call pageio_done for read-ahead page
  }
  else {   /* Page is already in memory */
    if( page does not refer to correct vnode/offset )
      /* it was stolen at interrupt level */
      goto tryagain
    lock page, add to return list
  }
  return page list
}
```

Figure 5.4: *Algorithm for ufs_putpage( )*

```
ufs_putpage( )
inputs: vnode, offset, length, flags
outputs: pages written to disk as side effect
{

  for (all pages in page range ) {
    if( page is locked OR page is gone
        OR page not associated with this vnode )
      continue  /* ignore this page */
    if( freeing or invalidating a page ) {
      if( page is locked OR page is copy-on-write)
        continue /* ignore this page */
      if( page is in transit )
        sleep( page I/O completes )
    }
    /* Process page */
    if( page is modified )
      write to disk /* Page will be freed/invalidated
                     * after I/O completes */
    else if( B_FREE flag )
      place page on freelist
    else if( B_INVAL specified ) {
      place page at head of freelist
      set page vnode pointer to null
    }
  }
}
```

- *biodone( )* — is called by device driver interrupt service routines when an I/O operation is complete. It sets the *B_DONE* bit, and wakes up any processes that are sleeping on the passed buffer.

- *pageio_done( )* — is called to free a buffer previously allocated by *pageio_setup( )*, but only after a synchronous write has completed. A function wishing to synchronously write pages, takes the following steps:

  - call *pageio_setup( )* to allocate a buffer header.

  - call the device driver *strategy( )* function to initiate the write to disk.

  - call *biowait( )* to suspend process execution until the write operation has completed. The device driver interrupt service routine will wake the process once the data has been written.

- call *pageio_done( )* to free the buffer header.

On the other hand, a process performing an asynchronous write takes the following steps:

- call *pageio_setup( )* to allocate a buffer header and mark it *B_ASYNC*.

- call the device driver *strategy( )* function to initiate the write, and then return. The function that initiated the write now thinks that the write is complete, so it continues its normal processing.

- after the operation completes, the device driver interrupt routine calls *biodone( )* to wake up any processes that may be sleeping on the buffer.

5.5 Read and write file I/O

The *read* and *write* system calls are the means by which a process reads and writes files. Their operation depends on what type of file is being operated on. This section looks at how *read* and *write* perform I/O to files in the file system. The functionality of the operation varies between file system implementations. This section examines how I/O is achieved on files in a *ufs* file system. However, the principles embodied in the *ufs* file system can be applied to other file system types.

5.5.1 Data structures for *read* and *write*

The *read* and *write* system calls use two data structures to record information about their progress. The *uio* structure (Table 5.5) holds the information about where the data is being copied, and how much of it has been copied so far. The *iovec* structure is contained within the *uio* structure, and holds pointers to the user data. The interesting fields in the *uio* structure are:

- *uio_offset* — holds the current file offset. A read operation starts reading from this offset, and a write operation starts to write at this offset.

- *uio_fmode* — these flags specify the modes that the file was opened with by the user (for example, *O_RDONLY*, *O_NDELAY*, and so on).

- *uio_limit* — limits the size of files by specifying the maximum file offset that can be written (*ulimit*). If a process attempts to exceed this offset, the write operation will fail and *EFBIG* is returned.

- *uio_resid* — holds the number of bytes to transfer. The data copied in a single *read* or *write* system call often requires multiple I/O requests. For example, if the user requests a read of 16K bytes from an 8K byte block file system, then at least two read I/O operations are needed internally to satisfy the single 16K byte request. As each I/O request completes, this field is reduced by the number of bytes transferred. When it reaches zero, the I/O operation is complete and the system call returns.

- *uio_iov* — is an array of *iovec* structures that hold pointers to the user data being read or written.

- *uio_iovcnt* — specifies how many elements are in the *uio_iov* array.

Table 5.5: *I/O structures*

struct uio (uio_t)	
Element	Description
*struct iovec *uio_iov*	User I/O buffers
int uio_iovcnt	Number of I/O buffers
unsigned long uio_offset	File offset for I/O
short uio_segflg	Specifies address space
short uio_fmode	File access flags
unsigned long uio_limit	Maximum file offset (from *ulimit*)
int uio_resid	Bytes remaining to be copied
struct iovec (iovec_t)	
Element	Description
caddr_t iov_base	Pointer to user buffer
int iov_len	Length of user buffer

An *iovec* structure is used to point to an area of user data that is being read or written. It has two fields: a pointer to the data, and a field specifying its length. The *iovec* is used for *scatter/gather* I/O operations (see *readv* and *writev* below).

5.5.2 The *read* and *write* system calls

This section describes the actions taken for the *read* and *write* system calls when applied to a file residing on a *ufs* file system.

- *read( )* — when a *read* system call is issued, the following actions are carried out:

  - The file descriptor is looked up in the file table (see § 6.2.1), returning an error if the file is not found. An *iovec* is created based on the arguments passed by the user, and a *uio* structure is set up to point to it.

  - The *vnode* associated with the file table entry is locked; this means that only a single process can update the *vnode*. Any other processes that want to read or write the file will sleep until the lock is released.

  - The *ufs_read( )* function (Figure 5.5) is called to read in data from the file. The call to *segmap_getmap( )* allocates an address in kernel virtual memory. The call to *uiomove( )* (see § 5.2.3) copies data from the kernel virtual address where the page of the file was mapped, into buffers in user-space pointed to by the *iovec* contained in the *uio* structure. *uiomove( )* operates by copying data into the first *iovec*. When it is full, it copies the data into the second *iovec*, and so on until all *iovec* structures have been filled.

At the lowest level, *uiomove( )* copies data between the kernel page and the user page. The first time the kernel page is accessed, there will be a page fault causing the data to be read in. The same may happen if the user page is accessed thus the copy will usually find that both pages are resident, and the data will be copied from the file into the user program.

Figure 5.5: *Algorithm for ufs_read( )*

```
ufs_read( )
inputs: vnode pointer, uio pointer, flags
output: uio updated as side effect
{
  do {
    /* Set up mapping for page that holds desired data */
    kernel_addr = segmap_getmap( vnode, offset )
    /* Copy data from kernel to user */
    call uiomove( kernel_addr, uio )
    call segmap_release
  } while NOT error AND uio_resid > 0
  update vnode access time
}
```

- *write( )* — The *write* system call operates in a similar fashion to *read* except that data is transferred in the opposite direction. In a *ufs* file system, the function *ufs_write( )* (Figure 5.6) performs the disk update. Again, the real work is done by the *segmap* operations. The *uiomove( )* function copies the data from the *iovec* supplied in the system call into the kernel page created by *segmap_getmap( )*. When the data has been copied, a call to *segmap_release( )* causes the page containing the data to be written to disk.

5.5.3 The *readv* and *writev* system calls

The system calls *readv* and *writev* are used to read and write data with a single system call, between a file and multiple buffers in a program. For example, a program might want to write to a file a message header followed by some message text. By using *writev* the data is written with a single system call. The programmer initializes the first element of an *iovec* to point to the header data structure. The second element is initialized to point to the message body. The *iovec* and its size are passed as arguments to *writev*, and the data is written in a single transaction.

An alternative method is to issue two *write* system calls: one for the header and one for the data. Another method is to combine the header and body into a single buffer and write it with a single *write* system call. However, in most circumstances, *writev* will be more efficient; a single system call reduces the context switching load on the system, and can also reduce the amount of paging since the pages involved are less likely to be stolen during its execution. In the two *write* case, the pages may

Figure 5.6: *Algorithm for ufs_write( )*

```
ufs_write( )
inputs: vnode pointer, uio, flags
outputs: error code, data is written as a side effect
{
  do {
    if( write offset in UIO is too great )
      return EFBIG error
    lock vnode
    /* ufs_bmap will ''automatically'' extend the file.
     * The disk addresses * it returns are ignored */
    call ufs_bmap for vnode/offset
    unlock vnode
    kernel_addr = segmap_getmap( vnode, offset )
    /* Copy data from user to kernel - may cause page faults */
    call uiomove( kernel_addr, uio )
    /* Segmap release will free the kernel pages. As a result, the
     * updated page is written to disk */
    call segmap_release
  } while NOT error AND uio_resid > 0
  update vnode access time
  return error code
}
```

be stolen between the first and second *write* calls, which will considerably increase the execution time. However, the single *write* case also has disadvantages: the data must be copied twice, first from the header and body into the single buffer, and then from the buffer to the kernel. This second copy increases the execution time of the *write*, and can cause unnecessary paging activity.

Both the *readv* and *writev* system calls have three parameters: the file being accessed, an array of *iovec* structures, and the length of the array. These system calls copy the contents of the *iovec* between user and kernel address space. The kernel's *iovec* array has a fixed size of 16 elements on most systems. This limits the number of elements in the user-supplied array to 16. If the array is larger than this, *EINVAL* is returned. When the *iovec* has been filled in, these system calls proceed in the same way as the *read* and *write* system calls.

5.6 Device drivers

The subject of device driver design is the subject of a book in itself (see [Egan, Teixeira 1988] and [Pajari 1992]), but for completeness we provide a brief discussion of device driver functionality, and highlight the facilities provided for device driver designers under UNIX System V Release 4.

A device driver is the means by which a process can interface to a device. Normally, a device is a peripheral component having some physical connection to the machine hardware — for example, CD-ROM, tape drive, SCSI controller, Ethernet controller, and so on. However, it may be a fictitious component that performs like a device and/or presents itself like a device; a RAM resident disk springs to mind, although the UNIX bit bucket (*/dev/null*) can be classed as a device also. A device driver associated with a non-physical device is called a pseudo device driver.

5.6.1 Special files

For the purpose of the rest of this chapter we will discuss only two types of special file: block special and character special.

All devices (including memory) are represented by special files stored in the file system. A high-level discussion of special files, devices, and the method by which a process interfaces with them is given in § 2.5.3 and § 2.11 respectively.

The interface between the kernel and device driver is called the *Driver Kernel Interface* (DKI). At the end of this chapter we discuss the DKI and some of the functions it contains.

A special file has no associated data per se. It is simply an abstraction of a device. A special file is created with the *mknod* system call, which simply makes an entry in the directory entry for the special file being created and marks it according to its special file type. *mknod* is used to create *block, character* or *pipe* special files. Pipe special files are referred to as "named-pipes" and are discussed in § 2.5.6 and § 7.10.

Since devices are usually permanent, their associated special files are usually permanent too. That is, once created they are rarely ever removed. Furthermore, apart from pipe special files, *mknod* will allow only super-user to create them. Generally, a special file is created for a device when the device and its associated device driver are first installed. So most special files are pre-installed into the file system by the vendor.

All special files usually reside in the */dev* directory although they can conceptually be created anywhere within the UNIX file system tree. In most cases a command called *mknod(1M)* is used and internally it uses the *mknod* system call. For example, on the author's system, the command:

```
mknod /dev/dsk/sc4d2s3 b 32 33
```

requests that a block special file is to be created to represent the third partition (slice) on the second disk of the fourth SCSI disk controller. The *b* argument specifies a block special device, and 32 is the major device number that specifies which type of device it is. Major numbers are preconfigured numbers that the system uses to index into a device switch table — in this case, the *bdevsw[]* table (see § 5.6.3) since it is a block special file. In the above example, the major number 32 represents the SCSI disk driver. The parameter, 33 is the minor device number, which is decoded by the device driver itself. In this case, the SCSI disk driver recognizes it to mean the third partition on the second disk of the fourth controller. It can be seen that the major and minor device number specify exactly which disk partition is being accessed; the name could be anything, but it is usually chosen to reflect some symbolic likeness to the actual device name.

5.6.2 Driver functions

When a program issues an *open* system call on a special file, the system passes control to its associated device driver *open* function. Subsequent calls to *read* and *write* on that special file result in the system passing control to the device driver *read* and *write* functions, to transfer data between the program and device. This paradigm is not true for all system calls, since a device driver represents only a handful of system services. Furthermore, the system does not require a device driver to support all possible services (although without an *open* function defined in the driver, a process can never directly associate with it). It can be seen that a device driver designer must define the functions that represent the system services for which his or her device driver supports. We will learn what these functions are in the following sections.

The kernel configuration software enforces a naming convention for device driver functions. The name is formed from two parts; a prefix and a suffix. The prefix is always a unique identifier for the driver — for example, a SCSI device driver may use the prefix *scsi_*. The suffix is the name of the function, such as *strategy, open, close, read, ioctl* and so on. Thus, the *strategy( )* function for this *scsi_* driver is called *scsi_strategy( )*, the open function is called *scsi_open( )*, and so on. When the driver is being configured into the kernel the configuration process expects the function names in the driver to conform to this convention.

Device driver designers often implement both block and character functionality into a single set of device driver functions, so there is a single device driver for both block and character interfaces controlling the same device. However, some functions in the driver are useful only to block drivers while others are useful only to character drivers. Additionally, the system is normally configured so that the major and minor numbers of block special files are the same as the major and minor numbers of their associated character special files.

5.6.3 Device driver data structures

The operating system holds an entry point for each configured device in a device switch table. The device switch table for block devices is called *bdevsw[ ]*. Similarly, the device switch table for character devices is called *cdevsw[ ]*. Thus, a block device driver has an entry in *bdevsw[ ]* and a character device driver has an entry in *cdevsw[ ]*. If the device driver is both block and character, then it has an entry in both device switch tables. Each entry in *bdevsw[ ]* is a *bdevsw* structure (Table 5.6). Similarly, each entry in *cdevsw[ ]* is a *cdevsw* structure (Table 5.7).

When a device is being accessed by a process the system uses the major number of its associated special file to index into its relevant device switch table. Suppose a block special file with major number 32 is being accessed; the kernel uses this

Table 5.6: *Struct bdevsw*

Element	Description
int (*d_open)( )	Device open function
int (*d_close)( )	Device close function
void (*d_strategy)( )	Read or write a block
void (*d_print)( )	Error message print function
int (*d_size)( )	Function to give partition size
int (*d_ioctl)( )	I/O control function
char *d_name	Device name
int *d_flag	Device flags

Table 5.7: *Struct cdevsw*

Element	Description
int (*d_open)( )	Device open function
int (*d_close)( )	Device close function
int (*d_read)( )	Read data from device
int (*d_write)( )	Write data to device
int (*d_ioctl)( )	Perform I/O control operation
int (*d_mmap)( )	Address range check for *mmap*
int (*d_segmap)( )	Set up mapping for *mmap*
int (*d_poll)( )	Poll device for I/O
struct streamtab *d_str	Device functions for STREAMS
char *d_name	Device name
int *d_flag	Device flags

number to index the 33rd entry in *bdevsw[]*. An operation is then performed by making an indirect function call using the function pointers defined in that *bdevsw[]* entry. For example, to call the *read* function for a block device, the following code fragment could be used:

```
error = (*bdevsw[major].d_read)(device, uio, credentials)
```

The fields in the device switch tables are described as follows:

- *d_open,* — pointer to the function used to open and close the device.

- *d_read, d_write* — pointer to the functions used for *read* and *write* system calls for the device. They perform the actions needed to copy the data between the process and the device.

- *d_strategy* — pointer to the *strategy( )* function for the device. A *buf* structure is passed to it as a parameter; the buffer contains the data to be read from or written to the device. (Used by block device drivers only.)

- *d_print* — pointer to the device print function, which is called by the kernel to print out error messages associated with the device, on the system console. (Used by block device drivers only.)

- *d_size* — pointer to the size function, which is used to find the number of sectors in a disk partition. For example, when read or write operations are being carried out the operating system can quickly detect an attempt to read or write beyond the end of the partition. (Used by block device drivers only.)

- *d_ioctl* — pointer to the function used for the *ioctl* system call for the device. This is used for control operations on the device, which are recognized and defined only by the device driver itself.

- *d_segmap* — pointer to the function used to map device memory into the address space of a process. For example, the on-board memory in an Ethernet controller card that can be accessed by both the CPU and the card itself. (Used by character device drivers only.)

- *d_mmap* — pointer to the function used by the *mmap* system call to check that an address being used falls within the range of addresses mapped by the device. (Used by character device drivers only.)

- *d_poll* — used by the *poll* system call for the device. This function is called to check if a polled event has taken place. (Used by character device drivers only.)

- *d_str* — points to the device's *streamtab* entry. STREAMS devices have this field filled in, but have empty entries for the other functions (*read*, *write*, and so on). This field is not used by non-STREAMS devices.

- *d_name* — pointer to a string containing the name of the device driver.

A device driver may also define an interrupt service routine, which is configured into the kernel separately; it does not have an entry in a device switch table. The function of the interrupt service routine is to handle interrupts for the device that the driver controls. For example, it must take the necessary steps to process an interrupt and to notify processes associated with the device of the event.

A device driver that does not support a particular operation must nevertheless specify *nodev( )* in the field of its entry in the relevant device switch table. For example, a parallel printer driver does not usually support the *read* system call, and so *nodev* is defined for its *d_read* function pointer field. *nodev( )* is a function that simply returns *ENODEV*, meaning that the operation is not supported by the device. Sometimes the device driver supports a function, but the function does not do anything special. For example, the *open* function in the driver for */dev/mem* does not do anything — it simply returns 0 indicating success. However, an *open* function must be provided so that a process can associate itself with the device. The kernel provides the function called *nulldev( )* for this purpose, which is used similarly to *nodev( )*. It is illegal to have the value zero as the function pointer in the device switch table. If, for example, the *open* function is specified as zero, a kernel error will occur when the open function is called, causing the system to panic. The *d_poll* function pointer is an exception to this rule; if it is null, the generic file system poll function *fs_poll( )* is called. This will always return a value saying that the device is ready for I/O.

Figure 5.7: *Device driver open( )*

```
int scsi_open(devp, flag, otype, credp )
  dev_t *devp ;
  int flag ;
  int otype ;
  cred_t *credp ;
```

5.6.4 Device driver *open* function

System calls for devices are implemented using the *vnode* operations of the *snode* (see § 6.9.1), so when a special file is opened an *snode* is assigned to the calling process to represent that file with. For example, when the *open* system call is applied to a character special file it calls the function *spec_open( )*; this in turn looks up the entry for the device in *cdevsw[]*. As an indirect result of this, the device driver open function associated with the special file is called (see § 6.9).

A device driver *open* function is called with four parameters (Figure 5.7) and they are explained as follows:

- *devp* — points to a data object containing the major and minor device numbers of the device being opened.

  A STREAMS device driver can choose to select a *clone* of the device that it represents by obtaining a different minor device number to represent it with, thus overriding that supplied in the function call parameters (see § 7.4.2 and 7.9.4). In such a case, the driver returns the new minor device number via the *devp* pointer.

- *flag* — is a bit mask indicating whether the device is to be opened for reading, writing, or both.

- *otype* — allows the driver to keep a count of the number of times it has been opened, and for what purposes. The following values are used:

  - *OTYP_BLK, OTYP_CHR* — indicates that the device is being opened as a block device (*OTYP_BLK*) or as a character device (*OTYP_CHR*). These values allow the driver writer to write an open function that recognizes the mode of operation (i.e., if it is to operate in character mode or block mode) and can direct its processing accordingly.

  - *OTYP_MNT* — indicates that the file is being opened as a result of a *mount* system call.

  - *OTYP_SWP* — indicates that the device is being opened as a swap device.

  - *OTYP_LYR* — indicates that the driver has been opened internally, perhaps by itself or perhaps by another driver.

The kernel increments the *otype* counter for each *open* (or *mount*) done on a device controlled by the driver. The counter is subsequently decremented as each process disassociates itself from the device (or when *umount* is used on it). Note that the driver's *open* function is called for every *open* operation requested on the device, while the driver's *close* function is called only by the process that last closes it. A device with a counter greater than zero is in use and is therefore busy. If the device is a disk then the driver maintains a counter for each partition on the disk. If one of these counters is associated with a partition containing a file system, then it indicates whether the file system is mounted. When the file system is first mounted, the counter is incremented and for each subsequent open done on a file within that file system the kernel increments the counter again.

The *mount* system call (§ 6.6.4) calls the block device *open* function when it attempts to associate the device containing the file system with the VFS mount list (see § 6.6.2). Thus, a device driver associated with a mounted file system always has an *otype* count greater than zero. Note that *mount* will fail if the counter is not zero since it assumes that the device is busy.

When the *umount* system call calls the device driver *close* function, it should result with a zero counter. If the counter is greater than 1 when an attempt to unmount the file system is made, the *umount* system call will fail since it assumes that there is still a file open — a busy file system cannot be unmounted. Since the *otype* counter is decremented by the kernel only for each *close* (or *umount*) done on the device, it can be seen that a *close* that renders the count equal to zero is, in fact, the last close done on the device.

If the driver open function is called with $OTYP\_LYR$ specified, it can assume that it is being called by another driver open function and so it has no associated special file; in other words, it is a layered driver not directly called by a process. Therefore, instead of incrementing the counter, the driver need only set a flag to indicate that a layered open has occurred. The flag is subsequently cleared when the layered driver is closed.

- *credp* — points to a credentials structure for the process that issued the open request (see § 4.11.5).

These flags allow a driver to carry out an orderly cleanup when it is being closed, or allow it to prevent certain kinds of open. For example, a block device driver may wish to prevent the device being opened for mounting if it is already being used as a swap device.

Operations carried out by a device driver open function are often hardware dependent. For example, a block device driver for a disk would typically do the following:

- Decode the *devp* argument to yield the controller number, the disk number and the partition number.

- If another process is currently opening the device, sleep until that open has completed. Then set the flag indicating that an open of this device is currently underway.

- If it is the first time the partition is being opened, read the drive parameters from the disk (usually partition zero). This contains the information about the disk geometry and its partition table.

The partition table is held on the disk, so it can be updated online and it contains the information about the size and start position of each partition within the disk.

The disk device driver dynamically allocates a private data structure for each disk drive and for each partition within the drive. The disk drive parameters and partition information are then read into these data structures for later use.

- The *otype* information is used to update the count of how many times the disk partition has been opened.

- The dynamic data structures that the driver uses to communicate with its controller are allocated.

- The open-in-progress flag is cleared and any processes that are asleep waiting for the open to complete are woken up.

5.6.5 Device driver *close* function

The device driver close function is called when the last process associated with the device issues a *close* system call. However, in the case of a block special file, the *close* may be the result of an *umount* system call. A block device driver close function for a disk typically does the following:

- Calculate controller, disk and partition numbers based on the *devp* argument.

- End the association between the user process and the device, and prepare the device and device driver so that it is ready to be opened again.

- The driver busy flag is set. If other processes wish to open or close the device, they will be forced to sleep. The driver then waits for any outstanding disk requests to complete, after which the dynamically allocated private data structure associated with the device is freed and the busy bit is cleared. Any processes that are waiting to open or close the device are awoken.

5.6.6 Device driver interrupt service routine

Interrupt handling service routines are one of the most machine-specific areas in the kernel so there are no hard rules about the functionality of their internal processing. Furthermore, the means by which a driver interrupt service routine is called, and the parameters passed to it, vary with each vendor's implementation.

Interrupt service routines are called by the low level interrupt handling mechanisms which are discussed in § 4.9.2 and § 4.9.7. An interrupt may occur at any time and it may not necessarily have any relation to the process that caused it. For example, consider a disk driver that issues a read instruction in the context of a process that issues a *read* system call. After posting the I/O instruction to the disk controller, the driver puts the process to sleep until the data is read in. When the data arrives, the disk controller will interrupt the processor and the disk driver interrupt service routine will be brought into service. However, the interrupt will normally arrive while the processor is executing in the context of another process.

For this reason, a device driver interrupt service routine must always obey the following rules:

- It must never assume a process's context is current.

- It must never reference or manipulate the currently running process's user-area (i.e., the kernels global *u* area) either directly or indirectly via another function call.

- It must never call *sleep( )* or call other functions that may result in the process being put to sleep.

- It must never lower the CPU interrupt priority level below the vectored interrupt level that the interrupt service routine was originally called with.

- It must never call itself or call other functions that may result in it calling itself.

There are two types of interrupt service routine: *vectored* and *polled* — their implementation depends on the system's bus architecture and also the facilities provided by the processor. Most machines implement vectored interrupts but on machines that do not support them, interrupt service routines are polled. During the interrupt poll, each handler returns a value to the kernel to indicate if it should poll another interrupt service routine. As each handler is invoked, it must determine if the interrupt was destined for it (i.e., if it was generated by a device associated with the driver) and if so, it must handle the interrupt.

On machines that implement vectored interrupts, all interrupts are handled by a single interrupt handler which determines the interrupt source. It, in turn, calls the relevant interrupt handling function according to the interrupt type.

Whatever method is used, when the handler is invoked it must take the necessary steps to process the interrupt as quickly as possible. In most cases the interrupt is generated when an I/O transaction has completed so the interrupt handler must notify the sleeping process of the event. To do this, character device interrupt service routines call *wakeprocs( )* or *wakeup( )* to wake up sleeping processes. Block driver interrupt service routines call *biodone( )* to set the *B_DONE* flag in the buffer and to wake up processes waiting for it to become available.

5.7 Block device drivers

A block device has associated with it a *block device driver*, which is characterized by a set of functions that implement the block device interface.

Block devices are hardware devices that provide random access to blocks of data, and are mainly used to access disk partitions. For example, when a disk partition is used to hold a file system, a command such as:

```
mount -F ufs /dev/dsk/sc4d2s3 /mnt
```

is used to associate the partition with a particular directory in the UNIX file system tree — in this case */mnt*. In this case, when files under the directory */mnt* are accessed, the block device driver will be called to physically read or write the files data.

The set of functions and data structures that comprise a block device driver are described in the following sections, and for the purpose of the examples, we have used the function name prefix of *scsi_*.

5.7.1 Device driver *strategy* function

The main interface to a block device driver is through its *strategy( )* function. It is responsible for carrying out the physical block read and write operations on the device. It is called with a single parameter, the buffer that is to be read or written.

A driver's *strategy* function is called indirectly via its entry in the *bdevsw[ ]* table (see § 5.6.3). It may also be called directly or indirectly (via *physiock( )* see § 5.7.4) by the *read*, *write* and *ioctl* interfaces in the character driver. This facility allows the driver designer to write a single device driver that implements both block and character functionality. However, unlike character drivers which perform raw I/O directly between user address space and kernel address space and hence may use the user-area to determine the details of the I/O request, a block driver is passed a buffer that details the I/O operation instead. Furthermore, a characteristic of the block device driver interface is that the paging system is used to cache data blocks of a file, and the paging mechanism calls the device driver *strategy( )* function to read or write the data. However, the nature of the caching mechanism means that not every *read* or *write* system call results in a physical read or write. This means that the block device driver *strategy( )* function may be called in the context of a process that did not directly call it. So, like the interrupt service routine, a driver *strategy( )* function must never use the global *u* area and must never assume the concept of a currently running process.

The *strategy( )* function (Figure 5.8) interacts with its associated controller to ensure that the data represented by the buffer is transferred to or from the device.

Figure 5.8: *Block device strategy( )*

```
int scsi_strategy(buffer)
  struct buf *buffer ;
```

Consider a disk device driver that implements two data structures per configured disk drive. The data structures are stored in an array indexed by their minor number. The first data structure is used for a *work-queue* and contains *request headers*. The request headers hold the information needed by the disk controller to carry out the transfer. Requests in the work-queue are the requests currently being worked on by the controller. The request headers have a flag that indicates if they are busy. The flag is set when a request is initiated and cleared when it completes. The design is such that there are only two request headers for each configured disk.

The second data structure is used for a *pending-request-queue*. It contains a list of buffers waiting to be placed on the work-queue. When the work-queue is full, buffers are chained onto the pending-request-queue. As a place become available on the work-queue, the buffer is moved from the pending-request-queue to the work-queue. This is done by associating a buffer with a request header.

The function *scsi_strategy( )* performs the following tasks:

- It calculates the controller, disk and partition numbers from the *b_edev* field in the buffer.

- It verifies that the device has been opened and that the request falls within the bounds of the partition.

- It links the buffer to the pending-request-queue.

- If the work-queue has space available, the first request on the pending-request-queue is moved to the work-queue. By writing to the disk controller registers, the controller is told that there is a new item in the work-queue to be processed.

After initiating the I/O request, *scsi_strategy( )* returns. If the I/O is synchronous, the caller sleeps on the address of the buffer, waiting for the *B_DONE* bit to be set. For asynchronous I/O requests, the caller simply continues processing.

5.7.2 Block device *read* and *write* functions

read and *write* system calls can be applied to block special files, despite the lack of *read* and *write* functions support by block device drivers.

There are two ways in which this can be done. The first is by issuing *read* and *write* system calls to the block special file. The second is by using the *raw I/O* interface — a process issues a *read* or *write* system call to the character special file associated with the block device. So, for each disk partition, there is both a block and character special file, and associated block and character device driver to control them.

System calls for devices are implemented using the *vnode* operations of the *snode* (see § 6.9), so as a result of issuing a *read* or *write* system call on a special file, the *spec_read( )* or *spec_write( )* function is called. The algorithm for *spec_read( )* is shown in Figure 5.9. A *read* from a block special file operates the same way as a *read* from a regular file. That is, *segmap_getmap( )* is called to set up a kernel address into which the data will be read. Then *uiomove( )* is called to copy the data from kernel space to user space. As a side effect of this copy, the data from the file is read in via the page-fault mechanism. Finally, *segmap_release( )* is called to free the kernel pages that were allocated. The operation of *spec_write( )* on a block special file is similar to that for a *write* on a regular file and is so is not discussed.

5.7.3 Raw disk I/O

For raw disk I/O, page caching and the paging mechanism are not used; the data is read or written directly between the device and user address space. Thus, raw disk I/O avoids the need to copy between kernel address space and user address space.

Figure 5.9: *Algorithm for spec_read( )*

```
spec_read( )
inputs: snode, uio structure, flag, credentials
outputs: error code, data read in as side effect
{
  if( snode is for a character special device ) {
    look up device in cdevsw
    if( it is a STREAMS device )
      call strread to process the read /* See Chapter 7 */
    else
      call character device specific read function
    return
  }
  do { /* At this point, it must be block special. */
    /* Set up mapping for page that holds desired data */
    kernel_addr = segmap_getmap( vnode, offset )
    /* Copy data from kernel to user */
    call uiomove( kernel_addr, uio )
    call segmap_release
  } while NOT error AND uio_resid > 0
  return ;
}
```

Each *read* or *write* system call results in a physical disk transfer. Raw I/O, coupled with synchronous writes is often used by database management systems. They control when data is read or written to or from the disk, and perform disk updates only when necessary. However, they achieve a gain in application performance because data need only be copied once.

Raw disk I/O is achieved using character special files with associated character device driver software. However, a driver that is implemented with both block and character functionality will use indirect calls to the block driver *strategy( )* function via *physiock( )* to achieve the physical I/O operation. As an example, consider the typical *read* and *write* functions of a disk driver that implements both block and character functionality. Since it controls a disk, the main use of the driver will be via its block interface, but for the following scenario assume that the *read* or *write* is done via its character interface. It might do the following (see also Figure 5.10):

- Calculate the controller, disk and partition information.

- Check that the read or write falls within the bounds of the device (if not, return *EIO*).

- Call the function *physiock( )*, passing to it the name of the block device driver *strategy( )* function, and the information about the I/O operation to perform — for example, whether the system call being serviced is a *read* or a *write*.

Figure 5.10: *Example driver read( ) and write( ) functions using strategy( )*

```
/*
 * dvr_read and dvr_write
 *
 * Uses dvr_strategy for RAW I/O
 */
dvr_read(dev)
int dev;
{
    physiock(dvr_strategy, NULL, dev, B_READ, nblocks, uio_p);
}


dvr_write(dev)
int dev;
{
    physiock(dvr_strategy, NULL, dev, B_WRITE, nblocks, uio_p);
}
```

Using this scheme, the kernel can call the driver *strategy( )* routine directly (via *bdevsw[ ]*) in the case of a *read* or *write* on a block special file, or it can call the driver *read* or *write* functions directly in the case of a *read* or *write* operation on a character special file. In either case, the driver *strategy( )* routine is called in the long run to perform the actual physical I/O.

5.7.4 The *physiock( )* function

The operation of *physiock( )* is shown in Figure 5.11. It is only ever called by the character driver *read* and *write* routines. Its purpose is to validate and verify the I/O request and perform an unbuffered physical I/O operation via the block driver *strategy( )* function.

If the second argument to *physiock( )* is non-NULL, then it points to a buffer structure describing the I/O request. Otherwise, *physiock( )* allocates a buffer header from the physical I/O buffer freelist (*pfreelist*, see § 5.3.2). The address field in the buffer header is initialized to point to the memory area specified in the *read* or *write* system call arguments. The block device *strategy( )* function is called, and *physiock( )* sleeps until the I/O request has completed. This means that the *strategy( )* function will physically transfer the data to or from the disk or user address space directly.

The *physiock( )* function takes 6 arguments which are described as follows:

- *strategy* — a pointer to the device driver block device *strategy( )* function.

- *buf* — a pointer to a *buf* structure describing the I/O request. If NULL, the buffer is allocated internally from *pfreelist* and returned when the I/O operation completes.

Figure 5.11: *Algorithm for physiock( )*

```
physiock( )
inputs: strategy function, read/write flag, uio, device information
outputs: zero if successful
         or error code for errno; reads/writes as side effect
{
   if( beyond end of device OR write would cross end of device)
     return ENXIO error

   if( read crosses end of device )
     reduce read count to read up to the end of the device

   allocate a buffer header from physical buffer freelist

   for( all iovecs in the uio structure ) {
     while( iovec length field > 0 ) {
       /* fill in fields in buffer  */
       address field = base address from iovec
       count field = count from iovec
       calculate disk address from uio->offset field
       call as_fault to page in and lock user pages that are
       referenced in this I/O operation
       call block device strategy function
       sleep until buffer done flag is set /* io is complete */
       unlock user pages
       wakeup processes sleeping on the buffer
       update counts in uio
     }
   }

   place buffer on physical buffer freelist
   return success or error code
}
```

- *dev* — expanded device major and minor number.

- *rwflag* — flag — either *B_WRITE* or *B_READ* depending on the operation being done.

- *nblocks* — maximum number of blocks that the device can support.

- *uio_p* — pointer to a *uio* structure describing the user space associated with the I/O request.

5.8 Character device drivers

The character special file interface allows a process to perform I/O via the character device driver without passing through the buffer cache. Character devices fall into two categories: STREAMS or non-STREAMS based character devices. STREAMS devices are character devices that are accessed via the STREAMS mechanism. A STREAMS device is distinguished by having a value in the d_str field in its entry in $cdevsw[]$ (see § 5.6.3). The descriptions that follow in this chapter assume that non-STREAMS devices are being used. For more information on STREAMS, see Chapter 7.

The original purpose of the character device driver scheme was to provide an interface to the system console, modems, terminals and networking hardware. However, the STREAMS mechanism has superseded the basic character device driver for this type of application, although graphics hardware, disk and tape devices are often implemented with character device driver interfaces. The character driver allows a process to access data in the hardware by using the $read, write$ or $mmap$ system calls.

The following subsections describe the operations of the various character driver functions, with the exception of the $mmap()$, which is described in § 5.9.

5.8.1 Character device $read$ and $write$ functions

The driver $read$ and $write$ functions manage the transfer of data between the process issuing the call and the device.

The major device number is looked up in the $cdevsw[]$ table. If the entry has a d_str field, then STREAMS processing is carried out, otherwise it calls the device driver specific $read$ or $write$ function.

A pseudo code example for a character driver $read$ function is shown in Figure 5.12. The device being accessed has a 256 byte memory mapped buffer. (That is, accessing a particular 256 byte area of memory will access the device's buffer.) The $read$ and $write$ functions copy the data between the process and the device in 256 byte chunks. The $uiomove()$ function makes it easier for the driver writer to transfer data from a device into the process that issued the call.

5.8.2 Device driver $ioctl$ function

The $ioctl$ system call provides an interface to device drivers that cannot be provided through the normal $read$ and $write$ interfaces. For example, an asynchronous line device driver provides the $ioctl$ function so that a process can alter the state of the modem-control outputs. These outputs cannot be easily controlled using the $read$ and $write$ system call interface.

The $ioctl$ system call has three arguments: a file descriptor, a command (or request) to perform, and an optional argument to that command. The file descriptor must be an open descriptor obtained from a previous $open, creat$ or dup system call. The command and argument parameters are defined by the driver; the

Figure 5.12: *Character device driver I/O*

```
#define DEVICE_ADDRESS   ... /* Hardware address of buffer */
#define DEVICE_BUFFER 256  /* Size of buffer */

int dvr_read( dev, uio, cred )
...
{
  return devrw(dev, uio, cred, UIO_READ)
}

int dvr_write( dev, uio, cred )
...
{
  return devrw(dev, uio, cred, UIO_WRITE)
}

/* Common function for read and write. */
int dvr_rw( dev, uio, cred, uioflag )
...
enum uio_rw uioflag ;
{
  int error = 0 ;
  check minor device number
  check credentials
  /* Call uiomove to transfer DEVICE_BUFFER sized pieces */
  while(uiop->uio_resid != 0 AND !error ) {
    n = MIN(uiop->uio_resid, DEVICE_BUFFER) ;
    /* uiomove reduces uio_resid. */
    if( uiomove( DEVICE_ADDRESS, n, uioflag, uio) )
      error = EFAULT ; /* uiomove got an address fault */
  }
  return error
}
```

command is selected from a list of control functions that the device driver knows about, and the optional argument is used to supply any additional information to the command. The kernel passes all three arguments through to the driver unchanged. The device driver *ioctl* function (Figure 5.13) is looked up in the *cdevsw[]* table in the same way as the *read* or *write* functions. Its arguments are explained as follows:

- *device* —the major and minor device number of the device being accessed.

- *command* — specifies which operation to perform. If the driver does not recognize the command, it must return *EINVAL*.

Figure 5.13: *Character device ioctl*

```
int dvr_ioctl(device, command, argument, mode, credentials, retval)
  dev_t *device ;
  int command ;
  int argument ;
  int mode ;
  cred_t *credentials ;
  int *retval ;
```

- *argument* — is used to pass data between the process in user-mode and the driver in kernel-mode.

- *mode* — specifies which flags were used to open the special file associated with the device. The driver may use this information to find out if the device was opened for reading or for writing.

- *credentials* — pointer to an area holding the user credentials of the process issuing the call.

- *retval* — is used for the *ioctl* system call return value. The driver must return the value zero for success, or an error code (see Appendix A) for failure. However, a successful *ioctl* command might also wish to provide a return value for the system call. For example, if the *ioctl* calculates how many characters are available for reading from the device, it is convenient to pass this number back as the return value of the system call. To do this, the driver fills in the value in the area pointed to by the *retval* argument.

The examples that follow show how an example character device driver, called *dvr_*, uses *ioctl* commands to achieve the same results as the *read* and *write* functions described in the previous section. Real device drivers use the same mechanism for exchanging device control and status information between the user process and the device. Note that the *ioctl* facility is not restricted to character drivers only (see Table 5.6).

An extract from a program that operates in user-mode is shown in Figure 5.14. It uses the *ioctl* system call to read data from the *dvr_* device. The definitions for *DVRREAD* and *DVRWRITE* follow the convention for *ioctl* command names. The construct ('B'<<8) is an attempt to ensure that the *ioctl* command value will be unique. Using unique commands reduces the risk of error if the command is applied to the wrong device type. For our example, we will assume that the letter *B* is not being used by another driver, so these values are sure to be unique.

Before issuing the *ioctl* system call, a *dvr_ioctl_struct* structure is filled. It contains a pointer to a buffer where the data is to be read into, and an integer specifying how many characters to read. The device driver code for processing the *ioctl* is shown in Figure 5.15.

The function *copyin* is used to copy the contents of the *dvr_ioctl_struct* structure from user address space into the driver buffer in kernel address space. If the user

Figure 5.14: *Using ioctl — user-side*

```
/* Define read, write command values usually in a header
 * file shared with the driver code */
#define DVRREAD  (('B'<<8) | 1 )
#define DVRWRITE (('B'<<8) | 2 )
/* This structure passed in/out for read/write commands */
struct dvr_ioctl_struct {
  int dvr_len ;    /* Length of buffer for read/write */
  unsigned char *dvr_buffer ; /* Date buffer for read/write */
}
...
/* User program to read data from device using ioctl */
unsigned char buffer[256] ;
struct dvr_ioctl_struct di ;
...
  di.dvr_len = 256 ;
  di.dvr_buffer = buffer ;
  if( ioctl( fd, DVRREAD, &di ) == -1 )
    error
  else {
    di.dvr_len says how much was read
    process contents of buffer
  }
```

specified an illegal address, *copyin( )* returns a non-zero value which makes the driver return the *EFAULT* error code. Page faults in the user address space are handled automatically by the paging mechanism.

After calculating the amount of data to transfer, the driver copies the data from the hardware device (at the address *DEVICE_ADDRESS*) to the buffer that the user program specified. A second *copyout( )* is used to write back the amount of data transferred. The *copyout( )* function works the same as *copyin( )*, except that the data is copied from the kernel address space to the user address space. Page faults and addressing errors are handled the same way as for *copyin( )*.

The driver *ioctl* function returns zero, indicating that it completed successfully. In this example, the *retval* parameter is not used. Before the driver *ioctl* was called, the return value was initialized to zero. This means that the user process will receive a return value of zero if the *ioctl* is successful.

5.8.3 Character device *poll* function

The *poll* system call is used to query a device or a stream to see if it is ready for an I/O operation. The operation of the *poll* system call, its parameters and the data structures used, are described in § 7.9.9.

Figure 5.15: *Handling ioctl — driver-side*

```
dvr_ioctl(device, command, argument, mode, credentials, retval)
  dev_t *device ;
  int command ;
  int argument ;
  int mode ;
  cred_t *credentials ;
  int *retval ; {
  int available ;
  struct dvr_ioctl_struct kdi ;

  /* Get data from user space to kernel space in buffer 'kdi' */
  if( copyin( argument, &kdi, sizeof kdi ) )
    return EFAULT ;
  available = amount of characters we can read from the device
  available = min( available, kdi.dvr_len ) ; /* find minimum */

  /* Copy data from device to user buffer */
  if( copyout( DEVICE_ADDRESS, kdi.dvr_buffer, available ) )
    return EFAULT ;
  /* Fill in length field and return whole structure to user */
  kdi.dvr_len = available ;
  if( copyout( &kdi, argument, sizeof kdi ) )
    return EFAULT ;
  return 0 ; /* Success! */ }
```

When the *poll* system call is applied to a character device, the device driver specific *poll* function (see Figure 5.16) is called with five arguments. They are described as follows:

- *dev* — holds the major and minor device number of the device being polled.

- *events* — specifies the events being polled for (see § 7.9.9).

- *anyyet* — specifies how many of the file descriptors being examined have events pending.

- *reventsp* — events pending on the file are returned through this pointer.

- *phpp* — points to a *pollhead* list described below.

The character device *poll* function checks if any of the events requested in the *events* parameter have occurred. If so, the corresponding bits are set in the variable to which *reventsp* points. If there are no events pending, then this value is cleared.

When the device is initialized, the driver should allocate a *pollhead* structure for each of its configured minor devices. In the example of Figure 5.16, they are held in an array, and indexed by the minor device number. The *pollhead* contains a linked

Figure 5.16: *Character device poll*

```
/* There is one pollhead for each minor device */
struct pollhead dvr_pollheads[ NMINOR ] ;

dvr_poll(dev, events, anyyet, reventsp, phpp )
 dev_t dev ;
 short events ;
 int anyyet ;
 short *reventsp ;
 struct pollhead *phpp ;
{
 calculate minor device number
 if( there are events pending ) {
   set bits in *reventsp for these events
   return 0
 } else {
   /* No events pending. */
   set *revents to zero
 }
 if( anyyet == 0 ) {
   /* set text */
   *phpp = &dvr_pollheads[ minor device number ] ;
 }
 return 0 ;
}
```

list of processes that will be awoken when the driver detects that an event has occurred on this minor device.

If the value of *anyyet* is zero, it means that the *poll* system call has not yet found any file descriptors with events pending. If the minor device being polled has no events pending either, it must fill in the value pointed to by *phpp* with a pointer to the private *pollhead* structure for this device. The process that issued the *poll* system call will be chained onto this list, and will sleep until data is available.

When there are no events pending on the minor device, the calling process sleeps. When the device driver detects that data has become available, it must wake all processes that are sleeping on the file descriptor. It does this by calling the *pollwakeup()* function, giving the *pollhead* pointer for the device as argument. The *pollwakeup()* function makes all the processes on this list runnable, so that they can each detect whether the file descriptor has events available.

5.9 The *mmap* system call

The *mmap* system call allows a process to map the contents of a file into its address space, so that instead of using the *read* and *write* system calls it uses pointers to access the files data. To do this, it combines elements of the memory management subsystem, the I/O subsystem, and the file subsystem.

mmap creates a new segment and attaches it to the process's address space. The new segment is associated with an already open file descriptor. Access to the file proceeds as if it were a data segment in the process. When the new segment is accessed, the data is read in from the file by using the normal page fault mechanism.

An *mmapped* file works as follows. A process maps the file and accesses its contents via the new data segment. Any changes will be made to the memory page mapping this part of the file (at the particular *vnode/offset*).

If another process accesses the same part of the file, it will be accessing the same *vnode/offset* and will, therefore, share the same physical memory page. As a result, any changes made to the file by one process are seen immediately by all others. Any modified pages will eventually be written to the disk; for example, by *fsflush*, *pageout*, or when the last process closes it.

The example in Figure 5.17 shows two functions that achieve the same result: they both open the file for reading and writing, read the 24th record, alter it, and then write it back again. The first function uses the *read*, *write* and *lseek* system calls while the second function uses *mmap*.

Figure 5.17: *Using mmap*

```
/* Structure of the file */
 struct record {
   unsigned char contents[256] ;
   unsigned accessed ;
 } ;

 /* Access the file using read, write, lseek.
  * error checks omitted for clarity. Record numbering
  * starts at zero
  */
 function1( )
 {
   int fd ;
   struct record r ;
   fd = open( "file", O_RDWR, 0 ) ;
   lseek( fd, 24 * sizeof(struct record), SEEK_SET ) ;
   read( fd, &r, sizeof(struct record)) ;
   /* alter fields of r */
   r.contents = data for this field
   r.accessed = data for this field
```

```
    /* Move back to correct point in file */
    lseek( fd, 24 * sizeof(struct record), SEEK_SET ) ;
    write( fd, &r, sizeof(struct record) ) ;
    close(fd) ;
}

/* Access it using mmap. Error checks omitted, record
 * numbering starts at zero
 */
function2( )
{
    int fd ;
    struct record *rp ;
    int len = the length of the file
    fd = open( "file", O_RDWR, 0 ) ;
    rp = mmap((caddr_t) 0, len, PROT_READ|PROT_WRITE,
            MAP_SHARED, fd, 0 ) ;
    /* Update the file, simply by altering memory location */
    rp[24].contents = data for this field
    rp[24].accessed = data for this field
    close(fd) ;
}
```

Figure 5.18: *Declaration for mmap*

```
caddr_t mmap(addr, len, prot, flags, fd, offset )
    caddr_t addr ;
    size_t len ;
    int prot ;
    int flags ;
    int fd ;
```

The *mmap* system call takes five parameters (see Figure 5.18), which are described as follows:

- *addr* — specifies the address within the program that the file is to be mapped into. If the address is zero, the operating system selects a suitable address to use and returns it in the system call return value. Programmers writing portable applications should make use of this facility. On many implementations the address is chosen so that there is an unmapped page either side of the mapped segment. This means that references beyond the bounds of the segment will generate a fatal error, leading to early detection of bugs in the user program. If the address is non-zero, it must be aligned to a page boundary otherwise the system call will fail.

When the address is non-zero, it is taken as a hint to *mmap* about which virtual address to use for the mapped segment.

- *len* — specifies the length of the segment. This value must be less than or equal to the length of the file, which means that it is not possible to extend a file with *mmap*. It is possible to call *mmap* with *len* greater than the file size, but the process will receive a *SIGSEGV* signal when it attempts to reference beyond the end of it. (Note that the file size is rounded up to the nearest page boundary; any data read between the end of file and the page boundary will read back as zeros; furthermore, data that is written into this area is not written back to the file.)

- *prot* — specifies how the segment will be accessed. The value is a bitmask formed from the values *PROT_READ*, *PROT_WRITE* and *PROT_EXEC*, meaning the segment can be read, written or executed. Note that usually the implementation automatically sets *PROT_READ* if *PROT_WRITE* or *PROT_EXEC* is set. The value can also be *PROT_NONE*, meaning that the pages in the map are inaccessible. If the process accesses the segment while its protection is *PROT_NONE*, it will receive a *SIGSEGV* signal.

- *flags* — specifies how the segment is to be used. The value is a bitmask formed from the values *MAP_SHARED*, *MAP_PRIVATE* and *MAP_FIXED*. If *MAP_SHARED* is specified, the mapping is shared with other processes that map the same part of the file so that any changes made to the data will be seen by other processes when they access this file. If *MAP_PRIVATE* is specified, no changes to the mapped file will be seen by other processes that access the file. Also, in this case, no changes made to the segment will ever be written back to the file. It is illegal to specify both shared and private mappings in the same call. Finally, if *MAP_FIXED* is specified, the system will attempt to map the data exactly at the address specified by the *addr* parameter. If it is not possible, the error code *EINVAL* will be returned.

- *fd* — is the file descriptor of an open file.

- *offset* — gives the offset in the file at which the mapping must start. This value must be aligned to a page boundary.

Note that not all file system types support the *mmap* facility. Furthermore, even if a file system type supports it, some file types do not allow it (see Table 5.8). For example, is impossible to *mmap* links, directories, FIFOs and STREAMS devices. A disadvantage of using *mmap* in place of *read* and *write* is that it will not allow a process to extend the size of a file, so it is only useful where the file has already been created. However, the advantages far outweigh this inconvenience:

- *mmap* is usually more efficient in use because a copy operation is avoided when the data is read or written; the data is read straight into a page and then accessed directly from that page, whereas a *read* system call reads the data into a kernel page which is then copied to user space.

- *mmap* is more convenient since a process can reference the contents of a file with pointers.

Table 5.8: *Availability of mmap( )*

File	File Type				
System	Regular	Char	Block	Directory	Link
s5	•				
ufs	•				
nfs	•				
rfs	•		•		
specfs		•	•		
fifofs					
bfs					
proc					

- *mmap* reduces the context switching load because only a single system call is made, whereas with the *read* and *write* interface a system call must be made for every I/O operation.

- *mmap* provides a shared memory facility; many processes can access a file using *mmap* and data written by one process can be read by another, without the data being copied to and from disk in the meantime.

Note that when a file has been mapped, the data is written back to the file when a *sync* occurs, or when the last process closes the file (see § 6.5.2). A process wishing to force an update of the mapped file must issue the *fsync* system call on the file. This guarantees that when the call is complete the data will have been written to the disk.

5.9.1 Block device and regular file *mmap*

The *mmap* implementation for regular files is quite simple. The steps to achieve the mapping of a file resident in a *ufs* file system are described below:

- The *mmap* system call itself does very little work. It validates the parameters and then calls the *vnode*-specific mapping function by calling *VOP_MAP( )* (see § 6.3.3). The *VOP_MAP( )* function does all the hard work, returning the address at which the segment was mapped. This address is returned by *mmap* as the result of the system call.

- When the file being mapped is on a *ufs* file system, the mapping is set up by *ufs_map( )*. The functions for the other file system types operate similarly. The function starts by validating the parameters and the *vnode* for the file being mapped. The system function *map_addr( )* is called. This calculates a suitable address at which to map the segment.

- *as_map( )* is called. This function takes the address at which a new segment should be mapped, and creates a segment that will be mapped to that address. The length of the segment is given in the *mmap* system call. The arguments passed to it by *ufs_map( )* cause *as_map( )* to create a new *segvn* segment. This new segment is associated with the *vnode* of the file being mapped. At this point, the new segment is set up at a virtual address in the process's address space, and the system call returns.

- The next phase occurs when the newly allocated segment is accessed. The first access incurs a page fault. The page fault software looks up the segment being addressed. In this case, it is a mapped segment, and the segment operations associated with the segment specify that *segvn_faultpage( )* must be called. As a result, a page is allocated and its contents are read from the file. (See § 3.6.1 for a description of how *segvn_fault( )* operates.) If the segment is marked as *MAP_PRIVATE*, and the segment is writeable, the first write will cause an anonymous page to be created. Remember that anonymous pages are accessible only to the process that created them. Anonymous pages are always associated with a swap *vnode*, so no changes made to the page will ever be written back to the file from which the page data originated.

For block special files that are mapped, instead of calling *ufs_map( )*, the mapping function for special files (*spec_map( )*), is called. This function checks that the length of the mapped segment is less than the length of the device. It then calls *as_map( )*, and a *segvn* segment is set up in the same way as described above.

5.9.2 Character device *mmap* function

The *mmap* system call is implemented differently for character devices. The *mmap* interface allows a user program to directly access memory that is on board a memory-mapped device. For example, a frame store will provide memory on its controller for the image being displayed. If the driver makes this memory available to a user program, the overhead of passing the data through the kernel is greatly reduced.

Each character device driver must provide its own *mmap* function which is used to check whether an address falls within the range of addresses mapped by the device. Character device drivers have the option of providing their own *segmap( )* function. If they specify *nodev( )* as the *segmap* function, then the generic function *spec_segmap( )* is used (see below).

The implementation of *mmap* on character devices is supported by the *segdev* segment type. The *segdev* operations that take part in the character driver *mmap* system call are described below (see Figure 5.19).

- *mmap( )* — calls *VOP_MAP( )*, which results in a call to *spec_map( )* because the file being mapped is a character special file.

- *spec_map( )* — is the *snode* specific mapping function. If the mapping is *MAP_PRIVATE*, the system call fails. This is because it is impossible to create private copies of device memory. The device-specific *map* function is called to ensure that each page in the mapped range is valid, *as_map( )* is then called.

- *as_map( )* — arguments to *as_map( )* indicate that it must create a *segdev* segment for the newly mapped segment. The function *segdev_create( )* does this.

Figure 5.19: *Character device mmap*

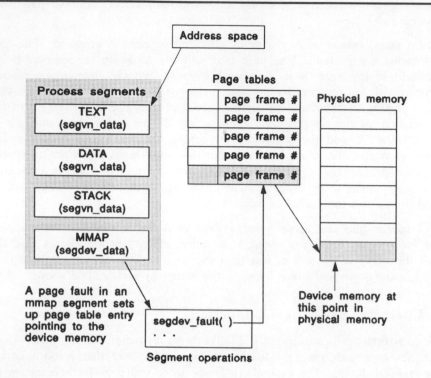

- *segdev_create( )* — creates and initializes the *segdev* segment. The private data structure contains information about which device is being mapped, and a pointer to the device-specific map function. Assuming all was set up correctly, the system call returns.

- *segdev_fault( )* — is called when the program accesses addresses within the device segment. It calls the device-specific map function to check that the address is valid. There is an area of memory in the device that can be accessed by using the *mmap* system call. This memory will appear at a certain physical address, and there will be a physical page number corresponding to it. The *segdev_fault( )* function creates a page table entry that contains the physical page number of the device memory. This has the effect of mapping the virtual address directly into the device's memory space. Note that this page is always valid, and present in memory, and cannot be stolen by the page stealer.

The device driver-specific *mmap* function is called to validate addresses. Pseudo code for an example driver *mmap* function is shown in Figure 5.20. The function is called with three arguments:

- *dev* — holds the major and minor device numbers of the device being accessed.

- *offset* — holds the offset into the device being accessed.

- *prot* — specifies the access mode required. It has the values *PROT_READ, PROT_WRITE* or *PROT_EXEC*.

In operation, the function checks that the given offset lies within the range of physical addresses mapped by the device. If the address is valid, the page number corresponding to that address is returned, otherwise it returns -1. The page frame number is calculated with the macro *btoc( )* (meaning byte-to-click) which converts a byte value into a page number.

Figure 5.20: *Character device mmap*

```
int dvr_mmap( dev, offset, prot )
  dev_t dev ;
  off_t offset ;
  int prot ;
{

  /* Check we are within bounds of the device */
  if( offset < 0 OR offset > DEVICE_BUFFER )
    return -1 ;

  /* DEVICE ADDRESS is the physical address of the device buffer
   * btoc = "byte to click" - gives the page frame number that
   * includes the given byte. Defined in sysmacros.h
   */
  return btoc(DEVICE_ADDRESS - offset) ;
}
```

5.10 Example character driver: mm

UNIX System V Release 4 provides a driver called *mm*, which gives a character device interface to the system memory. The *mm* driver supports four different minor device numbers. When the operating system is installed, four character special files are created, corresponding to the four minor device numbers. They are:

- */dev/mem* — provides an interface to the physical memory on the system. If a program reads from offset zero in this file, it will read the contents of the first byte of physical memory in the system.

- */dev/kmem* — provides an interface to the physical memory used by the kernel. Programs such as **crash(1M)** (see Chapter 9) or **netstat(1M)** need to read data held in the kernel and */dev/kmem* provides this access. If a program reads the first byte of this file, it reads the contents of the first byte of the kernel memory.

Without this interface, programs would have to know where in physical memory the kernel code and data start. Programs such as **crash(1M)** extract kernel data by using the *nlist(3E)* subroutine on */stand/unix* to obtain the kernel address of the variable of interest. *lseek* is then used to move to this offset followed by a *read* to extract the data from */dev/kmem* (an example of this is given in § 4.8.6).

- */dev/null* — is the system *bit bucket* or *rat whole*. Data written into this file disappears. It is used when you want to discard the output from a program. When the file is read, the system call always returns a count of zero.

- */dev/zero* — provides an infinite supply of zeros. When a program requests a read of 256 bytes from this file, it will receive 256 zeros. If the file is written to, the data is discarded.

The following describes the operation of the functions that comprise the *mm* driver. Where necessary, the functions check the minor device number to decide which of the four devices is being accessed.

- *mmopen( )*, *mmclose( )* — there is no special processing to do when these devices are opened. They simply return zero, indicating success.

- *mmread( )*, *mmwrite( )* — the following actions are performed, depending on the device being accessed:

  - */dev/mem* — the value in *uio_offset* specifies the physical memory address to access. The function checks that this address is valid and that the user is not trying to read from a hole in physical memory. If all is well, the function *uiomove( )* is called to copy the data between the physical memory address and the buffer in user address space.

  - */dev/kmem* — the value in *uio_offset* specifies the offset into kernel memory to use. The offset is once again checked to ensure that it does not reference a hole in the address space. If the offset is valid, the data transfer between user address space and kernel address space is made by calling *uiomove( )*.

  - */dev/null* — if the file is being read, a count of zero is returned. If the file is being written, the function adjusts the counts in the passed *uio* structure to make it appear that all the data has been written. (*uio_offset* is incremented by the size of the write, and *uio_resid* is set to zero.)

  - */dev/zero* — the function contains a buffer containing a block of zeros. When the file is being read, *uiomove( )* is called to copy the data from this buffer into the user address space.

- *mmmmap( )* — when this function is called, the parameter *offset* is the offset into the segment being mapped. The return value is the page number of the memory being accessed. The various devices are mapped as follows:

  - */dev/mem* — specifies the physical memory address being accessed. The address is checked to ensure that it does not reference a hole in physical memory. The function then converts the supplied offset into a page number, and the page number is returned.

- /dev/kmem — specifies the kernel address to be mapped. If the address is not a valid kernel address, or if it coincides with a hole in memory, the function returns a failure code. If the address is correct, it is converted to a page number and returned.

- /dev/null — the function always returns -1 when this file is mapped. This means that the mmap system call will fail for this file.

- /dev/zero — the function mmmmap( ) will never be called for this file (see below).

- mmsegmap( ) — the mm driver provides a segmap function, called indirectly by the mmap system call. It must initialize the segment mapping functions for the device. When mmap is called for the files /dev/mem, /dev/kmem or /dev/null, mmsegmap( ) then calls spec_segmap( ) to set up the segment and its mappings.

  Mapping /dev/zero is a special case. When this file is mapped, mmsegmap( ) calls as_map( ) which creates a segvn segment having no associated vnode. This means that as each page in the segment is accessed, the page will be created, filled with zeros, and allocated swap space. This method provides an alternative way for a process to allocate memory.

5.11 The Device Driver Interface and Driver Kernel Interface

The Device Driver Interface (DDI) and the Driver Kernel Interface (DKI) specify the means by which device drivers and the UNIX System V Release 4 kernel interact with each other. The interface specifies the functions a device driver must provide so that it can be called by the kernel, the functions in the kernel that a device driver may call, and the data structures used for the data exchange.

The DDI/DKI is provided to document the interfaces and to help software developers improve the portability of their drivers. If a driver is written with this interface it will be more easily portable to another machine that runs UNIX System V Release 4. The DDI/DKI interface also helps highlight the areas of a driver that are non-portable. If the areas of non-portability are known, they can be anticipated when a port is being attempted.

A driver interacts in three different ways with its hardware and software environment:

- Kernel to driver, and driver to kernel — this interface consists of the driver functions that are called by the kernel to implement system calls. For example, the driver-specific open function is called in response to the open system call. There is also a set of documented kernel subroutines that a driver is allowed to call — for example, the wakeprocs( ) function. The DDI/DKI specification concentrates on this interface.

- *Driver to hardware* — the means by which a driver interacts with device hardware is completely machine dependent. The device driver software usually includes an interrupt service routine; this forms part of the driver to hardware interface. The C Language specification of the interrupt service routine is specified by the DDI/DKI, but the remaining parts of the driver to hardware interface fall outside the scope of the DDI/DKI specification.

- *Driver to system boot procedures* — and driver to system configuration mechanism. The means by which a device driver is incorporated into the system, and the method by which a device driver makes itself known to the system at boot-time are, once again, completely machine dependent.

The DDI/DKI specification concentrates on the first of these interfaces. Its provision clearly improves the portability of device drivers. However, while there are many manufacturers, each with their own hardware platforms, the remaining two interfaces will always remain machine-specific. Fortunately, manufacturers are recognizing the need to encourage third parties to develop products for their machines, so they are improving the documentation of the machine-specific areas.

The DDI/DKI reference manual is divided into sections that are similar to the sections of the UNIX Programmer's Reference Manual:

- Section 2 describes the entry points to a driver that are called by the kernel. These are equivalent to the system calls section in the Programmer's Manual.

- Section 3 describes the kernel subroutines that are called by the driver. These are equivalent to the C library functions described in the Programmer's Manual.

- Section 4 describes the data structures that are passed between the driver and kernel, and are equivalent to the file formats section in the Programmer's manual.

Information in the DDI/DKI listed in the previous paragraph falls into a further three categories:

- *Processor specific functions* — also called the Device Driver Interface (DDI). This is the machine specific set of functions. Each manufacturer provides its own DDI specification. There is no guarantee that facilities in the DDI of one manufacturer will be in the DDI of another. However, manufacturers are encouraged to document their DDI so that driver writers isolate the machine specific parts of their drivers. Facilities in this category have their manual entry given as *facility*(D*x*D), for example: *int(D2D)*, *hdeeqd(D3D)* and *hdedata(D4D)*.

- *Processor independent functions* — supported in the current release of UNIX System V Release 4 and to be supported in future releases. These facilities are intended to be machine independent, and manufacturers are supposed to provide these functions with their releases of UNIX System V Release 4. The facilities in this category have their manual entry given as *facility*(D*x*DK). For example: *open(D2DK)*, *rmalloc(D3DK)* and *uio(D4DK)*.

- *Processor independent functions* — whose interfaces may change in future releases of UNIX. These functions should be provided by manufacturers who deliver UNIX System V Release 4. In future releases, these facilities may be altered or removed. Manual entries for this group of facilities are given as *facility*(D*x*K). For example: *segmap(D2K)* and *hat_getkpfnum(D3K)*.

The DDI/DKI specification provides the following recommendations to improve the portability of drivers:

- Driver code should not access the user-area directly, nor directly alter other operating system data structures. Previously, drivers had to alter the user-area directly to adjust I/O counts. However, if the structure of the user-area is changed, drivers will no longer be binary compatible.

- Drivers should not directly manipulate the fields in the data structures described in section 4 of the DDI/DKI specification. Where possible, the functions from section 3 should be used instead. This reduces problems if the field names or the sizes of these data structures are changed in future releases.

- The header file *ddi.h* must be included by device drivers, and it must be the last header file included before the body of the program code. This is because many kernel functions are implemented as C Language macros. The header file undefines some of these macros, thereby forcing the compiler to use the equivalent functions. The benefit of this is that the operation of the function can be changed, and binary compatibility maintained.

The sections that follow summarize the facilities described in each of the three sections of the DDI/DKI specification. Many of the functions have been described elsewhere in this book, in which case references to the descriptions are given.

Note that the documentation of the DDI function set cannot be easily standardized because manufacturers are free to put whatever they want into their DDI specification. In the sections that follow, DDI functions appear in the following references:

- The DDI/DKI specification for the AT&T 3B2 (the UNIX System V Release 4 porting base) [AT&T 1990e].
- The DDI/DKI specification for Intel Processors [USL 1992a].

These functions will be referred to as *commonly available functions*.

5.11.1 DDI/DKI section 2

The D2DK functions shown in Table 5.9 have all been described earlier in this chapter, except for the functions *srv( )* and *put( )*, which are described in Chapter 7.

The functions in Table 5.10 are part of the DDI set of functions, but they are commonly available.

The *init( )* and *start( )* functions are provided by device drivers that need to initialize or start the device. Both perform the same task: to set up any initial state of the device. The initialization operations that might be carried out by these functions are:

Table 5.9: *Functions in D2DK*

Function	Description
chpoll( )	Implement *poll* system call for character device
close( )	Close a device
ioctl( )	Device I/O control function
open( )	Implement *open* system call for a device
print( )	Displays driver error messages
put( )	Process a message in a stream
read( )	Implement *read* system call for a device
srv( )	Process messages held on a STREAMS queue
strategy( )	I/O function for block device
write( )	Implement *write* system call for a device

Table 5.10: *Functions in D2D*

Function	Description
int( )	Handle an interrupt from a device
init( )	Device hardware initialization function
size( )	Give the size of the device
start( )	Device software initialization function

- initialize device driver data structures;
- allocate memory used for *rmalloc( )*;
- set up any virtual address mappings for the device;
- initialize other static data areas.

The functions are called from the kernel *main( )* function as the system boots. The kernel has two tables: *io_init[]* and *io_start[]*. When a driver is configured into the kernel, its *init( )* and *start( )* functions are placed into these tables. The kernel *main( )* function calls each function in both tables after it has initialized the memory subsystem, but before it has mounted the root file system. At the time these functions are called, there is no user context, no root file system, and no scheduling system. This means that these functions must not go to sleep.

The *mmap( )* and *segmap( )* functions are in the DKI specification, meaning they might not be supported in their current form in future releases of UNIX System V Release 4.

5.11.2 DDI/DKI section 3

The functions from D3DK are the machine independent functions that are called by device drivers (Appendix E summarizes them).

In the DDI/DKI guidelines, we said that you should not access kernel state information, and that some macros have been reimplemented as functions. Using functions to access data means that the implementation of the data or data structure can be hidden from the programmer. This in turn makes the driver more portable and maintainable because the manufacturer can change the implementation, but the driver writer is insulated from the changes. The paragraphs below show some of the functions provided that make this concept possible.

- *drv_getparm( )* — reads kernel state information. In particular it is used to return the values of: *lbolt* (the time in *HZ* since the system was last booted), the current process group identifier, the process table pointer, the process identifier, the session identifier and the time of day clock. The function looks up the data from the correct place in the kernel address space, and returns its value. Without this call, drivers would need to access the user-area directly. If the manufacturer changes the definition of the *user* structure, then problems may occur. If, on the other hand, the driver uses *drv_getparm( )* to access these fields, then the manufacturer will hide the implementation changes within this function.

- *drv_priv( )* — checks whether a given credential's structure is for a privileged user. It replaces the *suser( )* function in earlier releases.

- *makedevice( )* — creates a *dev_t* from a major and minor device number so that the implementation of *dev_t* can be changed. Conversely, *getmajor( )* and *getminor( )* extract the major and minor numbers from a *dev_t*.

- *max, min* — these two functions have traditionally been implemented as macros. The DDI/DKI now provides them as functions. *max( )* returns the larger of two specified integers, and *min( )* returns the lesser of the two.

- *uiomove( )* — described earlier in this chapter. Before *uiomove( )* was available, driver writers had to access the user-area directly when they wanted to update I/O counts.

Table 5.11: *Functions in D3D*

Function	Description
dma_pageio( )	Breakup I/O request into smaller units
etoimajor( )	Change external to internal major number
getemajor( )	Get external major number
geteminor( )	Get external minor number
hal_getkpfnum( )	Get page frame number for virtual address
itoemajor( )	Change internal to external major number
kvtophys( )	Get physical address for kernel virtual address
physiock( )	Raw I/O request
vtop( )	Change virtual to physical address

The commonly available machine dependent functions are summarized in Table 5.11. They are described as follows:

- *dma_pageio( )* — was supplied with the 3B2 porting base to make raw disk I/O transfers more efficient. Other suppliers have provided this function, even though they may not need to, However, providing it aids portability. When raw disk I/O is performed by *physiock( )* (see § 5.7.3) the buffer being written is at an arbitrary address in user space. The DMA controller used for the floppy and hard disks in the 3B2 works best when the data is aligned to a sector-sized boundary, and when it is performing I/O in chunks of one page. If the user buffer is already aligned correctly, it is output directly. If not, a kernel buffer with the correct alignment is allocated, and the user data is copied to the new buffer. The I/O is then performed using the new, correctly aligned buffer. The function takes the device *strategy( )* function and a buffer pointer as its arguments.

- *physiock( )* — performs raw disk I/O. It is described in § 5.7.4.

- *etoimajor( )*, *getemajor( )*, *getminor( )*, *itoemajor( )* — in previous versions of UNIX System V, the major and minor device numbers were each 8 bits, and they were packed together into a 16 bit word (usually a C Language *short* variable). Under UNIX System V Release 4, the device numbers are held in a *dev_t* variable, which is often implemented as a 32 bit integer. The minor device number is held as 14 bits, and a further 8 bits are used for the major device number. *dev_t* is often referred to as the "expanded device type", since it allows many more minor devices than before.

Table 5.12: *Data structures in D4DK*

Structure	Used for	Chapter
buf	Block I/O requests	5
cred	User ID information	4
datab	Holding STREAMS data	7
free_rtn	Holding message-free function	4
iovec	User-kernel I/O request	5
map	*rmalloc( )* and *rmfree( )*	5
module_info	STREAMS driver information	7
msgb	STREAMS message header	7
qband	STREAMS band information	7
qinit	STREAMS queue procedures	7
queue	STREAMS queue	7
streamtab	STREAMS driver information	7
uio	User-kernel I/O request	5

Many drivers were written for earlier releases, and may eventually be ported to UNIX System V Release 4. In earlier releases, some manufacturers got around the 256 minor device number limit by using multiple major device numbers for a device. Devices were created with different major device numbers (the external major device number) but they all mapped onto the same device driver entry in the device switch tables (the internal device number). Even under this scheme, each major device could support only 256 minor devices, but the driver could support many more. This has been recognized in UNIX System V Release 4, and functions are provided to do this mapping; for example, the functions *etoimajor( )* and so on give a machine independent interface to the device number mapping.

- *vtop( )*, *kvtophys( )* — these two functions are used to get a physical address corresponding to a virtual address. For example, where the driver must initiate DMA transfers, it must know the physical address corresponding to a virtual address.

5.11.3 DDI/DKI section 4

Section 4 of the DDI/DKI specifies the structures used to pass data between the kernel and the device driver, and they are summarized in Table 5.12. The data structures are described elsewhere in this book.

5.12 Exercises

5.1   Explain the following concepts:

- regular file
- block device
- character device
- major device number minor device number

5.2   By what means does the kernel bring the benefits of virtual memory to the file I/O subsystem?

5.3   The old buffer cache mechanism has been retained in UNIX System V Release 4. What purpose does it serve, and why is it still needed?

5.4**   Consider the following structure and variable declarations:

```
struct buf {
  char *x ;
  int size_x  ;   /* Holds size of string in x */
  char *y ;
  int size_y  ;   /* Holds size of string in y */
} ;

struct buf b1 = {
            "Hello there", 12,
            "How are you", 12
          } ;
```

Write a program that uses the *read* and *write* system calls to exchange these structures between your program and a file. Write a second program that uses the *readv* and *writev* system calls to achieve the same result. Which runs more quickly and why?

5.5   How does the kernel associate a file name such as */dev/dsk/sc0d0s2* with a particular block device driver?

5.6***   Write a RAM disk driver. That is, write a block special device driver that manages an area of memory as if it were a disk drive.

5.7   Explain the difference between block and raw disk I/O. Under what circumstances would you use raw I/O instead of block I/O?

5.8**   Write a program that performs random-access I/O with 256 byte data blocks. Compare the performance of this program on regular and raw device files.

5.9**   Design a character device driver and a user program that allows a process to put itself to sleep at an arbitrary address. The driver should also allow the process to wake up other processes that are sleeping. The operation to perform, the address to sleep at, and the address to wake up should be passed as command line arguments to your program. Extend the driver so that you can send any signal to any process. Hint: use the *ioctl* interface.

5.10*   Implement a subroutine called *mread* that performs the same operation as the *read* system call. However, *mread* should use *mmap* to retrieve the data from the file.

5.11   Give a reason why the *write* system call cannot be implemented to use *mmap*.

5.12   Why does the DDI/DKI re-implement a number of macros as functions? For example *max()* and *min()* used to be macros, but now they are functions. Why are functions used to access system variables and data structures, instead of directly accessing them? For example *drv_getparm()* reads the values of certain kernel variables.

5.13   What is */dev/mem* used for?

5.14   Assume that one process is reading a file with *mmap* and another is using *write* on the same file. How does the reading process acknowledge the changes made by the writing process?

CHAPTER 6

File management subsystem

I never could make out what those damned dots meant.
— Lord Randolph Churchill

6.1 Introduction to the file management subsystem

Probably the most important role of any operating system is to provide a file system that is consistent, orderly, and easily accessible. Most important, it should provide a very high-level of security and data integrity.

The UNIX System V Release 4 file management subsystem is responsible and is held accountable for any action or operation that results in a file being accessed. Its responsibilities far outweigh those of any other module in the operating system, and include:

- *Data integrity* — it must maintain a consistent view of a file (including its administrative information) while it is being manipulated by the operating system. It must identify which parts of a file are stored in main memory, and which parts are stored on disk. It must keep track of processes associated with an open file, and respond to a process when it closes a file.

- *File administration* — it must keep track of a file's data blocks on disk. It must manage the administration of disk packs, partitions, and the file systems containing files stored within them.

- *Access permissions* — it must ensure that a user wishing to perform an operation on a file has sufficient permission to enact the operation.

- *System call compliance* — it must govern the use of all system calls related to the manipulation of files and file systems. For example, it must ensure that *open, close, read, write, ioctl, mkdir, link,* and so on are used correctly.

- *Coordination of file access* — it must maintain a list of open files in case multiple processes perform operations on the same file.

- *Mandatory file and record locking* — it must govern the use of locks used between cooperating processes.

335

This chapter presents a low-level technical discussion on how the UNIX System V Release 4 operating system manipulates and manages files and file systems by using a file system type independent interface. High-level concepts are described in Chapter 2.

Figure 6.1: *Process open file table*

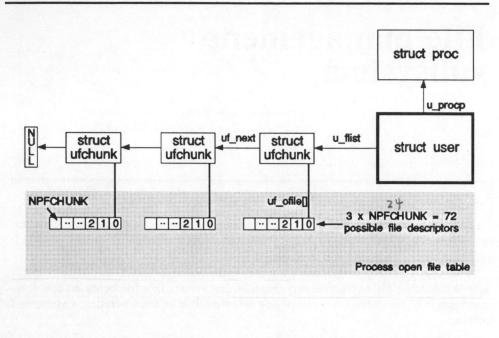

6.2 Associating with a file

To access a file (of any kind) a process must first open it by using any one of the *open, creat* or *pipe* system calls which will be discussed later. For now, it is only important to understand that these system calls return an integer referred to as a *file descriptor* which is used to pass to other system calls as an abstraction of the file being manipulated. No successful operation can be performed on a file unless a valid file descriptor has first been obtained.

This section describes the data structures and algorithms that manage the opening and closing of files on behalf of the user process.

6.2.1 The process open file table

The user-area of each active process maintains a field called *u_flist*. It contains a list of *ufchunks* that are inherited from the parent in *newproc( )*. The contents of a *ufchunk* structure are shown in Table 6.1.

Each *ufchunk* structure accommodates up to *NFPCHUNK* file descriptors. Whenever a file descriptor is assigned to a process, a free element in a *uf_ofile[]*

Table 6.1: *Struct ufchunk*

Element	Description
*struct file *uf_ofile[NFPCHUNK]*	Array of pointers into the system file list
char uf_pofile[NFPCHUNK]	Flags set by *fcntl* system call
*struct ufchunk *uf_next*	Pointer to the next *ufchunk* in the list

array is also allocated. The constant *NFPCHUNK* is normally set to 24, so there is room for 24 file descriptors in a single *ufchunk* structure. Initially the *u_flist* contains a single *ufchunk* structure. If the currently running process attempts to open a file and all elements in the *uf_ofile[]* array are assigned, the system allocates another *ufchunk* structure and attaches it to the list headed by *u_flist*. File descriptors are then allocated from the *uf_ofile[]* array in that *ufchunk* structure instead. It is clear that file descriptors are allocated dynamically to a process in multiples of NFPCHUNK. The value of a file descriptor is used by the kernel to index into one of the *uf_ofile[]* arrays within a *ufchunk* structure maintained by *u_flist* in the user-area (see Figure 6.1). The *user* structure member *u_nofiles* keeps a count of the number of file descriptor elements allocated to the currently running process. It is incremented by *NFPCHUNK* every time a *ufchunk* structure is allocated. If three *ufchunks* are on the list, there is room for 3 x *NFPCHUNK* (72) file descriptors, and *u_nofiles* is set to reflect this account.

Table 6.2: *Struct file (file_t)*

Element	Description
*struct file *f_next*	Pointer to the next entry on the list
*struct file *f_prev*	Pointer to the previous entry on the list
ushort f_flag	Specifying mode of *open*. For example, file is open for reading only (*O_RDONLY*), or open with no-delay set (*O_NDELAY*), and so on.
cnt_t f_count	Reference count. Number of *uf_ofile[]* pointers pointing to this same file table entry.
*struct vnode *f_vnode*	Pointer to the *vnode* structure for this file
off_t f_offset	Read/write character count offset within the file
*struct cred *f_cred*	Pointer to the credentials of the process that owns this file (i.e., the user)

6.2.2 The system open file table

Each element in *uf_ofile[]* is a pointer to a *file* structure. When a file descriptor is allocated to a process, a *file* structure pointer in one of the process's *uf_ofile[]* arrays is allocated. The allocated pointer points into the *system open file table*. The system open file table is a doubly linked list of *file* structures (Table 6.2) headed by the global variable *file*. Each *file* structure on the list represents an open file, and they are allocated on a per *open* basis. That is, when a process successfully calls *open* on a file, a new *file* structure is allocated and then appended to the list. A call to *pipe* results in the allocation of two *file* structures on the list: one for the reading end of the pipe and one for the writing end (the *pipe* system call is discussed in § 7.10.2).

The system call *dup* duplicates a file descriptor obtained from a previous successful *open*. The allocation of a file descriptor returned by *dup* also causes the allocation of a *file* structure pointer from one of the process's *uf_ofile[]* arrays. Since the two file descriptors represent the same open file, they both point to the same *file* structure in the system open file table (the *dup* system call is described in more detail later).

Figure 6.2: *System open file table*

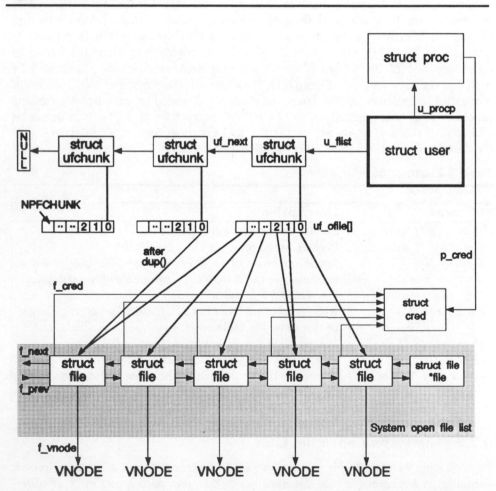

Section 2.7 mentions that file descriptors 0, 1 and 2 are normally assigned to a process during its creation. They represent the input, output and error output channels associated with the login terminal. However, the system makes no

assumption about the allocation of file descriptors, and file descriptors 0, 1 and 2 are allocated simply because they are inherited from the parent's open file table set up by **ttymon(1M)**. Although it is rare, it is quite legal for a process to be created with an empty open file table, although it will still have at least one *ufchunk* structure assigned to it. This situation may arise if no open files were being maintained by the parent when the child was created.

Nevertheless, in most cases file descriptors 0, 1 and 2 are assigned because **ttymon(1M)** had opened the special file representing the terminal for reading which resulted in the allocation of descriptor 0 representing *stdin*. It also opened the same special file for writing which resulted in the allocation of descriptor 1 representing *stdout*. It then duplicated descriptor 1 with the *dup* system call which resulted in the allocation of descriptor 2 representing *stderr*. Remember that a *file* structure is allocated on a per *open* basis. Since descriptors 1 and 2 are associated with the same "opening" of the file (the login terminal), both their associated file pointers in the *uf_ofile[]* array point to the same *file* structure on the system open file table. Figure 6.2 shows these three descriptors (the first three elements of the first *uf_ofile[]* array). Note that the elements representing descriptors 1 and 2 are pointing to the same *file* structure.

Each *file* structure on the list holds the information about an open file. When a process is switched in, the system references files that the process has open by using the file pointers stored in the *uf_ofile[]* arrays. For example, the *vnode* associated with descriptor 0 may be referenced as:

```
u.u_flist.uf_ofile[0]->f_vnode;
```

The *vnode* associated with the 25th descriptor may be referenced as:

```
u.u_flist.uf_next->uf_ofile[0]->f_vnode;
```

The members of the *file* structure are explained as follows:

- *f_next, f_prev* — pointers used to traverse backwards and forwards through the systems open file table.

- *f_flag* — contains the flags set when the file was opened. These flags correspond to those given in the second argument to *open*. For example, O_RDONLY, O_APPEND, O_CREAT, and so on.

- *f_count* — counts the number of references to this open file. For example, in the case of file descriptors 1 and 2 described above, the reference count in this *file* structure is 2 because the second two elements in the first *uf_ofile[]* array point here. A call to the *close* system call decrements the associated open *file* structure *f_count*. Thus, the C statement:

```
close(1);
```

results in *f_count* for this *file* structure being set to 1 in this case.

- *f_vnode* — this pointer points to the file system independent *vnode* associated with this open file. *vnodes* are discussed in § 6.3.

- *f_offset* — the current byte offset (with respect to 0, the beginning of the file) in the file. It corresponds to the offset returned from the system call *lseek* (§ 6.3.3). If the file is a special file, the *f_offset* variable is not used.

- *f_cred* — this pointer points to the process's credentials structure. It is the same credentials structure pointed to by the *proc* structure member, *p_cred*. The information stored in it defines the credentials of the user whose process has this file opened.

6.2.3 File allocation operations

If a process wants to open a file, the kernel must do the following:

- Allocate space for a new *file* structure from main memory.

- Place the new *file* structure on the system open file table headed by *file*.

- Find an empty *uf_ofile[]* slot in a *ufchunk* structure on the process's *u_flist*. This may mean allocating a new *ufchunk* if there are no *uf_ofile[]* slots available.

- Arrange for the pointer in the *uf_ofile[]* array to point to the newly allocated *file* structure on the system open file table.

- Return a file descriptor to reference the previously found slot in the process's *uf_ofile[]* array.

If the user wishes to perform an operation on a file, he or she must pass the open file descriptor representing the file to the relevant system call. For example, to read 10 integers from a file called *myfile* the C program sequence might look like this:

```
#define   MAXBUF   (sizeof(int) * 10)
int fd;
char buf[MAXBUF];


. . . .
if( (fd = open("myfile", O_RDONLY)) < 0 ) {
    perror("myfile");
    exit(1);
}

/* read 10 integers else exit with message */
if( read(fd,buf,MAXBUF) != MAXBUF ) {
    fprintf(stderr,"could not read %d integers\n",MAXBUF);
    exit(1);
}
. . . .
```

In this example, the *open* system call is used to obtain a file descriptor *fd* which is subsequently passed to *read* to read the data. Thus, given a valid open file descriptor, the system can find the relevant *file* structure in the system open file table. To do this, the kernel uses five subroutines which will be discussed in the following section.

6.2.4 File descriptor allocation

A file descriptor can be obtained with any of the *creat, open, dup* or *pipe* system calls. Internally, these system calls result in calling a function called *ufalloc( )*, which allocates a user file descriptor from one of the process's *uf_ofile[]* arrays. Note that the *fcntl* system call *F_DUPFD* switch also results in calling *ufalloc( )*.

Unless specified otherwise, file descriptors are always assigned sequentially, from the lowest available file descriptor. In other words, if the process opens five files, the first five slots in the first *uf_ofile[]* array are assigned. If the process subsequently closes the file associated with file descriptor 0, the first slot in *uf_ofile[]* becomes available by the next open. Thus, at the next successful open descriptor 0 is assigned, not descriptor 5.

ufalloc( ) takes two arguments. The first argument is an integer specifying the lowest value of the file descriptor required. The new file descriptor must be greater than or equal to this value. The second argument is a pointer that points to where the new file descriptor value will be stored.

Generally, the user does not care about the value of a file descriptor, all that is required is the first one available. Otherwise, the user wants the next lowest valued file descriptor. Therefore, it is clear that the first argument to *ufalloc( )* is almost always zero. This tells *ufalloc( )* to start from zero and search forward through all the *uf_ofile[]* arrays maintained by the process until a free slot is found. However, in a similar fashion to the *dup* system call, the *F_DUPFD* switch supported by the *fcntl* system call allows the process to obtain a duplicate file descriptor. Its value is the lowest available, but greater than or equal to that specified in its calling parameters. Figure 6.3 gives the algorithm for *ufalloc( )*.

However, *ufalloc( )* does not allocate a *file* structure nor place it on the system open file table. This is done by a function called *falloc( )* (see Figure 6.4). *falloc( )* expects four arguments: a pointer to a *vnode* associated with the file, a set of flags to place into *f_flag*, a pointer to a *file* structure pointer which will be assigned to the address of a newly allocated *file* structure, and a pointer to an integer to store the new file descriptor.

Three other functions are used in conjunction with *ufalloc( )* and *falloc( )*, as follows:

- *getf(int fd, file_t *fp)* — uses the supplied file descriptor *fd* to find its associated *uf_ofile[]* slot. It then arranges for the supplied pointer *fp* to point to the *file* structure pointed to by the pointer at that location.

- *setf(int fd, file_t *fp)* — uses the supplied file descriptor *fd* to find its associated *uf_ofile[]* slot. It then arranges for the pointer in that slot to point to the *file* structure pointed to by *fp*.

- *unfalloc(file_t *fp)* — removes the *file* structure pointed to by *fp* from the system open file table. It then frees the memory associated with it.

Figure 6.3: *Algorithm for ufalloc( )*

```
ufalloc( )
input:  start — starting value of next lowest available
            file descriptor
        fdp — integer pointer to store the new file descriptor
output: zero on success
        non-zero on error
{
   /*
    * enforce resource limits for number of open files.
    */
   if( "start" is greater than the soft user resource limit )
      return EMFILE         /* too many open files */

   while(1) {
      find the next lowest unused uf_ofile[] slot in the
       - process's current u_flist starting from "start".

      if(an entry was found) {
         assign index of file descriptor to "fdp"
         return(0);
      }

      /*
       * at this point there were no empty slots found
       * so we must allocate another ufchunk
       */
      allocate another ufchunk from the system memory pool.
      if( no memory available )
         return ENOMEM

      add NFPCHUNK to u.u_nofiles
      place the new ufchunk on the process's u_flist
      /* try again */
   }
}
```

Figure 6.5 shows the pseudo code for the *dup* system call. It is a good example of how these functions work.

6.2.5 File descriptors inherited from the parent

All file descriptors that are open in the parent are inherited by the child when the child is created. This is done in *procdup( )* (called from *newproc( )* — see § 4.12.2).

Figure 6.4: *Algorithm for falloc( )*

```
falloc( )
input: vp — pointer to the vnode associated with the file
       flag — modes used to open the file with
       fpp — pointer to a "file" structure pointer
       fdp — integer pointer to store the new file descriptor
output: zero on success
        non-zero on failure
{

    try to allocate a file descriptor /* ufalloc( ) */
    if( error )
      return error value returned from ufalloc( )

    try to allocate memory for a new "file" structure
    if( no memory available ) {
      print message to console
      "KERNEL: Could not allocate file table entry"
      return ENFILE              /* File table overflow */
    }

    add the new file structure to the system open file table

    call setf( ) to put the file pointer address into the
     - uf_ofile[] table

    initialize file structure reference count (f_count = 1)
    set f_flag to "flag"
    set f_vnode to "vp" /* possible (struct vnode *)NULL */
    increment reference to cred structure
    set f_cred to point to cred structure /* u.u_procp->p_cred */
    set "fpp" to point to the new file structure
    set "fd" to point to the new file descriptor

    return success
}
```

Both child and parent share the same file descriptors including *file* structures representing the parent's open files in the system open file table. The child inherits a duplicate copy of the parent's *u_flist* and all the *ufchunk* structures associated with it. This means that the reference count for each *file* structure maintained by the parent must be incremented when the child is created, and this is done in *newproc( )*. Since the child and parent share the same file descriptors, they also share the same open file characteristics. That is, if the parent has opened the file in

Figure 6.5: *Algorithm for dup( )*

```
dup( )
input:   uap — pointer to area containing argument list
         rvp — pointer to a return value structure
output:  zero on success
         non-zero on failure
{
        fp = get the file pointer for the user supplied
        - file descriptor /* getf( ) */

        fd = obtain and allocate the next lowest file
        - descriptor /* ufalloc( ) */

        if( error getting fp OR error getting fd )
           return error

        set the uf_ofile[] entry for the new file descriptor
        - to point to the same place as fp  /* setf(fd, fp) */

        increment the reference count for this file structure
        place fd in the return value structure

        return success or failure code;
}
```

read-only mode (O_RDONLY), the child cannot write to it. In addition to this, the file's current file pointer offset is shared (f_offset). This means that if the child reads 10 bytes from the beginning of the file, a subsequent read initiated by the parent will start reading from the 11th byte in the file. If the child seeks back to the beginning of the file, the value of f_offset for that file will be zero for both parent and child.

6.2.6 The *open* and *creat* system calls

The internal function handler for both of these system calls is called *copen( )*. That is, after being called by *systrap( )*, the *open( )* or *creat( )* system call handler calls *copen( )* to do the system call processing. A boolean flag passed down as an argument specifies which system call to process. Basically, a call to *creat(pathname, mode)* is equivalent to:

        open(pathname, O_WRONLY | O_CREAT | O_TRUNC, mode);

copen( ) begins by validating the set of flags passed down from the system call handler (see Table 6.3). *falloc( )* is then called to allocate a file descriptor from one of the process's *uf_ofile[]* arrays. It also allocates a *file* structure for the new open

Table 6.3: *Flags defined in <sys/fcntl.h> used by the open system call*

Flag	Description
O_RDONLY	Open for read-only
O_WRONLY	Open for write-only
O_RDWR	Open for reading and writing
O_NDELAY	Non-blocking I/O
O_NONBLOCK	Non-blocking I/O (*POSIX* compliant)
O_APPEND	Always write to the end of the file
O_SYNC	Do synchronous I/O on write
O_CREAT	Create file if it does not already exist
O_TRUNC	Truncate file to zero on open (no effect on *FIFO*)
O_EXCL	Exclusive open
O_NOCTTY	Do not allocate controlling *tty* (*POSIX* compliant)

file and then places it into the system open file table. The function *vn_open( )* is then called. This function resolves the pathname via *lookupname( )* and obtains a *vnode* for the final component specified in the path (§ 6.8.2). The *vnode* is then attached to the *f_vnode* pointer in the previously allocated *file* structure.

If *vn_open( )* is handling a *creat* system call, it passes control to a function called *vn_create( )*. It, in turn, results in a call to *VOP_CREATE( )* which makes a new directory entry for the file, allocates a file system dependent *inode* for it, and initializes the *inode* with the user specified attributes. Otherwise, if *vn_open( )* is handling an *open* system call, and the file is being opened for writing, a test is done to ensure that the *open* operation fails if the file being operated on is a directory (directory type files cannot be written to). A further test is done to see if the file system that the file resides on will allow the operation to take place. For example, if it is mounted in read-only mode, writing is prohibited. A test is then done to ensure that the process has the correct permission to perform the requested operation by calling the file system type dependent *vnode* operation, *VOP_ACCESS( )*, which determines the file's accessibility. Finally, *VOP_OPEN( )* is called to allow the file system type dependent code to perform any administration associated with the file system, to render the file or device open for the requesting process.

6.3 The file system independent *vnode*

The kernel separates file system type dependent functionality from file system type independent functionality with a data structure called *vnode* [Kleiman 1986]. The *vnode* is partly the result of an effort to make the UNIX System V kernel independent of file system type.

A *vnode* is the kernel's generic abstraction of a file. It is therefore the focus of all file activity carried out by the operating system. The term *vnode* comes from "virtual node" as opposed to *inode* which comes from "index node". Just to set the books straight, they have nothing in common although they are very much related to each other (see § 6.10).

6.3.1 Allocating a *vnode*

Unlike the system open file table, which maintains a *file* structure on a per open basis, a *vnode* is allocated on a per file basis. That is, any number of processes may be associated with the same *vnode* but each process that has opened the file associated with the *vnode* maintains its own *file* structure on the system open file table. Note, however, that not all *vnodes* maintained by the system are associated with a process's open file table; the system must often allocate a *vnode* to work with while carrying out an operation that references a file. For example, a *vnode* may be allocated by the *exec* mechanisms if there is a need to page in data from an *a.out* file.

 vnodes are allocated by the file system dependent code. They are not maintained by any list and are allocated dynamically when needed from the system main memory pool. Once allocated, the *vnode* is attached to the data structure pointer associated with the cause of the *vnode* allocation and it remains resident in main memory until the system decides that it is no longer needed. For example, in the case of the *file* structure maintained by the system open file table, the *f_vnode* pointer points to its associated *vnode*. Similarly, if the file is associated with a process image (i.e., it is an *a.out* file that has been *execed*) then the segment mapping for the parts of the file that are in memory is done via a *vnode* pointer (*vp*) in the *segvn_data* structure (§ 3.4.9).

 All operations that must be done to a file are done via its associated *vnode*. The *vnode* is used to reference the file. Therefore, any process that opens a file must also reference its associated *vnode*. When a process requests an operation on a file (for example when *opening* it), the file system type independent code passes control to a file system type dependent function to carry out the operation. If the file system type dependent function finds that a *vnode* representing the file is not in main memory, it allocates a new *vnode* for it.

 The system accesses a file via its associated *vnode* regardless of what type of file it is or what type of file system the file is stored on. The kernel has no concept of a file's structure and so it relies on the information stored in the *vnode* to describe the file. Thus, the *vnode* associated with a file holds all the administration information pertaining to it (Table 6.4).

6.3.2 *vnode* operations

The *v_op* pointer in the *vnode* structure points to its associated *vnodeops* structure. The *vnodeops* structure describes what operations can be done to the file associated with the *vnode*. The system maintains one *vnodeops* structure for each file system type configured into the operating system. Thus, a *vnodes v_op* pointer points to the *vnodeops* structure associated with its file system type implementation. The *vnodeops* structure contains a pointer to a function for each operation supported by the file system (Table 6.5). For example, when a process opens a file, it results in the

Table 6.4: *Struct vnode (vnode_t)*

Element	Description
u_short v_flag	Bitmask flags (see below)
u_short v_count	Count of reference to this *vnode*
*struct vfs *v_vfsmountedhere*	Pointer to *vfs* structure; used only if the *vnode* is associated with a directory that is a mount point
*struct vnodeops *v_op*	Pointer to a structure describing the file system type dependent operations that can be done to this file
*struct vfs *v_vfsp*	Pointer to the virtual file system structure describing this file's associated file system
*struct stdata *v_stream*	Pointer to associated stream if *vnode* represents a STREAMS device
*struct page *v_pages*	Pointer to *struct page* list for this *vnode*
enum vtype v_type	*vnode* type (see below)
dev_t v_rdev	Major and minor device number of special file, if this *vnode* represents a special file
caddr_t v_data	Pointer to file system type specific data structure (i.e., *struct inode*)
*struct filock *v_filocks*	Pointer to *filock* list for this *vnode* (file and record locking structures)
Flags (*v_flag*)	**Description**
VROOT	*vnode* is associated with the root of its file system
VNOMAP	*vnode* is associated with a file that cannot be mapped or faulted
VDUP	File should be *duped* rather then opened; this is pertinent to the */dev/fd* file system type only
VNOSWAP	File cannot be used as part of the virtual swap device
VNOMOUNT	File cannot be hidden by a mounted file system
VISSWAP	*vnode* is part of the virtual swap device
Type (*v_type*)	**Description**
VNON	No *vnode* type specified
VREG	*vnode* represents a regular (normal) file
VDIR	*vnode* represents a directory type file
VBLK	*vnode* represents a block special file
VCHR	*vnode* represents a character special file
VLNK	*vnode* represents a symbolic link file
VFIFO	*vnode* represents a pipe special file
VXNAM	*vnode* represents a XENIX shared data segment
VBAD	*vnode* represents a bad file (not currently used)

invocation of the function that *vop_open* points to.

The designers of a file system are responsible for defining its functionality. Therefore, they define the file (*vnode*) operations pertinent to its design. It is not mandatory for a file system to support a particular operation on a file, but if it does so, the kernel assumes that that operation will be carried out as expected by that particular file system type. It makes no assumption about the procedures required for the operation. From this, it is obvious that the file system type dependent code for performing operations on a file are hidden within the *vnodeops* structure.

The file system type independent code for accessing an operation defined in a file's associated *vnodeops* structure is implemented as a set of macros defined in <*sys/vnode.h*> (also shown in Table 6.5). These macros are independent of file system type since the *vnode* pointer given as an argument to the macro allows the system to trace which *vnodeops* structure the operation is to be carried out from.

6.3.3 File system type dependent *vnodeops* functions

This section discusses the file system type dependent *vnode* operations. It explains what the kernel assumes each function will do and where it is used by the file system type independent parts of the kernel.

Each file system type implementation must define a *vnodeops* structure. It must assign each member function pointer to its corresponding file system type dependent *vnode* operation also defined by the file system type implementation. If the file system type does not support a specific operation, it must nevertheless assign an appropriate function to do the minimum required of it. In most cases, such functions either do nothing or return an error value to the effect that it is not supported.

Many of the functions described are closely related to their corresponding system calls. In most cases, they are called as a result of the system call associated with the operation being invoked.

The functions that form the *vnodeops* structure members are explained in their macro form. Note that the operation performed by a particular function is implementation dependent. The kernel makes no assumptions about what has to be done to achieve the desired action for the *vnode* being manipulated:

- *VOP_OPEN* — corresponds to the *open* system call. It renders the file or device open for use by the requesting process and performs any required internal file system administration associated with the open — for example, manage locks, update tables, and so on. It is called whenever the kernel must perform an operation that involves accessing a file — for example, while carrying out an *exec* of an *a.out* file, when a process issues the *open* system call, to create a memory *core-dump* in the file system, if a swap file is added to the virtual swap device, if a file system is mounted, and so on.

- *VOP_CLOSE* — corresponds to the *close* system call. The *vnode* maintains a reference count that is incremented for each *VOP_OPEN()*. Each time *VOP_CLOSE()* is called, the reference is decremented. The process that renders the count equal to zero (the last process to close the file) makes the file finally closed.

Table 6.5: *Struct vnodeops and related macros (vnodeops_t)*

vnodeops element	Related macro	Description of operation
int (*vop_open)( )	VOP_OPEN	Open a file
int (*vop_close)( )	VOP_CLOSE	Close a file
int (*vop_read)( )	VOP_READ	Read from a file
int (*vop_write)( )	VOP_WRITE	Write to a file
int (*vop_ioctl)( )	VOP_IOCTL	Perform I/O control
int (*vop_setfl)( )	VOP_SETFL	Set file status flags
int (*vop_getattr)( )	VOP_GETATTR	Get file attributes
int (*vop_setattr)( )	VOP_SETATTR	Set file attributes
int (*vop_access)( )	VOP_ACCESS	Determine file accessibility
int (*vop_lookup)( )	VOP_LOOKUP	Lookup file name in name cache
int (*vop_create)( )	VOP_CREATE	Create a file
int (*vop_remove)( )	VOP_REMOVE	Remove a file
int (*vop_link)( )	VOP_LINK	Link a file
int (*vop_rename)( )	VOP_RENAME	Rename a file
int (*vop_mkdir)( )	VOP_MKDIR	Make a new directory
int (*vop_rmdir)( )	VOP_RMDIR	Remove a directory
int (*vop_readdir)( )	VOP_READDIR	Read directory entry
int (*vop_symlink)( )	VOP_SYMLINK	Create a symbolic link
int (*vop_readlink)( )	VOP_READLINK	Read contents of a symbolic link
int (*vop_fsync)( )	VOP_FSYNC	Flush pending data for file to disk
void (*vop_inactive)( )	VOP_INACTIVE	Release the inactive *vnode*
int (*vop_fid)( )	VOP_FID	Get unique file identifier
void (*vop_rwlock)( )	VOP_RWLOCK	Sleep until *inode* lock is free
void (*vop_rwunlock)( )	VOP_RWUNLOCK	Wake up process sleeping on lock
int (*vop_seek)( )	VOP_SEEK	Test if file is seekable
int (*vop_cmp)( )	VOP_CMP	Compare two *vnodes*
int (*vop_frlock)( )	VOP_FRLOCK	Perform file and record locking
int (*vop_space)( )	VOP_SPACE	Free space associated with *inode*
int (*vop_realvp)( )	VOP_REALVP	Get real *vnode* from *vnode* pointer
int (*vop_getpage)( )	VOP_GETPAGE	Get pages from *a.out*
int (*vop_putpage)( )	VOP_PUTPAGE	Flush pages associated with *vnode*
int (*vop_map)( )	VOP_MAP	Map file into address space
int (*vop_addmap)( )	VOP_ADDMAP	Increment count of mapped in pages
int (*vop_delmap)( )	VOP_DELMAP	Decrement count of mapped in pages
int (*vop_poll)( )	VOP_POLL	Test if poll event has taken place
int (*vop_dump)( )	VOP_DUMP	Currently unused
int (*vop_pathconf)( )	VOP_PATHCONF	Implement POSIX *pathconf* support

Table 6.6: *Vnode operations supported by each file system type*

Vnodeops	ufs	specfs	s5	rfs	procfs	nfs	namefs	fifofs	fd	bfs
vop_open	•	•	•	•	•	•	•	•	•	•
vop_close	•	•	•	•	•	•	•	•	•	•
vop_read	•	•	•	•	•	•	•	•	•	•
vop_write	•	•	•	•	•	•	•	•		•
vop_ioctl	•	•	•	•	•	•	•	•		•
vop_setfl	•	•	•	•	•	•	•	•		•
vop_getattr	•	•	•	•	•	•	•	•	•	•
vop_setattr	•	•	•	•	•	•	•	•		•
vop_access	•	•	•	•	•	•	•	•	•	•
vop_lookup	•		•	•	•	•	•	•	•	•
vop_create	•					•			•	•
vop_remove	•		•	•		•				•
vop_link	•		•	•		•	•			•
vop_rename	•		•	•		•				•
vop_mkdir	•		•	•		•				
vop_rmdir	•		•	•		•				
vop_readdir	•		•	•	•	•			•	•
vop_symlink	•		•	•		•				
vop_readlink	•		•	•		•				
vop_fsync	•	•	•	•	•	•		•		•
vop_inactive	•	•	•	•	•	•		•	•	•
vop_fid	•		•	•		•	•	•		•
vop_rwlock	•		•	•	•	•	•	•		•
vop_rwunlock	•		•	•	•	•	•	•		•
vop_seek	•	•	•	•	•	•	•	•	•	•
vop_cmp	•	•	•	•	•	•	•	•	•	•
vop_frlock	•		•	•		•	•	•		•
vop_space	•		•	•		•				•
vop_realvp		•				•	•	•		
vop_getpage	•	•	•	•		•				
vop_putpage	•	•	•	•		•				
vop_map	•	•		•		•				
vop_addmap	•	•	•	•		•				
vop_delmap	•	•	•	•		•				
vop_poll	•	•	•	•	•	•	•	•		•
vop_dump										
vop_pathconf	•	•	•	•		•	•	•	•	•

- *VOP_READ* — corresponds to the *read* system call. Data is read from the file associated with the *vnode*. Parameters passed to this function are: a pointer to the location where the data is to be read into, and an offset into the file being read.

- *VOP_WRITE* — corresponds to the *write* system call. Data is written to the file associated with the *vnode*. Parameters passed to this function are: a pointer to the location of the data being written, and an offset into the file where data is to be written to.

- *VOP_IOCTL* — corresponds to the *ioctl* system call. It performs a variety of control functions on the file associated with the *vnode*.

- *VOP_SETFL* — is called by the *fcntl* system call when the *F_SETFL* (set file status flags) switch is used. The file flags (*f_flag*) are passed as a parameter to this function so that they can be validated.

- *VOP_GETATTR, VOP_SETATTR* — used to obtain, or set, specified attributes associated with a file. In the case of the *s5* and *ufs* file systems the information is obtained from, or set in, the file's *inode* — for example, the *stat* system call collects its information using *VOP_GETATTR()*.

  The *vnode* member pointer *v_data* points to the file system type specific data object associated with a file. Thus, *vnodes* associated with files on an *s5* or *ufs* file system use this pointer to reference the file's *inode*.

  Attributes associated with a file are collected and set by setting the required attribute bits in the *va_mask* member of a *vattr* structure (see Table 6.7). The address of this structure is then passed to the function associated with the required operation. In the case of a *VOP_GETATTR()* operation, the structure is filled with data obtained from the file's *inode*. In the case *VOP_SETATTR()*, the contents of the structure are assigned to the file's *inode*.

- *VOP_ACCESS* — whenever the kernel has to access a file, it first checks if the process has the right to do so by calling this function to determine the file's accessibility. If the process is allowed to access the file, success is returned, otherwise it returns failure. For example, if the file system that stores a file is mounted read-only, any attempt to write to it will make this function fail. Similarly, any process that attempts to open a file without the correct credentials will also make this function fail. This includes the case where a process tries to *exec* a new program image.

- *VOP_LOOKUP* — supplied with a file name, this function obtains a pointer to its associated *vnode*. This may require file system type dependent directory lookup operations and file system type dependent *inode* to *vnode* translations.

  A *vnode* that is associated with a special file (or device) has a *shadow-special-vnode* (or *snode*) associated with it. This *snode* contains another *vnode* which is used to reference a private copy of data associated with the device.

  If the *vnode* obtained by this function is associated with a special file, then its *snode* is consulted to find a real *vnode* associated with the device. The *specfs* file system and the *snode* are discussed in § 6.9.

Table 6.7: *Struct vattr (vattr_t)*

Element	Description
long va_mask	Bitmask of the following attributes to set or get
vtype_t va_type	Type of *vnode*
mode_t va_mode	File access modes
uid_t va_uid	Owner's UID
gid_t va_gid	Owner's GID
dev_t va_fsid	ID of device containing a directory entry for this file
ino_t va_nodeid	Node ID (i.e., *inode* number)
nlink_t va_nlink	Number of references to file
u_long va_size	Size of file in bytes
timestruc_t va_atime	Time of last access
timestruc_t va_mtime	Time of last modification
timestruc_t va_ctime	Time file was created
dev_t va_rdev	Device the file represents for special files
u_long va_blksize	Fundamental block size used by the file system
u_long va_nblocks	Number of held (allocated) blocks on the device
u_long va_vcode	Version code for supporting cache consistency between file servers

- *VOP_CREATE* — corresponds to the *creat* system call. It creates the file and adds a new directory entry corresponding to its specified file name. However, directories themselves are not created (see *VOP_MKDIR*). A *vattr* structure is passed down so that the file system dependent routines can determine if the process is allowed to perform the *VOP_CREATE* operation.

  Both *s5* and *ufs* file system type dependent functions allocate an *inode* for the new file if it does not already exist. Otherwise, the file is truncated to zero length. The file's *v_data* member is then set to point to the new *inode*. If the file is a device represented by a special file in the file system (i.e., a node having a major and minor number), it is allocated a *shadow-special-vnode* (*snode*) (see Figure 6.6). Note that as a result of the *inode* allocation, the *vnode* is automatically created. The *vnode* forms part of the file system dependent *inode*.

- *VOP_REMOVE* — corresponds to the *unlink* system call. It removes the directory entry for the file. Usually, the *inode* number in the directory entry associated with the file is zeroed and its entry in the directory name lookup cache is removed.

- *VOP_LINK* — corresponds to the *link* system call. It creates a new directory entry for the existing file and increments that file's *inode* link count by one. The function must verify that the process has the correct credentials to carry out the operation. For example, only super-user is allowed to make a link to a directory file.

  Link files created by this function are known as *hard-links*. A hard-link can be created only within the file system associated with the *inode*. That is, the link

Figure 6.6: *File system independent vnode and related structure pointers*

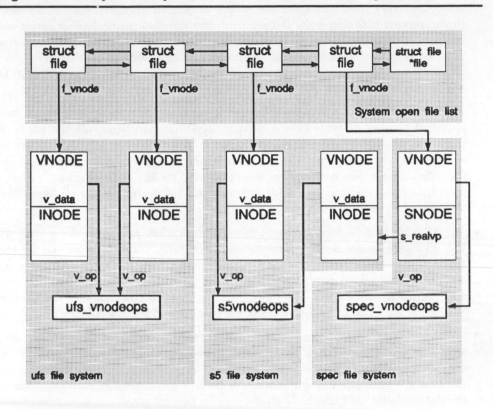

cannot connect with a file in another file system regardless of that file system's type. Note that the new link does not use up an *inode* but it does use up a directory entry.

- *VOP_RENAME* — corresponds to the *rename* system call. It renames a file or moves it to a new location. The function is given the *vnode* and directory entry name of the source file, and the *vnode* and directory entry name of the target (i.e., the destination). Apart from verifying that the process has the correct credentials to carry out the operation, the following operations are typically required:

```
unlink(target);
link(source, target);
unlink(source);
```

- *VOP_MKDIR* — corresponds to the *mkdir* system call. It creates a new directory in the file system associated with the *vnode*. The new directory is assigned an *inode* and linked to its parent directory. Therefore, by default, a newly created directory has a reference count of 2.

- *VOP_RMDIR* — corresponds to the *rmdir* system call. It deletes an existing empty directory from within the file system associated with the *vnode*. References to the removed directory are flushed from the directory name lookup cache and its associated *inode* is freed. However, if one or more processes are associated with the directory, then the directory remains intact (although un-writeable) until all references to it have been closed. If the directory is a mount point (§ 6.6.1), any attempt to remove it will fail and *EBUSY* is set in *errno*.

- *VOP_READDIR* — corresponds to the *getdents* system call. It reads a user specified number of bytes from a directory type file associated with the *vnode*. A pointer is passed which is set to point to the read data. Since each file system type defines its own directory structure implementation, the data read must be formated into a file system type independent directory data structure called a *struct dirent*. This structure holds information that is common to all file system type directory entries. For more information, see *dirent(4)*.

- *VOP_SYMLINK* — corresponds to the *symlink* system call. It creates a symbolic link file to a target file that may or may not exist. Link files created by this function are known as *soft-links*. A soft-link can connect with a file in another file system if required. A new directory entry is created for the symbolic link file and an *inode* is allocated for it. The target filename (i.e., the pathname of the file that the link is supposed to be linked to) is stored as text in the symbolic link file itself.

- *VOP_READLINK* — corresponds to the *readlink* system call. It reads the data stored in the symbolic link file associated with the *vnode* (i.e., the path of the target file). The function is not meant to be used to read the data stored in the file that the symbolic link references. A pointer to an area in user space where the data is to be read into is supplied.

- *VOP_FSYNC* — corresponds to the *fsync* system call. It copies all pages held in memory that are associated with the file (referenced by the *vnode*) to its storage device. The result is that both the in-memory copy and the on-disk copy of the pages are synchronized. The copy is done synchronously. That is, this function does not return until the I/O operation has completed.

- *VOP_INACTIVE* — when the kernel has finished using a *vnode* it is said to be inactive. An inactive *vnode* has a zero reference count.

  While executing a procedure, the kernel may need to allocate a temporary work *vnode*, but if an error condition arises during the procedure, the kernel must deallocate it. The kernel deallocates a *vnode* via a function called *vn_rele( )*, which simply decrements the *vnode* reference count (*v_count*). If the reference count reaches zero, the *vnode* is no longer active and *vn_rele( )* calls *VOP_INACTIVE( )* so that the file system type dependent routines can write the *inode* associated with the *vnode* out to disk and, if necessary, truncate and deallocate the file. The procedure for this involves an asynchronous write to the physical medium of the memory pages associated with the *vnode* and then they are put on the page freelist for later use.

- *VOP_FID* — NFS requires a generated *inode* number for each file that it manipulates. The NFS server uses this to detect accesses to files that no longer exist. This function may be called to generate a unique "file ID" for this purpose, but may also be called to generate a unique file ID for internally representing an exported directory hierarchy. An exported directory is recognized by the system as a shareable resource. It may be used by a remote machine as a mountable file system.

  The file ID is generated from information stored in the *inode* associated with the working *vnode* (i.e., the file being manipulated or the directory being exported).

- *VOP_RWLOCK* — when a process requests the kernel to read or write to a file, the kernel temporarily locks the file until the requested operation has completed. To lock a file, the kernel asks the file system independent functions to prevent access to it. This is done with *VOP_RWLOCK()*. The *inode* associated with the *vnode* is locked. If the *inode* is already locked, it is marked "wanted" and the process is put to sleep until the *inode* becomes unlocked. Additionally, if the *vnode* is associated with a virtual swap device, the current process's *p_flag* member is marked *SSWLOCKS* and its *p_swlocks* member is incremented. This signifies that the process has swap locks and so prevents it from being swapped out.

- *VOP_RWUNLOCK* — the *inode* associated with the *vnode* is unlocked. If there are processes asleep waiting for the *inode* to become unlocked, they are woken up. If the *vnode* is associated with a virtual swap device, its *p_swlocks* member is decremented. If it reaches zero, the *SSWLOCKS* flag is cleared. This signifies that the process has no swap locks and so, if necessary, it can be nominated by the scheduler to be swapped out.

- *VOP_SEEK* — corresponds to the *lseek* system call. Its purpose is to test if the file is seekable using the supplied offset. For example, both *s5* and *ufs* file systems implement this function as a test to see if the supplied file offset is valid. If the specified offset is less than zero, the function returns failure, setting *errno* to *EINVAL*. Otherwise the function succeeds and the system call continues to realign the file pointer to reflect the new offset.

- *VOP_CMP* — simply compares the equality of two *vnodes*.

- *VOP_FRLOCK* — any of the following switches specified in the second argument to *fcntl* results in a call to *VOP_FRLOCK()*: F_SETLK, F_GETLK, F_SETLKW, F_RSETLK, F_RGETLK and F_RSETLKW. This function is used by *fcntl* to implement file and record locking. It also provides an interface that allows the lock manager to support a file system independent file and record locking scheme using the client server paradigm (see *lockd(1M)*).

  A stateless file server such as NFS [Sandberg 1987] normally uses this facility to manipulate locks on files. Each site runs its own lock manager daemon which operates in either client or server mode. File and record locking requests are then communicated between client and server with Remote Procedure Calls

(RPC) [RFC 1057]. A lock manager operating in *server* mode accepts lock requests made on behalf of a client process via a remote lock manager, or on behalf of a locally running process via the kernel. A lock manager operating in *client* mode accepts lock request from a locally running process and forwards them to a remote lock manager.

Locking a file prevents multiple processes from modifying it simultaneously. Locks may be placed on an entire file or on individual segments within it. More details on file and record locking are given in the next section.

- *VOP_SPACE* — is called by the *fcntl* system call if the *F_FREESP* switch is used. Storage space associated with a section of the file described by the *vnode* is freed according to the information given in an *flock* structure pointed to by the third argument of *fcntl* (see Table 6.8). Note that *l_type* in the *flock* structure is not used with the *F_FREESP* switch. Furthermore, only the special case of *l_len == 0* is presently supported with this switch, meaning free to the end of file (see *fcntl(2)*).

Table 6.8: *Struct flock (flock_t)*

Element	Description
short l_type	File segment locking type (see below)
short l_whence	Flag indicating *l_start* offset
off_t l_start	Byte offset in file from position *l_whence*
off_t l_len	Byte count of section (0 = up to end of file)
long l_sysid	Used with *F_GETLK* only (see *fcntl(5)*)
pid_t l_pid	Used with *F_GETLK* only (see *fcntl(5)*)
Lock type (*l_type*)	Description
F_RDLCK	Read lock (shared)
F_WRLCK	Write lock (exclusive)
F_UNLCK	Unlock

- *VOP_REALVP* — if there is a real *vnode* associated with the *vnode* pointer, this function obtains a pointer to it. For example, if the *vnode* is associated with a special file represented by an *snode*, this function returns the real *vnode* associated with it.

- *VOP_GETPAGE* — obtains the pages in a file that map to a specified range. It is usually called by the page fault handling mechanisms. For example, *segvn_fault( )* calls *VOP_GETPAGE( )* to bring in pages from the file to main memory.

- *VOP_PUTPAGE* — is the complement of *VOP_GETPAGE( )*. That is, it writes modified (dirty) pages (originally obtained by *VOP_GETPAGE( )*) back to the device. A flag parameter passed down to this function specifies whether the pages should be written back asynchronously and also whether they should be marked invalid once the write back operation has completed.

This function is normally used by the *pageout* process. The *pageout* process nominates (actually, steals) pages that have already been allocated to processes, to make them available to others. It does this to overcome the situation where no free pages are available. Before the pages are stolen, their contents are flushed out to secondary storage by *VOP_PUTPAGE( )*.

- *VOP_MAP* — maps a specified portion of the file associated with the *vnode* into the calling process's address space. It is used by the *mmap* system call and the *exec* mechanisms to map-in portions of a file, an *a.out*, or shared library associated with the *vnode*. If mappings in the address range specified are already mapped into the process's address space, they are removed with *as_unmap( )*. *as_map( )* is then called to establish new mappings in the process's address space (see § 5.9).

- *VOP_ADDMAP* — if the memory management routines (i.e., *as_map( )*) create and attach a new segment to the process's address space (*segvn_create( )*), they must inform the *vnode* of the new mapping with *VOP_ADDMAP( )*. This must be done by a *vnode* operation because the number of page mappings for a file are stored in the *inode* associated with the *vnode*.

- *VOP_DELMAP* — in contrast to *VOP_ADDMAP( )*, this function is used by the memory management routines to inform the *vnode* that a segment has been detached from the calling process's address space (i.e., *segvn_unmap( )*).

- *VOP_POLL* — corresponds to the *poll* system call. It returns any events of interest that may have occurred for the file descriptor associated with the *vnode* (see § 7.9.9).

- *VOP_DUMP* — currently unused; however, we assume that it would be used to "dump" a specified number of blocks from a given address to the file associated with the *vnode*.

- *VOP_PATHCONF* — implements the *fpathconf* and *pathconf* system calls on the specified *vnode*. They are derived from the POSIX standard which provides a mechanism for obtaining configurable pathname parameters (see *fpathconf(2)* for more information).

6.4   File and record locking

The UNIX System V Release 4 operating system provides two forms of file and record locking: *mandatory* and *advisory*. Their purpose is to provide the synchronization between cooperating process's accessing the same file's data simultaneously. The following sections describe how these file and record locking mechanisms are implemented.

6.4.1 Advisory locking

The *fcntl* system call provides the programmer with file and record locking facilities. A library function called *lockf(3C)* is also provided which implements similar facilities although its underlying mechanisms use *fcntl*.

A lock may be placed on a whole file or on portions (segments) of it. To place a lock, the programmer specifies a byte offset in the file that the lock is to start from, and a count of bytes from that position, which the lock is to extend. Thus, to lock an entire file the programmer specifies that the lock begins at byte zero and extends to the end of the file.

The system allows a process to lock a file only if the file being referenced is not already locked (permissions permitting). If the file is locked, the process requesting the lock is put to sleep until the lock is removed — recall the previous discussion of *VOP_FRLOCK( )*. An option with *fcntl* allows the programmer to lock a file without blocking. That is, the programmer can specify that the system call is to return if the file is locked rather than wait for it to become unlocked. The programmer can also specify if a lock is to be enforced for *writes, reads,* or both. *fcntl* is also used to remove a lock.

A read lock prevents another process from placing a write lock on the locked area within the file. However, several read locks can be placed within the file so long as their segments do not overlap. On the other hand, a write lock is exclusive. That is, it prevents another process from placing a read or write lock on the file. Furthermore, only one write lock is allowed on a segment but the write lock is not allowed if the segment already has a read lock on it. Of course, none of these operations can be performed on a file unless a valid file descriptor has first been obtained for it (i.e., via *open, creat* etc). The file must be opened with the correct modes before a read or write lock can be placed on a segment within it. For example, to place a write lock on a file, the file must first be opened for writing. Similarly, to place a read lock on a file, the file must first be opened for reading.

Locking services provided by *fcntl* are useful only if the programmer implements them in his or her programs. Therefore, if cooperating programs are expected to access or modify the contents of the same file, this locking service is recommended. It is because of this that the locking features of *fcntl* are collectively referred to as *advisory file and record locking*. However, an advisory lock, as its name implies, is "advisory". That is, a program (if programmed to do so) may ignore the lock and read or write the data regardless.

6.4.2 File and record locking in the *vnode*

The *vnode* member pointer *v_filocks* points to a linked list of *filock* structures. Each *filock* structure on the list represents a record lock set in the file associated with the *vnode*. *filock* structures on the list are ordered by the starting byte offset of the lock in the file. The *filock* structure is complicated because it consists of several data types. Thus, it is shown in its declared form in Appendix B.

The members of the *filock* structure are described as follows:

- *prev, next* — these pointers link *filock* structures together on a doubly linked list. The list may be associated with the *vnode* via the *v_filocks* member, or with the system sleep locks list headed by a pointer called *sleeplcks*. The system sleep lock list holds *filocks* belonging to processes that have been put to sleep waiting for a lock to become free. When the lock is removed, the process is awoken and the *filock* is moved from the system sleep lock list to the *vnode* list associated with the file. *filock* structures put on a list managed by the *vnode* represent successful locks placed on the file associated with that *vnode*.

- *wakeflg* — so that it can recognise that a process has been put to sleep because of a lock, the system sets the *wakeflg* variable in the *filock* associated with the lock. When the lock is removed, the *wakeflg* is checked. If it is set, *wakeup( )* is called to wake the sleeping process.

- *pid, sysid* — to avoid deadlock situations, processes have their *pid* and *sysid* members set. *pid* is set to the process ID of the process that set the lock. *sysid* is set to the system ID associated with the process that set the lock. The process that set the lock, puts to sleep a process wanting the lock. If the process wanting the lock is the same process that set the lock, putting it to sleep will cause a deadlock. Thus, when *fcntl* is called, the system determines whether a deadlock condition is imminent. If it is, the process wanting the lock is not put to sleep and *fcntl* returns *EDEADLK*.

  The *F_SETLK* switch used with *fcntl* allows a process to set a lock without blocking. That is, if a lock already exists the system call will return immediately with a value of -1 and *errno* will be set to *EACCES*. This allows the process to detect a blocking situation.

- *set* — an *flock* structure describing the characteristics of the lock. For example, it describes the lock type and start and end offsets of the lock within a file.

Note that both *pid* and *sysid* variables are stored in a structure called *blk*. The *blk* structure and *wakeflg* form a union data type called *stat*, defined as a member within the *filock* structure.

6.4.3 Mandatory locking

As well as advisory locking, the system provides a mandatory locking mechanism. The only difference between the two is that for mandatory locks the system enforces the record locking mechanisms on the occurrence of each I/O operation on the file. That is, if either *read* or *write* system calls are made, and mandatory locks are enforced on the file, the system first determines whether the process can access the file according to the type of record lock set within it. Therefore, with mandatory locks, the system governs access to a locked record according to the lock type at the time the I/O operation is performed, whereas with advisory locks access is governed by cooperating processes operating in user-mode using the *fcntl* locking service.

At the cost of additional overhead, mandatory locks provide an extra and more secure form of synchronization. However, if multiple processes are expected to perform atomic *reads* or *writes* on a record within a file, it is recommended that those processes are made to cooperate with each other using advisory locks instead of depending on any mandatory locks that may or may not be enforced. The reasons for this will become evident presently.

As we said before, the system determines whether mandatory locks are enforced on a file at the time an I/O operation is performed. However, the decision to enforce mandatory locking depends on the access permissions set on the file. For mandatory locks to be enforced, the file must be a regular file with the set-group-ID on execution bit set on, and the execute bit for the group must be turned off (see Table 2.3). Note that all these conditions must be met before mandatory locking is enforced, otherwise record locks placed on the file will be advisory only. To change the modes of a file to enforce mandatory locking the program must use the *chmod* system call. An example of this is given in Figure 6.7. The command, *chmod(1)* can also be used to do this:

```
$ ls -l creb
-rw-r--r--   1 ayla    clan            12345 Feb 21 11:04 creb
$ chmod +l creb
$ ls -l creb
-rw-r-lr--   1 ayla    clan            12345 Feb 21 11:04 creb
```

Note that it is not good practice to have execute permissions set on a file that is also expected to have record locks set. This is because the system does not obey record locking set on a file while executing it.

6.4.4 Lock resource and accounting

The system updates system-wide accounting information for record locks that are created or removed. This information is referenced by the global variable *flckinfo* (see the *flckinfo* structure in Table 6.9). In addition to this, the tuneable parameter *FLCKREC* specifies the maximum number of file and record locks that can be active at any one time. That is, if *flckinfo.reccnt* is greater than this imposed limit, the system fails to create the lock.

6.5 The virtual file system

When the kernel has to access a file, it uses a file system type independent interface, which is implemented as a set of macros beginning with *VOP_*. It allows the system to carry out operations on a file without knowing what type of file system the file is stored under. Such flexibility is achieved via the implementation of the file system type independent *vnode*. However, the underlying mechanism of each *vnode* operation is dependent on the file system type implementation associated with the file being referenced by the *vnode*. Thus, to perform an operation on a file, the kernel is implemented with a mechanism that allows it to execute a file system type dependent function to carry out an operation without knowing what that function is called or what it does.

Figure 6.7: *An example of how to turn mandatory locks on*

```
#include <sys/types.h>
#include <sys/stat.h>

#define fmodes   st_buf.st_mode

/*
 * turn mandatory locking on.
 * Zero if success else non-zero on error
 */
man_locks_on(fd)
int fd;
{
    struct stat st_buf;

    /* file must be open */
    if( fstat(fd, &st_buf) )
        return -1;

    /* file must be regular */
    if( ! S_ISREG(fmodes) )
        return 1;

    /* turn off execute permission for the group */
        fmodes &= ~S_IXGRP;

    /* turn on set-group-ID bit */
    fmodes |= S_ENFMT;

    /* now change the file with given modes */
    if( fchmod(fd, fmodes) )
        return -1;

    return 0;
}
```

In a similar fashion to the *vnode* interface, under UNIX System V Release 4, all operations that are done on a file system are also conducted through a single interface that allows the system to carry out operations on a file system without knowing its construction or type. Such flexibility is achieved with the virtual file system (*VFS*).

Since the kernel is independent of file system type or construction, it is flexible enough to accommodate future file systems as they become available. For example,

Table 6.9: *Struct flckinfo*

Element	Description
long reccnt	Count of record locks currently in use
long rectot	Count of records locks used since system boot

it should be relatively easy to implement a non-UNIX file system under the *VFS* so long as one knows what one is doing. Note however, that while the *VFS* caters for several file manipulation techniques, certain file system type implementations may not fit its template.

A high-level discussion of file systems and the file system interface that is supported under UNIX System V Release 4 is given in § 2.4.4 and § 2.4.5. The following sections describe the implementation of the *VFS* and its interface.

6.5.1 Virtual file system switch table (VFSSW)

To configure a file system type into the operating system, it must have an entry in the system *virtual file system switch (vfssw)* table. The *vfssw[]* table is an array of *vfssw* structures (Table 6.10) each representing a particular file system type.

Table 6.10: *Struct vfssw (vfssw_t)*

Element	Description
*char *vsw_name*	String containing file system type name
*int (*vsw_init)( )*	Pointer to file system initialization function
*struct vfsops *vsw_vfsops*	Pointer to file system type dependent operations
long vsw_flag	Flags (currently unused)

The *vfssw[]* table (Figure 6.8) is implementation dependent because each vendor decides what file systems are supported on their implementation of the operating system. For example, many vendors support an *s5* or *ufs* file system but not both. Other implementations may implement both. Note, however, that because the operating system is independent of file system construction, it has no concept of the underlying format of a particular file system. Thus, programs that manipulate file systems must be prepared to understand the underlying construction of several file system types. They must also be prepared to recognise a file system that is not supported and print out an error message to that effect. For example, the administration utility **mkfs(1M)** is used to format and create a file system. It is implemented with a runtime switch that allows the user to specify what file system type to construct.

File system types that are likely to be used more often than others should be placed nearest to the top of the table so that algorithms scan through the table to access them more quickly. For example, to assist with file system hardening, the *fsflush* daemon (see *VFS_SYNC*) is brought into action each second to flush cached data (i.e., the buffer cache, in-core *inodes*, and mapped in pages) to its storage media. One would hope that locally attached devices are flushed before those that

Figure 6.8: *An example of a virtual file system switch table (vfssw[])*

```
struct vfssw vfssw[] = {

   /* element zero in the table is arbitrarily invalid by default*/
   { 0, 0, 0, 0 },

   { "spec",    specinit,    &spec_vfsops,  0 },   /* SPEC */
   { "vxfs",    vx_init,     &vx_vfsops,    0 }    /* Veritas */
   { "cdfs",    cdfsinit,    &cdfs_vfsops,  0 },   /* CD ROM */
   { "ufs",     ufsinit,     &ufs_vfsops,   0 },   /* UFS */
   { "nfs",     nfsinit,     &nfs_vfsops,   0 },   /* NFS */
   { "fd",      fdfsinit,    &fdfsvfsops,   0 },   /* FD */
   { "fifo",    fifoinit,    &fifovfsops,   0 },   /* FIFO */
   { "namefs",  nameinit,    &nmvfsops,     0 },   /* NAMEFS */
   { "proc",    prinit,      &prvfsops,     0 },   /* PROC */
   { "s5",      s5init,      &s5_vfsops,    0 },   /* S5 */
   { "rfs",     rf_init,     &rf_vfsops,    0 },   /* RFS */
   { "bfs",     bfsinit,     &bfs_vfsops,   0 },   /* BFS */
   { "xnam",    xnaminit,    &xnam_vfsops,  0 },   /* Xenix */
   { "dos",     dosinit,     &dos_vfsops,   0 },   /* MS-DOS */

};
```

are remotely attached since flushing remote devices probably takes considerably longer to complete.

During system initialization, the VFS initialization function *vfsinit( )* is called, which in turn calls each configured file system type's *vsw_init( )* routine. These functions are file system type specific and are responsible for initializing the internal working environment for their file system type.

6.5.2 File system type dependent VFS operations

The third element in the *vfssw* structure (*vsw_vfsops*) is a pointer to a *vfsops* structure (see Table 6.11) that describes the operations that can be done to a specific file system type. It contains several function pointers, each pointing to a file system type specific function defined by the file system type implementation. These functions are called when the kernel needs to perform an operation on a file system. For example, when a request to mount a file system is made, the function that *vfs_mount( )* points to for the file system being manipulated is invoked.

Like the *VOP_* macro suite used by the *vnode* interface, VFS operations are implemented with a suite of macros prefixed with *VFS_* and defined in *<sys/vfs.h>*. The first argument to these macros is a pointer to the *vfsops* structure pertaining to the file system being manipulated. Thus, they provide a file system type independent interface to the file system type dependent routines.

It is not mandatory for a file system type to support a particular VFS operation. However, if it does, the kernel assumes that that operation will be carried out as expected by that particular file system type. It makes no assumption about what procedures are required to carry out the operation. Thus, it can be seen that the file system type dependent code for performing operations on a file system is hidden in the *vfsops* structure.

Table 6.11: *Struct vfsops and related macros (vfsops_t)*

vfsops element	Related macro	Description of operation
int (*vfs_mount)( )	VFS_MOUNT	Mount a file system
int (*vfs_unmount)( )	VFS_UNMOUNT	Unmount a file system
int (*vfs_root)( )	VFS_ROOT	Get the file system root *vnode*
int (*vfs_statvfs)( )	VFS_STATVFS	Get file system statistics
int (*vfs_sync)( )	VFS_SYNC	Flush file system buffers
int (*vfs_vget)( )	VFS_VGET	Get vnode from *file ID*
int (*vfs_mountroot)( )	VFS_MOUNTROOT	Mount the root file system

Table 6.12: *VFS operations supported by each file system type*

Vfsops	ufs	specfs	s5	rfs	procfs	nfs	namefs	fifofs	fd	bfs
vfs_mount	•		•	•	•	•	•		•	•
vfs_unmount	•		•	•	•	•	•		•	•
vfs_root	•		•	•	•	•	•		•	•
vfs_statvfs	•		•	•	•	•	•		•	•
vfs_sync	•	•	•	•	•	•	•	•		•
vfs_vget	•		•							•
vfs_mountroot	•		•							

We will now discuss the file system type dependent VFS operations, what the kernel assumes each function will do, and where it is used by the file system type independent parts of the kernel.

Each file system type implementation must define a *vfsops* structure. It must assign each member function pointer to its corresponding file system type dependent VFS operation also defined by the file system type implementation. If the file system type does not support a specific operation, it must nevertheless assign an appropriate function to do the minimum required of it. In most cases, such functions either do nothing or return an error value to the effect that it is not supported.

In some cases, an operation is closely related to its corresponding system call and is usually called as a result of the system call associated with the operation being invoked.

The functions that form the *vfsops* structure members are explained in their macro form. Note that the operation performed by a particular function is file system type implementation dependent. The kernel makes no assumptions about what is to be done to achieve the desired action for the file system being manipulated:

- *VFS_MOUNT* — corresponds to the *mount* system call. The *mount* system call is used to request a specified file system to be mounted onto a specified directory mount point.

    After resolving the pathnames of the supplied directory mount point and obtaining a *vfs* structure for the file system about to be mounted, *VFS_MOUNT( )* is called to instantiate the mount and incorporate the specified file system into the global file system tree. File system specific data structures and variables that are managed by the particular file system implementation may be initialized in this function — for example, in-core *inode* tables, superblocks, directory hash lists, and so on. It must also resolve the pathname of the special file being mounted, and confirm that the file system can in fact be mounted and that the user trying to mount the file system has super-user privileges. For more information see **mount(1M)**. Mounted file systems and the system's *vfs* list are discussed in the next section.

- *VFS_UNMOUNT* — corresponds to the *umount* system call. It performs any file system specific operations required before the file system is unmounted. For example, it may be necessary to flush buffers associated with the file system — *inode* caches, superblock, and so on. The function must also deallocate space associated with data structures that were allocated for the file system when it was mounted.

    Before this function is called, all directory name lookup cache entries (see § 6.7) for files contained in the file system while it was mounted are purged, even if the subsequent call to *VFS_UNMOUNT( )* fails.

- *VFS_ROOT* — if the pathname translation algorithms encounter a *vnode* that has been covered by a mounted file system while resolving a pathname, it will have to go through the directory tree in the file system associated with that mount point. This allows the system to transparently indirect to the *vnode* associated with the root of a mounted file system. But before this can be done, the *vnode* associated with the root of the file system must be sought. Thus, *VFS_ROOT( )* obtains the root *vnode* of the file system being manipulated. Pathname resolution is discussed in § 6.8.

- *VFS_STATVFS* — is used by the *ustat, statvfs* and *fstatvfs* system calls. *ustat* obtains information about a file system. It fills a *ustat* structure (see Table 6.13) for which space is reserved in user space.

    The *statvfs* and *fstatvfs* system calls are used in a similar fashion. However, they fill a *statvfs* structure instead. A *statvfs* structure (see Table 6.14) is a method of describing generically a mounted file system's superblock. That is, the *statvfs* structure can be used to obtain information from any file system type so long as it is already mounted.

Table 6.13: *Struct ustat*

Element	Description
daddr_t f_tfree	Total number of free blocks
o_ino_t f_tinode	Total number of free *inodes*
char f_fname[6]	String containing name of the file system
char f_fpack[6]	String containing name of the file system volume

Table 6.14: *Struct statvfs (statvfs_t)*

Element	Description
u_long f_bsize	Fundamental file system block size
u_long f_frsize	Fragment size (if supported)
u_long f_blocks	Total number of blocks on file system specified in units of *f_frsize*
u_long f_bfree	Total number of free blocks available specified in units of *f_frsize*
u_long f_bavail	Number of available free blocks to non-superuser specified in units of *f_frsize*
u_long f_files	Total number of *inode*
u_long f_ffree	Total number of free *inodes*
u_long f_favail	Number of free *inodes* for non-superuser
u_long f_fsid	File system id (currently device number)
char f_basetype[FSTYPSZ]	String containing the name of the file system type
u_long f_flag	Bit-mask of flags (see below)
u_long f_namemax	Maximum file name length
char f_fstr[32]	File system specific string
Flags (*f_flag*)	**Description**
ST_RDONLY	File system is mounted read-only
ST_NOSUID	*setuid/setgid* semantics not supported
ST_NOTRUNC	Long file names are not truncated

The *VFS_STATVFS( )* function is used to obtain the file system specific information and convert it into the generic file system independent information described by the *statvfs* structure.

For more information about these system calls see [AT&T 1990h].

- *VFS_SYNC* — corresponds to the *sync* system call but is also used by the *fsflush* daemon. It flushes any pending I/O to the file system associated with the passed *vfs* pointer. Note in Table 6.12 it can be seen that all currently supported file system types support a *VFS_SYNC( )* function. This is because a file system sync must never fail. Thus, at the very least, *VFS_SYNC( )* must be made to return success to the caller even if the file system has no superblock or in-core *inode* table to flush i.e., *procfs* and *fifofs*.

Besides passing a pointer to the *vfs* structure associated with the file system that the *sync* operation is to be performed on, a flag is passed down. This flag is meant to be interpreted in the file system type dependent *vfs_sync()* function handler; it specifies whether a complete or partial flush is to be done. A partial flush involves flushing the cached attribute information only (i.e., in-core *inodes*). A complete flush also involves flushing all in-core buffers and the file system super block. The latter is done for all file systems, regardless of file system type when a *sync* system call is made. A partial flush is done each second by the *fsflush* daemon.

fsflush is a system process started at system boot. It is awoken each second[1] in *clock()* to flush cached data to its storage device. This includes the system's buffer cache, in-core *inode* cache and mapped-in memory pages. To bring some form of data integrity to the UNIX file subsystem implementation, the designers chose to flush the in-core *inode* tables of each file system each second from *fsflush*. This mechanism is known as "file system hardening".

- *VFS_VGET* — given a *file ID*, this function returns the *vnode* associated with it. For more information, refer to the discussion of *VOP_FID* in § 6.3.3.

- *VFS_MOUNTROOT* — file systems that can be mounted as a *root* file system must define this function. The root file system forms the beginning of the UNIX file system hierarchy. That is, it contains the root "/" of the UNIX file system tree. All other file systems mount onto a mount point with a pathname that references the beginning of the root file system. During system initialization, the kernel automatically mounts the root file system onto an in-core mount point. Therefore, without it, the system cannot start.

  VFS_MOUNTROOT() is passed a flag that explains why the function was called. It must interpret the condition of the flag and direct its execution as follows:

  - *ROOT_INIT* — initializes and mounts the root file system, which is described to the kernel by a configurable variable called *rootfstype*. It is a character pointer that simply holds a *NULL* terminated string containing the name of the file system type that holds a valid root file system — for example, *"ufs"* or *"s5"*. If this variable is not set, the system scans through the *vfssw[]* table during system initialization seeking a file system that supports a *vfs_mountroot()* operation. Once the root file system type is known, the initialization procedure can select its *vfssw[]* entry. It then follows the *vsw_vfsops* pointer to find its *vfs_mountroot()* function. The function is then called with an argument of *ROOT_INIT*.

  - *ROOT_REMOUNT* — the root file system is remounted, usually automatically by the system startup procedures if the root file system is found to be

---

1   *The rate (in seconds) at which fsflush is brought into action is tuneable.*

inconsistent during system initialization.

Earlier versions of the UNIX operating system used to prompt the administrator with the message:

"** BOOT UNIX (NO SYNC!) ****"**

if an inconsistency was found in the root file system while checking it. Unfortunately, in order to check the root file system, it had to be mounted so that the *fsck(1)* command itself could be located (although it was not formally mounted as such, it was implicitly mounted during the kernel boot procedure). Therefore, if an inconsistency was found on the root file system during system initialization, there were complications. It was considered too dangerous to continue any further and the above message was printed to the console in the hope that the user would obey its instructions. The best action to take was to press the reset button or pull the power plug without performing a *sync(1)*. Otherwise disastrous consequences could occur, hence the message to boot UNIX without syncing. If this action was not taken, any in-core buffers that were subsequently flushed to the file system, which may have been generated from information read from the original inconsistent root file system, could overwrite the work done by *fsck*. In severe cases, it rendered the root file system unreadable.

In such cases, one had to boot from some other medium such as a bootable tape because, the UNIX *a.out* file resided on the root file system which was inaccessible because of the damage and so the UNIX kernel could not be loaded. Typically, the system behaved as if a hardware problem was the cause. Once UNIX was booted off the tape, an attempt was made to fix the broken file system but alas, quite often it was unsuccessful. The next action was to reinstall the operating system and restore it to its working state from backups.

Under UNIX System V Release 4, the procedures are much less drastic. First of all the UNIX operating system *a.out* file resides in a separate file system called */stand/unix* (a *bfs* file system type). This allows the system to initialize separately from the root file system. Secondly, it is now possible to query a file system for its state via the **fsck(1M)** command, which reads the superblock of the file system to be checked. Normally, a bit is set in the superblock of a file system when it is mounted. The bit is then reset when the file system is unmounted (i.e., when the system is shut down). If the bit is set in the superblock when an attempt to mount it is done, it is assumed that the file system was not unmounted properly and thus it is "dirty".

During system initialization, an attempt is made to mount the "root" file system whether it is dirty or not. Once mounted, the */sbin/bcheckrc* startup script is run in user-mode to query its status. If it is dirty, it is assumed to be inconsistent and an attempt is made to fix it (while it is mounted) with **fsck(1M)**. If successful, it is remounted by executing **uadmin(1M)**. This command uses the *uadmin* system call to remount the (now fixed) root file system. The *uadmin* system call calls *VFS_MOUNTROOT( )* with the argument *ROOT_REMOUNT*. The file system type dependent *vfs_mountroot( )* operation must then take whatever action is necessary to remount the root file system.

- *ROOT_UNMOUNT* — when the system is shut down, the shutdown procedure unmounts all locally mounted file systems except the root file system. The final program run is normally */sbin/uadmin* and carried out as the final task of */sbin/init* as the result of a request to change to init state zero. This results in a call to the *uadmin* system call to unmount the root file system. The *uadmin* system call calls *VFS_MOUNTROOT()* with the argument *ROOT_UNMOUNT*.

    On return to the *uadmin* system call from *VFS_MOUNTROOT()* the system is halted and sometimes rebooted automatically, depending on the arguments given to **uadmin(1M)** and what is supported by the hardware.

6.6 The UNIX file system hierarchy

So far in this chapter we have discussed how the kernel manipulates files with *vnodes*, and how it accommodates different file system types with the virtual file system. However, we have yet to discuss the implementation specific details of the UNIX file system structure as a total file system hierarchy. This section concentrates on these details.

The UNIX file system hierarchy consists of several different file systems. A file system is a structured hierarchy of files and directories residing on some physical medium — usually a fixed disk, but it may be implemented on some other device such as CD ROM. In some cases a file system may be implemented as a remote resource accessible over a network — for example, NFS and RFS. Others may be implemented as a pseudo file system such as a RAM disk.

File systems that reside on disk are generally stored on a non-removable device that is divided into several logical partitions, each implemented as a separate file system. This is typical for small installations such as UNIX PCs or workstations. In large installations, a physical disk may contain a single file system on its own. Some installations may use disk striping to implement a file system across multiple disks and partitions. Whatever the implementation, a file system is a logical unit that may be integrated into one physical unit collectively called the UNIX File system hierarchy. Figure 6.9 depicts an installation with two internal hard disks, with each disk partitioned into separate file systems. Note that this diagram is only an example. The configuration of a UNIX system differs widely from one installation to another even when originally set up by the vendor. Once out in the field, the system configuration is usually changed by the system administrator to suit the application. Note also that the partition named "boot" is not a file system. We have shown it here because in most cases it is implemented as a reserved area of the disk that contains boot programs. The partition named "swap" is reserved for the system's swap space as described in § 3.8.4; this is not a file system either. The bottom half of the diagram shows how these individual file systems may be put together to form a complete UNIX file system hierarchy.

Figure 6.9: *Example of hard disk partitioning and file system placement*

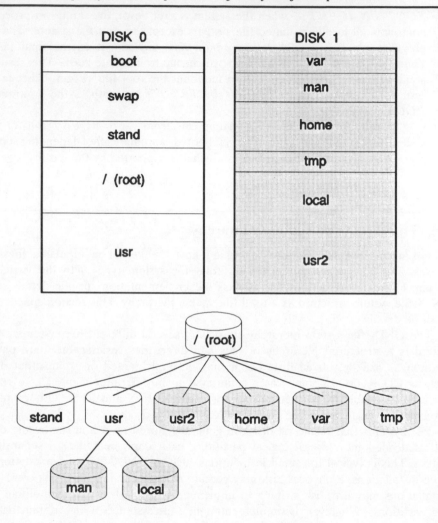

6.6.1 Mountable file systems

File systems such as those described above may be thought of as "packs" that can be attached to, or detached from, the main UNIX file system tree. Each file system contains its own file system hierarchy of files and directories, but when all file systems are attached to each other they form one large file system.

Apart from the root file system, which always forms the root of the UNIX file system tree, a file system can, conceptually, be attached anywhere within the main UNIX file system hierarchy. The point at which a file system is attached is called a *mount-point*. A mount-point is any directory within the main file system tree. For example, the diagram labeled B in Figure 6.10 represents a file system called "man". This file system contains a hierarchy of directories containing files that represent the

Figure 6.10: *Mounting a file system*

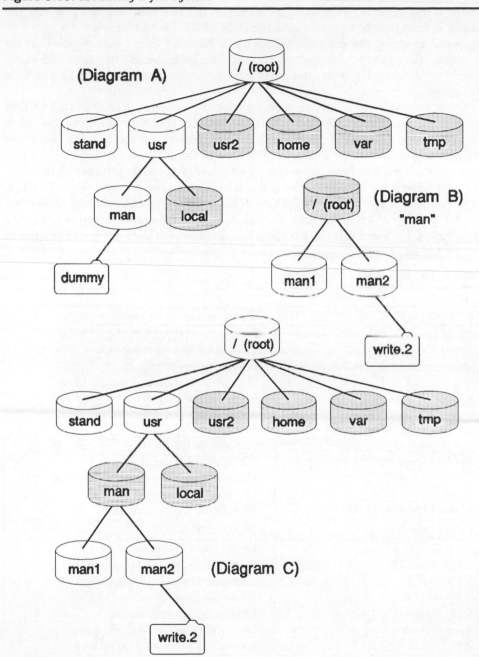

on-line manual pages for the UNIX operating system. However, on its own, this file system is inaccessible. Therefore, to reference the file named *write.2* in this file system, it must first be mounted onto the main UNIX file system labeled A.

In this example, the main file system has a directory called *man*, which contains a single file called *dummy* which can be referenced by the pathname, */usr/man/dummy*. However, the directory *man* is also a mount-point for the *man* file system.

Once mounted, the directory *man* contains the directory hierarchy that formed the root of the "man" file system. Conceptually, the *man* directory has been covered by the "man" file system and the file *dummy* cannot be seen any more although it still exists. The end result is shown in the diagram labeled C. Note that once a file system has been mounted, its attachment is totally invisible to the user. The user cannot detect if he or she is accessing files on one file system or the other. The effect is a single consistent file system hierarchy. This example also shows that it is not good practice to mount a file system onto a non-empty directory since files contained in a covered directory become inaccessible until the covering file system is unmounted again.

Table 6.15: *Struct vfs (vfs_t)*

Element	Description
*struct vfs *vfs_next*	Pointer to next VFS in the VFS list
*struct vfsops *vfs_op*	Pointer to VFS operations
*struct vnode *vfs_vnodecovered*	Pointer to *vnode* that this
	file system is mounted on top of
u_long vfs_flag	Flags (see below)
u_long vfs_bsize	Native block size
int vfs_fstype	File system type index
fsid_t vfs_fsid	File system ID
caddr_t vfs_data	File system private data
dev_t vfs_dev	Expanded device number of mounted VFS
u_long vfs_bcount	I/O count for accounting
u_short vfs_nsubmounts	Immediate sub-mount count
Flags (*vfs_flag*)	Description
VFS_RDONLY	Read-only VFS
VFS_MLOCK	Lock VFS so that subtree is stable
VFS_MWAIT	Someone is waiting for lock
VFS_NOSUID	*setuid* disallowed
VFS_REMOUNT	Modify mount options only
VFS_NOTRUNC	Does not truncate long file names
VFS_UNLINKABLE	*unlink(2)* can be applied to root

6.6.2 The system's VFS mount list

The kernel's generic abstraction of a file system is the file system type independent *vfs* structure (Table 6.15). The *vfs* structure contains generic information which the kernel uses to manipulate a file system in a file system type independent way.

For each active (mounted) file system maintained by the system, an associated *vfs* structure is allocated and held on a linked list. The list is called the *vfs-mount-list* (previously known as the *mount-table*) and is headed by a *vfs* structure named *root* which, in turn, is referenced by a pointer called *rootvfs*. The vfs-mount-list is used by the kernel to administer any file systems that are mounted. A file system that is not mounted is not known to the operating system, even if that file system coexists on the same physical device as those file systems that are mounted.

The *root vfs* contains the information about the root file system that is mounted automatically by the kernel at boot time. Once mounted, the root file system cannot be unmounted unless the system is being shut down via the *uadmin* system call. The fields in the *vfs* structure are described as follows:

- *vfs_next* — points to the next *vfs* structure on the vfs-mount-list. This pointer is *NULL* in the last *vfs* structure on the list.

- *vfs_op* — points to the file system's *vfsops* structure defining the operations that can be done on this VFS.

- *vfs_vnodecovered* — points to the *vnode* of the directory mount point covered by this file system. This is used during pathname resolution (discussed later).

- *vfs_flag* — a bitmask containing specific operational flags. For example, the flags may indicate whether the file system is mounted in read-only mode, or locked to prevent access to it during a *mount* or *umount*.

- *vfs_bsize* — specifies the logical block size that the file system was created with. The logical block size is the number of bytes read or written by the operating system in a single I/O operation.

    The operating system imposes limitations and consequences that concern a file system's block size. If the file system's logical block size encompasses several physical (512 byte) device blocks, the kernel assists disk I/O performance by reading and writing several physical device blocks of data at a time in order to manipulate them as a single logical block. This means that a single I/O request results in several physical blocks of data being transferred.

    Internally, the kernel works with logical blocks. On an *s5* file system, these may be in increments of 512, 1024 or 2048 bytes. On an *ufs* file system, they may also be in increments of 4096 or 8192 bytes. The size of a logical block is consistent across a whole file system and is dependent on how the file system was created with the **mkfs(1M)** command. However, this gain in disk I/O performance must be weighed against the possible wastage of disk space. A file is assigned a logical disk block to store its data with. If the file is larger than the size of a logical block, subsequent logical blocks are assigned to it until the data is stored. If there is residual space for more data past the end of the file in the last assigned logical block, that space may be wasted. For example, consider an *s5* file system that is created with a logical block size of 1024 bytes. Let us say that this file system contains 10000 files, each containing a single byte of data. The total disk space taken up by these files is 10 Mbyte although the data stored is only 10000 bytes! (Note that the *ufs* file system supports "fragments". This allows a disk block to be further broken down into smaller fragments than a physical disk block, thus reducing the implied potential disk space wastage.)

From this it can be seen that a file system used to contain mostly large files, benefits from using a large logical block size. However, if the file system is used to contain mostly small files (i.e., less than the smallest logical block size), then it is best to create the file system with the smallest logical block size.

The maximum size of a logical block is 8192 bytes although this constraint is file system implementation dependent. The minimum size of a logical block is the size of a physical device block (512 bytes).

- *vfs_fstype* — holds the value of the index into the *vfssw[]* table associated with this file system's type.

- *vfs_dev* — holds the *major* and *minor* numbers of the mounted device.

- *vfs_fsid* — contains a unique file system identifier made from an array of two long integers defined in an *fsid* structure (*fsid_t*). The first element contains a representation of the external *major* and *minor* numbers (as in *vfs_dev*) associated with the device that the file system resides on (see *makedevice(D3DK)* in [AT&T 1990e]). Note that the *minor* number is set to zero during file system initialization and is filled in with the real *minor* number when the file system is mounted. The second element contains the same value as that stored in *vfs_fstype*. Both *vfs_fstype* and *vfs_fsid* are initialized and set up within the file system switch *vsw_init()* function at boot time.

The function of the *fsid* structure is to provide a unique ID with which to represent a file system across a network. The ID should be unique to all machines since it is used by the lock manager daemon.

- *vfs_data* — points to an arbitrary file system type dependent data structure defined by the file system type implementation. This data structure is known only to the file system implementation, so it is often referred to as a "private file system data structure". It normally contains such things as a pointer to the file system's root *vnode*, a pointer to the file system's superblock in memory, and other file system type dependent information (Figure 6.11). For example, the *ufs* file system uses this area for storing *quota* information as well as the *vnode* and superblock pointers described above. Quota information enforces resource limitations that may have been set with the *quotactl* system call (see *quotactl(2)*).

- *vfs_bcount* — this variable holds a count of the number of *read and write* operations performed on the file system since it was mounted.

- *vfs_nsubmounts* — represents a count of file systems mounted under this one.

Figure 6.11: *VFS related data structures and pointers*

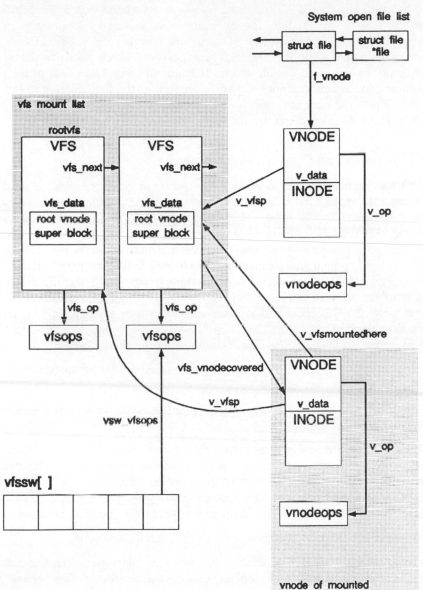

6.6.3 The *vnodes* association with the *vfs* structure

Every *vnode* that is associated with a file maintains a pointer called *v_vfsp* which points to the file's associated *vfs* structure. A *vnode* associated with a directory that is being used as a file system mount point also maintains a pointer called *v_vfsmountedhere* which points to the *vfs* structure covering the *vnode*. Likewise, a *vfs* structure maintains a pointer called *vfs_vnodecovered* which points to the *vnode* of the directory mount point the file system is mounted onto. The *vnode* of the root of the mounted file system can normally be referenced as the first element in the file system type dependent data structure pointed to by *vfs_data*. Figure 6.11 shows how these pointers and data structures are implemented.

6.6.4 The *mount* and *umount* system calls

In § 2.4.2 it was mentioned that to make a file system active (accessible) it must be mounted onto the main UNIX file system hierarchy. The attachment is done with the *mount* system call. In most cases, **mount(1M)** is used for this purpose. Internally, it uses the *mount* system call to achieve its result. However, programs that have reason to mount a file system such as a network file server may also make use of the *mount* system call. Once mounted, files in the mounted file system become available to the user. References to the directory that the file system is mounted onto are directed to the root of the mounted file system instead. Note that the system only allows a process that runs with super-user privileges to *mount* or *umount* a file system.

To achieve the attachment, the *mount* system call does the following:

- Obtains a *vnode* for the directory that the file system will be mounted onto from the directory name lookup cache.

- Ensures that the specified directory mount point is not already being used as a mount point for another file system.

- Sets up a pointer to the file system type dependent operations structure for the specified file system type (the default is the *root* file system type). This can be obtained by indexing into the file system switch table (*vfssw[n].vsw_vfsops*). However, depending on the specified system call arguments, it may be necessary to find the *vfssw[]* entry from the specified file system type number or name.

- Allocates and initializes a *vfs* structure for the mounted file system.

- Covers the directory mount point with the mounted file system. This causes all entries in the directory name lookup cache that represent files below the mounted-on directory to be purged.

- Calls the file system specific *vfs_mount()* routine via *VFS_MOUNT()* to read the superblock of the file system into memory so that the file system dependent routines can administer it. The superblock of a file system is file system type specific. It contains the critical data associated with the file system (see § 2.4.1).

This function also resolves the pathname of the special file being mounted by obtaining a *vnode* for it from the directory name lookup cache. It also allocates the file system type dependent *vfs* private data structure and attaches it to the *vfs_data* pointer associated with the newly allocated *vfs*.

- Logically attaches the physically separate file system to the main UNIX file system hierarchy by ensuring that the newly allocated *vfs* structure is added onto the system's *vfs* mount list (headed by *rootvfs*). The *vnode* that represents the mounted-on directory is covered by setting the *v_vfsmountedhere* pointer in the mounted-on *vnode* to point to the new *vfs* structure and by setting the *vfs_vnodecovered* pointer to point to the mounted-on *vnode*.

- Finally, the *vfs_nsubmounts* counter is incremented in the *vfs* structure associated with the mounted-on *vnode*.

To unmount a file system, the *umount* system call is used. Note that traditionally, the "n" has always been missing in this system call name. To perform a *umount*, the system basically reverse-engineers what was set up by the *mount*:

- The first requirement for the *umount* operation is to find the address of the mounted file system's associated *vfs* structure by using the information given in the system call arguments. The *umount* system call takes a single argument — a pointer to a pathname to unmount. However, to make things complicated, the user may specify this as the pathname of the block special device that represents the mounted file system or the pathname of the directory mount point used by it. In either case, the system obtains a *vnode* for the specified pathname by doing a lookup in the directory name lookup cache. The resulting *vnode* can then be used to decipher which type of pathname the user supplied. For example, if the *v_flag* is marked with *VROOT*, it can be assumed that the *vnode* is associated with the root of its file system, so that the address of its associated *vfs* structure can be found by referencing *v_vfsp*. Otherwise, the system must search through the *vfs* mount list trying to find a *vfs* with a *vfs_dev* member that matches the *v_rdev* member of the *vnode*.

- All entries in the directory name lookup cache that represent files in the mounted file system are purged since they are not needed any more.

- *VFS_SYNC()* is called on the mounted file system so that any in-core buffers associated with the file system are written out (flushed) to its device — for example, the superblock, *inodes* and any delayed-write buffers.

- The file system type dependent *vfs_unmount()* routine is then called via the *VFS_UNMOUNT()* macro. It is within this function that the user's credentials are checked to make sure that the user has super-user privileges. (In the authors' view, this really should have been the first thing checked in the *umount* system call handler).

  This function ensures that there are no files open in the file system. If files are open, the system call returns -1 and *errno* is set to *EBUSY*. Otherwise, it continues to free any file system type dependent data structures associated with the mounted file system; for example, its private data structure (*vfs_data*).

- The *vfs_nsubmounts* counter is decremented in the *vfs* structure associated with the directory mount point.

- The *vfs* associated with the mounted file system is removed from the system's *vfs* mount list and deallocated.

Once the file system is successfully unmounted, the directory mount point that the file system was mounted onto reverts back to itself. That is, if a user references files in that directory, he or she will reference files belonging to that directory, not those stored under the hierarchy of the previously mounted file system.

Note that to prevent simultaneous access to the file system while it is being mounted or unmounted, the system automatically locks the *vfs* structure while these operations are carried out. A process that finds it locked receives -1 with *errno* set to *EBUSY*.

6.7 The directory name lookup cache

The *directory name lookup cache* (dnlc) is a mechanism that allows the file system type dependent algorithms to gain quick access to a file's *vnode*. It is based on code originally written by Robert Elz in Melbourne, Australia, and first showed up in 4.2BSD. It is used during pathname traversals; that is, when resolving a pathname, the name of the file is used to look up an entry associated with the file in the dnlc. If no entry is found, one is created for it. If, however, an entry is found, the information obtained from the cache lookup contains several pieces of information about the file which may be useful to the file system type dependent functions. For example, it contains a pointer to the *vnode* associated with the file itself, a pointer to the file's parent directory *vnode*, a pointer to a string containing the name of the file, and a pointer to the file's credentials structure.

The dnlc is initialized in *main( )* at system boot. From then on it is managed by a Least Recently Used (LRU) algorithm where frequently accessed files are most likely to retain an entry within the cache, and less frequently accessed files are most likely to have their cached entries re-used if there are no free cache entries available.

The cache itself is a table made up from *ncache* structures (Table 6.16) that are dynamically allocated during the initialization procedure (*dnlc_init( )*). The table is appropriately called *ncache*. Its size is dependent on a variable called *ncsize* which in turn is set to 100 plus the value of the *proc* table tuneable parameter, *NPROC*.

Each allocated *ncache* structure is linked into a table called *nc_hash[]* that contains *NC_HASH_SIZE* entries (currently 8). Each element in the table contains a doubly linked list of *ncache* structures associated with cached entries. To index into the table, a hash value is used which is built up from the file's name and the address of its parent directory *vnode*. Hence its name — "directory name lookup cache". Besides being linked into the hash table, *ncache* structures are linked onto an LRU

Table 6.16: *Struct ncache*

Element	Description
*struct ncache *hash_next*	Pointer to the next entry in the hash list
*struct ncache *hash_prev*	Pointer to the previous entry in the hash list
*struct ncache *lru_next*	Pointer to the next entry in the LRU list
*struct ncache *lru_prev*	Pointer to the previous entry in the LRU list
*struct vnode *vp*	Pointer to the *vnode* of the file
*struct vnode *dp*	Pointer to the *vnode* of the file's parent dir
char namlen	Length of file name
char name[NC_NAMLEN]	Name of the file
*struct cred *cred*	Pointer to the file's credentials

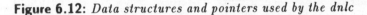

Figure 6.12: *Data structures and pointers used by the dnlc*

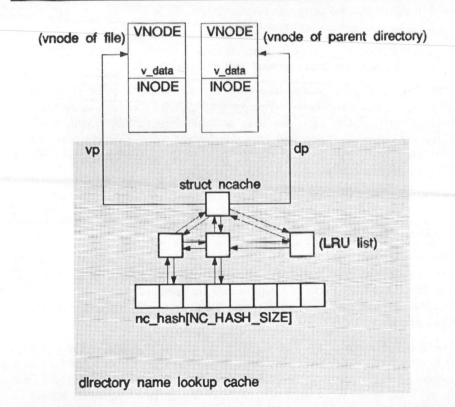

directory name lookup cache

list to determine which *ncache* structure will be used next for new cache entries.

The dnlc is good for most purposes but does not pretend to benefit every case. In particular, files that have names longer than some specified maximum are not cached at all. The maximum file name size used by the dnlc under UNIX System V Release 4 is defined by a constant called *NC_NAMLEN* (currently 15).

The following dnlc functions are implemented:

- *dnlc_init( )* — called from within *main( )* to initialize the dnlc. This includes allocating space for each element in *ncache[ ]*, and placing them all on the LRU list. Since there are no cached entries yet, all hash links in the table are set to point to themselves.

- *dnlc_enter( )* — creates a new dnlc entry from the given file name, *vnode* pointer, parent directory *vnode* pointer, and *cred* pointer. Reference counts in both *vnodes* and the *cred* structure are incremented so that they will not be removed by some other module in the system.

- *dnlc_lookup( )* — returns a pointer to a *vnode* associated with a given cached file name. If no entry is found, then *(vnode_t *)NULL* is returned.

- *dnlc_search( )* — searches for a cached entry. It returns a pointer to the found *ncache* structure associated with a given file name. Otherwise, *(ncache *)NULL* is returned to signify that no entry was found.

- *dnlc_remove( )* — by using the specified file name and parent directory *vnode* pointer to hash into *nc_hash[ ]*, it searches (via *dnlc_search( )*) for a matching entry. The entry found is then removed with *dnlc_rm( )*.

- *dnlc_rm( )* — is passed a pointer to an *ncache* entry which is to be purged from the directory name lookup cache. The removal includes the deletion of the hash list link, deletion of the LRU list link, decrementing reference counts in the *vnode*, parent directory *vnode*, and *cred*. Finally, the *ncache* structure associated with the removed entry is inserted into the head of the LRU list and its hash list pointer is re-initialized to point to itself.

- *dnlc_purge( )* — goes through the entire *ncache[ ]* table, deleting all entries.

- *dnlc_purge_vp( )* — goes through the entire *ncache[ ]* table, deleting all entries that reference the given *vnode*.

- *dnlc_purge_vfsp( )* — goes through the entire *ncache[ ]* table, deleting a specified number of entries that reference the given *vfs* structure pointer. If the specified count is zero, all entries associated with the *vfs* are removed.

  This function is used by *umount*; once a file system is unmounted, there is no need to cache file and directory names stored within it.

- *dnlc_purge1( )* — removes a single cached entry (the first found on the *ncache[ ]* table) in an effort to reclaim its *inode*. It is normally used to free an *inode* if a file system's *inode* freelist is emptied (commonly known as an "*inode* table overflow"). The *inode* associated with the *v_data* pointer in the *vnode* cannot be freed while the *vnode* itself is still in use. But since the dnlc increments the reference count in the *vnode* when the cache entry for it is created, the *inode* associated with it is held. By purging the cache entry, the *vnode* reference count is decremented. This provides a better chance for the *vnode* to be thrown away, allowing its *inode* table entry to be freed.

6.8 Pathname resolution

The system resolves a pathname to obtain the resulting *vnode* that is to be operated on. For example, consider the *mount* system call. Two parameters required by the system call are the pathname of a directory mount point and the pathname of a block special file to mount onto that directory mount point. To perform the mount successfully, these pathnames must first be broken down into individual objects (file names) so that their associated *vnodes* can be sought. The *mount* operation can then take place by using members in those *vnodes* to connect the specified file system at the specified directory mount point in the main UNIX file system hierarchy (see Figure 6.11).

Table 6.17: *Struct pathname (pathname_t)*

Element	Description
char *pn_buf	Pointer to the pathname to traverse
char *pn_path	Pointer to the remaining portion of pathname
u_int pn_pathlen	Length of remaining pathname

6.8.1 The *pathname* data structure

System calls that operate on a pathname do so by constructing a *pathname* structure (Table 6.17). This is the internal data object manipulated by the pathname resolving algorithms. Components of a pathname are delimited by a slash "/" and the pathname specified in *pn_buf* is traversed until the final component in the path is reached. At first, *pn_path* points to the same location as *pn_buf* which remains unchanged. Starting with the first component in *pn_path*, each component is translated and removed with the resulting pathname being placed back into *pn_path*. This is then repeated until the final pathname is resolved. If a symbolic link is encountered during the traversal, the data within the symbolic link (the new pathname to traverse) is used to build a new *pathname* structure to work with. This is then traversed in the same way that the original pathname was traversed until the final pathname is reached.

6.8.2 Pathname resolving functions

The system has two functions for performing pathname resolution:

- *lookupname()* — allocates and populates a *pathname* structure and passes it to *lookuppn()* to resolve the pathname.

- *lookuppn()* — traverses the pathname specified in the given *pathname* structure until the pathname is resolved (see Figure 6.13). The final pathname component is then left in *pn_path* in the passed *pathname* structure. The function completes by filling a *vnode* structure (via *VOP_LOOKUP()*). This *vnode* represents the file specified in the final component of the supplied pathname.

This function is the main routine in pathname translation. It handles multiple component pathnames separated by slashes "/". If a component in the pathname is the directory mount point of a mounted file system, the system silently redirects the traversal through that file system instead of through the current directory hierarchy. If a component in the pathname is a symbolic link, the new pathname is read in from the symbolic link file and the traversal is reset to begin at the start of the new pathname.

Figure 6.13: *Algorithm for lookuppn( )*

```
lookuppn( )
input:   pnp — pointer to pathname structure containing pathname
                 to lookup.
         followlink — flag to specify if symbolic links should
                 be followed or not.
         compvpp — pointer to the vnode to store component
         dirvpp — pointer to the area to store component's parent
                 directory vnode.
output: zero on error
        non-zero on success
{
  increment "namei" /* sysinfo accounting */

  start traversal at the current directory /* u.u_cdir */

begin-loop:
  if ( pathname length is zero  )
    return error

  if (the first character of pathname is '/') {
    remove the slash character from the pathname
    start traversal at the processes root directory
    /* u.u_rdir or rootdir depending on chroot(2) */
  }

next-loop:
  get a copy of the next component in the pathname to work with
  now remove that component from the pathname

  if (the component is zero length) {
    /* assume pathname maybe  '/.' or '.' */
    select current directory
    return success
  }
```

```
/* for backward pathname resolution */
if (the component is '..') {
  while(1) { /* handle '../../../..'
      if (this is the top level root directory)
        goto skip;
      if (this is the root of a new file system)
        select the directory that this file system is mounted onto
      else
        break
  }
}

/* get the vnode for the directory specified by the component */
if (VOP_LOOKUP( ) == error)
  return error
/* traverse mount points */
while (v_vfsmountedhere is not NULL) {
  if (an umount is in progress) {
    sleep until the umount has completed
    continue;
  }
  /*
   * transparently redirect to the vnode of the
   * root of that file system
   */
  VFS_ROOT( );
  break;
}

if (this component is a symbolic link && followlink is set) {
  allocate a new pathname structure
  read the symbolic link file data into the new pathname
  goto begin-loop;
}
skip:
  if (no more components) {
    if(parent directory is wanted)
      set pointer to vnode of parent directory
    if(last component wanted)
      set pointer to vnode of last component
    return success
  }
  /* assume more components yet at this point */
  remove the trailing slash
  goto next-loop;
}
```

6.9 The special file system (*specfs*)

The *specfs* file system is not a file system per se. That being said, it is implemented as a file system. Furthermore, it has its own entry in the *vfssw[]* table. However, the user is not aware of its existence because he or she cannot see or make use of it. It is not mountable, there is no way to obtain status information about it via the *ustat*, *statvfs* or *fstatvfs* system calls, it has no programmable interface, and it has no device associated with it. So what is the purpose of the *specfs*?

At the file system implementation level, it is a common interface to devices via special files stored in the file system — any file system. At the kernel level, it is a method of translating a *vnode* that represents a special file into a *vnode* that represents a device.

Consider the following scenario: a process opens a file in the current directory called *my-device*. This file happens to be a character special file that represents a device of some form. Furthermore, it resides on a *ufs* file system. The *open* system call on the file results in a call to *lookuppn()* in order to resolve its pathname and obtain its represented *vnode*. Within *lookuppn()* a call to the file system type dependent *vop_lookup()* operation is made to get the *vnode* associated with the file from its file system. This is done by calling the file system type independent *VOP_LOOKUP()* macro. The first parameter to this macro is the *vnode* of the directory that the file resides in. In this case it is the *vnode* of the current directory obtained by referencing *u.u_cdir*. From this, the *VOP_LOOKUP()* macro can follow the *v_op* pointer in the *vnode* to its *vnodeops* structure. Control can then be passed to the file system type dependent *vop_lookup()* function.

In this scenario, the resulting *vnodeops* function is called *ufs_lookup()* because the special file *my-device* happens to reside on a *ufs* file system. It, in turn, uses a *vnodeops* structure called *ufs_vnodeops* to describe the *ufs vnode* operations.

Within *ufs_lookup()*, the directory name lookup cache is consulted. If *my-device* is found in the cache, its cached *vnode* is used. Otherwise, the *vnode* of the directory is used to search for the given file name in the directory file itself by converting the *v_data* pointer in the directory *vnode* into a *ufs* file system specific *inode*. (Remember that the *vnode* member pointer, *v_data* points to a private file system type specific data object; in this case a *ufs inode*). The directory blocks associated with that *inode* are then searched for an entry that matches *my-device*. If a matching entry is found, its *inode* is read in from disk. The *vnode* associated with *my-device* can then be extracted from its *inode* (the concept of *inodes* is discussed in § 6.10).

Once the file's *vnode* has been located it can be passed back to *copen()*. *VOP_OPEN()* is then called to do any file system specific open operations on the file (in both *ufs* and *s5* file systems; this operation does nothing except return success for reasons that will become evident in a moment). *copen()* then finalizes the *open* system call protocol by attaching the *f_vnode* pointer in the *file* structure (previously allocated to represent the file with), to the *vnode* returned by *VOP_OPEN()* (§ 6.2.2).

However, the problem with this scenario is that the *vnode* returned by *ufs_lookup()* would be the one associated with the special file in the file system.

Since the special file represents a device in that file system, the *open* system call ought to pass control to the *open* routine in the device driver controlling that device. To overcome this problem, the system uses a data structure called *snode*.

Table 6.18: *Struct snode*

Element	Description
struct snode *s_next	Pointer to next *snode* on the list
struct vnode s_vnode	*vnode* associated with this *snode*
struct vnode *s_realvp	Pointer to the *vnode* in the file system (if any)
struct vnode *s_commonvp	Pointer to the common device *vnode*
ushort s_flag	Flags, see below
dev_t s_dev	Device that this *snode* represents
dev_t s_fsid	File system identifier
daddr_t s_nextr	Next byte read offset (read-ahead)
long s_size	Block device size in bytes
time_t s_atime	Time of last access
time_t s_mtime	Time of last modification
time_t s_ctime	Time of last attributes change
int s_count	Count of opened references
long s_mapcnt	Count of mappings of pages
Flags (*s_flags*)	**Description**
SLOCKED	*snode* is locked
SUPD	Update device access time
SACC	Update device modification time
SWANT	Another process is waiting for this *snode*
SCHG	Update device change time

6.9.1 The shadow-special-vnode (*snode*)

Every *vnode* that is associated with a special file also has an associated *shadow-special-vnode* (or *snode*). An *snode* can represent a special file in *any* file system and one is maintained for each active special file in the running system.

The *snode* contains a private copy of information associated with the device being manipulated (see Table 6.18). For example, it contains a reference count of opens done on the device, a byte offset of the next byte to be read from the device, a *vnode* to manage the device with, and so on.

The main difference between the *vnode* associated with the special file in the file system and the *vnode* in the *snode* associated with the device is that they use different sets of *vnode* operations. The *vnode* associated with the special file uses the *vnodeops* structure for the file system it is stored in, whereas the *vnode* associated with the device uses the *vnodeops* structure for the special file system — *spec_vnodeops*. *vnode* operations defined in *spec_vnodeops* operate on devices.

To allow several special files to map to the same device, the system uses a "common" *snode* to represent the underlying device (see Figure 6.14). It also maintains an *snode* for each name by which the device is known in the file system (these are allocated when the file is opened).

The *snode* maintains a pointer (*s_commonvp*) to point to the *vnode* of a common *snode*. This *snode* is common to all other *snodes* accessing the same device. The process that first opens the device creates the *snode* that is used to contain the common *snode* (besides creating the *snode* representing the special file). If another process opens the same device, it shares both *snodes* with the originator. If the originator exits, both *snodes* remain intact until all references to the device are removed (i.e., the device remains open until the last *close* is done on it). If, however, a process uses a different special file to access the same underlying device, a new *snode* is allocated to represent that special file although its *s_commonvp* pointer is set to point to the same common *vnode* associated with the underlying device.

Getting back to the open *my-device* scenario: if the *vnode* obtained by *VOP_LOOKUP()* is associated with a special file, its *snode* is consulted to find the *vnode* associated with the device. That *vnode* is then returned to *copen()* instead of the one referencing the special file in the file system. This indirection is done by calling a *specfs* function called *specvp()* (Figure 6.15). Given the *vnode* of a special file, it extracts the *vnode* associated with the device from its associated *snode*. If, on the other hand, an *snode* does not exist for it, then one is created and initialized for it and that is used instead.

snodes are hashed into a table of linked lists indexed via a combination of their device major and minor numbers. Thus, *specvp()* hashes into the table to find the list to work with. It then goes through each *snode* on the list via the *s_next* pointer. If an *snode* with a matching *vnode* is found, and they both have the same type with matching device major and minor numbers, that *vnode* (referenced by *s_vnode*) is returned.

The end result is that on return to *copen()* in our scenario, the call to *VOP_OPEN()* results in a call to *spec_open()* instead of *ufs_open()*. Since ordinary files require no special processing by the file system type dependent *vop_open()* routines they generally do nothing except return success. On the other hand, *spec_open()* passes control to the *open* routine in the device driver associated with the device. This is done by indexing into the device switch table (*bdevsw[]* if the device is a block special, *cdevsw[]* if it is character special) with the supplied major device number (the device switch table is discussed in Chapter 5). For example, to pass control to the open routine in a character device driver, *spec_open()* does the following:

```
maj = getmajor(dev);
if (cdevsw[maj].d_str) {    /* process STREAMS device */
  stropen(arg1, arg2, ...);
  ...
} else {                 /* process a non-STREAMS device */
  (*cdevsw[maj].d_open)(arg1, arg2, ...);
  ...
}
```

Figure 6.14: *The shadow-special-vnode (snode)*

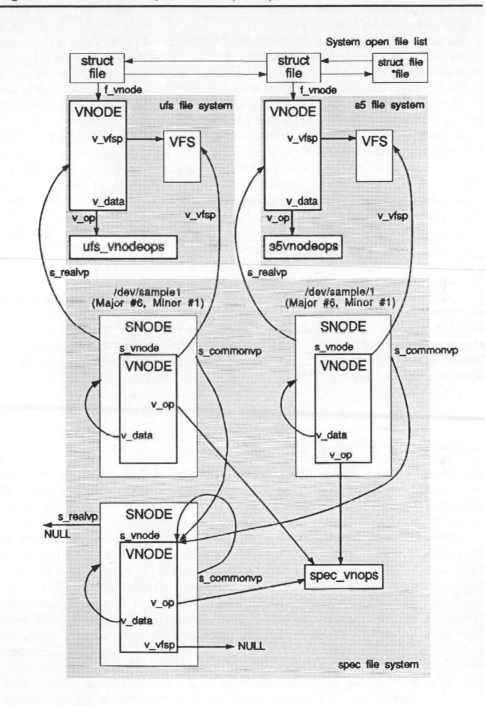

Note that a STREAMS device has the *d_str* field set in its *cdevsw[]* entry. This tells *spec_open( )* to call *stropen( )* (see § 7.9.3). Otherwise, the function pointed to by *d_open* in its *cdevsw[]* entry is called.

So far, our discussion on the *specfs* has been confined to the *open* system call. However, it should be understood that the *specfs* is brought into action every time a *vnode* that has an associated *snode* is accessed. That is, if the system needs to access a *vnode* that has a *shadow-special-vnode*, that *vnode* is replaced with the *vnode* in the shadow-special-vnode. From then on, any access to the file represented by the original *vnode* is directed through the *specfs*.

It is clear that the *specfs* implementation allows any file system type to be independent of the kernel's file-system/device-interface paradigm. A file system implementor does not have to be concerned about how special files will be interpreted, only how they are implemented. Furthermore, since all operations on a special file are directed through the *specfs*, there is no need to design any file system dependent *vnode* operation for handling them.

6.9.2 The *fifo* file system *(fifofs)*

If *specvp( )* finds that the *vnode* of the special file is associated with a FIFO, then *fifovp( )* is called (Figure 6.15) to find the *vnode* associated with the stream that represents the FIFO. The processing for this is similar to *specvp( )* except that the *vnode* returned uses the FIFO *vnode* operations *(fifo_vnodeops)* instead of the *specfs vnode* operations *(spec_vnodeops)*. FIFOs are represented by their own file system type *(fifofs)* but since they are implemented with STREAMS, the FIFO operations are discussed in § 7.10.1.

6.10 Concept of the *inode*

Historically, a file on the UNIX system is described by an object called an *inode*. An *inode* (index node, interior node, information node, and so on) describes a file and its owner, and contains the information about the location of the data blocks associated with the file on its storage medium.

Under UNIX System V Release 4, the *inode* is the file system type dependent abstraction of a file. The kernel's abstraction of a file is done through the file system type independent *vnode* interface. The *v_data* pointer in the *vnode* is used to locate the file system type dependent private data structure associated with the file that the *vnode* represents. Unlike previous versions of UNIX System V, it is not mandatory to implement a file system that uses *inodes*. However, a data structure of some form must be used to tie the *vnode* to its associated file type. In most ˉcases, the *v_data* pointer in the *vnode* is used to locate the file's *inode*, but if the file system type associated with the *vnode* does not implement *inodes*, it points to some other data structure that may be used to describe its file type to the operating system. However, it can be seen that whatever data type it is, it remains as an information-node *(inode)*, that is used to describe a file.

Figure 6.15: *Algorithm specvp( )*

```
specvp( )
input:  vp — pointer to vnode associated with file
        dev — expanded major/minor device number of device
        type — the type of file being accessed
        cr — pointer to cred describing file attributes
output: pointer to vnode describing the device
{

  if( the vnode type is a pipe (VFIFO)) {
    pass control to the fifo file system to get the vnode
    return the vnode associated with the pipe
  }

  /* assumes the vnode is associated with a device */

  index into snode hash table to find snode list for this dev
  traverse through each snode on the list {
      if( the vnode for the file matches the vnode in the snode )
          return the vnode in the snode
  }

  /* no snode found so create one for it */

  allocate memory for a new snode and initialize
      its file attributes
  arrange for new vnode in the snode to use spec_vnodeops
  arrange for v_vfsp in the new vnode to point to original
      vnodes v_vfsp
  arrange for new snode to point to the file's original vnode
  set the new vnode type to that of the original vnode

  if( the original vnode is block or character special ) {
    get or create and initialize a common snode from
        the hashed snode table and arrange to have it
        pointed to by the new vnode
  }

  place new snode into the snode hash table
  return the vnode in the snode

}
```

As an example, consider the *specfs* file system described in the previous section. It does not implement *inodes* but uses the *v_data* pointer in the *vnode* to point to an *snode*. Thus the *snode* is the *specfs* private data structure for containing the information associated with a device. However, only the *specfs* file system understands what an *snode* is. The kernel has no concept of any data abstraction that may be implemented by a file system type, it acknowledges only a *vnode*.

Since many file system types are implemented under UNIX System V Release 4, there are many abstractions of an *inode*. For example, the *ufs* file system type implements the *ufs_inode*, the *s5* file system type implements the traditional *inode*, and so on. It is not within the scope of this book to describe each file system type and its private data type. We will leave this for the subject of another book. However, the following section does cover to some extent the layout of a *ufs* file on disk. In any case, both *s5* and *ufs* file system types have been discussed in detail in other texts. For more information on the *s5* file system implementation, see [Bach 1986]; for more about the *ufs* file system, see [Leffler, McKusick, Karels, Quarterman 1988].

6.10.1 Layout of the file and *inode* on disk

A file held in a file system on disk traditionally consists of the following:

- *inode* — the actual structure of an *inode* is file system implementation dependent. But normally, it is used to describe the characteristics of a file such as the information about its owner, its access permissions, number of links, where it is stored, and so on.

- *data blocks* — data blocks for a file are held in a disk partition. The position of the data block in the disk partition is called its *disk address*. The low-level disk driver uses the disk address of a data block to retrieve the contents of that block from where it resides in the partition.

In a *ufs* file system, the layout of a file, its *inode* and its associated data blocks is shown logically in Figure 6.16. Following the information pertaining to the file itself are the data block numbers. The first 12 block numbers directly refer to the addresses of blocks on the disk containing the actual file data. So on an 8K byte block file system, these 12 direct-blocks can accommodate:

$$8192 * 12 = 98,304 \text{ bytes}$$

When a file requires more data blocks than the 12 direct-blocks, the file system must use disk blocks to hold the addresses of the remaining data blocks in the file. These are called indirect-blocks. In a *ufs* file system, the *inode* itself holds the addresses of three indirect-blocks in addition to the 12 direct-blocks. These three indirect-blocks are used for single, double, and triple-indirect-blocks. An indirect-block on an 8K byte block file holds the addresses of 2048 disk blocks. So a file using all 2048 addresses in the single-indirect-block means that it can accommodate:

$$8192 * (12 + 2048) = 16,875,520 \text{ bytes}$$

If the file uses more than 2060 blocks, the 14th block number in the *inode*

Figure 6.16: *Layout of a ufs file on disk*

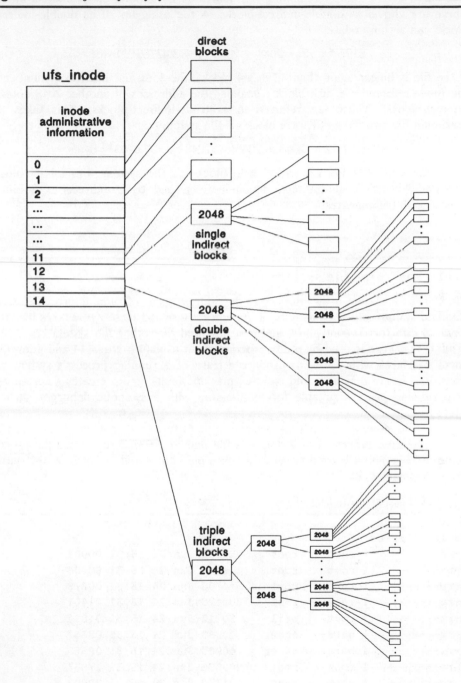

references a disk block containing the addresses of another 2048 indirect-blocks. These are known as double-indirect-blocks. A file using up all its double-indirect-blocks can accommodate:

$$8192 * (12 + 2048 + 2048^2) = 3.43766^{10} \text{ bytes}$$

If the file is bigger again than 4,196,364 blocks, the 15th and last block number in the *inode* references a disk block containing the addresses of another 2048 double-indirect-blocks. These are referred to as triple-indirect-blocks. This takes the maximum file size for an 8K byte block *ufs* file system to:

$$8192 * (12 + 2048 + 2048^2 + 2048^3) = 7.0403^{13} \text{ bytes}$$

Thus, the size of a file on an 8K byte block *ufs* file system with all its blocks allocated (direct, single-indirect, double-indirect, and triple-indirect) is 8 billion blocks or 70 trillion bytes.

6.11 The */proc* file system *(procfs)*

The */proc* file system is an interface to the address space of running processes using standard system calls such as *read, write, open, close* and *ioctl*. */proc* takes its name from its directory mount point, and it is mounted like other file system types with **mount(1)**. */proc* is used by utility programs such as **ps(1)**, **truss(1)** and **gcore(1)**; **truss** interfaces with */proc* to produce a trace of a running process's system call execution, received signals, and incurred machine faults. **gcore** creates a core-image of a running process suitable for examination with a symbolic debugger such as **sdb(1)**.

Each file name in */proc* has a decimal value (1 to 29999) that represents the PID of its associated process. For example, a file named "00378" represents the process whose PID is 378. Figure 6.17 shows an example of a partial listing from the output of the **ls -l** command.

Figure 6.17: *Partial listing of /proc*

```
$ ls -l /proc
-rw-------   1 root     root      327680 Jun 24 15:31 00001
-rw-------   1 root     root           0 Jun 24 15:31 00004
-rw-------   1 root     root      544768 Jun 24 15:31 00378
-rw-------   1 root     root      389120 Jun 24 15:31 01401
-rw-------   1 root     mail       90112 Jun 24 15:31 01834
-rw-------   1 berny    other      40960 Jun 24 15:31 08567
-rw-------   1 berny    other      40960 Jun 24 15:31 08568
-rw-------   1 root     root      208896 Jun 24 15:31 17657
-rw-------   1 root     root      331776 Jun 24 15:31 22003
```

Since files in the /proc file system represent processes, the discussion that follows refers to them as processes unless specified otherwise.

A process that is opened for reading can only be read. On the other hand, a process that is opened for both reading and writing allows the calling process to control the behaviour of the process being manipulated. As with ordinary files, entries in /proc have access permissions, so a process without the necessary privileges cannot read or modify another process's image.

Data can be transferred between the address space of the controlling process and the address space of the process being manipulated by applying the *lseek* system call followed by a *read* or *write*; *lseek* is used to position the file pointer at the desired virtual address (note that only "mapped-in" virtual addresses are accessible).

The most interesting form of process manipulation is performed through the *ioctl* system call, and the *ioctl* commands for /proc are shown in Table 6.19 (for a more detailed description of these commands see **proc(4)** in [AT&T 1990h]). The program shown in Figure 6.18 gives an example of how to use the /proc interface. In this example, a *prstatus* structure (see Table 6.20) is read-in for each process found by using the *PIOCSTATUS* command. The processing of this structure is left for the reader.

6.11.1 /proc implementation

Table 6.6 lists the *vnode* operations that can be applied to files in the /proc file system, and Table 6.12 lists the *VFS* operations that can be applied to the /proc file system itself.

The procedure for processing files in /proc is the same as for ordinary files except that the *vnode* operations that are executed are those for *procfs* (i.e., those defined in the *prvnodeops* structure). Consider the following scenario: a process opens a file in the /proc directory called *00378*. The *open* system call results in a call to *lookuppn()* in order to resolve the file's pathname and obtain its represented *vnode*. Within *lookuppn()* a call to the file system type independent *VOP_LOOKUP()* macro is made to get the *vnode* associated with the file from its file system. The function *prlookup()* is called because the file *00378* happens to reside in the /proc file system. Once the *vnode* is located it is cached in the *dnlc* and used to perform other system call operations on the file as necessary. For example, if the user issues an *ioctl* system call on the file, the system follows the *v_op* pointer in the *vnode* to get to its associated *vnodeops* structure (in this case *prvnodeops*). The *prioctl()* function is then called as a result of calling *VOP_IOCTL()*, to carry out the *ioctl* processing.

Note that there is no device driver associated with the /proc file system even though it supports the *ioctl* system call semantics.

Table 6.19: *Ioctl system call commands for /proc*

Constant	Description
PIOCSTATUS	Get the process status information
PIOCSTOP	Direct the process to STOP
PIOCWSTOP	Wait for process to STOP
PIOCRUN	Make the process runnable
PIOCGTRACE	Get traced signal set
PIOCSTRACE	Set traced signal set
PIOCSSIG	Set current signal
PIOCKILL	Send a signal to the process
PIOCUNKILL	Remove a pending signal
PIOCGHOLD	Get held signal set
PIOCSHOLD	Set held signal set
PIOCMAXSIG	Get maximum signal number
PIOCACTION	Get process's signal actions
PIOCGFAULT	Get traced hardware fault set
PIOCSFAULT	Set traced hardware fault set
PIOCCFAULT	Clear the current fault (if any)
PIOCGENTRY	Get traced system call entry set
PIOCSENTRY	Set traced system call entry set
PIOCGEXIT	Get traced system call exit set
PIOCSEXIT	Set traced system call exit set
PIOCSFORK	Set child inherits trace flags on fork
PIOCRFORK	Reset above
PIOCSRLC	Set clear all trace flags on last close
PIOCRRLC	Reset above
PIOCGREG	Get process registers
PIOCSREG	Set process registers
PIOCGFPREG	Get floating-point registers
PIOCSFPREG	Set floating-point registers
PIOCNICE	Set process's nice priority
PIOCPSINFO	Get **ps(1)** information
PIOCNMAP	Get number of active memory mappings
PIOCMAP	Get currently active memory mappings
PIOCOPENM	Open mapped object for reading
PIOCCRED	Get process credentials
PIOCGROUPS	Get supplementary groups
PIOCGETPR	Read process's *proc* structure
PIOCGETU	Read process's *user* structure

Figure 6.18: *Example program using /proc*

```
/*
 * Example program using /proc interface
 */
#include <stdio.h>
#include <fcntl.h>
#include <sys/types.h>
#include <sys/stat.h>
#include <sys/errno.h>
#include <dirent.h>
#include <sys/signal.h>
#include <sys/fault.h>
#include <sys/syscall.h>
#include <sys/procfs.h>
```

```
main(argc, argv)
int     argc;
char    **argv;
{
    struct prstatus pinfo;    /* process status info structure */
    struct dirent *dirent;
    DIR *dirp;
    char pathname[15];
    int pathlen;

    strcpy(pathname, "/proc");

    /* Open the /proc directory (see directory(3C)) */
    if ((dirp = opendir(pathname)) == NULL) {
        fprintf(stderr, "%s: cannot open /proc directory\n", argv[0]);
        exit(1);
    }

    strcat(pathname,"/");
    pathlen = strlen(pathname);

    /* Search the directory for each active process */
    while (dirent = readdir(dirp)) {
        int    fdproc;    /* file descriptor for /proc/XXXXX */

        /* don't need . and .. */
        if (dirent->d_name[0] == '.')
            continue;
```

```
        /* tack on the file/pid name */
        strcpy((pathname + pathlen), dirent->d_name);

    tryagain:

        if ((fdproc = open(pathname, O_RDONLY)) < 0) {
            /* no permission to read this process */
            perror(pathname);
            continue;
        }

        /* read in the status for this process */
        if (ioctl(fdproc, PIOCSTATUS,  &pinfo) < 0) {
            int    olderrno = errno;

            close(fdproc);
            switch(olderrno) {
               case ENOENT:
                  /* possible that process went away */
                  break;
               case EAGAIN:
                  /* interrupted system call */
                  goto tryagain;
               default:
                  perror(fdproc);

            }
            continue;
        }
        close(fdproc);

        /* process the prstatus structure here */
        ...
        ...
    }

    closedir(dirp);
    exit(0);

    /* NOTREACHED */
}
```

Table 6.20: *Struct prstatus (prstatus_t)*

Constant	Description
long pr_flags	Process flags (see below)
short pr_why	If stopped, reason why (see below)
short pr_what	More detailed reason (cause)
siginfo_t pr_info	Information associated with signal or fault
short pr_cursig	Current signal
short pr_pad	Padding to long (unused)
sigset_t pr_sigpend	Set of other pending signals
sigset_t pr_sighold	Set of held signals
struct sigaltstack pr_altstack	Alternate signal stack information
struct sigaction pr_action	Action for current signal
pid_t pr_pid	Process ID
pid_t pr_ppid	Parent process ID
pid_t pr_pgrp	Process group ID
pid_t pr_sid	Session ID
timestruc_t pr_utime	Process user cpu time
timestruc_t pr_stime	Process system cpu time
timestruc_t pr_cutime	Sum of children's user times
timestruc_t pr_cstime	Sum of children's system times
char pr_clname[8]	Scheduling class name
long pr_filler[20]	Reserved for future (unused)
long pr_instr	Current instruction
gregset_t pr_reg	General registers
Flags (*pr_flags*)	**Description**
PR_STOPPED	Process is stopped
PR_ISTOP	Process stopped on an event of interest
PR_DSTOP	A stop directive is in effect
PR_ASLEEP	Process is sleeping in a system call
PR_FORK	Inherit-on-fork is in effect
PR_RLC	Run-on-last-close is in effect
PR_PTRACE	Process is being controlled by *ptrace*
PR_PCINVAL	PC refers to an invalid virtual address
PR_ISSYS	System process
Flags (*pr_why*)	**Description**
PR_REQUESTED	Debugger requested stop
PR_SIGNALLED	Stopped on receipt of a signal
PR_SYSENTRY	Stopped on system call entry
PR_SYSEXIT	Stopped on system call exit
PR_JOBCONTROL	Job control stop
PR_FAULTED	Stopped on a fault

6.12 Exercises

6.1   Given a *vnode*, how does the system locate its file system dependent VFS operations structure?

6.2   Describe the difference between the *falloc( )* and *ufalloc( )* functions. Why are they not combined as a single function?

6.3   Describe the data structure that an *inode* is attached to.

6.4***   Outline the design of a simple file system that supports a single file type with pseudo code. Describe its *vnode* operations.

6.5   Describe the *vnode* operation used to determine whether a process is allowed to associate itself with a file.

6.6   Which parts of a file can a lock be placed?

6.7   Describe what is meant by "advisory" locking.

6.8*   Supposing you designed a new file system type and you wanted to install it into the VFS system. Describe the steps necessary to accomplish this task.

6.9   Given the name of a special file — */dev/dsk/sc0d0s0* for example — describe how the system locates the special files *snode* and also how it locates its device driver handling functions.

6.10*   Why and how does *spec_open( )* differentiate between a STREAMS device and a non-STREAMS device? How does a clone device fit within this scheme?

6.11   Assuming that no errors are generated, how many file descriptors will the following program have open? How many *ufchunks* are needed?

```
   . . .
   . . .
main( ) {
     int x;
     for( x = 0; x < 72; x++ )
       open("/dev/null", O_RDONLY);
     pause( );
}
```

6.12   When a file system is mounted with the *mount* system call, how does the system associate the newly mounted file system with the rest of the file system hierarchy?

6.13   What is the *vfs_data* pointer used for in the *vfs* structure?

6.14   How does the directory name lookup cache benefit the operating system?

6.15** In § 6.11.1, we mentioned that the */proc* file system supports the *ioctl* system call even though it does not have an associated device driver. How is this possible?

PART 3

Additional Facilities

CHAPTER 7

Streams

Still glides the Stream, and shall forever glide;
The Form remains, the Function never dies.
— William Wordsworth

7.1 Introduction

Computers normally communicate with each other over a network, and they use a network protocol to describe the way data is transmitted. The network protocol is run over network hardware by which the network protocol messages are physically transmitted. Network protocols usually have layered architectures, and most protocols in use today fit into the ISO 7 Layer Model [Day, Zimmerman 1983] — for example, TCP/IP and ISO/OSI protocols.

To implement any particular protocol or set of protocols requires appropriate hardware and software. The software consists of a set of device drivers that control the hardware, a set of protocol processing routines that implement the network protocol, and a set of user interface programs and libraries that access the protocol so that applications can be written to access the network. Before the advent of STREAMS, each implementation of a network protocol had to do all the work itself. That is, the software writers had to provide the device drivers, the protocol processing routines, the user interface software, and any extra infrastructure needed to support the software. This meant that there was little scope for "mixing and matching" software components from different manufacturers. The software was also less portable, since each manufacturer provided a different communications environment.

The 4.2BSD version of UNIX introduced *sockets* [Leffler, McKusick, Karels, Quarterman 1988]. The operating system provided an infrastructure in which network protocols could be implemented. It provided memory management facilities, a set of system calls for accessing network software, an object-oriented framework for the network protocols themselves, and a formalized device driver interface. The *sockets* mechanism was primarily used to implement the TCP/IP protocols for the ARPA Internet. The device driver interface made it possible for the operating system to support a wide range of network controllers. *sockets* are widely used for the implementation of TCP/IP on UNIX systems and have been ported to many implementations of UNIX System V. Although it is possible to implement other protocols within the *sockets* mechanism, it was not often done.

Figure 7.1: *Networking protocols*

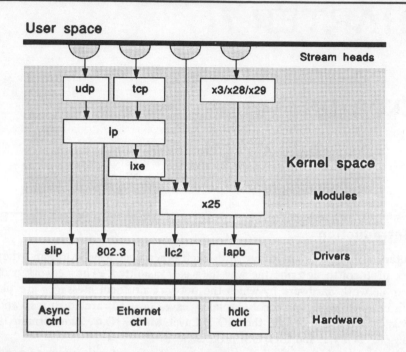

An alternative infrastructure for providing network protocols is STREAMS, originally designed by Dennis Ritchie [Ritchie 1984a] and first released in UNIX System V Release 3.0. STREAMS provides an environment in which communications protocols can be developed. It consists of a set of system calls, kernel functions and data structures. With this environment it is easier to write modular and reusable code. The code is also simpler because many of the support functions the programmer needs are provided by the STREAMS infrastructure.

The collection of protocols in a machine is often referred to as a *protocol stack*. A typical example of a protocol stack is shown in Figure 7.1. The computer in the diagram can connect to a host via an Ethernet, or to a host via a serial line. In this case, both the serial line and the Ethernet use the TCP/IP protocols. There is also an X25 connection, which if required, can also use TCP/IP over a wide area network. If this stack was implemented with STREAMS, each of the boxes would be implemented as a *module*, and the interconnection facilities of STREAMS would enable the modules to be connected together in the manner shown. The STREAMS environment provides the memory management facilities required to create messages that can be passed between the modules. It also arranges scheduling, so that the various modules are executed at the correct time. Furthermore, STREAMS provides an interface between kernel and user address space.

The implementation in the diagram came from three sources. One manufacturer provided the TCP/IP elements, another the X25 elements, and a third the IXE (name given to a module that places IP datagrams into X25 packets and vice versa

[RFC 877]). This was only possible because of the portability of the STREAMS modules and the relative ease of interconnecting them.

Under UNIX System V Release 4, the STREAMS mechanism has other uses besides network protocols. For example, the processing module called *ldterm* implements the line discipline characteristics of the traditional UNIX system terminal driver. (see *termio(7)* and *termios(2)*) This module provides the driver for asynchronously connected terminals.

A benefit of a STREAMS module is that it can be inserted into several types of stream. For example, the *ldterm* module can be inserted into a stream associated with a network connection so that processes think they are running with a physical terminal instead of a network connection. This concept is illustrated in Figure 7.2, where there are three processes, each of which thinks that it is talking to a terminal when in fact they are talking to an X25 connection, a terminal connection and a TCP/IP connection respectively.

Figure 7.2: *Use of ldterm*

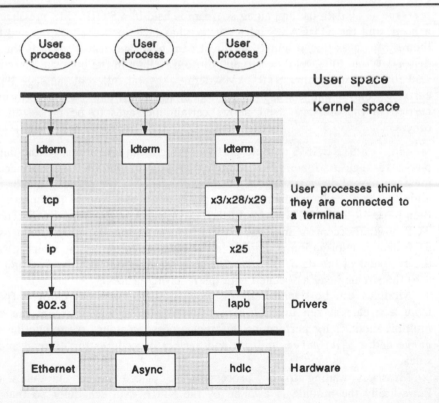

In earlier releases of UNIX, *named-pipes* and *software-pipes* used file system buffers to store the data being read or written. Under UNIX System V Release 4 they are implemented by using STREAMS. Two advantages of this are: the program accessing the pipe can change the amount of buffering in it, and modules can be pushed into them, so that piped data can be processed before reaching the other end.

So what is STREAMS? It is a set of data structures, a set of functions, and a philosophy. The combination of these elements allow software developers to write networking software in a defined framework. Since many developers use the same framework, their code works more easily with other software and is more easily ported to other machines. The main features of STREAMS are described as follows:

- *stream* — a stream consists of a *stream head* and a data path that connects between a stream head and a STREAMS device driver. The stream head provides the interface between kernel address space and user address space (the operations of the stream head are described in § 7.9). The device driver takes messages from the stream and converts them into a form suitable for the device hardware. In the opposite direction it takes information from the device hardware and constructs messages that are sent upwards towards the stream head.

- *message* — all data passing along a stream is held in a STREAMS *message* called a *msgb*, and the STREAMS infrastructure has facilities for allocating and freeing them. Messages that originate in the stream head and travel towards the device driver are said to travel downstream; those travelling in the opposite direction are said to travel upstream. STREAMS defines several different message types for carrying control and status information along the stream, and a priority field carried in the message itself allows certain messages to be processed before others.

- *module* — a STREAMS module performs processing operations on the data as it passes through a stream. For example, the TCP module in Figure 7.1 accepts a message passed down to it from the stream head (via the process in user-mode), adds the TCP header information to the front of the data in the message, and then passes it to the IP layer for further processing. In the opposite direction, the TCP module accepts a message passed to it from the IP module, and uses the TCP header information contained in the message to determine which process is the recipient of the data. The module then removes the TCP header, and passes it to the stream head associated with the receiving process.

Modules can be dynamically inserted (pushed) onto or removed (popped) from a stream at run time by a user-mode process, and a stream can contain multiple modules for performing different processing steps. A module has a *read queue* and a *write queue*, and *put* and *service* procedures for its read and write sides.

Messages waiting to be processed are placed in the module's queue. Periodically the module is awoken by the STREAMS scheduler so that it can process messages waiting on its queue. The amount of data waiting in the queue is used as the basis for the flow-control calculations. Each module has two queues: one for upstream, and one for downstream. The module's *put* and *service* procedures process messages passing along the stream. When a module wishes to pass data to a neighbouring module, it invokes the *put* procedure of the neighbouring module to allow a message to be passed quickly along the stream.

The *put* procedure of a module always checks the flow-control status of the neighbouring module. If flow-control says that the module is not blocked, the *put* procedure of the neighbour is called. If, however, the neighbour is blocked by flow-control, the message is placed on the queue of the next module via the *putq( )* function, which informs the STREAMS scheduler that the neighbour module has messages waiting in its queue. Later, the STREAMS scheduler will call the neighbour module's *service* procedure to process the messages waiting on its queue.

- *flow-control* — the STREAMS flow-control mechanism is voluntary, and it works only if modules are written to take account of it. Each module contains separate upstream and downstream high and low water marks that are used for flow-control. The function *canput( )* is called by a module to test the flow-control of the adjacent module. If it returns TRUE, the *put* procedure of the next module is called so that the message is processed immediately. If, however, FALSE is returned, the message is placed into the current module's queue to be processed later by its *service* procedure. Eventually this module's queue will reach its high water mark causing the previous module to store messages in its queue, and so on. In this way, flow-control backs up in the system, rather like the way drains back up when they are blocked.

  Eventually, the module causing the blockage will process enough messages to take the amount of data in its queue below its low water mark. When this occurs, STREAMS schedules the previous module's *service* procedure, allowing the previous module to remove some messages from its queue. This mechanism is called *back-enabling a queue*.

- *multiplexor* — some streams consist of several modules strung together one below the other but this linear arrangement is not suitable for all applications. For example, in Figure 7.1, data for the IP module comes from both the UDP and TCP modules. A module with multiple connections above or below it is called a multiplexor. The IP module in the diagram is an example of an *upper multiplexor* because it has multiple streams above it (on its upper surface). In the same diagram, the X25 module drives multiple devices, depending on the destination of the packets; this is an example of a *lower multiplexor* because it has multiple streams below it (on its lower surface). Multiplexors are constructed by using special pseudo-device drivers and the STREAMS functions for linking multiplexors.

The previous paragraphs have discussed the STREAMS facilities — but how are they used?

When you buy STREAMS-based software, you will need to link your operating system kernel with the drivers and modules provided by the software package. You will also get a set of application libraries and administration tools. A STREAMS driver is identified as such in the kernel so that when it is opened (using the *open* system call) the kernel will allocate a stream head and establish a connection to the driver.

The **mknod(1M)** command creates the file system entry that will be used by processes to connect with the driver. For example, consider a TCP/IP implementation that uses a special file called /dev/tcp for its interface. When this is opened, the kernel notes that it is a STREAMS driver, and sets up a stream head. STREAMS multiplexors also have file system entries, but the open is processed slightly differently.

STREAMS connections are set up by first opening the STREAMS device driver — for example, by opening /dev/tcp. The program must then insert modules in the correct order into the stream with the *I_PUSH* STREAMS *ioctl* command. Usually, the software vendor provides library routines that open the correct device and then push the modules in the correct sequence.

Once the stream has been set up, data can be sent via combinations of the *read*, *write*, *getmsg* and *putmsg* system calls. The software vendor's documentation describes the format of the messages that must be sent, and defines the sequences of system calls recognized by the software.

The following sections describe the implementation and operation of STREAMS in detail. For more information on STREAMS data structures and interfaces see [AT&T 1990d].

Figure 7.3: *Structure of STREAMS messages*

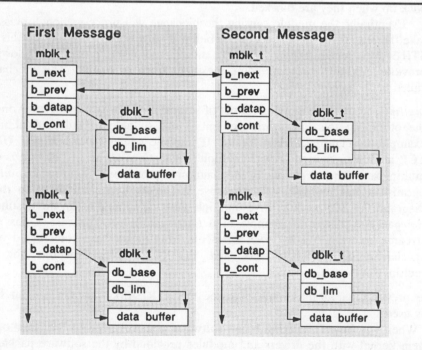

7.2 STREAMS data structures

UNIX System V Release 4 offers a feature called *Extended Fundamental Types* or
EFT (see § 2.16). Whether EFT is used or not depends on whether the C language
preprocessor constant _STYPES is defined. If it is, STREAMS data structures are
binary compatible with those under UNIX System V Release 3. If _STYPES is not
defined, EFT is used. Whether EFT is used or not makes no difference to the
facilities available to the programmer. However, without EFT the implementation is
made clumsy because extra fields must be squashed into the old data structures.
Throughout the discussion, we assume that EFT is *not* being used.

7.2.1 STREAMS messages *(msgbs)*

All data and control information passing along a stream is held in STREAMS
messages. A STREAMS message consists of three parts, the first of which is the
msgb (mblk_t), which is the message header. A *msgb* is allocated by a user-mode
program when it needs space for data that is to be passed along a stream. The
second part is the data block, or *datab (dblk_t)*, which holds pointers to the data.
Finally, there is the data area, which is simply an area of memory for storing the
message data itself. The relationship between these parts is shown in Figure 7.3.

Note that the *msgb* has three pointer fields, called *b_next*, *b_prev* and *b_cont*.
The first two fields link messages together on a module's queue. The *b_cont* field
allows a single logical message to be made up of many parts. As you will see when
you look at the stream head, the STREAMS environment encourages you to write
modules where the first block of a message contains control information, and
subsequent parts contain data.

Table 7.1: *Struct msgb (mblk_t)*

Element	Description
*struct msgb *b_next*	Next message on queue
*struct msgb *b_prev*	Previous message on queue
*struct msgb *b_cont*	Next block in message
*unsigned char *b_rptr*	First unread byte in buffer
*unsigned char *b_wptr*	First unwritten byte in buffer
*struct datab *b_datap*	The data block

The fields of a *msgb* are shown in Table 7.1 and are explained as follows:

- *b_next, b_prev* — hold messages in a module or driver's message queue on a
  doubly linked list. These fields are not manipulated directly by the module
  designer.

- *b_cont* — links together *msgbs* that constitute a single logical message.

- *b_rptr* — points to the first unread byte in the buffer. Module designers manipulate this field directly. The value is incremented as bytes are read from the buffer.

- *b_wptr* — points to the first unwritten byte in the data buffer. It is directly manipulated by the module designer as data is written into the buffer.

- *b_datap* — points to the *datab* associated with the message. The format of a *datab* is described below.

Table 7.2: *Struct datab (dblk_t)*

Element	Description
*struct free_rtn *frtnp*	Used internally by STREAMS (see § 7.7.1)
*unsigned char *db_base*	First byte of buffer
*unsigned char *db_lim*	Last byte plus one in buffer
unsigned char db_ref	Count of messages using this block
unsigned char db_type	Message type (see below)
unsigned char db_band	Priority band
unsigned char db_iswhat	Message status
unsigned short db_flag	Data block flag
caddr_t db_msgaddr	Back pointer to *msgb*
Message type (*db_type*)	**Description**
QNORM	Normal priority message
QPCTL	High priority control message

Each *msgb* points to a *datab* (see Table 7.2). Its members are explained as follows:

- *frtnp* — the function *esballoc()*, described in § 7.7.1, allocates STREAMS messages that point to a private data buffer. *esballoc()* is passed a data structure that holds the routine for freeing the data area, and this information is pointed to by *frtnp*. If *esballoc()* is not used, the STREAMS memory allocators use *kmem_alloc()* and *kmem_free()* to allocate and free the data part. In this case, these fields are unused.

- *db_base* — points to the base of the data area.

- *db_lim* — points one byte past the end of the buffer and is used for limit checks on the size of the buffer.

- *db_ref* — multiple message headers can refer to the same data block and this field holds a count of the number of *msgbs* pointing to a *datab*. If the count falls to zero, the data associated with the *datab* is released, and the *datab* is placed on the *datab* freelist.

- *db_type* — holds the message type (see Table 7.3 and Table 7.4).

- *db_band* — messages that belong to a particular priority band for flow-control. Priority bands are described below.

Each STREAMS message has a type describing what sort of message it is (Table 7.2). Message types are broken down into two categories: *normal* and *priority*. Priority messages are automatically placed at the front of a module's queue.

Table 7.3: *Normal message types*

Type	Usage (values < *QPCTL*)
M_DATA	Used for passing data to and from user address space.
M_PROTO	Used for protocol and control information. This can also be passed to and from the user program.
M_BREAK	When this is received by a driver, it will send a break on the medium the driver is controlling.
M_CTL	Used to pass data between drivers and modules. Allows for inter-module communication.
M_DELAY	Sent to a driver to request a real-time delay in output processing. The data buffer contains the delay time.
M_IOCTL	Used for passing the data associated with STREAMS *ioctl( )* calls, as described in *streamio(2)*.
M_PASSFP	Used by stream heads to pass file pointers to each other.
M_RSE	Reserved message type for future STREAMS internal use.
M_SETOPTS	Sent by modules or drivers, it alters some of the characteristics of the stream head.
M_SIG	Used by modules and drivers to send a signal to a process. The stream head takes the signal number from the data part of the message and sends the signal to the process.

Modules use *M_DATA* messages for passing data to and from user programs. When the stream head receives an *M_DATA* message from downstream, the data is passed on to the user. Similarly, data written by the user is copied into *M_DATA* messages by the stream head and passed downstream. Similarly, modules use *M_PROTO* messages to pass control information to and from the user program. Thus, a control message goes into an *M_PROTO* message block and data goes into an *M_DATA* message block. Both the *getmsg* and *putmsg* system calls allow the user to specify control and data messages.

Other message types specify the format of the data buffer for the message. For example, the first byte of the data buffer in an *M_SIG* message specifies the signal number to send to the process, or the first byte of the data buffer in an *M_ERROR* message is used to specify an error number to return to the user. Similarly, in an *M_IOCTL* message the data buffer contains an *iocblk* structure. The formats of the data buffer for the different message types are described fully in [AT&T 1990d].

Normal messages are subject to flow-control, but this is not so for priority messages (although, they will still be placed in queues because some modules do not have *put* procedures — they always process messages from their own queue). However, in network protocols certain data messages must be processed before others. In TCP/IP networks such messages are often called *out-of-band* data and in OSI networks they are called *expedited data*. The STREAMS environment uses the

Table 7.4: *Priority message types*

Type	Usage (values > *QPCTL*)
M_COPYIN	Sent by a module or a driver to request the stream head perform a *copyin( )*. Used for *ioctl* processing.
M_COPYOUT	Sent by a module or a driver to request the stream head perform a *copyout( )*. Used for *ioctl* processing.
M_ERROR	Sent by drivers or modules to indicate an error. After receiving this, most STREAMS system calls fail with the error code specified in the data part of this message.
M_FLUSH	Requests that drivers and modules discard messages waiting in their queues.
M_HANGUP	Sent by drivers, it indicates that no more data from the device can be read or written. The stream head allows only reads of messages in transit, after that, reads return 0, indicating no more data.
M_IOCACK	Indicates successful processing of *ioctl* requests.
M_IOCNAK	Indicates unsuccessful processing of *ioctl* requests.
M_IOCDATA	Used by the stream head to pass in the data requests by an M_COPYIN message.
M_PCPROTO	Similar to M_PROTO, but passes priority data.
M_PCRSE	Reserved for future use.
M_PCSIG	Priority version of the M_SIG message.
M_READ	Sent by the stream head when the user program issues a *read( )* call.
M_STOP	Requests a device stops its output.
M_START	Requests a device start its output.
M_STARTI	Requests a device start its input.
M_STOPI	Requests a device stop its input.

db_band field in the *datab* to support this mechanism (see also [Rago 1989]). By using two bands, 0 and 1, a simple out of band scheme can be implemented. Ordinary messages use band 0 and expedited messages use band 1. While messages are being queued, priority messages always go to the front of the queue, band 1 messages go behind priority messages, and band 0 messages go behind band 1 messages, as shown in Figure 7.4. The STREAMS mechanism allows for 256 message bands.

7.2.2 STREAMS *queue* structures

As we have seen, an active stream consists of a stream head, a set of modules, and a device driver. For each stream head, pushed module, and opened device driver, the kernel allocates two *queue* structures. A *queue* provides a place to hold messages and allows the kernel to know which processing routines to apply to a message as it passes through a module.

Figure 7.4: *Priority messages and message bands*

Message arrival sequence

1	normal	2	normal	3	normal	4	priority	5	priority
band 0		band 0		band 1					
M_DATA		M_DATA		M_DATA		M_FLUSH		M_ERROR	

4	priority	5	priority	3	normal	1	normal	2	normal
				band 1		band 0		band 0	
M_FLUSH		M_ERROR		M_DATA		M_DATA		M_DATA	

Message processing sequence

STREAMS *queues* are always allocated in pairs. One queue is always the read-side or upstream *queue*, the other is always the write-side or downstream *queue*. Allocation in pairs allows the functions that process data on the read side to find the write side queue and vice versa. Figure 7.5 shows the *queue* structure and its relation to other STREAMS data structures.

The fields in the *queue* structure are summarized in Table 7.5 and are explained as follows:

- *q_qinfo* — points to the *qinit* structure that holds information on the processing routines for the queue (see Table 7.6).

- *q_first* — points to the first message to be processed on the queue.

- *q_last* — points to the last message to be processed on the queue.

- *q_next* — points to the next queue in the stream.

- *q_eq* — points to the *extended queue* information (described below).

- *q_ptr* — an active module or driver needs a private data area to hold the current state of the module or device. The *q_ptr* field in the *queue* points to the private data.

- *q_count* — holds the number of bytes of data in the messages waiting on the queue.

- *q_flag* — holds information about the state of the queue.

- *q_minpsz, q_maxpsz* — hold the minimum and maximum message sizes accepted by the queue. Only the stream head takes notice of these values. When data is being passed into a module via the *write* system call, the stream head breaks the data into *q_maxpsz* chunks. The stream head rejects writes that contain less than *q_minpsz* bytes of data.

- *q_hiwat, q_lowat* — hold the high and low water marks, for flow-control.

Figure 7.5: *Relationship between STREAMS data structures*

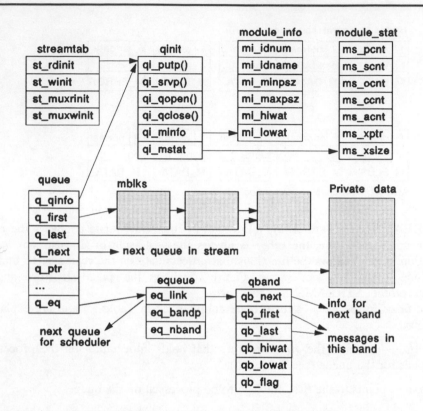

The *q_qinfo* field in each queue points to a *qinit* structure (Table 7.6) containing the module's procedures, configuration, and statistical information. The elements of this structure, are explained as follows:

- *qi_putp* — points to the module's *put* procedure. The operation of this procedure and of the others held in the *qinit* structure is described in later sections.

- *qi_srvp* — points to the modules *service* procedure.

- *qi_qopen* — points to the procedure called each time the module is opened or pushed into a stream.

- *qi_qclose* — points to the procedure called each time the module is closed or popped from the stream.

- *qi_minfo* — points to a data structure containing module information (*module_info*) that is used when the stream is created.

- *qi_mstat* — points to a data structure containing state and statistical information (*module_stat* — see Table 7.11) for the module. For example, it holds a count of the number of times each of its procedures are called.

Table 7.5: *Struct queue (queue_t) non-EFT version*

Element	Description
struct qinit q_qinfo	Information structure for the queue
struct msgb *q_first	Head of queued messages
struct msgb *q_last	Tail of queued messages
struct queue *q_next	Next queue in this stream
struct equeue *q_eq	Extended queue structure
_VOID *q_ptr	Private data pointer
ushort q_count	Number of bytes in queue
ushort q_flag	Queue state
short q_minpsz	Minimum packet size queue will accept
short q_maxpsz	Maximum packet size queue will accept
ushort q_hiwat	High water mark for flow-control
ushort q_lowat	Low water mark for flow-control

Table 7.6: *Struct qinit*

Element	Description
int (*qi_putp)()	Put procedure
int (*qi_srvp)()	Service procedure
int (*qi_qopen)()	Open procedure
int (*qi_qclose)()	Close procedure
int (*qi_qadmin)()	Admin procedure (not currently used)
struct module_info *qi_minfo	Module information structure
struct module_stat *qi_mstat	Module statistics structure

A new facility included in STREAMS under UNIX System V Release 4 is the priority band mechanism. The data structures to support this are the *equeue* (extended queue — Table 7.7) and *qband* (Table 7.8). The fields of the *equeue* structure are described as follows:

- *eq_link* — points to the next queue in the list waiting to be run by the STREAMS scheduler. The STREAMS scheduler is described in § 7.8.3.

- *eq_bandp* — points to the priority band information for the queue.

- *eq_nband* — holds the number of priority bands for the queue.

Each priority band in a queue maintains separate high and low water marks for flow-control, and pointers to the first and last messages in that priority band. All this information is held in the *qband* structure and its fields are described as follows:

- *qb_next* — points to the next *qband* structure.

- *qb_count* — the number of bytes of data currently queued on the band.

- *qb_first, qb_last* — pointers to first and last *msgbs* queued on the band.

- *qb_hiwat, qb_lowat* — hold the high and low water marks for the flow-control mechanism. Each priority band has separate high and low water marks for flow-control.

Table 7.7: *Struct equeue*

Element	Description
*struct queue *eq_link*	Next *queue* structure for scheduling
*struct qband *eq_bandp*	Band's flow-control information
unsigned char eq_nband	Number of priority bands

Table 7.8: *Struct qband (qband_t)*

Element	Description
*struct qband *qb_next*	Next priority band
unsigned long qb_count	Number of bytes queued
*struct msgb *qb_first*	First queued message in this band
*struct msgb *qb_last*	Last queued message in this band
unsigned long qb_hiwat	High water mark for flow-control
unsigned long qb_lowat	Low water mark for flow-control
unsigned long qb_flag	Flags (see below)
Flag (*qb_flag* **)**	**Description**
QB_FULL	Band is considered full
QB_WANTW	Someone wants to write to band
QB_BACK	Queue has been back-enabled

From this, it is clear that the *equeue* structure contains the priority band information (*qband*) that really should be in the *queue* structure, but to prevent jeopardizing the binary compatibility of STREAMS modules and drivers in previous versions of the software, it cannot be added to it. However, if expanded fundamental types are used, the fields of the *qband* structure are in fact incorporated into the *queue* structure itself (see Table 7.9).

7.2.3 The *module* structures

Each STREAMS *module* compiled into the system has an associated *module_info* structure (Table 7.10), which describes a module's queue configuration and initialization information. Its fields are described as follows:

- *mi_idnum* — each STREAMS module and driver is given a unique identifier which is used by the STREAMS logging driver to identify the STREAMS module on which tracing is to be performed (see *strlog(D3DK)*).

Table 7.9: *Struct queue (queue_t) EFT version*

Element	Description
*struct qinit *q_qinfo*	Information structure for the queue
*struct msgb *q_first*	Head of queued messages
*struct msgb *q_last*	Tail of queued messages
*struct queue *q_next*	Next queue in this stream
*struct queue *q_link*	Next queue structure for scheduling
*_VOID *q_ptr*	Private data pointer
ulong q_count	Number of bytes in queue
ulong q_flag	Queue state
long q_minpsz	Minimum packet size queue will accept
long q_maxpsz	Maximum packet size queue will accept
ulong q_hiwat	High water mark for flow-control
ulong q_lowat	Low water mark for flow-control
*struct qband *q_bandp*	Band's flow-control information
unsigned char q_nband	Number of priority bands

- *mi_idname* — each module or driver is given a unique name, used when the module is pushed onto a stream.

- *mi_minpsz, mi_maxpsz* — these hold the initial minimum and maximum packet sizes that are accepted by the module.

- *mi_hiwat, mi_lowat* — hold the high and low water marks used by the STREAMS flow-control mechanism. Under the original STREAMS implementation, these items were declared as *short* (usually meaning they are 16 bit quantities). Under UNIX System V Release 4, with EFT in effect, they are enlarged to be *unsigned long* (usually 32 bit quantities). The rationale for this change is that under the old implementation the flow-control mechanism could break when large quantities of data were queued, since the variables for the high and low water marks were only 16 bits, and could wrap around, giving false counts.

Table 7.10: *Struct module_info*

Element	Description
ushort mi_idnum	Module's number
*char *mi_idname*	Name of the module
short mi_minpsz	Minimum packet size
short mi_maxpsz	Maximum packet size
ushort mi_hiwat	High water mark for flow-control
ushort mi_lowat	Low water mark for flow-control

The minimum and maximum packet sizes and the flow-control information are held in both the *queue* structure and the *module_info* structure in the *qinit* that also forms part of the *queue* structure. The *module_info* holds the default values for a particular module type; when the *queue* is initialized, it takes the values from the *module_info* structure. Subsequent STREAMS *ioctl* system calls can be used to alter the packet size and flow-control values. When this occurs, the values in the *queue* structure are changed.

Additionally, each *qinit* structure contains a pointer to a *module_stat* structure (Table 7.11). This is intended to hold statistical counts of how often the various procedures of each module are called. However, these fields are only updated if the corresponding procedure updates the count itself.

Table 7.11: *Struct module_stat*

Element	Description
long ms_pcnt	Count of calls to *qi_putp( )* procedure
long ms_scnt	Count of calls to *qi_srvp( )* procedure
long ms_ocnt	Count of calls to *qi_qopen( )* procedure
long ms_ccnt	Count of calls to *qi_qclose( )* procedure
long ms_acnt	Count of calls to *qi_qadmin( )* procedure
*char *ms_xptr*	Pointer to module private statistics
short ms_xsize	Length of module private statistics buffer

7.2.4 Initialization of module data structures

The *qinit* and *module_info* data structures for a module or driver must be configured with suitable initialization information; an example is given in Figure 7.6.

In the example, it is clear that all data structures and functions are declared *static*. This helps avoid name clashes, and makes it easier to integrate new software into an existing kernel. The only publicly accessible data object that a STREAMS module or driver needs to declare is a *streamtab* structure (see Table 7.12), and one is compiled into the system for each configured module type. A *streamtab* contains four pointers to *qinit* structures; one each for the read queue, write queue, and read and write sides of a multiplexor. When a STREAMS module or driver is configured into the system, the module switch table (*fmodsw[]* — see § 7.15) or character device switch table (*cdevsw[]* — see § 5.6.3) must be modified to include an entry that points to the *streamtab* structure for the new driver or module.

7.3 STREAMS modules

A STREAMS module is used to perform intermediate processing on data passing between a device driver and a stream head. *ldterm* is an example of a frequently used module; it provides first-level processing of the data typed by users at their

Figure 7.6: *STREAMS data structure initialization*

```
/* Sample module initialization */
static int sampleopen(),sampleclose();
static int samplerput(),samplewput();

static struct module_info samplerinfo {
  0x1234,        /* Module id number */
  "sample"       /* Module name */
  0,             /* Min packet size */
  256,           /* Max packet size */
  0,             /* Lo water mark */
  1              /* Hi water mark */
} ;
static struct module_info samplewinfo {
  ... same as for samplerinfo
} ;

static struct qinit rinit = {
  samplerput,    /* Read put routine */
  NULL,          /* We have no read service routine */
  sampleopen,    /* Open function */
  sampleclose,   /* Close function */
  NULL,          /* We have no admin function */
  &samplerinfo   /* Point to module info */
  NULL           /* We have no statistics structure */
} ;

static struct qinit winit = {
  samplewput,    /* Write put procedure */
  NULL, NULL,    /* No write service, no open.. */
  NULL, NULL     /* .. no close, no admin functions */
  &samplewinfo,  /* Point to module info */
  NULL           /* We have no statistics structure */
} ;

/* The streamtab is pointed to by cdevsw, and is the only
 * publicly visible data structure in this file */
struct streamtab sampleinfo = {
  &rinit,    /* Point to read side initializers */
  &winit,    /* Point to write side initializers */
  NULL, NULL /* We are not a multiplexor */
} ;
/* Rest of file is the code to implement the STREAMS module */
```

Table 7.12: *Struct streamtab (used in cdevsw[] and fmodsw[])*

Element	Description
*struct qinit *st_rdinit*	Read queue initialization
*struct qinit *st_wrinit*	Write queue initialization
*struct qinit *st_muxrinit*	Multiplexor read side initialization queue
*struct qinit *st_muxwinit*	Multiplexor write side initialization queue

terminal. For example, it handles back space, line delete, character mapping, operating speed, and so on.

A module is activated when a process pushes it onto a stream. This is done by issuing a STREAMS *I_PUSH ioctl* system call with a parameter that specifies the name of the module to push. When a module is pushed, the kernel allocates it a pair of *queue* structures and initializes them with the module's *module_info* data. The queues are then linked into the stream, and the *open* procedure of the module is called to perform any initial processing. As messages pass up and down the stream, the *put* and *service* procedures are called to process the data. If the process exits, dies, or issues a STREAMS *I_POP ioctl*, the kernel invokes the module's *close* routine to perform any final processing. It then unlinks the queues from the stream and frees them. The module is thus deactivated.

Figure 7.7: *Open declaration*

```
static int
sampleopen( q, dev, flag, sflag, cred )
   queue_t *q ;
   dev_t *dev ;
   int oflag, sflag ;
   cred_t *cred
```

7.3.1 Open procedures

The declaration for a STREAMS module or STREAMS driver *open* procedure is shown in Figure 7.7. Note that the argument list is distinctly different from that used in a normal device driver *open* function (see § 5.6.4). Furthermore, the *open* procedure for a STREAMS driver is called through an entry in *cdevsw[]*, whereas the *open* procedure for a STREAMS module is called through an entry in *fmodsw[]* (see § 7.15). An *open* on a STREAMS driver takes place when a user-mode process issues the *open* system call on a character special file that represents a STREAMS device. A subsequent *ioctl* system call on that file using the *I_PUSH* switch is used to push a module onto the open stream. This results in the invocation of that modules *open* procedure.

The argument *q* is a pointer to the read queue of the module or driver. For modules, the *dev*, *oflag* and *sflag* parameters can be ignored, although for drivers these values are important: *dev* points to an area containing the major and minor number of the special file associated with the stream (i.e., the device) and *oflag* describes the modes used to open the stream — for example, *FNDELAY*, *FREAD* and *FWRITE*. (Note that *FAPPEND*, *FCREAT* and *FTRUNC* are redundant when using STREAMS devices.) The use of *sflag* is described in § 7.4.2. The *cred* pointer is used to pass in the credentials of the process that issued the open; this information is useful for imposing access permissions if required (see § 4.11.5).

A STREAMS *open* procedure performs the processing required when the module or driver is initiated. For example, a module normally maintains state information in an area pointed to by *q_ptr*, which is allocated and set up when the module is first pushed onto the stream. Take, for example, *ldterm*; its *open* routine checks the value of *q_ptr*, and if it is not *NULL* the module assumes that it is already open and so returns to the caller. Otherwise, the *ldterm* private storage area is allocated and initialized to contain the information about the terminal's input and output modes, output row and column, baud rate, and so on.

The STREAMS environment imposes some rules on STREAMS module and driver handling procedures. In particular, if an *open* procedure wants to *sleep()* it must do so with *PCATCH* set, or at priority *PZERO*. This ensures that the *sleep()* will return to the *open* procedure (see § 4.6.13). The full set of rules is given in the *Design Guidelines* section of [AT&T 1990d].

7.3.2 Put procedures

The module's *put* procedure performs the processing steps on messages passing through it. When a *put* procedure finishes processing a message it calls the *put* procedure of the next module along the stream (this is done via a function called *putnext()*), allowing the message to pass quickly along the stream in a continuous processing sequence. Figure 7.8 shows the C language declaration for an example *put* procedure.

Figure 7.8: *Put declaration*

```
static int
samplerput( q, mp )
   queue_t *q ;
   mblk_t *mp ;
```

The first parameter is a pointer to the queue, the second points to the message block being processed. A *put* procedure must conform to the STREAMS rules in order to work properly. It is the programmer's responsibility to ensure the rules are obeyed:

- Priority messages should be processed immediately. If the module does not process a priority message directly (i.e., if it is destined for the stream head or another module), it should pass it immediately to the next module by using *putnext()*.

- For normal messages, the module should check the flow-control status of the next module in the stream. If it is not blocked (see *flow-control* in § 7.1), the message should be processed and passed on to the next module with *putnext( )*.

- If the next module is blocked by flow-control the message should be put into the queue of the current module by using the *putq( )* function. After calling *putq( )*, the module should return. Later, the *service* procedure for the module will process the queued messages.

Pseudo-code for a typical *put* procedure is shown in Figure 7.9. When a module is executed, it does not necessarily run in the context of the process for which the data is intended. This is in contrast to a STREAMS *open* which always executes in the context of the process performing the *open*. In other words, the time spent processing the data as it passes through a stream is charged to an arbitrary process rather than to the process performing the transaction. However, the STREAMS processing will eventually be shared amongst all processes. This leads to two additional constraints on module design. First, a module may not *sleep* waiting on a resource. If it did so, it would put to sleep an arbitrary process, and this must never happen. (For example, if a user's shell were put to sleep in a STREAMS module, waiting on an event that never occurs, that user's shell will be hung for ever!) The second restriction is that a module may not access the systems global *u area*. Since a module runs in the context of an arbitrary process, the information in the *u area* is meaningless.

   There are two types of module. The first queues all messages, and only processes them via its *service* procedure. Such modules have *putq( )* specified as their *put* procedures. In practice, however, modules are designed with both *service* and *put* procedures. The second type of module has no *service* procedure. Such modules can never put blocked messages onto their queue. However, this does not defeat the flow-control mechanism. When a module executes *canput( )* it searches the stream for the next module with a *service* procedure, and uses its state as the basis for the flow-control calculations. The stream head always has a *service* procedure, so flow-control is always guaranteed to work. Modules that perform simple translations of the data are sometimes written without a *service* procedure.

7.3.3 Service procedures

Whenever a module finds that the next module is blocked by flow-control, it stores messages in its own queue. At a later stage, upstream flow-control is relaxed. When the STREAMS scheduler sees this, it calls the module's *service* procedure to process the backlog of messages waiting in its queue. A *service* procedure must perform the following steps:

- Retrieve the first message from the queue via *getq( )*. If it is a priority message, process it immediately and pass it on to the next module.

- If it is a normal message, check for flow-control. If the next module is blocked, put the message back onto its queue again (this time via *putbq( )*) then return since no more processing is possible.

Figure 7.9: *Example put procedure*

```
static int
samplerput( q, mp )
  queue_t *q ;
  mblk_t *mp ;
{
  ...
  if ( mp->b_datap->db_type >= QPCTL ) {
    ...
    /* Process priority message */
    ...
    putnext( q, mp ) ;
    return ;
  }
  if ( canput(q->q_next) ) {
    ...
    /* Process normal message */
    ...
    putnext( q, mp ) ;
  } else {
    /* Put message on our own  queue because upstream is blocked. */
    putq( q, mp ) ;
  }
}
```

- If the next module is not blocked, process the message and pass it along the stream with *putnext( )*.

- Repeat the above steps until all messages on the queue are processed or until it is blocked by flow-control in the next module along the stream.

When a modules *service* procedure is called, it is called with a single parameter; a pointer to the queue to be processed (see the example in Figure 7.10).

Note that the *service* procedure must exit only when *canput( )* fails (because of flow-control) or when there are no more messages on the queue. Otherwise, it will defeat the STREAMS scheduling mechanism; there will be messages stuck on the queue, but neighbouring modules may call the module's *put* procedure. This means that messages will be processed later before those that are stuck in the queue.

7.3.4 Message processing

put and *service* procedures must do something with all messages passed to them. They do not have the option of ignoring them. Messages that are not handled by the module itself are passed on, otherwise they are processed by the module and then passed on if necessary.

Figure 7.10: *Example service procedure*

```
static int samplersrv( q )
  queue_t *q ;
{
  mblk_t *mp ;
  /* Get all messages from queue */
  while ( ( mp = getq(q) ) != (mblk_t *)0) {
    if( mp->b_datap->db_type >= QPCTL ) {
      ...
      /* Process priority message */
      ...
      putnext(q, mp) ;
      return ;
    }
    if ( canput(q->q_next) ) {
      ...
      /* No flow-control, so process message and pass it on */
      ...
      putnext( q, mp ) ;
    }
    else {
      /* Flow-control, so we put it back and exit */
      putbq( q, mp ) ;
      return ;
    }
  }
}
```

Figure 7.11 shows the typical skeleton code used by a module. Generally, a module is written with a switch statement that recognizes and manipulates the different message types. The processing code for *M_DATA* and *M_PROTO* messages perform whatever data manipulation the module is designed to do. The write-side procedures of a module may need to recognize and process *M_IOCTL* messages (discussed in the next section). Modules with *service* procedures must recognize and process *M_FLUSH* messages, which may be generated at the stream head or driver. They instruct modules to discard any data they are queueing. Such messages are often generated in response to an error condition, where existing data in the stream must be cleared out.

7.3.5 Processing *ioctl*

Calls to *ioctl* are the means by which control information is passed between a user-mode process and a device driver. STREAMS supports two types of *ioctl*: *I_STR* and *transparent*. *I_STR ioctl* commands are those described in *streamio(7)*; the

Figure 7.11: *Typical message processing code*

```
/* this module does not process priority messages
 * so pass them on immediately */
if( mp->b_datap->db_type >= QPCTL) {
  putnext( q,mp ) ;
  return ;
}
/* We process many types of normal message.. */
switch( mp->b_datap->db_type ) {
case M_DATA:
  do what this module does to data, and then pass it on
  check for flow-control and putnext or putq accordingly
  return ;
case M_PROTO:
  /* these may carry information we must process.. */
  ...
  check for flow-control and putnext or putq accordingly
  return ;
case M_IOCTL:
  perform ioctl processing, see § 7.3.5
case M_FLUSH:
  check which queue is to be flushed
  call flushq to clear it
  return ;
default
  check for flow-control then putnext or putq accordingly
}
```

second parameter of the system call always has the value *I_STR*, and the third parameter (the data argument) must always point to a *strioctl* structure (see § 7.9.7). Most *I_STR* commands are interpreted at the stream head, the remainder are packaged into *M_IOCTL* messages and passed down the stream.

Transparent *ioctls* are provided for source code compatibility with earlier releases of UNIX. Traditionally, many device drivers were not written for STREAMS, but were written as character device drivers, which always had their own class of *ioctl* commands. For example, serial line drivers traditionally support the set of *ioctls* described in *termio(7)*. Transparent *ioctls* allow the code for a program to remain unchanged after the underlying driver has been recoded for STREAMS.

STREAMS modules and drivers process *I_STR* and transparent *ioctls* in different ways:

- *I_STR* — *ioctls* are associated with two data structures. The first is the *strioctl* structure, which is populated by the program in user address space (Table 7.13).

Table 7.13: *Struct strioctl*

Element	Description
int ic_cmd	Command to perform
int ic_timout	*ioctl* timeout period
int ic_len	Size of data buffer
char *ic_dp	Address of data buffer

Table 7.14: *Struct iocblk*

Element	Description
int ioc_cmd	Command to perform
o_uid_t ioc_uid	User ID of process
o_gid_t ioc_gid	Group ID of process
unsigned ioc_id	ID of this *ioctl*
unsigned ioc_count	Size of the data field
int ioc_error	*ioctl* error code (for *errno*)
int ioc_rval	System call return value

Figure 7.12: *Issuing an I_STR ioctl*

```
struct strioctl s ;
...
s.ic_cmd = XYZZY ;   /* Fill in command field, XYZZY
                      * is a value recognised by the module */
s.ic_timout = 0 ;   /* Timeout value for the ioctl */
s.ic_len = ...   ;   /* Length of data buffer */
s.ic_dp = ...    ;   /* Fill in address of your buffer */

if( ioctl(fd, I_STR, &s ) == -1 )
  unsuccessful
else
  successful
```

The second is the *iocblk* structure, which is used internally by STREAMS in kernel address space (Table 7.14). Figure 7.12 shows how the *I_STR ioctl* command is used.

When the *ioctl* system call is issued the stream head recognizes the *I_STR* command, and so constructs an *M_IOCTL* message whose data block holds an *iocblk* structure. The message has attached to it an *M_DATA* message whose data block holds the user data — the stream head copies the contents of the *strioctl* from user address space via the *ic_dp* pointer. The *M_IOCTL* message is then passed down the stream. This means that it will be examined by the write-side procedure of every module in the stream including the driver. As each module processes the message, it examines the command stored in the *ioc_cmd* field of the *iocblk*. If the command is not recognized by the module, it passes on the message to the next module in the stream, and so on. If, however, the command is recognized, the module performs the necessary processing then changes the message type to *M_IOCACK* and passes it up the read side of the stream (towards the stream head) with a function called *qreply( )*. Figure 7.13 shows a module code fragment for processing *ioctl* requests. For the sake of demonstration, this module generates a negative acknowledgement for commands that it does not recognize, although such requests are usually passed on unchanged.

Figure 7.13: *Module ioctl processing*

```
/*
 * This function is called from samplewput when
 * it receives an M_IOCTL message
 */
sampleioctl(q, mp)
  struct queue *q ;
  mblk_t *mp ;
{
  struct iocblk *ip ;
  /* Point to the command structure */
  ip = (struct iocblk *)mp->b_rptr ;
  switch( ip->ioc_cmd ) {
  case XYZZY:
     process the ioctl
     mp->b_cont->b_rptr points to the user data
     mp->b_datap->db_type = M_IOCACK ;
     ip->ioc_count = 0 ;
     qreply( q, mp ) ;
     return ;
  default:
     /* Unknown ioctl */
     mp->b_datap->db_type = M_IOCNAK ;
     qreply(q, mp) ;
     return ;
  }
}
```

If there is no data to be passed back to the user program, a module must set the *ioc_count* field in the *iocblk* structure to zero. If this field is non-zero, the stream head copies this number of bytes from the accompanying *M_DATA* message back into user address space. The field, *ic_dp* in the user supplied *strioctl* structure points to the buffer that will receive the data.

A driver processes *M_IOCTL* messages in the same way as for a module. However, if a driver receives an unknown command or detects some sort of error while processing the *ioctl*, it changes the message type to be *M_IOCNAK*, fills in the error code field, then passes the message back up the stream towards the stream head.

- *transparent* — *ioctl* processing is more complicated. With an *I_STR ioctl*, the user program specifies the length of the data in the *ic_len* field of the *strioctl* structure. The stream head uses this to copy in and out the correct amount of data. With a transparent *ioctl*, the user program knows the size of the data, as does the STREAMS driver or module. However the stream head does not know the length of the data, so it cannot copy the correct amount in and out. For example, assume the following appeared in a program:

```
result = ioctl( fd, TCSETA, &t ) ;
```

This is an *ioctl* system call described by *termio(7)*. The item *t* is a *struct termios* and has a certain size. However, only the program and the STREAMS *ldterm* module know the type of the structure and its size; the stream head does not.

On the other hand, the stream head does know that an *ioctl* has been performed on the stream, so it creates an *M_IOCTL* message. The command field of the *iocblk* structure contains the value *TCSETA*, and the *count* field contains the special value *TRANSPARENT* to indicate that a transparent *ioctl* is being performed (*TRANSPARENT* is defined in the header file *sys/stream.h*). The *M_DATA* message attached to the *M_IOCTL* message contains the third parameter of the *ioctl* call. Generally this is the address of the data area in user space that accompanies the *ioctl*.

The STREAMS environment uses three message types and two data structures to support transparent *ioctls*. The message types are: *M_COPYIN, M_COPYOUT* and *M_IOCDATA*. The data structures are the *copyreq* (Table 7.15) and *copyresp* (Table 7.16) structures. The processing steps performed by a module for a transparent *ioctl* are as follows:

- The module receives the *M_IOCTL* message, recognizes the command and recognizes that it is a transparent *ioctl*.

- If the *ioctl* requires data to be copied in from user address space, the module creates an *M_COPYIN* message with the data part containing a *copyreq* structure whose fields specify the address (*cq_addr*) and length (*cq_size*) of the data to be copied. This message is sent back upstream to the stream head.

- The stream head receives the *M_COPYIN* message and in response creates an *M_IOCDATA* message whose data part contains a *copyresp* structure. The data is then copied from user address space into an *M_DATA* message attached to the newly created *M_IOCDATA* message in kernel address space. This is then passed back downstream to the module.

- The module receives the *M_IOCDATA* message and processes the data. Eventually, when the *ioctl* processing is complete, the module changes the message type to *M_IOCACK* and passes it back upstream with *qreply( )*.

Copying data out to user address space operates similarly, except that an *M_COPYOUT* message is used instead of *M_COPYIN*.

Table 7.15: *Struct copyreq*

Element	Description
int cq_cmd	Original *ioctl* command
o_uid_t cq_uid	User ID of process
o_gid_t cq_gid	Group ID of process
unsigned cq_id	*ioctl* sequence identifier
caddr_t cq_addr	Address of data in user-space
unsigned cq_size	Size of user data
*mblk_t *cq_private*	Module's private information

Table 7.16: *Struct copyresp*

Element	Description
int cp_cmd	Original *ioctl* command
o_uid_t cp_uid	User ID of process
o_gid_t cp_gid	Group ID of process
unsigned cp_id	*ioctl* identifier
caddr_t cp_rval	Return value from system call
*mblk_t *cp_private*	Module's private information

The module processing for transparent *ioctls* is greatly complicated by this repeated exchange of messages. When the first *M_IOCTL* message is received, the module creates the *M_COPYIN* request and sends it upstream. However, the module cannot just wait for the data to arrive, it must return. Some time later, the data is copied in from user space and an *M_IOCDATA* message is created, and the module's write *put* procedure is called once more. The appearance of an *M_IOCDATA* message means that the module "knows" it was halfway through processing the *ioctl*. The module may need to send repeated *M_COPYIN* requests using the *cq_private* field of the *copyreq* structure to maintain its internal state information. The fields of interest in the *copyreq* structure are:

- *cq_cmd* — the original *ic_cmd* field from the *iocblk* structure.

- *cq_addr* — holds the address in user address space from which to copy the data.

- *cq_size* — the number of bytes to be copied.

- *cq_private* — points to an *mblk_t* by which the module holds state information.

The interesting fields in the *copyresp* structure are:

- *cp_cmd* — the original *ic_cmd* field from the *iocblk*.

- *cp_rval* — the status of the request. Zero denotes that the copy-in was successful, non-zero denotes that there was an error and that the copy-in failed (for example, the user may have specified an illegal address from which to copy the data).

For efficiency, when allocating a message block to hold the initial *M_IOCTL* message, the stream head ensures that the data block is big enough to hold an *iocblk*, *copyreq* or *copyresp* structure. This allows a single message to be used for all the up-and-down stream activity; the stream head and the module simply reuse the same message, changing the type field and the data as required.

Figure 7.14 gives an example of a module that requires an *M_COPYIN* message. The processing steps performed in this example are as follows:

- The user-mode process issues the system call:

$$\text{ioctl(fd, TCSETA, \&t)}$$

- The example module reads in a *termios* structure from the address specified in the system call arguments (**&t**). The data in this structure is used by the *ioctl* processing code to set certain operational characteristics.

- The private field is not used here because there is no state information. The appearance of an *M_IOCDATA* message is the result of an *M_COPYIN* message that was sent earlier.

When the *ioctl* is issued, the stream head generates an *M_IOCTL* message and sends it downstream. The user-mode process is then blocked until the *ioctl* is acknowledged, or the *ioctl* times out. This means that there is never more than one *ioctl* currently active on a stream at one time, which makes the processing of *ioctls* a little easier. For example, an *M_COPYIN* message will only ever apply to the *ioctl* active on the stream. If multiple *ioctls* were allowed, additional code would be needed to match the *M_COPYIN*, *M_IOCACK*, and *M_IOCNAK* messages to a particular *ioctl* message in the stream.

7.3.6 Flush handling

All STREAMS drivers and modules must handle *M_FLUSH* messages. They are generated by the stream head, modules or drivers, usually in response to some error condition that requires the removal of any messages stored in the stream. For example, an error condition detected by a driver may mean that it is necessary to clear out all messages currently stored in the read side of the stream. In this case, the driver creates an *M_FLUSH* message and sends it up the read queue, telling all modules to discard messages on their queue. This is done by calling a function called *flushq( )*.

Figure 7.14: *Use of M_COPYIN*

```
struct copyresp *cresp ;
struct termio *t ;
struct copyreq *creq ;
struct iocblk *ip ;
...
case M_IOCTL:
  ip = (struct iocblk *)mp->b_rptr ;
  switch (ip->ioc_cmd) {
  case TCSETA:
    if( ip->ioc_count != TRANSPARENT )
        error   /* TCSETA is always transparent ioctl */
    /* Reuse mblock for copyin request */
    mp->b_datap->db_type = M_COPYIN ;
    mp->b_wptr = mp->b_rptr + sizeof(struct copyreq) ;
    /* Fill in copy request block fields.. */
    creq = (struct copyreq *)mp->b_rptr ;
    creq->cq_size = sizeof(struct termio) ;
    creq->cq_flag = 0 ;
    qreply( q, mp) ; /* Send request back upstream */
    return ;  /* Nothing more to do at this time..*/
  default: /* Not our ioctl, so pass it on */
    putnext( q, mp) ;
    return ;
  }
case M_IOCDATA:
  /* This is the result of an earlier M_COPYIN */
  cresp = (struct copyresp *)mp->b_rptr ;
  switch( cresp->cp_cmd ) {
  case TCSETA: /* Message is meant for us.. */
    if( cresp->cp_rval )
      error  /* the copyin from user space failed */
    /* point to the data copied from user-space */
    t = (struct termios *)mp->b_cont->b_rptr ;
    ...  /* Process the data */
    mp->b_datap->db_type = M_IOCACK ;
    fill in rptr, wptr with iocblk information
    qreply(q, mp) ; /* Send ACK back upstream */
    return ;
  default:
    putnext( q, mp ) ; /* Message for another module.. */
    return ;
  }
```

The first data byte in an *M_FLUSH* message specifies which queues are to be flushed. Therefore, when an *M_FLUSH* message is received, the module or driver must decode the first byte of the data pointed to by *b_rptr* in the *mblk_t* to compute the arguments it must use to call *flushq( )*. It takes the following values:

- *FLUSHR* — flush only the read queue.

- *FLUSHW* — flush only the write queue.

- *FLUSHRW* — flush both read and write queues.

- *FLUSHBAND* — flush the messages in a particular band; the second byte in the data part of the *M_FLUSH* message specifies which band.

As an example, a fragment of code for handling *M_FLUSH* messages is given in Figure 7.15. Note that the option byte is a bit field, and that the code tests whether the read or write bits in the option byte are set.

Figure 7.15: *M_FLUSH processing*

```
/* This is the write put function.. */
char option, band ;
...
case M_FLUSH:
  /* Handle M_FLUSH message */
  option = *mp->b_rptr ;
  if ( option & FLUSHR )
    flushq( RD(q), FLUSHDATA ) ;   /* Flush read queue */
  if ( option & FLUSHW )
    flushq( q, FLUSHDATA ) ;
  /* Pass onto next module */
  putnext( q, mp ) ;
```

7.3.7 Close procedures

The close procedure for a module is called either when the module is removed from the stream with the *I_POP ioctl*, or when the last *close* is performed on the stream. The declaration for an example close procedure is shown in Figure 7.16.

The procedure arguments are: a pointer to the queue being closed, the flags by which the original *open* was called, and a pointer to the process's credentials structure.

A module or driver's *close* procedure must free any dynamically allocated resources and clear any held state information. The rules for close processing are the same as those for open processing (see *Design Guidelines* in [AT&T 1990d]).

Figure 7.16: *Close declaration*

```
static int
sampleclose( q, flag, cred )
  queue_t *q ;
  int flag ;
  struct cred *cred ;
```

7.4 STREAMS drivers

It is sometimes difficult to describe the term "driver" since it might refer to a STREAMS-based device driver (which may or may not include STREAMS modules), or to the lowest module in a stream (the module that interfaces with the device). Therefore, throughout the following sections, the term "driver" will be used to refer to either STREAMS module or driver unless specified otherwise.

Except for pseudo device drivers, a driver interfaces directly with physical hardware. It manipulates registers, processors, memory, and so on, to perform input and output operations between the device it controls and the rest if the machine hardware. For example, the 802.3 driver shown in Figure 7.2 interfaces directly with the Ethernet controller.

A STREAMS driver is a special type of STREAMS module and is the last module in the stream. A STREAMS driver is more complex than a module because it has more work to do and a greater set of rules to obey. It must process all messages that it receives from upstream; it does not have the option of passing on messages to the next module. The driver is further complicated with the task of taking data from within a STREAMS message and passing it on to the physical device. In the opposite direction, it must take data from the device and passes it into the stream towards the stream head. It must also provide an interrupt service routine to handle interrupts generated by the device when it is ready to send or receive data.

To illustrate the key points of STREAMS driver processing, we will use a hypothetical hardware device and examine its associated driver. The hypothetical device converts data generated in the computer to a serial form that is sent over an RS232 communication line. Data received from the line is converted into a form that is readable by the computer. The device consists of a simple serial controller chip with four separate communication channels, each having a status register and an on board memory mapped data buffer. Each channel can be referenced by simply reading or writing its address.

Writing a byte of data into a buffer will cause that character to be transmitted along its associated serial link. In the opposite direction, data received on a serial link is placed into its associated register, and can be read by the processor. Each status register has two bits in it. The first, called *TXE*, is set when the transmitter is empty. This indicates that another character can be written to the buffer. When a character is placed in the transmitter, TXE is cleared and remains clear until the character has been transmitted, at which point TXE is set again. The other bit is called *CR*, meaning that a character has been received and can be read by the processor. Once the processor reads the character from the buffer, *CR* is cleared again and remains clear until another character is received.

The processor is normally busy doing other chores, so when the serial communications chip sets either *CR* or *TXE*, it generates an interrupt to tell the processor that it needs servicing. This results with the device driver interrupt service routine being called with the minor device number of the interrupting device as parameter (i.e., the channel number).

7.4.1 Configuration and linking

The code for the device driver follows the general form of a module, and has already been described. For device drivers, the following additional items are needed:

- a mapping between the interrupt generated by the device and the interrupt service routine in the device driver must be made.

- the special device files must be created so that processes can associate with the device.

- the kernel must be configured and rebuilt to include the device driver.

The detailed steps for configuring a driver into the kernel are vendor dependent (see Appendix E of [AT&T 1990d]).

7.4.2 Driver open

There are two possible ways to open a STREAMS driver: normal open and clone open. Which method is used depends on how the device driver is written and how the system is configured. Our example serial device has four channels, and each channel is identified by its own minor device number. For our example, assume that the serial device driver has major number 42, and that the STREAMS clone driver has major device number 3.

For normal opens, four special files are created, each having their own minor device numbers 0 to 3; they each share the same major number 42 (see Table 7.17).

Table 7.17: */dev entries for normal open*

Filename	Major#	Minor#
/dev/ser0	42	0
/dev/ser1	42	1
/dev/ser2	42	2
/dev/ser3	42	3

When a process wants to use one of the channels, it opens one of these special files using the *open* system call. This results in the kernel passing the minor number of the device to the *open* procedure in the special file's associated device driver. The driver uses this number to determine which channel it is operating with. In this case the process opening the device must be aware of the free channels available to it. In order to do this, it must attempt to open the first device; if that fails it is assumed that the device is busy, and so it attempts to open the next device, and so on until a free channel is found.

If, however, the device is configured as a clone device, the device driver itself selects the minor device number at the time the device is opened. That is, the driver is responsible for finding the free channel, allowing the process to simply open the clone device.

To configure a clone device, its associated special file must use the major device number of the STREAMS clone driver. Its minor number is then used as the major number of the actual device driver to use (see Table 7.18).

Table 7.18: */dev entry for clone open*

Filename	Major#	Minor#
/dev/ser	3	42

Figure 7.17: *Serial device structures*

```
#define NSERDEV 4  /* Number of channels */
typedef struct {
  queue_t *q    ; /* Back pointer to owning queue */
  mblk_t *outq ; /* Data block being written to device */
  caddr_t status; /* Addr of hardware status register */
  caddr_t buffer; /* Addr of hardware buffer */
} serdev_t ;
serdev_t serdevs[NSERDEV] ; /* Holds the device info */
```

Figure 7.17 shows the data structure used by our example driver, and Figure 7.18 shows example code for a normal device *open* procedure. There is one *serdev_t* structure for each channel held in an array called *serdevs[]*. Each structure contains a back pointer to the queue on which the device is attached. The *mblk_t* pointer *outq* is used by the output routines when writing data to the device. The structure also contains the addresses of the status register and data buffer for the channel that it represents.

The arguments to the driver *open* procedure are the same as those for a module *open* procedure. The procedure first checks *sflag*. If it is set, the user-mode process has attempted a clone open which is not accepted by this version of the driver *open* procedure. Otherwise, it checks that the minor device number is supported by the driver. The STREAMS environment allocates one queue for each minor device that is opened. Subsequent opens of the same minor device use the same queue. However, this example driver allows only one process to associate with a serial communications channel, so it allows only one open at a time per channel. To do this, the procedure checks if q->q_ptr is non-zero. If it is, the driver knows that the

Figure 7.18: *Code for normal open*

```
static int
seropen( q, devp, flag, sflag, credp )
  queue_t *q ;
  dev_t *devp ;
  int flag, sflag ;
  cred_t *credp ;
{
  dev_t minor ;
  serdev_t *sd ;
  if (sflag)  /* User tried a clone open .. */
    return ENXIO ; /* .. not allowed */
  minor = getminor(*devp) ;
  if ( minor < 0 OR minor >= NSERDEV ) /* Check minor is in range.*/
    return ENXIO ;
  /* STREAMS gives us 1 queue per minor, and we allow only
   * one open per minor in this example */
  if( q->q_ptr )
    return EBUSY ; /* Device currently in use */
  sd = &serdevs[minor] ;
  sd->q = q ;
  ...           /* Fill in remaining fields in sd */
  ...           /* Initialize the hardware device */
  q->q_ptr = (char *)sd ;    /* Fill in private data field */
  WR(q)->q_ptr = (char *)sd ; /* Also on the write side */
  return 0 ;
}
```

minor device has already been opened, and so it rejects a second open attempt. Otherwise, the driver assumes the channel is free; the fields of the *serdevs[]* structure (indexed by the minor device number) are initialized, and *q->q_ptr* is set to point to it. A real device driver usually requires much more initialization of the physical hardware than shown here.

When a clone driver *open* procedure is called, the parameter *sflag* is set to the value *CLONEOPEN* allowing the driver code to detect that a clone open is being done. The code for our serial device clone *open* procedure is shown in Figure 7.19. In this case it searches *serdevs[]* for a free channel. If there are none free, an error is returned. Otherwise, the index of the free channel is used as the minor device, and this is returned to the caller in *devp*.

7.4.3 Driver close

The driver *close* procedure is similar to that of a module; it frees any dynamically allocated resources associated with the device.

Figure 7.19: *Code for clone open*

```
static int
seropen( q, devp, flag, sflag, credp )
  queue_t *q ;
  dev_t *devp ;
  int flag, sflag ;
  cred_t *credp ;
{
  int i ;
  dev_t minor;
  if( sflag != CLONEOPEN )        /* Only allows clone open */
    return ENXIO ;
  /* Search for free device */
  for( i = 0 ; i < NSERDEV ; i++ )
    if( serdevs[i].q == (queue_t *) 0 )
      break ;
  if( i >= NSERDEV )
      return ENXIO ; /* No free devices */
  minor = i ;
  /* Set everything up, as for normal open */
  ...
  /* Return the minor device number we selected to caller */
  *devp = makedevice( getmajor( *devp ), minor ) ;
  return 0 ;
}
```

The close code for the serial driver is shown in Figure 7.20. The code takes the *serdevs* structure pointer held in the queue private data structure (*q->q_ptr*), and marks it as free. In a real driver, if there is a physical device associated with it, the processing required to disassociate the process from the hardware may also be carried out.

7.4.4 Driver input

The input processing of a STREAMS driver consists of two parts: an interrupt service procedure and a read *service* procedure.

A driver interrupt service routine is brought into action when its associated device generates an interrupt. Usually, it checks if there is room in the driver's read queue, and if there is, the data from the device is put there. The act of putting the data on the driver's read queue means that its *service* procedure will be called by the STREAMS scheduler. The second part of input processing is in the *service* procedure itself. It processes the data, and then passes it on to the next module upstream.

Figure 7.20: *Driver close code*

```
static int serclose( q, flag, cred )
  queue_t *q ;
  int flag ;
  cred_t *cred ;
{
  serdev_t *sdp ;
  if ( ! q->q_ptr ) {
    /* Something is horribly wrong here.. */
    cmn_err( CE_WARN, "Closing a closed device" ) ;
    return ENXIO ;
  }
  sdp = (serdev_t *)q->q_ptr ;
  /* Setting q field to nil marks the device
   * as deallocated */
  sdp->q = (queue_t *)0 ;
  ... /* Perform any necessary hardware operations */
  return 0 ;
}
```

The input processing for our example serial driver follows this pattern. It uses *canput( )* (via *serdevread( )*) to see if the read queue has room for the data. If it has, a message block is allocated and the data is placed on that queue. If it has no room, the input side is blocked by flow-control, and the input data is simply discarded. A more sophisticated driver would attempt to exert flow-control on the hardware to prevent it from sending more data. The interrupt routine calls *cmn_err( )* if it gets input from a device that has not been opened (see Appendix D of [AT&T 1990d]).

Our example driver interrupt service routine handles both read and write interrupts from the serial controller. When it is invoked, it examines the status register to compute its mode of processing (i.e., whether to read or write) and calls the functions *serdevread( )* or *serdevwrite( )* appropriately. The read *service* procedure for the driver simply takes the data from the queue and passes it upstream (see the code for the sample driver *service* procedure shown in Figure 7.10). The example code for our serial driver interrupt service routine is shown in Figure 7.21.

7.4.5 Driver output

The output side of our example serial device driver consists of three parts: an interrupt service routine, a write *put* procedure and a write *service* procedure.

The device interrupts the processor when it is ready to receive the next output character. This results with the invocation of the driver's interrupt service routine, which detects that *TXE* is set and so calls *serdevwrite( )* to *qenable( )* the write

Figure 7.21: *Driver interrupt service routine*

```
/*
 * Calling of the interrupt procedure
 * is system dependent. Here, we get
 * the minor device as argument
 */

int serdevintr( minor )
  int minor ;
{
  serdev_t *sd ; /* Info structure for interrupting device */
  queue_t *q ;   /* Queue that will receive data */
  sd = &serdevs[minor] ;
  q = sd->q ;

  if( !q ) {
    /* Interrupt from non-open device: error */
    cmn_err( CE_WARN, "Unexpected interrupt" ) ;
    return ;
  }

  if ( sd->status & CR )
    serdevread(q) ; /* Read a character */

  if( sd->status & TXE )
    serdevwrite(WR(q)) ;

  return ;
}

void serdevread(q)
  queue_t *q ;
{
  mblk_t *mp ;
  char ch ;
  /* Try to put the data on the queue, if not,
   * silently discard it.. */

  if( canput(q) ) {
    mp = allocb( 1, BPRI_LO ) ;  /* Alloc buffer for data */
    if ( !mp )
      error /* no buffer  */
    ch = sd->buffer ;   /* get char from hardware */
    mp->b_wptr++ = ch ; /* into the msgb */
```

```
    putq(q, bp) ;          /* put on read-side queue */
  }
}

void serdevwrite(q)
  queue_t *q ;
{
  qenable(q) ;   /* see § 7.6.3 */
}
```

---

queue. This instructs the STREAMS scheduler to execute the drivers write *service* procedure.

The write *service* procedure does all the work. It takes characters one at a time from the *msgbs* on its queue and passes them to the device. It does this by taking a *msgb* from the front of the queue, outputting the character stored within it, and then putting the *msgb* back on the queue. Under normal circumstances, a message is put back on a queue only when the downstream module is blocked by flow-control. When the downstream blockage is released, the queue is enabled and the *service* procedure runs once more. Obviously, with a driver, there is no downstream module that can enable the queue. However, when the character has been output by the device, it generates another interrupt which invokes the interrupt service routine, and so the queue is once again enabled so that it can output the next character. For convenience of processing, the *service* procedure calls the STREAMS utility function *pullupmsg( )*. This function makes a single *msgb* from a group of *msgbs* that are linked together with their *b_cont* pointers (remember that *b_cont* links together *msgbs* that constitute a single logical message — see § 7.2.1). Eventually, the *service* procedure takes the last character from the last *msgb* on the queue and writes it to the device. This makes the device generate an interrupt and the queue is once again enabled. However, this time, when the *service* procedure calls *getq( )* it returns *NULL* which indicates that there is no more data on the queue. As a result, the queue is marked by STREAMS as empty.

Since this is a driver and not a module, the driver's write *put* procedure simply calls *putq( )* for *M_DATA* messages, which always puts a messages back onto its own queue ready to be processed by the write *service* procedure (see § 7.3.4). Therefore, when the driver's write *put* procedure is next invoked (as a result of another character coming down the stream) STREAMS will automatically schedule the queue, and the driver's write *service* procedure will then run and output the next character.

The code for the write *service* procedure is shown in Figure 7.22.

Figure 7.22: *Driver write service procedure*

```
int serdevwsrv(q)
  queue_t *q ;
{
  mblk_t *mp ;
  char ch ;
  serdev_t *sd ;
  sd = (serdev_t *)q->q_ptr ; /* Get output device info */
  mp = getq(q) ; /* Get first message */
  if( mp == (queue_t *)0)
    return ;  /* Nothing to do. Next putq will enable us */
  switch( mp->b_datap->db_type) {
  default:
    error - we only queue M_DATA messages
  case M_DATA:
    if( mp->b_cont )
      pullupmsg(mp, -1) ; /* Put into 1 msgb */
    ch = mp->b_rptr++ ;   /* This is the char to output */
    if( mp->b_rptr == mp->b_wptr )
      freeb(mp) ;  /* We have processed all data in this message */
    else
      putbq(q,mp) ;   /* Put it back for later */
    sd->buffer = ch ; /* Write it to the hardware */
    break ;
  }
  return ;
}
```

7.5 Multiplexors

A multiplexor is a special type of STREAMS module that has multiple streams connected to it. The multiplexing module routes STREAMS messages between connected streams. For example, in Figure 7.1 both the IP and X25 modules are multiplexors. The IP module routes packets into or out of the SLIP and 802.3 drivers; the X25 module routes packets into or out of the LLC2 and LAPB drivers.

The code for a multiplexor is more complex than for normal STREAMS modules because message routing is required. For example, the X25 driver in Figure 7.1 must decide whether outgoing packets are destined for LAPB or LLC2. Conversely, it must know which stream to send incoming packets to. The multiplexor is split into two halves, the upper and lower. Both the upper and lower parts have their own *read, write, put* and *service* procedures. The upper half processes requests to and from the stream head, and the lower half processes requests to and from the modules linked below the multiplexor towards the driver. The STREAMS flow-control mechanism works badly with multiplexors, and compounds their complexity.

The next section shows how multiplexor configurations are built; sections following this show how a multiplexor works. The X25 driver in the following examples is imaginary; it is not a description of a real X25 driver, although real X25 drivers and other real multiplexors use similar principles to those described.

7.5.1 Building the multiplexor

Before a STREAMS multiplexor configuration can be used it must be built and configured at run-time. Multiplexors are provided with a *daemon* process that builds the multiplexor configuration and maintains it for the life of the system. For this example, we describe how the X25 multiplexor module shown in Figure 7.1 is set up. First, we assume that there are three /*dev* entries; two for the LAPB and LLC2 drivers and one for the X25 module interface driver. The code for the configuration *daemon* is shown in Figure 7.23.

The first three calls to *open* simply open each of the drivers. The first *I_LINK ioctl* links the LLC2 driver below the X25 module so that the X25 module can now pass messages down into the LLC2 driver. This is followed by a second *I_LINK ioctl* which links the LAPB driver below the X25 module also. The *daemon* process must now wait forever. If it did not, it would exit, and the multiplexor would be automatically dismantled by the operating system. The *daemon* executes the *pause* system call which means it will wait until a signal is delivered to it (in effect, it waits forever, because no-one is likely to send a signal). User processes can now open /*dev/x25* in the normal way, but the module for X25 is written in such a way that it can use the facilities of the drivers linked below it.

In the STREAMS environment, special steps are taken to create a multiplexor. When the three drivers are opened by the *daemon*, each is allocated a *queue* pair and a stream head (the operations of the stream head are discussed in § 7.9). The *qinit* structure for the driver's read queue is initialized to point to the driver's read queue initialization structure (see *st_rdinit* in Table 7.12). Similarly, the *qinit* structure for the driver's write queue is initialized to point to the driver's write queue initialization structure (*st_wrinit*). This is shown in more detail in Figure 7.24. Above the driver is the stream head which also has a queue pair. The queues point to the *qinit* structures for the stream head (*strdata* and *stwdata*).

The *I_LINK* ioctl modifies the stream head data structure associated with the driver being linked underneath (called the linked driver). The stream head in the linked driver is altered so that it points to the *muxrinit* and *muxwinit* fields in the multiplexor (see Figure 7.25). The only difference at this stage between the multiplexing driver and the ordinary driver is that the multiplexor has the *muxrinit* and *muxwinit* fields in the *streamtab* entry initialized.

In Figure 7.1, the stream heads of the LAPB and LLC2 modules will be altered to point to the processing routines held in the data structures *x25muxrinit* and *x25muxwinit*.

Figure 7.23: *Multiplexor construction*

```
int x25, lapb, llc2 ;
int lapb_muxid, llc2_muxid ;
/* Error checks have been omitted for clarity */

/* Open the devices to get a file descriptor
 * for each device.  */
x25 = open( "/dev/x25", O_RDWR ) ;
lapb = open( "/dev/lapb", O_RDWR ) ;
llc2 = open( "/dev/llc2", O_RDWR ) ;

/* First, put llc2 under x25 */
llc2_muxid = ioctl( x25, I_LINK, llc2 ) ;

/* Then put lapb under x25 */
lapb_muxid = ioctl( x25, I_LINK, lapb ) ;

/* Configure lapb and llc2 with driver specific commands */
...
/* Process must still exist to keep the mux open, so wait forever */
pause( ) ;
```

Figure 7.24: *Data structures before I_LINK*

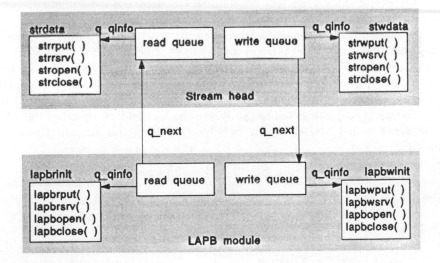

Figure 7.25: *Data structures After I_LINK*

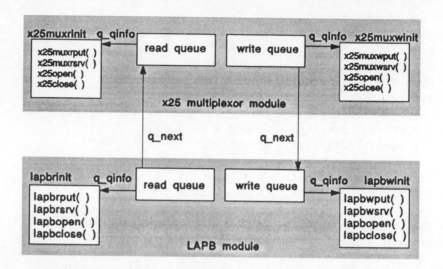

7.5.2   Multiplexor data structures

The STREAMS environment provides little support for developers of multiplexing drivers. Driver writers must develop their own facilities for routing and control of packets across a multiplexor.

This section presents data structures that are used in our example X25 driver to support configuration and routing through a driver. These data structures do not form part of the UNIX System V Release 4 source code distribution, but are presented simply to show how a driver could be written.

Our sample X25 driver needs an addressing scheme that allows a process to communicate with another process on another machine across a Wide Area Network (WAN). To do this, each machine is assigned its own address that is unique to all other machines on the network. An address consists of two parts, a *subnetwork address* and a *host address*. The subnetwork address identifies a Local Area Network (LAN) connected to the WAN; the host address specifies the address of a machine in a LAN. Examples of addresses using this scheme are given in Table 7.19.

Table 7.19: *Addressing scheme for our X25 multiplexor*

Address	Subnet Part	Host Address Part
A.26245690063030	A	26245690063030
B.23424420015318	B	23424420015318

When the example driver is running it must direct data from the lower stream to the correct upper stream, and a routing table is used for this purpose (see Table 7.20). The driver's in-core version of this table is described by the declarations shown in Figure 7.26.

Table 7.20: *Sample multiplexor routing table*

x25mux_routes[]		
muxid	**queue**	**subnet**
1	0xC0014580	A
2	0xC00145C8	B

Figure 7.26: *Routing table declaration*

```
struct x25_routing_entry {
    int muxid ;          /* Holds the muxid of the lower stream */
    queue_t *lower ;   /* Queue of the lower stream */
    subnet_t subnet ; /* Subnet address of the lower stream.
                        * Assume appropriate declaration of subnet_t */
} ;
/* Multiplexor's routing table */
#define X25_ROUTE_SIZE 0
struct x25_routing_entry x25mux_routes[X25_ROUTE_SIZE] ;
```

Each machine connected to the network supports several logical connections using a single physical connection. These logical connections are called *virtual circuits*. When data is transmitted across a link it is transmitted in packets. Each packet contains an identifier for the particular virtual circuit the data is destined for (for a full discussion of packet switched networks, see [Halsall 1988]). In X25 networks, this identifier is called the *logical channel number* (LCN). When our example multiplexor module receives data from the driver below it, it must determine which upper stream to send the data to. The LCN in the incoming data determines which upper stream queue to send the data on. The mapping between queues and LCNs is performed by the multiplexor using the *lcn_mapping[]* table (see Table 7.21). The C language declaration for the LCN mapping table is shown in Figure 7.27.

Table 7.21: *Sample multiplexor channel mapping*

lcn_mapping[]		
upper queue	**lower queue**	**LCN**
0xC0015010	0xC001CDE0	1
0xC001A2B4	0xC001CEE8	2
0xC001BBF4	0xC001F000	3

Figure 7.27: *Channel mapping declarations*

```
#define LCN_PER_DRIVER 256
struct x25_channel_map {
  queue_t *upper ;     /* Upper queue */
  queue_t *lower ;     /* Lower queue */
  int lcn ;            /* Logical Channel Number */
} ;
struct x25_channel_map lcn_mapping[LCN_PER_DRIVER];
```

A user-mode process (such as the configuration *daemon*) must pass data to the multiplexor and drivers in a suitable form. One way to achieve this is to define a set of *ioctl* commands (§ 7.3.5). An alternative is to use *M_PROTO* messages. Our example driver uses *M_PROTO* messages to convey information to the multiplexor for configuration and control. Each control message consists of an *M_PROTO* message linked to an *M_DATA* message. The first word of the data block in the *M_PROTO* message contains a value that indicates the command to execute. The data block of the attached *M_DATA* message contains the data associated with the command. Any *M_DATA* messages sent to the multiplexor are assumed to be data for transmission to the drivers. The structure of the control messages is shown in Figure 7.28. Our example multiplexor uses two control messages. The first is a *ROUTING* message for setting the subnet address of the LAPB or LLC2 drivers; the second is a *CONNECT* message for when the process requests a connection to a remote host.

Figure 7.28: *Sample multiplexor control messages*

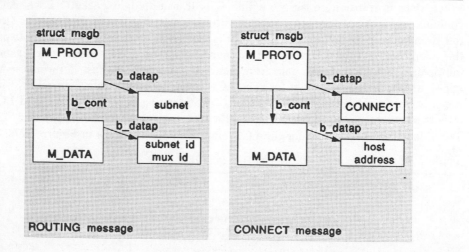

7.5.3 Multiplexor open

Our sample X25 multiplexor is a clone device. When the operating system boots, the configuration *daemon* is started. It opens the X25 multiplexor, getting minor device zero, which it uses for configuring the multiplexor (the driver will only accept *I_LINK ioctl* commands on minor device zero). Other processes will not be able to configure the X25 multiplexor because the control stream has already been claimed by the configuration *daemon*. The open routine for our X25 multiplexor is shown in Figure 7.29.

Figure 7.29: *Multiplexor open*

```
queue_t *x25mux_controlqueue = 0 ;

static int x25_muxopen(q, devp, flag, sflag, credp )
  queue_t *q ;
  dev_t *dev ;
  int flag ;
  int sflag ;
  cred_t *credp ;
{
  dev_t minor ;
  if( !x25mux_controlqueue ) {
    /* First open, so this is the control stream */
    x25mux_controlqueue = q ;
    minor = 0 ;
  } else
    minor = next free minor device number

  *devp = makedevice( getmajor( *devp ), minor ) ;
  return 0 ;
}
```

The open routine checks if it is the first open on the device. If so, it returns minor device number 0 and fills in the global variable *x25mux_controlqueue* (used for validating *I_LINK ioctls*). Otherwise, another free minor device number is sought and returned to the caller. Note that the *q->q_ptr* field is initialized later when a *CONNECT* message is received.

7.5.4 Multiplexor write side

The upper write side of the multiplexor handles data coming from the user program and passes the data to the lower side. The code fragment in Figure 7.30 shows how *x25mux_uwput( )* processes *I_LINK ioctl* messages. The code checks that the *I_LINK* has been issued on the control channel. If not, an *M_IOCNAK* message is sent back upstream to indicate the error. The code then finds a free entry in

Figure 7.30: *Processing I_LINK*

```
x25mux_uwput(q, mp)
...
struct iocblk *iocptr ;
struct linkblk *linkptr ;   /* see Table 7.31 */
struct x25_routing_entry *x ;
struct x25_channel_map *xce ;
...

case M_IOCTL:
  /* Process M_IOCTL messages */
  iocp = (struct iocblk *)mp->b_rptr ;

  switch( iocp->ioc_cmd ) {
  case I_LINK:
    /* Check that it is the control queue */
    if ( q != x25_control_queue ) {
        error  /*  send back M_IOCNAK message */
        return ;
    }
    linkptr = (struct linkblk *)mp->b_cont->b_rptr ;
    x = pointer to a free slot in x25mux_routes
    /* Save muxid and queue fields */
    x->muxid = linkptr->l_index ;
    x->lower = linkptr->l_qbot ;
    /* Subnet address is not filled in yet
     * because we dont know what it is.. */

    /* Create an x25mux_channels structure to hold
     * the mappings between LCN and upper queues,
     * and make q->q_ptr in the lower driver point to it */
    xce = (struct x25_channel_map *)allocb(
                sizeof(struct x25mux_channels)
                * LCN_PER_DRIVER, BPRI_LO) ;
    error check omitted
    q->q_ptr = (char *)xce ;

    /* All ok, so perform qreply/M_IOCACK processing */
    ...
    return ;
  ...
}
```

x25mux_routes[] to hold the routing information. This table is used by the multiplexor for data coming down the write side of the driver to determine which lower stream to use for the connection. After the routing information has been filled in, an array of *x25_channel_map* structures is dynamically allocated. Each lower stream is assigned one of these so that the lower read side processing routines in the multiplexor can determine the upper stream associated with a particular virtual circuit.

Figure 7.31: *Processing I_UNLINK*

```
int muxid ;
...
case M_IOCTL:
  /* Process M_IOCTL messages */
  iocp = (struct iocblk *)mp->b_rptr ;
  switch( iocp->ioc_cmd ) {
  case I_UNLINK:
    linkptr = (struct linkblk *)mp->b_cont->b_rptr ;
    /* We need to find lower queue to unlink */
    muxid = linkptr->l_index ;
    x = address of entry in x25mux_routes whose muxid
        field is the same as muxid
    /* Zero fields in lower queue, zero out routing
     * table entry */
    if( x->queue->q_ptr )
       freeb( x->queue->q_ptr ) ;
    x->queue = (queue_t *)0 ;
    ...
    qreply() ; /* Acknowledge the message */
    ...
    return ;
  }
```

The configuration *daemon* uses *I_UNLINK* (see Figure 7.31) when it dismantles the multiplexor. It passes down the *muxid* of the module to unlink. The multiplexor code searches its routing table for the entry corresponding to the *muxid* and clears the routing data for that driver.

The upper write *put* routine for the X25 multiplexor must also handle *M_PROTO* messages. The code fragment from *x25mux_uwput()* that handles *M_PROTO* messages is shown in Figure 7.32.

The configuration *daemon* issues the driver-specific *ROUTING* message to set up the routing table entry. The entries in the routing table associate the queue of a lower stream with a subnetwork address and a STREAMS *muxid*.

A user program issues a *CONNECT* control message when it wants to establish a connection to another host in the network. The upper write *put* procedure uses

Figure 7.32: *Multiplexor M_PROTO processing*

```
x25mux_uwput(q, mp)
...
struct x25_routing_entry *x ;
struct x25_channel_map *xce ;
queue_t *lower ;
int type ;
...
case M_PROTO:
  type = *(int *)(mp->b_rptr) ;
  switch (type) {
  case ROUTING:
   /* Routing set up on control stream */
   if( q != x25_control_queue )
      return error /*  discard message */
   /* Get muxid and subnet from the M_DATA block
    * attached to this message */
   subnet = mp->b_cont->b_rptr ...
   muxid  = mp->b_cont->b_rptr ...
   x = address of x25mux_routes entry that corresponds to muxid
   fill in subnet address into x->subnet field
   return ;

  case CONNECT:
    /* Connect request */
    if( q == x25_control_queue )
       return error /*  discard message */
    get subnet address from mp->b_cont->b_rptr
    x = address of x25mux_routes entry that corresponds
        to the subnet address
    xce = (struct x25_channel_map *)x->lower->q_ptr ;
    l = find empty slot for this connection in xce
    /* Fill in channels for this driver */
    xce[l].upper = q ;
    xce[l].lower = x->lower ;
    xce[l].lcn   = l ;
    /* Fill in q_ptr on upper side to point to the
     * entry. Allows us to send data down without
     * looking up the route and LCN mapping each time */
    q->q_ptr = (char *)xce ;
  ...
 } /* end switch */
```

Figure 7.33: *Multiplexor upper write service procedure*

```
static int
x25uwsrv(q)
  queue_t *q ;
{
  mblk_t *mp ;
  queue_t *lower ;

  /* Find queue down to driver */
  lower = ((struct x25_channel_map *)(q->q_ptr))->lower ;
  while( (mp = getq(q)) != NULL ) {
    /* If room, send to lower side */
    if( canput( lower ) )
      putq(lower) ;
    else
      putbq( q, mp ) ;
  }
  return 0 ;
}
```

the subnetwork identifier held in the *CONNECT* request message to determine which driver (lower stream) to send the data to. The subnetwork identifier is looked up in the routing table, which yields the *queue* of the lower level driver. The message is then put on that queue for transmission to the driver.

The upper write *put* procedure also receives *M_DATA* messages, which are used to hold the data to be sent to the network. The *put* procedure simply places all *M_DATA* messages on the queue using *putq( )*.

The upper write *service* procedure is shown in Figure 7.33. It simply takes data from the queue and passes it onto the associated lower queue.

The lower write *service* procedure for the module takes the messages from its queue and passes them down to its driver. However, the lower write *service* procedure also has to implement flow-control across the multiplexor. In a non-multiplexing driver, when *getq( )* returns *NULL* the STREAMS scheduling mechanism schedules the *service* procedures of previous modules in the stream. This is called back-enabling. The lower write *service* procedure cannot back-enable any other module automatically because there are no modules above it.

When the queue empties, the lower write *service* module enables all the upper queues that pass data into this lower side, which means that all the upper write queues will be run and they will generate more data for the lower side. The code for the lower write *service* procedure is shown in Figure 7.34.

The routing through a multiplexor is complicated but Figure 7.35 shows how the data structures fit together. Note that although the example multiplexor shown is hypothetical, the principles it embodies appear in commercially available STREAMS implementations of X25 and other networking protocols.

Figure 7.34: *Multiplexor lower write service procedure*

```
static int
x25mux_lwsrv(q)
   queue_t *q ;
{
  x25_channel_map *xce ;
  mblk_t *mp ;
  int i ;
  /* Get messages from queue and pass them on */
  while( (mp = getq(q)) != NULL ) {
    if( canput(q->q_next) )
      putnext(q, mp) ;
    else {
      putbq(q, mp) ;
      return 0 ;
    }
  }
  /* At this point, getq returned NULL, so try
   * to generate trade from above */
  xce = (x25_channel_map *)q->q_ptr ;
  for( i = 0 ; i < LCN_PER_DRIVER ; i++ ) {
    /* Check that lcn is in use */
    if( xce->lcn != -1 )
      /* Schedule the queue that feeds me */
      qenable( xce->upper ) ;

    xce++ ; /* Point to next entry in table */
  }
  return 0 ;
}
```

7.5.5 Multiplexor read side

The multiplexor lower read side contains only a *put* procedure; it has no *service* procedure, which means that there is no flow-control in the upstream direction through this multiplexor. If the lower read *put* procedure cannot pass the data up to the upper side, it simply discards the packet. A real multiplexor normally implements some form of flow-control protocol. For example, when the upper queue starts to get full, it could send down a flow-control request message, asking the remote end to stop sending data.

It is difficult to design a lower read *service* procedure to use the STREAMS flow-control mechanism. When the lower read *service* procedure is reading its queue, it gets messages destined for many upper queues. Normally, when it detects that it cannot put a message on the next queue, a *service* procedure must put the

Figure 7.35: *Multiplexor routing data structures*

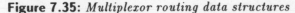

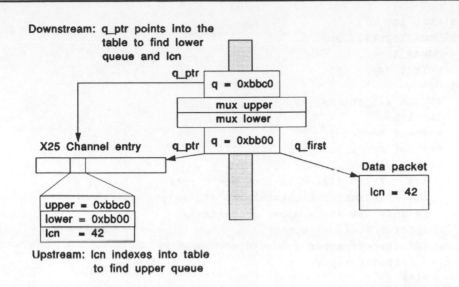

message back on its queue and then return. However, this option is not available in a multiplexor, because there may be other messages in the lower read queue destined for upper queues that are *not* blocked by flow-control. If the *service* procedure were to put the message back and then return, these messages would not be delivered during this queue run.

The solution in this case is to examine each message in the queue and then pass on those which are destined for upper queues if they are not blocked by flow-control. However, none of the real drivers researched for this book use this technique. Instead, they simply discard incoming packets.

The code for the multiplexor lower read *put* procedure is shown in Figure 7.36. It is similar to that of the *put* procedure described in § 7.3.2. The only difference is that the multiplexor code must look up the correct upper queue in its routing table.

This multiplexor has no upper read *put* procedure because it is not needed. Data passing along the read side is routed by the lower read side to the correct upper queue, but no further processing of the message is needed, so it can be passed directly to the next module above the multiplexor.

7.5.6 Multiplexor close

The multiplexor close routine has very little work to do. It simply has to clear the entry in the channel mapping table so that the lower side routines will know that the connection has been broken. The code for the close function is shown in Figure 7.37.

Figure 7.36: *Multiplexor lower read put procedure*

```
static int
x25mux_lrput(q, mp)
  queue_t *q ;
  mblk_t *mp ;
{
  struct x25_channel_map *xce ;
  int lcn ;
  queue_t *upper ;
  switch( mp->b_datap->db_type ) {
  case M_DATA:
    lcn = value filled in from mp->b_rptr ;
    xce = (struct x25_channel_map *)q->q_ptr ;
    /* Work out where upper queue is */
    upper = xce[lcn].upper ;
    if( canput( upper ) )
      putnext( upper ) ;
    else {
      freemsg(mp) ; /* Drop the packet */
      return 0 ;
    }
  case ... /* Process other message types */
  } /* end switch */
}
```

7.6 STREAMS utility functions

The STREAMS environment provides the many utility functions that support module, driver and multiplexor writers. They are very briefly summarized as follows:

- *adjmsg( )* — trims bytes from the front or back of a message.

- *allocb( )* — allocates a combined message and data block (*mblk_t*). The message block returned is of type *M_DATA*.

- *backq( )* — obtains a pointer to the previous queue in a stream.

- *bcanput( )* — tests for flow-control in a particular priority band.

- *bufcall( )* — calls a specified function (usually *timeout( )*) when buffers become available.

- *canput( )* — tests flow-control.

- *copyb( )* — allocates a message block and then copies data from one message block to the new block.

Figure 7.37: *Multiplexor close procedure*

```
static int
x25mux_close( q, flag, credp )
  queue_t *q ;
  int flag ;
  cred_t *cred ;
{
  struct x25_channel_map *xce ;
  xce = (x25_channel_map *)q->q_ptr ;
  xce->lcn = -1   ; /* LCN not in use */
  xce->upper = (queue_t *)0 ; /* No upper queue anymore */
  q->q_ptr = (char *)NULL ;
  WR(q)->q_ptr = (char *)NULL ;
  return 0 ;
}
```

- *copymsg()* — similar to *copyb()*, but follows the *b_cont* fields to copy the all components of the message.

- *datamsg()* — tests if a message is a data message — that is, *M_DATA*, *M_PROTO*, and so on.

- *dupb()* — duplicates the message header, so that two messages point to the same data block.

- *dupmsg()* — like *dupb()*, but operates on all message blocks in the message.

- *enableok()* — marks a queue as being ready to be *qenabled*.

- *esballoc()* — allocates a message header, pointing to a data block supplied by the caller.

- *flushband()* — removes all queued messages in a specified priority band.

- *flushq()* — removes (flushes) all messages from a queue.

- *freeb()* — frees a message block.

- *freemsg()* — frees all messages in a message block (via *freeb()*).

- *getadmin()* — finds the pointer to the *qi_qadmin()* function for a module.

- *getmid()* — looks up a module id.

- *getq()* — gets a message from a queue.

- *insq()* — inserts a message at a given point in a queue.

- *linkb()* — links a message to the *b_cont* pointer of another message.

- *msgdsize( )* — counts the number of bytes in *M_DATA* blocks attached to a message.
- *noenable( )* — stops a queue from being scheduled by the STREAMS scheduler.
- *OTHERQ( )* — macro returning the sibling of a given queue. Returns the read queue if given a write queue, and vice versa.
- *pullupmsg( )* — puts data from message into a single data block.
- *putbq( )* — puts a message back on a queue.
- *putctl( )* — puts a control message onto a given queue.
- *putctl1( )* — like *putctl( )*, but allocates a message with a 1 byte data block attached.
- *putnext( )* — passes a message to the next queue in a stream.
- *putq( )* — puts a message on a queue.
- *qenable( )* — enables a queue for scheduling.
- *qreply( )* — passes a message along a stream in the opposite direction.
- *qsize( )* — counts the number of messages on a queue. (But *not* the number of bytes in those messages.)
- *RD( )* — macro giving the read side of a given queue.
- *rmvb( )* — takes a message block out of a message.
- *rmvq( )* — takes a message out of a queue.
- *splstr( )* — sets processor interrupt level to a value suitable for protecting critical regions of STREAMS code.
- *strlog( )* — passes message to the STREAMS logging device.
- *strqget( )* — queries the information from the *queue* and *module_info* structures.
- *strqset( )* — sets the information held in the *queue* and *module_info* structures.
- *testb( )* — sees if a buffer of a given size is available for allocation.
- *unbufcall( )* — cancels an earlier *bufcall( )* request.
- *unlinkb( )* — removes the first message in a message block.
- *WR( )* — macro giving the write side of a given queue.

7.6.1 STREAMS memory allocation functions

The STREAMS environment uses two functions for memory allocation: *allocb( )* and *esballoc( )*. The declarations for these functions are shown in Figure 7.38.

Figure 7.38: *Declarations for allocb( ) and esballoc( )*

```
struct msgb *allocb( size, priority )
  int size ;
  unsigned int priority

struct msgb *esballoc( base, size, priority, freeinfo )
  unsigned char *base ;
  int size, priority ;
  frtn_t *freeinfo ;

/* Last parameter to esballoc() */
typedef struct free_rtn {
  void (*free_func)() ; /* Freeing function */
  char *free_arg;       /* Argument to give to free function*/
} frtn_t ;
```

allocb( ) is used by STREAMS drivers and modules to allocate memory for a combined message header and data block (*mblk_t*). The *size* parameter specifies the number of bytes needed; the *priority* parameter is not used but retained for compatibility with earlier versions of STREAMS. It used to indicate the priority of the allocation request — *BPRI_LO, BPRI_MED* and *BPRI_HI* (see § 7.7.2). If memory cannot be allocated, *allocb( )* returns a null pointer, otherwise it returns a pointer to a *msgb*, which has a message block type of *M_DATA*. The allocated *msgb* should be returned to the operating system with *freemsg( )* or *freeb( )*. If *allocb( )* returns *NULL*, the caller can request (via *bufcall( )* — see Figure 7.39) for a particular function to be called later when memory becomes available.

esballoc( ) performs similarly to *allocb( )*. That is, it allocates a message header and attaches a data buffer to it. The difference between them is that the parameter *base* is supplied by the programmer and is the address of the data buffer to attach to the message header. Again, the parameter *priority* is not used. The parameter *size* informs the STREAMS environment how big the user-supplied buffer is. The caller must fill in the structure pointed to by *freeinfo* with the name of the function that will free the buffer, and the arguments to give to the function when it is called. This information is stored in *frtnp* in the data block header (see § 7.2.1).

esballoc( ), at first sight, seems to be a redundant function. Why would a programmer want to supply his or her own buffer? One reason is that many I/O controller cards provide areas of memory that can be accessed by both the computer and the card itself. This type of memory is called *dual-ported* memory. It is often used to pass data between the I/O controller and the main processor. When a device driver wants to pass data into main memory, it normally allocates a memory buffer by using *allocb( )* and then copies the data from the card into the buffer. By using *esballoc( )* instead, the device driver need not copy the data from the dual-ported RAM since the message header points directly to the data held on the card.

A second reason is that a module or driver sometimes wants to know when the stream head has processed a message. The driver or module allocates a buffer, then uses *esballoc( )* to attach the buffer to a message header and to attach a function to the message that will be called when the message is freed. Some time later the message is freed, and the attached function is called, which informs the driver that the message has been processed. The kernel *socket* module (§ 7.14.2) uses this facility to be certain that out-of-band data has been passed to the process.

The functions *freeb( )* and *freemsg( )* deallocate STREAMS messages. Both functions take a single argument, *bp*, which is a pointer to the message to delete. *freeb( )* deallocates a single message. That is, it will not follow the *b_cont* pointer in the message. Any other messages are left intact, but possibly with nobody pointing to them. Conversely, *freemsg( )* traverses the *b_cont* pointer, freeing everything it finds. If these functions detect that the message block was allocated with *esballoc( )* they call the function pointed to by *frtnp* in the message block.

Figure 7.39: *Declaration of bufcall( )*

```
int bufcall( size, priority, function, argument )
  unsigned size ;
  int priority ;
  void (*function)() ;
  long argument ;
```

testb( ) has the same arguments as *allocb( )* and determines whether an *allocb( )* might be successful. It checks if there is enough memory for the allocation, but does not actually allocate memory. It returns non-zero if there is enough memory, zero otherwise. Unfortunately, a successful return from *testb( )* does not guarantee that a subsequent *allocb( )* will be successful because the free memory might be stolen at interrupt level by another part of the kernel. Like *allocb( )* the argument *priority* is not used, but is retained for backward compatibility. *bufcall( )* calls the specified function with its argument when a buffer of specific size becomes available. This is commonly used by a module processing routine to give itself a second chance at processing a message.

When a module needs a data buffer for storage, but *allocb( )* fails, it calls *bufcall( )*, passing its own function name and queue as arguments. Later, when a buffer becomes available, the module routine will be called again, so it gets another chance to process the data. An example of a read *service* procedure that does this is shown in Figure 7.40.

The information about the function to call is stored by the kernel in a stream event table. Each outstanding *bufcall( )* uses an entry in this table. If the table fills, *bufcall( )* will fail and the function will not be called when buffers become available.

The *unbufcall( )* function cancels a *bufcall( )* request. The argument to this function must be the address of the table entry allocated by the kernel to hold the *bufcall( )* information. A successful call to *bufcall( )* returns this address.

Figure 7.40: *Using bufcall( )*

```
int samplersrv(q)
    queue_t *q ;
{
  mblk_t *mp, newmp ;
  ...
  while( (mp=getq(q)) != (mblk_t *)0 ) {
    ...
    if( canput(q->q_next) ) {
      /* Get message header */
      newmp = allocb( HDRSIZE, BPRI_LO ) ;
      if( newmp == (mblk_t *)0 ) {
        /* put back the message we got.. */
        putbq( q, mp ) ;
        /* Call service procedure later ERROR CHECK OMITTED */
        bufcall( HDRSIZE, BPRI_LO, samplersrv, q ) ;
        return ; /* Give up for now, bufcall will re-call us */
      }
      fill in fields in newmp
      /* join the two, and pass them on */
      linkb( newmp, mp ) ;
      putnext( q, mp ) ;
    }
    ...
  }
  return ;
}
```

7.6.2 Queue manipulation functions

Figure 7.41 shows the declarations for the queue manipulation functions $getq( )$, $putq( )$, and $putbq( )$. These functions have been used widely in this chapter, so by now it should be clear how they are used.

There are two extra functions in Figure 7.41 that we have not seen before: $insq( )$ and $rmvq( )$. The first is used to insert a message at a specified place in the queue. This allows the programmer to place messages where needed on the queue. The function $rmvq( )$ does the opposite: it removes a message from the queue. One use of these functions is for discarding messages at the lower side of a multiplexor when the upper side (which they are queued for) is closed down.

Both functions update the flow-control variables associated with the queue. That is, when $rmvq( )$ is used to take a message out, the queue count (q_count) is reduced by the number of bytes in the message. Similarly, $insq( )$ adds bytes to the queued data count.

Figure 7.41: *Queue control functions*

```
mblk_t *getq(q) /* Retrieve message from front of queue */
  queue_t *q ;

int putq( q, bp ) /* Put message at back of queue */
  queue_t *q ;
  mblk_t *bp ;

int putbq( q, bp ) /* Put message at front of queue */
  queue_t *q ;
  mblk_t *bp ;

int insq( q, emp, mp ) /* Insert message at position in queue */
  queue_t *q ;
  mblk_t *emp, mp ;

int rmvq( q, mp ) /* Delete message from middle of queue */
  queue_t *q ;
  mblk_t *mp ;
```

Figure 7.42: *Flow-control function declarations*

```
int bcanput(q,band)   /* Test for flow-control */
  queue_t *q ;
  unsigned char band ;

int canput(q)         /* Test for flow-control */
  queue_t *q ;

void enableok(q)      /* Permit scheduling of queue */
  queue_t *q ;

void noenable(q)      /* Forbid scheduling of queue */
  queue_t *q ;

void qenable(q)       /* Schedule queue */
  queue_t *q ;
```

7.6.3 Flow-control functions

The flow-control functions are *canput( )*, *bcanput( )*, *enableok( )*, *noenable( )* and *qenable( )* (see Figure 7.42). Of these, *canput( )* has already been described.

bcanput( ) is similar to *canput( )* except that the second parameter specifies the priority band to test against. *noenable( )* prevents a queue from being run; even if it becomes empty, the STREAMS scheduler will not run the *service* procedure for the queue. *enableok( )* undoes the work of *noenable( )*. It tells the STREAMS scheduler that this queue is once more eligible to have its *service* procedure run. Finally, *qenable( )* is called to tell the STREAMS scheduler to run the queue. However, the *service* procedure of the queue is not run immediately — the queue is simply linked into the list of runnable queues. The *service* procedures for all queues are called from the kernel routine *runqueues( )*, which is called just before a system call returns to user-mode (see § 7.8.3).

7.7 STREAMS memory management

The STREAMS memory management implementation is surprisingly simple and elegant, which is in stark contrast to the memory management scheme for STREAMS under UNIX System V Release 3. It uses a single internal data type, the *mdbblock* structure (Table 7.22), to manage the message header, data block header and data buffers.

Table 7.22: *Struct mdbblock*

Name	Description		
struct mbinfo *msgblock	struct mbinfo		
	mblk_t *m_mblock void (*m_func)( )	Message header Function that allocated to the message header	
struct dbinfo *datblk	struct dbinfo		
	dblk_t *d_dblock	Data block part of the structure	
char databuf[FASTBUF]	Buffer for the data. *FASTBUF* is set so that the size of an *mdbblock* is 128 bytes		

7.7.1 allocb( ) and esballoc( )

The *allocb( )* function operates in two modes depending on the value of *size* (see Figure 7.38):

size < FASTBUF   — get an *mdbblock* from the freelist. The first element of the freelist is pointed to by the variable *mdbfreelist*. If there are no entries on the freelist, then one is allocated with *kmem_alloc( )*. The values in the message and data block header are set to point to the buffer attached to the *mdbblock*.

size > FASTBUF   — the same steps for getting a *mdbblock* are carried out. However, *kmem_alloc( )* is called a second time to allocate the data buffer. The pointers in the message and data block headers are adjusted to point to the buffer obtained from *kmem_alloc( )*.

In both cases, the function returns a null pointer if the call to *kmem_alloc( )* is unsuccessful.

When a message block is freed by *freeb( )* or *freemsg( )*, the data buffer is deallocated by calling *kmem_free( )* if necessary. The *mdbblock* is then placed onto the freelist pointed to by *mdbfreelist*.

The function *esballoc( )* works similarly: an *mdbblock* is allocated. However, instead of using an internal buffer, or allocating one from the operating system, the function sets up the data block pointers to point to a caller-supplied buffer. It also fills in the *frtnp* field in the data block to save the information about the deallocation function.

7.7.2 Comparison of old and new allocation schemes

The STREAMS memory allocator under UNIX System V Release 3 (also called *allocb( )*) used a table containing fixed quantities of fixed-sized buffers. Table 7.23 shows a typical STREAMS memory arrangement under UNIX System V Release 3. On that system, a request for a buffer of size *n* was satisfied by allocating a buffer of the next largest size. So, for example, a 72 byte request was fulfilled with a 128 byte buffer. All requests were given an allocation priority, which was either *BPRI_LO, BPRI_MED* or *BPRI_HI*. Usually, buffers with low priority were requested. Low priority requests failed when 80% of the buffers from a required class were allocated. Similarly, medium priority requests failed when 90% of the buffers from a required class were allocated. Finally, high priority requests failed when all the buffers from a required class were allocated. The thresholds (80% and 90%) for the buffer classes were given by the values of *strlofrac* and *strmedfrac*.

The size of each buffer class, the number of buffers in it, and the values of *strlofrac* and *strmedfrac* were configurable by the system administrator. However, they could not be changed without rebuilding the kernel. This allocation mechanism had the following disadvantages:

- Requests for a particular size of buffer were satisfied from the appropriate buffer size class, or the next size higher if there were none of the required sized buffers available. This meant that buffer allocations could fail, even if memory in the STREAMS buffer pool was available.

- Most STREAMS modules and drivers allocated buffers at low priority. If no buffers were available, the routine either called *bufcall( )* or returned an error. In practice, 20% of all STREAMS memory was wasted! (Since *strlofrac* had been reached, the remaining buffers in that memory class were available only for medium or high priority allocation requests.) System administrators could alter *strlofrac* and *strmedfrac*, but they rarely did.

Table 7.23: *STREAMS buffer pool under UNIX System V Release 3*

Buffer class and size	Number of Pools	Number in *BPRI_LO*	Extra in *BPRI_MED*	Extra in *BPRI_HI*
4 bytes	2048	1638	205	205
16 bytes	1024	820	102	102
64 bytes	1024	820	102	102
128 bytes	128	102	26	26
256 bytes	64	51	13	13
512 bytes	32	26	3	3
1024 bytes	20	16	2	2
2048 bytes	10	8	1	1
4096 bytes	10	8	1	1
Total bytes	221184			
strlofrac	80%			
strmedfrac	90%			

- It was time-consuming to tune the number of STREAMS buffers to the right values. The system administrator had to monitor the use of the STREAMS buffers and then tune them accordingly by trial and error. Each change was time-consuming, requiring a kernel rebuild and system reboot On many systems, STREAMS memory parameters remained set at their factory default settings, and so STREAMS did not run efficiently, and memory was wasted by being allocated to buffers that were not used.

- The allocation priority scheme was difficult to use and brought no benefit when STREAMS was running low on memory. If a low priority request failed, then making a medium or high priority request simply delayed the inevitable problem of dealing with failed calls to *allocb( )*. The difficulty of coding for this situation meant that it was rarely used.

The UNIX System V Release 3 STREAMS memory allocation scheme did have some good points:

- It was easy to implement. All the message headers for the various sized blocks were held in an array. Allocation and deallocation was easy, the allocator simply set a flag saying the item had been allocated.

- The allocation scheme protected the operating system from bugs in modules, and from drivers that made them lose STREAMS memory buffers. Buffers are usually allocated, passed along the stream and then freed. If a bug is encountered, a module or driver may lose its pointer to the buffer, which means that a buffer has been allocated by *allocb( )* but is never freed by *freeb( )*. In other words, the buffer is lost. The result is that after a while, calls to *allocb( )* fail, the requestor issues a *bufcall( )* and then waits for a buffer to become available. Unfortunately, it will wait forever, because by now all the buffers have been lost. However, only the STREAMS part of the kernel is hung. Other operating systems services will still function, so the system administrator has a chance to discover the problem and fix it.

The new STREAMS memory allocation scheme has several advantages over the old scheme:

- The memory resources applied to STREAMS are automatically tuned to the STREAMS memory load. If there is a lot of STREAMS activity going on, more memory is allocated to STREAMS. As the STREAMS memory load decreases, the amount of memory allocated to STREAMS reduces. Message and data block headers are never explicitly deallocated; they are put onto their freelist. Periodically the function *strgiveback* scans the freelists, returning a proportion of the headers to the operating system (see § 7.9.2).

- The priority allocation scheme has been abandoned; it was a design idea that looked good on paper, but did not work in practice.

- The new memory allocation scheme is less wasteful of memory; the unit of memory allocated is the same size as that requested, and not the next fixed size.

Under the new allocation scheme, the system has only limited protection against drivers or modules that lose buffers. As buffers are lost, more system memory is consumed in creating new ones. Eventually, all memory is used up and the system cannot do anything useful, which leads to a "hung" system. The only facility in STREAMS that limits the use of memory, occurs in the stream head. It checks a STREAMS memory high water mark. If too much memory is being used by STREAMS, user programs are not allowed to write any more data into a stream.

7.8 STREAMS scheduling and flow-control implementation

Flow-control and scheduling mechanisms are closely interrelated. They are also influenced by other parts of the kernel such as the memory management routines, and the system call mechanism. The following subsections describe how the variables and data structures for flow-control and scheduling are used, and how the individual procedures work together.

7.8.1 Flow-control variables

The flow-control mechanism uses the q_flag bitmask in the *queue* structure to hold state information. The flag values are described as follows (see also Table 7.24):

- $QENAB$ — set by *qenable( )* and cleared when the *service* procedure is run by *runqueues( )*.

- $QWANTR$ — set by *getq( )* when it tries to take a message from the queue but finds the queue empty, indicating that a *service* procedure wants to read from the queue. The flag is cleared when *getq( )* takes a message from the queue.

Table 7.24: *Values of q_flag in the queue structure*

Value	Description
QENAB	Queue has been enabled by *qenable( )*
QWANTR	A service procedure wants to *getq( )* from this queue
QWANTW	A service procedure has done *canput( )* for this queue and found that it is full
QFULL	The queue is full
QNOENB	Queue has been disabled by *noenable( )*

- QWANTW — set by *canput( )* when it detects that the queue being tested is above its high water mark. It indicates that a function is trying to put data into the queue. The flag is cleared when the quantity of data in the queue falls below the low water mark.

- QFULL — set when *putq( )* or *putbq( )* make the queued data count exceed the high water mark by putting a message on the queue. The flag is cleared when the data count falls below the high water mark.

- QNOENB — set by *noenable( )* and cleared by *enableok( )*.

Several variables are used by the scheduling and flow-control mechanisms. They fall into two categories, Boolean variables and list variables. The Boolean variables prevent the kernel from trying to do two things at the same time. The list variables link together items that are waiting for something to happen. Table 7.25 summarizes their function. The description of the Boolean variables explain what the variable means when it is set. When it is unset, it has the opposite meaning.

7.8.2 Flow-control procedures

There are seven procedures that a STREAMS module or driver uses to manage queue flow-control. Their operation is described as follows:

- *qenable( )* — performs the following tasks:

  - Checks whether the queue to be enabled has a *service* procedure; if not, it returns to the caller.

  - Checks the QNOENB bit in *q_flag*. If it is set, the queue cannot be enabled, so it returns to the caller.

  - Checks the QENAB bit in *q_flag*. If set, the queue has already been enabled, so it returns to the caller.

  - Sets the QENAB bit in *q_flag*.

  - Links the queue into the tail of the list of scheduled queues (*qtail*).

  - Sets *qrunflag* by calling the macro *setqsched( )*.

Table 7.25: *Flow-control variables*

Boolean variables	
Variable	**Description**
char qrunflag	There is at least 1 enabled queue
char queueflag	The function *queuerun( )* is running
char strbcflag	There is enough free memory, so the *bufcall( )* functions must be run
char strbcwait	Someone has called *bufcall( )*, but there is not yet enough free memory to let the function execute
List variables	
Variable	**Description**
*struct queue *qhead*	Pointer to first queue in list of scheduled queues
*struct queue *qtail*	Pointer to last queue in list of scheduled queues
struct bclist strbcalls	List of *bufcalls* pending execution
*struct queue *scanqhead*	Head of the STREAMS scan queue
*struct queue *scanqtail*	Tail of the STREAMS scan queue
*struct seinfo *sefreelist*	List of free stream events used for scheduling *bufcall( )* and *poll*
*struct seinfo *secachep*	Pointer to secret store of stream events for when times get hard and memory is low
struct strinfo Strinfo[]	Keeps track of allocated stream events

- *noenable( )*, *enableok( )* — these two functions simply set or clear the *QNOENB* bit in the queue flag.

- *getq( )* — the algorithm for *getq( )* is shown in Figure 7.43. It shows how the back-enable mechanism works. The term "back-enable" refers to the procedure of finding a previous queue that feeds data, to the current queue and then enabling it. A back-enable is done in two situations; when the current queue becomes empty, or if another module or driver found the queue full previously but now it has drained below its low water mark.

- *putq( )*, *putbq( )* — these two functions are similar, they both put a message at the "right place" in the queue. *putbq( )* (Figure 7.44) puts the message at the back of the queue, whereas *putq( )* puts it at the front. The "right place" in the queue depends on the message type and the message priority band. Given a priority message, *putq( )* puts it after the last priority message but before the ordinary messages in the queue. Similarly, *putbq( )* puts an ordinary message back into the queue after all the priority messages but before the ordinary messages. (The order of messages in a queue are shown in Figure 7.4.)

Note the circumstances in which the queue is enabled. When the queue receives its first message after being empty, it is enabled; this is a good policy because a *service* procedure generally passes on a batch of messages to the next queue. That queue is then enabled and runs after the current *service* procedure exits.

Figure 7.43: *Algorithm for getq( )*

```
getq( )
  inputs: queue — pointer to queue
  outputs: pointer to msgb
{
  if( first item on queue is NULL ) {
    want to read from this queue so mark it QWANTR
    set back-enable flag
  }
  else {
   if( count of bytes stored in queue is less than
       queue high water mark )
     /* Allow previous queues to give us data */
     clear QFULL flag in this item

   if( count of bytes stored in queue is less than
       or equal to queue low water mark ) {
     set back-enable flag
     clear QWANTR in this item and remove it from the queue
     set this item as last message on the queue
   }

   if( back-enable flag set and QWANTW is set ) {
     /* Someone wants to write to us, and we have the space */
     find a previous queue to back-enable and enable it
   }
  }
  return item on the queue ;
}
```

A queue is *always* enabled when a priority message is placed on to it so that it can be processed more quickly. However, a deadlock condition could occur if a module puts a priority message back on to its own queue. If the *service* procedure puts the priority message back on its queue because it cannot pass it along, the *service* procedure exits; but putting the priority message back on the queue makes it enabled again. The STREAMS scheduler finds this queue in its run-queue list, so it calls the *service* procedure again. The *service* procedure gets the same message, but since the conditions have not changed the message is put back. This cycle continues indefinitely, giving the appearance that the system is hung. This problem does not occur when normal priority messages are put back.

- *bufcall( )* — called when a module or driver needs memory, but the call to *allocb( )* fails, indicating there is none. It allocates a *strevent* structure (Appendix D) and stores in it: the size of the request, the function to call, and the argument

Figure 7.44: *Algorithm for putq( ) and putbq( )*

```
putq( )/putbq( )
  inputs: queue — pointer to queue
          bp — msgb to put on the queue
  outputs: none
{
  /* The only difference between putq and putbq
   * is how they find the correct place in the queue
   */
  find correct place in queue for bp
  insert bp at this point
  recalculate q_count
  if( q_count > queue high water mark )
    /* means that canput will fail on this queue */
    set QFULL flag

  if( bp is a priority message )
    /* Enable queue for priority message regardless of
     * whether noenable has been called previously */
    enable this queue

  if( QNOENB clear AND QWANTR is set )
    /* Someone wants to read this queue, and we have
     * just put some data in it, so schedule it.. */
    enable this queue
}
```

to pass to the function. The *strevent* structure is then linked into the list pointed to by *strbcalls* (see Table 7.25). The flag *strbcwait* is then set to tell *kmem_free( )* that someone is waiting for memory. When *kmem_free( )* sees this, it in turn, sets *qrunflag* which tells the kernel to call *runqueues( )* as soon as possible. *runqueues( )* processes the *bufcall( )* list.

7.8.3 The STREAMS scheduler

The *runqueues( )* and *queuerun( )* functions form the STREAMS scheduler. They are described together because *runqueues( )* is the only function that calls *queuerun( )*.

runqueues( ) is called by the functions: *strread( )*, *strwrite( )*, *strioctl( )*, and *strgetmsg( )*. These are the kernel system call handlers for STREAMS. They call *runqueues( )* so that the data they generate is processed as soon as possible, and before a context switch is made. *runqueues( )* is also called after a context switch, but before returning to user-mode. (The points at which *runqueues( )* is called were chosen to ensure that the STREAMS environment is processed as fully as possible before returning to user-mode.)

Both the *runqueues()* and *queuerun()* functions traverse the list of enabled queues and call their *service* procedures. *runqueues()* checks if there are any enabled queues and if there are, it calls *queuerun()* to process them. *queuerun()* (see Figure 7.45) performs three distinct tasks:

- It checks the stream-head scan queue list (*scanqhead*), and processes any messages found there.

- It processes the *bufcall()* list; *strevents* are removed from the list one by one and their event handling procedures are called to deal with the event. The number of cells in the list is counted. Only this number of events is processed in a single pass to stop it from looping indefinitely when memory is low. (The event handling procedure called by *bufcall()* might issue another *bufcall()*, adding another event to the end of the list and so on.) Only functions that are likely to get memory are triggered. So before scanning the list, *kmem_avail()* is called to calculate the amount of free memory, and *all* functions requesting less than this amount are called; they each must fight for whatever is left.

- The list of scheduled queues is scanned, and the *service* procedure of each scheduled queue is called.

Note that the *bufcall()* list is processed before the enabled queues list. In fact, *bufcall()* is typically called from a *service* procedure like this:

```
bufcall( size, BPRI_LO, qenable, q)
```

In this case, *qenable()* is called as part of the *bufcall()* processing, and the *service* procedure for the enabled queue is called shortly after as part of the *service* procedure processing.

7.9 Operation of the stream head

The stream head forms the bridge between the system calls that communicate with the stream such as *read, write* and *ioctl,* and the internal STREAMS environment. The stream head consists of a set of data structures and functions that work together to do the necessary processing to pass messages into and out of the STREAMS environment. The operation of the stream head is described in a top-down fashion; first, we describe the data structures and variables, followed by a description of the high level routines such as *strread()* and *strwrite()* which perform I/O between user address space and the STREAMS environment operating in kernel address space. Finally we describe the functions that support these routines.

7.9.1 Stream head data structures

When a STREAMS device is opened for the first time, a stream head is dynamically allocated for it. Subsequent opens on that stream reference the same stream head.

Figure 7.45: *Algorithm for queuerun( )*

```
void queuerun( )
inputs: none
outputs: none
{
 /* Process scan queue head list */
 for all stream heads in scanqhead list {
   unlink first item
   if queue has message waiting
     pass message along
 }

tryagain:   /* Process bufcall events list and queues */
   if (kernel memory subsystem indicates there is enough
     - memory to run some bufcall routines) {

     for each bufcall event on the list {
       if( there is enough memory for it to run ) {
         remove the bufcall item from the list
         call event handling procedure /* deal with event */
         free up space associated with used item
       }
       else size of memory wanted is too big so
         put event to the back of the list
     }

   } /* end if */

   if ( still have events on bufcall list )
       indicate to the kernel memory subsystem that we still
       - have bufcall events waiting

   /* Now process scheduled queues */
   for each scheduled queue on the qhead list {
     clear QENAB flag
     call its service procedure /* if any */
     remove it from the list
   }

   if (the kernel memory subsystem indicates there is newly
     - available memory)
       goto tryagain ;
}
```

Thus the same stream head is made to associate with each process that opens the stream. The stream is pointed to by the *snode* associated with the device's special file (see § 6.9.1).

Table 7.26: *Struct stdata (stdata_t): the stream head*

Element	Description
*queue_t *sd_wrq*	Write queue for the stream head
*mblk_t *sd_iocblk*	Message to return for *ioctl*
*struct vnode *sd_vnode*	Back pointer to *vnode*
*struct streamtab *sd_strtab*	Stream head processing functions
long sd_flag	State of the stream head (see below)
long sd_iocid	Sequence identifier of active *ioctl*
ushort sd_iocwait	Number of processes awaiting *ioctl*
*struct pid *sd_sidp*	Controlling session identifier
*struct pid *sd_pgidp*	Controlling process group
ushort sd_wroff	Write offset
int sd_rerror	Read error code
int sd_werror	Write error code
int sd_pushcnt	Number of modules pushed in stream
int sd_sigflags	Signal flags
*struct strevent *sd_siglist*	List of processes to receive *SIGPOLL*
struct pollhead sd_pollist	List of poll wakeup functions
*mblk_t *sd_mark*	Pointer to marked message
int sd_closetime	Time to wait to let queue drain when closing
clock_t sd_rtime	Time to forward held message
Flags (*sd_flag*)	**Description**
IOCWAIT	*ioctl* in progress
RSLEEP	Process sleeping, waiting to read data
WSLEEP	Process sleeping, waiting to write data
STRPRI	Priority message waiting at stream head
STRHUP	Stream is hung up
STWOPEN	Stream head *open* in progress
STPLEX	Stream is part of a multiplexor
STRISTTY	Stream is a terminal
STRDERR	*M_ERROR* for read received by stream head
STWRERR	*M_ERROR* for write received by stream head
STRCLOSE	Stream is waiting for *strclose* to complete
SNDMREAD	Send *M_READ* message when a *read* is issued
STRHOLD	Coalesce written messages

The stream head is described by the *stdata* structure (Table 7.26). The fields of this structure are summarized as follows:

- *sd_wrq* — points to the stream head write queue. Although the stream head has a write queue, it does not queue messages in it or process them with its *service* procedure. Instead, the write queue is used to hold messages that are being compacted by the stream-head buffering mechanism. The operation of this buffering feature is described in § 7.9.8.

- *sd_iocblk* — points to a message block used by the STREAMS *ioctl* processing code to hold the result of the *ioctl* before it is passed to the user (see § 7.9.7).

- *sd_vnode* — points back to the *vnode* for the stream.

- *sd_strtab* — points to the *streamtab* for the stream head. The stream head itself has read and write queues and *put* and *service* procedures that work in much the same way as those of a module or driver.

- *sd_flag* — the stream head state flag bitmask. It holds information about the state of the stream head (see Table 7.26).

- *sd_iocid* — holds the current *ioctl* identifier. Only one *ioctl* is ever active on a stream at any one time, and each *ioctl* is given a unique identifier so that the stream head can tell if *ioctl* reply messages arriving at the stream head actually relate to the currently outstanding *ioctl*.

- *sd_siglist* — contains a pointer to a linked list of processes that must be sent a *SIGPOLL* signal when a particular stream head event has occurred.

- *sd_pollist* — is a *pollhead* structure containing a pointer to a linked list of poll wakeup triggering functions associated with processes that issued a *poll* system call against the stream head (see the description of *poll* in § 7.9.9).

7.9.2 Limiting STREAMS memory

When data is copied from user space to kernel space, the stream head uses *allocb( )* to allocate a message block and buffer to hold the data. Under UNIX System V Release 4 there is nothing to prevent *allocb( )* from using up all kernel memory. However, the stream head functions that copy data from processes in user-mode into the STREAMS environment make some attempt to limit memory use.

A variable called *Strcount* holds the total amount of memory that has been dynamically allocated by STREAMS, and the variable *strthresh* is used as the limiting value for STREAMS dynamic memory allocation. *strthresh* is a configurable variable defined in the *master.d/sad/space.c* file ("sad" refers to the Streams Administrative Driver — see **sad(7)**). A *strthresh* value of zero gives STREAMS no memory limit.

Each STREAMS system call handler that copies data into STREAMS from user space (*strwrite( )*, *strputmsg( )*, *strioctl( )*) checks that *Strcount* is less than *strthresh*. If it is greater, the system call fails with the error *ENOSR*, meaning "no more STREAMS resources". If *strthresh* is set to zero, or super-user is issuing the call, this check is not performed.

STREAMS messages are allocated by *allocb( )*, which in turn uses *kmem_alloc( )* to allocate memory for the message header and the message data. When the message is freed, the message data is deallocated by *kmem_free( )*, but the message header is placed on the freelist. This can be wasteful if STREAMS memory use is decreasing; a portion of the system memory is locked up, providing message headers that are stuck on the freelist.

The function *strgiveback( )* is called once a second (via a *timeout( )*). Its purpose is to give message headers back to the operating system when the STREAMS memory load is decreasing. Internally, the function keeps a count of the average number of message headers in use. Every time the function is called, it recalculates the average based on the previous average and the number of blocks in use. If this number is less than the average, *strgiveback( )* removes 12.5% of the message headers from the freelist and returns them to the operating system with *kmem_free( )*.

The effect is that when the number of message blocks is rising, *strgiveback( )* does nothing. But when it is falling, *strgiveback( )* returns memory to the operating system.

7.9.3 Opening a stream

When a process issues an *open* system call on a character special file, the kernel determines (from its *cdevsw[]* entry associated with the special file's major number) whether to pass control to a STREAMS device driver or an ordinary device driver. Thus, a process does not consciously open a stream. A process issues an *open* system call like this:

$$fd = open("/dev/x25", O\_RDWR) ;$$

The pathname given in the *open* is looked up in the file system with the file system dependent *vnode* lookup operation *VOP_LOOKUP( )* (see § 6.8). In this case, the lookup sees that */dev/x25* is a character special file and so it returns a *shadow-special-vnode* (*snode*). The file system dependent *vnode* open operation (*VOP_OPEN( )*) is then called. Since the *vnode* is associated with an *snode* because it is a device special file, the function *spec_open( )* is called, which looks up the major device number in *cdevsw[]* (see § 6.9.1). If the *cdevsw[]* entry has the *d_str* field set, *stropen( )* is called to set up the stream. (The processing of STREAMS clone devices is described in the next section.)

- *stropen( )* — is called with four arguments: a pointer to a *vnode* to represent the device, a variable holding a pointer to the major and minor device numbers, a flags argument, and a pointer to a credentials structure associated with the process. *stropen( )* (Figure 7.46) takes one of the following two paths:

    vp->v_stream != 0 — means that another process has already opened this device and created the stream. Thus, the *vnode* already points to this stream. If the stream head *STWOPEN* flag is set (indicating that another open is in progress), *stropen( )* sleeps on the stream head. After waking up, the *open* functions for all the modules in the stream are called. (This means that the *open* function of a module is called each time the stream is opened.) After this, any process that is sleeping while waiting for the open to complete is awoken.

vp->v_stream == 0 — in this case, it is the first open of the stream. A memory check is carried out to make sure that STREAMS is not using too much memory (described in the previous section). A queue pair and a stream head are then allocated; the stream head (*stdata_t*) is initialized and the *STWOPEN* flag is set; *vp->v_stream* is then set to point to it. The *q_ptr* fields in the queue pair are also set to point to the stream head.

If the *vnode* is really a FIFO, the stream head *streamtab* pointer (*sd_strtab*) is altered to point to the FIFO *streamtab* structure, which means that different stream head processing routines are executed (see § 7.10).

The stream head queues are attached to the driver with *qattach()*, and the driver *open* routine is called.

Any configured modules that need to be automatically pushed into the stream are pushed; STREAMS provides a module autopush facility allowing the administrator to configure a list of modules to be automatically pushed onto a stream when it is first opened. This is done with a utility called **autopush**, which interfaces with the STREAMS subsystem through the **sad** driver using specific *ioctl* commands. Each successful *ioctl* configures an automatic module push for a specific device (see **autopush(1M)** and **sad(7)**).

Finally, the *STWOPEN* flag is cleared, and processes sleeping on the stream head are awoken.

7.9.4 Opening a clone device

A STREAMS clone device, as we have already said, automatically generates its minor device number each time the device is opened. Clones are implemented via a STREAMS device driver called the *clone device driver*, together with special coding in *spec_open()* (see also **clone(7)**). A special file that represents a cloned device has the same major number as the STREAMS clone driver but its minor number is used to select its real driver. For example, assuming the STREAMS clone major number is 3, and the major number for the X25 clone device is 42, then */dev/x25* is created with major number 3 and minor number 42.

The sequence of events to open a clone device is as follows:

- The same steps are taken as for a normal open: the function *spec_open()* is called which in turn calls *stropen()*.

- *stropen()* creates a stream and calls the device's open procedure. In this case, *clnopen()* is called because a clone device is being opened.

- Within *clnopen()*, the minor device number is used to index into *cdevsw[]*, which yields a pointer to the *streamtab* structure for the real driver.

  The queue pair for this stream currently point to the clone device open procedure. These are changed so that they point to the open procedure of the real device instead.

  The open procedure for the real driver is called with the *CLONEOPEN* flag set, telling the driver to select a replacement minor device number which is eventually returned to the process in user-mode.

Figure 7.46: *Algorithm for stropen( )*

```
stropen( )
  inputs: vp — pointer to vnode
          devp — pointer to expanded device number structure
          flags — open system call modes set by user
          vp — pointer to credentials for the process
  outputs: error status
{
  queue_t *q ;

  /*
   * See if stream was created by previous
   * open of this device
   */
  if( stream head pointer in the vnode is not NULL ) {
    go to sleep if stream_head is busy
    call open function for all modules in the stream
    wake up all processes that are sleeping on the stream head
    return
  }

  /* First open of this stream */
  allocate and initialize a queue pair and stream head

  /* set stream head processing function */
  if( vnode is a FIFO )
    function is set to FIFO operation
  else
    function is set to streamtab for this driver from cdevsw[]

  attach stream head queue to streams driver
  for each module to autopush
      push the module and call its open routine

  wake up all processes that are sleeping on the stream head
  return
}
```

- On return to *spec_open( )*, if it finds that a clone open had occurred a new *snode* is created to associate the stream with the process. Its *vnode* pointers are set to point to the new stream head, and the stream head pointers are adjusted to point back to the *vnode* in the *snode*. Finally, the *v_stream* pointer in the original *vnode* (the one associated with the clone device) is set to zero, indicating that no stream is attached to it. This leaves the clone device looking like it had never been opened, and so the next open of the clone device will force it to create a new stream.

7.9.5 Writing to a stream

A process writes data into a stream with the *write* system call. For example, when the process issues this system call:

```
count = write( fd, buf, nbytes ) ;
```

the kernel looks up the file's associated *vnode* and the file system dependent *vnode* write operation is called (*VOP_WRITE( )*). Since all devices are represented by an *snode*, the *spec_write( )* procedure is called. This in turn calls *strwrite( )* (see Figure 7.47).

Using the minimum and maximum packet size constraints, *strwrite( )* attempts to allocate STREAMS message buffers and copy the data from user space into the allocated message buffer. The message buffers are then passed to the *put* procedure of the next module downstream.

strwrite( ) sleeps when the downstream modules are blocked by flow-control, when STREAMS uses too much memory, or when *allocb( )* fails to allocate space for the data.

A message hold feature is provided that improves the performance of STREAMS when the process issues many small writes. The message hold feature is enabled if the system administrator has changed the variable *strhold* to be non-zero, and if the stream head flag *STRHOLD* is set by a module. (The *ldterm* tty line discipline module does this.)

The message hold feature exploits the fact that *allocb( )* allocates a buffer with a data size that is always equal to or greater than *FASTBUF*. The buffer is allocated, and the data copied into it. *strwrite( )* then checks to see if another write of the same size can be fitted into the same buffer. If it can, the buffer is held temporarily on the stream head write queue, a timeout is started (usually 10ms), and the stream head is linked into the *scanqhead* list. One of three things will then happen:

- A second write occurs with a data portion that is small enough to fit into the remaining portion of the saved buffer. The data is put into the buffer and sent downstream. Since two writes have been sent downstream in one message, the optimization is successful.

- A second write occurs with a data portion that is too big to fit into the remaining portion of the saved buffer. The saved message is sent downstream followed by another message holding the data of the second write.

- No second write occurs so the timeout expires. The timeout processing performed by *queuerun( )* scans the *scanqhead* list and sends downstream any messages held on the stream head write queues whose timeouts have expired.

Figure 7.47: *Algorithm for strwrite()*

```
strwrite()
inputs: vp — pointer to vnode
        uiop  user I/O pointer
        crp — pointer to credentials structure
{
  do { /* until all data has been written */
    go to sleep if downstream is blocked by flow-control

    /* deal with messages on the write queue first */
    if( enough space in message for a write ) {
        copy data from user space into message
        return if enough space in message for another write
        /* In the hope of further buffering */
    }

    else { /* deal with held messages */
      get data from user space into a newly allocated message

      /* deal with held messages */
      if( message hold feature is on and STRHOLD flag is set ) {
        if(enough space in message for another write )
          link stream_head onto scanqhead and start timeout
        return  /* In the hope of further buffering */
      }
    }
    unlink held message from queue

    /* now send message down stream */
    pass message to put procedure of next queue

  } while( there is data to be written ) ;
}
```

7.9.6 Reading from a stream

The function *strread()* is the system call handler for *read* when applied to a stream. It, in turn relies on the stream head read *put* procedure called *strrput()*.

In the following discussion we use the term *relevant processes*. It refers to processes that have issued a *read*, *write*, *poll* or *ioctl* system call on the stream, or have issued the *I_SETSIG ioctl* in order to receive a *SIGPOLL* signal when certain events occur. There are many points at which *strrput()* must wake up these processes, or send them a *SIGPOLL* signal. This operation is described as: "the relevant processes are woken up or signalled." See also § 7.9.9 "Polling a stream", and § 7.9.7 "Stream *ioctl*" for explanations of how streams are polled and how processes can elect to receive the *SIGPOLL* signal.

strrput( ) handles all message types and their processing is described as follows:

- *M_DATA, M_PROTO, M_PCPROTO, M_PASSFP* — after checking the message type, the message is placed on the stream head read queue. If the message is an *M_PCPROTO* the *STRPRI* flag is set in the stream head, indicating the presence of an *M_PCPROTO* message. If this bit is already set, indicating that an *M_PCPROTO* message is already present, the new message is discarded. The relevant processes are then woken up or signalled. The pseudo code for the part of *strrput( )* that handles these messages is given in Figure 7.48.

- *M_ERROR* — when this message type is received, the first byte of the message is put into the stream head (*sd_rerror*) and the *STRDERR* flag is set. The second byte is placed in *sd_werror* and the *STWRERR* flag is set. If the error code in the message has the special value *NOERROR* the corresponding error flag is not set. However, if the error flag is set, a read or write will fail, and the value returned to the process in *errno* is taken from *sd_rerror* or *sd_werror*. The error condition prevents all further reads and writes to the stream until it is closed, or the stream head receives a *NOERROR* code in an *M_ERROR* message. The relevant processes are then awoken or signalled. Finally, an *M_FLUSH* message is sent downstream to discard all data queued in the stream.

- *M_HANGUP* — if this message is received, the stream head is marked *hung up*. Any subsequent reads from the stream will return zero, any writes will fail with the *EIO* error code. As with the other message types, the relevant processes are awoken or signalled.

- *M_SIG, M_PCSIG* — these messages send signals to a process group. The first byte of the message contains the number of the signal to send. For an *M_PCSIG* message the signal is sent immediately. For an *M_SIG* message it is placed on the read queue and the signal is sent when the message is read from the queue by *strread( )*. If the signal is *SIGPOLL* it will be sent only to processes that requested it with the *I_SETSIG ioctl*. Other signals are sent to a process only if the stream is associated with the control terminal (see § 7.11.2).

- *M_FLUSH* — when this message is received, all data queued in the stream is flushed.

- *M_IOCACK, M_IOCNAK, M_COPYIN, M_COPYOUT* — are not meaningful at the stream head unless an *ioctl* has been issued.

  If the message type is *M_IOCACK* or *M_IOCNAK*, it is discarded if: an *ioctl* on the stream is already in progress, a return message (an error) is pending for the caller, or the *ioctl* message is out of sequence (see *strdoioctl( )* in the next section). The same qualifying procedure is applied to *M_COPYIN* and *M_COPYOUT* messages except that they are not discarded; instead, they are converted to *M_IOCDATA* messages (they hold the stream head response to the *M_COPYIN* or *M_COPYOUT* request) and are sent back downstream with the error code set to 1, indicating failure of the request. Otherwise, the message is placed in the stream head (*sd_iocblk*) and the process that issued the *ioctl* is awoken.

- **M_SETOPTS** — contains a *stroptions* structure (Table 7.27) used to alter stream head characteristics such as the maximum and minimum packet sizes and so on. The format and use of this message type is described in Appendix B of [AT&T 1990d].

Table 7.27: *Struct stroptions*

Element	Description
ulong so_flags	Options to set (see below)
short so_readopt	Read option
ushort so_wroff	Write offset
long so_minpsz	Minimum read packet size
long so_maxpsz	Maximum read packet size
ulong so_hiwat	Read queue high water mark
ulong so_lowat	Read queue low water mark
uchar_t so_band	Band for water marks
Flags (*so_flags*)	**Description**
SO_ALL	Set all options
SO_READOPT	Set mode for *read* system call
SO_WROFF	Set write offset into *write* system call data
SO_MINPSZ	Set minimum stream head queue packet size
SO_MAXPSZ	Set maximum stream head queue packet size
SO_HIWAT	Set flow-control high water mark
SO_LOWAT	Set flow-control low water mark
SO_MREADON	Generate *M_READ* messages in *read*
SO_MREADOFF	Disable *SO_MREADON*
SO_NDELON	Set non-STREAMS semantics for NDELAY reads/writes
SO_NDELOFF	Set STREAMS semantics for NDELAY reads/writes
SO_ISTTY	Tell the stream it is acting as a terminal
SO_ISNTTY	Tell the stream it is not acting as a terminal
SO_TOSTOP	Stop on background writes to the stream
SO_TONSTOP	Do not stop on background writes to the stream
SO_BAND	Set water marks in a priority band
SO_DELIM	Messages are delimited
SO_NODELIM	Turn off delimiters
SO_STRHOLD	Enable *strwrite* message coalescing

- **M_IOCTL** — It does not make sense to receive one of these messages at the stream head, so rather than quietly discarding it, a response is generated by converting it into an *M_IOCNAK* message, which is then sent back up the stream.

Other types of STREAMS messages received at the stream head by *strrput( )* are silently discarded. (The function *freemsg( )* is called to deallocate the message.)

Figure 7.48: *Part of algorithm for strrput( )*

```
...
switch( message type )
case: M_PROTO or M_PCPROTO or M_DATA or M_PASSFP
  if (M_PCPROTO AND STRPRI is set in stream head) {
     freemsg /* already have 1 M_PCPROTO in the queue */
     return
  }
  if (RSLEEP bit set in stream head flags) {
     /* Someone is sleeping in read, waiting for data */
     wakeup stream head write queue
  }
  put message onto queue
  if( M_PCPROTO message ) {
    if( S_HIPRI bit set in stream_head->sd_sigflags )
       send SIGPOLL to all processes on sd_siglist
    if( POLLPRI set in ph_events in stream head )
       wakeup processes on sd_pollist
  } else if( this message is first on queue ) {
    if( S_INPUT bit set in stream_head->sd_sigflags )
       send SIGPOLL to all processes on sd_siglist
    if( POLLIN set in ph_events in stream head )
       wakeup processes on sd_pollist
  }
  return
... handle other message types
```

The algorithm for *strread( )* is shown in Figure 7.49. It waits for data to arrive in the stream head read queue and as the data arrives, it is copied into user space. This continues until the read count has been satisfied. Receipt of a zero length message makes the *read* terminate prematurely and the number of characters returned will be less than that asked for in the *read* system call. The following stream head read options alter the way *strread( )* works. They can be set by using the *I_SRDOPT ioctl* command (see *streamio(7)*):

- *RNORM* — the default mode. This is the normal byte-stream mode were message boundaries are ignored; *strread( )* returns data until the read count has been satisfied or a zero length message is received.

- *RMSGN* — the *read* will return when either the count is satisfied, a zero length message is received, or a message boundary is encountered. If there is any data left in a message after the read count has been satisfied, the message is placed back on the read queue. The data will be read on a subsequent *read* call.

Figure 7.49: *Algorithm for strread( )*

```
strread( )
inputs: vnode pointer
        user I/O pointer
        credentials structure
outputs: error code
{

  for( ;; ) {    /* forever */

    while( no data at the stream head queue ) {
      send M_READ message downstream if necessary
      go to sleep until message arrives on write queue
    }

    /* We now have a message */
    if( message type is M_DATA ) {
      return if zero length message
      copy data from message to user space
      free parts of message that have been copied
      if( message discard mode )
        free remainder of message
      else
        put remainder of message back on queue

      if( I/O count satisfied )
        return
    }

    if( message type is M_PROTO ) {
      if( protocol message is being read as data ) {
        convert message to M_DATA
        put back on queue
        continue
      }
      free the message
      return EBADMSG error code
    }
    ...
  } /* end for loop */

}
```

- *RMSGD* — similar to *RMSGN* but data that remains in a message after the read count has been satisfied is discarded.

Normally, a *read* from a stream will only work correctly with *M_DATA* messages. However, the following modifiers may be ORed with the above options to change the way control messages are interpreted by the stream head:

- *RPROTNORM* — *M_PROTO* messages make *read* return with the *EBADMSG* error code (default).

- *RPROTDAT* — *M_PROTO* messages are converted to *M_DATA* messages, which means they are read correctly.

- *RPROTDIS* — *M_PROTO* messages are discarded.

7.9.7 Stream *ioctl*

ioctl requests issued on a stream are handled by the functions *strioctl( )* and *strdoioctl( )*. As with *read* and *write*, the process issues an *ioctl* against an open file descriptor that is associated with a stream, for example:

```
result = ioctl(fd, I_STR, &striocbuf ) ;
```

The processing steps are the same as for the other system calls; the file system dependent *vnode* ioctl operation is called (*VOP_IOCTL( )*), and in this case it is *spcc_ioctl( )*, which in turn detects that the file descriptor refers to a stream, and so calls *strioctl( )*.

There are 29 different *ioctl* requests understood by *strioctl( )*; they are documented in *streamio(7)* and summarized in Table 7.28.

strioctl( ) consists of a large *switch* statement that directs processing according to a user specified *ioctl* command. Many of the commands are handled by the function *strdoioctl( )* described shortly. The algorithms described below are for the shaded items shown in Table 7.28:

- *termio(7) ioctls* — the group of terminal control *ioctls* described in *termio(7)* are all recognised by *strioctl( )*. The command is encapsulated in a *strioctl* structure before being passed down the stream so that when a user program issues the following:

```
result = ioctl( fd, TCSETAW, &termiostruct ) ;
```

the encapsulation makes it look as if the user issued the following STREAMS *ioctl* instead:

```
strioc.ic_cmd = TCSETAW;
strioc.ic_dp = &termiostruct;
...
result = ioctl( fd, I_STR, &strioc );
```

The *strioctl* structure is then passed to *strdoioctl( )* for further processing.

Table 7.28: *STREAMS ioctls*

Name	Description
I_PUSH	Push a module into the stream
I_POP	Pop a module from a stream
I_SETSIG	Receive a *SIGPOLL* signal when particular events occur
I_FDINSERT	Pass in information about a stream
I_STR	Generic STREAMS module *ioctl*
I_SENDFD	Send file descriptor down a stream
I_LINK	Create a multiplexor
I_PLINK	Create persistent link
I_LOOK	Get name of module below stream head
I_FLUSH	Flush messages from the stream
I_FLUSHBAND	Flush a particular message band
I_GETSIG	Show events that will generate a *SIGPOLL*
I_FIND	Say if a particular module is present in a stream
I_PEEK	Read first message from stream without consuming it
I_SRDOPT	Set read mode
I_GRDOPT	Get read mode
I_NREAD	Count data bytes in the stream head queue
I_SWROPT	Set the write mode
I_GWROPT	Get the write mode
I_RECVFD	Retrieve file descriptor sent by *I_SENDFD*
I_LIST	List all modules in a stream
I_ATMARK	See if stream head message has been marked
I_CKBAND	Check if message of a particular band is at the stream head
I_GETBAND	Get priority band of first message at stream head
I_CANPUT	Check if a given band is writable
I_SETCLTIME	Set the time that STREAMS will wait whilst closing a stream
I_GETCLTIME	Get the STREAMS close time
I_UNLINK	Dismantle a multiplexor
I_PUNLINK	Disconnect persistent link

- I_PUSH — The pseudo code for this *ioctl* command is given in Figure 7.50. the STREAMS memory limit and the number of pushed modules are checked. If either is exceeded, the call fails. The module name is looked up in the module switch table (*fmodsw[]*). If it is found, the function waits until any open in progress completes. The *STWOPEN* flag is then set in the stream head to force any other opens of this stream to wait. The module is then linked into the stream with *qattach()*, and the module's *open* procedure is called. Finally, the *STWOPEN* flag is cleared, and any processes sleeping on the stream head are awoken.

- I_POP — calls *qdetach()*, which calls the module close procedure, and removes the module from the stream.

Figure 7.50: *Processing I_PUSH*

```
/* part of strioctl */
case I_PUSH:
 check STREAMS memory and number of pushed modules
 return if error

 if( module name is NOT in fmodsw )
   return error EINVAL
 while( STWOPEN flag set in stream head )
   sleep (stream head) ;
 set stream head STWOPEN flag /* Forces others to sleep */
 call qattach to link in module and call open procedure
 if ( STRISTTY  flag set in stream head )
   make this stream control terminal
 clear STWOPEN flag in stream head
 wakeprocs( stream head )
 return
```

Table 7.29: *Events causing SIGPOLL*

Event	Description
S_INPUT	Any message *except M_PCPROTO* received
S_RDNORM	Ordinary message (ie non priority) received
S_RDBAND	Expedited message (band > 0) received
S_HIPRI	Priority message received
S_OUTPUT	There is space to write another message
S_WRNORM	Same as S_OUTPUT
S_WRBAND	There is space to write an expedited message
S_MSG	An M_SIG message containing SIGPOLL received
S_ERROR	An M_ERROR message received
S_HANGUP	An M_HANGUP message received
S_BANDURG	Send SIGURG instead of SIGPOLL if S_RDBAND is set and a priority message reaches the stream head

- *I_SETSIG* — when the process issues the *I_SETSIG ioctl*, it means that it wishes to be sent a *SIGPOLL* signal whenever certain events occur. The events are specified as bits in the argument to the *ioctl* and are summarized in Table 7.29. The stream head contains a pointer called *sd_siglist*, which in turn holds a list of *strevent* structures (see Appendix D) containing two fields: the process ID, and event flags. The event flags is a bit mask representing the events that cause a signal to be sent. The process ID indicates which process is to receive the signal. The stream head read processing routines use this list to determine which processes must be signalled when a message is received at the stream head.

- *I_FDINSERT* — this *ioctl* allows the user-mode program to create an *msgb* that contains the *queue* pointer for the bottom of a stream, as shown in Figure 7.51. A process might want to do this when passing information to a multiplexor. The facility is also used by the socket and TLI interface libraries. A message is sent down the control stream, containing the *queue* pointer of another stream. The multiplexor receives this message and can use it to send data up the other stream. The advantage of this scheme is that a programmer need only manipulate file descriptors. The advantage for the driver writer is that the *queue* pointer is passed down as part of the message, so the driver itself does not have to convert a file descriptor into a *queue* pointer.

  This *ioctl* command is passed a *strfdinsert* structure as a parameter. It contains two *strbuf* structures which are used to create the control and data parts of a message (see *putmsg* in § 7.9.8). It also contains an offset and a file descriptor. If the file descriptor is associated with an open stream, the *queue* pointer for the bottom of that stream is placed at the specified offset in the control part of the message. The message is then passed down the stream.

Figure 7.51: *Operation of I_FDINSERT*

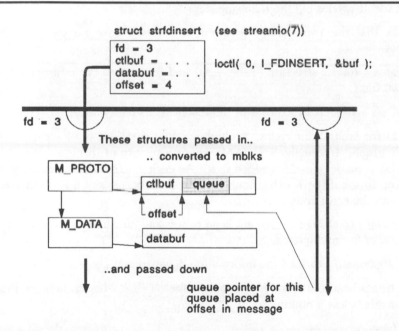

- *I_STR* — this *ioctl* command passes in module and driver specific *ioctls*, as described in § 7.3.5. The *strioctl* structure is copied in from user space and passed to *strdoioctl( )*.

- *I_SENDFD* — passes file descriptors between stream heads. The argument to the *ioctl* is a *strrecvfd* structure that holds the file descriptor value itself. The data is retrieved at the other end of the stream by the *I_RECVFD ioctl*. (The stream head puts this information into an *M_PASSFP* message.)

With this command, *strioctl( )* assumes that the stream on which the message is being sent is a STREAMS pipe, which means that by following the *q_next* pointer it comes to the other stream head. The *M_PASSFP* message is placed directly on the remote stream head; no intervening modules or drivers will see the message. When the stream is closed or flushed, and there is an *M_FLUSH* message on the queue, its associated file descriptor is closed.

This mechanism is used by the kernel in the implementation of STREAMS based pipes (see in § 7.10).

Table 7.30: *Struct linkblk*

Element	Description
*queue_t *l_qtop*	Lowest level write queue of upper module stream
*queue_t *l_qbot*	Highest level write queue of lower module stream
int l_index	Unique index or ID of lower stream

- *I_LINK* — the purpose and operation of the *I_LINK ioctl* is described in § 7.5.1. In summary, it is used to establish a link between a module or driver and a multiplexor. It carries out the following steps:

  - Checks that the two streams involved in the link have no error conditions present.

  - Allocates a *linkblk* structure (Table 7.30) and fills it with the information about the two links.

  - Initializes a *strioctl* structure with the *linkblk* as its data buffer.

  - Checks for multiplexor cycles. Multiplexor configurations must form a directed acyclic graph. Internally, STREAMS keeps a picture of this graph and when a new link is made, a node is added to it. As each *I_LINK* is issued, the graph is checked to see if the *I_LINK* could make a cycle occur; and if it could, the *ioctl* fails with the error code *EINVAL*.

  - Calls *setq( )* to change the stream head processing functions in the lower stream to those of the multiplexor.

  - Calls *strdoioctl( )* to send the information downstream.

  - The stream head of the lower stream sets the *STPLEX* flag to indicate that this stream sits below a multiplexor.

  - The function *wakeprocs* is called to wake up any processes sleeping on the stream head.

  - Finally, the link index (*l_index*) is returned to the caller. Note the *l_index* field is used as the return value of the system call. It is a unique identifier used to disconnect the multiplexor with *I_UNLINK*.

- *I_PLINK* — creates a permanent link that works in much the same way as a regular link. The difference is that the controlling process can exit and still leave the multiplexor intact. (The *muxid* must be saved so that the stream can be dismantled if necessary.)

strdoioctl( ) passes an *M_IOCTL* message downstream and waits for an acknowledgement. It ensures that only one *ioctl* is active on the stream. The pseudo-code for this function is given in Figure 7.52. Note that the sequence number (stored in *sd_iocid* in the stream head) is used to distinguish between different *ioctl* messages. Its value is taken from a system global variable (a long data type) called *ioc_id* which is incremented each time an *ioctl* message is sent downstream by *strdoioctl( )*. This ID allows the stream head to tell if *ioctl* reply messages arriving at the stream head relate to the currently outstanding *ioctl*.

7.9.8 *putmsg* **and** *getmsg*

These two system calls provide a message interface to the STREAMS environment. *putmsg* takes buffers specified in user address space, encapsulates them into STREAMS messages, then passes them into a stream. *getmsg* does the opposite: it takes messages from a stream and decapsulates them into user buffers.

putmsg and *getmsg* are called with four parameters: a file descriptor, a set of flags, a control buffer and a data buffer. The control and data buffer arguments are pointers to *strbuf* structures (Table 7.31) describing the data to send, or specifying an area to receive data. The processing for both system calls is described as follows:

- *putmsg* — calls *msgio( )* to copy the user specified control and data buffer structures into kernel address space, which in turn calls *strputmsg( )* to send the message downstream.

  strputmsg( ) checks that the STREAMS memory limit has not been exceeded, and also that the minimum and maximum packets size constraints are met. Downstream flow-control is tested, and *strputmsg( )* sleeps until downstream flow-control is relaxed. *msgbs* are then allocated and the message data copied into them; the data from the control buffer is placed in an *M_PROTO* message and the data from the data buffer is placed in an *M_DATA* message (see Figure 7.53). The process may be put to sleep whilst the data is being copied, or whilst waiting for the message blocks to be allocated. Finally, the message is passed downstream.

  strputmsg( ) ensures that the *msgb* allocated for the control part of the message is at least 64 bytes long so that a module or driver has a better chance of reusing the *M_PROTO* message. If a message is reused, processing is more efficient because the calls to *freemsg( )* and *allocb( )* can be avoided.

- *getmsg* — is similar in operation to *putmsg( )* except that data travels in the opposite direction (i.e., from kernel space to user space). *msgio( )* is called, which validates the stream packet size constraints and copies in the control and data *strbuf* structures from user space. *strgetmsg( )* (see Figure 7.54) is called to wait for upstream messages to arrive and to copy the data buffers from them into the user supplied control and data buffers.

Figure 7.52: *Algorithm for strdoioctl( )*

```
strdoioctl()
  inputs: stream head, struct strioctl
  outputs: error indicator
{
  allocate buffer to hold the struct iocblk
  - and the user data
  fill in data fields in iocblk
  copy in user data to iocblk
again:
  while( IOCWAIT flag set in stream head )
    sleep( stream head ioctl ) /* Someone has ioctl outstanding */
  set IOCWAIT flag in stream head
  assign sequence number to ioctl
  put message downstream and call runqueues()

  /* This will timeout after ic_timout seconds, (code not shown) */
  while( no ioctl response received at stream head )
    sleep( stream head )
  clear iocwait
  wakeprocs( stream head ioctl ) /* Let other sleepers go */

  /* At this point, we have a message.. */
  switch( ioctl response message ) {
  case M_IOCACK:
    copy data back to user and return
  case M_IOCNAK:
    get error code from message
    copy error code back to user and return
  case M_COPYIN:
    allocate M_IOCDATA buffer for user data
    copy data from user space into buffer
    pass message downstream
    goto again
  case M_COPYOUT:
    copy data to user space
    send M_IOCDATA downstream as acknowledgement
    goto again
  }
  return
}
```

Table 7.31: *Struct strbuf*

Element	Description
int maxlen	Maximum size of a buffer. Used by *getmsg* to avoid going beyond the end.
int len	Length of data in message. Used by *putmsg* to make sure that all the user data gets copied into the kernel.
*void *buf*	Pointer to the user data area.

Figure 7.53: *Operation of the putmsg system call*

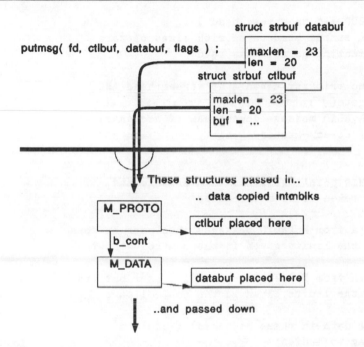

7.9.9 Polling a stream

The *poll* system call is a multiplexing I/O mechanism. Given a set of open file descriptors, *poll* can be used to notify the caller when an event of interest occurs, or to identify which file descriptors are ready to be read from or written to. This is especially useful where a process reads from multiple inputs (see, for example, Figure 7.55).

When a program uses *poll*, it specifies the events of interest in an array of *pollfd* structures (see Table 7.33). For each element in the array, *poll* examines a set of given file descriptors for the occurrence of an event of interest (specified in the *events* field). When the events of interest occur, *poll* returns to the caller; the results of the system call are stored in the *revents* field to indicate to the caller which events took place. The events that can be polled for (see Table 7.32) clearly

Figure 7.54: *Algorithm for strgetmsg( )*

```
strgetmsg( )
 inputs: stream head pointer
         strbuf structures for the control and data messages
 outputs: error code
{

  if( STRDERR set in stream head )
    return error code

  if( STRHUP set in stream head )
    return strbuf structures with sizes of zero
    - indicating no data was read

  while( no priority message at stream head AND
         getq( ) returns no data from read queue ) {
    send M_READ message downstream if necessary
    sleep( stream head )
  }

  /* At this point, we received a message and
   * have taken it from the queue
   */
  copy data from M_PROTO messages into user buffers
  - up to the limits given in the control strbuf

  copy data from M_DATA messages into user buffers
  - up to the limits given in the control part

  if( more data in these messages) {
   set flag to indicate
   MORECTL or MOREDATA /* see getmsg(2) */
  }

  if( first message on queue is now M_SIG )
    send SIGPOLL to processes on stream head sig list

  if( first message on queue is now M_DATA)
    wakeup anybody polling this stream

  return flag
}
```

Figure 7.55: *Using poll*

```
/* Illustrate how to poll for input */
#include <stropts.h>
#include <poll.h>

#define NF 10
struct pollfd serial_pollfd[ NF ] ;
int serial_fd[ NF ] ; /* Holds the fd of each line */
...
/* set up data structure prior to poll */
for( i = 0 ; i < NF ; i++ ) {
  serial_pollfd[i].fd = serial_fd[i] ;
  serial_pollfd[i].events = POLLIN; /* Only interested in input */
}
err = poll( serial_pollfd, NF, INFTIM ) ;
error check omitted

/* Poll completed, examine each revents.. */
for( i = 0 ; i < NF ; i++ ) {
  if( serial_pollfd[i].revents & POLLIN ) {
     cc = read( serial_fd[i], buf, count ) ; /* fd is ready */
     ...
  }
  check for errors etc
}
...
```

Table 7.32: *Poll events*

Event	Description
POLLIN	Any input except high priority messages
POLLRDNORM	Normal data message (not expedited) is available
POLLPRI	High priority message is available
POLLOUT	Normal data message can be written
POLLWRNORM	Normal data message can be written
POLLWRBAND	Expedited message may be written
POLLERR	An error occurred in the stream
POLLHUP	The stream has been hung up
POLLNVAL	The *fd* was not that of an open file

indicate that *poll* was designed primarily with STREAMS in mind. (The events shown in the shaded area of the table are those that might be set in *revents* by *poll* — for example, when an error occurs.)

Table 7.33: *Poll data structures*

Element	struct pollfd
	Description
int fd	File descriptor
short events	Events requested
short revents	Events returned
Element	struct polldat
	Description
struct polldat *pd_next	Next in list
struct polldat *pd_prev	Previous in list
struct polldat *pd_chain	Other *fds* in this call
short pd_events	Events we are looking for
struct pollhead *pd_headp	Back pointer
void (*pd_fn)( )	Function to call when event occurs
long pd_arg	Argument to pass to function
Element	struct pollhead
	Description
struct polldat *ph_list	List of *polldat* structures (pollers of this file)
struct polldat *ph_dummy	Dummy pointer

Any file descriptor can be polled. The action taken depends, in principle, on the file's type. For ordinary files, *poll* always indicates that the file is available for input and output. For pipes and streams, *poll* calls *strpoll( )* to determine which events have occurred. Finally, for non-STREAMS device drivers, the driver implementor decides the effect of *poll* on the file (see § 5.8.3).

The implementation of *poll* relies on three data structures and three support functions. The data structures, summarized in Table 7.33, are as follows:

- *struct pollfd* — holds the file descriptor, the events wanted and the events found.

- *struct polldat* — these are dynamically allocated by *poll* to hold the information supplied by the user in the system call arguments. They also contain a pointer to a function to call when the desired events occur on the file descriptor, and pointers to link the *polldat* structures together.

- *struct pollhead* — is the head of a list of *polldat* structures.

The three support functions are:

- *pollrun( )* — called to wake up a single process that is sleeping on *pollwait*, which informs it that an event being polled for has occurred.

- *polltime( )* — is placed in the system *callout*. When the timeout occurs, this function is called to wake up a process that is sleeping on *pollwait*.

- *pollwakeup( )* — this function notifies the system when an event occurs so that it can wake up processes sleeping in *poll*. It is called with two parameters, a *pollhead* list and an *event*. The list is scanned, and each process waiting for the given event has its associated function called (this is always *pollrun( )*). By calling *pollwakeup( )*, all processes waiting for events on a particular file descriptor are made runnable.

The *poll( )* function uses the *p_pollflag* bitmask in the *proc* structure to control its operation as follows:

- *SINPOLL* — indicates that the kernel is processing a *poll* request. It is cleared by *pollrun( )*. When the flag is cleared it indicates that data arrived on a file descriptor while *poll* was processing a different file descriptor. When *poll* notices the flag has been cleared, it examines the file descriptors again to find out which ones now have data available.

- *SPOLLTIME* — indicates that the *poll* timeout is running. When the timeout occurs, the flag is cleared, indicating to *poll* that the timeout expired.

The algorithm for *poll* is given in Figure 7.56. When a STREAMS file descriptor is not ready for data, a *polldat* structure is added to the *sd_pollist* in the stream head. When data subsequently arrives at the stream head, *pollwakeup( )* is called which wakes up only those processes that are polling this stream head.

For each file descriptor that is checked, the file system dependent *vnode* poll operation is called (*VOP_POLL( )*). For STREAMS, this function is called *strpoll( )*. The *strpoll( )* function checks output events by examining the first queue below the stream head. If the queue is not blocked, the output events bits are set in the value returned to the caller. For input events, it checks on the messages waiting at the stream head. If there are messages waiting to be read at the stream head, an input events bit is set in the value returned to the caller.

7.9.10 The *Strinfo* array

In previous versions of UNIX System V, STREAMS used statically allocated data structures. That is, space was set aside for them during system initialization; they were then allocated as necessary from a static array of each data structure type.

In UNIX System V Release 4, all STREAMS data structures are dynamically allocated. Dynamic allocation is more flexible because memory is not wasted; it is allocated only when needed. However, when things go wrong, dynamically allocated resources are very hard to track down. For example, consider a badly written STREAMS module that is losing *msgbs*. That is, instead of deallocating them with *freemsg( )*, their *msgb* reference pointers are overwritten. Eventually, the system will grind to a halt because there is no more memory available. (Remember that all routines that write into STREAMS, such as *putmsg* and *write* check the STREAMS memory use limit.)

Figure 7.56: *Algorithm for poll( )*

```
poll( )
  inputs: fdp — array of pollfd structures,
          nfds — count of pollfd structures,
          timo — timeout value
  outputs: modified array of pollfd structures
{
  allocate space for pollfd array and polldat structures
  chain polldat structures together
  copy data from user space into pollfd array
again:
  for( all pollfd structures passed in ) {
    call file system dependent vnode poll operation for the fd
    if( fd is ready ) {
      update pollfd array
      goto gotone
    }
  }
  /* poll unsuccessful if we get here */
  if( poll timeout not expired )
    call timeout( polltime ) /* set up time out */

  sleep( waiting for fd to become available )
  /* either fd became available, or the timeout expired */
  goto again

gotone:
  copy pollfd array back to user space
  free pollfd array and polldat structures
}
```

Under UNIX System V Release 3, *msgbs* of various sizes were each held in their own array. Thus, it was quite easy to see when *msgbs* of a particular size had all been used. Furthermore, it was possible to inspect each *msgb* because it was stored in an array. This provided a mechanism for the system to determine which module or driver had last used it.

Under UNIX System V Release 4, examining the contents of a dynamically allocated *msgb* is much harder. *msgbs* are no longer elements in an array, but allocated by *kmem_alloc( )*, so if a module loses an *msgb* it is lost forever. Debugging this type of environment is therefore much harder.

Similar problems apply to other dynamically allocated STREAMS resources. The designers of UNIX System V Release 4 anticipated this problem, and provided the *Strinfo[]* array. This array links together, and keeps a count, of all dynamically allocated STREAMS data structures. Each element is a *strinfo* structure (see

Table 7.34) containing two fields:

- *sd_head* — points to an *info* data structure list header (described in a moment).

- *sd_cnt* — counts the number of data structures allocated for this entry; it is incremented and decremented as data structures of the type pointed to by *sd_head* are allocated and freed.

Additionally, a global variable called *Strcount* keeps a count (in bytes) of all STREAMS allocated resources. Note that the constants shown in Table 7.34 are used to index into *Strinfo[]* for a particular data structure list type.

Figure 7.57: *The Strinfo[] array*

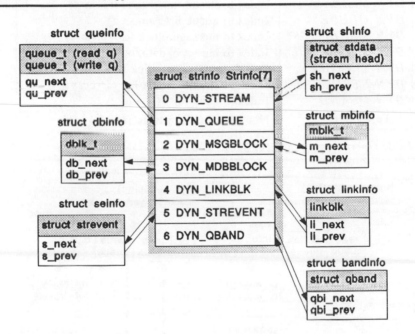

Figure 7.57 shows the complete set of dynamically allocated STREAMS structures and how they link into *Strinfo[]*. Each dynamically allocated structure is encapsulated in an *info* structure. For example, stream heads (or *stdata* structures) are encapsulated in *shinfo* structures, *queue* structures are encapsulated in *queinfo* structures, and so on. Each of these *info* structures contain a pair of pointers for linking the item into the *Strinfo[]* array.

Note that implementations of the *Strinfo[]* array vary. For example, *msgbs* and *databs* are linked into this list only if the kernel is compiled with the *DEBUG* preprocessor flag set. This gives production kernels a runtime benefit because it avoids the need to link and unlink *msgbs* from the lists each time a buffer is allocated and freed. However, when problems occur it is harder to find out what went wrong.

It can be seen then, that when anything goes wrong, a debugging program can follow the links from the lists in *Strinfo[]*, allowing all dynamically allocated data structures to be found (for example, you can use **crash(1M)** to examine them).

Table 7.34: *Struct strinfo*

Element	Description
*void *sd_head*	Head of data structure list
int sd_cnt	Total number of data structures allocated
Constant	**Description**
DYN_STREAM	Index to stream head list (*stdata_t*)
DYN_QUEUE	Index to queue list (*queue_t*)
DYN_MSGBLOCK	Index to message block list (*mblk_t*)
DYN_MDBBLOCK	Index to message/data/buffer list (*dblk_t*)
DYN_LINKBLK	Index to multiplexor link block list (*linkblk*)
DYN_STREVENT	Index to stream events list (*strevent*)
DYN_QBAND	Index to qband list (*qband_t*)
NDYNAMIC	Number of elements in *Strinfo[]* array

Figure 7.58: *Operation of qattach()*

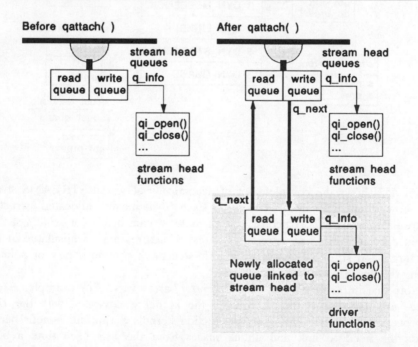

7.9.11 *qattach( )* **and** *qdetach( )*

When a module or driver is opened, *qattach( )* is called to set up a queue pair for the driver or module and to call its open function. One of the parameters to *qattach( )* is an existing queue pair below which the new queue pair will be linked. The processing steps are as follows (see also Figure 7.58):

- Allocate a new *queue* pair.

- Find the *streamtab* for the driver or module from its *cdevsw[ ]* or *fmodsw[ ]* entry.

- Adjust the pointers in the new queue pair and the existing queue pair so that they point to each other (i.e., link them into the stream).

- Initialize the queue pair *qinit* structures (they hold information about the processing routines for the queues — minimum and maximum packet sizes, high and low water marks, and so on (see Table 7.6)).

- Call the *open* procedure of the newly attached module or driver.

- If the device information changed as a result of the open, then *qattach( )* realizes that this was a clone open. The *q_qinfo* pointer is adjusted to point to the *streamtab* for the driver that was actually opened.

The function *qdetach( )* performs the opposite set of operations. It unlinks the queue from the stream, calls the module or driver *close* function and then deallocates the queue.

7.10 STREAMS-based pipes and FIFOs

In the following discussion, the terms "named-pipe" and "FIFO" are used interchangeably.

There are two types of pipes: software-pipes and named-pipes. Software-pipes are created with the *pipe* system call, and named-pipes are created with the *mknod* system call. Both system calls create a FIFO I/O mechanism. That is, a read from one end of the pipe accesses the data written to the other end of it on a first-in-first-out basis. (The notion of named-pipes is also introduced in § 2.5.6.)

Named-pipes allow processes to communicate with each other. Usually, one process opens a named-pipe for reading, and another opens it for writing. Data written by one process is then read by the other. A good example of this is the line printer spooler. It controls access to print devices by listening on the read end of a named-pipe for incoming print requests. When a user wants to print a file, he or she invokes the line printer interface program, **lp(1)** which communicates with the spooler by writing to the write end of the named-pipe. The spooler then queues the print job which is eventually sent to the print device.

Since named-pipes are created with *mknod* they have entries in the file system (for example, **mknod(1M)** uses this system call). Thus, they use up a directory entry and are assigned an *inode*. When file system operations are carried out on a named-pipe, the FIFO-specific *vnode* operations are used.

Software pipes, on the other hand, have no entry in the file system, and since they have no associated name, they cannot be opened for use with the *open* system call.

The *pipe* system call sets up two file descriptors, one for the writing end of the pipe and one for the reading end. They are used to set up an interprocess communication channel between related processes with a common parent. A process that uses *pipe* usually performs the following operations to set up the communication path through a pipe:

- Calls *pipe* to create the pipe. This sets up two file descriptors in user address space, one for the reading end, and one for the writing end.

- Calls *fork* to clone the process. There are now two processes, both of which have copies of the open file descriptors. The process that writes to the pipe must close the read end, and the process that reads the pipe must close the write end. If this is not done, the pipe is registered as having two readers and two writers so that if the reading process dies, the writing process will not receive a *SIGPIPE* signal when it next tries to write to the pipe.

The implementation does not allow a module to be linked under a FIFO, nor does it allow a FIFO to become the control terminal for a process.

7.10.1 FIFO operations

FIFOs are implemented by a separate file system type called *fifofs*. The *fifofs* defines a *vnodeops* structure (*fifo_vnodeops*) containing a set of file system dependent *vnode* operations that operate on named-pipes. These operations are summarized as follows:

- *fifo_open( )* — A FIFO's *vnode* keeps a count of readers and writers operating on the pipe. As soon as there is both a reader and a writer, the pipe is opened for use. Otherwise the system call will block if an open for reading is attempted without a writer, or an open for writing is attempted without a reader.

  Once successfully opened, *fifo_open( )* (Figure 7.59) alters the stream head write queue pointers so that *q_next* points to the read queue. This means that whenever data is written to the stream, the data is "passed down", and ends up on the read queue of the same stream head. This loop-around queue configuration is shown in Figure 7.60.

- *fifo_write( )* — the pseudo code for *fifo_write( )* is shown in Figure 7.61. Note that it calls *strwrite( )* to send the data. If the data cannot be sent, *strwrite( )* returns the error code *ESTRPIPE*, which tells *fifo_write( )* that the stream is blocked, making it sleep on the write queue of the stream. If an attempt is made to write to the pipe without there being a reader, or the pipe is broken because the reader disappears (i.e., the reading process exits or is killed), the operation returns *EPIPE* in *errno* and *SIGPIPE* is sent to the caller. Otherwise, the data is written and *fifo_write( )* issues a *wakeprocs( )* to wake up any processes sleeping on the read queue of the stream.

Figure 7.59: *Algorithm for fifo_open( )*

```
fifo_open()
  inputs: FIFO-vnode pointer, read/write indicator
  outputs: updated vnode
{
  if( reading the fifo ) {
    wakeup processes waiting for a reader
    /* can't open for reading without a writer */
    /* so wait for someone to open for writing */
    if( there is no writer )
      sleep until writer appears
  }
  if( writing the fifo ) {
    /* can't open for writing without a reader */
    /* so wait for someone to open for reading */
    if( there is no reader )
      sleep until reader appears
  }

  call stropen to create and open a stream
  set max packet size & flow-control parameters
    so that PIPE_BUF bytes can be written

  if( first open of the FIFO )
    set q_next on write side to point to read queue
  increment open count in the vnode
}
```

Figure 7.60: *Operation of fifo_open( )*

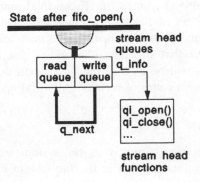

Figure 7.61: *Algorithm for fifo_write()*

```
fifo_write()
  inputs:  vnode pointer, details of io to perform
  outputs: error code
{
  if( no readers )
    post SIGPIPE and return EPIPE error code

  while( strwrite() returns error code ESTRPIPE ) {
    if( no readers )
      post SIGPIPE and return EPIPE error code
    sleep( stream head write queue )
  }
  update vnode access & modification times
  wakeprocs( stream head read queue )
  return error code
}
```

- *fifo_read()* — the algorithm for *fifo_read()* is very similar to *fifo_write()*. The function loops, calling *strread()* to get the data from the stream. When *strread()* has no data available, it returns the error code *ESTRPIPE*. The function then sleeps on the read queue of the stream, waiting for data to arrive. After getting the data, the *vnode* access and modification times are updated, and *wakeprocs()* is called to wake up processes sleeping on the stream head write queue. If an attempt is made to read from the pipe without there being a writer, or the pipe is broken because the writer disappears (i.e., the writing process exits or is killed), the operation returns *EPIPE* in *errno*.

- *fifo_close()* — if the pipe is open for reading, the reader count is decremented; if it is open for writing, the writer count is decremented. A count of processes that have opened the pipe is also decremented. If the total number of opens falls to zero, all readers and writers of the pipe are awoken, and the stream is freed. Processes that are awoken will run when they are next scheduled. Any further reads or writes will detect that the pipe stream has disappeared. Writers will receive *SIGPIPE*, readers will be able to read only data buffered in the stream, after which they will receive a count of zero bytes, indicating the FIFO is closed.

7.10.2 Pipe operations

Named-pipes are created by users (mostly by the system administrator) with the **mknod(1M)** command; they then remain in the file system until removed and can be opened and closed by arbitrary processes that have relevant access permission. In contrast, software-pipes are created and opened at the same time with the *pipe* system call (see Figure 7.62). When processes using a software-pipe exit, the pipe is automatically deallocated. A software-pipe is a mechanism that can only be used by processes having a common parent; the pipe is always created in the parent, and the file descriptors for the pipe are always inherited by its children.

When a pipe is created by the *pipe* system call, two file table entries are created (see § 6.2.4), and their index is returned as two file descriptors.

Figure 7.62: *Algorithm for pipe( )*

```
pipe( )
  inputs: none
  outputs: error code
{
  allocate and initialize two vnodes
  set their vnode type to VFIFO /* (v_type) */

  allocate and initialize two file table entries
  /* Both descriptors are opened for reading and writing */

  allocate two stream heads and attach to each vnode via v_stream

  adjust the stream head queues so that the write queue
  - of one points to the read queue of the other

  generate a unique inode number and assign it to
  - both vnodes

  return pipe file descriptors in rval_t /* see § 4.9.5 */
}
```

Two *vnodes* are also allocated; their *v_type* field is set to *VFIFO*, which distinguishes the pipe as a software-pipe rather than a named-pipe. Additionally, two streams are created and linked together (see Figure 7.63). Note that this contrasts with named-pipes which have only one stream head.

There is no software-pipe open operation; both ends of a software-pipe are opened as the by-product of a successful *pipe* system call. The software-pipe read and write operations are the same as those for a named-pipe, but the software-pipe close operation is slightly different. It performs all the steps of the named-pipe close operation described above, plus the following:

- It sends an *M_HANGUP* message to prevent all I/O on the other end of the pipe.

- It calls *qenable( )* on the other end of the stream to cause it to process the *M_HANGUP* the next time *queuerun( )* is called.

- It closes the stream at the end of the pipe associated with the file descriptor specified in the *close* system call.

Figure 7.63: *Situation after a pipe system call*

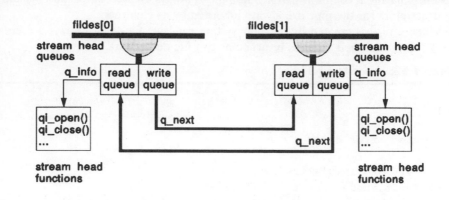

After one side of the pipe has been closed, reads continue to obtain data buffered in the pipe. Once the dada has been consumed, subsequent reads return zero. A subsequent write returns the *EPIPE* error code, and the process also receives a *SIGPIPE* signal.

7.11 STREAMS terminals

Traditionally, a user logged in to the UNIX system through a teletype terminal such as the Digital Equipment VT100, which was connected to the computer via an RS232 serial link and operated in full duplex mode. Data could be sent simultaneously from the terminal to the computer and vice versa. The original UNIX terminal interface was developed to suit this method of user interaction. In contrast to this, many other operating systems worked in half duplex mode (block-mode). That is, character echo was handled by the terminal itself, and complete screenfuls of data were transmitted between the terminal and computer.

Today, a user can choose from a variety of methods to establish a session with a UNIX system — for example, X terminals, PCs, networked UNIX systems, such as workstations, and so on. However, the basic model of "using a terminal" to access a UNIX system remains [Goodheart 1991].

Asynchronous terminal I/O on previous versions of UNIX was handled by the *terminal driver* (*tty*), which provided the following *line discipline* facilities:

- *Canonical processing* — characters are buffered, and simple line editing keys such as erase and line delete are processed until a complete line is received.

- *Signal generation* — certain input characters tell the driver to send a signal to the controlling process. For example, the Control-C character sequence can be configured to send a *SIGINT* signal to the process.

- *Flow-control processing* — output to the terminal is stopped or started with the *XON/XOFF* protocol.

- *Raw mode* — characters are passed directly to the application without being processed.

The complete set of facilities provided by the terminal driver is documented in *termio(7)* under UNIX System V Release 3. This interface is referred to as *termio*.

The *termio* interface was originally developed to drive directly connected terminals, but did not cater for users accessing the system via remote terminals connected over a network. For example, locally connected users can alter the operating characteristics of their login terminal by using the **stty(1)** command. This results in a *termio ioctl* system call to the device driver controlling the terminal. However, this cannot be achieved by remotely attached terminals using *termio* because network drivers did not (and still do not) support it. This problem was solved under UNIX System V Release 3 with a *pseudo terminal* driver that emulated the facilities of the *termio* interface (§ 7.13.1).

Some vendors provide "intelligent" terminal controllers that have the *termio* interface implemented in software within the controller. This frees the kernel from the lengthy processing of each character — instead the controller passes the processed data to the kernel.

So far we have discussed two different implementations of the *termio* interface that can coexist in the same system. Different implementations can lead to problems because each one might interpret the *termio* interface specification slightly differently; for example, a program that works correctly on a directly connected terminal may not when work from a networked terminal.

UNIX System V Release 4, has alleviated this problem with a STREAMS module that implements the *termio* interface, and by making all terminal connections STREAMS-based. Therefore, regardless of the method of accessing the system, all *termio*-style processing is handled by STREAMS. This module is called *ldterm*. The following sections look at the *ldterm* interface.

Table 7.35: *Struct termios*

Element	Description
unsigned c_iflag	Input mode bits
unsigned c_oflag	Output mode bits
unsigned c_cflag	Control mode bits
unsigned c_lflag	Local mode bits
char c_cc[NCCS]	Control characters

7.11.1 Using *ldterm*

UNIX System V Release 4 describes the terminal interface in two places: *termios(2)* describes as set of line control functions and their return values, and *termio(7)* gives details of the terminal driver characteristics and *ioctl* interface. To change the terminal modes, a user program reads the current terminal state into a *termios* structure, alters the values to those desired, and then writes them back.

The *termios* structure is summarized in Table 7.35. The fields are used as follows:

- *c_iflag* — input control bit mask. For determining whether parity is checked on input, whether XON/XOFF flow-control is used, and so on.

- *c_oflag* — output control bit mask. For controlling output delays after carriage return, line feed or newline and so on.

- *c_cflag* — character control bit mask. For selecting word size, number of stop bits, whether hardware flow-control is used, and so on.

- *c_lflag* — line control bit mask. For determining whether characters are echoed, whether erase processing is performed (canonical mode), whether signals are sent on receipt of certain character sequences, and so on.

- *c_cc[]* — in canonical mode, an action is carried out for the control characters described in this array. They are represented by the constants shown in Table 7.36.

Table 7.36: *Termios control characters*

Constant	Default (ASCII)	Description
VEOF	^D	End of file
VEOL	NULL	Alternate end of line character
VERSE	#	Erase
VINTR	DEL	Send *SIGINT* signal
VKILL	@	Delete line
VQUIT	^|	Send *SIGQUIT* signal
VSTOP	^S	Suspend output (XOFF)
VSTRT	^Q	Restart output (XON)
VSUSP	^Z	Send *SIGTSTP* signal
VEOL2	NULL	2nd alternate end of line character
VSWTCH	^Z	Used by shell layers **shl(1)**
VDSUSP	^Y	Send *SIGTSTP* on foreground process read
VREPRINT	^R	Reprint line
VDISCRD	^O	Discard output until *VDISCRD* typed again
VWERSE	^W	Erase preceding word
VLNEXT	^V	Perform no special processing on next character
VMIN	(decimal) 4	Minimum read in raw mode
VTIME	(decimal) 5	Wait time in raw mode
NCCS		Size of *c_cc[]* array

Figure 7.64 gives an example extract of a program that manipulates the terminal's operating characteristics. Note that the modes are explicitly set because the program wants to define *exactly* how the device will react. Normally the existing terminal modes are read with *tcgetattr(2)*, they are then modified to suit those desired, and then reset with *tcsetattr(2)*. (Although *tcgetattr(2)* and *tcsetattr(2)* are

documented system calls, they are, in fact, implemented as library functions which use *termio(7)*.)

Figure 7.64: *Use of termios structure*

```
/* Code fragment to alter terminal modes. In this example
 * the program is talking to a device that is sending
 * ''International Alphabet #2'' codes at 50 bits/second
 */


...
struct termios t ;
t.c_iflag = BRKINT ; /* Send SIGINT if break occurs */
t.c_oflag = OPOST ;
t.c_cflag = CS5 | CREAD ; /* 5 bit chars, enable receiver */
t.c_lflag = ISIG | TOSTOP | ICANON ; /* Signals, canonical input */

/* Set speed to 50 baud in termio structure */
cfsetispeed( &t, B50 ) ;
cfsetospeed( &t, B50 ) ;

/* Update line itself.. (also sets speed) */
if( tcsetattr( teleprinter, TCSADRAIN, &t ) == -1 )
    error occurred
```

7.11.2 Job control

Job control is a facility derived from 4BSD and used by the UNIX shell (see **ksh(1)**) to provide a certain amount of control over which processes can access the user's control terminal. The following concepts are used in the discussion that follows:

- *Control terminal* — the terminal from which a process is started. Job control facilities and characters that generate signals are processed only if they come from the control terminal associated with the process.

- *Process group* — Each process has a process identifier and a process group identifier (see also § 4.11.3). When a signal is sent to a process group leader (a process having a group ID the same as its process ID), the signal is sent to all processes in that process group. Each stream data structure (and therefore, each terminal connection) contains a process group identifier. When a stream is being used as the control terminal, it only allows a process to read it if the process group ID of the stream head matches the group ID of that process. An example of process groups is shown in Figure 7.65.

- *Foreground and background processes* — a foreground process can read from its control terminal. Its process group ID will be the same as that stored in the stream head of its control terminal. A background process has a process group ID that differs from that stored in the stream head of the control terminal.

Figure 7.65: *Process groups*

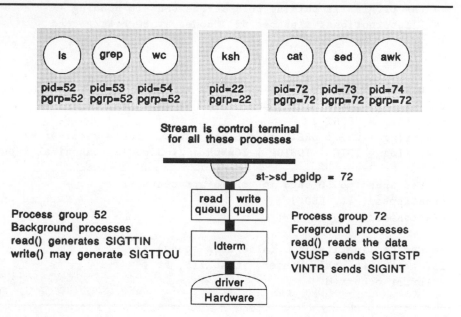

Consider the following scenario: A user enters a command known to take a long time to complete, so he or she runs it as a background task (by adding the **&** character to the end of the command line). The process starts, and the shell prompt comes back straight away; the user can do other work (say, for example, edit a file) while the long job runs concurrently in the background. After some minutes, the long job has to read some data from the terminal. It stops (that is, its execution is paused) because it cannot read from the terminal, since it is a background job. The user notices this, so types `^Z`. This causes the foreground process (the editor) to stop, passing control to the user's shell which now has two stopped jobs: the long process and the editor. By typing:

    fg %1

the long job is brought into the foreground — that is, it can read data from the terminal. The user types in the data needed by the long job, which then runs to completion. Eventually, the shell prompt comes back, but the user still has the editor stopped. By typing:

    fg

once more, the editor comes into the foreground, and the user continues editing.

Other shells implement the job control mechanism in a similar way (see **csh(1)**). The following kernel facilities allow a programmer to implement job control:

- *setpgid* — sets the process group ID.

- *tcsetpgrp* — sets the process group ID in a stream head. The shell brings a process group into the foreground by switching a stream head to a process group.

- *waitid* — allows a process to detect when one of its children changes state. The shell uses this system call to detect when its child processes stop after receiving the stop signals shown below.

- *SIGSTOP* — this signal makes a process stop; that is, when it receives the signal it is put into the state *SSTOP*. The process does not exit, but it will not execute any more; it is no longer scheduled to run. It becomes eligible to run again when it receives the *SIGCONT* signal. A process cannot catch or ignore this signal, although it can catch those described below.

- *SIGTSTP* — this signal is issued when the user enters the *VSUSP* character. It has the same effect as the *SIGSTOP* signal.

- *SIGTTIN* — when a process tries to read from its control terminal, but the control terminal is attached to another process group, the process receives a *SIGTTIN*. That is, the signal is sent if a background process tries to read from the terminal. It has the same effect as the *SIGSTOP* signal.

- *SIGTTOU* — this signal is sent if the *TOSTOP* bit has been set by a *termio ioctl* and a process tries to write to its control terminal while the control terminal belongs to a different process group. That is, the signal is sent if a background process tries to write to the terminal.

Figure 7.65 shows two process groups accessing their control terminal. The shell and kernel interact to set up the process groups and to perform job control as described below:

- The first process group is started. It contains three processes; the first is made process group leader (with the *setpgid* system call), and the others are assigned to the process group. The terminal is associated with the group via the *tcsetpgrp* system call. All processes are invoked, and the shell executes *waitid*, waiting for something to happen.

- The user types the ^Z sequence at the terminal.

- The sequence is received by *ldterm*, which finds that the *VSUSP* character has been entered. *ldterm* sends an *M_PCSIG* message to the stream head. The stream head sends the *SIGTSTP* signal to the process group, and all processes in the group stop.

- The *waitid* executed by the shell returns because the processes stopped. The shell issues a new prompt, and switches the terminal to its own process group so that it can receive input.

- The user enters the command string for the second group of processes. The shell makes the first process in the group the process group leader, and places the other members into the same process group. *tcsetpgrp* is issued to switch the terminal to this new group, and the shell executes *waitid* once more.

- The first process group could have continued running in the background if the user had entered the shell's built-in command **bg**. If any of the processes tried to read the terminal, they would have been stopped by a *SIGTTIN* signal.

- The second process group runs to completion and exits. The *waitid* returns, and the shell switches the terminal back to its own process group allowing the user to type in a new command. If the user enters the shell's built-in command **fg**, the terminal is switched to the first process group by using *tcsetpgrp*. The shell restarts the processes by issuing the *kill* system call to send a *SIGCONT* to the members of the process group.

7.11.3 The *straccess( )* function

The *straccess( )* function (Figure 7.66) tests whether the process can access its control terminal. It is called by the stream head functions *strread( )*, *strwrite( )*, *strioctl( )*, *strputmsg( )*, and *strgetmsg( )*.

If a process attempting to write to the control terminal is running in the background, *straccess( )* sends it a *SIGTTIN* signal causing it to stop. It will remain stopped until it receives *SIGCONT*. Thus, the process will block until the process is once more in the foreground.

7.12 Implementation of *ldterm*

ldterm is a STREAMS module that implements the terminal interface described in *termio(7)*. However, its implementation is cumbersome and complicated because new facilities were added to it without removing old ones, and because there are very many different ways to connect terminals to a UNIX system. The sections that follow explain the major functional units of *ldterm*.

7.12.1 Data structures in *ldterm*

The *ldterm* module uses an *ldterm_mod* structure (see Table 7.37) to store the current state of the connection, and to buffer messages that are being assembled in canonical input mode. The structure is dynamically allocated when the module is pushed into the stream, and the modules *open* function sets *q_ptr* to point to it.

Note that the *t_modes* and *t_dmodes* fields define the division of work between *ldterm* and the driver (see § 7.13.2).

Figure 7.66: *Algorithm for straccess( )*

```
/* called by strread, strwrite, strioctl, strgetmsg, strputmsg */

straccess()
  inputs: stream head pointer, read/write access information
  outputs: error code
{

  for( ever ) {
    if( stream is not control terminal OR
        stream is a FIFO OR
        stream is foreground)
      return OK  /* process may access stream */

    /* Allocate stream to a different process
     * group, i.e., call the process in the background
     */
    if( control terminal deallocated )
      /* user has hung up */
      send SIGHUP to process group
    else if( access mode is READ )
      send SIGTTIN to process group
    else if( access mode is WRITE ) {
      if( TOSTOP termio mode is set )
        send SIGTTOU to process group
      else
        return OK /* background write to terminal is OK */
    }
  }
}
```

7.12.2 *ldterm* read side

Data is passed up into *ldterm* from a STREAMS device driver, or from another module. *ldterm* has both a read *put* and a read *service* procedure. The following operations are handled in the read *put* procedure:

- *Break processing* — when a serial line device driver detects a break on the line, it sends an *M_BREAK* message upstream, which is recognised by the read *put* procedure. Depending on the terminal modes in force, the read *put* procedure either sends an *M_SIG* message upstream to generate a *SIGINT* signal, or sends an *M_DATA* message upstream containing a null character.

- *M_CTL processing* — handles the negotiation with intelligent controllers (§ 7.13.2).

Table 7.37: *Struct ldterm_mod (ldtermstd_state_t)*

Element	Description
mblk_t *t_savbp	Pointer to *msgb* holding this item
struct termios t_modes	Modes that *ldterm* processes
struct termios t_amodes	Modes that the user has set
struct termios t_dmodes	Modes that the driver processes instead of *ldterm* processing them
unsigned t_state	State flags (see below)
int t_line	Line number on terminal
int t_col	Terminal output column
int t_rocount	Number of characters echoed since last write
int t_rocol	Column of first echoed character since last write
mblk_t *t_message	Current message being built
mblk_t *t_endmsg	Last *msgb* in current message
int t_msglen	Size of current message
mblk_t *t_echomp	Pointer to message being echoed
int t_rd_request	Bytes requested by *M_READ*
int t_id	Timer ID used for *VTIME*
Flag (*t_state*)	**Description**
TS_XCLUDE	Only one open allowed
TS_TTSTOP	Output has been stopped by receipt of XOFF character
TS_TBLOCK	Input has been stopped by sending XOFF character
TS_NOCANON	Another module is doing canonical processing for us

- *XON/XOFF protocol* — for I/O flow-control as described in § 7.12.7.

- *Processing of special characters* — takes place as described in § 7.12.6.

Additionally, the following flags set in *c_iflag* of the *termios* structure cause *ldterm* to perform the following character conversions:

- *INLCR* — received newlines are converted to carriage return characters. Similarly, carriage returns are mapped to line feeds if *ICRNL* is set.

- *IUCLC* — upper-case characters are converted to their lower-case equivalents.

- *ISTRIP* — the top bit in all characters is zeroed.

Data messages that contain special characters such as *XON/XOFF* (or signal generating characters) are processed immediately. All other messages are placed on the queue where they will be processed by the read *service* procedure, which performs the following operations:

- *M_HANGUP* — this message is an indication from the driver that the connection to the terminal has been lost. The *service* procedure flushes its own queue, and creates an *M_FLUSH* message to clear out the data from the read and write sides of the stream. The *M_HANGUP* is then passed upstream.

- *Canonical Mode* — processing is handled in the *service* procedure, which includes echoing of characters, quoting of characters, erase of characters, and erase of lines.

- *XON processing* — when the input queue falls below its low water mark, the *XON* character is sent to the terminal so that it can send more data.

7.12.3 *ldterm* **write side**

On the write side, *ldterm* has only a *put* procedure. If the flag *OPOST* is clear, it means no output processing is to be performed, and the messages are simply passed to the next module down. If *OPOST* is set, messages are processed; for example, if *OLCUC* is set, lower-case characters are converted to upper-case.

The write side must process *M_READ* messages. These are sent down by the stream head when a process issues a *read* system call while the terminal is operating in raw mode. This is described in § 7.12.8.

7.12.4 *ldterm ioctl*

All *ldterm ioctls* are sent downstream in *M_IOCTL* messages. A process sets the terminal modes by issuing the *TCSETA ioctl*, and passes in a *termios* structure containing the modes to set. The *termios* structure is encapsulated in the *M_IOCTL* message. The *ioctl* processing code takes the data from this *termios* structure and copies it into the *t_amodes* field of the *ldterm_mod*. The *M_IOCTL* is then passed downstream to the driver.

The *TCGETA ioctl* is used to read the current state of the line. When this appears on the write side of *ldterm*, no action is taken — it is passed straight on to the driver. The driver does whatever processing is required, and then sends the message back up the read side as an *M_IOCACK* message. When it appears in the read *put* procedure, *ldterm* copies the *t_amodes* structure into the *M_IOCACK* message. The message eventually reaches the stream head, which copies the data from the *M_IOCACK* message into the *termios* structure in user address space.

7.12.5 **Character input**

This section describes the passage of characters from a terminal through the *ldterm* module. Assume that *ldterm* is working in canonical mode, characters are echoed, and that the erase character is CONTROL-H. The user, sitting at the terminal types in the following keystrokes:

> k,⇐mj<CR>

where ⇐ indicates that a backspace was typed and <CR> means carriage return. The processing steps are:

k   The terminal reads the letter from the keyboard and transmits it over the serial line to the serial line driver on the UNIX system. Nothing appears on the screen yet because the terminal is in full-duplex mode with echoing performed by the UNIX system. The serial line hardware on the UNIX system passes the character to the serial line device driver. This puts the letter into an *M_DATA* message and calls the read *put* procedure of *ldterm*. Character translations are performed if necessary and the message is placed on the queue for the *service* procedure

The next time the *service* procedure runs, it takes the message containing the **k** from its queue. An *msgb* is allocated and attached to *t_message* in the *ldterm_mod* for this queue. It is then placed into the newly allocated buffer.

The character is now ready to be echoed. So the *service* procedure allocates a buffer and attaches it to *t_echomp* in the *ldterm_mod* for this queue. Output processing checks are then performed on the character before it is placed in the echo message, which is then detached from *t_echomp*, and passed to the write *put* procedure of the next module below *ldterm*. When the message appears at the driver, the character is then echoed on the terminal screen.

, The same steps are performed as for the **k** above.

⇐ Processing the backspace is the same as above, until the *service* procedure sees that it has received the *VERSE* (erase) character. The pointers in the *t_message* buffer are adjusted so that the comma is deleted, and the sequence backspace-space-backspace is echoed to rub out the character on the terminal screen.

m The **m** is processed as for other letters, and occupies the place in the buffer formerly taken by the comma.

j The same steps are performed as for **k**.

<CR> Since *ICRNL* is set, the read *put* procedure converts the carriage return to a line-feed before placing it in the queue. The *service* procedure detects the end of line character in the message. The newline is placed into the buffer being assembled in *t_message*. This message now contains the complete string "kmj<NL>". The message is passed upstream, the pointer *t_message* is zeroed, and a new *msgb* attached to it. This new buffer will be used to hold data for the next line being assembled. The newline is echoed back to the user.

The user program issues a *read* system call to receive this data. When *ldterm* is working in canonical mode the stream head read option is set to "message non discard mode", meaning that a *read* will return when a message is received at the stream head. That is, if the read requested 256 bytes, it would return a value of 4 if a 4 byte message was received by the stream head.

At first sight, *ldterm* seems grossly inefficient as there is so much processing to be done for each character received. However, optimization is possible. First, the device driver might deliver more than one character in each message block. If three characters are received in a message block, all three are echoed back in the same message. Secondly, the read *service* procedure runs only when the kernel is about to return to user-mode. This means that many data messages might accumulate on the queue before the *service* procedure is run. (One message is passed upstream for each line of input.) Thirdly, when an intelligent controller is used in canonical mode, *ldterm* receives whole lines from the intelligent controller and passes them straight up towards the stream head.

7.12.6 Special character I/O

This section explains how special characters are handled on input and output. The input characters considered are ^C which normally causes an interrupt to be generated, and ^D which is normally the end of file indicator. For output, we show how the tab character is printed, and how tab delays are implemented.

^C   The character is processed in the *ldterm* read *put* procedure. It finds that the *VINTR* character has been read, and so an *M_SIG* message is allocated and sent upstream. This will make the stream head send a *SIGINT* to the current foreground process group. The character is then echoed if the *ECHOCTL* bit is set (see *termio(7)*).

^D   The read *put* procedure places the message containing the character onto the queue. It notices that *VEOF* has been received, and so the line being assembled is passed upstream (without the *VEOF* being added to it). If necessary, the character is echoed. If the *VEOF* is received at the end of a line, the characters received so far are sent upstream, and the user program will *not* detect end of file. On the other hand, if the *VEOF* is received as the first character of the line, a zero length message is sent upstream. The user program that has issued a *read* receives zero, which indicates end of file.

TAB   If *XTABS* is set, tabs must be converted to spaces by the output processing code. The tab character is replaced by space characters. By using the columns counter, the correct number of spaces are output to position the cursor at the next tab stop. If *XTABS* is not set, the tab character is output unchanged.

If *TABDLY* is set, *ldterm* must provide a delay after sending a tab character. This delay is required by some mechanical teleprinters. It is normally achieved by sending two null characters; the transmission time of the two nulls is sufficiently long enough to let the teleprinter carriage move.

If the *NOFILL* flag is set, *ldterm* must wait for a few milliseconds after sending the tab character. It does this by creating an *M_DELAY* message and sending it downstream to the serial line driver. The driver receives the message and delays for the number of clock ticks given in the message. The delay is achieved by the driver setting a timeout and then returning control to the operating system. When the timeout expires, the driver processing continues.

7.12.7 Flow-control

Flow-control between a computer and a serial line is often performed with the *XON/XOFF* protocol (see § 4.3.1 of [Halsall 1988]). Normally, *XON* is the ASCII character Control-S and *XOFF* is the ASCII character Control-Q. In a *termios* structure, the value of *XON* is stored in *VSTRT*, and *XOFF* is stored in *VSTOP*.

Flow-control can operate in two directions: Output flow-control occurs when the computer sends output to the terminal too fast. The terminal sends the *VSTOP* character to stop the computer sending more data. When it is ready for more data, it sends *VSTART* and the computer resumes transmission. Input flow-control works the other way. The computer sends a *VSTOP* to stop the terminal sending data too fast.

Output flow-control is handled by the read *put* procedure in *ldterm*. When the *VSTOP* character is received, an *M_STOP* message is sent back downstream to instruct the driver to stop sending output. When the terminal is ready, it sends the *VSTART* character. The read *put* procedure receives the *VSTART*, and sends an *M_START* message to the driver to resume transmission.

Input flow-control is handled similarly. The read *put* procedure checks the amount of data in the queue. When it goes above a high water mark, an *M_STOPI* message instructs the driver to tell the terminal to stop sending data (a serial driver sends the *VSTOP* character). When enough data has been processed to take the queue level below a low water mark, an *M_STARTI* message is sent downstream to instruct the driver to tell the terminal to resume transmission.

7.12.8 VMIN & VTIME input

When the terminal is set into raw mode, characters are passed upstream unchanged. No signals are generated, and no line editing or buffering is performed. Characters are, however, echoed if *ECHO* is set.

When the switch to raw mode occurs, the stream head is set so that message boundaries are ignored, and *strread( )* will keep collecting data until the count has been satisfied. If a zero length message is received by *strread( )* the read is terminated, and a count of characters received so far is returned. (This value is less than that demanded by the read, and is called a *short count*.) A switch to raw mode also changes the stream head state so that *M_READ* messages are generated for each read system call.

In the following discussion, we refer to *VMIN* and *VTIME* in the context of their constant values which are used to index into the *c_cc[]* array in the *termios* structure (actually, elements 4 and 5 respectively). For example, if we say *VMIN=0* we actually mean *termios.c_cc[VMIN] = 0*.

To demonstrate the use of *VMIN* and *VTIME*, assume that the user program issues either:

```
count = read( fd, buf, 256 ) ;
```
or
```
count = read( fd, buf, 1 ) ;
```

The paragraphs below look at the possibilities. Note that in the examples *VTIME* is set to 3 or 0, implying a timeout of 0.3 seconds or no timeout. *VTIME* always specifies a delay in tenths of a second:

VMIN=0, VTIME=0   As characters are received from the terminal they are sent upstream immediately by the read *service* procedure. When a read system call is issued, an *M_READ* message is sent downstream and received by the write *put* procedure in *ldterm*, which sends a zero-length message upstream. The zero-length message terminates any read in progress. If there are no characters at the stream head, the read returns a count of zero. Otherwise, a single character read returns the value 1 immediately, and a read of 256 returns a short count.

VMIN=0, VTIME=3   When the read is issued, the write *put* procedure initiates a 0.3 second timeout. Characters received during the timeout are sent upstream immediately. A read for single characters returns them one by one as they are received; a read for 256 characters returns a short count. If no character is received during the timeout period, a zero length message is sent upstream and the read terminates.

VMIN>=1, VTIME=0   This gives no timeout. Characters received from the terminal driver are buffered in the *t_message* by the read *service* procedure in *ldterm*. When the buffer size is greater than or equal to *VMIN* the characters are sent upstream. A read for 256 characters returns a count of *VMIN* when the group of characters arrives at the stream head. A read for a single character returns the *VMIN* group of characters one at a time.

VMIN=1, VTIME=3   Each character is passed upstream immediately by the read *service* procedure. The timeout never gets started. All reads return each character as it is received.

VMIN>1, VTIME=3   As characters are received by the read *service* procedure they are buffered. When the number of characters is greater than or equal to *VMIN* they are sent upstream. Reads return as each group of characters reaches the stream head. After the first character is received the timeout is started; 0.3 seconds later, the timeout triggers. Any buffered characters are sent to the stream head and the timeout restarted. If the timeout triggers, and no characters are received during the timeout interval, a zero length message is sent to the stream head to terminate any outstanding read. A read for 256 characters is guaranteed to get at least one character. It returns a short count if no character is received during a 0.3 second period. A read of 1 character waits indefinitely until the character is received.

The strange behaviour of *VMIN* and *VTIME* make it difficult for software writers to handle terminal input efficiently. In many cases, they read a character at a time from the terminal in raw mode. This is not efficient because of the high overhead of context switching each time the read system call is used. To read terminal input in larger units, the best course is to set *VMIN* high, set *VTIME* to a suitable value, and then poll for input. The reading process will sleep until the poll indicates that data is ready at the stream head.

Setting *VMIN* to a high value means that characters are buffered in *ldterm*, and they are sent upstream when *VMIN* is reached, or when the timeout expires, so that when input is coming in fast, large reads are done. When input is slow, single character reads are done. However, there is still a drawback when characters are coming in slowly, there is a delay of at least 0.1 seconds before they are read.

7.13 Other terminal issues

The terminal I/O mechanism of UNIX System V Release 4 supports *pseudo terminals* and intelligent serial device controllers. These are discussed in the following sections.

7.13.1 Pseudo terminals

A pseudo terminal allows a process to behave as if it was the control terminal of another process. That is, the controlled process believes that it is talking to a terminal although it is really talking to another process that emulates the terminal.

A pseudo terminal consists of two halves, a *master* and a *slave*. The controlling process writes data to the master side and the controlled process reads it from the slave side. In the opposite direction, the controlled process writes data to the slave side, and it is read by the controlling process from the master side. Figure 7.67 gives an example of processes connected via a pseudo terminal.

Figure 7.67: *Pseudo-tty construction*

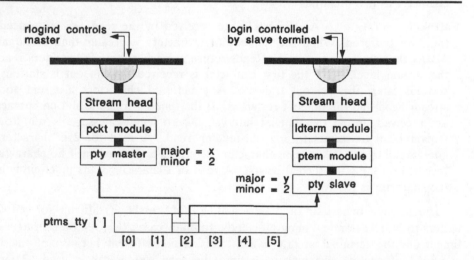

The master device driver is a STREAMS clone device and the slave device driver is a non-clone device. When the master side is opened, the driver open routine allocates a *pt_ttys* structure (see Table 7.38) from an array called *ptms_tty[ ]*, which holds pointers to the write queues for both master and slave sides. The size of this array is configurable by the system administrator, and governs the number of available pseudo terminals.

The master side uses a clone open, which means the open function selects the minor device number itself. That is, the offset in the *ptms_tty[]* array is used as the minor device number.

The controlled process opens the slave side and uses the library routine *ptsname(3C)* to obtain the name of the slave terminal to open. The open function in the slave driver puts the slave side write queue pointer into the *ptms_tty[]* array. In order to connect with the master side, the process opening the slave must use the same minor device number as the master.

Table 7.38: *Struct pt_ttys*

Element	Description
unsigned pt_state	Status of master/slave pair (see below)
*queue_t *ptm_wrq*	Master's write queue pointer
*queue_t *pts_wrq*	Slave's write queue pointer
*mblk_t *pt_bufp*	Pointer to zero byte *msgb* (control only)
pid_t tty	Process ID of controlling terminal

Status (pt_state)	Description
PTLOCK	Master/slave pair is locked
PTMOPEN	Master side is open
PTSOPEN	Slave side is open

Data flow through the pseudo terminal is now simple. The write functions in the master side pass their data onto the read queue of the slave side, and vice versa.

In order to make pseudo terminals work correctly, UNIX System V Release 4 provides three modules to use with pseudo terminals:

- *ptem* — emulates a serial line device driver (see *ptem(7)*), which processes and acknowledges the following *ioctls* (see also *termio(7)*): *TCSETA, TCSETAF, TIOCGWINSZ, JWINSIZE, TCSBRK, TCSETAW, TCGETA, TCSETS, TCSETSF,* and *TCSETSW*. If the user program sets the line speed to zero (to hang up the line), *ptem* sends a zero length message downstream. A process reading the zero length message treats this as the end of file. The messages *M_STOP* and *M_START* are also processed and the module is pushed below *ldterm*. A stream consisting of *ldterm* above *ptem* behaves exactly as if a terminal was connected to it.

- *pckt* — messages such as: *M_PROTO, M_PCPROTO, M_STOPI, M_STARTI, M_STOP, M_START, M_READ, M_FLUSH, M_DATA* and *M_IOCTL* STREAMS messages are "packetized". Messages passing upstream are converted to *M_DATA* messages and have an *M_PROTO* message placed at their head. The first four bytes in the *M_PROTO* message hold the original message type. The converted message is passed upstream. In the downstream direction, messages are passed unchanged. This module allows the process on the master side of the pseudo terminal to recover the messages sent by the slave terminal. The process issues a *getmsg* and can determine what messages were sent by the slave side. If this module is *not* pushed, most of the above messages are deleted by the stream head in the master side of the terminal.

- *ttcompat* — This module allows programs that use the 4.3BSD terminal *ioctl* interface to work correctly under UNIX System V Release 4. The module maps the 4.3BSD *ioctls* into the equivalent *termios* format. (For a description of the 4.3BSD terminal interface, see § 9.3 of [Leffler, McKusick, Karels, Quarterman 1988].) The UNIX System V Release 4 terminal *ioctls* are documented in *termio(7)* and *termios(2)*.

To see how the pieces fit together, we will look at how the **rlogind(1M)** program sets up a pseudo terminal.

    rlogind is the server process that provides a remote login facility via **rlogin(1)**. **rlogin** is used to log in to another machine in the network. On the remote machine the **rlogind** program is invoked. **rlogind** sets up a pseudo terminal, controls the master side itself, and runs **login(1)** on the slave side. The following steps are taken to establish the pseudo terminal:

- The master side of the pseudo terminal is opened.

- The slave side of the terminal is opened.

- *ptem*, *ldterm*, and *ttcompat* are pushed into the stream on the slave side.

- *pckt* is pushed into the master side.

- *fork* is called to create a child process.

- The child process closes both the master side of the pseudo terminal and the network connection, and it makes the slave terminal its control terminal. It then alters its file descriptors so that *stdin, stdout* and *stderr* relate to the slave side of the terminal. Finally, it *execs* the **login** program.

- The parent process closes the slave. Data from the master side of the terminal is read with *getmsg* and sent to the network. Conversely, data is read from the network with *read* and sent to the master terminal with *write*.

7.13.2 Intelligent controllers

The *ldterm* module can work with an intelligent serial controller, which has its own processor, and supports the on-board *termio(7)* interface. Only characters that are processed are passed upstream. (This works in canonical mode only; for raw mode, all characters are passed upstream.)

    When *ldterm* is opened or pushed into a stream, it creates an M_CTL message and sends it to the driver. The data part of the message contains an *iocblk* structure containing the value MC_CANON_QUERY in its *ioc_cmd* field.

    The driver receives the M_CTL message. It places its reply in the *ioc_cmd* field and sends the message back up the read side of the stream. The reply is then processed by the read *put* procedure in *ldterm* and may be one of the following:

- MC_NO_CANON — the driver performs no canonical processing.

- *MC_DO_CANON* — the driver performs canonical processing of the data. In this mode, *ldterm* passes the data traffic unchanged.

- *MC_PART_CANON* — the driver does partial canonical processing. The data block attached to the reply message contains a *termios* structure. The bits set in this structure indicate what canonical processing is to be performed by the driver. For example, a controller that handles *XON/XOFF* flow-control and parity bit stripping has the *ISTRIP*, *IXON* and *IXANY* bits set in *c_iflag*. Thus, when data is flowing through *ldterm* it will never strip parity or process *XON/XOFF* characters.

7.14 STREAMS networking support

STREAMS provides a framework for writing networking software. Externally, this software uses standard protocols such as TCP/IP or X25, but for flexibility, portability and interoperability between modules, the software uses an internal protocol. This internal protocol specifies how messages are passed between the different internal layers in the software. An interface library is provided to allow programmers use of its facilities.

In UNIX System V Release 4 the internal interface is called the *Transport Service Interface* (TSI). There are two other interface libraries: the *Transport Layer Interface* (TLI) and the *socket library*, and they are summarized in the following sections. (For an excellent discussion on how to program sockets and the TLI see [Stevens 1990]. See also [AT&T 1990f]). The positioning of these networking interface modules is shown in Figure 7.68.

7.14.1 Transport service interface

A *service interface* specifies the interaction between adjacent layers in a multi-layer networking protocol. In UNIX System V Release 4, the TSI specifies the interface between a *transport user* (TU) and the *transport provider* (TP). A transport user is a program that uses a network to communicate with another program. A transport provider is a set of networking protocols.

The TSI corresponds exactly to the transport layer (layer 4) in the OSI reference model. The correspondence is so close that the names of the commands and responses are the same as those used by the ISO to describe the layer 4 interface. For a discussion of service interfaces in general, and the ISO/OSI transport layer, see Chapter 6 of [Halsall 1988].

The TSI is made up of a set of data structures called *message primitives*, which are passed between the TU and TP. Messages sent by the TU are specified in Table 7.39, and those sent by the TP are specified in Table 7.40.

Each message type has a C language data structure associated with it. For example, the *T_CONN_REQ* message is sent in a *T_conn_req* structure, as shown in Table 7.41. The structures corresponding to other message types are not shown, but are defined in the header file *sys/tihdr.h*.

Figure 7.68: *Networking interfaces*

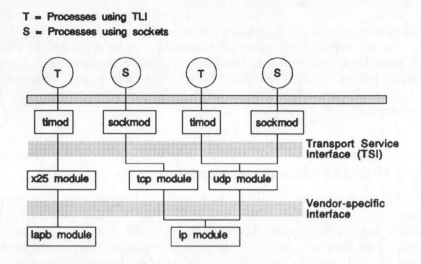

T = Processes using TLI
S = Processes using sockets

Table 7.39: *Messages initiated by transport user (TU)*

Name	Description
T_CONN_REQ	Make outgoing connection
T_DISCON_REQ	Disconnect current connection
T_DATA_REQ	Send data
T_EXDATA_REQ	Send expedited data
T_INFO_REQ	Information request
T_BIND_REQ	Bind to an address
T_UNBIND_REQ	Unbind from an address
T_UNITDATA_REQ	Send a datagram
T_OPTMGMT_REQ	Change options
T_ORDREL_REQ	Disconnect current connection "in an orderly fashion"
T_CONN_RES	Accept incoming connection

The message primitives are sent along the stream in *M_PROTO* or *M_PCPROTO* messages. Any data associated with the message primitive is placed in the message buffer after the message itself. Most of the message primitives contain *offset* fields which are used to indicate whereabouts in the message the data starts. User data sent across the connection is sent along the stream via *M_DATA* messages.

It is beyond the scope of this book to discuss the internal operation of the TSI protocol, but the general principle can be seen from the following example.

To initiate a connection, the TU sends a *T_CONN_REQ* message to the TP. The fields of the *T_CONN_REQ* specify the address of the remote system. The TP receives the message and initiates the connection. While the connection is being set up, the TU waits. Once the connection is established, the TP sends a

Table 7.40: *Messages initiated by transport provider (TP)*

Name	Description
T_CONN_IND	Indication of incoming call
T_CONN_CON	Confirmation of outgoing connection
T_DISCON_IND	Connection has been disconnected
T_DATA_IND	Incoming data
T_EXDATA_IND	Incoming expedited data
T_INFO_ACK	Acknowledgment of information request
T_BIND_ACK	Acknowledgment of successful bind
T_ERROR_ACK	Used when a message primitive failed or was sent out of sequence
T_OK_ACK	Sent when a message primitive was successfully processed
T_UDERROR_IND	Datagram error
T_OPTMGMT_ACK	Acknowledgment of option change
T_ORDREL_IND	Remote has requested orderly release
T_UNITDATA_IND	Incoming datagram

Table 7.41: *struct T_conn_req*

Element	Description
long PRIM_type	Always set to T_CONN_REQ
long DEST_length	Length of destination address
long DEST_offset	Offset to destination address
long OPT_length	Length of options
long OPT_offset	Offset to options

T_CONN_CON message back to the TU. On receipt of this confirmation, the TU can start to send data on the connection. Other message primitives are handled in a similar manner.

A programmer could use the TSI specification to write a program that used *getmsg* and *putmsg* to interface to a transport provider. However, programming this interface is difficult and error-prone because the interface is complicated. The TLI and socket interface libraries, which simplify access to the TSI are summarized in the following two sections.

7.14.2 Socket interface

The socket interface library makes UNIX System V Release 4 compatible with the 4.3 BSD *socket* interface [Vessey, Skinner 1990] and makes it easier to port 4.3 BSD-based applications to UNIX System V Release 4.

The socket interface library is supplemented by a STREAMS module for holding state information about the connection, which must be preserved across *fork* and *exec* system calls. The subroutine calls in the library send and receive messages via the TSI, as explained in the paragraphs below. The major routines in the socket library are summarized in Table 7.42 and are described below (see also Section 3N of [AT&T 1990h]):

- *socket( )* — creates an endpoint for a communication channel and returns a suitable file descriptor. After creating the socket, a program must bind an address to the socket and then initiate a connection to the remote system. Alternatively, after binding an address, it must listen for incoming connections. A parameter to the call determines which file to open (for example, */dev/tcp* for a TCP connection). The file is opened, and the socket module pushed into the stream. Finally, an *ioctl* is issued which is understood by the socket module as an instruction to configure the protocol being used on the stream. The open processing for the socket module sets the stream head options so that *M_PROTO* messages are discarded. This feature is used by *read* and described further in this section.

- *bind( )* — binds a socket to an address. The parameters to the call specify the address to which the socket will be bound. The subroutine takes the bind parameters and issues a *TI_BIND ioctl*. This *ioctl* is interpreted by the socket module. It sends a *T_BIND_REQ* down the stream to the transport provider such as the TCP module. The *T_BIND_REQ* message specifies how many outstanding connection requests (backlog) will be queued by the transport provider before incoming calls on this address are rejected. This field is set to zero by *bind( )*, meaning that all calls will be rejected (but see the description of *listen( )* below). The transport provider does whatever is necessary to process the bind, and sends a *T_BIND_ACK* upstream. The acknowledgement is processed by the socket module, which saves the address that was bound in the structure pointed to by the *q_ptr*. Finally, the *ioctl* is acknowledged.

  The processing of bind requests could have been done more simply by sending the *T_BIND_REQ* directly into the stream via *putmsg*. However, implementing it as an *ioctl* means that only one *bind( )* can ever be processed at a time.

- *connect( )* — initiates a connection on a socket. The parameters to the call specify the remote machine to connect with. The subroutine encapsulates the parameters into a *T_CONN_REQ* message, sends it into the stream with *putmsg*, then issues a *getmsg* to receive the reply. If the connection was successful it receives a *T_CONN_CON* message, otherwise an error code is returned. The socket module processes the connect request message and marks the socket state to show that a connect has been issued but not yet acknowledged. The message is passed downstream to the transport provider, which establishes the connection and sends a *T_CONN_CON* message upstream. The socket module processes this message by saving the peer address, marking the connection as connected, and then passing the message upstream. The call completes when the *T_CONN_CON* has been received.

- *listen( )* — is called after a *bind( )* or *connect( )* but before an *accept( )*. The manual says that this subroutine listens for connections on a socket. In fact, it specifies how many pending connections (backlog) will be queued in the lower levels of the software while the process waits for a connection in *accept( )*. If the *backlog* is set to three, then the lower levels of the software will queue up three pending connections. If a fourth arrives, it will be rejected. The socket module processing for *listen( )* is clumsy; it sends a *T_BIND_REQ* downstream, specifying the supplied *backlog* parameter. This value is interpreted by the transport provider, which begins to queue incoming calls sent to this address. The calls are then processed by the *accept( )* subroutine. However, if the specified backlog is non-zero, the socket module, first unbinds the socket, and then rebinds it to the same address in order to reset the backlog correctly.

- *accept( )* — when a process wants to receive incoming call requests it issues an *accept( )* call. When the call returns, it means that an incoming connection has been accepted from a remote machine. A new file descriptor is returned, which will be used by the process for I/O on the connection. The *accept( )* subroutine issues a *getmsg* to receive a *T_CONN_IND* message. If it does not receive one, it returns an error. Otherwise, it opens a new stream with a variant of the *socket( )* call. It then issues an *I_FDINSERT ioctl* (see Figure 7.51). The control buffer for this message contains a *T_CONN_RES* message, which contains a pointer to the queue of the stream on which the data for the connection will be accepted. This is set by the stream head before passing the message downstream. The message is received by the socket module, which copies the source and destination addresses and other state information into the new queue specified in the *T_CONN_RES* message. The message is then passed downstream. The transport provider ensures that the data travelling on the connection is passed to the new queue.

- *write* — a write to a socket behaves in the same way as a write on a normal stream: the data is encapsulated in an *M_DATA* message by the stream head and passed downstream. The socket module does no special processing for these messages. If there is space downstream, the message is passed on, otherwise it is queued and passed down by the *service* procedure.

- *read* — as with *write*, the *read* system call behaves the same way as for a read on a normal stream. No special processing is performed on *M_DATA* messages. Data messages sent upstream by a transport provider consist of an *M_PROTO* message that encapsulates an *M_DATA* message containing the data. When this type of message reaches the stream head, the *M_PROTO* header is unlinked and discarded. If *M_PROTO* messages were not discarded, then a *read* will fail with the error code *EBADMSG*. A *read* cannot read *M_PROTO* messages unless suitable stream head options have been set.

7.14.3 Transport layer interface

The Transport Layer Interface provides an alternative method for accessing network facilities. The interface is protocol independent, in contrast to the socket interface which is heavily biased towards the Internet Protocols. The TLI is similar to the socket library because it has a set of interface subroutines and a STREAMS module.

Table 7.42: *Major socket library functions*

Function	Description
accept	Accept a connection on a socket
bind	Associate an address with a socket
connect	Make a connection on a socket
listen	Specify queue length for incoming call requests
socket	Create a STREAMS-based communication endpoint
getpeername	Get address of remote socket
getsockname	Get address to which a socket is bound
getsockopt	Get socket options
recv	Receive a message through socket (similar to *getmsg*)
send	Send a message through a socket (similar to *putmsg*)
select	Provides similar function to *poll*

Table 7.43: *Major TLI functions*

Element	Description
t_open	Open a transport endpoint
t_bind	Associate transport endpoint with an address
t_connect	Set up a transport connection
t_listen	Wait for an incoming connection request
t_accept	Accept an incoming connection request
t_snd	Send data over a transport connection
t_rcv	Receive data from a connection
t_close	Close a transport connection
t_getstate	Get current state of a connection
t_listen	Listen for incoming connections
t_optmgmt	Control transport layer options

The TLI exchanges messages with transport providers that conform to the TSI. The major functions in the TLI are summarized in Table 7.43, and are described as follows:

- *t_open()* — similar to *socket()*, it establishes an endpoint for communication. It opens the STREAMS device driver specified by the user and pushes the TLI module, *timod*, into the stream.

- *t_bind()* — similar to *bind()*, it sets the address of the transport endpoint. It issues an *ioctl* that is processed by *timod*. The module creates a *T_BIND_REQ* message that is sent downstream and processed by the transport provider. The *ioctl* is acknowledged when the *T_BIND_ACK* is received from the transport provider.

- *t_connect()* — similar to *connect()*, it initiates a connection to a remote machine. The parameters to the call specify the destination.

- *t_listen()* — similar to *listen()*, it issues a *getmsg* in the hope of receiving a connection indication message (*T_CONN_IND*).

- *t_accept()* — similar to *accept()*, it is issued by a process that wishes to accept incoming calls. However, it operates slightly differently to *accept()*, which automatically gets a new endpoint; with *t_accept()* the application decides if it is to use a new descriptor. The incoming call request is received by *t_listen()* and accepted by *t_accept()*. The process must either accept the call on the endpoint that issued the listen, or open a new transport end point and bind the endpoint to an address. The new endpoint can be used for the data transfer.

- *t_snd()* — this subroutine is the preferred method for sending data into a TLI connection. The data is sent into the stream via *putmsg*; the control part contains a *T_DATA_REQ* message, and the data part contains the data being sent. No special processing is done.

- *write* — in principle, it is possible to issue a write to the file descriptor returned by a call to *t_open()*. The data will be passed to the transport provider unmodified. However, the transport provider may have packet size constraints in force. If a process issues a write that is too large the request will be rejected by the transport provider. The *t_snd()* function is used instead, because it breaks the messages up into chunks if necessary.

- *t_rcv()* — this subroutine reads data from the transport connection. Data arrives at the stream head as an *M_PROTO* message encapsulating an *M_DATA* message, which contains the data. The subroutine issues a *getmsg* to retrieve the data, which is automatically copied into the process's data buffer.

- *read* — if the process issues a *read* system call on a file descriptor issued by *t_open()*, the first message that arrives at the stream head will make the read fail with an *EBADMSG* error code. The TLI does not alter the stream head state to allow a *read* to succeed.

A disadvantage of the TLI is that a process cannot issue *read* and *write* directly, which creates a problem for certain kinds of network server applications. Normally, a network server sets up the communication channels. It then *forks* and *execs* a back-end process to do the real work. The server alters the file descriptors for the back-end so that its standard input and output are the network connections. The back-end acts in the traditional UNIX way: it reads from its standard input, writes to its standard output, and so on.

The *tirdwr* module allows this form of server/back-end to be written. The server establishes the connection; once established, it pushes the *tirdwr* module into the streams that will be used as standard input and output by the back-end.

The *tirdwr* module allows the use of *read* and *write* system calls on a TLI endpoint; for *write*, it places a *T_DATA_REQ* header on the front of the message. Similarly, for *read*, it removes *T_DATA_IND* from the front of the messages.

7.15 STREAMS module configuration

Similar to STREAMS drivers, which are configured into *cdevsw[]* (see § 5.6.3), STREAMS modules are configured into *fmodsw[]* — the operating system's "module switch table". Each entry in the table is a *fmodsw* structure (see Table 7.44) described as follows:

- *f_name* — holds the module's unique null terminated name, for use when it is pushed onto a stream. Its maximum length is *FMNAMESZ* bytes (currently 8).

- *f_str* — points to the module's public *streamtab* data object (see § 7.3) describing its queue initialization information.

Table 7.44: *Struct fmodsw*

Element	Description
char f_name[FMNAMESZ+1]	The module name
struct streamtab *f_str	Pointer to private queue initialization info
int *f_flag	Module flags (same use as for *cdevsw[]*)

7.16 Exercises

7.1   Describe the differences between a *module, driver* and *multiplexor.*

7.2   How does STREAMS benefit suppliers and users of networking software?

7.3   What purpose is served by a module's *put* and *service* procedures? Why do some modules provide both procedures, and others only one?

7.4   Why are *put* and *service* procedures not allowed to sleep? What problems would occur if they did?

7.5   Why does it make no sense for *put* and *service* procedures to access the user-area for the currently running process?

7.6   Explain why STREAMS allows only a single *ioctl* to be active in a stream.

7.7   Many processes might simultaneously issue an *ioctl* to the same stream. How does STREAMS manage this, bearing in mind that only a single ioctl is active? How could STREAMS be modified to allow multiple *ioctls* to be active in a stream?

7.8   Explain the processing steps for opening a clone device.

7.9*   Device */dev/ser1* is a STREAMS device. Process A opens it and then pushes *ldterm* into the stream. Processes B and C then open the same file:
- How many streams are created?

- How many streams contain the *ldterm* module?
- How often is the *ldterm* open function called?

Process A then issues an *I_POP ioctl* to remove *ldterm* from its stream:

- How many streams are there now?
- How many instances of the *ldterm* module are there now?
- How often is the close procedure for *ldterm* called?

7.10*** Design a STREAMS module that compresses data passing downstream, and uncompresses data passing upstream. The module should operate correctly in the case of memory allocation failures.

7.11*** Extend the design of the compression module so that it does data encryption instead. (Assume you have a function that encrypts the data for you.) The module must allow a process to enter an encryption key. In the opposite direction, it should decrypt the data, using the same key.

7.12 Describe the transparent *ioctl* facility. How does it differ from the STREAMS *I_PUSH* facility?

7.13 A driver can use *esballoc( )* to make a message block point to a data buffer held on an I/O card. Why does this only work for data coming from the card into memory and not in the other direction?

7.14** Write a STREAMS loop-around driver. That is, a STREAMS driver that passes data received on the downstream side back to the upstream side. Test this driver to ensure that it allows two processes to exchange data.

7.15*** Write a STREAMS driver and a subroutine that uses the semantics of the *pipe* system call.

7.16 Write a program that uses *poll*, scans multiple inputs, and writes the data to a log file. The log file should indicate the input the data came from.

7.17 How does a shell such as **ksh(1)** manage job control?

7.18 What purpose does *ldterm* serve?

7.19 Explain what pseudo terminals are used for, and how they work. Explain why STREAMS also provides the *pckt* and *ptem* modules.

7.20** Write a *curses(3X)* program that enables you to run two or more shells on a single terminal. The shells should be controlled via a pseudo terminal. Design it so that screen-based applications such as **vi** operate correctly.

7.21 Explain why both the socket and TLI libraries require a STREAMS module.

7.22 Why does UNIX System V Release 4 provide both a socket and a TLI networking library? If you were writing a new networking application, which would you use? Justify your choice.

7.23 Why is it not possible to use *read* and *write* on the file descriptors returned by the *t_open( )* subroutine call? What does a program do to rectify this?

CHAPTER 8

Interprocess communication

And I began to hear the voice of Jehovah saying: "Whom shall I send, and who will go for us?" And I proceeded to say "Here I am! send me".

— Isaiah 6:8

8.1 Introduction to interprocess communication

Every multitasking operating system provides a set of facilities that allow processes to communicate with each other: information is exchanged between the operating system and running processes, or between one running process and another. The various methods are given different names depending on which literature you read. The different types of interprocess communication (IPC) facilities fall into three categories which we will call: *message queues, event flags* and *shared resources*. These are described briefly as follows:

- *message queues* — provide a generalized message-passing scheme; a set of processes wishing to communicate make a connection to a message queue having a unique identifier. Arbitrary data is then encapsulated and passed along the queue in messages, the format of which is defined either by the operating system or by the cooperating processes themselves.

  Message queues provide a reliable buffering mechanism for messages. That is, all messages are delivered, and in the sequence they were sent. The size of buffering is system dependent; on UNIX systems it is configurable. In UNIX System V Release 4 the facility is referred to as *IPC message queues* or simply as message queues. Besides message queues, similar functionality is provided by pipes, STREAMS and FIFOs.

- *event flags* — tell a process that a certain event has occurred. A flag is set by either process or operating system to indicate an event, and other processes use it to determine that the event has occurred. Data is seldom communicated with the event flag; it simply indicates the event. When event flags are used to control access to a resource, they are often referred to as *semaphores*. UNIX System V Release 4 provides two event flag mechanisms that use signals and semaphores.

528

- *shared resources* — are the commonest method of exchanging data between processes. There are many different ways to provide processes with access to one resource; the most common is to use files to hold the data to be shared.

    Many operating systems have facilities that enable processes to share areas of memory by mapping a portion of physical memory into their address space. UNIX System V Release 4 allows processes to share data by using files, and it also provides a shared memory interface.

8.1.1 IPC operation permissions

Message queues, semaphores and shared memory segments are referred to here as *IPC resources*.

An IPC resource has two unique identifiers associated with it: *key* and *id*. They are described as follows:

- *key* — is analogous to a file name, and is used to identify exclusively an IPC resource. Cooperating processes wishing to access the same IPC resource must use the same key. The key is implemented as an integer, so, like file descriptors, processes use integers to identify the IPC resource they wish to access.

    The C library provides the function *ftok( )* (see *stdipc(3C)*) to generate keys. This takes a filename and an integer as parameters and generates a key from them. Cooperating processes use *ftok( )* to generate identical keys; the key it returns is based on the file's *inode* number, so if the file is deleted and re-created, the key generated by *ftok( )* will change. If *ftok( )* is not used, cooperating processes simply agree on a hard-coded value for the key. However, this scheme is not recommended since another process might accidentally try to use the same IPC resources, which could lead to chaos.

- *id* — is analogous to a file descriptor. When a program attaches to an IPC resource, the system call returns the *id* (an integer). Subsequent system calls use the *id* to identify the IPC resource being used.

Table 8.1: *Struct ipc_perm*

Element	Description
uid_t uid	User ID of resource owner
gid_t gid	Group ID of resource owner
uid_t cuid	User ID of resource creator
gid_t cgid	Group ID of resource creator
mode_t mode	Resource access modes
unsigned long seq	Sequence number
key_t key	Global resource key

The operating system uses permissions to restrict access to the IPC resources. Each process is free to create an IPC resource, but once created the permissions restrict access to it. When an IPC resource is created, it has associated with it an access mode similar to that used when accessing a file. That is, the access mode has fields to restrict the read and write permission for the owner, the owner's group and the rest of the world. The permissions relevant to an IPC resource are held in an *ipc_perm* structure (see Table 8.1) whose fields are described as follows:

- *uid, gid* — the user ID and group ID of the current owner of the resource. A privileged process can change these fields with the *IPC_SET* control operation to allow non-privileged processes to access the resource.

- *cuid, cgid* — the user ID and group ID of the creator of the resource. These fields remain constant throughout the life of the resource.

- *mode* — the access modes of the resource. The permission bits are the same as those used for a file (see § 2.10.2).

- *seq* — a resource usage sequence counter. Each time the resource is freed, the sequence number is incremented. This field ensures that resource IDs are unique.

- *key* — holds the key for the resource.

8.2 Semaphores

The dictionary defines a semaphore as "a signalling apparatus that is upright and has arms that move up and down". The example familiar to most of us is the old-fashioned railway line signal. When the arm is horizontal, the train must stop. When it is at an angle, the train can go. This type of signal usually moves back to the horizontal position as soon as the train passes the signal to prevent the following train entering the section of track before the signal person is ready for it. For night use, the signal arm had a light that shone red for stop or green for go.

This analogy was presumably in the mind of whoever first described the computer use of semaphores. In an operating system, semaphores provide a function similar to that of railway signals.

A semaphore has an integer value associated with it, and it has two operations:

P   In simple terms, a P operation means "wait for signal to go green, pass the signal, signal automatically goes to red". This operation is also referred to here as *semaphore claim*.

A P operation is used when the process wants to enter a critical section, which it cannot do if the value of the semaphore is zero. The process waits until the semaphore is greater than zero; then it decrements the semaphore value and enters the critical section.

V   In simple terms, a V operation means "set the signal to green."

A V operation is used when a process leaves a critical section. The semaphore value is incremented.

The semaphore P and V operations must be atomic. That is, no interrupts must occur while they run, otherwise processes could find the semaphore values in an inconsistent state. In UNIX, these facilities are implemented as system calls, which means that they are atomic from the user's point of view.

Semaphores are used in operating systems in two main areas: *mutual exclusion* and *producer consumer*.

- *Mutual exclusion* — prevents two processes accessing the same data at the same time. If two processes are accessing a shared resource, the data could become inconsistent. A means must be provided whereby only one process at a time can access shared resources. For files, most operating systems provide a file-locking mechanism, but semaphores may also be used. When the resource to be locked is initialized, its associated semaphore is initialized to one. When the first process wishes to access the resource, it carries out a P operation, meaning that it is entering the critical section. The semaphore protecting the resource is set to zero. A second process wanting to access the data will find the semaphore at zero, and so it must wait. When the first process has finished with the data, it performs the V operation on the semaphore, meaning that it has left the critical section, and that the other process can lock the data and enter its critical section.

- *Producer consumer* — used by cooperating processes: one generates data, the other uses the data. Many contemporary database systems work in this way. The user produces a database query that is consumed by the database lookup software. This in turn produces results that are consumed by the database front end and displayed to the user. Producer consumer relationships use semaphores to indicate that data is available. When the producer is initialized, the semaphore is set to zero, meaning that no data has been produced yet. When the consumer starts, it performs a P operation, meaning enter critical section, or "consume some data". When the producer has some data available, it can perform the V operation; the consumer can then proceed to consume the data.

In both these situations a single binary semaphore controls access to a single resource. However, there are extensions to the basic semaphore concept.

The semaphore value need not be just zero and one. If it is a positive integer, the value can be used to indicate how much of a resource is available. For example, if a buffer pool contains 20 buffers, the semaphore that protects the buffer pool is initialized to 20. Each time a process takes a buffer, it performs a P operation, which decrements the semaphore value. However, processes block only when the semaphore count falls to zero, indicating that the pool is empty. When a process has finished with the buffer, it performs the V operation, which increments the semaphore value, indicating that the resource is available.

Sometimes a process has to perform a P operation on multiple semaphores to claim multiple resources. For example, if a process has to access a buffer and a shared memory segment, it must perform a P operation on two semaphores. A naive implementation would first claim the buffer, then the free memory. However, this could lead to a deadlock if the process's claim to the buffer prevents another process from releasing its claim for free memory. Implementations of multiple semaphore claim take "all or nothing". That is, all semaphores are claimed at once. If one is blocked, none of the others are claimed.

A process might claim a buffer, but then die because it receives a signal; it cannot perform a V operation because it is dead. Thus, a semaphore implementation should provide the means to undo a semaphore claim.

The UNIX System V Release 4 implementation of semaphores allows all the above operations. That is, it allows simple semaphores for mutual exclusion and producer consumer, multi-valued semaphores for controlling access to pooled resources, and multiple semaphore claim in a single operation.

8.2.1 Semaphore initialization and control

In UNIX System V Release 4 a semaphore identifier refers to a group of individual semaphores specified in the system call arguments at the time they are allocated. To implement a simple semaphore operation, a group size of one is specified. If, however, multiple semaphore claims are to be performed in a single operation, a group of semaphores must be specified. Each semaphore group has a data structure called *semid_ds*, which holds the IPC permissions, the semaphores themselves, and their access time information. Individual semaphores in a group are represented by the *sem* structure. Both the *semid_ds* and the *sem* structures are summarized in Table 8.2.

Table 8.2: *Semaphore structures*

struct semid_ds	
Element	Description
struct ipc_perm sem_perm	Permissions
*struct sem *sem_base*	Pointer to semaphore array
unsigned short sem_nsems	Number of semaphores in the group
time_t sem_otime	Time of last operation
time_t sem_ctime	Time of last change
struct sem	
Element	Description
unsigned short semval	Current value of semaphore
pid_t sempid	Process that did the last operation
unsigned short semncnt	Count of processes waiting to perform P operation
unsigned short semzcnt	Count of processes waiting for *semval* to be zero

The system calls *semget* and *semctl* perform initialization and control operations on semaphores.

- *semget()* — is called with three parameters: a semaphore key, the number of semaphores to allocate for that key, and a flags value. The flags contain the semaphore permission modes ORed with one of the following:

  - *IPC_PRIVATE* — if set, a private semaphore is initialized i.e., the key is ignored. Private semaphores are useful if the process is going to *fork* later.

The private semaphore will be usable by both parent and child processes. Other processes, however, will not have access to the *id* or the key for this semaphore, so they are completely unable to access it.

- *IPC_CREAT* — if set, and the semaphore with the given key does not exist, it is created. If it is clear, and the semaphore does not exist, the system call returns the *EEXIST* error code in *errno*.

The value returned by *semget* is the identifier, or *semid*, that the program must use when it issues other semaphore system calls. Note that once a semaphore is created, it persists until such time that it is deallocated or until the operating system is next rebooted. Even if a process exits, its semaphores remain in the kernel. Thus if a program is not careful about allocating and deallocating semaphores, the operating system eventually exhausts its supply of semaphores. The command **ipcs(1)** indicates the IPC resources that are in use, and the command **ipcrm(1)** deletes unwanted IPC resources.

Figure 8.1: *Arguments to semctl*

```
/* Union used for argument. */
union semun {
    int value;            /* For SETVAL command */
    struct semid_ds *b;   /* For IPC_STAT and IPC_SET */
    unsigned short *a;    /* For GETALL/SETALL command */
};

int
semctl( semid, semnum, cmd, arg )
    int semid;
    int semnum;
    int cmd;
    union semun arg;
```

- *semctl( )* — performs miscellaneous control operations on a group of semaphores. In particular it can be used to do the following:
  - Get or set the values of the individual semaphores.
  - Query the fields in the *semid_ds*.
  - Set certain fields in the *semid_ds*,
  - Delete the semaphore group.

The system call takes four arguments, as shown in Figure 8.1. The *cmd* parameter specifies the operation to be carried out as follows:

- *GETVAL* — returns the value of a semaphore in the group. The *semid* and *semnum* specify the semaphore to read. (Note that semaphores are numbered from zero.)

- *SETVAL* — sets the value of the semaphore to the value in the parameter *arg.value*.

- *GETPID* — returns the *sempid* field from the *semid_ds*, allowing the process to find out who last altered the semaphore values. This, for example, allows a producer to know which consumer is consuming.

- *GETNCNT, GETZCNT* — returns the value in the *semncnt* or *semzcnt* fields of the *semid_ds*. It can be used to get an idea of how many processes are blocked on the resource controlled by the semaphore.

- *GETALL* — fills the array pointed to by *arg.a* with the values of all the semaphores in the group specified by the *semid* argument.

- *SETALL* — allows the program to set all the values in the semaphore group. The semaphores in the group have their value set by the corresponding value in *arg.a*.

- *IPC_STAT* — reads the *semid_ds* for the semaphore group. The data is put into the buffer pointed to by *arg.b*.

- *IPC_SET* — the *uid*, *gid* and *mode* fields in the *semid_ds* for the semaphore are set with the corresponding values from *arg.b*. This command succeeds only if the process is privileged, or if the effective user id of the process is the same as the *uid* or *cuid* fields in the *semid_ds*. It allows a program to give a semaphore away, but not to get it back again.

- *IPC_RMID* — removes the semaphore group and all data structures associated with it.

Table 8.3: *Struct sembuf*

Element	Description
ushort sem_num	Number of semaphores in group to operate on
short sem_op	Operation to be performed
short sem_flg	Flags that modify the operation

8.2.2 Using semaphores

Operations on a group of semaphores are carried out by the *semop* system call, which provides an interface for manipulating semaphores in the most general way imaginable. Such generality makes the system call complicated. The example in Figure 8.2 shows how *semop* is used. It is called with three arguments, which are described as follows:

- *semid* — identifies the semaphore group to operate on.

- *sops* — an array of *sembuf* structures (see Table 8.3) that specifies which operations are to be performed on which semaphores in the group.

- *nsops* — specifies how many *sembuf* structures are in the *sops* array.

The following description explains what happens when *semop* is applied to one semaphore in the group. However, the specified operation is applied to each of the semaphores given in the *sops* argument. The system call succeeds only when it has performed *all* the semaphore operations. If it succeeds for some semaphores in the group and not others, a deadlock might ensue. Three types of operation can be specified depending on the value in the *sem_op* field:

< 0   is used to enter a critical region. For the P operation, *sem_op* has the value -1. The notation *abs(sem_op)* gives the absolute value of *sem_op*. If the semaphore value is greater than or equal to *abs(sem_op)*, *abs(sem_op)* is subtracted from the value of the semaphore. Otherwise, *abs(sem_op)* is less than the semaphore value and the process sleeps. It wakes up when *abs(sem_op)* is once more greater than or equal to the semaphore value.

> 0   is used to leave a critical region. For the V operation, *sem_op* has the value 1. In general, the value of *sem_op* is added to the value of the semaphore.

= 0   is used to wait for the value of the semaphore to fall to zero. If the semaphore is zero, the system call returns immediately, otherwise it sleeps until the value becomes zero.

The semaphore operation is modified by the values in the *sem_flg* field. The following two values can be used:

- *IPC_NOWAIT* — if set, the process will not sleep waiting to perform the specified operation. Instead, the system call returns -1 immediately, and *errno* is set to *EAGAIN*.

- *SEM_UNDO* — if set, a semaphore undo operation is performed when the process exits. Each semaphore has a *semadj* value associated with it for adjusting the value of the semaphore when the process dies. If the value of the semaphore is reduced by *x*, then *x* is added to the *semadj* value. Conversely, if it is increased by *y*, then *y* is subtracted from the *semadj* value. When the process exits, the value in *semadj* is added to the value of the semaphore, which has the effect of undoing any outstanding semaphore operations. The example in Figure 8.2 sets the *SEM_UNDO* flag so that the semaphore is properly reset should the process dies while executing its critical section.

8.3 The implementation of semaphores

IPC facilities in UNIX System V Release 4 are directly inherited from UNIX System V Release 3. As a result, IPC resources are all statically allocated, whereas most other kernel data structures are dynamically allocated, so the system administrator has a raft of tuneable parameters that must be tweaked in order to meet the needs of applications running on the machine.

Figure 8.2: *Example of semaphore use*

```
/* Example code to protect a critical region using
 * P and V operations on a semaphore. Note that only
 * one process should initialize the semaphore.
 */

#include <sys/types.h>
#include <sys/ipc.h>
#include <sys/sem.h>

/* Get semaphore id and initialize it to one. */
int init( key, what )
key_t key;
int what;
{ int retval;
  /* Allocate and create semaphore */
  if( (retval = semget( key, 1, 0777 | IPC_CREAT )) == -1 )
    process an error
  else {
    /* Initialize semaphore zero to "what" */
    if( semctl( retval, 0, SETVAL, what ) == -1 )
      process an error
  }
  return retval;
}

/* P(s) -- enter critical region */
void P(s)
int s;
{
  struct sembuf sb;
  sb.sem_num = 0;
  sb.sem_op = -1;         /* P operation - decrement semaphore */
  sb.sem_flg = SEM_UNDO; /* Semaphore claim undone if we die */

  /* Attempt to decrement the semaphore. Sleeps until operation
   * has been completed.
   */
  if( semop( s, &sb, 1 ) == -1 )
    process an error
  return;
}
```

```
/* V(s) -- leave critical region */
void V(s)
int s;
{
  struct sembuf sb;
  sb.sem_num = 0;
  sb.sem_op = 1;          /* V operation - increment semaphore */
  sb.sem_flg = SEM_UNDO; /* Semaphore claim undone if we die */
  if( semop( s, &sb, 1 ) == -1 )
    process an error
  return;
}

main( )
{
  int s;
  ...
  s = init(key, 1); /* Assume key is initialized elsewhere */
  ...
  P(s);                   /* Start critical section */
  perform critical operations
  V(s);                   /* End of critical section */
  ...
}
```

The tuneable parameters are copied into the global *seminfo* structure, which is referenced by the semaphore routines to check the semaphore allocation limits. Table 8.4 shows the fields of the *seminfo* structure, the tuneable parameters that the administrator can tune, and the global variables used by the semaphore system. The *seminfo* structure, and its related tuneable parameters, are used to size various statically allocated tables compiled into the kernel. To change them, the administrator alters the relevant parameters then rebuilds the kernel. The tuneable parameters are explained as follows:

- *SEMMNI* — controls the number of active semaphore groups in the system (equivalent to the number of unique semaphore keys in use). *SEMMNI* specifies the number of elements in an array of *semid_ds* structures called *sema[]*, which is used to allocate to each active semaphore group.

- *SEMMAP* — controls the size of the allocation map used for the individual semaphores in the group. When a semaphore is allocated, the individual semaphores are allocated from the semaphore memory pool with *rmalloc()*. Semaphores are allocated from an array of *map* structures called *semmap[]*; the size of this array is given by *SEMMAP*. If the map size is too small, *rmfree()* reports errors on the console, saying that items are being lost from the map. The solution is to increase the size of the map until the problem goes away. (*rmalloc()* and *rmfree()* are described in § 3.9.4.)

Table 8.4: *Semaphore information*

Element	Tuneable	Description
	*Struct seminfo*	
semmap	*SEMMAP*	Number of entries in *rmalloc* map used for semaphores
semmni	*SEMMNI*	Total number of semaphore groups available
semmns	*SEMMNS*	Total number of semaphores available
semmnu	*SEMMNU*	Total number of undo structures
semmsl	*SEMMSL*	Maximum number of semaphores in a group
semopm	*SEMOPM*	Maximum number of operations in a single call
semume	*SEMUME*	Number of semaphore undos a single process may perform
semusz	-	Number of bytes in undo structures
semvmx	*SEMVMX*	Maximum value of a semaphore
semaem	*SEMAEM*	Maximum value to adjust a semaphore by on exit

Variable	Description
	Semaphore global variables
struct semid_ds sema[ ]	Array of semaphore data structures
struct sem sem[ ]	Poll from which semaphores are allocated
struct map semmap[ ]	Allocation map used by *rmalloc*
struct sem_undo *sem_undo[ ]	Per process semaphore undo group
struct sem_undo semu[ ]	Pool of semaphore undo structures
struct seminfo seminfo	Semaphore information structure
struct sem_undo *semfup	Freelist of undo structures (points into *semu[ ]*)

- *SEMMNS* — controls the total number of semaphores in the system. They are held in a global array called *sem[ ]*, and are allocated from it using *rmalloc( )*. If a program issues a *semget* to create a semaphore group containing 10 semaphores, 1 *semid_ds* and 10 *sem* structures are allocated.

- *SEMMNU* — specifies the number of undo groups in the system. These are held in a global array called *semu[ ]*, which contains at least *SEMMNU*SEMUME* entries, and is divided up into *SEMMNU* groups, each of which contains *SEMUME* undo structures. Each process that sets a *SEM_UNDO* flag is given a block containing *SEMUME* undo entries (see also Figure 8.4).

- *SEMUME* — specifies the maximum number of undo operations a process can maintain (see *SEMMNU*).

- *SEMMSL* — specifies the maximum number of semaphores in a single group. If a program attempts to allocate more than *SEMMSL* semaphores, the *semget* system call fails with the *EINVAL* error code.

- *SEMOPM* — specifies the maximum number of semaphore operations in a *semop* system call. If the program attempts more than *SEMOPM* operations, the *semop* call will fail with the error code *E2BIG*.

- *SEMVMX* — specifies the greatest value a semaphore can have and prevents it from wrapping round. (If it is incremented too many times, it will become negative.) If a process attempts a V operation, and the value of the semaphore would go above *SEMVMX*, the call fails, and the error *ERANGE* is returned.

- *SEMAEM* — specifies the maximum amount by which a semaphore will be adjusted on exit. If a semaphore has the *SEM_UNDO* flag set, and an operation is performed that would make the adjust on exit value exceed *SEMAEM*, the operation fails with the error code *ERANGE*.

8.3.1 Semaphore support functions

The functions that administer IPC resources rely on two common functions to allocate the resource data structures and to check the access permissions on the resource. They are described as follows:

- *ipcget( )* — is called to allocate the data structure for the IPC resource. For example, it is called by *semget* to allocate a *semid_ds*, by *shmget* to allocate a *shmid_ds*, and by *msgget* to allocate a *msqid_ds*. It is called with seven parameters:

  - *key, flag* — the same as the arguments *key* and *flag* from the *semget*, *shmget* or *msgget* system calls.

  - *base, count, size* — specify the location of the data structures, how many of them there are, and their size. *ipcget( )* searches this list for a free data structure, or for a data structure that matches the key.

  - *status* — a pointer to an integer. The caller uses it to find the result of the *ipcget( )*. If the status is returned as zero, it means that an entry matching the key was found. Otherwise, it indicates that a new entry was created.

  - *ipcpp* — when an entry in the table is found, a pointer to the table entry is returned to the caller via this parameter.

  The return value of *ipcget( )* is set to zero on success, otherwise it indicates an error code. This function deals with two separate cases:

  IPC_PRIVATE   When this bit is set in the flags argument, the data structure table is searched for a free entry. If one is found, the values in the *ipc_perm* are initialized, and the entry is marked as allocated.

  ~IPC_PRIVATE   When this bit is clear, the function searches the table for an allocated entry that matches the key, and if one is found, *ipcpp* is made to point to it. The contents of *status* are set to 1, and the function returns successfully. If the entry is not found, but the *IPC_CREAT* flag was set, a new entry is used and initialized.

- *ipcaccess( )* — whenever a semaphore, shared memory or message operation is attempted, the kernel must check that the desired operation is allowed, and *ipcaccess( )* performs this validation. It is called with three parameters that specify the IPC permissions of the resource to be accessed, the modes of access required, and the process's credentials. The super-user is always allowed to access the resource; otherwise, the desired operation is checked against the permission bits stored in the IPC permission structure. Note that if owner read/write permission is set, the creator or the current owner of the resource can access it. Similarly, if group read/write permission is set, processes in the same group as the creator of the resource can access it, and so can processes in the same group as the owner of the resource.

8.3.2 Semaphore initialization

Most semaphore data structures and arrays are sized by their associated tuneable parameters when the system is built. This simplifies the semaphore initialization procedure because most of it is done automatically by the compiler. The remaining initialization is performed by *seminit( )*, which is called in *main( )* as the system boots. *seminit( )* does the following:

- The semaphore pool is initialized by calling *rminit( )* to create the semaphore map containing the number of entries given by *seminfo.semmap*.

- *rmfree( )* is called so that the map shows that all the semaphores are deallocated.

- The semaphore undo structures are linked together, and the variable *semfup* (see Table 8.4) is initialized to point to the first element in the *semu[ ]* freelist.

8.3.3 Semaphore allocation

The system call handler for *semget* is called *semget( )*. It, in turn, calls *ipcget( )* to locate the *semid_ds*, or to allocate a new one. If a new *semid_ds* is allocated, then a group of semaphores are allocated from the semaphore map.

8.3.4 Semaphore operations

Operations on a semaphore are performed by the *semop* system call, which is handled by the kernel function called *semop( )* (see Figure 8.3). *semop( )* loops through all semaphores in the group specified in the function call arguments. It will succeed only if it is able to perform *all* the specified operations in one go. If any operation fails, it undoes the operations already performed. For example, if it successfully decrements the first and second semaphores, but fails on the third, it adds back the values to the first and second semaphores (leaving them unchanged from their original values). The process sleeps, waiting for the third semaphore to be increased. Eventually another process increases the third semaphore, and this process is awoken. The function loops again, decrementing the first and second semaphores, and, possibly the third.

Note that performing multiple operations on multiple semaphores can slow the system considerably. Consequently, some database systems running under UNIX

Figure 8.3: *Algorithm for semop( )*

```
semop( )
inputs: semaphore id, semaphore operations, count
outputs: error code
{
loop:
  for( all semaphores to operate on ) {
    if( V operation ) { /* Semaphore being increased */
      if( SEM_UNDO is set ) update semaphore adjustment value
      add value to semaphore
      wake processes that are sleeping on the semaphore
    } else if ( P operation ) { /* Semaphore being reduced */
      if( semaphore value is greater than zero ) {
        OK to decrement it
        if( SEM_UNDO is set ) update semaphore adjustment value
        subtract value from semaphore
      }
      /* We were unable to decrement the semaphore. */
      sleep( semaphore value becomes > zero );
      goto loop;
    } else {
      /* Operation is "wait for semaphore = zero" */
      if( semaphore is not zero ) {
        sleep( semaphore value becomes zero );
        goto loop;
      }
    }
  } /* End for all semaphores in operation */
}
```

implement their own semaphore scheme instead.

8.3.5 Semaphore undo

Semaphore operations carried out by a process can be undone if it dies; the semaphores claimed by the process will be automatically unclaimed.

For each semaphore that has the *SEM_UNDO* flag set, and is accessed by a process, the kernel maintains a *shadow value*, which tracks the changes made to a semaphore's value. For example, if the semaphore is reduced by 2, the shadow value is increased by 2, and vice versa. If the process exits, the shadow value is added back to the value of the semaphore so that the last semaphore operation is undone.

Consider a semaphore that has the value 10. A process performs a P operation (enter critical section), so it decrements the semaphore to 9. Since this is the first time a *SEM_UNDO* flag has been specified by the process, the shadow value is incremented to 1 when the P operation is performed (initially it is set to zero). If the process dies in its critical section, the shadow value is added back to the semaphore, making the value 10 once more. If, however, the process completes its critical section, it performs a V operation, which adds 1 to the semaphore and takes 1 away from the shadow. The semaphore is now 10 and the shadow value 0. If the process exits now, adding the shadow value of 0 leaves the semaphore unchanged, as it should because the process has no semaphore claims outstanding once it completes its critical section.

Figure 8.4: *Semaphore undo structures*

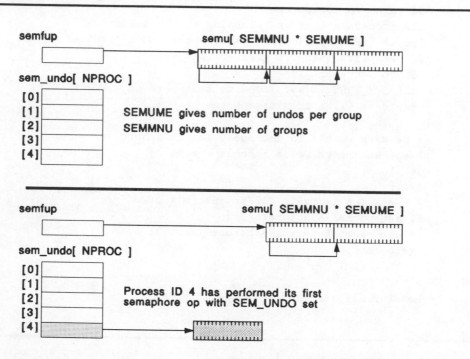

Table 8.5: *Struct sem_undo*

Element	Description
*struct sem_undo *un_np*	Points to the next group of undo structures
short un_cnt	Number of entries in the group currently in use
short un_aoe	Shadow value (also called adjust on exit value)
unsigned short un_num	Semaphore number
int un_id	Semaphore identifier (semid)

A semaphore-undo relies on the *sem_undo* structure shown in Table 8.5. (See also Figure 8.4.)

sem_undo[] is an array of pointers each pointing to a group of undo structures used by each process and is sized by *NPROC*, so that there is one entry for each process regardless of whether it uses semaphores or not. The *semu[]* array holds the systems pool of undo structures and a group of *SEMUME* undo structures is allocated for each process that sets the semaphore *SEM_UNDO* flag. *SEMMNU* specifies how many groups there are (it also specifies how many processes can perform undo operations), and *SEMUME* specifies how many different semaphores a process may undo.

Shadow values are manipulated by a function called *semaoe( )* (semaphore adjust on exit), which is called if *SEM_UNDO* is set and the semaphore value is about to be updated. The first time a process performs a semaphore operation with the *SEM_UNDO* flag set, a group of *sem_undo* structures is allocated from *semu[]*, and the entry corresponding to this process in the *sem_undo[]* table is set to point to this group. The first of the undo structures is filled in with the semaphore identifier, the semaphore number, and the shadow value. Subsequent operations on the semaphore update the shadow value. An operation on a different semaphore results with the allocation of a new undo structure from the group. Note that a process is only ever allocated a single group of undo structures. Therefore, semaphore operations that specify *SEM_UNDO* will fail if the process attempts to undo too many.

When a process exits, the semaphore function *semexit( )* is called by *exit( )* to perform any semaphore cleanup operations for the process. *semexit( )* looks up all the undo entries for the process, and adds the shadow value to the semaphore. The process's group of *sem_undo* structures is then linked back into the freelist headed by *semfup*, and the corresponding entry in *sem_undo* is set to zero.

8.4 Message queues

Before the advent of STREAMS, message queues provided the only reliable message passing interface. For programs developed under UNIX System V Release 4, however, STREAMS-based pipes and FIFOS provide a much better interprocess communication mechanism. However, to be compatible with programs developed on earlier versions of UNIX System V, message queues are still supported.

8.4.1 Message initialization and control

Messages are passed between processes via a message queue, which is identified by a message queue identifier (*msqid*). All messages that pass between communicating processes are linked into the queue. When a message is sent, it is linked to the back of the queue, and when a message is read, it is unlinked from the front of the queue.

Message queues are allocated with the *msgget* system call, which takes two parameters: a key and a flag. The key identifies which message queue to use, and has the same use as the semaphore key described in § 8.1.1. The flag contains the

Table 8.6: *Struct msqid_ds*

Element	Description
struct ipc_perm msg_perm	IPC permissions
*struct msg *msg_first*	Points to the first message on this queue
*struct msg *msg_last*	Points to the last message on the queue
unsigned long msg_cbytes	Number of bytes in the queue
unsigned long msg_qnum	Number of messages held in the queue
unsigned long msg_qbytes	Maximum number of bytes that can be queued
pid_t msg_lspid	Process id that performed last *msgsnd*
pid_t msg_lrpid	Process id that performed last *msgrcv*
time_t msg_stime	Time at which last message was sent
time_t msg_rtime	Time at which last message was received
time_t msg_ctime	Time at which *msqid_ds* was last changed

message queue access permissions and modes such as *IPC_PRIVATE* and *IPC_CREAT*. The flag parameter works the same as for semaphores, and is described in § 8.2.1.

The *msgctl* system call alters the IPC permissions for a message queue. It is called with three parameters:

- *msqid* — the key for the message queue.

- *cmd* — the command to perform (see below).

- *buf* — a pointer to a *msqid_ds* structure (Table 8.6) holding the results of an *IPC_STAT* command, or holding the values to set for the *IPC_SET* command.

Three commands can be specified:

- *IPC_STAT* — copies the *msqid_ds* held in the kernel into the user buffer pointed to by *buf*.

- *IPC_SET* — alters fields in the kernel *msqid_ds* for the given message queue. The argument *buf* points to the *msqid_ds* from which the values are taken. Only the fields *msg_perm.uid, msg_perm.gid msg_perm.mode* and *msg_qbytes* can be altered. The value of *msg_qbytes* may be reduced by any user, but can be increased only by the super-user.

- *IPC_RMID* — removes the message queue and all the messages held on it. Only the super-user, the creator, or the owner of the message queue may delete a particular message queue.

8.4.2 Using messages

Two system calls *msgsnd* and *msgrcv* are used to send and receive messages. They are documented in *msgop(2)*. Figure 8.6 gives an example program that initializes, sends and receives messages.

Figure 8.5: *Msgsnd and msgrcv*

```
int msgsnd( msqid, msgp, msgsz, msgflg )
  int msqid;
  const void *msgp;
  size_t msgsz;
  int msgflg;

int msgrcv( msqid, msgp, msgsz, msgtyp, msgflg )
  int msqid;
  const void *msgp;
  size_t msgsz;
  long msgtyp;
  int msgflg;
```

The function prototypes for these system calls are shown in Figure 8.5. The parameters are used as follows:

- *msqid* — specifies the message queue on which to send the message.

- *msgp* — points to the message to send. The message is free format, that is, the sender and receiver decide the format of the data in the message. The only constraint is that the first field of the message must be a positive integer, which defines the message type. The receiver can request that only messages of a particular type are received.

- *msgsz* — for *msgsnd* this parameter specifies the size of the message being passed. For *msgrcv*, it gives the maximum size of the received message. If the flag *MSG_NOERROR* is set, and a message is received that is larger than *msgsz*, the message is silently truncated to *msgsz*. Otherwise, a message that is too large makes *msgrcv* fail with the error code *E2BIG*.

- *msgtyp* — used only with *msgrcv*. It specifies which type of message to receive. If the value is zero, the first message is taken from the queue, otherwise *msgrcv* searches for the next message on the queue with the given type.

- *msgflg* — modifies the behaviour of the send and receive calls. If *IPC_NOWAIT* is set, the process does not block when the queue is full and a *msgsnd* is attempted, or when the queue is empty and a *msgrcv* is attempted.

8.5 The implementation of message queues

Message queue tuneable parameters can be configured by the system administrator. Obviously, to take effect, the operating system must be rebuilt and rebooted. The fields of the *msginfo* structure have the same names as their corresponding tuneable parameters and the system global variable *msginfo* holds this information. The

Figure 8.6: *Sending a message*

```
#include <sys/types.h>
#include <sys/ipc.h>
#include <sys/msg.h>
#include <stdio.h>

/* Our message format */
struct message {
  int type;
  int data;
};

/* Send a message on a queue */
sender( id, data )
int id;
int data;
{
  struct message message;
  message.type = 1;
  message.data = data;
  return msgsnd( id, &message, sizeof message, 0 );
}

/* Receive a message from a queue */
int receiver( id )
int id;
{
  struct message message;
  message.type = 1;
  if( msgrcv( id, &message, sizeof message, 0, 0 ) == -1 ) {
    perror( "msgrcv" );
    exit(2);
  }
  return message.data;
}

main()
{
  int id, r1, r2;

  /* Connect to, and allocate the message queue */
  if((id = msgget( ftok("msgex.c",0), IPC_CREAT | 0777 )) == -1) {
    perror( "msgget" );
    exit(1);
```

```
    }

    /* For true IPC, you would have sender and receiver in
     * different processes.
     */
    sender( id, 42 );
    sender( id, 43 );

    r1 = receiver(id);
    r2 = receiver(id);

    printf( "Receiver receives: 1st %d, 2nd %d\n", r1, r2 );
    return 0;
}
```

Table 8.7: *Message information*

Element	Tuneable	Struct msginfo Description
		Struct msginfo
		Description
msgmap	*MSGMAP*	Size of *rmalloc( )* map for message data
msgmax	*MSGMAX*	Largest message size allowed
msgmnb	*MSGMNB*	Maximum number of bytes on a message queue
msgmni	*MSGMNI*	The number of message queues
msgssz	*MSGSSZ*	Size of message allocation unit
msgseg	*MSGSEG*	Number of message segments
msgtql	*MSGTQL*	Number of message headers

Variable	Message global variables Description
	Message global variables
	Description
struct map msgmap[]	Map used by *rmalloc( )*
struct msqid_ds msgque[]	Message queue array
struct msg msgh[]	Message headers
struct msginfo msginfo	System tuneable message information structure
*struct msg *msgfp*	Message header freelist (points into *msgh*)
paddr_t msg	Message storage buffer managed by *msgmap*

tuneable parameters and the global variables used by the message system are summarized in Table 8.7, and a description of the parameters follow:

- *MSGMAP* — memory used to hold queued messages is allocated from a message pool (*msgmap[]*) with *rmalloc( )* and deallocated with *rmfree( )*. This parameter specifies the size of the message pool.

- *MSGMAX* — specifies the maximum size of a message. If a process attempts to send a message larger than this, *msgsnd* fails with the error code *EINVAL*.

- *MSGMNB* — specifies the maximum number of bytes that can be queued in a single queue.

- *MSGMNI* — the message queue data structures are held in a statically allocated array (*msgque[]*). One entry from this array is used for each active message queue. The size of this array is given by *MSGMNI*.

- *MSGSSZ, MSGSEG* — control the size of the message buffer. The total number of bytes available for all messages in the system is given by the product *MSGSSZ*MSGSEG*. Memory to hold messages is allocated from the pool in units of segments, rather than in units of bytes. If the segment size is 8 bytes, a 4 byte message will use 1 segment, and a 12 byte message will use two segments. The size of a segment is given by *MSGSSZ* and the number of segments by *MSGSEG*.

- *MSGTQL* — each message in the system has a message header, which is allocated from a global array of *msg* structures (see Table 8.8) called *msgh[]*. The size of this array is given by the parameter *MSGTQL*.

    Note that the *msg_spot* field specifies the segment number of the first segment in the message. It is used internally when the segments of the message are returned to the free pool.

Table 8.8: *Struct msg*

Element	Description
struct msg *msg_next	Pointer to the next message in the queue
long msg_type	The message type
ushort msg_ts	The message size
short msg_spot	The message map address

8.5.1 Message initialization

Initialization of the message queue structures is done mostly by the compiler when the kernel is built. Any remaining initialization is performed by *msginit()*, which is called in *main()* when the system boots. *msginit()* does the following:

- The data area that forms the message pool is allocated with *kmem_alloc()*. The size of the pool is given by the product *MSGSSZ*MSGSEG*.

- The global variable *msg* is set to point to the pool.

- The message map is initialized by *rminit()* and the free space is initialized by *rmfree()*.

- All the message headers are linked together onto the message header freelist.

8.5.2 Message allocation

The system call handler for *msgget* is called *msgget( )*. It operates in the same way as *semget( )* but uses a different data structure pool. It calls *ipcget( )* to allocate a *msqid_ds* from the message queue array. The fields of the message queue are initialized, and the message identifier is returned to the process that made the system call.

Figure 8.7: *Message operations*

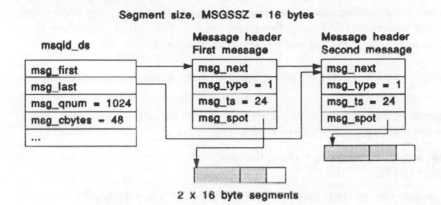

2 x 16 byte segments

8.5.3 Message operations

The system call handlers for *msgsnd* and *msgrcv* are described as follows:

- *msgsnd( )* — The structure of messages in a queue is shown in Figure 8.7. To send a message, the following operations are carried out.

  - The parameters given in the system call are validated: the message queue is looked up, the size of the message being sent is compared with *MSGMAX* and the access permissions are checked. The message type is copied in from user-space and validated. If any of these tests fail, the system call returns an error code.

  - The size of the queue is checked. If there is no space on the queue for the message being added, the action taken depends on the flag *IPC_NOWAIT*. If it is set, the system call returns immediately with the error code *EAGAIN*. If it is clear, then the process sleeps until there is enough space in the queue for the message.

  - The function then attempts to allocate a message header. If there are no message headers available, it sleeps or returns, depending on the value of *IPC_NOWAIT*, as described above.

- The next step is to allocate from the message buffer pool a buffer large enough to hold the message. If there is not enough space for the message, the process once more sleeps or returns, depending on the value of *IPC_NOWAIT*. Before returning, however, it deallocates the message header allocated previously.

- At this point, the function has ensured that there is enough space in the queue, that it has a message header, and that there is a message buffer. It copies the message data from user space into the message buffer, and links the buffer to the header. The header is then linked to the end of the message queue. If any processes are sleeping, waiting for data to appear in the queue, they are awoken by calling *wakeprocs( )*. Finally, the access time and the other accounting fields in the *msqid_ds* are updated and the system call returns.

- *msgrcv( )* — carries out the following steps to read a message from a message queue:

  - The queue is looked up, and the other system call parameters validated. If any of the tests fail, the system call exits and returns error.

  - If there are no messages to receive, the process sleeps or returns, depending on the value of *IPC_NOWAIT*.

  - The processing of the message queue depends on whether the *msgtyp* arguments is less than, equal to, or greater than zero:

    < 0   Starting from the first message on the queue, *msgrcv* performs a linear search for the first message with a type less than the absolute value of *msgtyp*.

    = 0   The first message on the queue is used.

    > 0   The function performs a linear search for the first message with a message type equal to the value of *msgtyp*.

  - If the search was unsuccessful, the system call sleeps or returns, depending on the value of *IPC_NOWAIT*. If a suitable message is found the message data is copied to user space and the used data buffer is returned to the message buffer pool.

  - The message header is then unlinked from the queue and returned to the header pool, and any processes that are waiting for a header are awoken. Finally, the queue counts and the access time information in the *msqid_ds* is updated.

8.6 Shared memory

Shared memory is exactly what its name implies: an area of memory that is shared between two or more processes. A shared memory segment has a certain size and physical memory address. Processes that want to access the shared memory segment attach the segment to their address space by using the *shmat* system call, which sets up a virtual address in the process that references the shared memory segment. Other processes do the same, so that many processes can access the same area of physical memory.

The segments of a process, such as the *text, data* and *stack*, are not normally persistent. That is, they do not stay in memory when there is no process to access them. For example, when a process exits, its *data* and *stack* segments are deleted from memory. A *text* segment may be deleted when there are no more copies of the program running. Shared memory segments are different: they persist in the system until the shared memory identifier is removed, and there are no more processes attached to it, or the system reboots.

The advantage of using shared memory for interprocess communication is speed. It is very quick to exchange data between two processes: one process simply writes the data into memory and the other reads it. Database systems use shared memory to exchange queries and results between the user-interface client programs and the database servers. The disadvantage is that processes must take steps to ensure that they synchronize access to the memory. For example, the database server must know when the client has finished writing its query into the shared memory because it cannot process the query until all the data has been written.

8.6.1 Shared memory data structures

The *shmget* system call converts an IPC key to a shared memory identifier (*shmid*). It has three parameters:

- *key* — specifies the IPC key used to identify the shared memory segment.

- *size* — specifies how large the shared memory segment must be. If the *shmget* references an existing shared memory segment, and the size parameter is greater than the actual size of the segment, the system call fails with the *EINVAL* error code.

- *shmflg* — gives the flags for the system call, and contains the access modes for the segment and the mode bits such as *IPC_PRIVATE* and *IPC_CREAT*. The access modes define which processes are allowed to attach to the shared memory segment. If a process has neither read nor write permission for the segment, it will not be able to attach to it. If a program attempts to write to a read-only shared memory segment, it will be killed with a *SIGSEGV* signal.

Each shared memory segment is described by a *shmid_ds* structure, which is summarized in Table 8.9. Four of its fields are described as follows:

Table 8.9: *Struct shmid_ds*

Element	Description
struct ipc_perm shm_perm	IPC permissions structure
int shm_segsz	Size of this segment
*struct anon_map *shm_amp*	Pointer to the anon map for this segment
ushort_t shm_lkcnt	Count of times this segment is locked
pid_t shm_lpid	ID of last process to perform a *shmop*
pid_t shm_cpid	Creator's process ID
long shm_nattch	Count of processes attached to this segment
ulong_t shm_cnattch	Holds the same value as *shm_nattch*
time_t shm_atime	Time last *shmat* was done
time_t shm_dtime	Time last *shmdt* was done
time_t shm_ctime	Time of last *IPC_SET shmctl* command

- *shm_perm* — holds the IPC permissions structure.

- *shm_segsz* — specifies how big the segment is, in bytes. The size can be any value, up to the maximum shared memory segment size. There is no need to align the size to a page boundary.

- *shm_amp* — the kernel uses anonymous pages for shared memory segments. This field is used in the kernel to point to the *anon_map* which in turn points to the anonymous pages that comprise the segment.

- *shm_lkcnt* — counts the number of processes that have issued the *SHM_LOCK* command to lock the pages of the shared memory segment in memory.

The contents of the *shmid_ds* are obtained from the kernel with the *shmctl* system call. It has three parameters:

- *shmid* — the shared memory identifier for the segment that was returned by an earlier call to *shmget*.

- *cmd* — the command (or operation) to perform (see below).

- *arg* — the argument to the command to perform.

The *shmctl* system call understands five commands:

- *IPC_STAT* — reads the *shmid_ds* into the buffer pointed to by *arg*.

- *IPC_SET* — alters the values of some of the fields in the *shmid_ds.shm_perm*. The only fields that can be changed are: *uid*, *gid* and *mode*. Note that changing the mode does not affect processes that already have the segment attached. If the mode is changed from read-write to read-only, processes that still have the segment attached can still read and write the segment. However, the next process that attempts to attach the segment will be affected by the new permissions.

- *IPC_RMID* — removes the shared memory identifier from the system. Processes that still have the shared memory segment attached can still use it. The pages disappear only when the last process detaches from the segment. However, no new processes will be attached to it. If another process attempts to attach to the segment (using the same key) it will result with the creation of a new segment.

- *SHM_LOCK* — locks the pages of the segment in memory. It can only be performed by the super-user. Pages that are locked are never swapped.

- *SHM_UNLOCK* — undoes the effect of *SHM_LOCK*. That is, the pages are unlocked, and so are eligible for swapping.

8.6.2 Using shared memory

To use a shared memory segment, a process must first call *shmget* to get a shared memory identifier. The shared memory segment is then attached to the process's address space with *shmat*. When the process no longer needs to access the shared memory segment, it calls *shmdt*. These system calls are documented under *shmop(2)*.

The *shmat* system call takes three arguments, as follows:

- *shmid* — the shared memory identifier returned by the *shmget* system call.

- *shmaddr* — specifies the virtual address at which the shared memory segment must be attached. If this is zero, the system is free to choose a virtual address. The address chosen is implementation dependent. If this value is non-zero, it allows the program to specify the address at which the segment is to be mapped. If the flag *SHM_RND* is set, the address is rounded down to a multiple of the system parameter *SHMLBA* (the system memory page size or low boundary address multiple). The kernel, however, will not allow arbitrary addresses. Normally, the resultant address must be aligned to a page boundary, and the address must lie in user space.

- *shmflg* — there are two flags that can be specified. The flag *SHM_RND* was described above. The flag *SHM_RDONLY* specifies that the segment is to be attached read-only. Attempts to write to the segment will result in the process being killed with a *SIGSEGV* signal.

The *shmdt* system call takes a single parameter that gives the virtual address of the shared memory segment to detach. If the process attempts to access the segment once it is detached, it will receive a *SIGSEGV* signal. The example shown in Figure 8.8 shows how two processes share data by using a shared memory segment, and how a semaphore is used to synchronize the access.

The producer and consumer example uses two semaphores to control access to the shared memory segment. The consumer semaphore indicates whether the shared memory buffer is available to producers; the producer semaphore indicates that the data has been written to the buffer.

The consumer program operates in a continuous loop. First, it performs a V operation on the consumer semaphore to indicate that the shared memory buffer is free. It then performs a P operation on the producer semaphore, forcing the consumer to wait until the producer has generated some data. When the P

Figure 8.8: *Producer and consumer*

```
/* Shared memory example -- consumer */
...
...

struct exchange {
  char buf[256]; /* The data that is passed */
  int seq;        /* Sequence number filled in by client */
};

unsigned char *shminit( key )
key_t key;
{
  int shmid;
  unsigned char *retval;
  if( (shmid = shmget( key, sizeof(struct exchange),
              0666|IPC_CREAT)) == -1 ) {
    perror( "shmget" );
    exit(5);
  }
  if( (retval = shmat( shmid, (unsigned char *)0, 0 ))
              == (unsigned char *)-1 ) {
    perror( "shmat" );
    exit(6);
  }
  return retval;
}

/* This is the main function for the consumer program */
main( )
{
  struct exchange *e;
  int producer, consumer;
  consumer = seminit( ftok("consumer", 0), 0 );
  producer = seminit( ftok("producer", 0), 0 );
  e = (struct exchange *)shminit( ftok("memory", 0) );
  for( ;; ) {
    V(consumer);       /* Let him produce some more */
    P(producer);        /* Wait for the data */

    /* Process the data */
    printf("Data received:%s, sequence: %d\n",e->buf, e->seq);

  }
```

```
    /* NOTREACHED */
}


/* This is the main function for the producer program */
...
main( )
{
  struct exchange *e;
  int producer, consumer, i;

  allocate producer, consumer semaphores and shared memory segment

  for( i = 0 ;; i++ ) {
    P(consumer);        /* Wait for the buffer */

    /* Fill in sequence number and buffer */
    e->seq = i;
    sprintf( e->buf,"Message %4d from producer %d\n",i,getpid( ) );

    V(producer);        /* Tell consumer to take the data */
  }
  /* NOTREACHED */
}
```

operation completes, the consumer knows that there is data waiting in the shared memory buffer. The example code simply prints the data. When the consumer has finished processing the data, the loop starts again.

The producer program also runs in a continuous loop. It first performs a P operation on the consumer semaphore. This forces the producer to wait until the shared memory buffer is free. When the P operation completes, the producer writes its data into the shared memory buffer. Once the data has been written, it performs a V operation on the producer semaphore, indicating to the consumer that the data is available. The producer program then runs through its loop once more.

The two programs exchange data using a shared memory segment. They define the *exchange* structure to describe the format of the data passed between them. Both programs declare a pointer variable that points to this structure. This pointer is initialized to point into the shared memory segment. The programs then use their pointer, to write directly to, or read directly from the shared memory segment.

8.7 The implementation of shared memory

The shared memory system is controlled by four tuneable parameters that are held in a global *shminfo* structure variable. This structure has four fields: *shmmax, shmmin, shmmni*, and *shmseg* which are initialized from the following tuneable parameters:

- *SHMMAX* — specifies the largest shared memory segment allowed.

- *SHMMIN* — specifies the minimum size of a shared memory segment.

- *SHMMNI* — configures the number of shared memory identifiers in the system.

- *SHMSEG* — configures the maximum number of shared memory segments that a single process can attach to.

The implementation of shared memory uses anonymous pages. The anonymous pages that comprise the segment are pointed to by an *anon_map* structure. The map uses a reference count to keep track of how many processes are referencing the pages. When the reference count falls to 1, the *anon_map* and its associated pages are freed. While the reference count is greater than 1, the pages are kept, even if no process is attached to the segment. The reference count on a shared memory segment is altered by the following:

- *shmget* — when the segment is first created, the reference count is initialized to 2.

- *shmat* — each attach to a shared memory segment increments the reference count.

- *fork* — when a process forks, the reference count for each shared memory segment attached to the process is incremented because there is now an extra process attached to each of the segments.

- *shmdt* — each detach of a segment decrements the reference count.

- *exit* — when a process exits, the reference counts on each of its shared memory segment are decremented.

- *exec* — when a process issues the *exec* system call, the process detaches from all its shared memory segments. Therefore, the reference counts are all decremented.

- *IPC_RMID* — when the shared memory identifier is removed, the reference count is decremented. Removal of the identifier prevents any new processes attaching to the segment. However, the segment remains until all other processes have detached from it.

Table 8.10 shows how the value of the reference count varies as system calls are performed on a shared memory segment.

The kernel must keep track of the shared memory segments attached to a process so that it can update the reference counts. The field *p_segacct* in the *proc* structure holds a linked list of *segacct* structures, which locate the shared memory segments of the process. The fields of the *segacct* are shown in Table 8.11 sorted in address order, with the lowest addresses first.

Table 8.10: *Shared memory reference count*

Operation	Reference Count	Description
shmget	2	Segment is created, reference count initialized
shmat	3	1st process attaches the segment
shmat	4	2nd process attaches the segment
shmdt	3	1st process detaches segment
exit	2	2nd process exits. No processes have the segment attached now
shmat	3	3rd process attaches
shmdt	2	3rd process detaches
IPC_RMID	1	3rd process issues *shmctl* to delete the segment ID The pages of the segment will be deleted

Table 8.11: *Struct segacct*

Element	Description
struct segacct *sa_next	Pointer to next *segacct* for this process
caddr_t sa_addr	Virtual address at which the segment is mapped
size_t len	Gives the size of the segment
struct anon_map *sa_amp	Points to the *anon_map* for this segment

8.7.1 Initialization and control of shared memory

A shared memory segment is allocated with the *shmget* system call. The parameters to the call were described above, and are shown in the example in Figure 8.8. The system call handler for *shmget* is called *shmget( )*, which performs the following tasks:

- The function *ipcget( )* is called to lookup the *shmid_ds* associated with the key. If the segment already exists, a pointer to it is returned. If it is an existing segment, *shmget* checks that the size requested in the system call is the same as the current size of the segment.

- The size of the requested segment is checked against *SHMMIN* and *SHMMAX*. If the size is outside these bounds, the system call fails with the error code *EINVAL*.

- Swap space for the segment is reserved, and the *anon_map* structure is dynamically allocated. The reference count in the *anon_map* is set to 2.

- The remaining fields in the *shmid_ds* are initialized.

The shared memory system uses the system call *shmctl* to alter the contents of a shared memory data structure, detach a segment, or to lock a shared memory segment. The following points describe how *shmctl* performs its operations:

- *IPC_RMID* — the shared memory identifier is looked up in the global table *shmem*. This lookup operation gives the *shmid_ds* for the segment being removed. The reference count for the anonymous map is decremented. If the value falls to 1, the *anon_map* and its associated pages are freed. The fields in the *shmid_ds* are cleared, to indicate that the shared memory segment is no longer in use.

- *SHM_LOCK, SHM_UNLOCK* — lock or unlock the pages of the segment in memory. The *shmid_ds* for the segment is looked up. The function scans through the segments attached to the address space of the process until it finds the one that contains this shared memory segment. It then calls *as_ctl( )* to lock or unlock the pages in memory. The locking is performed in the same way as the *MC_LOCK* command of the *memcntl* system call (see § 3.10.2). Only the super-user is allowed to perform these operations.

Figure 8.9: *Algorithm for shmat( )*

```
shmat( )
inputs: shm identifier, address, flags
outputs: address or error code
{
  convert shmid to pointer to shmid_ds
  call ipcaccess to check access permissions
  check there are less than SHMSEG segments attached to this process
  if( address == 0 ) {
    /* The system allocates the address */
    call map_addr to allocate an address
  } else {
    /* Use the supplied address */
    if( SHM_RND flag specified )
      truncate address to SHMLBA
    if( address is already mapped OR
        NOT in user space OR
        NOT aligned to a page boundary )
      return EINVAL error
  }
  set up arguments for segvn_create
  call as_map to create the segment
  add segacct accounting record to current process
  update shmid_ds access time information
  return address at which segment is mapped
}
```

8.7.2 Attaching shared memory

The pseudo code for *shmat* is shown in Figure 8.9. After performing the access and parameter checks, the function calls *as_map( )* (§ 3.5) to find a suitable address at which to map the segment. If, on the other hand, the caller supplied an address at which the segment must be mapped, checks are carried out to ensure that the address is valid. Finally, *as_map( )* is called to create a *segvn* segment. It is created so that pages are created and filled with zeros when they are accessed for the first time.

8.7.3 Detaching shared memory

The function *shmdt( )* detaches a shared memory segment from the address space of a process. It takes the following steps:

- The *segacct* list for the process is searched to check that the address supplied in the call to *shmdt( )* is the address of a shared memory segment. If the address does *not* apply to a shared memory segment, the system call fails with the *EINVAL* error code.

- The function *as_unmap( )* is called to destroy the address mappings in the process that refer to the shared memory segment.

- The *segacct* record for the shared memory segment is removed from the *p_segacct* list for the process.

- The reference count in the *anon_map* for the shared memory segment is decremented. If the reference count falls to 1, the *anon_map* is deleted, and the corresponding pages are freed.

- If the shared memory segment still exists, then the access times in the *shmid_ds* are updated.

8.8 Exercises

8.1   Why must semaphore operations be atomic?

8.2   Why does the operating system provide the semaphore undo facility? What problems would occur if it was not provided?

8.3   What facilities does UNIX System V Release 4 provide for exchanging data between processes? Which facility would you use for:
- passing queries to a database server?
- passing back the results from a database server?
- passing 12 byte messages from a serial line to a message-switching process?

- passing the output from one process to the input of another?
- passing print jobs to the print spooler?

8.4*   Write client and server programs that pass megabytes of data from the client to the server using:

- message queues
- shared memory
- pipes
- FIFOs
- files

Which is the most efficient method? Which is the easiest?

8.5   Why do shared memory segments need some form of locking scheme to synchronize access?

8.6*   Design a scheme to allow a single server and multiple clients to exchange data by using a shared memory segment. Make sure that access to the memory is properly synchronized. The synchronization scheme should use shared memory, *not* semaphores. Describe the facilities you would use to overcome a deadlock condition and data corruption.

8.7   Why is the count on a shared memory segment increased when a process *forks*, but decreased when it *execs*?

8.8   When an IPC resource is created with the *IPC_PRIVATE* flag set, no other process can access the key to the resource. What is the purpose of this flag?

8.9   How can processes guarantee unique resource keys? What problems could occur if keys are not unique? What is the drawback with the UNIX System V Release 4 key generator?

CHAPTER 9

Crash

Nitwit ideas are for emergencies. You use them when you've got nothing else to try. If they work, they go in the Book. Otherwise you follow the Book, which is largely a collection of nitwit ideas that worked.

— Larry Niven and Jerry Pournelle, *The Mote In God's Eye*

9.1 Introduction to crash

One of the sad facts of life is that no computer system runs forever; all computer systems crash from time to time due to hardware or software failures. Usually, hardware failures are fatal: the computer will not run any more when one of its key components fails. The solution to a hardware failure is to replace the failed component. Your system downtime depends on how quickly you can get the spare part to the machine. Fault-tolerant computer systems greatly reduce their downtime by duplicating all their hardware components such as CPU, disk and memory. However, even fault-tolerant computers are not invincible, and they sometimes crash due to multiple hardware failures, or a hardware failure caused by external factors.

Software failures are harder to deal with than hardware failures: you cannot provide a "software uninterruptable power supply", it is not so easy to replace failed software with a new component, and most suppliers do not write their software twice, to give you "fault-tolerant software." Software bugs, therefore, are a fact of life. The problem for operating system developers is to detect operating system bugs as they occur, and to limit the damage to your data when a bug occurs.

The UNIX operating system designers have taken steps to minimise the impact of kernel bugs. Throughout the operating system code there are frequent *assertion* points, and many *data integrity* checks. If an assertion or data integrity check fails, the system *panics*.

When a UNIX system panics, it tries to crash in a controlled way. This controlled crash consists of writing the contents of memory to a disk partition, and then rebooting the operating system. The data saved in the crash partition can be examined post mortem, in an attempt to find out what caused the panic.

Assertion checks are made with a C Language *ASSERT( )* macro. It is illegal to dereference a null pointer, and so a typical check on a pointer is coded as:

```
ASSERT( ptr != 0 );
```

Assertion tests like this are placed in critical places throughout the kernel software. The assertion test always assumes a true condition, so in this case, if *ptr* is not equal

561

to zero, then processing continues as normal. If, however, *ptr* is null, the assertion fails, and the system will panic.

There are many other points in the kernel where data integrity checks are made. If the data check fails, the function *cmn_err( )* is called. Depending on the severity of the data corruption, the system panics, but even if the data corruption is recoverable, a message is normally printed on the console.

The kernel contains approximately 370,000 lines of C and assembler code. Within this there are nearly 1700 assertions, over 600 non-fatal calls to *cmn_err( )*, and more than 250 calls to *cmn_err( )* that panic the system.

Despite the efforts of the designers, there are bugs that will not be caught by the assertions or data integrity checks. When you hit this type of bug, you lose: processes might hang, the operating system might hang, or worse, the operating system might continue processing corrupt data.

This leaves the question of what to do when your system crashes. Hardware failures are easier to deal with. When they occur, an engineer is called to find out what is broken, and a replacement part is installed. This option is not available with operating system software failures: most people reboot their system and then wonder what happened. If your system simply hung, and you rebooted it to get it working again, there is probably nothing you can do to get the problem resolved. Your operating system vendor cannot help you because there is no information that you can give to help the vendor fix the problem. The only thing you can do is hope that it is fixed "in the next release".

If you can get a crash dump you stand a chance. Analysis of the dump sometimes yields enough information for you to file a bug report with your operating system supplier. Eventually this will be fixed, and issued in a later release. The time taken to provide the fix depends on how easy it is to reproduce the problem in the lab, how easy it is to understand what happened, and how easy it is to fix (but often, it relies on how interested the supplier is in fixing it!). In the meantime, the dump may give you enough information to avoid the problem. In all other cases, you have to live with the problem.

The following two examples illustrate how crash dumps are dealt with in real life.

- Sometimes you have to live with the problem. A customer buys a copy of UNIX for his PC from a local computer store, and did not pay for software support. Approximately 3 to 6 weeks after installing the system, something went wrong with the keyboard driver; some of the keys failed to work properly. The problem occurs religiously every 3 to 6 weeks, and the only solution is to reboot the system. The chances of getting it fixed are zero because he did not pay for support or upgrades, and he also has no useful data to give the supplier.

- Sometimes the vendor is responsive: A user uses a UNIX system to run a mail network. Sometime between 3 and 6 months after a reboot, the network software hangs, although other parts of the operating system still work. The only way to cure the hung software is to reboot the system, so the system is forced to panic via some console sequence. The forced panic generates a crash dump. Analysis of the dump showed that STREAMS buffers were being lost. The workaround was to increase the STREAMS buffers: this bought the supplier 6-12 months in which to fix the problem. Within a few days, the module that was losing the buffers was identified, fixed, and incorporated into the next release.

The remainder of this chapter looks at the **crash(1M)** program and how it is used. Note that **crash** is a machine dependent program; a manufacturer might add features to **crash** to suit the data structures that have been added to the kernel when the software was ported. For this book, we have used the version of **crash** distributed with MIPS-based kernels.

Finally, if you are a user of a UNIX system but do not have access to the source code, you will find it difficult to get more than basic information from **crash**.[1]

9.2 Getting started

When the kernel panics, it requires an area on the disk in which to dump the contents of memory. On many systems dumps are placed in the swap partition, on others a special partition is reserved. A kernel variable (often called *dumpdev*) holds the major and minor device numbers of the dump device.

When the system boots, it checks the crash partition to see if a dump has been written there. If so, the dumped data is copied into a file in the directory */var/adm/crash*. The first memory image is saved in a file called *core.1*, the second in *core.2*, and so on. A copy of the kernel taken from */stand/unix*, is also saved in the same directory, in the files *unix.1*, *unix.2*, and so on.

Note that a crash dump is a "memory image". Therefore, if your system is fitted with 192 Mbyte of memory, you need at least 192 Mbyte of disk space to hold a crash dump. If there is not enough space in the file system when the dump is written, you will only get a partial dump, in other words, you lose!

To examine a crash dump image, change to the directory where the dumps are saved and enter the command:

```
crash  -d  core.1  -n  unix.1
```

The -d option allows you to choose the image to examine. If this is not specified, **crash** assumes that you want to examine an image of the currently running kernel, thus it defaults to */dev/mem*. The -n option allows you to specify a *text* file namelist containing the symbol table information corresponding to the chosen crash dump — it defaults to */stand/unix*. If a different crash dump image is to be examined, its corresponding namelist file must be supplied. If you are logged in as *root*, you can examine a snapshot image of the currently running kernel by invoking **crash** without arguments. This is the same as entering the command:

```
crash  -d  /dem/mem  -n  /stand/unix
```

crash is an interactive command line interpreter, thus it issues a prompt and you enter commands. The **crash** prompt is the character ">" and the following options

---

1 *Unless, of course, you have an understanding of the magic in the garden!*

are available to subcommands within **crash**:

! *shell-command*   Allows you to pipe the output from a **crash** command into a shell command. For example, the command:

   proc ! pg

   lets you see the process table listing, one screen at a time. Remember that **crash** uses the ! symbol instead of the more traditional | symbol for piping its output.

-e   Displays every entry in a table. Usually, commands print only the entries in a table that are in use.

-f   Forces the command to display a data structure in full. Usually, commands print only the important fields of a data structure.

-p   Makes the command interpret its address arguments as physical addresses. Usually they are treated as virtual addresses and are looked up in the page tables.

-s *slot*   Forces process-related commands to use the given process table slot instead of the default slot.

-w *file*   Redirects the output of the command into the given file.

To find out what commands are available in **crash** you type the ? character. Figure 9.1 shows an example of the output.

The **crash** command is the subject for a book in itself. Thus, it is not within the scope of this book to describe each and every command and facility provided by it. We have, however, given examples of the commands that we felt were the important and most frequently used ones.

For simplicity, each command is shown with a short form synopsis of its arguments similar to that used in the UNIX Reference Manual. Appendix F gives a listing of all the available **crash** commands and includes a long form synopsis of their arguments and syntax.

It is not possible to explain how to use **crash** to solve every problem you will encounter: just as you cannot learn to ride a bicycle by reading a book — you have to go away and ride — so it is with **crash**. However, the following three steps may improve your technique:

• The first command you always use with **crash** is stat, which prints out the kernel print buffer. The kernel print buffer holds those last *n* bytes of output that were written to the console, to allow you to read the *exact* message that appeared on the console when the system paniced. If you are dealing with the support organization of your vendor, they will usually ask for this information, so that they can tell quickly if you have run into a known bug.

• The second step is to look through the process table to see which process was running at the time of the crash — that is, the one that provoked the bug (unless the kernel crashed whilst processing an interrupt, in which case the process running then was simply an innocent bystander).

Figure 9.1: *Output from ?*

```
> ?
as            fnode         pcb           stream
async         fs (vfssw)    prnode        strstat
b (buffer)    gdp           proc          t (trace)
base          help          pty           trace
buf (bufhdr)  hrt           q (quit)      ts
buffer        i (inode)     qrun          tsdptbl
bufhdr        inode         queue         tsproc
c (callout)   kmastat       quit          tty
callout       l (lck)       rcvd          u (user)
class         lck           rd (od)       user
dbfree        linkblk       rduser        ui (uinode)
dblock        m (vfs)       redirect      uinode
defproc       major         resource      v (var)
dis           map           rtdptbl       var
dispq         mbfree        rtproc        vfs
ds            mblock        s (stack)     vfssw
evactive      mode          search        vnode
evmm          mount (vfs)   size          vtop
f (file)      nm            sndd          ?
file          od            snode         !cmd
findaddr      p (proc)      srmount
findslot      page          stack
```

- The third step is to examine the kernel traceback for the process, to show what functions were active in the kernel at the time of the crash. Once it points you in the direction of the problem, you will use other commands as necessary to examine the kernel data structures. Eventually, you may discover what went wrong.

9.3 Symbols

The **crash** program is not a symbolic debugger like **dbx(1)** or **sdb(1)**, but a tool for examining kernel memory. When **crash** is invoked, it opens its input file in read-only mode — so it is not a peek-and-poke type facility. Therefore, you cannot write to locations, set break points, and so on. It does, however, provide a number of commands for manipulating symbolic information. There are, for example, commands to convert between addresses and symbolic names, to dump memory in a variety of formats, and to disassemble the code. The symbol manipulation commands are shown in Table 9.1 and are described below.

Table 9.1: *Symbol commands*

Command	Description
dis	Disassemble instructions
od	Dump memory in a variety of formats
size	Print size of a table element
findslot	Find table and position of an address
findaddr	Find address of position in table
nm	Find address corresponding to symbolic name
ds	Find symbolic name corresponding to address

SYNOPSIS dis [-a] *start count*

Disassembles instructions, starting at the address *start*, for *count* instructions. The start address can be given as a symbolic name, or as a hexadecimal address. The count is always assumed to be decimal. Disassembly is used mainly to help you understand how functions have been called, and where the arguments to those functions have been stored. On the MIPS implementation, for example, if you are trying to work out where the arguments to the functions are stored, you have to disassemble the first few instructions in each function to find out how large the stack frame is. (That is, you have to see by how much the stack pointer has been moved by the function being called.) Figure 9.2 gives an example from an Intel-based system.

Figure 9.2: *Output from* dis

```
> dis read 5
  read              pushl   %ebp
  read+1            movl    %esp,%ebp
  read+3            incl    0xd00b1100              [sysinfo+5c]
  read+9            pushl   $0x1
  read+b            call    0x018 <d0089f38>        [rdwr]
```

SYNOPSIS od [-*format*] [-*mode*] *start* [*count*]

Produces an "octal dump" from *start* printing out *count* items. The *mode* parameter specifies whether the data is to be printed in long, short or byte-sized quantities. The *format* parameter takes the following values:

-c   Prints the data as characters. Non-printing characters are printed using a "\" prefix.

-d   Prints the data as decimal numbers.

-x   Prints the data as hexadecimal numbers.

-o Prints the data as octal numbers.

-a Prints the data as ASCII characters. If the character is non-printing, nothing is output for that character.

-h Prints the data in hexdump format. That is, each line starts with an address, followed by four four-byte hexadecimal numbers, followed by the ASCII character representations of those numbers.

This command is used to print out the data contained in a variable, structure, or buffer, as shown in Figure 9.3.

Figure 9.3: *Output from* od

```
> od -h putbuf 20
  d0108238: 746f740a 72206c61 206c6165 206d656d    .total real mem
  d0108248: 38203d20 35373532 740a3633 6c61746f    = 8257536.total
  d0108258: 61766120 6d206c69 3d206d65 34303720    avail mem = 8704
  d0108268: 36313239 4e550a0a 53205849 65747379    9216..UNIX Systo
  d0108278: 2f56206d 20363833 656c6552 20657361    m V/386 Release
```

SYNOPSIS `size [-x] [`*structure*`]`
Prints the size of the given structure. If the argument -x is given, the size is printed in hexadecimal. If no arguments are given, the command prints out the list of structures whose sizes are known. This command is useful for examining arrays of structures. If you know the structure size, you will know where the boundaries between the individual elements are. If a C Language compiler is installed on your system, the system header files will also be installed in */usr/include/sys*, and you can consult them for the definitions of system data structures. This makes it possible to break down the output of commands such as `size` and `od` into structures and fields.

SYNOPSIS `findslot` *address*
The address given is looked up, and the table and slot number that correspond to this address are printed. This command will only look up items in the tables printed by the `size` command. For example, if there is a function call in the kernel, and its argument is a pointer to a process, you can use the `findslot` command to see which process is being passed. Conversely, if `findslot` reports an error, you know that the function was passed an illegal pointer. The example in Figure 9.4 shows a valid process table address, followed by an illegal process table address.

SYNOPSIS `findaddr` *table slot*
Prints the address of the given *slot* in the table. This operation complements the one performed by `findslot` and is shown in Figure 9.4.

Figure 9.4: findslot *and* findaddr

```
> findslot 0xd00b1ed8
  proc, slot 10, offset 0

> findslot d009a81c
  no match for io_kexit in sizetable

> findaddr proc 10
  d00b1ed8
```

SYNOPSIS ds *address*

Looks up the address in the symbol table, to give the name of the symbol closest to the given address. The address of the symbol will be less than or equal to the argument *address*. This command determines which variables are being accessed. The od command prints out hexadecimal values, the ds command shows you which variables are being referenced. For example, when the *rmalloc( )* map used by the IPC primitives overflows, the starting address of the table is printed on the console. From ds you can see which table has overflowed, as shown in Figure 9.5.

Figure 9.5: *The* ds *and* nm *commands*

```
> ds 0xd00b0b04
  msgmap    + 0

> nm msgmap
  msgmap    d00b0b04    bss
```

SYNOPSIS nm *symbol*

Gives the address of the given symbol, to show where a variable or function is stored in memory. For example, if you want to know where *msgmap* is stored, issue the command shown in Figure 9.5.

9.4 Processes

There are seven **crash** commands that deal with processes, the process table and the user-area; they are summarized in Table 9.2. The commands proc, u, and as are each described in their own subsection because they are frequently used and present a copious amount of information.

Table 9.2: *Process commands*

Command	Description
proc	Print entries from the process table
defproc	Set the default process
as	Print the address space of a process
u	Print the user-area
pcb	Print the process control block
dispq	Print the scheduler queues
class	Display the scheduler classes

SYNOPSIS   class *slot*
Prints information about the available scheduler classes i.e., the contents of the *class* array (see § 4.6.6). The command output is shown in Figure 9.6.

Figure 9.6: *Output from* class

```
> class
  SLOT      CLASS     INIT FUNCTION      CLASS FUNCTION
  0         SYS       800e25e0           8024c330
  1         RT        8010f6b0           80255290
  2         TS        80148c10           802668e4
> ds 800e25e0
  sys_init+0 [../disp/sysclass.c: 91, 0x800e25e0]
```

The sample output shows that the system has three priority classes called *SYS, RT* and *TS*. The ds command shows that the initialization function for the system class is *sys_init( )*. The information between the brackets in the output gives the source code filename and line number that corresponds to the address 0x800e25e0, so that users who have the appropriate source go quickly to the definition of *sys_init( )*. We could follow this further into the class functions. The value 8024c330 is the pointer to the *classfuncs* structure that holds the system scheduler class functions. If new priority classes are added, they appear in this table.

SYNOPSIS   dispq *slot*
Prints out the dispatcher queues described in § 4.6.4. In the example output in Figure 9.7, the priority queues are idle, so they all hold the value zero. Only runnable processes are placed into the dispatcher queues: processes that are sleeping, and the process that is currently running do not appear in the queues. At the moment the example output was generated, the system was idle, and **crash** was the only running process. The remaining processes were all sleeping, waiting for something to do. As a result, the dispatch queues are all empty. When there are processes ready to run, the fields in the dispatcher queue will hold the addresses of the runnable process's *proc* structures. The slot number is both the index into the dispatch parameter table, and the priority of the runnable process.

Figure 9.7: *The* dispq *command*

```
> dispq
  SLOT      DQ_FIRST      DQ_LAST      RUNNABLE COUNT

    0           0            0              0
    1           0            0              0
  ...
  158           0            0              0
  159           0            0              0
```

SYNOPSIS pcb [*process*]

Prints the process control block of the given process. If the process is not specified, the pcb of the currently running process is printed. The pcb holds the information that must be restored when a context switch takes place. On the MIPS implementation, it is stored as the first part of the user-area (see Figure 9.8).

Figure 9.8: *Output of the* pcb *command*

```
> pcb
  resched: 0, bd_epc: 0, bd_cause: 0, bd_ra: 0, bd_instr: 0
  softfp_pc: 0, fpc_csr: 0, fpc_eir: 0, ownedfp: 0
  sstep: 0, ssi_cnt: 0:, bp[0] = 0,0, bp[1] =  0,0
  regs: (S0-S7, SP, FP, PC, SR)
    804ff600   00000002   0000f73d   806225b8
    00000000   800ced2c   ffffede4   00000020
    ffffecd8   ffffede0   8008460c   00000001
```

The MIPS *pcb* contains some useful information. The field *resched* is set to 1 when the time slice for this process expires. The numbers at the bottom are the processor general registers that are saved across a context switch; on the MIPS they are labeled *S0-S7*. The stack pointer (SP), program counter (PC) and status register (SR) are saved in the pcb. You can use these registers to see where the process will continue execution when it is rescheduled. In this example we see that execution will resume at the address 0x8008460c, and that the stack pointer will be set to 0xffffecd8. If necessary, we can use this information to generate a traceback to see what this process was doing prior to being switched. The *FP* register is no longer used by MIPS compilers; instead, one of the general registers is saved in this position (see the discussion of the stack frame in § 9.5). The fields that start *bd_* are no longer used. The fields referring to *fp* hold the contents of the floating point coprocessor. Whenever a process is context-switched, the registers in the floating point processor are saved in the pcb. Finally, the line containing *bp[0]* contains information used when the process is being single-stepped by the debugger. The contents of the pcb are defined in the system include file *pcb.h*.

SYNOPSIS defproc *slot*
Sets the current default process slot. Commands such as trace and proc display information about the process in the default slot. Therefore, if you are interested in the process in slot 15, you enter the command:

defproc 15

9.4.1 The proc command

SYNOPSIS proc [-r] *slot* ... *#pid* ...
Prints entries in the process table. The default display gives a one-line listing for all processes in the process table. The long form listing prints most of the information contained in the *proc* structure. The option -r displays only the entries for runnable processes. If numeric arguments are given, the command prints the entries for the selected positions in the process table. If *#pid* is used, the information for the process with the given process-ID is printed.

The listing in Figure 9.9 is an excerpt from the output of the short form proc command.

Figure 9.9: *The proc command*

```
> proc 0 1 9 10 11 23 25 44 45
PROC TABLE SIZE = 2000
SLOT ST PID PPID PGID  SID UID PRI CPU  EVENT    NAME     FLAGS
   0 s    0    0    0    0   0  99   0 8028cf81 sched    load sys
                                                         nwak lock
   1 s    1    0    0    0   0  60   0 fffff000 init     load jctl
   9 s  254  253  253  253   0  71   0 805a5a00 swapped
  10 s   87    1   87   87   0  73   0 8029f044 inetd    load
  11 s   22    1   22   22   0  60   0 8026700c voliod   load sys
  23 s  325    1  325  325   0  73   0 80d4b600 sac      load jctl
  25 s  237    1  237  237   0  73   0 8029f044 lpsched  load nowait
  44 s 1096    1 1096 1096   0  69   0 80d01800 swapped
  45 p 1253 1096 1096 1096   0  59   6          crash    load
```

The fields of the output have the following meanings:

- *PROC TABLE SIZE* — the maximum process table size, taken from the tuneable parameter *NPROC*.

- *SLOT* — the index into the process table, also called the slot number.

- *ST* — the process status, taken from the *p_stat* field in the process structure. The following values are printed:

    s   process is sleeping, waiting on an event.

r   process is runnable, and is waiting in one of the run queues.

i   process is in the *SIDL* state, a temporary state used whilst the process is being created.

z   process is a zombie process. This means it has exited, but the parent process has not executed a *wait* to collect the exit status.

t   process is stopped as a result of being run under debugger control, or a result of a *SIGSTOP* signal.

p   process is the currently running process.

In the sample output, the process in slot 45 was the currently running process. All the other processes are sleeping.

- *PID, PPID, PGID, SID* — the process ID, process ID of the parent, the process group to which the process belongs, and the session identifier for the process. From the sample output we can see that process 45 has its parent in slot 44. These two processes are in the same process group. The process in slot 44 is the shell from which **crash** was invoked.

- *UID* — the real user ID of the process. In the example, all processes are owned by root. The effective user ID is printed by the `proc -f` command.

- *PRI* — the process priority, used for scheduling. Its value is taken from the *p_pri* field in the process structure.

- *CPU* — the recent CPU usage of the process; this measure is used by the scheduler. The value is incremented each time a clock interrupt occurs while the process is using the CPU and it is divided by two every second.

- *EVENT* — the event on which a process is sleeping. The event is normally the address of a data structure, so it is often possible to use the `ds` command to get a symbolic name for the event on which a process is sleeping. If the process is not sleeping, this field is empty.

- *NAME* — the name of the process. Note that a swapped process has no user-area available since it is stored in swap space. Thus, the process's program name cannot be determined. In this case, the name "swapped" is given.

- *FLAGS* — the values in the process flags field, *p_flag*. The possible values for this field are summarized in Table 9.3.

The long form of the `proc` command prints out most of the fields of the process structure. The sample output is shown in Figure 9.10. The first three lines are the same as those printed by the short form command. Many of the fields are self-explanatory, and the labels in the output are similar to their corresponding field names in the *proc* structure. The important fields are explained as follows:

- *as* — the base address of the process's address space. The contents of the address space are printed by the `as` command, described below.

Table 9.3: *Process flags*

Value of p_flag	Shown as	Description
SLOAD	load	Process is in memory
SULOAD	uload	Only the user-area is in memory
SSYS	sys	Process is a system process (permanently resident)
SLOCK	lock	Process is locked in memory (cannot be swapped)
STRC	trc	Process is being traced
SNWAKE	nwak	Process will not be awoken when it receives a signal
SPOLL	poll	Process is polling a stream
SPRSTOP	prst	Process has been stopped through /proc
SPROCTR	prtr	Signals and system calls are being traced through /proc file system
SPROCIO	prio	I/O to this process is occurring though /proc. The process is therefore not runnable.
SPRFORK	prfo	Child processes will inherit tracing flags from /proc
SPROPEN	prop	Someone has opened the process via /proc
SRUNLCL	runl	Process will run when the last close from /proc occurs
SNOSTOP	nstp	Process is sleeping, so stop is not allowed (from debugger etc.)
SPTRX	ptrx	Process is running under the control of *ptrace(2)*
SASLEEP	aslp	The process is asleep during a call to *sleep( )*
SUSWAP	uswp	User-area of the process is being swapped
SNOWAIT	nowait	Children will not become zombies when they die
SJCTL	jctl	Process will receive *SIGCLD* signal when its children stop or continue
SVFORK	vfrk	Process was created by the *vfork* system call
SSWLOCKS	swlk	Swap locks are held by this process
SXSTART	xstr	*SIGCONT* or *ptrace* has made the process runnable
SPSTART	pstr	Process was made runnable via /proc

- *Session* — the session ID, and the major and minor device numbers of the control terminal (*ctty*). If there is no control terminal, a "–" is printed.

- *sig* — the signals waiting to be delivered to the process. This is a bitmask: when a bit is set, the signal corresponding to the bit is delivered to the process. Remember that there are 32 signals, thus there is one bit for each signal type.

- *cursig* — the current signal being handled by the process.

- *link* — the *p_link* field that chains together processes on the scheduler queue. The other fields, *parent, child,* and *sibling* point to the process's relatives.

- *link* — the second line marked link; gives the slot number in the process table of the process pointed to by *p_link*.

Figure 9.10: *Output from proc -f*

```
> proc -f 25
PROC TABLE SIZE = 2000
SLOT ST PID PPID PGID SID UID PRI CPU EVENT      NAME     FLAGS
  25  s 237    1  237 237   0  73   0 8029f044 lpsched load nowait
        Session: sid: 237, ctty: -
        Process Credentials:uid: 0, gid: 0, real uid: 0, real gid:0
        as: 80ff2c50
        wait code: 0, wait data: 0
        sig: 0, cursig: 0, clktim: 0
        link: 806c6200  parent: 80ff2200
        child: 806c6200 sibling: 808b9000
        link: 22
        utime: 9        stime: 21       cutime: 3       cstime: 7
        ubptbl:  0:   f6c760  1:   f6d760  2:   f6e760
        6:       7 7:       2  8: 802668e4
        epid: 237, sysid: 0, rlink: 0
        srwchan: 0, trace: 0, sigmask: 0,        hold: 0
        whystop: 0, whatstop: 0
        class: 2, clfuncs: 802668e4
        clproc: 80feeb60
        aiocount: 0, aiowcnt: 0
```

- *utime, stime, cutime, cstime* — the user and system CPU times for the process, and the cumulative user and system times for its children.

- *ubptbl* — the page table entries for the user-area. The example gives a maximum eight entries in this table, so the user-area will hold a maximum eight pages. The format and meaning of page table entries is described in § 3.6.2.

9.4.2 Hints for the proc command

This section looks at some of the problems that can be solved by judicious use of the proc command. All the examples come from real-life situations, although we forced the crash dumps for some of the examples since the machine from which they were taken was able to do this.

If the operating system hangs, you cannot use the **crash** program on the running system. In order to find out why it is hung, it is vital to be able to force a panic, so that a crash dump can be generated for inspection. You should consult your vendor to see if this facility is provided on your machine. The list of possibilities given below is not exhaustive.

- *Symptom* — the system performance fell to zero, and output from the **sar(1M)** command showed 95% system time, 5% user time. The proc command in **crash** showed that there were 300 processes all sleeping on the same address. (That is, the proc output showed that 300 processes all had the same *EVENT* value.) The ds command showed that they were all sleeping on a variable defined in a device driver supplied by the application vendor. Every time a piece of data was available in the driver, it called *wakeprocs( )*. This made all 300 processes runnable, but only one of them got the data, the rest went back to sleep. This constant *wakeup( )* and *sleep( )* of 300 processes used all the processor time, which prompted the application vendor to redesign the driver.

- *Symptom* — very poor response time. Output from the **sar(1M)** command showed that system and user times were even, and there was no idle time. The proc command in **crash** showed there was a large number of a particular process running — 90, of a total 100 processes. The proc command showed that these 90 processes all had the same parent process. Inspection of the program showed that the process was locked in a loop forking child processes.

- *Symptom* — the system was apparently hung, although some processes were obviously still running. The proc command showed that none of the stuck processes were runnable. They were all sleeping at different addresses, but they were addresses of STREAMS queues. Further investigation with the trace command (described in § 9.5.3) showed that the processes were all sleeping in the function *strwaitq( )*. The most likely reasons for this was a network failure, or the exhaustion of STREAMS buffers. The problem was, in fact, caused by a bug in a STREAMS module that was losing STREAMS buffers instead of deallocating them. Eventually, the network drivers were unable to allocate any new buffers, so the processes slept forever, waiting for data to be sent up from the network.

    In general, you can use proc, together with the *EVENT* fields and the output of the trace command to see if your system is hung due to a loss of resource. Knowing where your system is hung allows you to tune the kernel so that it will not run out of that resource. This may seem like a work-around but it might be your only choice!

    Note, however, that it is *not* normally a bug to have many processes sleeping at the address *pollwait*. When processes issue the *poll* system call, they all sleep on the same address. However, when the data is available the operating system wakes up only those processes that need the data; it does not issue *wakeprocs( )* to wake all the processes.

- *Symptom* — users were unable to start any more processes because the process table was full. Increasing the size of the process table simply delayed the onset of the problem. Analysis with **crash** showed that the table was full of zombie processes all waiting to have their exit status collected by the *init* process. For some reason *init* was not performing a *wait* to collect the information. The proc output gave the process priorities and these showed that the database front-end programs had a high priority, the database back-end programs had a lower priority, and *init* had a very low priority. The system was also overloaded: **sar** showed no idle time.

The priority mismatch meant that users of the system were creating work faster than the database could process it. When they logged out, they created a zombie process, but due to the workload there was always a higher priority process ready to run, so *init* never had time to clean up all the zombies. The priority mismatch was caused accidentally by an application startup script. The solution was to increase the priorities of *init* and the database back-end programs.

- *Symptom* — processes showed negative execution times for user and system time. By using the `proc -f` command you can see the user and system times used by a process. These are driven by the kernel variable *lbolt* which is incremented for each tick of the clock. This variable is usually implemented as a 32 bit signed integer, which means it will eventually become a negative number when the top bit is set. The system had been running so long that *lbolt* went negative, making processes show negative user and system times. Since *lbolt* is a 32 bit signed integer, and it is incremented at 100 Hz, it goes negative after 5965.23 hours. At 60 Hz, you have 9942.05 hours.

9.4.3 The u command

SYNOPSIS u *slot*
Prints the user-area for the process in the given slot. If no arguments are given, the user-area for the current default process is printed. Figure 9.11 shows the long-form listing of the user-area.

Figure 9.11: *Display of the user-area*

```
> u -f
PER PROCESS USER AREA FOR PROCESS 25
PROCESS MISC:
        command: lpsched, psargs: /usr/lib/lpsched
        proc slot: 25    start: Tue Feb 29 14:59:13 1993
        mem: cd, type: fork su-user
        proc/text lock: none
        vnode of current directory: 803b8008,
        vnode of root directory: 803d0198,
OPEN FILES AND POFILE FLAGS:
        [0]: F 0x80f91680, 0             [1]: F 0x80f916c0, 0
        [2]: F 0x80c6d840, 0             [3]: F 0x80be2280, 2
FILE I/O:
        u_base:         0, file offset: 0, bytes: 0,
        segment: data, cmask: 0000
RESOURCE LIMITS:
        cpu time: unlimited/unlimited
        file size: unlimited/unlimited
        swap size: 134217728/134217728
```

```
              stack size: 16777216/16777216
              coredump size: 33554432/33554432
              file descriptors: 2048/2048
              address space: 134217728/134217728
              file mode(s):
SIGNAL DISPOSITION:
               1:   ignore   2:   ignore   3:   ignore   4: 421698
               5: 421698    6: 421698    7: 421698    8: 421698
               9:  default  10: 421698   11: 421698   12: 421698
              13:   ignore  14: 4213cc   15: 4210e0   16: 421698
              17: 421698   18:   ignore  19: 421698   20: 421698
              21: 421698   22: 421698   23:  default  24:   ignore
              25:  default  26:   ignore  27:   ignore  28: 421698
              29: 421698   30:   ignore  31:   ignore  32:  default
         nshmseg: 0
         bsize: 0, qsav: f73c, error: 0
         ap: fffff27c, u_r: 0, pbsize: 0
         pboff: 0, rablock: 0, errcnt: 0
         tsize: 0, dsize: 0, ssize: 0
         arg[0]: 100dc000, arg[1]: 2, arg[2]: ffffffff
         arg[3]: bfe0a7c0, arg[4]: 4001d8ec, arg[5]: 4
         ar0: fffffef40, ticks: 470c
         pr_base: 0, pr_size: 0, pr_off: 0, pr_scale: 0
         ior: 1, iow: 0, iosw: 0, ioch: 681
         sysabort: 0, systrap: 0
         entrymask: 00000000 00000000 00000000 00000000
                    00000000 00000000 00000000 00000000
                    00000000 00000000 00000000 00000000
                    00000000 00000000 00000000 00000000
         exitmask:  00000000 00000000 00000000 00000000
                    00000000 00000000 00000000 00000000
                    00000000 00000000 00000000 00000000
                    00000000 00000000 00000000 00000000


         EXDATA:
         vp:  - , tsize: 0, dsize: 0, bsize: 0, lsize: 0
         magic#: 413, toffset: 0, doffset: 0, loffset: 0
         txtorg: 0, datorg: 0, entloc: 5fc46acc, nshlibs: 0
         execsz: c1
         tracepc: 0


         RFS:
         syscall: 0


         SIGNAL MASK:
            1: 0            2: 0            3: 0            4: 0
```

```
        5: 0            6: 0            7: 0            8: 0
        9: 0           10: 0           11: 0           12: 0
       13: 0           14: 0           15: 0           16: 0
       17: 0           18: 0           19: 0           20: 0
       21: 0           22: 0           23: 0           24: 0
       25: 0           26: 0           27: 0           28: 0
       29: 0           30: 0           31: 0           32: 0
       sigonstack: 0, sigflag: 0, oldmask: 0
       altflags: disabl , altsp: 0, altsize: 0
```

The fields of interest printed by the u command are described as follows:

- *command, psargs* — the contents of the *u_comm* and *u_psargs* fields in the user-area. When the process starts, the last part of the file pathname for the executable file is copied into the *u_comm* field, and the arguments to the *exec* system call are put into the *u_psargs* field. (Note that only the first *PSARGSZ* characters from the command arguments are written into this field.) In the example, it is clear that the process in slot 25 is **lpsched**, and that the only argument (argument 0) was the string "/usr/lib/lpsched".

- *proc slot* — the slot number for the process in the process table. The adjacent field labeled *start* gives the time that the process started running.

- *mem* — the number of pages used by the process. When the process is running, the value is updated on the occurrence of every clock tick. The value is printed in hexadecimal, therefore the process in Figure 9.11 is using $0xcd$ pages (205 pages in decimal).

- *type* — the type of the process. The values printed are based on the value of *u_acflag*. The type will be *fork* if the process resulted from the *fork* system call, or *exec* if the process carried out an *exec* after it was created. If the type also shows *su-user*, it means the process is a set-user-ID process.

- *lock* — indicates which parts of the process are locked in memory. The following values are possible:

  - none — no parts of the process are locked in memory.

  - txtlock — the process text is locked in memory.

  - datlock — the process data is locked in memory.

  - proclock — the whole process, including the user-area, is locked in memory.

- *vnode* — the two *vnode* fields give the addresses of the *vnodes* for the current working directory and the root directory of the process. Normally, the root directory of a process is the root directory of the file system. This value changes, however, if the *chroot* system call is executed. The values are taken from the *u_cdir* and *u_rdir* fields in the user-area.

- *OPEN FILES AND POFILE FLAGS* — this section of the listing gives the file descriptor numbers, the flags and the pointers into the file table for the open files used by the process. In UNIX System V Release 4 the first group of open files are held in the user-area, the rest are dynamically allocated and chained together (see § 6.2.1). The number in square brackets gives the file descriptor number. Adjacent to this is the address of its associated *file* structure followed by the flags with which the file was opened. The flags can be interpreted by consulting the include file *fcntl.h*. In Figure 9.11 the first three file descriptors are opened read-only, and the fourth is open for read and write access.

- *FILE I/O* — shows the status of the current I/O operation. If all fields are zero, there is no I/O in progress. Otherwise, *u_base* gives the virtual address of the buffer in the process which is the source of a write or the destination of a read. The *file offset* gives the current offset in the file at which the I/O is taking place, and *bytes* shows how many bytes remain to be transferred.

- *segment* — taken from the *u_segflg* field. The value mirrors the *uio_segflg* field in the *uio* structure that describes the type of I/O in progress. Two values are shown: *data*, meaning that the I/O is between kernel and user space; or *sys*, meaning that the I/O is between two kernel addresses. For example, when data is being read from a file into the buffer cache, the I/O is between the file and a kernel address. In this case, the segment is specified as *data*.

- *cmask* — the value of the *u_cmask* field that holds the file creation mask bits. This value is set by the *umask* system call.

- *RESOURCE LIMITS* — the soft and hard resource limits that apply to the process; they are altered with the *ulimit* system call. The output also contains the *file mode(s)*, which have nothing to do with resource limits but shows the file modes that apply to the current I/O operation. This value is filled in only by a device driver that was written for UNIX System V Release 3 and has been built into the UNIX System V Release 4 kernel. A native UNIX System V Release 4 driver will not use this field.

- *SIGNAL DISPOSITION* — shows which signals are set for their default action, which signals are ignored, and which have signal handlers. A field is given for each of the 32 signals. The example in Figure 9.11 contains numbers such as 421698, which represent signals that have handlers installed. These numbers are the virtual addresses (in the process) of the functions that catch the signals. If the symbol table of the executable file has not been stripped (see **strip(1)**), the **nm(1)** command or a debugger can be used to find out the signal handler's name. Table 4.33 in § 4.10.1 shows the mapping between signal numbers and their signal names.

- *bsize* — some device drivers (notably the *s5* file systems) fill in the *u_bsize* field with the block size of the storage device. This is shown in *bsize*.

- *qsav* — prints the *u_qsav* field. Many file operations, such as *open* and *close*, call *setjmp()* to save a copy of the current execution environment. If the system call is interrupted, the kernel does a *longjmp( )* back to this saved environment by using the information saved in *u_qsav*. The value printed by **crash** is the value of the first element of the data saved by *setjmp( )* (see also § 4.9.9).

- *error* — the value of the *u_error* field. When a system call fails, the error code is placed in this field, which is used to fill in *errno* in the user-mode text.

- *ap* — the value of the *u_ap* pointer, which points to the arguments for the current system call. When a system call is made, *u_ap* is initialized to point to the argument array, *u_arg[ ]* in the user-area.

- *u_r, pbsize, pboff, rablock, errcnt* — these fields are described as being obsolete. They might, however, be filled in by some device drivers. If so, *u_r* holds the return value from the system call, *pbsize* gives the number of bytes in the block for an I/O operation, *pboff* gives the offset in the block for I/O, *rablock* gives the disk address of the read-ahead block and *errcnt* gives the system call error count.

- *tsize, dsize, ssize* — when a program is running normally, these fields are set to zero. However, if the program suffers an error that forces it to core dump, these fields are filled in with the number of pages in the text, data and stack segments. They are then used elsewhere to ensure that the resource limit for the crash dump size is not exceeded.

- *arg[0]* — the arguments to the current system call are held in the *arg* array, which is sized by the system call with the most arguments. In Figure 9.11, we see that the maximum is six arguments.

- *ar0* — when a system call is made on a MIPS processor, this field points to the exception frame, which holds the information needed to restore the context once the system call completes. Other processors use a similar mechanism, and this field points to the equivalent information.

- *ticks* — holds the value of the kernel timer *lbolt* at the time the process was started. This timer is set to zero when the system boots, and is incremented for every clock tick. It is used for process execution time accounting; when an accounting record is generated, the elapsed time for the process is calculated by subtracting *u_ticks* from the current value of *lbolt*.

- *pr_base, pr_size, pr_off, pr_scale* — these fields (stored in the user-area) store the arguments that are passed to the *profil* system call.

- *ior, iow, iosw, ioch* — the counts *ior* and *iow* count how many buffered read and write operations have been performed. Each time *bread( )* or *bwrite( )* is called, the appropriate count is incremented. The value *ioch* gives the total number of bytes read and written by the process. The field *iosw* is not used in UNIX System V Release 4.

- *sysabort* — when a process is being traced via */proc*, this variable may be set in the user-area (*u_sysabort*). If it is, the current system call will abort, behaving as if it had received a signal (the value is checked when the process is made runnable, and acted upon when it next runs).

- *systrap* — if this value is non-zero, it means system calls are being traced through the */proc* file system. If the value is zero, system calls are not being traced. The values in *entrymask* and *exitmask* specify which system calls are being traced.

- *entrymask, exitmask* — a mask of the system calls that will cause the process to stop on entry, and stop on exit. The values used in these fields are defined in the *procfs.h* include file.

- *EXDATA* — this section prints out useful information about the executable file from which the process was started. The following information is printed:

  - *vp* — the *vnode* associated with the file.

  - *tsize dsize, bsize* — the size of the *text, data* and *bss* segments of the program.

  - *lsize* — the size of the library segment.

  - *magic* — the *magic number* of the executable file.

  - *toffset, doffset, loffset* — the offsets in the executable file of the start of the text, initialized data, and library segments.

  - *txtorg, datorg* — the start addresses in memory of the text and data segments.

  - *entloc* — the entry location for the program.

  - *nshlibs* — how many shared libraries are used.

  - *execsz* — the size, in pages (clicks), of the executable. The value is printed in hexadecimal.

  - *tracepc* — the value of the saved trace program counter. The interrupt handler in *ttrap.s* saves a copy of the program counter in *u_tracepc* if it notices that the process is being traced; *u_tracepc* holds a saved copy of the PC to return to. When a stack exception is handled, a trace trap check is done. If *u_tracepc* is found to be non-zero but not equal to the value of the program counter that the stack fault occurred on, then the stack fault occurred while processing a trace exception. In this case, *SIGTRAP* is posted to the process, which is handled by the process on its return to user-mode.

- *syscall* — is used by RFS servers to keep track of the system calls being made on behalf of their clients. It holds the number of the system call being executed.

- *SIGNAL MASK* — the system call *sigaction* is used to install a signal handler. One of the parameters to the call, *sa_mask*, specifies the set of signals that must be blocked while the signal handler is executing. The *sa_mask* for each signal is stored in the *u_sigmask* field of the user-area. The **crash** output (Figure 9.11) shows the signal mask for each signal. That is, it shows which signals will be blocked when a signal handler is running.

- *sigonstack* — the value of a bitmask for which a bit is set for each signal processed on an alternate stack. In other words, if a bit is set in this mask, its corresponding signal will be taken on the alternate stack (see *sigaction* and *sigaltstack* in § 4.10.4).

- *sigflag, oldmask* — the value of the *u_sigflag* field. If this field is non-zero, the process has previously executed a *sigsuspend* system call, and is waiting for a signal. The *u_sigoldmask* field holds the signal mask that will be installed when the process starts running after *sigsuspend* completes.

- *altflags* — the status of the alternate signal stack. **crash** will either print *disabl,* meaning that the alternate stack has been disabled, or *onstak,* meaning that a signal handler is currently running on the alternate stack. The state information is held in the *u_sigaltstack* field in the user-area.

- *altsp, altsize* — the alternate signal stack base address and its size as installed by the *sigaltstack* system call.

9.4.4 Hints for the u command

The u command can be used to good effect when examining a post mortem crash dump, or when examining a running system. Three hints are given for both cases and a hint is also given for finding the pages that contain the user-area and the kernel stack for any particular process.

- On some UNIX systems, the kernel stack and the user-area share an area of memory, with the user-area at the bottom and the kernel stack growing down from the top. This area of memory is usually two or three pages, and is sufficient to accommodate kernel stack growth. In such a system, the kernel stack may grow into the user-area; if the kernel is executing deeply nested function calls, and higher priority interrupts occur, the stack may grow so large that it overflows into the user-area. If this happens, the system will eventually crash. If the fields at the end of the user-area are corrupted, it is likely that the kernel stack has grown into it. This corruption will be obvious in the output of the u command, and it can be double checked against the *user* structure definition in the header file *user.h.* Unfortunately, the size of the kernel stack is not normally tuneable: it is fixed by the vendor.

- The user-area of the process that was running at the time of the crash shows which program was running. If the same program is responsible for repeated crashes, you can deduce that the program somehow provoked the kernel into crashing. Knowing this allows you to fix the program, or not run it until the problem is fixed.

- If the system crashes whilst executing a system call associated with a file (such as *open, close, read* or *write*), the kernel stack trace for the process executing at the time of the crash identifies the system call it was executing. The arguments to this system call are in the *arg[x]* fields in the user-area. This information, along with the open file table held in the user-area, will show you which file was being accessed at the time. This might provide clues about the cause of the crash.

- When **crash** is used on a running system, the u command can be useful in tracing odd process behaviour. The file table shows you which files are open by a particular process. If the process is hung, the `trace` command and the file table often give information about where and on which file the process is hanging. For example, if the process is waiting for input from a FIFO, the stack trace will tell you it is executing a *read*, the system call arguments will tell you which file descriptor is being read, and the file and *vnode* tables will tell you exactly what type of file is being read.

- Sometimes processes are written to handle signals, but they do not handle the signals as expected. The u command shows you the disposition of all signals at run time. This might point out errors in the coding of the program.

- A user found that he could not successfully increase the file size limit for a process. Investigation using the u command showed that the **login(1)** program on his system was setting the file size limit to a low value. Armed with this information, he discovered that this feature was documented, and so he was able to reconfigure login to set a higher file size limit.

Sometimes you need to inspect the memory of the user-area. For example, you may need to look up a field in the user area that is not displayed by the u command. To do this you must first find the address of the user-area. The kernel will either contain a symbol *u* that you can look up using the nm command, or it will be at a fixed virtual address, which you can find in the include file *user.h*. For example, on one MIPS implementation, it is always found at the virtual address 0xfffff000. The user-area is always mapped to the same virtual address, regardless of which process is running. Assuming the process is in slot 25, you use the vtop command (virtual to physical) to look up the physical address of the user-area for that process, and then the od -p command to display the page of data. Note that the user-area for a process that is swapped out cannot be examined. Furthermore, if you use od to display bytes from the virtual address of the user-area, it will display the user-area for the default process (defproc).

```
> vtop -s25 0xfffff000
  virt 0xfffff000 -> phys 0xcca000

> od -p -x 0xcca000 0x400      /* Prints 1024 * 4byte words */
  ...
```

9.4.5 The as command

SYNOPSIS as *slot ...*
This command prints the address space information from the *as* structure for a given process. If no process is specified, the address space of the current process is printed. Note that the *as* and *seg* structures are not defined in */usr/include/sys*. The long form output is shown in Figure 9.12. The output of the *as* command is implementation dependent because it is hardware dependent and therefore vendor

Figure 9.12: *Output of the* as *command*

```
> as -f 25

PROC  KEEPCNT         SEGS      SEGLAST   MEM_CLAIM  FLAGS
SLOT
 25         0   0x80bd4f60   0x80bd4f60       1559
   LOCK         BASE     SIZE       NEXT         PREV      OPS        DATA
      0   0x00400000   331776  0x80bd4da0  0x806c05e0  segvn_op  0x804ff120
      0   0x10000000    73728  0x80761400  0x80bd4f60  segvn_op  0x804ff520
      0   0x10012000  9363456  0x806c05e0  0x80bd4da0  segvn_op  0x80fd37d4
      0   0x4001c000     8192  0x80bd4f60  0x80761400  segvn_op  0x806c0890
```

defined. For example, on one MIPS implementation, the fields *KEEPCNT*, *FLAGS*, and *LOCK* are always zero because their corresponding *as* structure members are not used. The fields that are interesting in the output are described below:

- *PROC SLOT* — the slot number in the process table of the process owning this address space.

- *SEGS, SEGLAST* — pointers to the first and last segments that comprise the address space.

- *MEM_CLAIM* — the value of the *a_rss* field in the process's associated *as* structure giving the number of memory pages claimed by the process (i.e., its resident set size).

Each segment in the process's address space is linked together in a doubly linked list. The information about each segment, taken from its associated *seg* structure, is shown in the output and is described as follows:

- *BASE, SIZE* — the virtual address of the base of the segment, and its size in bytes.

- *NEXT, PREV* — the values of the next and previous *seg* structure pointers in the list of segments comprising the process's address space.

- *OPS* — the value of the segment operations field for the segment. In the *seg* structure, the *s_ops* field is a pointer to the segment operations. This pointer is looked up in the symbol table, and the symbolic name for the operations is printed (note that only the first 8 characters are displayed). In the sample output of Figure 9.12, the pointers are to *segvn_ops*, indicating that they are *segvn* segments. If no symbol is found for the corresponding segment operation, its value is printed in hexadecimal.

- *DATA* — the address of the private data structure for the segment. In the example output, the address of the *segvn_data* structure is given since this is the private data structure associated with *segvn* segments.

The benefit of the *as* command should be obvious: it allows you to see which segments are attached to the process, and which virtual addresses they are mapped to. This information is useful when you are trying to figure out the meaning of addresses in your program. The example in Figure 9.12 shows that the process has four segments. From this output we can postulate that the first segment is the text segment for the process, the second is the data segment of the process, the third is likely to relate to a shared library, and the fourth to the process's stack. However, to confirm this, you would have to inspect the fields in the *segvn_data* structures for these segments.

9.5 Kernel stack

For crash dumps, the kernel stack holds the key to understanding what the system was doing when it crashed. It contains information about which kernel functions were active, and the values of the local variables in those functions. The functions that were active were in some way responsible for the system crashing — either they crashed the system due to a bug, or they crashed the system because they were given corrupt data. It is vital, therefore, to understand the kernel stack and how it works.

The next two sections describe how the C Compiler on the MIPS processor uses the stack, and show how the kernel stack on a MIPS processor is laid out. Hints are given on how to understand the C Compiler and kernel stack on other processors. The **trace** command prints out the contents of the kernel stack, and often gives you all the information you need; it is described in § 9.5.3. Finally, § 9.5.4 describes how to print the kernel stack in hexadecimal, and gives a method for constructing a traceback by hand. This is sometimes needed when there are exception frames on the kernel stack — the **trace** command will not traverse them, so you have to do it by hand.

9.5.1 C Language stack

The C Language does not specify how the language itself should be implemented. At the implementation level, it does not specify how functions are called or how their arguments are passed. This leaves compiler writers free to exploit the architecture of the machine. However, nowadays, manufacturers are keen to develop computer systems that are binary compatible with other machines using the same processor, reducing the cost of providing software. To assist with this, USL provides the *System V Application Binary Interface* (ABI) (see [USL 1992b]). There is a separate ABI for each processor type, so that if you have an application written for the MIPS processor ABI, it will run without recompilation on any other machine that conforms to the MIPS ABI. However, it will not run on one that conforms to another processor ABI, for example, the Intel ABI.

The ABI covers many different areas but of interest here are the C Language calling conventions.

This section describes how C Language functions are called on systems that conform to the MIPS ABI. The specification for this is given in the *MIPS Processor Supplement* [USL 1991]. For the calling conventions used on other processors, you should consult the relevant ABI supplement (see [USL 1990 a,b,c,d]).

Figure 9.13: *MIPS stack frame*

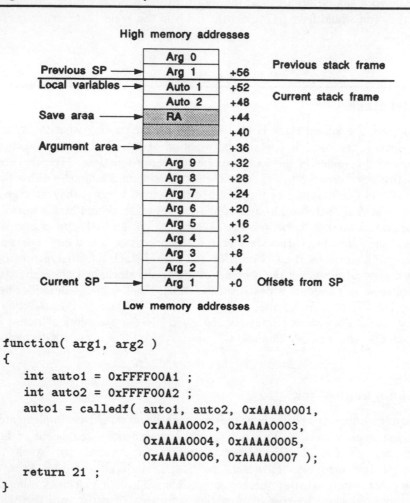

```
function( arg1, arg2 )
{
    int auto1 = 0xFFFF00A1 ;
    int auto2 = 0xFFFF00A2 ;
    auto1 = calledf( auto1, auto2, 0xAAAA0001,
                     0xAAAA0002, 0xAAAA0003,
                     0xAAAA0004, 0xAAAA0005,
                     0xAAAA0006, 0xAAAA0007 );
    return 21 ;
}
```

Figure 9.13 shows the code for a simple C Language function and its stack frame. The stack frame consists of three areas:

- *Local variables* — the highest addresses in the stack frame contain the local variables for the function. The first local variable is stored at the highest address in the stack frame, the second local variable at the second highest address, and so on.

Figure 9.14: *C Language call — MIPS assembler version*

Address	Op	Args	Comment
0x400240:	addiu	sp,sp,-56	Create stack frame
0x400244:	sw	ra,44(sp)	Save return address
0x400248:	sw	a0,56(sp)	Save arguments we were called with in
0x40024c:	sw	a1,60(sp)	callers stack frame
0x400250:	lui	t6,0xffff	Calculate initial value of auto1..
0x400254:	ori	t6,t6,0xa1	
0x400258:	sw	t6,52(sp)	.. and save it
0x40025c:	lui	t7,0xffff	Calculate initial value of auto2..
0x400260:	ori	t7,t7,0xa2	
0x400264:	sw	t7,48(sp)	.. and save it
0x400268:	lui	t8,0xaaaa	Set up top halves of temporary registers
0x40026c:	lui	t9,0xaaaa	
0x400270:	lui	t0,0xaaaa	
0x400274:	lui	t1,0xaaaa	
0x400278:	lui	t2,0xaaaa	
0x40027c:	ori	t2,t2,0x7	Create arg 9..
0x400280:	sw	t2,32(sp)	.. and place in register area
0x400284:	ori	t1,t1,0x6	Create arg 8..
0x400288:	sw	t1,28(sp)	.. and place in register area
0x40028c:	ori	t0,t0,0x5	.. create arg 7
0x400290:	ori	t9,t9,0x4	.. create arg 6
0x400294:	ori	t8,t8,0x3	.. create arg 5
0x400298:	lw	a0,52(sp)	Copy auto1 into arg1
0x40029c:	lw	a1,48(sp)	Copy auto2 into arg2
0x4002a0:	lui	a2,0xaaaa	Set up top halves of arg 3..
0x4002a4:	lui	a3,0xaaaa	.. and arg 4
0x4002a8:	sw	t8,16(sp)	place arg5 in register area
0x4002ac:	sw	t9,20(sp)	place arg6 in register area
0x4002b0:	ori	a3,a3,0x2	Fill in bottom half of arg 4..
0x4002b4:	ori	a2,a2,0x1	.. and arg 3
0x4002b8:	jal	calledf	Call the function
0x4002bc:	sw	t0,24(sp)	Branch delay slot. Save arg 7 in register area while jump address is fetched
0x4002c0:	sw	v0,52(sp)	Save return value in auto1
0x4002c4:	b	0x4002cc	Jump to function exit
0x4002c8:	li	v0,21	Fill in return value in branch delay slot
0x4002cc:	lw	ra,44(sp)	Recover the return address
0x4002d0:	addiu	sp,sp,56	Clear our stack frame
0x4002d4:	jr	ra	Return to caller
0x4002d8:	nop		

- *Register area* — if the function calls another function, it must first save some registers. For example, the return address register (*RA*) must be saved so that the program counter can later be restored to the point where the function was called. Additionally, the MIPS processor has a group of nine registers (*S0-S8*) called the *callee saved registers*. If a function intends to use these registers it must first save them, and before returning to the calling function it must restore them to their original values. If the function uses the floating point processor, it must save its associated registers also (*F20-F30* in the MIPS) before calling another function, and restore them on return too. Finally, a function that is returning to its caller does so by jumping unconditionally to the saved return address, *RA*. It can be seen that these registers are pushed onto the register save area and popped from it as necessary. On the MIPS processor, the register area is always aligned to an 8-byte boundary. In the example of Figure 9.14, only the return address register, *RA*, is saved.

- *Argument area* — the third area of the stack frame is used for building the arguments to called functions. On the MIPS processor, the minimum size of this area is four 32-bit words. If functions with more than four arguments are called, this area must be big enough to hold the arguments for the function that is called with the most arguments. In Figure 9.14, nine words have been reserved. The size of the argument area is adjusted so that the stack frame aligns to an 8-byte boundary.

A C Language function call on the MIPS processor proceeds as follows:

- The calling function evaluates the arguments to be passed to the called function. The first four arguments are passed in registers *A0-A3*, the remaining are passed in the argument area. The function call is made with the jump-and-link (*JAL*) instruction to place the address of the next instruction to execute in the return address (*RA*) register, and to jump to the start of the called function.

- The called function first reserves space on the stack for its stack frame by decrementing the stack pointer by the size of the stack frame. It then saves the *RA* in the register area.

- The called function accesses its first four arguments via registers *A0-A3*, although sometimes it has to save them — for example, when it is creating the arguments for a function it is going to call. When this happens the argument registers, *A0-A3*, are saved in the argument area of the *callers* stack frame. If the function is called with a variable number of arguments, it manipulates its arguments with the macros *va_start*, *va_arg*, and *va_end* from the header file *stdarg.h*. To operate successfully, these macros require the arguments to be held in memory. When these macros are used, the compiler arranges that the first four arguments are placed into the argument area automatically.

- In order to return, the function fills the *RA* register with the value that was saved in the stack frame. The stack pointer is then incremented by the size of the stack frame. Finally, a jump instruction is executed, jumping to the address held in the *RA* register.

- The return value from a called function is held in the register *V0*.

Figure 9.14 is an annotated MIPS disassembly of the function described in Figure 9.13. Note that the MIPS C calling sequence does not use a frame pointer. However, in the header files and the documentation, reference is often made to the *FP* register. In MIPS ABI conformant systems, the *FP* register is treated as the ninth callee-saved register.

Figure 9.15: *Kernel stack layout*

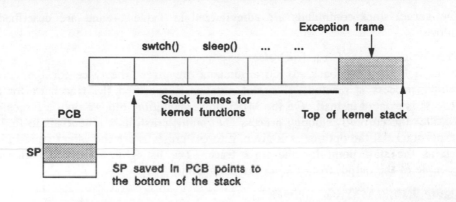

9.5.2 The kernel stack layout

Each process has its own kernel stack, which is used when the process is executing in kernel-mode (see § 4.2.6). The kernel stack is always mapped as part of the user-area of the process, but its exact layout is system dependent. The MIPS kernel stack layout is shown in Figure 9.15. When a process enters kernel-mode on the MIPS implementation, the kernel stack pointer is initialized and an exception frame pushed. The exception frame contains the information necessary to resume normal operation on return to user-mode. On other implementations, such as the Intel 80386, kernel-mode is entered via a *call gate* (see [Intel 1986a]), and the first part of the kernel stack contains the user-mode stack pointers, the system call arguments, and the user-mode return address.

Below the exception frame is the kernel stack proper. The kernel is written in C, and so conforms to the C calling conventions described in the previous section. Therefore, the contents of the kernel stack can be printed by following the stack pointer. The process control block contains the kernel stack pointer for the process, and so the kernel stack for a process is found by displaying its pcb. This is done with the *pcb* command (regardless of the processor architecture, if your version of **crash** has the pcb command, then it will display the kernel stack pointer). When the system crashes, the kernel stack pointer is saved in the pcb of the currently running process; this allows you to construct a traceback from the panic, and gives you a picture of the final moments of the life of the system.

Table 9.4: *Kernel stack commands*

Command	Description
trace	Print kernel stack trace
stack	Hexadecimal dump of kernel stack
pcb	Print process control block

9.5.3 Kernel stack commands

The kernel stack commands are summarized in Table 9.4 and are described as follows:

SYNOPSIS trace [-r] [-s] *slot*
Prints a kernel traceback. If no arguments are given, the trace for the current default process is printed. If a slot number is specified the traceback for that process is printed instead. On the MIPS implementation, the -r option forces it to consider the currently running process. Normally, **crash** uses a heuristic to find the kernel stack. If the option -s is given, it forces **crash** to use the values stored in the pcb as the start point for the stack trace. The listing in Figure 9.16 shows an example of the output from the trace command.

Figure 9.16: *The* trace *command*

```
> trace  25
  STACK TRACE FOR PROCESS 25: (lpsched)
  swtch+38 [../arch/machdep.c: 850, 0x8008460c]
  sleep+45c [../os/slp.c: 283, 0x8004f5ac]
  poll+4c8 [../fs/vncalls.c: 2094, 0x800ceb54]
  syscall+2ac [../arch/trap.c: 585, 0x800a3a38]
  VEC_syscall+3c [../arch/locore.s: 1400, 0x80031880]
```

The trace output shows the functions active for the process in slot 25 — the line printer scheduler. Clearly the process has executed a *poll* system call, and is waiting for an event to happen on one of the polled file descriptors. The line *swtch+38* gives the address at which execution will resume in the *swtch* function. Similarly, the location *sleep+45c* is the address at which the *sleep* function will resume execution. The items in square brackets refer back to the source files from which the kernel was compiled. Armed with this information, a support engineer will be able to access line 283 in the file *os/slp.c* to see where the call to *swtch* returns. The hexadecimal number in the brackets is the address of the instruction that will be executed.

SYNOPSIS stack [-u] [-k] *slot*
Produces a hexadecimal and ASCII dump of the kernel and interrupt stacks for the process in the given slot. If the option -k is given, the kernel stack is printed. Similarly, if the option -u is given, the user stack for the process is printed.

9.5.4 Kernel stack hints

In UNIX System V Release 4 the kernel stack for a process is always placed at a
fixed virtual address; on most implementations it is placed below the user-area and
the kernel stack grows downwards away from it. Thus, most systems preallocate a
fixed number of pages for the user-area and kernel stack. For example, an
implementation may use one page for the user-area and two for the kernel stack.
This information can be found with the `proc -f` command. The example listing in
Figure 9.10 shows that there are three valid entries for the `ubptbl`.

To print the kernel stack for a given process the `stack` command is used,
specifying the process slot of the process of interest. The pcb of the process holds
the kernel stack pointer in the *SP* field.

When **crash** is used on a running system, it will not print the kernel stack for the
currently running process. However, when you examine a post mortem crash dump
you will find that the currently running process caused the crash, so the kernel stack
and traceback for this process show the sequence of function calls leading to the
crash.

Figure 9.17: *Hand built stack trace*

```
> od -p a7d000 0x400
00a7d000: 2f6e6673 2f546578 742e6765 6e657269

. . .

00a7dcb0: 80ffe000 00000002 0000f73d 80536738
00a7dcc0: 00000000 800846dc 00000000 00000004
00a7dcd0: 100db000 30000008  800ad808  00000100  SP in swtch( )
00a7dce0: 0000000b 803b2f00 803b1c70 ffff390f
00a7dcf0: 00000000  8004f5ac                     RA from swtch( )
                     4001df58  802fddc4  SP in sleep( )
00a7dd00: 802afb48 100c3000 00001000 00000100
00a7dd10: 00000000 801b79e8 80536700 00000000
00a7dd20: 809f9600 800b0001 00000001  800ceb54  RA from sleep( )
00a7dd30: ffffede0 802f6228 00000000 00000001
00a7dd40: 8045f820 800ce984  802fddc4  0000011a  SP in poll( )
00a7dd50: 00000000 00001000 8053671c 800beef4
00a7dd60: 100c4000 100e7000 80f181e0 80255aa8
00a7dd70: 1000639c 00001000 00051000 800b8e84
00a7dd80: 80c559b4 8022d414 0000f73c 00000000
00a7dd90: 4001df58 4001df58 1000639c 100061dc
00a7dda0: 100063a4 00000001 00000000  800a3a38  RA from poll( )
00a7ddb0: 00000000 00000001 0000000d 0000000d
00a7ddc0: 00000000 100c3000 00051000 80ffe000

. . .

00a7deb0: 5e400000 00000000 0000000a ffffef24
00a7dec0: ffffee00 800a3a38 805476d8 800a3c8c
00a7ded0:  fffff27c  ffffef24 5e400000 30000008  SP in syscall( )
```

```
00a7dee0:  00000000  800a4024  100061dc  800a417c
00a7def0:  00000001  8003170c  00000000  80031880   RA from syscall( )
00a7df00:  00000000  00000000  8024c004  0000f73c
00a7df10:  0000f73d  4001df58  4001df58  1000639c
00a7df20:  100061dc  00000000  00000000  00000000
00a7df30:  000000fa  800bcfa8  80ffe000  00000000
00a7df40:  ffffef40  00000057  0000f73c  b000000c   SP in VEC_syscall( )
00a7df50:  10040000  00000057  00000000  100db000
00a7df60:  00000002  ffffffff  00000000  00000000
00a7df70:  00000001  00000001  00000000  5e400350
00a7df80:  5fc07350  40021c04  4001d558  00000000
00a7df90:  00000000  4001df58  4001df58  1000639c
00a7dfa0:  100061dc  100063a4  00000001  00400ada
00a7dfb0:  0007762c  00000000  00003500  5fe12550
00a7dfc0:  4001d5c8  0000000                        User space PC
                               0042d848  0000f73c   User space RA
00a7dfd0:  00000000  00000004  ffaf2000  00000020
00a7dfe0:  5fc35774  00ffffff  00200000  00002d02
00a7dff0:  ffffffff  ffff390f  00000000  5fc35770   End of Stack
```

```
> pcb 25                    PCB holds current stack pointer
resched: 0, bd_epc: 0, bd_cause: 0, bd_ra: 0, bd_instr: 0
softfp_pc: 0, fpc_csr: 0, fpc_eir: 0, ownedfp: 0
sstep: 0, ssi_cnt: 0:, bp[0] = 0,0, bp[1] =  0,0
regs: (S0-S7, SP,  FP, PC, SR)
  80ffe000  00000002  0000f73d  80536738
  00000000  800ced2c  ffffede4  00000020
  ffffecd8  ffffede0  8008460c  00000001
```

```
> vtop -s25 ffffecd8        find physical address of stack
virt 0xffffecd8 -> phys 0xa7dcd8
```

```
> ds 8008460c
swtch+38 [../arch/machdep.c: 847, 0x8008460c]
```

```
> dis swtch 2               find frame size, and position of RA
swtch+0 [../arch/machdep.c: 841, 0x800845d4]    addiu   sp,sp,-32
swtch+4 [../arch/machdep.c: 841, 0x800845d8]    sw      ra,28(sp)
```

```
> ds 8004f5ac
sleep+45c [../os/slp.c: 250, 0x8004f5ac]
```

```
> dis sleep 6
sleep+0 [../os/slp.c: 98, 0x8004f150]    addiu   sp,sp,-80
sleep+4 [../os/slp.c: 113, 0x8004f154]   lui     t6,0x802f
sleep+8 [../os/slp.c: 113, 0x8004f158]   lw      t6,-24732(t6)
sleep+c [../os/slp.c: 98, 0x8004f15c]    sw      s0,48(sp)
sleep+10 [../os/slp.c: 99, 0x8004f160]   lw      s0,-3368(zero)
```

```
sleep+14 [../os/slp.c: 98, 0x8004f164]  sw      ra,52(sp)

> ds 800ceb54
poll+4c8 [../fs/vncalls.c: 2001, 0x800ceb54]

> dis poll 3
poll+0 [../fs/vncalls.c: 1952, 0x800ce68c]   addiu  sp,sp,-392
poll+4 [../fs/vncalls.c: 1969, 0x800ce690]   lw     t6,-3368(zero)
poll+8 [../fs/vncalls.c: 1952, 0x800ce694]   sw     ra,100(sp)

> ds 800a3a38
syscall+2ac [../arch/trap.c: 492, 0x800a3a38]

> dis syscall 3
syscall+0 [../arch/trap.c: 475, 0x800a378c]   lw     v0,-3368(zero)
syscall+4 [../arch/trap.c: 473, 0x800a3790]   addiu  sp,sp,-112
syscall+8 [../arch/trap.c: 473, 0x800a3794]   sw     ra,44(sp)
```

The crash output in Figure 9.17 shows a hand-built stack trace. If you need to find out the values of the local variables in one of the active functions, you have to build the trace by hand to find out where in the stack the local variables are kept. The following steps produced the stack trace:

- The pcb command shows that the stack pointer (SP) was at 0xffffecd8, and the program counter (PC) was at 0x8008460c.

- The ds command shows that the address 0x8008460c is within *swtch( )*.

- The vtop command shows that the SP points into the page 0xa7dcd8. The page containing the stack contents was printed by using od -p a7d000.

- Disassembling the first few instructions of *swtch( )* shows that the stack frame size is 32 bytes, and the return address (RA) was stored 28 bytes along from the SP.

- Counting along 28 bytes from the SP gives the address 0x00a7dcf4, which contains the value 0x8004f5ac. The ds command shows that 0x8004f5ac lies within the function *sleep( )*. Counting along 32 bytes from the SP gives the value of the SP in the *sleep( )* function.

- The first few instructions of *sleep( )* are disassembled. The instructions show that the stack frame size is 80 bytes, and that the RA is 52 bytes along from the SP. The ds command shows that *sleep* was called from *poll( )*.

This process continues, showing that *sleep( )* was called by *poll( )*, that *poll( )* was called by *syscall( )*, and that *syscall( )* was called by *VEC_syscall* (functions that start *VEC_* on the authors' system are the lowest level assembler functions that handle system call exceptions). They do not have a C Language stack frame; their stack frame consists of an exception frame containing the information needed to return to user-mode once the system call is completed. On one implementation using the MIPS processor, the exception frame contains 48 long words. Close examination of its data structure definition shows that the item with index 40 is the PC in the user program and that index 34 is the RA into the user program, and that index 32 gives the SP.

Table 9.5: *File system commands*

Command	Description
file	Display an entry from the file table
vnode	Print a *vnode*
uinode	Display a *ufs_inode*
vfssw	Print the virtual file system table
vfs	Show the mounted file systems

9.6 Files

It is often useful to know which files are being accessed by the running processes. For example, if the system crashes as a result of a file system call, you can examine the file system data structures to see which file, and which type of file was being accessed at the time.

The following sections describe the output of the file system related commands, which are summarized in Table 9.5. Fewer hints are given in this section because the file system data structures play a smaller role in determining the causes of a crash. The main point of these commands is to allow you to build up a picture of the file system state at the time of the crash. Note that you cannot easily deduce the name of a particular file by using **crash** since the pathname information is lost as the directory structure is traversed at the time the file is opened. The best way to get a file's name is to note the *inode* number of file of interest, and then look it up in the file system with **ls(1)** or **ncheck(1M)**.

Figure 9.18: *The* file *command*

```
OPEN FILES AND POFILE FLAGS:
[0]: F 0x80de32c0, 0          [1]: F 0x80536700, 0
[2]: F 0x80536700, 0          [3]: F 0x80a9a600, 0


> file 0x80de32c0
ADDRESS   RCNT    TYPE/ADDR        OFFSET   FLAGS
80de32c0   1      UFS /8042ab38       2     read
```

9.6.1 The `file` command

SYNOPSIS `file` *address*

Print the contents of the *file* structure at the given address. The address may also be given as a slot number, in which case the file entry in that slot is displayed. The addresses of the file structures are held in the user-area. You use these addresses for the arguments to the file command as shown in Figure 9.18. The fields in the output have the following meanings:

- *ADDRESS* — the memory address of the *file* structure. The output in Figure 9.18 shows that file descriptors 1 and 2 both point to the same *file* structure; this is because they refer to the control terminal, and were created by the *dup* system call. File descriptor 0 is different because the standard input for that process was redirected from a file.

- *RCNT* — the reference count; it specifies how many file descriptors in the system reference this file structure. If a process *forks*, or if a file descriptor is duplicated by the *dup* system call, the reference count is increased. The reference count decrements whenever the file is closed.

- *TYPE/ADDR* — the file system type, and the address of the *vnode* structure that describes the file. The exact values of the type are file system dependent, but most systems will print: *S5* for System V file system, *UFS* for the Unix file system, *SPEC* for block and character devices, *FIFO* for named pipes and fifos, and *PROC* for entries in the */proc* file system. If **crash** does not know the file system type, it prints a question mark.

- *OFFSET* — the current value of the read/write character offset for the file.

- *FLAGS* — the value of the *f_flag* field. These values are set when the file is opened, or by the *fcntl* system call. The values printed are taken from the set: *read, write, appen, sync, creat, trunc, excl, ndelay*, and correspond to the values: *FREAD, FWRITE, FAPPEND, FSYNC, FCREAT, FTRUNC, FEXCL and FNDELAY.*

9.6.2 Examining *vnodes*

SYNOPSIS `vnode` *address*

Prints the information about the *vnode* at the given address. The output in Figure 9.19 shows the *vnode* associated with the address 0x8042ab38:

- *VCNT* — the *v_count* field; it specifies how many times the *vnode* has been referenced.

- *VFSMNTED* — the value of the *v_vfsmountedhere* field; if it is zero, the *vnode* is not a mount point. That is, there is no file system mounted on the *vnode*. If the value is non-zero, it contains the address of the *vfs* structure mounted at that point.

Figure 9.19: *Output from* vnode

```
> vnode 8042ab38
VCNT VFSMNTED  VFSP  STREAMP VTYPE RDEV VDATA VFILOCKS VFLAG
   5       0 80519e00      0  f     -  8042ab30      0
```

- *VFSP* — the value of the *v_vfsp* field, which is a pointer to the *vfs* structure for the file system that the file resides on.

- *STREAMP* — if the file is associated with a stream, this field (*v_stream*) contains the address of the stream head data structure. Otherwise, its value is zero.

- *VTYPE, RDEV* — the *vnode* type (*v_type*). The field has the value f, d, l, p or -, meaning: file, directory, symbolic link, FIFO (pipe) or unknown file type. For a *vnode* that is not yet associated with a file (i.e., during initialization), the value n is printed. If the file is a block or character special device, the letters b or c are printed, and the major and minor device numbers are printed in the *RDEV* field (*v_rdev*).

- *VDATA* — the contents of the *vnode* private data field (*v_data*). For file *vnodes*, it points to the file system type dependent in-core *inode* structure. For example, if a file resides in a *ufs* file system, the *vnode* data field points to a *ufs_inode* structure; if the file resides on an *s5* file system, the data points to an *s5 inode* structure, and so on. Whichever file system implementation, the file system type dependent in-core *inode* contains the *vnode* associated with the file. We can see this in the example: the address of the *vnode* is 0x8042ab38, and the data field points to 0x8042ab30, which is the in-core *ufs_inode* for the file. Note that only a portion of the in-core *ufs_inode* is stored permanently on the disk. (The *ufs_inode* is defined in the header file *ufs_inode.h*.)

- *VFILOCKS* — the contents of the *v_filocks* field. If it is non-zero, it points to the first file locking structure for the file.

  Unfortunately, there is no command for displaying file locking structures, so you must display them with the od command.

- *VFLAG* — the *v_flag* field. If the *vnode* is associated with the root of its file system, the word root is printed.

9.6.3 Examining *inodes*

There are five commands for printing a file's *inode* information, although again their presence depends on the file system types installed in your UNIX system. However, for the purpose of this discussion we will concentrate only on the *ufs* file *inode*. The five commands are:

- uinode — prints the *inode* information about a file in the *ufs* file system.

- prnode — prints the *inode* information about a file in the */proc* file system.

- snode — prints the *inode* information about a block or character special file.

- inode — prints the *inode* information about a file in the *s5* file system.

- fnode — prints the *inode* information about a FIFO.

SYNOPSIS uinode *address*
Prints the in-core *ufs_inode* at the given address. The address may also be a slot number, in which case the *ufs_inode* in that slot is printed.

Figure 9.20: *The* uinode *command*

```
> uinode -f 0x8042ab30
UFS INODE TABLE SIZE = 300
SLOT MAJ/MIN INUMB RCNT LINK  UID   GID    SIZE   MODE  FLAGS
  98   4, 9   242    5    1    207    1  4199084 f---744 rf
        FORW BACK AFOR ABCK
         297   -    -    -
        OWNER COUNT NEXTR
          3     0     0
     [ 0]: 1ce0    [ 1]: 1cf0    [ 2]: 1d00    [ 3]: 1d10
     [ 4]: 1d20    [ 5]: 1d30    [ 6]: 1d40    [ 7]: 1d50
     [ 8]: 1d60    [ 9]: 1d70    [10]: 1d80    [11]: 1d90
     [12]: 94e0

VNODE :
VCNT VFSMNTED   VFSP   STREAMP VTYPE RDEV VDATA    VFILOCKS VFLAG
  5       0 80519e00      0    f     -  8042ab30       0
> !ls -li /usr/book/chap9
   242 -rwxr--r-- 1 berny other 4199084 Jan 7 10:06 /usr/book/chap9
```

The output of this command (see Figure 9.20) consists of the following fields:

- *SLOT* — gives the position in the *ufs_inode* table at which the *inode* was found.

- *MAJ/MIN* — gives the major and minor device numbers of the block special device on which the file resides.

- *INUMB* — gives the disk *inode* number for the file. If you have access to the file system of the machine from which the crash dump was taken, you can work out the filename from the *inode* number. In the example of Figure 9.20, the file system on major device 4 and minor device 9 is the */usr/book* file system, and the inode with the number 242 has the name */usr/book/chap9*. The size of the file (seen with ls -li) matches that shown in the uinode printout, so we can be certain that the *inode* displayed corresponds to the file */usr/book/chap9*.

- *RCNT* — specifies how many times the *inode* has been referenced.

- *LINK* — specifies how many different directory entries points (link counts) are associated with this *inode*. If the file is a directory, the link count should be at least 2.

- *UID/GID* — prints the user and group IDs for the owner of the file.

- *SIZE* — prints the size of the file, in bytes.

- *MODE* — specifies the mode of the file. The first letter gives the file type (see the description of *VTYPE* above), the remaining fields give the permission bits. If the file has the set-user-ID bit set, the letter *u* is printed; if the set-group-ID bit is set, the letter *g* is printed.

- *FLAGS* — the status of the *inode* flags (see Table 9.6).

Table 9.6: *ufs_inode flags*

Output	Description
lk	*inode* is locked
up	File has been modified
ac	*inode* has been accessed
wt	A process wants to lock the *inode*
ch	*inode* itself has been modified
sy	Allocate blocks to file synchronously
wt	Process waiting on file lock
rf	The *inode* is being referenced
na	*getpage* will not update access time
md	The modification time has been set already
md	*inode* has been modified

- *FORW, BACK, AFOR, ABCK* — specify the slot numbers of the *inodes* linked to this *inode*. *FORW* and *BACK* are the forward and backward pointers used for linking *inodes* onto a hash list. Similarly *AFOR* and *ABCK* are used for linking *inodes* onto a freelist.

- *OWNER,COUNT* — if the *inode* is locked, *OWNER* specifies which process currently holds it locked, and *COUNT* specifies how many locks there are.

- *NEXTR* — holds the offset in the file of the next byte to read. This is used for read-ahead.

- *Direct blocks* — if the file is a regular file or a directory, the disk block addresses held within the *inode* are printed. Note that only the 12 direct block addresses are printed. The three indirect block addresses stored in the *inode* are not shown.

9.6.4 Mounted file systems

There are two commands related to file systems: vfssw and vfs.

SYNOPSIS vfssw *slot*
Prints the contents of the virtual file system switch table. If a slot number is given, only the entry in that slot is printed. The output from this command is shown in Figure 9.21.

Figure 9.21: *Output from* vfssw

```
> vfssw
FILE SYSTEM SWITCH TABLE SIZE = 13
SLOT    NAME      FLAGS
   1    spec        0
   2    vxfs        0
   3    cdfs        0
   4    ufs         0
   5    nfs         0
   6    fd          0
   7    fifo        0
   8    namefs      0
   9    proc        0
  10    s5          0
  11    rfs         0
  12    bfs         0
  13    xnam        0
  14    dos         0
```

The output consists of the slot number, the name of the file system type and its flags specified as a hexadecimal number showing the contents of the *vsw_flag* field in the *vfs* structure.

SYNOPSIS vfs *address*
Prints the contents of the mounted file system entry at the given address. The address can be given as a slot number, in which case the entry in that slot of the mounted file table is printed.

Figure 9.22 shows the output from this command. The figure shows a *vfs* entry, and the *vnode* associated with the underlying mount point. The fields in the output of the vfs command are:

- *FSTYP* — the file system type.

- *BSZ* — the block size used on the file system.

- *MAJ/MIN* — the major and minor device numbers of the device on which the file system is kept.

Figure 9.22: *Output from* vfs

```
> vfs 80519e00
 FSTYP  BSZ MAJ/MIN  FSID   VNCOVERED  PDATA     BCOUNT   FLAGS
   ufs 8192   4,9    100009 80448858   806aed60  2048     notr

> vnode 80448858
 VCNT VFSMNTED    VFSP     STREAMP VTYPE RDEV   VDATA     VFILOCKS VFLAG
   1  80519e00    80d09540       0 d      -     804486c0           0
```

- *FSID* — the file system ID. The exact meaning of the field is file system type dependent. For the *ufs* file system type, it holds the major and minor device numbers printed in hexadecimal. (In the example the bottom 18 bits give the minor device number, 9, and the remaining bits give the major device number, which is 100 in binary, or 4 in decimal.)

- *VNCOVERED* — the address of the *vnode* on which the file system is mounted. If you print out the information about the underlying *vnode*, the *VFSMNTED* field points back to the *vfs* entry; this is illustrated in the sample output.

- *PDATA* — the value of the private data pointer. For a *ufs* file system, it points to the superblock of the file system.

- *BCOUNT* — the number of blocks that have been read and written to the file system since it was mounted.

- *FLAGS* — Table 9.7 shows the values that can appear in this field, and the corresponding *vfs_flag* values.

Table 9.7: *VFS flags*

Value	Display	Description
VFS_RDONLY	rd	File system is mounted read-only
VFS_MLOCK	lck	VFS is locked
VFS_MWAIT	wait	A process is waiting for the lock
VFS_NOSUID	nosu	Set-user-ID bit is not honored
VFS_REMOUNT	remnt	Only mount options are changed
VFS_NOTRUNC	notr	Long file names are not truncated
VFS_UNLINKABLE	nolnk	It is possible to unlink the root

Table 9.8: *Memory commands*

Command	Description
kmastat	Show statistics for *kmem_alloc( )*
var	Show system configurable parameters
tune	Show system tuneable parameters structure
page	Print a *page* structure
vtop	Translate virtual to physical address

9.7 Memory

Since machine memory architectures are inherently implementation dependent, the **crash** command provides few facilities for examining memory-related data structures (see Table 9.8). In most cases, your only option is to consult their associated header files (if they are available!) and use the od command to display the data in byte form. In particular, tracing through virtual memory data structures involves traversing many data structures by hand, although the commands vtop and page provide some assistance.

The commands kmastat and mem show the state of dynamic memory, and map summarizes the mapping structure used by the kernel *rmalloc( )* functions. Finally, the var command allows you to display the tuneable system parameters that are held in the *var* structure.

The following subsections describe the memory related commands, and are followed by some hints on how they might be used.

9.7.1 Memory configuration commands

SYNOPSIS kmastat
This command takes no arguments; it prints the kernel memory allocator statistics, which are held in the data structure *kmeminfo*, defined in the header file *sysinfo.h*, and are updated each time the kernel memory allocator, *kmem_alloc( )* is called.

Figure 9.23: *Output from* kmastat

```
> kmastat
                total bytes  total bytes
size    # pools    in pools    allocated  # failures
-----------------------------------------------------
small   163         584192      470544    0
big     757        3100672     3042816    0
outsize   -              -      4845568    0
```

The output from this command is shown in Figure 9.23. The fields in the output are described as follows:

- *size* — gives the size of the allocated units. The small pool satisfies allocation requests for sizes between *MINASMALL* and *MAXASMALL*, the large pool satisfies allocation requests for sizes that are greater than *MAXASMALL* and less than *MAXABIG*. Allocation requests greater that *MAXABIG* are satisfied by allocating pages directly. Typically, these values are 16, 256 and 4192 bytes respectively.

- *pools* — specifies how many pools are in each of the size categories (see § 3.9.2).

- *total bytes* — specifies the number of bytes available to allocate in the size categories.

- *bytes allocated* — specifies how many bytes from the pools are allocated.

- *failures* — counts the number of times that allocation requests for memory from the pools have failed.

SYNOPSIS `var`

Whenever a tuneable parameter is referenced by the kernel, it takes its value from its corresponding variable defined in the *var* structure. Implementing the tuneables in a variable, rather than as defined constants, means that the whole kernel need not be recompiled every time a parameter changes. Instead, only the file that holds the parameters must be recompiled, after which the kernel is relinked. Each field of the *var* structure is initialized to the appropriate tuneable parameter value specified by the system administrator in the *stune* file when the kernel was built. For example, the field *v_call* is initialized by the parameter *NCALL*.

The values of the following fields in the *var* structure are printed:

- *v_buf, v_pbuf* — the configured number of buffers in the buffer cache, and the number of physical I/O buffers. These values are influenced by the tuneable parameters, *NBUF* and *NPBUF* respectively, and are described in § 5.3.

- *v_call* — the number of *callout* entries influenced by the *NCALL* tuneable parameter; that is, the number of entries that can be put into the timeout table (see § 4.8.3).

- *v_proc, v_maxup* — the maximum size of the process table, and the maximum number of processes that a single user is allowed to run. These values are influenced by the tuneable parameters, *NPROC* and *MAXUP* respectively.

- *v_maxsyspri* — the maximum priority that will be used by processes in the system-class. This value is influenced by the *MAXCLSYSPRI* tuneable parameter.

- *v_hbuf* — the number of hash lists for the buffer cache. The value must be a power of two; the higher it is, the smaller the number of hash lists. This value is influenced by the *NHBUF* tuneable parameter.

- *v_hmask* — the mask to apply to the buffer hashing function. Normally, this value must be one less than the value of *v_hbuf*.

- *v_sptmap* — the size of the *rmalloc( )* map used to allocate kernel virtual memory. If this map overflows, it becomes impossible to allocate kernel virtual space, and a characteristic warning message is printed on the console. This value is influcnced by the *SPTMAP* (system page table map) tuneable parameter.

- *v_maxpmem* — specifies, in pages, the maximum amount of physical memory to use. Normally the value is zero, meaning all physical memory is used.

- *v_autoup* — When a buffer is marked for delayed write and its age has reached *v_autoup* seconds, it is flushed to disk. This value is influenced by the *NAUTOUP* tuneable parameter.

Figure 9.24: *Output from* page

```
> page -e 6
PAGE STRUCTURE TABLE SIZE: 7494

SLOT KEEPCNT      VNODE       HASH      PREV      VPPREV FLAGS
          NIO      OFFSET                NEXT      VPNEXT
    8        0 0x803a6120 0x00000000 0x00000000 0x00000000 lock
           52         0               0x00000000 0x00000000
```

9.7.2 Virtual memory commands

The commands vtop and page print information about the virtual memory system. vtop is by far the most useful; it looks up a given virtual address (in the context of a particular process if necessary) and prints the corresponding physical address of the page of memory mapped by that page.

SYNOPSIS vtop [-s *process*] *address* ...
Converts a virtual address to a physical address. The output from this command is shown in § 9.4.4. If the address is a kernel virtual address, the kernel page tables are used to translate the address. If a process slot is given, the page tables for that process are used to translate the address. If no slot is given, the page tables for defproc are used.

vtop reports that there is no mapping for the specified address, if the page mapped by the virtual address, or one of the page table pages needed to map the address, are not resident in memory.

SYNOPSIS page *address* ...
Prints the contents of the *page* structure at the given address. If the address is given as a slot number, the *page* structure in that slot is printed. The output of the command is shown in Figure 9.24.

The *page* structure is described in Table 3.2, and the fields in the output of the page command correspond to the fields described in that table. Note that the pointer fields are printed as either a slot number or an address. If the number is in hexadecimal (that is, it starts with 0x), it specifies the address of the item being pointed to. If, however, it is printed in decimal, it is the slot number of the item. The possible values in the *FLAGS* column are shown in Table 9.9.

Table 9.9: *Page flags*

Value	Display	Description
p_lock	lock	Page is locked
p_want	want	A process wants this page
p_free	free	Page is on the freelist
p_intrans	intrans	I/O in progress for this page
p_gone	gone	Page has been released
p_mod	mod	Page is modified
p_ref	ref	Page is referenced
p_pagein	pagein	Page is being paged in
p_nc	nc	Do not cache this page
p_age	age	The page stealer has marked this page

9.7.3 The map command

SYNOPSIS map *name*
This command prints the contents of the map used by *rmalloc( )* with the given name. The *name* argument is the name of the map to print, such as *sptmap* or *msgmap*. (The command looks the name up in the symbol table to get the corresponding address.) An example of the output is shown in Figure 9.25.

Figure 9.25: *Example output from map*

```
> map sptmap

sptmap:
MAPSIZE: 1020    SLEEP VALUE: 0

SIZE      ADDRESS
   2      c0003
2020      c001c
2 SEGMENTS, 2022 UNITS
```

The example output shows that the system page table map (*sptmap*) is not heavily fragmented, and that there are 2022 units of space left in the map. The meaning of the address column is defined by the routines that use the map. In the *sptmap*, the address column shows the top 20 bits of the kernel virtual address. In the listing, there are two pages of kernel virtual memory free at the location 0xc0003000, and 2020 pages free starting at 0xc001c000. When kernel virtual space is allocated (for example, to hold page table pages), the routine *rmalloc( )* is called to allocate a page of virtual memory. From this map we can see that the next call will allocate the page at the address 0xc0003000. Note that this is a block of 4096 consecutive virtual addresses. When the addresses are used, a physical page is allocated to hold the data using the page fault mechanism.

9.7.4 Memory hints

This section contains three hints on how to use the memory-related commands when diagnosing system problems.

In contrast to earlier releases, UNIX System V Release 4 dynamically allocates most of its data structures. This means that processes are much more sensitive to memory allocation failure. When a process fails to allocate dynamic memory, the error code *EAGAIN* is returned. When this error is printed with the *perror( )* library routine, it prints the message "no more processes", which is misleading because this error code applies to three separate cases: when a *fork* fails because the process table is full, when the user is not allowed to create any more processes, or when a system call fails due to insufficient memory.

When a system starts to show many failures of this nature, it may indicate that the system has insufficient physical memory or swap space. The kmastat command can be used to check this; if it shows many failures, it may indicate that the load on the system is too great, and that more memory or swap space must be added.

The *sptmap* table may overflow as a result of many processes performing I/O; for example, STREAMS, file or IPC operations. It overflows because the table becomes too fragmented to hold an entry for a block of free space. In this situation, *rmfree( )* prints a message on the console giving the hexadecimal address of the map that overflowed. By using **crash**, you can find out which map overflowed, and with the **map** command you can examine it. The cure for this problem is to increase the map size.

The *vtop* command is invaluable for converting virtual addresses to physical. It mechanizes the task of looking up the page tables to find the physical address. It is important to remember, however, that when you want to examine the contents of a physical address, you must use the -p argument to the relevant command.

9.8 STREAMS

There are eight commands in **crash** for examining STREAMS data structures. They fall into two categories: commands for examining STREAMS memory, and commands for examining STREAMS data structures. They are summarized in Table 9.10.

The following sections describe the STREAMS memory and data structure commands. The hints section shows how to follow through a stream, how to

determine the modules that are present in a stream, and how to examine the data
queued in a stream; it also describes how to detect when STREAMS has run out of
memory.

Table 9.10: *STREAMS commands*

Command	Description
mblock	Print an *msgb*
dblock	Display contents of a *datab*
strstat	Show the STREAMS statistics
stream	Print a stream head
queue	Display a *queue* structure
qrun	Print a list of the runnable queues
linkblk	Print the *linkblk* table
pty	Display pseudo terminal state

9.8.1 STREAMS memory

SYNOPSIS mblock *address ...*
This command prints the fields of a *msgb* structure, as shown in Figure 9.26. The
argument specifies the address of the *msgb* to print. If no argument is given, *all*
msgb structures are printed. Note that with *msgb* and *datab* structures, there is no
concept of slot number; they are allocated dynamically with *kmem_alloc( )*, so **crash**
cannot look them up by slot number (the *msgb* and *datab* structures are described in
§ 7.2.).

The first line of the output displays the number of allocated *msgb* structures.
The remaining fields print the fields of the *msgb* structure:

- *NEXT, PREV* — the values of the *b_next* and *b_prev* pointers in the *msgb*, that
  link together successive messages in a queue.

- *CONT* — the *b_cont* field. This field links together the *msgb* structures that
  comprise a single message. In the example output there is no continuation block
  for the message.

- *RPTR, WPTR* — the *b_rptr* and *b_wptr* fields, which point to the positions in
  the buffer of the next characters to be read and written. In the example, these
  pointers are in a different block of memory than the *msgb* itself, which means that
  the data buffer was allocated separately by using *kmem_alloc( )*. (See the
  implementation of *allocb( )* in § 7.7.1).

- *DATAB* — points to the *datab* associated with the *msgb*. The example shows
  that the *datab* address is 44 bytes higher than that of the *msgb*. This shows that
  the *msgb* and *datab* were allocated together as an *mdbblock* (see § 7.7.1).

- *BAND* — the priority band to which the *msgb* belongs.

Figure 9.26: mblock *and* dblock *commands*

```
> mblock -f 8080ec00
MESSAGE BLOCK COUNT = 290
MBLKADDR    NEXT CONT   PREV     RPTR     WPTR    DATAB  BAND FLAG
8080ec00 80dcb700    - 8080e500 80daff00 80daffb9 8080ec2c   0
         FUNCTION
         -


> dblock 8080ec2c
DATA BLOCK TABLE SIZE = 269
DBLKADDR  SIZE  RCNT TYPE       BASE     LIMIT    FRTNP
8080ec2c  185    1 data      80daff00   80daffb9  -


> od -h 80daff00 0x34
80daff00: 0a574152 4e494e47 3a202f68 6f6d652c  .WARNING: /home,
80daff10: 202f6d6e 742f3635 304d622c 202f7573   /mnt/650Mb, /us
80daff20: 722f7372 63206172 65206e6f 74206175  r/src are not au
80daff30: 746f6d6f 756e7465 64206166 74657220  tomounted after
80daff40: 0a612062 6f6f742e 20546869 73206973  .a boot. This is
80daff50: 20626563 61757365 20746865 20737973   because the sys
80daff60: 74656d20 77696c6c 2068616e 6720696e  tem will hang in
80daff70: 20726562 6f6f7420 69660a69 74206861   reboot if.it ha
80daff80: 64207072 6576696f 75736c79 20637261  d previously cra
80daff90: 73686564 2e205468 65726566 6f72652c  shed. Therefore,
80daffa0: 206d6f75 6e742074 68656d20 62792068   mount them by h
80daffb0: 616e642e 0a0a0a0a 0a0d0a0d 0a0d0a0d  and.............
80daffc0: 00000000 00000000 00000000 00000000  ................
```

- *FLAG* — there are two values that can appear in this field. If *nl* appears, it means that the flag *MSGNOLOOP* is set. Messages with *MSGNOLOOP* set are never looped back to the write side of a stream. If *mk* appears, the flag *MSGMARK* is set, meaning that the stream head has marked the last byte of the message.

SYNOPSIS   dblock *address ...*

This command displays the *datab* at the given address. If no argument is printed, all *datab* structures are printed. The output of this command, shown in Figure 9.26, consists of the following fields:

- *DBLKADDR* — the address of the *datab*.

- *SIZE* — the size of the data portion of the *datab*. The size is initialized by *allocb( )* when the block is created.

- *BASE, LIMIT* — point to the start and end of the data buffer. Note that there may be more than *SIZE* bytes between the base and the limit when *allocb( )* uses a data buffer that is larger than the requested size.

- *RCNT* — the reference count for the *datab*. When messages are duplicated by *dupb( )*, the reference count on the underlying *datab* is increased. The data buffer will not be returned to the operating system until the reference count falls to zero.

- *TYPE* — the type of the *datab*. If the block is *M_PROTO*, the string "proto" is printed. Other types are printed similarly. (The message types are shown in Tables 7.3 and 7.4.)

- *FRTNP* — if the *datab* has a *free* function associated with it, its symbolic name is displayed.

The output in Figure 9.26 shows the contents of the *datab*, followed by an octal dump of the data buffer. The sample output was set up so that the data buffer would contain readable ASCII characters. The output shows that the read and write pointers correspond to the start and end of the buffer. This message was found on a queue that was subject to flow-control whilst trying to write to a terminal; the position of the pointers show that the service routine for that particular queue had not read any of the data from the buffer.

SYNOPSIS `strstat`
This command prints the STREAMS memory allocator statistics. A sample output from this command is shown in Figure 9.27. Note that the `strstat` command prints data for streams, queues, message blocks, link blocks and stream events. These data types will be referred to collectively as "item".

Figure 9.27: *STREAMS statistics*

```
> strstat
ITEM            CONFIG ALLOC  FREE    TOTAL   MAX  FAIL
streams            120   120     0     2654   129     0
queues             592   592     0    16436   608     0
message blocks     281   182    99   604871   883     0
data blocks        269   182    87   577775   698     0
link blocks          7     7     0        7     7     0
stream events        5     4     1     1723     5     0

Count of scheduled queues:   0

> od -d Strcount
8030a118:  0000137628

> od -d strthresh
802f0794:  0000000000
```

The rows in the output are self-explanatory; the columns have the following meanings:

- *CONFIG* — the number of configured items present in the system. In fact, they are dynamically allocated, so the number of items will have grown to the displayed level. When items are deallocated, they are either placed on a freelist, or returned to the kernel via *kmem_free( )*.

- *ALLOC* — the number of items in use.

- *FREE* — the number of free items. The sum of the allocated and free counts should be the same as the count of configured items.

- *TOTAL* — the number of times an item has been allocated since the system was booted.

- *MAX* — the allocation high-water mark that shows the maximum number of allocated items achieved so far.

- *FAIL* — the number of times a request for an item has failed.

The example in Figure 9.27 shows the values of *strthresh* and *Strcount*. The value of *strthresh* is zero, meaning that there is no limit on the size of STREAMS memory. The variable *Strcount* shows how much total memory has been allocated to STREAMS. If this value is close to *strthresh*, programs that use STREAMS are likely to suffer problems allocating STREAMS resources. If the value is very high as a percentage of system memory, the system will strike problems with allocating memory to processes.

In many cases, high STREAMS memory usage indicates problems, even on systems that carry heavy network or terminal traffic. Most STREAMS software writers set quite low buffering in their modules and drivers to limit the amount of data buffered in the stream. If a system is working correctly, it will reach a steady state of STREAMS memory use. High STREAMS use means that either a module or driver is losing buffers, or that the flow-control parameters for the system are set wrongly. In either case, the system will not run properly.

In UNIX System V Release 3, if the free count for message blocks fell below 80% of the configured value, it often indicated problems with STREAMS memory because very few drivers were robust in the face of STREAMS memory failures. Low memory also implied low performance. Similarly, if the free queue count fell to zero, no more STREAMS connections could be made. With UNIX System V Release 4 it is no longer a problem if the free counts are zero because if there are no free items, a new one is dynamically allocated when required.

Figure 9.28: *Stream and queue structures*

```
> u 57
...
OPEN FILES AND POFILE FLAGS:
       [0]: F 0x80dafcc0, 0                    [1]: F: 0x80bc4940,  0
       [2]: F 0x80ed7ec0, 0
...

> file 0x80bc4940
ADDRESS  RCNT    TYPE/ADDR       OFFSET  FLAGS
80bc4940  1      SPEC/80d9c604    4722f   write

> vnode 80d9c604
VCNT  VFSMNTED  VFSP   STREAMP  VTYPE   RDEV  VDATA    VFILOCKS VFLAG
 2        0    80e6fe40 80dcbe00   c     10,2 80d9c600            0

> stream  -f 80dcbe00
STREAM TABLE SIZE = 121
 ADDRESS      WRQ      IOCB    VNODE  PSHCNT RERR/WERR FLAG
80dcbe00 8084f248  802c1b24 80dcba04    3      0/0     rslp istty mnds
          SID       PGID    IOCBLK    IOCID  IOCWAIT
          1012      1012      0        6307     0
          WOFF     MARK  CLOSTIME
           0        0     1500
       SIGFLAGS:
       SIGLIST:
       POLLFLAGS:
       POLLIST:


> queue -f 8084f248
QUEUE TABLE SIZE = 586
 QUEADDR   MODULE     NEXT  LINK      PTR      RCNT FLAG
8084f248 strwhead 80e5c548    - 80dcbe00       0 us
          HEAD     TAIL MINP  MAXP     HIWT  LOWT BAND BANDADDR
           -        -    0     0        0     0    0       0
```

9.8.2 Queues and streams

SYNOPSIS stream *address* ...

This command prints the stream head data structure at the given address. If no address is given, all stream heads are printed. The output from this command (see the example in Figure 9.28) shows how to traverse from the user-area of a process to the stream head for a particular file. In the example, the stream being examined corresponds to the standard output of the process. The output from the stream command consists of the following fields:

Table 9.11: *Stream head flags*

Value	Display	Description
IOCWAIT	iocw	*ioctl* in progress
RSLEEP	rslp	A process wants to read the stream
WSLEEP	wslp	A process wants to write to the stream
STRPRI	pri	A priority message is at the stream head
STRHUP	hup	The stream is hung up
STWOPEN	stwo	The stream is waiting for its first open
STPLEX	plex	The stream is part of a multiplexor
STRISTTY	istty	The stream is a terminal
RMSGDIS	mdis	Stream is in read message discard mode
RMSGNODIS	mnds	Stream is in read message non-discard mode
STRDERR	rerr	Fatal read error, caused by *M_ERROR* message
STRWERR	werr	Fatal write error, caused by *M_ERROR* message
STRTIME	sttm	First part of timeout pending
STR2TIME	s2tm	Second part of timeout pending
STR3TIME	s3tm	Third part of timeout pending
STRCLOSE	clos	Stream is waiting for *strclose( )* to complete
SNDMREAD	mrd	*M_READ* messages will be sent
OLDNDELAY	ondel	SVR3 semantics used for tty reads in *O_NDELAY* mode
RDBUFWAIT	rdbfw	Stream head has issued *bufcall( )*
STRSNDZERO	sndz	Zero length messages may be sent
STRTOSTOP	tstp	Background writes to the stream will block
RDPROTDAT	pdat	Read *M_PROTO, M_PCPROTO* as data
RDPROTDIS	pdis	Discard *M_PROTO, M_PCPROTO* messages
STRMOUNT	mnt	Stream is mounted
STRDELIM	delim	Delimited messages will be generated
STRSIGPIPE	spip	Send *SIGPIPE* when it is impossible to write

- *ADDRESS* — the memory address of the stream head structure.

- *WRQ* — the pointer to the write queue for the stream. To find the corresponding read queue, you must calculate the size of the *queue* structure from the header files, then subtract this amount from the address of the write queue.

- *IOCB* — points to the *streamtab* containing the information about the stream head processing functions. The pointer to the current *iocblk* is displayed by the *IOCBLK* field.

- *VNODE* — points to the *vnode* associated with the stream head.

- *PSHCNT* — the number of modules pushed into the stream.

- *RERR/WERR* — the error codes that will be returned on the next attempted read from, or write to the stream. If these values are zero, no error has occurred.

- *FLAG* — the values of the stream head flags (see Table 9.11).

- *SID, PGID* — the session ID and the process group ID. The process and session IDs in the stream head determine which processes receive signals.

- *IOCBLK, IOCID* — point to the message associated with the current *ioctl*, and its identifier.

- *IOCWAIT* — the number of processes waiting to perform an *ioctl* on the stream.

- *WOFF* — the stream head write offset. When this value is non-zero, all writes performed at the stream head start at this offset in the message.

- *MARK* — the stream head pointer to a marked message.

- *CLOSTIME* — the time to wait to allow the queues to drain when the stream is being closed.

- *SIGFLAGS* — the list of events that make the stream generate a *SIGPOLL* signal. The list of flags is given in Table 7.29. If the *S_INPUT* flag is set, the string "input" is printed; other flags are printed similarly.

- *SIGLIST* — the list of processes that will receive the *SIGPOLL* signal. Each process has its own flags; the set of flags is printed alongside the process in the same format as the *SIGFLAGS* field.

- *POLLFLAGS* — the events that are being polled for, as shown in Table 7.32. If the flag *POLLIN* is set, the string "in" is printed; other flags are printed similarly.

- *POLLIST* — the contents of the list of *polldat* structures attached to the stream head (see § 7.9.9). For each item in this list, **crash** prints the poll flags that will trigger the entry, the function that is triggered, and the argument to pass to that function.

SYNOPSIS `queue` *address* ...
This command displays the contents of the queue at the given address. If no address is given, all *queue* structures are displayed. The output of this command is shown in Figure 9.28. The figure shows the write queue associated with the stream head. The output of the command contains the following fields:

- *QUEADDR* — the address of the queue structure.

- *MODULE* — the name of the module or driver to which the queue belongs. By traversing the queues in a stream, you can determine which modules have been pushed.

- *NEXT* — the address of the next queue in the stream. If this field is empty, the queue is at the end of the stream. That is, it is either a driver queue or the stream head read queue.

- *LINK* — if the queue has been scheduled, but not yet run, this field points to the next queue in the list of scheduled queues. If the field is empty, the queue is either being run or has not been scheduled.

- *PTR* — points to the private data structure for the queue. For stream head modules, this is a pointer to an *stdata* structure. To examine its contents, you must use the od command and then consult the header file *strsubr.h* to interpret the output.

- *RCNT* — the number of bytes queued in messages held on the queue.

- *FLAG* — the queue flags summarized in Table 9.12.

Table 9.12: *STREAMS queue flags*

Value	Display	Description
QENAB	en	Queue is scheduled
QWANTR	wr	Someone wants to read the queue
QWANTW	ww	Someone wants to write the queue
QFULL	fl	Queue is full
QREADR	rr	This is the read queue
QUSE	us	This queue is in use
QNOENB	ne	Calls to *putq( )* will not enable queue
QOLD	ol	Queue uses SVR3 open/close semantics

- *HEAD, TAIL* — point to the first and last messages held on the queue. By dereferencing them you can examine the data held in the queue. In the sample output, there is no data queued.

- *MINP, MAXP* — the minimum and maximum packet sizes accepted by the queue.

- *HIWT, LOWT* — the high and low water marks used by the STREAMS flow-control mechanism.

- *BAND* — the number of priority bands attached to the queue.

- *BANDADDR* — points to the flow-control information for the first priority band on the queue.

SYNOPSIS qrun
This command prints the list of scheduled queues. The output consists of a list of addresses of queues that have been scheduled.

SYNOPSIS linkblk *address* ...
This command prints the link block at the given address. If no address is given, all link blocks are printed. A *linkblk* structure is used to establish a link between a module or driver and a multiplexor. Figure 9.29 shows the output from this command. The following fields appear in the output:

- *LBLKADDR* — the address of the *linkblk* structure.

- *QTOP* — the address of the queue connected to the multiplexor. If *QTOP* is zero, this is a persistent multiplexor — that is, the multiplexor will exist even

Figure 9.29: *Link block table*

```
> linkblk
LINKBLK TABLE SIZE = 7
LBLKADDR     QTOP     QBOT FILEADDR     MUXID
80c61580        0 80728a48 809a9e80        7
80ff7a00        0 80f07a48 806af780        6
80b89c00        0 80b89448 80b89c40        5
80c61bc0        0 80b88348 80c61380        4
80b87300        0 80b88e48 80b87340        3
80b87e40        0 80b87b48 8053cd80        2
8053cf00        0 8053c848 80ce9700        1

> queue -f 80f07a48
QUEUE TABLE SIZE = 586
  QUEADDR  MODULE     NEXT     LINK       PTR   RCNT FLAG
  80f07a48  ip      80fff348          - 80314c74      0 wr us
  HEAD      TAIL     MINP     MAXP     HIWT    LOWT BAND BANDADDR
   -         -         0     8192     8192    1024    0        0
```

when no processes have the multiplexor open. If the value is non-zero, it points to the write queue of the lowest module in the stream above the multiplexor.

- *QBOT* — points to the stream below the multiplexor. The sample output shows that the highlighted multiplexor contains the *ip* module.

- *FILEADDR* — points to the streams associated *file* structure, which holds the information needed to find the stream head for the lower half of the multiplexor.

- *MUXID* — the multiplexor ID, which is the value returned when the *I_LINK ioctl* is successfully executed (see § 7.5.4).

9.8.3 STREAMS terminals

SYNOPSIS pty [-s] [-h] [-l] *address* ...
This command displays information about pseudo terminals in the system. If *address* is specified, the pseudo terminal (*pty*) structures at that address are printed. § 7.13.1 discusses pseudo terminals, and Figure 7.67 shows the modules in the stream. All pseudo terminals are associated with an entry in the table *ptms_tty[]*. The pty command displays information based on this table. Options to the command provide additional output:

-h displays, in addition to the fields from the *ptms_tty[]*, information about the *ptem* module pushed into the slave side of the pseudo terminal.

-s displays information about the *pckt* module pushed into the master side of the pseudo terminal.

Figure 9.30: *The* pty *command*

```
> pty -f -l -h -s
ptms_tty TABLE SIZE = 128
SLOT   MWQPTR   SWQPTR  PT_BUFP  TTYPID STATE
   0 80b72548 8057ff48 80e02680      113 mopen sopen
```

```
   RQSLOT   MODNAME   MODID DACK_PTR  RDQ_PTR  TTYPGID STATE
   29983299 ptem      43981 80bded80        0      113 inuse
   cflag:  b9600 cs8 cread hupcl
   Number of rows: 0        Number of columns: 0
   Number of horizontal pixels: 0  Number of vertical pixels: 0
```

```
   RQSLOT MODNAME   MODID  MESSAGE   ENDMSG    MSGLEN STATE
   29992888 ldterm    2989 80f3a480 80f3a480        0
   pointer to echo buffer          0
   output row 0     output column 0
   number of chars echoed 0 at column position 2
   number of bytes requested by M_READ 0
```

```
   Effective termios
   intr: ?          quit: ?          erase:        kill: ?
   eof/vmin: ?      eol/vtime:       eol2:         swtch:
   start: ?         stop: ?          susp: ?       dsusp:
   reprint: ?       discard: ?       werase: ?     lnext: ?
   iflags:  brkint ignpar istrip icrnl ixon
   oflags:  opost onlcr nl0 cr0 tab3 bs0 vt0 ff0
   lflag:   isig icanon echo echoe echok
```

```
   Apparent termios
   ...             similar output to Effective termios
```

```
   Driver's termios
   ...             similar output to Effective termios
```

```
   Line Discipline support for Multi-byte
   Code set indicator 0     bytes left for current character 0
   Bytes left to ignore 0   padding 0
   Pointer to array cols. 0 Pointer to m_blk for col. array 0
   Max. length count of an EUC. 1  bad EUC counter 0
   struct eucioc entries
   eucw[0] 1        eucw[1] 0        eucw[2] 0        eucw[3] 0
   scrw[0] 1        scrw[1] 0        scrw[2] 0        scrw[3] 0
```

```
   RQSLOT   MODNAME   MODID
   30004903 pckt      39064
```

-l   displays information about the *ldterm* module pushed into the slave side of the pseudo terminal.

The output from this command is shown in Figure 9.30. The command was invoked with all options specified. If fewer options are given, less output is produced. The diagram contains lines that divide the output into four sections. The first section is output by the `pty` command; the second section of the output results from the -h option; the third from the -l option; and the fourth from the -s option. The fields in the output are described as follows:

- *SLOT* — gives the position in the *ptms_tty[]* table occupied by the terminal. The slot number corresponds to the minor device number of the terminal. Therefore, slot 0 in the table corresponds to the terminal */dev/pts/0*.

- *MWQPTR, SWQPTR* — point to the write queues for the master and slave sides of the pseudo terminal.

- *PT_BUFP* — the master side of the pseudo terminal allocates a zero length message when the terminal is opened. This guarantees that it will be able to send the end of file (EOF) indication when the stream is closed, regardless of the current STREAMS memory use. This field points to the zero length message.

- *TTYPID* — the process group ID of the process that opened the master side of the pseudo terminal.

- *STATE* — the state of the pseudo terminal. Up to three values can be printed: *mopen* indicates that the master side of the pseudo terminal is open, *sopen* indicates that the slave side is open, and *lock* indicates that the pseudo terminal is locked.

The next group of fields in the output are generated by the -h option, and give information about the *ptem* module. This module implements the characteristics of a serial line device driver, and is described in § 7.13.1.

- *RQSLOT* — the slot number of the read queue of the *ptem* module in the slave side of the stream.

- *MODNAME* — the name of the module — always "ptem".

- *MODID* — the module ID for the *ptem* module.

- *DACK_PTR* — when this module is opened, it preallocates a message to acknowledge disconnection. The pointer to this message is displayed by the *DACK_PTR* field.

- *RDQ_PTR* — the value of *q_ptr* for the read queue in the *ptem* module.

- *TTYPGID* — the process group ID of the process that opened the master side of the pseudo terminal.

- *STATE* — the status of the *ptem* entry. The string "inuse" is the only value that will appear in this field.

- *cflag* — the terminal control structure, *termios*, contains a field *c_cflag* which controls the hardware control modes (see *termios(2)* and *termio(7)*). This information is held internally by the *ptem* module.

  The example output shows that the pseudo terminal speed is set to 9600 bits a second, 8-bit characters, receiver enabled, send hang up on close. Note that for a pseudo terminal the values have no real significance since the *ptem* module is not communicating with any hardware. They do, however, mean that a program connected via a pseudo terminal behaves in the same way as one connected via a real terminal.

- *Number of rows etc* — when a process issues the *TIOCSWINSZ ioctl*, the window size data is stored in the terminal driver; for pseudo terminals, the data is stored in the *ptem* module. The window size *ioctls* for terminals are described in *termio(7)*.

The next group of fields in the output are generated by the -1 option, and give information about the *ldterm* module.

- *RQSLOT* — the slot number of the read queue of the *ldterm* module in the slave side of the stream.

- *MODNAME* — the name of the module — always "ldterm".

- *MODID* — the module ID for the *ldterm* module.

- *MESSAGE, ENDMSG* — the values of the *t_message* and *t_endmsg* fields in the *ldterm_mod* structure, which point to the start and the end of the input message being built by *ldterm*.

- *MSGLEN* — the number of bytes in the input message being built by *ldterm*.

- *STATE* — the values of the flags set in the *t_state* field of the *ldterm_mod* structure. In the sample output none of the flags are set, but the values that might appear are shown in Table 9.13.

- *Pointer to echo buffer* — the address of the *msgb* that holds the characters being echoed.

- *Output row, column* — the row and column of the next character to output.

- *number of chars ...* — the count of characters echoed since the last line was output to the terminal, and the column at which the first character was output.

- *number of bytes ...* — the number of bytes requested by the current *M_READ* message.

- *Effective termios* — the internal settings of the *termios* structure (see § 7.11). The effective *termios* are the modes that are processed by the *ldterm* itself. They are held in the *t_modes* field in the *ldterm_mod* structure (see § 7.12.1).

- *Apparent termios* — the apparent *termios* are the modes set by the user program, and are taken from the *t_amodes* field in the *ldterm_mod* structure.

Table 9.13: *ldterm state flags*

Value	Display	Description
TS_XCLUDE	`xclud`	Terminal was opened for exclusive use
TS_TTSTOP	`tstop`	Output has been stopped by ^S
TS_TBLOCK	`blk`	Input has been stopped in *IXOFF* mode
TS_QUOT	`quot`	Previous input character was '\'
TS_ERASE	`erase`	*ECHOPRT* mode in force
TS_SLNCH	`slnch`	Service routine processes next character as literal
TS_PLNCH	`plnch`	Put procedure processes next character as literal
TS_TTCR	`ttcr`	NL is mapped to CR-NL
TS_NOCANON	`nocan`	Canonical processing performed by module below
TS_RESCAN	`rescn`	Mode of canonical processing changed, so re-process input queue
TS_RTO	`rto`	*VTIME* timer is started
TS_TACT	`act`	*VTIME* timer is active
TS_MEUC	`meuc`	Multibyte character sets are in use
TS_WARNED	`warn`	*ldterm* has written a message on the console warning about bad received multibyte characters

- *Driver's termios* — the *termios* that are processed by the driver. The output is taken from the *t_dmodes* field in the *ldterm_mod* structure.

- *Line discipline, etc* — The remaining fields in this section print the control fields used for processing multi-byte characters.

The final group of fields in the output is generated by the `-s` option; these give information about the *pckt* module.

- *RQSLOT* — the slot number of the read queue of the *pckt* module in the slave side of the stream.

- *MODNAME* — the module name — always "pckt".

- *MODID* — the *pckt* module ID.

9.8.4 STREAMS hints

Memory leakage from a STREAMS module containing a bug is a common cause of a system hang. Some vendors provide a facility to panic a hung system, forcing a crash dump. Examination of the crash dump will tell you if the system hung as a result of STREAMS memory leakage. The STREAMS statistics show that a large number of message blocks have been allocated, and *Strcount* will show a high percentage of system memory allocated to STREAMS. If you examine the processes in the system, you will find that they are sleeping in STREAMS-related functions such as *strwaitq( )*.

If it is not possible to force panic the system, you have to assume that it is going to happen, and then look for evidence before it does. To do this, run **crash** periodically, and check the STREAMS statistics and the value of *Strcount*. If they show that the STREAMS memory use increases constantly, it implies that a driver or module, somewhere in the system, is losing STREAMS buffers.

It is almost impossible to find the module causing the memory loss. Operating system vendors have an advantage: they can run debugging versions of the kernel that will monitor the buffers. Only by inspecting the *msgb* structures can you determine which function allocated them and, by implication, which function did not deallocate them properly.

Occasionally, it is necessary to traverse the STREAMS data structures in a crash dump, or in the running kernel. You usually do this when attempting to debug flow-control problems, or problems caused by stuck processes. The examples in this chapter show how to traverse a stream starting from the stream head, and how to view the data in the queue. The file-related commands allow you to find the stream head associated with a particular file descriptor.

9.9 Miscellaneous commands

Commands that do not fit into any obvious category are discussed in this section and summarized in Table 9.14.

Table 9.14: *Miscellaneous commands*

Command	Description
callout	Display the contents of the callout table
base	Useful calculation tool
search	Search for a word in memory

SYNOPSIS `callout`
This command prints the contents of the *callout[]* table, which holds functions that will be called at some point in the future (see § 4.8.3). Functions are placed in the table by the *timeout()* function. An example of the output generated by this command is shown in Figure 9.31. Note that the **crash** command prints the entries in the order they appear in the table, which is also the order in which they will be triggered by the *clock* function. The columns in the output are:

- *FUNCTION* — the name of the function to call. The sample output shows that the function *str2time()* will be the next function called, followed by *polltime()* and so on.

- *ARGUMENT* — the single argument that will be passed to the function when it is called.

Figure 9.31: *Output from* callout

```
> callout
FUNCTION          ARGUMENT    TIME  ID
str2time          8065d700     114  214431
polltime          80989800      35  1013095
tcp_slowtimo      00000000       1  1018124
ts_update         00000000       0  1018123
tcp_fasttimo      00000000       3  1018115
strtime           80c2fb00      28  223125
ip_slowtimo       00000000       0  1018125
polltime          80ff2600     219  1015115
schedpaging       00000000       1  1018110
wakeup            80f08801    1385  1013070
strgiveback       00000000      28  1011904
arptimer          00000000    3239  1017659
...
```

- *TIME* — the time in *HZ* that will elapse before the function is called. The output shows that *str2time( )* will be called in 0.114 seconds time. The time between each function call is incremental. Therefore, the second function, *polltime( )* will be called in 0.149 seconds time (0.114 + 0.035), and the third function, *tcp_slowtimo( )* will be called in 0.150 seconds (0.114 + 0.035 + 0.001), and so on.

- *ID* — the timeout ID. This value is used when a function is cancelled by the *untimeout( )* function. The timeout ID is incremented every time that *timeout( )* is called.

Some systems panic if the *callout[ ]* table overflows with the message "Timeout table overflow". The state of the *callout[ ]* table confirms the cause of the crash: the table will be full. Some systems avoid this problem by calling the function early to free a place in the table for a newly inserted function. These systems print warning messages on the console saying that the *callout[ ]* table is full. Note that the size of the *callout[ ]* table is tuneable, and its tuneable parameter value can be displayed with the **var** command.

The *callout[ ]* table fills for two reasons: it is either too small for the load placed on it, or there is a bug, and it is being filled in error. The first case is easy to solve: you increase the size of the table and the problem goes away. If increasing the table size does not help, you have a bug somewhere. The functions stored in the table may give a clue to the problem. For example, if most of the functions are *tcp_slowtimo( )*, it indicates that the tcp STREAMS module is filling the table.

SYNOPSIS **base** *number* | *(expression)*
This command prints its decimal argument in hexadecimal, decimal, octal and binary. If a number is given, that number is printed in the four bases. More usefully, an expression enclosed in brackets is evaluated and printed in the four

Figure 9.32: *Using* base

```
> base 0x803696c8
hex: 803696c8
decimal: -2143906104
octal: 20015513310
binary: 10000000001101101001011011001000

> base (0xffe18+72)
hex: ffe60
decimal: 1048160
octal: 3777140
binary: 11111111111001100000
```

bases, as shown in Figure 9.32. Numbers in the expression are assumed to be base 10, but hexadecimal numbers may be specified preceded with 0x, and octal numbers may be specified preceded with a leading zero.

This command is most useful when you want to do mixed base arithmetic. For example, on the MIPS processor the size of the stack frame is given in decimal, but the current stack pointer is given in hexadecimal. By using the base command you can calculate the position of the next stack frame.

Figure 9.33: *The* search *command*

```
> search 803696c8 callout 400
MASK = ffffffff, PATTERN = 803696c8, START = 802ff328, LENGTH = 400

MATCH AT 802ff720: 803696c8
```

SYNOPSIS search [-m *mask*] *pattern start length*
This command allows you to search an area of memory for a particular pattern. Each long word in the area of memory between *start* and *length* is compared with the pattern. Whenever a match is found, it prints the address at which the match occurred together with the value that was matched. If a *mask* is specified, each memory word is first ANDed with the mask before it is compared to the pattern. The mask has a default value 0xffffffff.

An example of the output is shown in Figure 9.33. The command is useful when trying to find a particular value in a limited area of memory. For example, if you know that the return address 0x803696c8 appears in the kernel stack, the search command will help you find the position. In the example output, the search was for a function address in the *callout[]* table, which is used to help find the other fields in the same structure.

Appendix A

System call error codes

Error Constant	Value	Description
EPERM	1	Not super-user
ENOENT	2	No such file or directory
ESRCH	3	No such process
EINTR	4	Interrupted system call
EIO	5	I/O error
ENXIO	6	No such device or address
E2BIG	7	Argument list too long
ENOEXEC	8	Exec format error
EBADF	9	Bad file number
ECHILD	10	No children
EAGAIN	11	No more processes
ENOMEM	12	Not enough core
EACCES	13	Permission denied
EFAULT	14	Bad address
ENOTBLK	15	Block device required
EBUSY	16	Mount device busy
EEXIST	17	File exists
EXDEV	18	Cross-device link
ENODEV	19	No such device
ENOTDIR	20	Not a directory
EISDIR	21	Is a directory
EINVAL	22	Invalid argument
ENFILE	23	File table overflow
EMFILE	24	Too many open files
ENOTTY	25	Not a typewriter
ETXTBSY	26	Text file busy
EFBIG	27	File too large
ENOSPC	28	No space left on device

Error Constant	Value	Description
ESPIPE	29	Illegal seek
EROFS	30	Read only file system
EMLINK	31	Too many links
EPIPE	32	Broken pipe
EDOM	33	Math arg out of domain of func
ERANGE	34	Math result not representable
ENOMSG	35	No message of desired type
EIDRM	36	Identifier removed
ECHRNG	37	Channel number out of range
EL2NSYNC	38	Level 2 not synchronized
EL3HLT	39	Level 3 halted
EL3RST	40	Level 3 reset
ELNRNG	41	Link number out of range
EUNATCH	42	Protocol driver not attached
ENOCSI	43	No CSI structure available
EL2HLT	44	Level 2 halted
EDEADLK	45	Deadlock condition
ENOLCK	46	No record locks available
Streams Errors		
ENOSTR	60	Device not a stream
ENODATA	61	No data (for no delay I/O)
ETIME	62	Timer expired
ENOSR	63	Out of streams resources
ENONET	64	Machine is not on the network
ENOPKG	65	Package not installed
EREMOTE	66	The object is remote
ENOLINK	67	The link has been severed
EADV	68	Advertise error
ESRMNT	69	Srmount error
ECOMM	70	Communication error on send
EPROTO	71	Protocol error
EMULTIHOP	74	Multihop attempted
EBADMSG	77	Trying to read unreadable message
ENAMETOOLONG	78	Path name is too long
EOVERFLOW	79	Value too large to be stored in data type
ENOTUNIQ	80	Given log. name not unique
EBADFD	81	File descriptor invalid for this operation
EREMCHG	82	Remote address changed
Shared Library Errors		
ELIBACC	83	Can't access a needed shared library
ELIBBAD	84	Accessing a corrupted shared library
ELIBSCN	85	.lib section in a.out corrupted

Error Constant	Value	Description
ELIBMAX	*86*	Attempting to link in too many libraries
ELIBEXEC	*87*	Attempting to exec a shared library
EILSEQ	*88*	Illegal byte sequence
ENOSYS	*89*	Unsupported file system operation
ELOOP	*90*	Symbolic link loop
ERESTART	*91*	Restartable system call
ESTRPIPE	*92*	If pipe/FIFO, don't sleep in stream head
ENOTEMPTY	*93*	Directory not empty
EUSERS	*94*	Too many users (for UFS)
BSD Networking Software argument errors		
ENOTSOCK	*95*	Socket operation on non-socket
EDESTADDRREQ	*96*	Destination address required
EMSGSIZE	*97*	Message too long
EPROTOTYPE	*98*	Protocol wrong type for socket
ENOPROTOOPT	*99*	Protocol not available
EPROTONOSUPPORT	*120*	Protocol not supported
ESOCKTNOSUPPORT	*121*	Socket type not supported
EOPNOTSUPP	*122*	Operation not supported on socket
EPFNOSUPPORT	*123*	Protocol family not supported
EAFNOSUPPORT	*124*	Address family not supported by protocol family
EADDRINUSE	*125*	Address already in use
EADDRNOTAVAIL	*126*	Can't assign requested address
BSD Networking Software operational errors		
ENETDOWN	*127*	Network is down
ENETUNREACH	*128*	Network is unreachable
ENETRESET	*129*	Network dropped connection because of reset
ECONNABORTED	*130*	Software caused connection abort
ECONNRESET	*131*	Connection reset by peer
ENOBUFS	*132*	No buffer space available
EISCONN	*133*	Socket is already connected
ENOTCONN	*134*	Socket is not connected
ESHUTDOWN	*143*	Can't send after socket shutdown
ETOOMANYREFS	*144*	Too many references: can't splice
ETIMEDOUT	*145*	Connection timed out
ECONNREFUSED	*146*	Connection refused
EHOSTDOWN	*147*	Host is down
EHOSTUNREACH	*148*	No route to host
EALREADY	*149*	Operation already in progress
EINPROGRESS	*150*	Operation now in progress
SUN Network File System		
ESTALE	*151*	Stale NFS file handle

Error Constant	Value	Description
XENIX error numbers		
EUCLEAN	*135*	Structure needs cleaning
ENOTNAM	*137*	Not a XENIX named type file
ENAVAIL	*138*	No XENIX semaphores available
EISNAM	*139*	Is a named type file
EREMOTEIO	*140*	Remote I/O error
EINIT	*141*	Reserved for future
EREMDEV	*142*	Error 142

Errno values defined in $<sys/errno.h>$

The following error code values are currently unused in the standard UNIX System V Release 4 kernel: 47-59, 72-73, 75-76, 100-119, and 141-142. For a more detailed description of these codes, see *intro(2)* in [AT&T 1990h].

These codes represent system call error numbers that are set in an external variable called *errno* in the user-mode text upon the occurrence of a system call error. See also *perror(3C), fmtmsg(3C)* and *strerror(3C)* in [AT&T 1990h].

Appendix B

filock structure

```
typedef struct filock {
   struct   flock set;    /* contains type, start, and end */
   union   {
      int wakeflg;    /* for locks sleeping on this one */
      struct {
         long sysid;
         pid_t pid;
      } blk;          /* for sleeping locks only */
   }   stat;
   struct   filock *prev;
   struct   filock *next;
} filock_t;
```

filock_t defined in <sys/flock.h>

Appendix C

siginfo structure

```
typedef struct siginfo {
  int   si_signo;          /* signal from signal.h   */
  int   si_code;           /* code from above   */
  int   si_errno;          /* orror from errno.h   */
  union {
    int   _pad[SI_PAD];       /* for future growth   */
    struct {         /* kill(), SIGCLD   */
      pid_t   _pid;       /* process ID      */
      union {
        struct {
          uid_t   _uid;
        } _kill;
        struct {
          clock_t _utime;
          int   _status;
          clock_t _stime;
        } _cld;
      } _pdata;
    } _proc;
    struct {   /* SIGSEGV, SIGBUS, SIGILL and SIGFPE   */
      caddr_t   _addr;        /* faulting address   */
    } _fault;
    struct {         /* SIGPOLL, SIGXFSZ   */
    /* fd not currently available for SIGPOLL */
      int   _fd;       /* file descriptor   */
      long   _band;
    } _file;
  } _data;
} siginfo_t;
```

siginfo_t defined in <sys/siginfo.h>

Appendix D

strevent structure

```
struct strevent {
    union {
        struct {
            struct proc    *procp;
            long           events;
        } e;    /* stream event */
        struct {
            void (*func)();
            long arg;
            int size;
        } b;    /* bufcall event */
    } x;
    struct strevent *se_next;
};
```

struct strevent defined in <sys/strsubr.h>

Appendix E

Streams D3DK functions

Function	Description	Chapter
adjmsg( )	Remove bytes from a STREAMS message	7
allocb( )	Allocate a STREAMS message	7
backq( )	Point to the previous queue	7
bcanput( )	Check for priority band flow-control	7
bufcall( )	Handle failure of *allocb*	7
canput( )	Check for space in a message queue	7
copymsg( )	Copy contents of a message to another message	7
datamsg( )	Check that message is a data message	7
dupb( )	Duplicate the header of a message	7
dupmsg( )	Create a duplicate of a message	7
enableok( )	Allow a queue to be scheduled	7
esballoc( )	Create message using user supplied buffer	7
esbbcall( )	Handle failure of *esballoc*	-
flushband( )	Remove messages from a priority band	7
flushq( )	Delete messages held on a queue	7
freeb( )	Deallocate a message	7
freemsg( )	Deallocate all the messages in a message block	7
getq( )	Retrieve message at the head of a queue	7
insq( )	Place a message into a queue	7
msgdsize( )	Say how much data is in a message	7
noenable( )	Stop a queue from being scheduled	7
OTHERQ( )	Return a pointer to a queue's partner	7
pullupmsg( )	Combine multiple message block into a single message	7
putbq( )	Replace a message on the front of a queue	7
putctl( )	Send a control message	7
putctl1( )	Send a single-byte control message	7
putnext( )	Pass a message along a stream	7
putq( )	Place message at the back of a queue	7

Function	Description	Chapter
qenable( )	Schedule a queue	7
qreply( )	Send a message in the opposite direction along a stream	7
qsize( )	Give the number of bytes queued	7
RD( )	Find read queue for a given queue	7
rmvb( )	Unlink a message block from a message	7
rmvq( )	Take a message out of a queue	7
strlog( )	Pass a message to the STREAMS logger	7
strqget( )	Get information from STREAMS data structures	7
strqset( )	Set information in STREAMS data structures	7
testb( )	Find out if *allocb( )* might succeed	7
unlinkb( )	Delete message block from start of message	7
WR( )	Find write queue for a given queue	7
bcopy( )	Kernel byte-copy function	-
biodone( )	Buffer processing after I/O completes	5
biowait( )	Wait for I/O to complete	5
bp_mapin( )	Allocate kernel virtual address for I/O	-
bp_mapout( )	Deallocate kernel virtual address for I/O	-
brelse( )	Free I/O buffer	5
btop( )	Convert bytes to pages (rounds down)	-
btopr( )	Convert bytes to pages (rounds up)	-
bzero( )	Zero memory	-
clrbuf( )	Clear fields in I/O buffer	-
cmn_err( )	Log message or panic	9
copyin( )	User-space to kernel data copy	5
copyout( )	Kernel to user-space copy	5
delay( )	Sleep for a specified time	-
drv_getparm( )	Read kernel variables	5
drv_hztousec( )	Convert HZ to microseconds	-
drv_priv( )	Get user credentials	-
drv_usectohz( )	Convert microseconds to HZ	-
drv_usecwait( )	Busy-wait for a short interval	-
freerbuf( )	Deallocate buffer header for raw I/O	-
geterror( )	Extract error number from I/O buffer	-
getmajor( )	Extract major device number from *dev_t*	5
getminor( )	Extract minor device number from *dev_t*	5
getrbuf( )	Allocate buffer header for raw I/O	-
kmem_alloc( )	Kernel memory allocator	3
kmem_free( )	Deallocate memory	3
kmem_zalloc( )	Allocate zeroed kernel memory	3
makedevice( )	Convert major and minor to *dev_t*	5
min( )	Determine the minimum of two numbers	5
max( )	Determine the maximum of two numbers	5

Function	Description	Chapter
page_numtopp( )	Get page pointer for given page number	3
page_pptonum( )	Get page frame number from given page	3
ptob( )	Convert pages to bytes	-
rmalloc( )	Allocate memory from private buffer	5
rmfree( )	Deallocate private memory buffer	5
rminit( )	Initialize private memory allocator	5
rmsetwant( )	Set wake up flag in memory pool	5
rmwant( )	Sleep, waiting for memory	5
sleep( )	Sleep	4
spl( )	Shut-out interrupts	4
timeout( )	Call function at a later time	4
uiomove( )	Move data between user and kernel	5
untimeout( )	Cancel a timeout	4
ureadc( )	Place a character into *uio* structure	-
useracc( )	Find out if user is allowed to access memory	-
uwritec( )	Get a character from a *uio* structure	-
wakeup( )	Wake a process up	4

Appendix F

Crash commands

Command	Description and syntax
as	address space structures [-e] [-f] [-wfilename] [proc[s]]
async	aio structures [-wfilename] [-f]
base	base conversions [-wfilename] number[s]
buffer	buffer data [-wfilename] [-b|-c|-d|-x|-o|-i] (bufferslot |[-p] st_addr)
bufhdr	buffer headers [-f] [-wfilename] [[-p] tbl_entry[s]]
callout	callout table [-wfilename]
class	class table [-wfilename] [tbl_entry[s]]
dbfree	free data block headers [-wfilename]
dblock	allocated stream data block headers [-e] [-wfilename] [[-p] dblk_addr[s]]
defproc	set default process slot [-wfilename] [-c | slot]
dis	disassembler [-wfilename] [-a] -c | st_addr [count]
dispq	dispq table [-wfilename] [tbl_entry[s]]
ds	data address namelist search [-wfilename] virtual_address[es]

Command	Description and syntax
evactive	active event queue [-wfilename] [-f] [event_name]
evmm	events memory management [-wfilename]
file	file table [-e] [-f] [-wfilename] [[-p] address[es]]
findaddr	find address for given table and slot [-wfilename] table slot
findslot	find table and slot number for given address [-wfilename] virtual_address[es]
fnode	fnode table [-e] [-f] [-wfilename] [[-p] tbl_entry[s]]
gdp	gdp structure [-e] [-f] [-wfilename] [[-p] tbl_entry[s]]
help	help function [-wfilename] function[s]
hrt	high resolution timers [-wfilename]
inode	inode table [-e] [-f] [-wfilename] [[-p] tbl_entry[s]]
kmastat	kernel memory allocator statistics [-wfilename]
lck	record lock tables [-e] [-wfilename] [[-p] tbl_entry[s]]
linkblk	linkblk table [-e] [-wfilename] [[-p] linkblk_addr[s]]
major	MAJOR table [-wfilename] [entry[ies]]
map	map structures [-wfilename] mapname[s]
mbfree	free message block headers [-wfilename]
mblock	allocated stream message block headers [-e] [-f] [-wfilename] [[-p] mblk_addr[s]]
mode	address mode [-wfilename] [v | p]
nm	name search [-wfilename] symbol[s]
od	dump symbol values

Command	Description and syntax
	[-wfilename] [-c|-d|-x|-o|-a|-h] [-l|-t|-b] [-sprocess] [-p] st_addr [count]
page	page structure [-e] [-wfilename] [[-p] tbl_entry[s]]
pcb	process control block [-wfilename] [[-u	-k] [process]	-i [-p] st_addr]
prnode	proc node [-e] [-wfilename] [[-p] tbl_entry[s]]
proc	process table [-e] [-f] [-wfilename] [([-p] [-a] tbl_entry	#procid)...	-r]
pty	pty structure [-e] [-f] [-wfilename] [-s] [-h] [-l] [([-p] tbl_entry)]
qrun	list of serviceable stream queues [-wfilename]
queue	allocated stream queues [-e] [-f] [-wfilename] [[-p] queue_addr[s]]
rcvd	receive descriptor [-e] [-f] [-wfilename] [[-p] tbl_entry[s]]
rduser	rcvd user table [-e] [-f] [-wfilename] [[-p] tbl_entry[s]]
redirect	output redirection [-wfilename] [-c	filename]
resource	resource list [-wfilename]
rtdptbl	real time dispatcher parameter table [-wfilename] [tbl_entry[s]]
rtproc	real time process table [-e] [-wfilename] [tbl_entry[s]]
search	memory search [-wfilename] [-mmask] [-sprocess] pattern [-p] st_addr length
size	symbol size [-x] [-wfilename] structure-name[s]
sndd	send descriptor [-e] [-f] [-wfilename] [[-p] tbl_entry[s]]
snode	special node [-e] [-f] [-wfilename] [[-p] tbl_entry[s]]
srmount	server mount list [-wfilename] [-p] srmount_addr[s]
stack	stack dump

Command	Description and syntax
	[-wfilename] [[-u | -k] [process] | -i [-p] st_addr]
stream	allocated stream table slots [-e] [-f] [-wfilename] [[-p] stream_addr[s]]
strstat	streams statistics [-wfilename]
trace	kernel stack trace [-wfilename] [[-r] [process] | -i [-p] st_addr]
ts	text address namelist search [-wfilename] virtual_address[es]
tsdptbl	time sharing dispatcher parameter table [-wfilename] [tbl_entry[s]]
tsproc	time sharing process table [-e] [-wfilename] [tbl_entry[s]]
tty	tty structures (valid types: pp, iu) [-e] [-f] [-wfilename] [-l] [-ttype [[-p] tbl_entry[s]] | [-p] st_addr]
user	u-area [-f] [-wfilename] [process]
uinode	inode table [-e] [-f] [-wfilename] [[-p] tbl_entry[s]]
var	system variables [-wfilename]
vfs	mounted vfs list [-e] [-wfilename] [[-p] address[es]]
vfssw	virtual file system switch table [-wfilename] [[-p] tbl_entry[s]]
vnode	vnode list [-wfilename] [-p] vnode_addr[s]
vtop	virtual to physical address [-wfilename] [-sprocess] st_addr[s]
?	print list of available commands [-wfilename]
!cmd	escape to shell

*Internal **crash** commands and syntax*

Note that **crash** is implementation dependent, so some commands may not be available and others may be implemented that are not defined here.

Appendix G

IEEE POSIX Suite

Standard	Description
P1003.0	Guide to the POSIX Open Systems Environment
P1003.1	Language Independent Specification
P1003.1a	New Extensions to P1003.1
P1003.2	Command Shell and Utilities
P1003.2a	User Portability Extensions
P1003.3.1	Test methods for P1003.1
P1003.3.2	Test methods for P1003.2
P1003.4	Real Time Extensions
P1003.4a	Threads
P1003.6	Security Extensions
P1003.7.1	Printer Administration
P1003.7.2	Software Administration
P1003.8	Transparent File Access (TFA)
P1003.10	Supercomputing Application Environment Profile (AEP)
P1003.11	Transaction Processing AEP
P1003.12	Protocol Independent Network Application Programming Interface (sockets and XTI)
P1003.13	Realtime AEP
P1003.14	Multiprocessing Application Support AEP
P1003.15	Batch Queuing Extensions
P1003.16	C Language
P1003.17	Directory Services
P1003.18	POSIX Platform Environment Profile
P1003.19	Fortran 90 bindings for P1003.1
P1003.20	Ada Real Time bindings for P1003.1
P1201.1	Window Interfaces for User Portability
P1201.2	Recommended Practice for Drivability
P1295.1	X Window System Modular Toolkit Environment

Standard	Description
P1295.2	(Based on OSF/Motif) X Window System Open Toolkit Environment (Based on Sun Microsystems Inc. Open Look)

Although not technically part of the POSIX standard the P1201 and P1295 windowing standard efforts are supervised by the IEEE Technical Committee on Operating Systems and meetings are frequently coordinated with POSIX groups.

For more information see [UniForum 1993].

BIBLIOGRAPHY

[AT&T 1990a] AT&T UNIX System Laboratories, Inc., *UNIX System V Release 4 System Administrator's Reference Manual*, Prentice Hall, Englewood Cliffs, NJ.

[AT&T 1990b] AT&T UNIX System Laboratories, Inc., *UNIX System V Release 4 System V Application Binary Interface, MIPS Processor Supplement*, Prentice Hall, Englewood Cliffs, NJ.

[AT&T 1990c] AT&T UNIX System Laboratories, Inc., *UNIX System V Release 4 Programmer's Guide: ANSI C and Programming Support Tools*, Prentice Hall, Englewood Cliffs, NJ.

[AT&T 1990d] AT&T UNIX System Laboratories, Inc., *UNIX System V Release 4 STREAMS Programmer's Guide*, Prentice Hall, Englewood Cliffs, NJ.

[AT&T 1990e] AT&T UNIX System Laboratories, Inc., *UNIX System V Release 4 Device Driver Interface/ Driver-Kernel Interface (DDI/DKI) Reference Manual*, Prentice Hall, Englewood Cliffs, NJ.

[AT&T 1990f] AT&T UNIX System Laboratories, Inc., *UNIX System V Release 4 Programmer's Guide: Networking Interfaces*, Prentice Hall, Englewood Cliffs, NJ.

[AT&T 1990g] AT&T UNIX System Laboratories, Inc., *UNIX System V Release 4 System Administrator's Guide* Prentice Hall, Englewood Cliffs, NJ.

[AT&T 1990h] AT&T UNIX System Laboratories, Inc., *UNIX System V Release 4 Programmer's Reference Manual*, Prentice Hall, Englewood Cliffs, NJ.

[Bach 1986] Maurice J. Bach, *The Design of the UNIX Operating System*, Prentice Hall, Englewood Cliffs, NJ.

[Bergen, Tolchin 1986] Eric S. Bergan, Stephen G. Tolchin, *Using Remote Procedure Calls (RPC) for a Distributed Clinical Information System*, Conference Proceedings of UniForum, Anaheim, CA.

[Bourne 1978] S. R. Bourne, *The UNIX Shell*, Bell System Technical Journal, July-Aug 1978.

[Cheng 1987] R. Cheng, *Virtual Address Cache in UNIX*, USENIX Association, Summer Conference Proceedings, Phoenix 1987.

[Comer 1988] Douglas E. Comer, *Internetworking with TCP/IP*, Prentice Hall, Englewood Cliffs, NJ.

[Courington 1985] Bill Courington, *The UNIX System: A Sun Technical Report*, Sun Microsystems, Inc., Mountain View, CA.

[Day, Zimmerman 1983] J.D. Day, H. Zimmerman., *The OSI Reference Model*, Proceedings of the IEEE, vol 71, pp 1334-1340, Dec. 1983.

[Deitel 1984] Harvey M. Deitel, *An Introduction to Operating Systems*, Addison-Wesley, Reading, MA.

[Egan, Teixeira 1988] Janet I. Egan, Thomas J. Teixeira, *Writing A UNIX Device Driver*, John Wiley & Sons, Inc., New York, NY.

[Gircys 1988] Gintaras R. Gircys, *Understanding and Using COFF*, O'Reilly & Associates, Inc., 981 Chestnut St, Newton, MA.

[Goodheart 1991] Berny Goodheart, *UNIX Curses Explained*, Prentice Hall, Englewood Cliffs, NJ.

[Gray 1991] Pamela Gray, *Open Systems: A Business Strategy for the 1990s*, McGraw Hill Book Company, Berkshire, UK.

[Halsall 1988] Fred Halsall, *Data Communications, Computer Networks and OSI*, Addison-Wesley, Reading, MA.

[Hansen 1973] Per Brinch Hansen, *Operating System Principles*, Prentice Hall, Englewood Cliffs, NJ.

[Intel 1986a] *80386 Programmer's Reference Manual*, Chapter 6 "Protection", Intel Corporation, Santa Clara, CA.

[Intel 1986b] *Introduction to the 80386 including the 80386 Data Sheet*, Intel corporation, Santa Clara, California.

[Intel 1987] *80386 System Software Writer's Guide*, Intel corporation, Santa Clara, California.

[Kay, Lauder 1988] J.Kay and P. Lauder, *A fair share scheduler*, Communications of the ACM, January 1988, Volume 31 Number 1.

[Kane, Heinrich 1992] Gerry Kane, J. Heinrich, *MIPS RISC Architecture*, Prentice-Hall, Englewood Cliffs, NJ.

[Kernighan, Pike 1984] Brian W. Kernighan, Rob Pike., *The UNIX Programming Environment*, Prentice Hall, Englewood Cliffs, NJ.

[Kernighan, Ritchie 1978] Brian W. Kernighan, Dennis M. Ritchie, *The C Programming Language*, Prentice Hall, Englewood Cliffs, NJ.

[Kleiman 1986] S. R. Kleiman, *Vnodes: An Architecture for Multiple File System Types in Sun UNIX*, USENIX Association, Summer Conference Proceedings, Atlanta 1986.

[Knuth 1968] Donald E. Knuth, *The Art of Computer Programming, Volume 1, Fundamental Algorithms*, Addison-Wesley, Reading, MA.

[Leffler, McKusick, Karels, Quarterman 1988] Samuel J. Leffler, Marshall K. McKusick, Michael J. Karels, John S. Quarterman. *The Design and Implementation of the 4.3BSD UNIX Operating System*, Addison-Wesley, Reading, MA.

[Libes, Ressler 1989] Don Libes, Sandy Ressler, *Life With UNIX A Guide for Everyone*, Prentice Hall, Englewood Cliffs, NJ.

[Lions 1977] John Lions, *A Commentary On The UNIX Operating System* and companion, *UNIX Operating System Source Code, Level Six*, Student course notes 6.602B and 6.657G, University of New South Wales, Sydney 1977.

[McKusick, Joy, Leffler, Fabry 1984] M. K. McKusick, W. N. Joy, S. J. Leffler, R. S. Fabry, *A Fast File System For UNIX*, ACM Transactions on Computer

Systems, Volume 2, #3, August 1984.

[Moran 1988] Joseph P. Moran, *SunOS Virtual Memory Implementation*, Sun Microsystems, Inc., Mountain View, CA.

[Nemeth, Snyder, Seebass 1989] Evi Nemeth, Garth Snyder, Scott Seebass, *UNIX System Administration Handbook*, Prentice Hall, Englewood Cliffs, NJ.

[Nohr 1993] Mary Lou Nohr, *UNIX System V Release 4 Understanding and Using ELF*, Prentice Hall, Englewood Cliffs, NJ.

[Organick 1972] E. I. Organick, *The MULTICS System*, Massachussets Institute of Technology Press, Cambridge, Massachussets.

[Pajari 1992] George Pajari, *Writing UNIX Device Drivers*, Addison-Wesley, Reading, MA.

[Peacock 1991] Jeffrey Peacock, *Dynamic Shared Libraries*, UNIX Review, vol. 9 No 5, pp. 37-44, May 1991.

[Rago 1989] Stephen Rago, *Out-Of-Band Communication in STREAMS*, USENIX Association, Summer Conference Proceedings 1989.

[Reinfelds 1990] Juris Reinfelds, *The First Port Of UNIX*, Australian UNIX Review, pp. 32-34, February/March 1990.

[RFC 877] John Korb, *A Standard for the Transmission of IP Datagrams over Public Data Networks*, Purdue, September 1983.

[RFC 1014] Sun Microsystems, Inc., *XDR: External Data Representation Standard*, June 1987.

[RFC 1057] Sun Microsystems, Inc., *RPC: Remote Procedure Call Protocol Specification, Version 2*, June 1988.

[Richards 1969] Martin Richards, *BCPL: A Tool for Compiler Writing and Systems Programming*, Proceedings of the AFIPS SICC Spring Joint Computer Conference 1969, vol 34, pp. 557-566.

[Ritchie 1977] D. M. Ritchie, *A New Input-Output Package*, addendum to the UNIX Programmer's Manual, Sixth Edition, Western Electric Company, 1975.

[Ritchie 1979] D. M. Ritchie, *PROTECTION OF DATA FILE CONTENTS*, United States Patent, Number 4,135,240, Jan. 16, 1979.

[Ritchie 1984a] D. M. Ritchie, *A stream input output system*, AT&T Bell Laboratories Technical Journal, Oct 1984, 63,8, Part 2, pp. 1897-1910.

[Ritchie 1984b] D. M. Ritchie, *The Evolution of the UNIX Time-sharing System*, AT&T Bell Laboratories Technical Journal, Oct 1984, 63,8, Part 2, pp. 1577-1594.

[Ritchie, Thompson 1974] D. M. Ritchie, K Thompson, *The UNIX Time-Sharing System*, Communications of the ACM, 17,7 July 1974. Revised and reprinted in Bell System Technical Journal, 57,6 July 1978, pp. 1905-1929.

[Sandberg 1987] Russel Sandberg, *The Sun Networked File System: Design, Implementation and Experience*, Sun Microsystems, Inc., Mountain View, CA.

[Stevens 1990] W. Richard Stevens., *UNIX Network Programming*, Prentice Hall, Englewood Cliffs, NJ.

[UniForum 1989] UniForum, *POSIX Explored: System Interface*, UniForum, Santa Clara, CA.

[UniForum 1993] UniForum, *Standards-Based Procurement Using POSIX and XPG*, UniForum, Santa Clara, CA.

[USL 1990a] AT&T UNIX System Laboratories, Inc., *System V Application Binary Interface — Intel 80386 Processor Supplement*, Prentice Hall, Englewood Cliffs, NJ.

[USL 1990b] AT&T UNIX System Laboratories, Inc., *System V Application Binary Interface — Motorola 68000 Processor Supplement*, Prentice Hall, Englewood Cliffs, NJ.

[USL 1990c] AT&T UNIX System Laboratories, Inc., *System V Application Binary Interface — Motorola 88000 Processor Supplement*, Prentice Hall, Englewood Cliffs, NJ.

[USL 1990d] AT&T UNIX System Laboratories, Inc., *System V Application Binary Interface — SPARC Processor Supplement*, Prentice Hall, Englewood Cliffs, NJ.

[USL 1991] AT&T UNIX System Laboratories, Inc., *System V Application Binary Interface — MIPS Processor Supplement*, Prentice Hall, Englewood Cliffs, NJ.

[USL 1992a] AT&T UNIX System Laboratories, Inc., *Device Driver Interface/ Driver-Kernel Interface (DDI/DKI) Reference Manual for Intel Processors*, Prentice Hall, Englewood Cliffs, NJ.

[USL 1992b] AT&T UNIX System Laboratories, Inc., *System V Application Binary Interface — Revised Edition*, Prentice Hall, Englewood Cliffs, NJ.

[Vessey, Skinner 1990] Ian Vessey, Glen Skinner, *Implementing Berkeley Sockets in System V Release 4*, USENIX Association, Winter Conference Proceedings 1990.

[X/Open 1987] X/Open, *Open Systems Directive: Overview*, X/Open Company Ltd, Berkshire, UK.

[X/Open 1988] X/Open, *X/Open Portability Guide, Issue 3*, Prentice Hall, Englewood Cliffs, NJ, August 1988.

INDEX

#! 261
1BSD 9
2BSD 9
3b2 26
4.2BSD 12, 62
4.3BSD 19
4BSD 9

A

accept 58, 522-3, 525
access permissions 46
activation record 147-8
address space hole 69
addupc 203
adjmsg 454
advisory locking 358
algorithm 89
    anon_alloc 89
    anon_decref 89
    anon_getpage 91
    anon_private 91
    brk 132
    checkpage 112
    clock 192
    clock_int 207
    core 262
    dispinit 274
    dup 342
    exece 259
    exit 266
    falloc 341
    fifo_open 498
    fifo_write 498
    fork1 253
    freeproc 271
    getq 466
    hat_pteload 102
    issig 236
    kmem_alloc 124
    kmem_free 124
    lookuppn 382

newproc 253
pagefault 107
page_find 91
page_get 91
pageout 112
page_reclaim 91
physiock 311
pipe 501
poll 493
psig 238
pswtch 164
putbq 466
putq 466
queuerun 469
sched 115
segvn_fault 94
segvn_faultpage 98
segvn_lockop 137
semop 540
setrun 190
shmat 558
sigtoproc 223, 225
sleep 183
spec_read 309
specvp 388
ssig 231, 233
straccess 508
strdoioctl 487
strgetmsg 489
stropen 474
strread 479
strwrite 476
swap_alloc 118
swtch 164
systrap 218
uadmin 277
ufalloc 341
ufs_getapage 293
ufs_putpage 293
ufs_read 298
ufs_write 298
u_trap 235
waitid 270

wakeprocs   188
allocation map   128
allocb   454, 456-8, 461-3, 467, 472, 476,
    487, 606-8
anon   88-9, 91, 94, 117-18, 127
anon_alloc   90
anon_decref   90-1
anon_free   91
anon_getpage   91
anon_private   91
anonymous page   85, 88
anon_zero   90
a.out   35, 39, 144-7, 202-3, 249, 261,
    263-5, 269, 274, 276, 346, 348, 357, 368
argc   261
argv   261
as   86-7, 104, 127
as_alloc   89, 277
ASCII   25
as_ctl   134-6, 558
as_fault   89, 107, 109
as_faulta   89
as_map   89, 107, 132-3, 277, 322-3, 327,
    357, 559
as_segat   89
ASSERT   561
as_swapout   117
as_unmap   132, 357, 559
AT&T   8
    UNIX System V   10
AT&T-IS   11
Australia   5-7, 9
autopush   474

B

B   5
backlog   523
backq   454
BadVAddr   105-6
B_AGE   291
B_ASYNC   292, 296
B_BUSY   290
bcanput   454, 460-1
bclnlist   112
BCPL   5
bdevsw   48, 300-2, 386
B_DONE   293, 295, 307, 309
Berkeley   9
    fast file system   33
    Software Distribution   9, 19
bfreelist   290
bfs   34, 48-9
bhdrlist   290
B_HEAD   290
Bill Joy   6, 9

bind   58, 522, 524
/bin/passwd   46
/bin/sh   22, 27
biodone   295-6
biowait   293, 295
block   282
    device driver   282
    device strategy   308
bmap   291-2
boot   26, 34, 48, 274
    banner   276
    block   26, 29
    partition   48
bootstrap   24
bootstrapping   273
B_PAGEIO   293
bpool   123-4
BPRI_HI   462
BPRI_LO   462
BPRI_MED   462
bread   292-3, 580
brelse   290-1
Brian Kernighan   4
brk   129, 131-3
BSD   9, 12, 29, 51
bss   146, 261, 276, 581
btoc   325
buddy system   121
bufcall   454, 456-8, 462-3, 465, 467-9
buffer   290
    allocation   290
    I/O   292
    mapping   291
bufhdr   291
B_WANTED   290-1
bwrite   292-3, 580

C

C   23
    Language   5-6, 8, 23, 25
    Language stack   585
    source code   26
caddr_t   183
calloc   129
callout   196, 602, 619-21
    table   196
canput   407, 422-3, 438, 454, 460-1, 464-5
cause register   105, 151
cdevsw   48, 301, 304, 313-14, 386, 388,
    418, 420, 473-4, 497
character   282
    device driver   282
    I/O   51, 282
checkpage   115
child   241

Chuck Haley 6
CL_ADMIN 176
class 166, 569
    dependent functions 175
    dependent interface 174
    table 166
cleanup 115
CL_ENTERCLASS 176
CL_EXITCLASS 176, 269
CL_FORK 176
CL_FORKRET 177
cl_funcs 175
CL_GETCLINFO 177
CL_GETGLOBPRI 177
client-server 61
cl_init 168
clkstart 192
clnopen 474
clock 110-12, 115-16, 179, 187, 193-7,
    199, 201-5, 207, 275, 367
    drift 205
    interrupt service routine 192
    priming 195
    resource limits 201
clock_int 194-5, 207
clone 304, 474
CLONEOPEN 474
CL_PARMSGET 177
CL_PARMSIN 177-8
CL_PARMSOUT 177
CL_PARMSSET 178
CL_PREEMPT 175, 178
cl_preempt 175
CL_PROCCMP 178
CL_SETRUN 178
CL_SLEEP 178, 186
CL_STOP 178
CL_SWAPIN 115, 179
CL_SWAPOUT 115, 117, 179
CL_TICK 179
CL_TRAPRET 180
CL_WAKEUP 180
cmn_err 438, 562
COFF 26, 144, 259
command 148
    as 23, 148
    bg 508
    cat 27, 43-4, 246
    cc 23, 148
    chown 27
    cp 27, 36
    cpp 23
    crash 129, 325-6, 496, 563
    csh 246, 507
    dbx 565
    dispadmin 168
    ds 129

edit 37
ex 9, 37
fg 506, 508
fmthard 31
format 31
fsck 30, 278, 368
fsdb 36
gcore 392
getty 63-4
grep 43-4, 142
inetd 50, 63-4
init 176, 247, 277
ipcrm 533
ipcs 533
ksh 505
ld 23, 148, 214, 264
listen 64
ln 38
lockd 355
login 21-2, 45, 64, 518, 583
lp 246, 497
lpsched 578
ls 27, 35, 594
mail 56
make 148
mkdir 27
mkfs 30-1, 362, 373
mknod 300, 408, 497, 500
mv 27
ncheck 594
netstat 325
nm 579, 583
passwd 46
pic 246
prof 203
ps 112, 393
quota 45
rlogin 56, 63, 518
rlogind 518
rm 27, 40
rmdir 27
rsh 63
sar 574-5
sdb 262, 392, 565
sh 8
shell 22-3
shl 504
strip 579
stty 503
tbl 246
telnet 56
troff 246
truss 392
ttymon 21, 42, 64, 248, 339
vedit 37
vi 9, 12, 37, 79, 102
view 37

command line interpreter 21
common object file format 144
communication facilities 51
concurrency 142
connect 58, 522, 525
context 154
    switch 154, 159-60, 165
    switching 25
controlling terminal 248
copen 344, 384, 386
copyb 454
copyin 315-16, 411
copymsg 455
copy-on-write 90-1, 95, 101, 106-7, 117,
    138, 177, 218, 252, 264
copyout 316, 411
copyreq 428-30
copyresp 428, 430
core 262-3
    dump 262, 348
    image 392
CP/M 3
CPU usage 44
crash 563
    ? 564
    as 583
    base 620
    callout 619
    class 569
    dblock 607
    defproc 571
    dis 566
    dispq 569
    ds 568
    file 595
    findaddr 567
    findslot 567
    kmastat 601
    linkblk 613
    map 604
    mblock 606
    nm 568
    od 566
    page 603
    pcb 570
    proc 571
    pty 614
    qrun 613
    queue 612
    search 621
    size 567
    stack 590
    stream 610
    strstat 608
    trace 590
    u 576
    uinode 597

var 602
vfs 599
vfssw 599
vnode 595
vtop 603
credentials 155, 249
ctty 573
_curbrk 132
curpri 162, 164
curproc 162, 164, 202, 207
currently running process 146
cylinder group 29

D

DARPA 9, 51, 54
data segment 79, 145-6, 252, 259, 261,
    265, 551
datab 409-10, 412, 606
datamsg 455
dblk_t 409, 496
DDI 52
DDI/DKI 329
ddi.h 329
DEBUG 495
DEC 76
demand paging 74, 105
Dennis M. Ritchie 4
desfree 110-11, 114
desscan 111-12
/dev 34
/dev/console 36
/dev/fd 34
device 47
    character 313
    close 306, 436
    ioctl 313
    mmap 322
    open 304
    poll 316
    pseudo 47
    streamtab 303
    switch tables 48
device driver 25, 36, 47, 51, 282
    data structures 301
    functions 301
    interface 52, 328
    interrupt service routine 306
    kernel 104
    mm 325
/dev/kmem 325-7
/dev/mem 303, 325, 327
/dev/null 300, 327
devp 304-6
/dev/prf 202
/dev/swap 48

dev_t 331-2
/dev/tcp 408, 522
/dev/tty 48
/dev/x25 442, 473-4
/dev/zero 327
directory 27, 354
    consistency check 30
    /dev 34
    format 35
    home 21
    mount point 30, 373
    mounted-on 377
    /proc 272
    structure 22, 27
    working 27
directory name lookup cache 378
dispdeq 163
dispinit 168, 274
dispq 161-3
DKI 52
dnlc 378, 393
    initialization 378
dnlc_enter 380
dnlc_init 378, 380
dnlc_lookup 380
dnlc_purge 380
dnlc_purge1 380
dnlc_purge_vfsp 380
dnlc_purge_vp 380
dnlc_remove 380
dnlc_rm 380
dnlc_search 380
DOD 53
dot 27
dot-dot 27
Doug McIlroy 7
dqactmap 163
dq_sruncnt 163
dq_srundec 163
dq_sruninc 163
Dr John Lions 6
drv_getparm 331
dumpdev 563
dupb 455, 608
dupmsg 455
dynamically-linked-shared-libraries 264
dynamic-link-loader 265

E

E2BIG 538, 545
EACCES 359
EAGAIN 535, 549
EBADMSG 482, 523, 525
EBUSY 354, 377-8
ECHILD 231, 270

ECHO 514
ECHOCTL 513
EDEADLK 359
EFAULT 316
EFBIG 296
effective user ID 250
EFT 64, 409
EINTR 187-8, 218, 230, 273
EINVAL 134, 230, 299, 314, 321, 355, 486,
    538, 547, 551, 557, 559
EIO 310, 478
ELF 26, 144, 259
enableok 455, 460-1, 465-6
end 132
ENODEV 303
ENOSR 472
entrymask 581
environment 213
envp 261, 277
EPIPE 498, 500, 502
ERANGE 539
esballoc 410, 455-8, 461-2
ESTRPIPE 498, 500
/etc/group 45
/etc/init 277
/etc/passwd 36, 43, 45-6, 250
Ethernet 54
etoimajor 332
event-identifier 183
events 317
event-type 181, 183
exec 525
exec_core 263
exec_func 259-60
execsw 145, 259, 263
executable 143
    a.out 143
    file 23
    format 143
    logical view 143
execute permission 45
execution 235
    errors 235
    fault 75
exit 265
exitmask 581
expedited data 411
Extended Fundamental Types 64, 409

F

falloc 341, 344
FASTBUF 461, 476
fastscan 111
fault 25, 94
    copy-on-write 91

fbuf   123-4
fcntl.h   345, 579
F_DUPFD   341
F_FREESP   356
FFS   33
F_GETLK   356
FIFO   34, 38, 41, 345, 388, 474
   creation   497
   operations   498
fifofs   34
fifo_open   498
fifo_read   500
fifo_vnodeops   388, 498
fifovp   388
fifo_write   498, 500
file   336
   access   40, 336
   access modes   45
   access permissions   22
   accessibility   46
   a.out   39, 143
   block-special   36, 48
   character-special   36, 48
   closing   41
   core   44, 262
   creation   40
   creation size   44
   definition   34
   descriptor   40, 42, 336
   descriptor allocation   341
   directory   35
   generic abstraction   345
   inode   50, 529
   I/O   282
   link   37
   management   26
   management subsystem   335
   mapped   85
   mapping   80
   memory mapped   39
   mmapped   319
   name size   33, 39
   named pipe   38
   ordinary   35
   protection   45-6
   record locking   41, 357
   record-locks   41
   regular   35, 47
   removal   39
   segments   144
   sharing   60
   special   36, 47-8, 248, 300
   structure   337
   symbolic link   38
file system   27
   bfs   34, 48, 368
   boot   34

bootable   29
busy   30
/dev/fd   34
dirty   30
fifofs   34, 366, 388, 498
format   30
hardening   362
initialized   31
installation   33
integrity   29
interface   32
management   25
mountable   30, 370
networked   62
NFS   33
nfs   33
/proc   34, 116, 188, 392
procfs   366
quota   374
remote   60
rfs   34
root   27, 31, 367, 376
s5   29, 33, 39, 45, 50, 289, 390,
   579, 596
specfs   34, 351, 384
structure   29, 33
super block   50
traditional   34
ufs   29, 33, 39, 45, 276, 289, 292,
   296, 322, 390
UNIX   35
unmount   30
virtual   32, 62
filock   359
first-in-first-out   38
flags register   151
flist   123
floating point register   151
flow of execution   142
flow-control   422
flushband   455
flushq   430, 432, 455
fmodsw   418, 420, 483, 497, 526
fmthard   31
fork   525
fork1   253
fork.s   253
format   31
frame pointer   151
free   129
freeb   455, 457-8, 462-3
freed   41
freemsg   455, 457-8, 462, 479, 487, 493
freeproc   255, 271-2
free_rtn   410, 456
F_RSETLKW   355
frtnp   410, 457-8, 462

fsck 30
fsdb 36
F_SETFL 351
F_SETLK 359
fsflush 169, 194, 277, 319, 362, 366-7
fs_poll 303
ftok 529
FTRUNC 421
FWRITE 421

G

GATE 214
GE-645 4
GEC 3
GECOS 3-4
General Electric Company 3
general purpose data register 151
getadmin 455
getblk 290-2
geteblk 290-1
getfreeblk 290-1
getitimer 194, 206
getmajor 331
getmid 455
getminor 331
getpage 292
getq 422, 440, 451, 455, 459, 464, 466
gettimeofday 194
getty 63-4
GID 22, 30
global variable u 148
group ID 22, 45
grow 131, 133, 216

H

handspread 276
hard link 352
hardware 25
    address translation 25, 86, 92
    clock 192
    interrupt 159
HASHSZ 245
HAT 92
hat 100, 104
hat_dup 104
hat_getpte 103
hat_pagesync 104
hat_pageunload 104
hat_pteload 102-4, 287
hat_swapout 104
hat_unload 287
Honeywell 3
hrestime 204

hrt_active 209
HZ 331

I

i386 26
icode 277
ICRNL 510, 512
IEEE 13
I_FDINSERT 523
I_LINK 442, 447, 486
ilist 29-30
index node 388
inetd 63-4
init 277, 329-30, 575
inode 10, 29-30, 32, 35-6, 38, 41, 45-6,
    50, 180-1, 194, 249, 288, 291, 345, 352,
    388, 390, 596
    concept 388
    link 38
    link count 352
    number 352
    table 380
insq 455, 459
Intel 80386 73-4
intelligent controllers 516
Interdata 6
    7/32 6
    8/32 8-9
interface 22
    interactive 22
    programmatic 25
    raw 37
    system call 25-6
    VFS 33
Internet protocol 54
interrupt 307
    polled 307
    vectored 307
interrupt exception 25, 105
interrupts 216
interval timer 206
intsx 216, 581
intsxk 216
I/O 42
    interface 42
    management 26
    redirection 41-2
    scatter gather 297
    stderr 42
    stdin 42
    stdout 42
iocblk 411
ioc_cmd 427, 518
ioc_count 427
ioc_id 487

io_init 330
io_start 330
IP 54
IPC 529
    id 529
    introduction 528
    key 529
    permissions 529
ipcaccess 539-40
IPC_CREAT 539, 544, 551
ipcget 539-40, 549, 557
IPC_NOWAIT 545, 549-50
ipc_perm 539
IPC_PRIVATE 539, 544, 551
IPC_RMID 556
IPC_SET 530, 544
IPC_STAT 544
I_POP 432
I_PUSH 408, 420
I_SETSIG 477
ISO 13
ISSIG 237
issig 186, 188, 236-8
I_STR 424-6
ITIMER_PROF 207, 209
ITIMER_REAL 207, 209
itimerval 207
ITIMER_VIRTUAL 207, 209
I_UNLINK 449, 486

J

job control 245
John Lions 7
Juris Reinfelds 6

K

Ken Thompson 3
kernel 24
    address space 283
    profiler 202
    stack 148, 585
kernel-mode 210
Kernighan 9
kmdaemon 127, 245, 275, 277
kmem_alloc 81, 119, 123-4, 127-8, 290-1,
    293, 410, 461-2, 472, 494, 548, 601, 606
kmem_avail 469
kmem_fast_alloc 123, 127
kmem_fast_free 123, 127
kmem_free 81, 119, 123, 127, 291, 410,
    462, 468, 473, 609
kmem_freepool 277
kprunrun 161-2, 164, 178-80, 190

k_trap 216, 236

L

lbolt 331, 576, 580
ldterm 405, 418, 421, 428, 476, 503,
    507-15, 517-19, 616-17
    character input 511
    data structures 508
    flow-control 513
    implementation 508
    intelligent controllers 518
    ioctl 511
    read side 509
    special character I/O 513
    VMIN & VTIME 514
    write side 511
least recently used 77
libc.so 263
link 37
    hard 37, 39, 46
    soft 38
    symbolic 38-9
linkb 455
linking 37
listen 58, 64, 522-3, 525
lock 357
    advisory 357
    mandatory 357, 359
    resource 360
lock manager 356
lockf 358
login 64
longjmp 187-8, 218, 273, 580
lookupname 345, 381
lookuppn 381, 384, 393
lotsfree 110-12
ls 35

M

machine 26
    architecture 26
    dependent 25
    runnable object 23
    virtual memory 25
main 192, 195, 203, 252, 254, 259, 261,
    274-5, 330, 378, 380, 540, 548
major 48, 53
major number 48
makedevice 374
malloc 129
mandatory locking 359
map 119, 128-9
map_addr 322

MAP_FIXED 321
MAP_PRIVATE 88, 321, 323
MAP_SHARED 88, 321
Massachussets Institute of Technology 3
master 516
master.d 27, 168, 172, 181-2, 196, 202
master.d/sad/space.c 472
max 331
MAXABIG 602
MAXASMALL 602
MAXBSIZE 283, 285, 287
MAXCLSYSPRI 182
maxpgio 112
MAXPID 243
maxrunpri 163, 180
MAXUP 255
mblk_t 409, 454, 457, 496
mboot 26
M_BREAK 509
MC_CANON_QUERY 518
MCL_CURRENT 136
MCL_FUTURE 136
MC_LOCK 138, 558
MC_LOCKAS 136
M_COPYIN 428-30, 478
M_COPYOUT 429, 478
MC_SYNC 137
M_CTL 518
MC_UNLOCK 138
M_DATA 411, 424, 426-8, 440, 446, 451,
    454-7, 482, 487, 509, 512, 517, 520, 523,
    525
mdbblock 461-2
mdbfreelist 461-2
M_DELAY 513
mdep 279
memcntl 84, 131, 134-6
memory 119
    allocation 119
    allocator 124, 275
    associative 72, 75, 95
    bank switching 70
    cache 73-4
    deallocator 120
    fault 221
    free 111
    hierarchical-storage 70
    hole 69
    management 24-5, 27
    mapped file 44
    multiple-level 70
    non-paged 119
    overlay scheme 69
    pages 71
    paging-in 75
    physical 24, 69
    physical address 70, 72

    registers 151
    shared 131
    structure 80
    usage 44, 141
    virtual address 70
    virtual addresses 70
    working set 75
M_ERROR 411, 478
message 549
    allocation 549
    initialization 548
    initialization and control 543
    operations 549
    queues 10, 543
    using 544
M_FLUSH 424, 430, 432, 478, 486, 510
M_HANGUP 501, 510
Microsoft Corporation 10, 12, 15, 19
Mike Lesk 6
min 331
MINASMALL 602
mincore 138
minor 48, 53
minor number 48
minpid 243, 245
M_IOCACK 427, 429-30, 478, 511
M_IOCDATA 428-30, 478
M_IOCNAK 428, 430, 447, 478-9
M_IOCTL 411, 424-6, 428-30, 487, 511, 517
MIPS 26
    exception 105-6
    KSEG2 96
    R3000 73, 75
    TLB 100
misc.s 277
MIT 3, 12
mkfs 30-1, 48
ml 27
mlsetup 83, 274
mm 325-7
mmmmap 326-7
mmopen 326
mmread 326
mmsegmap 327
mmwrite 326
/mnt 307
module 616
    ldterm 616-17
    pckt 614, 618
    ptem 614
    put procedure 406, 421
    service procedure 406
mon.out 203
mounted file system 599
mount-point 370
mount-table 373
M_PASSFP 485-6

M_PCPROTO 478, 520
M_PCSIG 478, 507
mpid 243
mprotect 138
M_PROTO 411, 424, 446, 449, 455, 482,
    487, 517, 520, 522-3, 525
M_READ 508, 511, 514-15
MS-DOS 3
msg 548
msgb 406, 409-10, 606, 617
msgdsize 456
msgh 548
msginfo 545
msginit 548
msgio 487
msgmap 547
MSG_NOERROR 545
msgque 548
M_SIG 411, 478, 509, 513
msqid 543
M_START 514, 517
M_STARTI 514
M_STOP 514, 517
M_STOPI 514
MULTICS 3-4
multiplexor 407
Murray Allen 6
muxrinit 442
muxwinit 442

N

named pipe 40, 405
NAME_MAX 39
ncache 380
nc_hash 378, 380
NC_HASH_SIZE 378
NC_NAMLEN 379
ncsize 378
networking features 51
new buffer cache 283, 285
newproc 176, 253-4, 258, 276-7, 336, 343
NFPCHUNK 336-7
NFS 12, 33, 61-2
nfs 33
nice 173
nlist 326
nodev 303, 323
noenable 456, 460-1, 464-6
NOERROR 478
NOFILL 513
not recently used 77
Novell, Inc. 18
NP_FAILOK 254
NP_INIT 254
NPROC 255, 543

nproc 255, 272
NP_SYSPROC 254
npwakecnt 164, 189
nscan 111-12, 115
NSIG 221, 223
nulldev 303

O

OLCUC 511
old buffer cache 283, 288
ONC 62
O_NDELAY 296, 337
Open Systems Interconnect 51, 56
OPOST 511
O_RDONLY 296, 337, 344
OSI 51, 56
OSMT/32 6
OTHERQ 456
OTYP_BLK 304
OTYP_CHR 304
OTYP_LYR 304-5
OTYP_MNT 304
OTYP_SWP 304
out-of-band data 411

P

page 83-5, 89, 94, 102-4, 115, 138
    allocation 91
    anonymous 88
    attributes 137
    clock 77
    clustering 76
    copy-on-write 90, 106, 138
    directory number 73
    dirty 77, 194
    fault 75-6, 89, 94, 107-8
    frame number 71, 81
    free 91
    initialization 81-2
    I/O 293
    klustering 76
    lazy creation 74
    locked 83
    mapping 100
    modified 77
    prefetch 76
    protection 87
    referenced 77
    stealer 76, 85
    stealing 111
    structure 83
    table 71, 96
    un-mapping 100

pageac_table 81, 83
pagedaemon 76
pagefault 106-9
page_find 91
page_get 90-1, 112
pageio_done 293, 295-6
pageio_setup 292-3, 295-6
pageout 76-7, 104, 110-12, 114-15, 169,
    194, 277, 293, 319, 357
pageprot 87
page_reclaim 91
paging system procedures 89
panic 561
parent 241
p_as 154, 268
password 21
pathname 381
    relative 27
    resolution 381
p_brkbase 132
p_brksize 132
PCATCH 187-8, 421
PCB 165
pcb 274, 570
pcb.h 570
PCC 8
PC_GETPARMS 178
p_child 243
p_cid 166
pckt 518
p_clfuncs 174
p_clktim 197
p_clproc 168, 170, 173, 176
p_cred 155, 249, 340
p_cstime 199
p_curinfo 238
p_cursig 225, 238-9
p_cutime 199
PDP-11 6-8
PDP-11/20 4
PDP-11/45 8
PDP-11/70 6
PDP-7 4
Perkin-Elmer 6
Peter Weinberger 32
p_flag 134, 155, 157, 163, 170, 173, 231,
    258, 355
pfreecnt 290
pfreelist 290, 311
pgsignal 224
p_hash 83
p_hold 225, 227-8, 233
physical page number 71
physiock 310-11, 332
PID 243
pid 359
pidhash 245, 274

p_ignore 225
PIOCRUN 188
PIOCSTATUS 393
pipe 34, 38, 40, 52
    named 40
p_italarm 209
pl 94
p_link 162, 183
plock 84, 131, 134-5
p_mod 83
P_MYPID 240
p_next 155
PNOSTOP 186, 188
pollhead 317-18
pollrun 493
polltime 619-20
pollwait 492, 575
pollwakeup 318, 493
port monitor 63
POSIX 13, 15
p_parent 243
p_pgidp 155, 246
p_pglink 246-7
p_pidp 155, 245-6
p_pollflag 493
p_ppid 247
p_pri 161-3, 170, 172-3
practive 155, 272, 274
PREEMPT 164
preempt 162-4, 175, 177-80
preemption 159
p_ref 83
PRFMAX 202
prioctl 393
priority 166
    class dependent functions 166
    class dispatch parameter tables
        168
    class groups 166
    class independent functions 163
    class independent variables 161
    dispatch queue 162
    level 170
    levels 181
priority class 569
prlookup 393
PRMPT 190
/proc 34, 155, 179, 188, 225, 245, 392,
    580
    implementation 393
proc 132
    structure 274
    user 149
procdir 274
procdup 257-8, 342
process 274
    0 274

1 247
accounting 26
active list 155
address space 34, 78, 86, 154
bss 148
child 176, 252
context of 145
creation 252
credentials 249
currently running 146
data 148
descriptor table 40
execution 142
execution modes 209
execution rights 45
execution state 155, 157
exit 236
flags 155
flow 142
functional state 155, 157
group 241
group leader 246
ID states 45
identification 243
image 35, 143, 147
job control 245
kernel-mode 145
life 141
light weight 192
management 24, 26
memory model 145
multi-threaded 192
open file table 336
orphaned 247
page tables 259
pageout 77
priority class 160, 166
real-time 169
resident set size 86
scheduling 160
sibling 252
sleeping 155, 180
stack 44, 148, 230
states 155
statistics 199
stopped 188
structure 153
subsystem 141
suspension 273
system-class 169, 182
table 81
terminates 265
termination 41, 265
text 148
time-shared 171
time-slice 160-1
user interface 47

user-area 146
user-mode 145
waiting for 269
wake up 188
zombie 265
processor 105
exceptions 105
execution level 197
execution mode 214
interrupt level 188, 192, 194
interrupt priority level 217
status register 151
type 25
procfs.h 581
proc.h 237
profiling 202
program 151
counter 151
execution 258
prot 87
protected mode 274
PROT_EXEC 138, 321
PROT_NONE 138, 321
PROT_READ 138, 321
PROT_WRITE 138, 321
p_sessp 248-9
pseudo terminal 503
pseudo terminals 516
p_sibling 243
p_sig 221, 223, 225, 238, 268
psig 228, 238-9, 262-3
p_siginfo 230-1, 238
psignal 223-4, 243
p_sigqueue 235
PSLEP 182, 273
p_stat 155, 162, 170, 173
p_stime 199
p_swlocks 355
pswtch 161-2, 164-5, 190
pte 99-105, 107, 109
ptem 517-18
ptms_tty 516-17, 614, 616
ptsname 517
pty 614
pullupmsg 440, 456
put 329
putbq 422, 456, 459, 465-6
putctl 456
putctl1 456
p_utime 199
putmsg 522
putnext 421-3, 456
putpage 292
putq 407, 422, 440, 451, 456, 459, 465-6
PWAIT 266, 270
PWB 5, 10
p_wchan 155, 183, 186, 188-9

p_wcode   268-70
p_wdata   268
PZERO   223, 421

Q

qattach   474, 483, 497
qband   415
qband_t   496
qdetach   483, 497
QENAB   465
qenable   440, 456, 460-1, 464-5, 469, 501
QNOENB   465-6
QNORM   410
QPCTL   410-11
qreply   427, 429, 456
qrunflag   465, 468
qsize   456
qtail   465
queue   442
   back-enabling   407
   enable   455
queuerun   465, 468-9, 476, 501
queue_t   496
quota   374
quotactl   374
quotas   45

R

raw disk I/O   309
RD   456
real time clock   26
real user ID   250
realloc   129
real-time class   169
reboot   277
record locking   357
regions   78, 86
resched   570
resident set size   584
resource   44
   limitations   44
   limits   201
   management policy   23
restoring environment   213
resume   165
rexit   266, 268-9
RFS   11, 34, 60, 64
Richard Miller   6, 8
Ritchie   4-6, 8, 51
rlogin   63
rmalloc   121, 128-9, 330, 332, 537-8, 547,
   568, 601, 603-4
rmfree   121, 128-9, 332, 537, 540, 547-8,

605
rminit   540, 548
rmvb   456
rmvq   456, 459
Robert Elz   8, 378
roff   4
root   23, 27
   partition   48
rootfstype   276, 367
ROOT_INIT   367
ROOT_REMOUNT   367-8
ROOT_UNMOUNT   369
rootvfs   373, 377
Ross Nelson   7
RPC   57, 62
rsh   63
RTBACKQ   170
rt_dptbl   169-71
RTRAN   170, 178-9
rt_swapin   179
rt_swapout   179
RT_TQINF   179
run queue   160
runin   187
runqueues   461, 464, 468-9
runrun   161-2, 173, 177-80, 189-90, 220

S

s5   29, 33, 36, 39, 45, 50
sad   472, 474
SAF   64
SA_NOCLDSTOP   230-1
SA_NOCLDWAIT   231, 271
SA_NODEFER   230
Santa Cruz Operation   10
SA_ONSTACK   230
SA_RESETHAND   230
SA_RESTART   218, 230
SA_SIGINFO   230-1, 236, 238
save   165
saving environment   213
/sbin/bcheckrc   368
/sbin/init   253, 266, 276-7, 279, 369
/sbin/inittab   277, 279
/sbin/uadmin   369
sbrk   129, 132
scanqhead   469, 476
SCCS   5
sched   115-17, 169, 179
schedpaging   111-12, 276
scheduler   115, 172
SCO   9
scratch register   151
security   45
seg   86-7, 93

seg_alloc 90
seg_attach 90
segdev 323
    operations 323
    segments 89
segdev_create 89, 323
segdev_fault 324
seg_free 90
segkmap 283, 285-7
segmap 282-3, 287, 327, 330
    operations 288, 298
    swap space 287
segmap_fault 287, 292
segmap_getmap 283, 286, 297-8, 309
segmap_release 287, 298, 309
segment 135
    lock 135
    locking operation 137
    operations 93
    segdev 323-4
    segkmap 285
    segmap 283, 323
    segvn 322-3, 327, 559, 584
segmentation 78
segmentation violation 101
segments 78, 80
seg_ops 87, 94
segvn 87, 132, 134, 283
    segments 89, 137-8
segvn_create 89, 132, 134, 357
segvn_data 86-7
segvn_fault 94, 109, 287, 292, 323, 356
segvn_faultpage 94, 323
segvn_lockop 134, 137
segvn_swapout 94, 117
segvn_unmap 357
sem 538
sema 537
semaoe 543
semaphore 10, 528, 530
    allocation 540
    claim 530
    implementation 535
    initialization 540
    initialization and control 532
    mutual exclusion 531
    operations 540
    producer consumer 531
    semadj 535
    support functions 539
    undo 541
    using 534
semexit 543
semfup 540, 543
seminit 540
semmap 537
semu 538, 543

SEM_UNDO 538-9, 541, 543
sem_undo 543
sendsig 238, 240
service 461, 472
service access facility 63
session 241
    leader 248
setbackdq 163, 178
setfrontdq 163, 178
set-group-ID 46
setitimer 206-7
setjmp 188, 215, 218, 220, 579-80
SETJUMP 215
setprocset 240
setq 486
setqsched 465
setrun 155, 178, 190
setsigact 231, 233, 271
set-user-ID 46
shadow-special-vnode 351-2, 385, 388, 473
shared 263
    libraries 263
    memory 10, 551
shared memory 551
    attaching 560
    detaching 559
    initialization and control 557
    using 553
shell 8, 22-3
shmat 134
shmctl 134
shmem 558
shmget 134
SHM_LOCK 552-3
shmop 134
SHM_RDONLY 553
SHM_RND 553
sibling 241
SIDL 155, 179, 572
sigaddq 235
siginfo 268
SIGMA 6
signal 221
    action 230
    disposition 186
    handle 223
    handler 221
    handling 225
    information 233
    mask 227
    pending 221
    posted 223
    posting 221, 240
    processing 236
    set 227-8
SIGALRM 197, 206, 221
SIG_BLOCK 228

SIGBUS 94
SIGCHLD 155, 181, 221, 231, 236,
    247, 265-6, 269-70
SIGCLD 572
SIGCONT 155, 225, 246, 270, 507-8,
    572
SIG_DFL 230
SIG_HOLD 227
SIGHUP 221, 249, 268
SIG_IGN 227, 231
SIGILL 221, 235, 262
SIGINT 226, 245, 279, 502, 504,
    509, 513
SIGKILL 225, 227, 230, 236, 238
SIGPIPE 498, 500, 502
SIGPOLL 471-2, 477-8, 482-4, 612
SIGPROF 206
SIGPWR 227, 230, 236
SIGQUIT 229, 262, 504
SIGSEGV 87, 94, 133, 221, 240,
    262, 321, 551, 553
SIG_SETMASK 228
SIGSTOP 227, 230, 236, 507, 572
SIGTRAP 581
SIGTSTP 245-6, 504, 507
SIGTTIN 236, 246, 507-8
SIGTTOU 246, 507
SIG_UNBLOCK 228
SIGURG 236, 483
SIGVTALRM 206
SIGXCPU 201-2, 221
SIGXFSZ 236
    system calls 226
sigsetops 227
sigset_t 227
sigstack 228
sigtoproc 223-5
SINCR 133
slash 27
slave 516
sleep 155, 178, 180, 182-4, 187, 190,
    237, 421, 572, 575, 593
sleep queue 183
sleeping process 180
sleeplcks 359
sleepq 183
SLOAD 115, 163-4, 179, 190, 274
SLOCK 134, 179
slowscan 111
smd_sm 285
SNA 51
snode 304, 309, 323, 351-2, 385-6, 471,
    473, 475
    common 385
SNOWAIT 164, 231, 271
SNWAKE 186
socket 58, 403, 521, 523-4

library 519, 521
soft link 354
software-pipe 405
SONPROC 157, 164, 179, 187, 201, 274
specfs 34, 388
special file 36, 300
special file system 384
spec_ioctl 482
spec_map 323
spec_open 304, 386, 388, 473-5
spec_read 309
spec_segmap 323, 327
spec_vnodeops 385, 388
specvp 386, 388
spec_write 309, 476
spl 217
splstr 456
spltty 217
splx 218
SPROCIO 163, 179
sptmap 604-5
SRUN 155, 157, 162, 164, 177, 179, 186,
    189
srunprocs 163
srv 329
SS_DISABLE 228
SSLEEP 155, 183, 189, 225
SS_ONSTACK 228
SSTOP 178, 186, 188-9, 507
SSWLOCKS 179, 355
SSYS 179, 274
stack 44
    frame 147-8
    growth 131-2
    kernel 148
    pointer 151
    segment 79, 145-6, 252, 259, 261,
        276
    user 147
stack segment 551
/stand 48
stand partition 48
/stand/unix 26, 148, 202, 274, 326, 368,
    563
start 329-30
startup 274
statically-linked-libraries 263
statically-linked-shared-libraries 264
stat_loc 270
status register 151
stdarg.h 588
stdata_t 496
stderr 42, 339, 518
stdin 42, 44, 339
stdio 6
stdio library 6
stdipc 529

stdout 42-4, 339
Steve Bourne 8
sticky bit 46
stop 178, 186
storage devices 31
STPLEX 486
str2time 619-20
straccess 508
strategy 292-3, 295-6, 301-2, 308, 310-11, 332
strbcalls 468
strbcwait 468
Strcount 472, 495, 609, 618-19
strdata 442
STRDERR 478
strdoioctl 478, 482, 486-7
stream 40
    bidirectional 40
    device 53
    head 53
    module 53, 55
    vnode 472, 475
stream.h 428
streamio 411, 424, 480, 482
STREAMS 11, 51
    architecture 52
    pipes 52, 59
    subsystem 51
streams 497
    attaching to a queue 497
    building the multiplexor 442
    close procedures 432
    configuration and linking 434
    data structures 409
    driver 407, 433
    driver close 436
    driver input processing 437
    driver open 434
    driver output processing 438
    FIFO operations 498
    flow-control 407, 464
    flow-control functions 460
    flow-control procedures 465
    flow-control variables 464
    flush handling 430
    ioctl 424, 482
    job control 505
    ldterm data structures 508
    ldterm implementation 508
    ldterm ioctl 511
    ldterm read side 509
    ldterm write side 511
    memory allocation 456
    memory limiting 472
    memory management 461
    message 406
    message processing 423

message structure 408
module 416, 418
multiplexor 407, 441
multiplexor close 453
multiplexor data structures 444
multiplexor open 447
multiplexor read side 452
multiplexor write side 447
networking support 519
open procedures 420
opening a clone device 474
pipe operations 500
pipes and FIFOs 497
polling 489
pseudo terminals 516
put procedures 421
putmsg and getmsg 487
queue 412
queue manipulation 459
read service procedure 437
reading 477
scheduler 407, 468
scheduling 464
service procedures 422
socket interface 521
stream head data structures 409
stream head operation 469
Strinfo array 493
terminals 502
transparent ioctl 428
Transport layer interface 523
Transport Service Interface 519
using ldterm 503
utility functions 454
writing 476
streamtab 303, 442, 472, 474, 497
strgetmsg 468, 487, 508
strgiveback 464, 473
STRHOLD 476
strhold 476
Strinfo 494-6
strioctl 468, 472, 482, 486, 508
strlofrac 462
strlog 416, 456
strmedfrac 462
stropen 388, 473-4
strpoll 492-3
STRPRI 478
strputmsg 472, 487, 508
strqget 456
strqset 456
strread 468-9, 477-8, 480, 500, 508, 514
strrput 477-9
strsubr.h 613
strthresh 472, 609
struct 117
    anon 86, 88-9, 91, 117-18, 127

anon_map 88, 552, 556-8
as 86-7, 89, 98, 104, 127, 154,
     283, 583
bdevsw 301
blk 359
bpool 123-4
buf 288, 290, 302
callo 196
cdevsw 301
class 166, 175
classfuncs 166, 175-6, 569
copyreq 429
copyresp 429
cred 155, 249-50, 275, 305
datab 410, 606
dirent 354
dispq 162-3
equeue 415-16
execsw 259, 261
fbuf 123-4
file 337, 339-41, 343, 345-6, 384,
     579, 595, 614
filock 358-9
flckinfo 360
flist 123
flock 356, 359
fmodsw 418, 526
fsid 374
hat 86, 98, 100, 104
hbuf 289-90
info 495
iocblk 424, 426, 428, 518
iovec 296-7, 299
ipc_perm 529-30
itimerval 207
kmeminfo 601
ldterm_mod 508, 511-12, 617
linkblk 486, 496, 613
map 119, 127-8, 537
mdbblock 461
module_info 414, 416-18, 420, 456
module_stat 414, 418
msg 548
msgb 409, 440, 606, 619
msginfo 545
msqid_ds 539, 543-4, 549-50
ncache 378, 380
page 83-4, 89, 94, 102-4, 115,
     138, 603
pageac 81-2
pathname 381
pid 155, 245-9, 252, 255, 272
polldat 492-3, 612
pollfd 489
proc 74, 81, 127, 132, 145-6, 148,
     153-5, 157, 161-3, 166, 168, 170, 172-4,
     183, 197, 199, 209, 221, 223-5, 227,

235, 241, 246-7, 255, 259, 265-6, 268-
     72, 340, 493, 556, 569
procset 240
prof 203
prstatus 393
prvnodeops 393
pte 99-104
pt_ttys 516-17
qband 415-16
qinit 413-15, 418, 442, 497
queinfo 495
queue 412-13, 416, 418, 420, 456,
     464, 495, 611-12
queue EFT 416
queue non-EFT 414
rtdpent 169-70
rtproc 170, 176, 179
rval 215
rval_t 215, 218, 233
seg 86-7, 89-90, 93, 583
segacct 556, 559
segmap_data 285
seg_ops 87, 94
segvn_data 86-7, 346, 584-5
sem 532, 538
sembuf 534
semid_ds 532-4, 537-40
seminfo 537
sem_undo 542-3
sess 248, 252
shinfo 495
shmid_ds 539, 551-2, 557-8
shminfo 555
sigaction 229-30, 238
sigaltstack 228
siginfo 230, 233, 235-6, 238, 270
sleepq 183
smap 283-5, 287
snode 385
statvfs 365
stdata 471, 495, 613
strbuf 485, 487
strdata 471
streamtab 418
strevent 467-8, 484, 496
strfdinsert 485
strinfo 495-6
strioctl 424-6, 428, 482, 485-6
stroptions 479
strrecvfd 485
swapinfo 117-18
sysent 215
termios 503, 511, 514, 519, 617
timestruc 204
timeval 207
tsdpent 172
tsproc 173, 176

ucontext   230, 238
ufchunk   336-7, 339-40, 343
ufs_inode   596
uio   296-7, 579
user   74, 145-6, 148, 153-5, 157,
        160, 201, 203, 209, 215, 225-6, 331,
        337, 582
ustat   365
utsname   275
vattr   351-2
vfs   32, 275, 365, 367, 372-3,
        376-7, 596
vfsops   363-5, 373
vfssw   32, 362
vnode   32, 248, 337, 346
vnodeops   346, 348, 384-5, 498
strwaitq   575, 618
strwrite   468-9, 472, 476, 498, 508
stune   602
stwdata   442
STWOPEN   473-4, 483
STWRERR   478
_STYPES   64, 409
SULOAD   258
Sun Microsystems, Inc.   33
Sun Microsystems, Inc   12
SunOS   12, 19, 51
super block   29, 37, 50
        backup   29
        multiple   33
super-user   23, 36
suser   331
SUSWAP   179
SVID   12, 14-5
SVR2   10
SVR3   11, 19
SVR4   12, 15, 19
SVVS   12-3
swap   117
        area   117-18
        space   90
        space management   117
swap_alloc   90
swapinfo   117-18
swapout   115, 117
swappable image   252
swapper   115
swapper process   115
swtch   161-3, 165, 178-9, 257
SXSTART   225
SYSCALL   214-15
syscall   593
sysent   215, 233, 253, 266
sysid   359
sysinfo.h   601
sys_init   182, 569
system   147

address space   147
call traps   214
class   169
clock   192
configuration   27
initialization   24-5, 48, 273
open file table   337
priority levels   181
resources   44
shutdown   23, 277
stack   165
wide statistics   200
system call   25
acct   200
adjtime   205-6
alarm   197, 207
brk   129, 132, 146
chdir   27
chmod   360
chown   38
chroot   27, 578
close   40-1, 43, 47, 53, 305-6,
        339, 348, 386, 420, 432, 497
creat   40, 336, 344-5, 352
dup   41-2, 44, 313, 338-9, 341-2,
        595
exec   42, 104, 177, 218, 252,
        258-61, 277, 346, 348, 351, 357, 521,
        556, 578
exece   258-9, 276-7
_exit   176, 236, 265-6, 268, 270
exit   41, 236, 240, 265-6, 268-9,
        543, 556
fcntl   41, 336, 341, 351, 355-6,
        358-9, 595
fork   41-2, 155, 176-7, 218, 241,
        252-5, 258, 498, 518, 521, 532, 556,
        578, 605
fpathconf   357
fstat   46
fstatvfs   30, 365, 384
fsync   37, 322, 354
getcontext   191-2
getdents   36, 354
getmsg   408, 411, 487, 517-18,
        521-3, 525
getpgid   249
getrlimit   44
ioctl   40, 47, 53, 188, 202, 303,
        313-16, 351, 392-3, 408, 411, 418, 420,
        424-30, 432, 446, 469, 471-2, 474, 477-
        9, 482-7, 503, 511, 518, 522-4
kill   221, 240, 243, 508
lchown   38
link   38, 352
lseek   319, 326, 340, 355, 393
lstat   38

memcntl 84, 131, 134-6, 558
mincore 138
mkdir 36, 49, 353
mknod 36, 49, 300, 497
mmap 104, 131, 301, 303, 313,
    319-24, 327, 330, 357
mount 30, 37, 304-5, 365, 373,
    376-7, 381, 392
mprotect 138
msgctl 544
msgget 539, 543, 549
msgop 544
msgrcv 544-5, 549-50
msgsnd 544-5, 547, 549
nice 172-4
open 40, 43, 47-8, 53, 202, 301,
    303-4, 327, 329, 336-40, 344-5, 348,
    384-6, 388, 393, 407, 420-2, 432, 434-5,
    442, 473-4, 483, 497-8, 508
pathconf 39, 357
pause 228, 231, 273, 442
pipe 40, 43-4, 59, 215, 336, 338,
    341, 497-8, 500-1
plock 84, 131, 134, 268
poll 64, 303, 316-18, 329, 357,
    465, 472, 477, 489, 492-3, 575, 590,
    593
priocntl 163, 166, 171, 173-4,
    176-8, 180
profil 203, 580
ptrace 146, 155, 572
putmsg 408, 411, 485, 487, 493,
    521-2, 525
quotactl 45
read 40, 47-8, 53, 80, 202, 283-4,
    296-9, 301-3, 308-10, 313-15, 319,
    321-2, 326, 329, 340, 351, 359, 393,
    408, 411, 477, 480, 482, 511-13, 518,
    522-3, 525, 583
readlink 38, 354
readv 297-9
rename 353
rmdir 36, 39, 354
sbrk 129, 132
semctl 532-3
semget 532-3, 538-40, 549
semop 534-5, 538, 540
setcontext 191-2, 230
setgid 22, 45-6, 259
setpgid 247, 507
setpgrp 247-9
setrlimit 44
setsid 249
setuid 22, 45-6, 259
shmat 134, 551, 553, 556, 559
shmctl 134, 552, 557
shmdt 553, 556, 559

shmget 134, 539, 551-3, 556-7
shmop 134, 553
sigaction 227-31, 233, 236, 238-9,
    271, 581-2
sigaltstack 228, 230, 582
sighold 227, 231
sigignore 231
signal 223, 227, 229-30, 233, 246
sigpause 231, 233, 273
sigpending 231
sigprocmask 227
sigrelse 231
sigsend 221, 240
sigsendset 240
sigsendsys 240
sigset 227, 230, 233
sigsuspend 225, 228, 273, 582
ssig 233
stat 38, 46, 351
statfs 30
statvfs 30, 365-6
stime 204
swapctl 278-9
symlink 38, 354
sync 37, 322, 366-8
sysinfo 200
tcgetattr 504-5
tcsetattr 504
tcsetpgrp 507-8
termios 617
time 204
times 199, 265, 269
uadmin 118, 277-9, 368-9, 373
ulimit 44, 132, 296-7, 579
umask 579
umount 30, 305-6, 365, 373, 376-7,
    380
unlink 39, 352
ustat 365
vfork 155, 252-4, 258, 572
wait 157, 199, 231, 236, 265-6,
    268-70, 572, 575
waitid 233, 269-71, 507-8
waitpid 269-70
waitsys 269-70
write 40, 47, 53, 80, 296-9,
    301-3, 308-10, 313-15, 319, 321-2, 329,
    351, 359, 393, 408, 413, 476-7, 482,
    493, 518, 523, 525, 582
writev 297-9
systrap 187-8, 213, 215, 218, 220, 223,
    233, 236, 253, 266, 268, 273, 344
SZOMB 157, 179, 265, 269-70

T

TABDLY 513
t_accept 525
task 142
T_BIND_ACK 522, 524
T_BIND_REQ 522-4
T_CONN_CON 521-2
T_CONN_IND 523, 525
T_CONN_REQ 519-20, 522
T_conn_req 519
T_CONN_RES 523
TCP/IP 9, 51, 54, 64
tcp_slowtimo 620
TCSETA 428
TCSETSW 517
T_DATA_IND 525
T_DATA_REQ 525
terminal 502
    driver 502
    ioctl 617
    pseudo 516
    pseudo terminal 503
termio 405, 425, 428, 482, 503, 508, 513,
    518, 617
termios 405, 430, 503, 510
testb 456, 458
text segment 79, 145-6, 148, 252, 259,
    261, 265, 276, 551
The Bible 8
Thompson 4-5
thrashing 77
threads 191
TI_BIND 522
TICK 204-5
tick 194, 201, 204, 275
tickdelta 205
tihdr.h 519
time 204
    getting 204
    setting 204
timed 206
timedelta 205
timein 197
timeout 194, 196-7, 473, 619-20
time-shared class 171
time-slice 160
timod 524
tirdwr 525
TLI 11, 55, 58, 519
t_listen 525
Tony McGrath 7
t_open 525
TOSTOP 246, 507
translation lookaside buffer 73
TRANSPARENT 428
Transport Layer Interface 55, 519, 523

transport provider 63, 519
Transport Service Interface 519
transport user 519
trap 25, 159, 214
    handling 161
t_rcv 525
TSBACKQ 174, 177
ts_dptbl 172-3
TSI 519
ts_kmdpris 181-2
TSKPRI 174, 178-80
ts_maxkmdpri 182
t_snd 525
ts_sleep 182
ttcompat 518
TTIPRI 181
ttrap.s 179-80, 193-4, 197, 203, 207,
    213, 215-17, 220, 235, 253, 581
tty 217-18, 502
    line discipline 502
    raw mode 503
ttymon 42, 64
tuneable 290
    BUFHWM 290
    FLCKREC 360
    GPGSLO 111, 115
    MAXCLSYSPRI 602
    MAXUP 255, 602
    MSGMAX 549
    MSGMNI 548
    MSGSEG 548
    MSGSSZ 548
    MSGTQL 548
    NAUTOUP 603
    NBUF 602
    NCALL 602
    NHBUF 290, 602
    NPBUF 290, 602
    NPROC 254, 378, 571, 602
    SEMAEM 539
    SEMMAP 537
    SEMMNI 537
    SEMMNS 538
    SEMMNU 538, 543
    SEMMSL 538
    SEMOPM 538
    SEMUME 538, 543
    SEMVMX 539
    SHMLBA 553
    SHMMAX 557
    SHMMIN 557
    SPTMAP 603
tuneable parameters 27

U

u area 146
uadmin 118
u_ap 215
u_arg 215
UCB 5-6
u_cdir 384
u_comm 261
ucontext 191
ufalloc 341
ufchunk 258, 268
ufchunks 336
u_flist 336-7, 340, 343
uf_ofile 337-41, 344
UFS 33
ufs 29-30, 33, 39, 45, 351
ufs_bmap 291-2
ufs_getapage 292-3
ufs_getpage 292
ufs_inode 390
ufs_inode.h 596
ufs_lookup 384
ufs_map 322-3
ufs_open 386
ufs_putpage 293
ufs_read 297
ufs_vnodeops 384
ufs_write 298
UID 22, 30
uio_iov 297
uiomove 287, 297-8, 309, 313, 326, 331
uio_offset 326
uio_resid 326
ulimit 132-3
u_lock 134-5
u_mem 201
unbufcall 456, 458
UNICS 4
UniForum 13
UniSoft UniPlus+ 10
University 5
    of California at Berkeley 5-6, 9
    of New South Wales 5, 7
    of Wollongong 6
UNIX 9
    32/V 9
    all-known-bugs-free 9
    AT&T 7
    Berkeley 9
    bit bucket 300
    bootstrapping 26
    Fifth Edition 5
    First Edition 5
    first version 4
    Fourth Edition 5
    history 3

    hybrid 7
    International 15
    kernel 24
    Ninth Edition 5
    porting 25
    Research 5
    Second Edition 5
    Seventh Edition 8-9
    Sixth Edition 5, 7
    Software Operation 15
    Support Group 9
    System 10
    System III 9
    System Laboratories, Inc. 25
    System V 10
    System V Release 2 10
    System V Release 3 11, 19
    System V Release 4 12, 15
    Time-Sharing 5
    V6 5-6, 9
    Version 7 8
unlinkb 456
u_nofiles 337
UNSW 5, 7, 9
    John Lions 6-7
untimeout 197, 620
u_procp 148, 154, 161-2
u_qsav 220
USDL 10
user 160
    access 63
    area 146-7
    ID 22, 45
    root 23
    stack 147
    structure 153
user.h 582-3
USG 9-10
u_sigaltstack 228
u_sigevpend 225
u_sigflag 228
u_signal 221, 225-6
u_signodefer 230
u_sigoldmask 228
u_sigonstack 228, 230
u_sigresethand 230
u_sigrestart 230
USL 25
USO 15
/usr 31
/usr/group 13
/usr/include/limits.h 39
/usr/include/sys 567, 583
/usr/include/sys/class.h 175
/usr/include/sys/signal.h 227
/usr/lib/libnsl_s.a 57
/usr/lib/librpcsvc.a 57

/usr/lib/libsocket.a 58
/usr/sbin/shutdown 279
/usr/src/uts/machine 26
u_stack 149
utlbmiss 105-7, 109
u_trap 216, 235
UUCP 59
/var/adm/crash 563

V

VDISCRD 504
VEC_syscall 593
VEC_tlbmiss 106, 108
VEC_tlbmod 106
VEOF 513
VERSE 512
Version 7 8
VFIFO 501
VFS 32, 62, 361-2
    mount list 305, 373
    operations 363
    table 32
vfs 26, 275, 398, 599
vfs.h 363
vfsinit 363
VFS_MOUNT 365, 376
vfs_mount 363, 376
vfs-mount-list 373, 377
VFS_MOUNTROOT 276, 367-9
vfs_mountroot 367-8
vfsops macros 364
VFS_ROOT 365
VFS_STATVFS 365-6
vfssw 276, 362-3, 367, 374, 376, 384
VFS_SYNC 362, 366, 377
vfs_sync 367
VFS_UNMOUNT 365, 377
vfs_unmount 377
VFS_VGET 367
VINTR 513
virtual 39
    address space 39, 78
    addressing 70
    file system 275, 361
    file system switch table 362
    machine 70
    memory 27, 39, 69
    memory mapping translation 165
    memory segment operation 282
    page number 71
    page offset 71
    to physical 71
virtual file system 32, 62, 275, 361
    interface 33
    switch table 32

VM 39
vm 27
VMIN 514-15
vn_create 345
vnode 26, 32, 62-3, 83, 85, 87-8, 91, 94,
    109, 117, 119, 153, 248, 259, 263, 268-9,
    283, 285-6, 288, 292, 323, 339, 345-6, 384,
    595
    allocation 346
    definition 345
    device 386
    file and record lock 358
    file system root 374
    hash list 85
    inactive 354
    interface 388
    lookup 473
    macros 348
    management 26
    mounted-on 377
    offset 283-7, 319
    operations 32, 346, 348, 384
    page 85
    shadow special 473
    stream 388
    supported operations 348
    swap 323
vnode.h 348
vnodeops 346
vnodes 117, 355
vn_open 345
vn_rele 354
VOP_ACCESS 345, 351
VOP_ADDMAP 357
VOP_CLOSE 348
VOP_CMP 355
VOP_CREATE 345, 352
VOP_DELMAP 357
VOP_DUMP 357
VOP_FID 355, 367
VOP_FRLOCK 355, 358
VOP_FSYNC 354
VOP_GETATTR 351
VOP_GETPAGE 94, 284, 287-8, 292, 356
VOP_INACTIVE 354
VOP_IOCTL 351, 393, 482
VOP_LINK 352
VOP_LOOKUP 351, 381, 384, 386, 393, 473
vop_lookup 384
VOP_MAP 322-3, 357
VOP_MKDIR 352-3
VOP_OPEN 345, 348, 384, 386, 473
vop_open 348, 386
VOP_PATHCONF 357
VOP_POLL 357, 493
VOP_PUTPAGE 119, 284, 292, 356-7
VOP_READ 351

VOP_READDIR   354
VOP_READLINK   354
VOP_REALVP   356
VOP_REMOVE   352
VOP_RENAME   353
VOP_RMDIR   354
VOP_RWLOCK   355
VOP_RWUNLOCK   355
VOP_SEEK   355
VOP_SETATTR   351
VOP_SETFL   351
VOP_SPACE   356
VOP_SYMLINK   354
VOP_WRITE   351, 476
VROOT   377
VSTART   514
VSTOP   514
VSTRT   514
VSUSP   507
vsw_init   363, 374
VTIME   508, 514-15

W

wait3   270
wait-channel   183
wakeflg   359
wakeprocs   128, 180-1, 183, 186-8, 190,
    327, 486, 498, 500, 550, 575
wakeup   183, 190, 359, 575
    non-preemptive   189
Western Electric Company   5
WR   456
wstat   270

X

X Window System   12
X.25   51
XDR   57, 62
XENIX   9-10, 12, 15
    System III   10
    System V   19
X/Open   13, 15, 18
    Portability Guide   14
XPG3   13
XTABS   513

Z

zombie   231, 265